Plutarch

Selected Lives and Essays

Translated from the Greek by
Louise Ropes Loomis

With an Introduction by
Edith Hamilton

Published for the Classics Club ® by

WALTER J. BLACK, INC. · ROSLYN, N. Y.

Contents

VOLUME ONE

Contents

VOLUME TWO

MAPS: ANCIENT GREECE, FRONTISPIECE, VOLUME ONE

ANCIENT ITALY, FRONTISPIECE, VOLUME TWO

ALEXANDER'S EMPIRE, VOLUME TWO, pp. 30-31,

by Philip Grushkin

Introduction

IN THE eleventh century of our era a bishop of the Byzantine Church made a prayer: "If, Lord, thou art willing in thy grace to save any Pagans from the wrath of God, I pray thee humbly to save Plato and Plutarch." Such truly good men, he said, and he gave the Lord to understand that he cared so much for them, he could not bear to have them lost forever.

That was some nine hundred years after Plutarch's death, and in the nine hundred years since, the bishop's opinion has never been challenged, only endorsed many times over down the ages. That prayer strikes the dominant note in all the tributes that have been paid to Plutarch. It is the note of personal affection, not often heard when a man's writing is appraised. Most good writers are admired; only a very few are loved. Who ever dreamed of feeling affection for Gibbon, or, for that matter, Thucydides or Tacitus? Who loves Stendhal or Flaubert or Proust or Henry James or Steinbeck or Hemingway? All these have seen in a very great degree men's misery and meanness and spiritual poverty; in some degree their pitifulness; but they have not seen them as lovable, they do not even like them. But there are writers who love mankind and in return mankind loves them. There is no other open sesame to that particular response on the part of readers. The bishop had a sure instinct; Plato possesses it as well as Plutarch. Horace stands with them. It is a mixed company. Chaucer belongs to it and Scott and Dickens and Burns and Charles Lamb and Trollope. Sir Thomas Browne, also, who always has a circle, small but very select, of true lovers. Anyone can fill out the list, but there is hardly a better guarantee of immortality than to be on it, and no one has a more assured place there than Plutarch. Only the other day a distinguished Greek scholar called him "the most widely beloved of all the literary treasures of Greece."

He was born a few years after the death of Christ, around the year 45, and he lived into the next century. Those fifty or sixty years are immensely important. They saw the entry into the world of the Christian Church. During them the Gospels were coming into existence and the new society was taking shape. When we think of the first century after Christ's death we are apt to see it dramatically. Two figures only engage our attention, the pure and radiant earliest Church of Christ and the Rome of Nero and Caligula. It is a strikingly dramatic contrast. On the one side are the Gospels and St. Paul's Epistles and the existence they point to of a society founded in purity and charity and faith, and on the other side accounts of cruelty and vice which have never been surpassed and seldom equaled in the long annals of history. On the stage of the world lofty goodness confronts atrocious wickedness.

The page of history thus unrolled looks, of course, very attractive, all in vivid colors or clearest blacks and whites, no dullness anywhere, no half-tones. The greatest writers of that period did not admit such. St. Paul did not see a gray world, nor yet the Roman writers who have left a record of the age. The two greatest, Tacitus and Juvenal, saw mankind sunk in an abyss of degradation, governed by tyrants run mad, and themselves given up to hideous cruelty as shown in the amphitheater, and monstrous vice as typified in Messalina. "An era of atrocities," Tacitus calls it. "Nothing but base servility and a deluge of blood shed by a despot in the hour of peace." Those whose dearest had just been put to death would "hasten to print kisses on the emperor's hand."

Juvenal was in full agreement. His world was a nightmare city where no one could drink a cup of wine without fearing poison, where "every street is thronged with gloomy-faced debauchees," and "never a one that does not have its Clytemnestra," where banquets celebrate unnatural and incestuous vice and spies abound "whose gentle whisper cuts men's throats."

The tragic power of Tacitus and Juvenal's blazing indignation and terrific vigor of expression have made this the familiar, one might say the popular, picture of the Roman world where the young Christian Church was beginning to live. It was endorsed to the full by the only contemporary

Christian writer who treated the subject. This is the author of the Book of Revelation, a most singular document, as unclassical as a document could well be, but in the author's Hebrew fashion, poles apart from the Latin fashion, he backed Tacitus and Juvenal with his own peculiar power of violent invective. He sees "that great city which reigneth over the kings of the earth and sitteth upon seven hills," as "the habitation of devils and of every foul spirit and a cage of every unclean and hateful bird," "full of the filthiness of her fornication." The book is written with a kind of somber grandeur which has ensured the long life of its contribution to the picture of the first century of the Roman Empire. "A black and shameful age," is Tacitus' summary, and deeply underlined as it is by Juvenal and Revelation it has been generally assented to by historians, especially Church historians. The triumph of Christianity over this blackness and shame has been celebrated by many writers.

To this sink of iniquity, this vilest city of Rome, during the reign of one of the worst of the emperors, Domitian, a young Greek came, not so very young, thirty-five, perhaps. His name was Plutarch and he came from a little town in Boeotia, Chaeronea, about halfway between Athens and Delphi. He was sent to Rome, he tells us, on public business, but one of his purposes while there was to give a series of lectures on philosophy, although he was obliged to deliver them in Greek because he had little Latin. This matter-of-fact statement comes to the reader with a shock of surprise. Where did he get his hearers? From among Tacitus' servile flatterers or Juvenal's gloomy-faced debauchees, to say nothing of the foul and unclean creatures of the Biblical writer? The pursuit of philosophy is hardly compatible with such characters, and certainly to lecture to them would seem not only a most unprofitable business, but dangerous as well. Indeed, one would suppose that no foreigner would willingly put himself in the power of such people for even a single day.

But all this portentous picture vanishes when Plutarch appears. He saw the city so differently that there seems no connection between his Rome and the black abode of crime and vice familiar to us. To him she was "the fairest of all the works of mankind," for all the peoples of the earth "an anchorage from the wandering seas," giving stability to a world which had never known it before. "For there now reigns among us a great peace and calm. Wars have ceased. Expulsions, seditions, tyrannies, are no more"—since Rome is Queen of the World. He also found the city "given to the liberal arts, where there are plenty of books and plenty of people who can remember what has escaped the pens of writers," pleasant, cultivated people who liked to tell him stories which had been handed down in their families about Caesar and Brutus and Mark Antony, and liked to listen to philosophy too. In Rome Plutarch lectured and studied and talked at his ease, living happily the student's life and the life of the man of the world.

One cannot but wonder if his writings ever fell into Tacitus' or Juvenal's hands. They were certainly in Rome when Plutarch gave those lectures. Possibly they met, the tragic historian, the bitter satirist, and the Greek to whom the world was a place full of interest and men generally likable and often admirable.

The contrast in the points of view is great. There is a good deal of contemporary backing for Tacitus and Juvenal. The Roman writers of the period were not optimists. But what the Greeks thought is very generally passed over. Plutarch is the only well-known Greek writer of that day and he is known chiefly as the author of the *Lives*. He has left us, however, a great deal besides, many writings which give an excellent idea of what he himself was like and his circle of friends and his home, and so what the Greeks of the day were like and the Greek point of view, an important matter for a true picture of the age. Plutarch was no eccentric genius. He was a steady-thinking, sober-minded man, obviously qualified to represent his countrymen. The reason that Greece saw things so differently from the way the great Latins saw them was due to a fundamental difference in the way the two countries looked at life. The Greek way and the Roman way came together only rarely, and that is an important fact in understanding this important period. The two great influences in the Western world, the Greek and the Roman, were at many points antagonistic, and the time was at hand when the Christian Church would inevitably choose between them.

About Plutarch himself, what kind of man he was, we know much, but about his life only a little. He was born, as has been said, in the year, or near the year, 45 A.D. and he died certainly after 106, for he speaks of Trajan's spending that winter on the Danube. The date of his death is usually assumed to be 119 or 120, but nothing that he did or that happened to him can be dated with complete accuracy.

He was born in Chaeronea where his family were well-considered people, and except for a time of study in Athens and one or perhaps two journeys abroad he spent his life there, going, however, often to Delphi, as he was attached to the oracle in some official capacity. He seems to have had a singularly peaceful and pleasant life, spent with an affectionate family and many friends, cultivated, traveled men, as we see them in his dialogues.

A letter we have to his wife when their little daughter died while he was away shows a genuine love for her, and he speaks often and warmly of his two brothers. He speaks also of his "numerous children," but the exact number we do not know. The little girl who died seems to have been his only daughter.

He quotes both his grandfather and his great-grandfather in the *Life of Antony*. One can deduce with some reason that he grew up in a household where the atmosphere was not provincial, where good talk went on and the affairs of the great world claimed attention. A story he tells about his father shows that he was a man who understood human nature. "I remember," he says, "that when I was still young I was sent with a companion on a deputation to the pro-consul [the Roman governor]. My comrade was unable to go on and I performed the commission alone. When I returned and was about to give an account of what had been done, my father bade me privately to be careful not to say *I* went, or *I* said, but *we* went and *we* said. In all my account I must give a full share to my companion." The father seems to have bequeathed his wisdom to the son. In a most difficult age Plutarch lived a pleasant life and died a peaceful death, the latter as striking proof in those violent times as could be given of ability to get on with people.

He had of course extraordinary abilities, but they were not such as in a happier age would have turned him naturally to books. If he had been able to choose his manner of life he would have disregarded the artist that was in him and gone into active affairs. Great writer though he was, his bent was strongly practical. He said of himself that he "did not so much understand matters through words as words through experience and knowledge of matters."

The *Lives* as they have come down to us have been changed from their original form. As Plutarch planned the work, it was to consist of a series of parallels, one Greek life and one Roman, followed by a comparison, but in our collection the comparison is lacking in a number of cases. Several single lives, too, have been added. Also, some of the parallels have been lost. In the long lapse of time, however, between Plutarch's day and ours, the wonder is that so much has been preserved, another proof of his great popularity.

The rest of his writings are grouped under the general title of *Moralia,* but they differ so much that no common name is appropriate. They are a collection of essays and letters and dialogues on most diverse subjects. The majority have to do with philosophy and ethics and religion, but they deal also with education and music and politics and archaeology and history and literature and mathematics and astronomy, and many other matters besides. Plutarch had an astonishing amount of information and almost everything in the world interested him. So he writes on Platonic Questions, and the Training of Children, and the First Principle of Cold, and the Three Sorts of Government, and the Virtues of Women, and Whether it is Good Manners to Talk Philosophy at Table (at his own table, he says, questions on history and poetry are always the second course) and Why Mushrooms are Produced by Thunder, and What God is Worshiped by the Jews, and Why Women Do Not Eat the Middle Part of a Lettuce— the list is encyclopedic. Socrates once told the young Theaetetus that to wonder was a very philosophic attitude of mind, and in that sense no one was ever a better philosopher than Plutarch.

His private life was eminently successful. Nothing emerges so clearly from his writings as his own sweet and kindly temper of mind. He knew how to create happiness around him, and the fact is a great tribute to him, for most men, even of far less ability than he, would have been dissatisfied and embittered and a trial to live with. A successful public life was impossible for Plutarch as for any Greek of the day. Greece was a humiliated conquered country, largely depopulated, desperately poor, commerce gone, agriculture in hardly better case, more shepherds than farmers on the land. A traveler in Greece, Pausanias, a few years after Plutarch's death, saw "shrunken or ruined cities, deserted villages, roofless temples . . . faint vestiges of places which had once played a part in history."

Rome treated the country fairly well. The Greeks had some measure of self-government; their education, their courts of law, were not interfered with. But over all was the Roman governor with full power to interfere if he chose, and Rome's taxation, tribute, it was called, from the conquered to the conqueror, could be crushing when an emperor needed money. The Roman idea of civilization. a world brought together by great laws and great roads, meant nothing to Greece. She was too poor to keep roads in repair and she had her own great system of law. That was the world Plutarch was born into. He says of his own province Boeotia, where once great Thebes had flourished, "She is mute, altogether desolate and forlorn," and he calls his native town, "a poor little place, where I remained willingly so that it should not become even less." We have a letter of his to a young friend urging him to enter public life to the degree open to a Greek, which throws a light on the way he looked at himself. He tells him, "You will have no wars to wage, no tyrants to put down, no alliances to consolidate. The utmost you can hope for is to abolish some petty abuse, fight some bad custom, revive some charitable foundation, repair an aqueduct, rebuild a temple, adjust a local tax." They are all duties well worth doing, he tells his friends.

There is sadness in the words coming from a man who must have been aware of great powers in himself, and there is a wonderful high courage too. Plutarch did just what he advised. He threw himself into the petty details of small town management, business of little moment and less interest. He said of himself that his neighbors often laughed at him when they saw him watching, for instance, while stone and mortar were measured out, but he would only say, "This is done not for myself, but for my country." That was the way he spent his life, "centered in the sphere of little things," but never despising them and never pitying himself. There is something here, some feeling, some ideal, which was not in Periclean Athens. Suffering may teach a profound lesson, and the mighty Greek spirit which had suffered so much had not lost its power to learn and to perceive new forms of excellence. When Plutarch declared that he who is faithful in that which is least may be fulfilling life's highest demands, he was Greece's far-sighted spokesman for a change that was beginning in the moral atmosphere of the world.

This conviction kept him from seeking a field fitted to his powers, in Rome, in Alexandria. He would stay in his own sorely stricken country and let nothing pass him that could help her. But his thoughts were not limited to one poor little town. He could send them where he pleased, soaring away with those who had not had to be content with humble duties in a lowly place, with men who had molded the world to their desires. Within that careful, patient guardian of Chaeronea's buildings and taxes and water supply there dwelt a passionate lover of great deeds, of heroic courage and splendid generosity, of magnificence in life and majesty in death. That was what turned Plutarch into a writer. He could not be an Aristides to lift Greece up by great statesmanship, or an Alexander to make her the mistress of the world. The time was long since over when a Greek could lead states or armies. But the time was never over for trying to help men to a loftier view of what it means to be a man. The mighty dead could teach that lesson. So Plutarch set himself to write his Lives. "It was for the sake of others," he says, "that I first began to write biographies, but I find myself continuing to do it for my own. The virtues of these great men serve me as a sort of looking-glass in which I may see how to adorn and adjust my own life. I can compare it to nothing but living daily with them . . . turning my thoughts happily and calmly to the noble."

Yet it cannot be said of him that he did not understand human nature and saw mankind far too favorably. It is true that he kept always the quality of mercy. Even Nero he would have spend only a short time in purgatory and then be given another chance, but he looked straight at the evil in men and he was perfectly aware that not one was righteous. In one essay he says, "If you will scrutinize and open up yourself you will find a storehouse of evils and maladies, not entering from abroad, but homebred, springing from vice, plenteous in passions. Wickedness frames the engines of her own torment. She is a wonderful artisan of a miserable life."

As a historian he has been drastically criticized for his romantic turn of mind; indeed, he is usually dismissed with a smile from the historians' domain as a mere storyteller. That is to do him an injustice. He was a first-rate storyteller, but his aim was not to please but to tell the truth, and he had a real power of critical judgment. In his lives of semi-mythical heroes like Theseus, Lycurgus, Romulus, and Numa, he is perfectly aware that his sources are "full of suspicion and doubt, being only poets and inventors of fables," and he asks his readers to "receive with indulgence the stories of antiquity." "So very difficult is it," he says, "to find out the truth of anything." He rejects all the marvelous tales reported of Alexander's death, which include one of his being poisoned by a deadly water cold as ice, distilling from a rock and kept in an ass's hoof "because it was so very cold and penetrating no other vessel would hold it." All such stories, he declares, are the inventions of writers who tried "to make the last scene of so great an action as tragical and moving as they could." Plutarch will have none of them. He gives word for word the meager and factual account in the court journal of the time, an undramatic record of a fever which increased for ten days and then proved fatal.

He did love those who could use life for grand purposes and depart from it as grandly, but he would not pass over weaknesses and vices which marred the grandeur. His hero of heroes is Alexander the Great; he loves him above all other men, while his abomination of abominations is bad faith, dishonorable action. Nevertheless he tells with no attempt to extenuate how Alexander promised a safe conduct to a brave Persian army if they surrendered, and then, "even as they were marching away he fell upon them and put them all to the sword," "a breach of his word," Plutarch says sadly, "which is a lasting blemish to his achievements." He adds piteously, "but the only one—". He hated to tell that story.

His aim was the truth, not brightly colored romances; but historic truth and artistic truth are not the same and Plutarch was an artist. He says that his purpose is to write lives, not histories, and he had a clear idea what the difference between the two was. A Life was a portrait, which Socrates once told a great painter must be a portrayal of the man's inner self, a revelation of what he really was. A History was an account of men's actions and fortunes irrespective of what the people were like who produced them. Economics and politics and the rise and fall of empires were the historian's concern; the biographer's was human beings. The two could not use the same methods. "The most glorious exploits," Plutarch says, "do not always furnish the clearest indications of virtue or vice in men; sometimes a mere expression, a jest, even, gives us their characters better than the most famous sieges, the bloodiest battles." These are history's material, but for himself, "I must be allowed to give my particular attention to the marks and indications of men's souls, as I endeavor to portray their lives."

In one passage he likens himself to a painter aware of an imperfection in the face he is painting, aware too that he must not leave it out, but above all that if he stresses it the likeness will be lost. So, he continues, he will follow the truth exactly in that which is excellent, but "not introduce faults officiously, if it be but out of tenderness for the weakness of human nature."

Debunking was odious to him, of course. The sharpest censure he was capable of was given to a writer who tried to pull a great man down from his pedestal. One such who had attacked the unfortunate general Nicias, forced against his will to lead the disastrous expedition against Sicily, was only trying, Plutarch says, to make himself out a better historian than Thucydides, and, he remarks coldly, "only succeeded in showing himself half-lettered and childish, accurately described in Pindar's lines,

"One who on his feet
"Would with Lydian cars compete."

Then he permits himself a little sarcasm, a weapon he rarely used: "This may be merely another indication of the admirable taste which makes him abuse Plato and Aristotle." "I myself," Plutarch declares, "will briefly recount the errors and faults of Nicias, because they illustrate his character under his many and great troubles." Also he will add to his biography "matters not commonly known, but found in old archives and on old monuments, not in order to collect useless bits of learning, but only those that make his disposition understood."

The deep seriousness which he brought to his work was founded on his religion, or, as he would have put it, on his philosophy. His profoundest conviction was that we needs must love the highest when we see it—but who can see it if there are none to show it, first, of course, in their lives, but, second only to that, in their words? The one he raised to a pedestal was the man who made it easy for people to believe in goodness and greatness, in heroic courage and warm generosity and lofty magnanimity. In humble virtues, too, patience that never wearies; readiness to forgive; kindness to an erring servant, to an animal. Plutarch was the first man to write about treating animals kindly. Below, far below, such men stood the historian, but the task of the latter was a high obligation none the less, since virtue unheralded must quickly be forgotten. "We are right," he says, "to blame those who misuse the natural love of inquiry and observation by expending it on unworthy objects. Every man is able to turn his mind easily upon what he thinks good. It is a duty to contemplate the best." St. Paul never came Plutarch's way—he seems not to have had any contact with Christianity—but if he had known him Plutarch would have endorsed with all his heart, "Whatsoever things are true, whatsoever things are pure, whatsoever things are lovely, if there be any virtue and if there be any praise, think on these things."

As a Greek, Plutarch had for his birthright the belief that men had within them "the mysterious preference for the best," and that they could strengthen it or weaken it, and he knew his own obligation. "Admirable actions," he writes, "can produce, even in the minds of those who only read about them, an eagerness which may lead them to imitate them. He who busies himself in mean occupations is his own evidence that he does not care for what is really good. The bare account of noble needs can make us admire and long to follow the doers of them. Moral good is a practical stimulus; it is no sooner seen than it inspires an impulse to follow it."

In all this Plutarch was the true representative of Greece. Plato was at his most Greek when he said that to describe the ugliness and weakness of men was to give only the appearance, not the truth, and that men's supreme duty was to trace out the examples—the forms—of excellence, which would enable them to choose the right pattern for their lives.

Plutarch's Lives is essentially a book of such patterns, models on which men may mold themselves, and, above all, be inspired to do so. What has made the book live for 1800 years is that Plutarch's spirit breathes through it and sweeps the reader along, a glowing sense of how great and how good greatness and goodness are, how wonderful human beings can be, how admirable are courage and the disdain of death and the high sense of honor and the contempt of the petty and the mean. Greatness is Plutarch's theme, not great fortune—he loves to depict a hero in adversity. "The truly noble and resolved spirit becomes more evident in times of disaster"; not great power, which he distrusts and disapproves, "such an unsociable solitary thing is power"; but great character: "Those who are great produce nothing little." Plato had said that men built on a grand scale sometimes stand forth because of the magnitude of their vices, not their virtues, and Plutarch's villains along with his heroes scorn the mean and what Schiller called, "Das was uns alle bändigt, das Gemeine." To such a villain he always gives full credit for any good in him. He says of Alcibiades whom he really detested for his arrogance and treachery, "He had such pleasant comely ways, he won over everybody. The charm of daily intercourse with him was more than any could resist."

Antony was the cause of terrible evils and Plutarch does not minimize a single one, but in the worst action of all his life he shows him to be pitied. At Actium when Cleopatra fled, Antony, "as if he had been part of her and must move wheresoever she went, abandoned those that were fighting and spending their lives for him, to follow her. She as he reached her fleet took him into her own ship. But without looking at her he went forward by himself to the prow and sat him down alone, covering his face with his hands, and there he remained for three days." This passage is an example of Plutarch's power to convey the significance of what is happening without a single comment. No one needs to have put into words what went on in Antony's mind as he sat there.

This is the literature of aristocracy. It belongs with the Morte d' Arthur. The grand manner is always there, in death as in life. Caesar's lieutenant, captured and offered his life, answers, "Caesar's soldiers give, but do not take, mercy," and he falls on his sword. Alexander, choked with thirst in a battle in the desert and offered a helmet full of water, refuses it because his soldiers need it as much as he. His enemy, Darius, dying on the field and given a cup of water by a Roman, says when he has quenched his thirst that the last extremity of his ill fortune is to receive a kindness and not be able to return it. Chivalry was first born in Plutarch's pages. When Alexander captures Darius' camp with his mother and wife and daughters, Arthur himself could not have improved upon his behavior. He provides for them royally and sends them word he will not enter their presence unbidden. He is a forerunner of Lancelot when, urged to attack the Persian army under the cover of the night, he cries, "I will not steal a victory."

Prudence and common sense are of course most useful and highly to be commended, but how delightful and thrilling it can be when they are splendidly dismissed by those who are willing to pay for the dismissal with their lives. Pyrrhus was near to conquering the Romans. His physician sent the Roman commander a letter in which he offered to poison Pyrrhus and so end the war. The Roman sent this letter to Pyrrhus and wrote him, "You are fighting honorable men who will not conquer by treachery." The Athenians during a fierce contest with Philip of Macedon surprised a messenger of his with letters. They opened them, except those to his wife, which they returned to him with the seals intact. "The grace and the gentleness of true greatness," Plutarch remarks. Pompey, despatched to Africa by the senate to bring back a shipload of corn with all speed to hungry Rome, upon being told by the sailors when the ship was loaded they could not set sail in such a storm, cried, "There is a necessity upon us to sail. There is no necessity upon us to live."

Such stories fill Plutarch's pages and make an appeal to some disdain within us all of the man who loves life most, some sense of pride as well, that human beings have been like that, since we too are human.

Our own greatest stories are built on Plutarch's model. The Charge of the Light Brigade is pure Plutarch.

> "Was there a man dismayed?
> Not though the soldiers knew
> Some one had blundered."

In other words, "There is no necessity upon us to live." Sir Richard Grenville, engaging the entire Spanish fleet with the little *Revenge,* belongs to Plutarch's company and he dies like one of them:

> "But he rose upon their decks and he cried,
> I have fought for Queen and faith like a valiant man and true;
> I have only done my duty as a man is bound to do.
> With a joyful spirit I Sir Richard Grenville die."

The Spaniards, too, who praised him to his face with their courtly foreign grace, are in the true Plutarchian tradition. The great conqueror shows magnanimity to the conquered. Alexander was "as gentle after victory as he was terrible on the field." When Aemilius Paulus was told that the leader of the enemy's forces had surrendered and had asked to be taken to him, he rose from his seat and accompanied by his friends went himself to meet him with tears in his eyes for a formidable opponent who had failed. The war with him had cost the Romans much, but a defeated foe ceased to be an enemy. "When the invincible and terrible Hannibal was vanquished," Plutarch says, "Scipio gave him his hand and put no hard article in the peace treaty, nor insulted him in his fallen fortune." The Victorian poets understood that point of honor as well as Plutarch did—learned it from him very likely along with Sir Thomas Malory. When "the Dane" was conquered in the Battle of the Baltic,

> "Outspake the victor then
> As he hailed them o'er the wave,
> Ye are brothers! Ye are men!
> And we conquer but to save:—
> So peace instead of death let us bring."

We seem today to be establishing a new tradition of the way the victor should treat the vanquished. If it is to prevail, Plutarch will be carefully censored along with the Victorians.

Plutarch called himself a Platonist. His bent of mind, however, was more Socratic than Platonic. He wanted to do what Cicero said Socrates had done, "bring philosophy down from heaven into the cities and the homes of men." In his hands, as he talked to his friends in Chaeronea, in Delphi, divine philosophy took on a pleasantly homely look. It was said of Socrates that to him knowledge, philosophy, was "action getting under way." That was exactly Plutarch's idea. Philosophy must work in daily life to guide and strengthen men in the path to virtuous action.

He stood at the beginning of a new era in religion and he felt that it was so and that he was part of it, but he did not let go of the old, of what he calls, "the ancient and hereditary faith." The different gods were merely different views of the one God, perfect in goodness, or perhaps they were different ways of trying to find Him. The myths he said were "to be tenderly treated," interpreted in "a spirit at once pious and philosophic." They are, he writes, the reflection of truth like "the rainbow which the mathematicians tell us is nothing else but an image of the sun, a reflection of his beams upon the clouds." Nevertheless he knew that the framework which always encloses religion was falling apart and a new frame had to be constructed.

A startling change was taking place before his eyes. A great religious institution was coming to an end, the oracles were failing. They had been very important. Through them men had had the assurance of direct communication with God. In great distresses and perplexities it was possible to find out from a god what should be done. They could get divine counsel at Delphi, at Argos, as far away as Ammon's temple in the Sahara. But everywhere oracles were ceasing to speak. Why? men were asking. Plutarch answers the question in a remarkable passage. He could be a clear, hard thinker on occasion. The oracle at Delphi, he points out, depended upon two things, the vapor in the Delphic cave and the priestess who spoke under its influence. Neither was divine. They operated according to natural law and were subject, as all things in nature, to change and decay. The power behind the oracles was God, but in speaking by means of them He used what was fallible and imperfect. His words came to men not directly, but through natural channels. "God," Plutarch sums up, "is not a ventriloquist."

A statement like that shakes the condescension with which we view the pre-Christian world. An infallible voice, an infallibly dictated Book—a large part of the western world today holds to the one or the other, each a manifestation of God's powerful ventriloquism.

A man who thought like this could not be superstitious. Plutarch had no tolerance for that particular form of human weakness. To him a superstition was not a mistaken belief, a kind of religious stupidity; it was an unmitigated evil, far worse than absolute disbelief. Atheism, he says, denies God, but superstition wrongs Him. It makes God evil or silly. It uses the very worst of all weapons, terror. It fills the world after death with "flaming fires and awful shapes and inexorable judges and horrible torments"; in this world it teaches people to practise absurd penances and self-torturing. Better far not to see God at all than see Him like that. "I had rather have it said that there was not and never had been such a fellow as Plutarch, than that he was fickle and vindictive and would pay you out for not calling upon him."

His religious creed was not complicated. A contemporary of his, the younger Pliny, wrote, "For man to help man is God," and to Plutarch that was certainly a clause in the definition. The life according to God was accepting an unconditional obligation to make things better for others wherever one was. But there was more than that. In an essay he wrote upon the delay of God in punishing the wicked he faced with candor and with courage the basic problem of religion, the problem of evil. He did not propose a solution. With our limited knowledge to try to understand God's ways was, he once said, like a man's looking at a painting and claiming to be able to explain how it was done because he had analyzed the colors and knew how they were mixed. Nevertheless, in God's slowness to punish there was a clue to understanding Him Himself. He gives people time to repent, and from Him we may learn patience with those who wrong us, and forgiveness.

Of course as a Platonist he believed in the reality and the eternity of the things not seen, but the Greeks for generations before him had been learning Platonic idealism through hard facts. Ever since Alexander's day they had been forced to see that the things that are seen are temporal;

they vanish, riches, power, empire, no matter how solidly founded, how mightily bulwarked, and only the splendor of the spirit endures.

The immortality of the soul necessarily followed or, rather, was bound up in this conception. Life and death, Plutarch says, are only the prelude to the great initiation. We are like those being initiated into the mysteries. At first they wander along tortuous ways and through wearisome mazes, which end in a shuddering passage through darkness full of terror. But then "a clear shining light comes to meet you; pure meadows receive you; there is song and dance and holy apparitions." In the letter he writes to his wife about the death of their little daughter, he says, "About that which you have heard, dear heart, that the soul once departed from the body vanishes and feels nothing, I know that you give no belief to such assertions because of those sacred and faithful promises given in the mysteries of Dionysus which we who are of that religious brotherhood know. We hold it firmly for an undoubted truth that our soul is incorruptible and immortal. We are to think [of the dead] that they pass to a better place and a happier condition. Let us behave ourselves accordingly, outwardly by an ordered life, while within all should be pure, wise, incorruptible."

"Is God so petty," he asks, "so attached to the trifling, that He will take the trouble to create souls if we have nothing divine in us, nothing that resembles Him, nothing lasting or sure, but all of us fades like a leaf?"

The unseen world was peopled for him with hosts of spirits, good and bad, but chiefly good. The bad were useful in lifting from God the burden of the responsibility for evil, and the good satisfied the human longing for a mediator between God's awful perfection and man's feeble wickedness. They were the spirits of good men who, Plutarch says, "have become able to share in the nature of God." They could draw near to men and help them. If a man persists on the path of excellence, he will become "able to hear this spiritual speech which fills all the air but can be heard only by those whose souls are pure."

Plutarch was not an original or profound thinker. He could not melt the old in the fire and fuse it into a new form. But he was typically Greek. In that age of confusion when the young Christian Church first confronted the classic world he could and did hold up the bright torch of the Greek spirit so soon to be darkened for centuries to come. Christianity in its beginnings was addressed to Greeks. The Gospels as we have them are in Greek. St. Paul wrote in Greek to Greek-speaking Christians. Plutarch never came into contact with the new religion; he knew nothing about Christianity, although his spirit was naturally Christian, as was said of Socrates. But when Christianity entered Greece it must have made converts of many men like Plutarch, spiritually minded, longing for light, men of strong mentality too. But, extraordinarily, the Church was never really influenced by Greeks. Two roads lay open to her, the Greek way and the Roman way and she took the Roman. It was a decisive choice, destined to affect fundamentally the course of Christianity.

The Greek was instinctively Socratic. He must reason and try to understand, always remembering that every conclusion was forever open to question and re-examination. Plutarch wanted men, he said, "to borrow reason from philosophy and make it the guide to religion." To the Romans reason and philosophy signified little. The will was the matter of importance, not the mind or the spirit. Obedience to authority and disciplined self-control were the Roman essentials—as became a nation which Livy said had been fighting for eight hundred years.

Christ had said, "Seek and ye shall find." Also, "And ye shall know the truth and the truth shall set you free," sayings easy for a Greek to understand, but very hard for a Roman. They were great organizers and an organization is not a place where individuals are encouraged to seek or to be free. Institutionalism was natural to the Romans and the Church took the Roman way.

The Greek trinity was goodness, truth, beauty. The Romans understood the first in what may be called a military sense. Goodness, virtue, was made up of high courage, unshaken fortitude, high honor, too, even when it interfered with military advantage, as a truly great soldier sees it, and, of course, patriotic devotion. They gave little thought to the other two, but beauty in especial was unimportant, a mere decoration to the very serious and difficult business of life. To Plutarch it was a revelation of God. "The World," he wrote, "is a most holy and divine temple into which man is introduced at birth, not to look at motionless images, but at those things which the mind of God has brought forth as the visible images of the invisible, sun, moon, stars, fresh-flowing rivers, earth the sustainer of all. Life is our initiation." St. Paul had said, "The invisible things of God are *seen*, being understood by the things that are made," a saying truly Greek and Plutarchian, but that was not the way the Roman mind went. The mediaeval writer who told those who sought to please God to put their hands before their eyes when they went out of doors, "especially in the spring time," was made in the Roman mold.

Gilbert Murray says, "Plutarch explains in his beautiful and kindly way that all religions are attempts toward the same goal." He really was that rare person, a man of perfect tolerance with deep religious convictions. He did not agree with either of the two chief philosophical schools of his day, the Stoic and the Epicurean, and he argued with them, but he did it like a Greek, reasonably, in a civilized manner, with no bitterness and no anathemas. The terrible *odium theologicum* which for hundreds and hundreds of years would distract and disgrace Christendom had not yet been born, but it would never find a home in Greece, and it would have been unimaginable to Plutarch.

It was quite in accordance with the Roman point of view. The Romans thought very poorly of human nature. It was tolerable only when it was submissive to strong control, and properly hated when it got out of control. The Greeks from the beginning had had a vision of the true light which lighteth every man that cometh into the world—"the divine," the *Odyssey* says, "for which all men long." "God knows," Plutarch says, "with how great a share of goodness souls come into the world, how strong is their nobility of nature which they derive from Him Himself. And that if they do break out into vice, corrupted by bad habits and bad companions, they may yet reform."

Christ's last prayer had been, Father, forgive them for they know not what they do. Plutarch would have understood that prayer.

What would it not have meant to the religion of Christ if Christians could have been learners as well as teachers of Greece! There would have been another criterion of the truth, not only creeds and *ipse dixits,* authoritatively promulgated and obediently accepted, but Plutarch's criterion—If we live here as we ought, we shall see things as they are, the Greek version of, The pure in heart shall see God

EDITH HAMILTON

Translator's Note

THE FIFTEEN LIVES OF ILLUSTRIOUS GREEKS AND Romans which make up the bulk of this work were chosen not only for their individual and intrinsic interest but also for their significance as illustrations of the course of Greco-Roman history, from its legendary beginnings in scattered, small, free commonwealths down to the stage of violent dissolution of the traditional fabrics of government and their replacement by imperial despotisms.

The Lives come in pairs, one Greek statesman and general matched in character and achievement with one Roman, concluding sometimes with a formal comparison of the two. There was space here for seven pairs and a single additional Life. For the last, the Life of Cato the Younger was chosen, as representing the blending of Greek and Roman influences in the final era of this history. Cato, an intensely patriotic Roman, was profoundly moved by Greek Stoic ideals and died rather than accept life as a gift from Caesar.

The Lives are translated in full, but the ten selections from Plutarch's miscellaneous essays, commonly known as the Moralia, are, with two exceptions, made up of excerpts. Seventy-seven of his essays are extant, in the form of letters, dialogues, lectures, and collections of anecdotes, many being lengthy discussions of topics briefly touched on in the Lives. Our selections are intended to show Plutarch's own opinion on sundry matters that still have an interest for us. Through them we may learn more of the urbane, tolerant Greek himself and of the things he and his friends talked about together.

In view of the fact that Plutarch's biographies are supposedly among the most attractive and diverting works of ancient literature, it is surprising that there exists no modern, inexpensive, and readable version in English of the whole fifty, nor of the essays. The so-called Dryden-Clough translation of the Lives, now generally used, dates back to the late seventeenth century and in spite of a mid-nineteenth century revision is still old-fashioned and ponderous in style and loose and often inaccurate in its rendering of the Greek. The early nineteenth century version of the Essays, revised by W. W. Goodwin, is, if anything more difficult reading and more inexact. I have taken suggestions from them when I could, but in all essentials the version here presented is new. The Greek texts used for the Lives were those of the Loeb Classical Library edition, B. Perrin, 1914-1926, and of the Teubner edition, Bernadakis, 1888-1896; for the Essays, those of the Loeb edition, Babbitt, Fowler and Helmbold, 1927- , and of the Teubner edition, Lindskog and Ziegler, 1914-1935.

LOUISE ROPES LOOMIS

PLUTARCH

SELECTED LIVES
AND ESSAYS

VOLUME ONE

Lycurgus

8TH TO 7TH CENTURY B.C.

1. NOTHING can be said of Lycurgus, the lawgiver of Sparta, which is not open to dispute. Historians differ as to his family, his travels, the manner of his death, but most of all as to the laws he made and the commonwealth he founded. They do not even agree as to the age in which he lived. Some say he flourished in the time of Iphitus,[1] and that together they brought about the Olympic truce. Aristotle, the philosopher, was of this opinion, and in confirmation cites the copper quoit preserved at Olympia, inscribed with Lycurgus' name. But Eratosthenes and Apollodorus and other chronologers, who reckon time by the reigns of the Spartan kings, argue that he lived years before the first Olympiad.[2] Timaeus [3] believes that there were two Lycurguses at Sparta at different times, and that one of them, who was more famous, was credited with the exploits of both. The elder of the two, according to him, lived not long after Homer, and some say he even saw Homer. That Lycurgus lived in the distant past is implied by a passage in Xenophon, where he

[1] Iphitus, king of Elis and son of Eurotas, one of the Argonauts, was credited with having founded or restored the Olympic games in 776 B.C. During these games a general truce was habitually observed throughout Greece.

[2] Strabo, the geographer, who lived about a century before Plutarch, thought that Lycurgus flourished around 900 B.C. The later Greeks reckoned time by Olympiads.

[3] No attempt is made in these notes to identify the numerous minor Greek and Latin poets, historians, and other writers to whom Plutarch refers as his authorities; in most cases nothing has come down save a bit of doubtful legend, or a few lines from their works, quoted by other men.

is spoken of as contemporary with the Heraclidae.[4] By descent indeed
even the latest kings of Sparta were Heraclidae too, but Xenophon seems
to mean by Heraclidae the immediate successors of Heracles.

In spite of this confusion, I shall endeavor to write a history of his life,
following the statements which are least contradicted and depending on
the authors who are most worthy of belief. The poet Simonides [5] says
that Lycurgus was not the son of Eunomus, but that both Lycurgus and
Eunomus were sons of Prytanis. Most writers, however, trace his gene-
alogy as follows: Aristodemus, Patrocles, Soüs, Eurypon, Prytanis,
Eunomus; and Eunomus had two sons, Polydectes by his first wife and
Lycurgus by his second wife, Dionassa. Dieutychidas says he was sixth
from Patrocles and eleventh from Heracles.

2. The most renowned of his ancestors was Soüs, for under him the
Spartans enslaved the helots,[6] and annexed a good part of Arcadia.
There is a story that Soüs, when surrounded by the Clitorians in a stony
and waterless place, agreed to restore his conquests, provided he and all
his men should drink of the nearest spring. After taking the usual oaths,
he called his soldiers together and offered his kingdom to the one who
would refrain from drinking. But not a man of them was able to refrain, and they all drank their fill. Soüs himself came last to the spring,
and, while the enemy still looked on, merely sprinkled his face, and
then marched off, refusing to yield up his conquests, because they had
not all of them drunk.

Although for these reasons he was much admired, his family was not
named for him but for his son Eurypon (for whom they were called
Eurypontides), because Eurypon first relaxed the despotic tradition of
the kingdom, seeking favor and popularity with the people. As a result,
the people grew bolder, and succeeding kings either incurred their hatred

---

[4] Xenophon, *Commonwealth of the Lacedaemonians*, X, 8. The Heraclidae were
supposed to be descendants of the mythical hero Heracles, who, with the Dorians,
conquered the Peloponnesus some eighty years after the fall of Troy.

[5] Simonides of Samos (c.660 B.C.) was one of the most quoted of early Greek poets,
though only fragments of his poems have been preserved. They all reflect a somber
view of life.

[6] The helots were a part of the original Achaean population of Laconia who were
reduced by their Dorian conquerors to subjection. The Spartans employed them as
farmers and to some extent as artisans.

by trying to use force on them, or weakly yielded to them, in an effort
to acquire popularity. So anarchy and confusion prevailed in Sparta for
a long time, and was, indeed, the cause of the death of the king who
was Lycurgus' father. He was trying to quell a riot when he was stabbed
with a butcher's knife, and left the kingdom to his elder son, Polydectes.

3.   But he too died soon after, and the succession, as all thought, fell
to Lycurgus. In fact, he reigned until it was found that his brother's
wife was with child. At this, he at once declared that the kingdom belonged to her child, if it were a male, and that he himself would exercise jurisdiction only as guardian. The Spartan name for the guardian
of an orphan king is *prodicus*. The queen, however, secretly made overtures to him, suggesting that she destroy her unborn child on condition
that he would marry her when he was king of Sparta. Although he
abhorred the woman's wickedness, he did not reject her proposal outright, but pretended to agree and accept it. He told her she should not
use drugs to procure an abortion, and thus injure her health and en-
danger her life; he himself would see to it that the child, as soon as
born, should be put out of the way. Thus he deluded her until her confinement, and as soon as he heard she was in labor, he sent watchers
and guards with orders, if it were a girl, to give it to the women, but if a
boy, to bring it to him, no matter what he happened to be doing.

It turned out that when he was at supper with the archons a boy was
born and the servant brought the child to him. Taking it in his arms, the
story is, he said to those around him, "Men of Sparta, a king is born to
you!" Then he laid him down in the king's seat, and called him Charilaus,
that is, Joy of the People, because all were filled with joy and with wonder
at Lycurgus' noble and just spirit. So he was ruler for only eight months
in all, but the citizens honored him on other counts. More, in fact, looked
up to him and were eager to do what he said because of his goodness than
because he was the royal guardian and held the power of the king. Some,
however, were jealous of him and tried to curtail his growing influence
while he was still young, especially the relatives and friends of the queen-
mother, who thought she had been insultingly treated. Her brother
Leonidas once boldly berated Lycurgus, saying he was sure he would be
king again, thus giving ground for suspicion and for an accusation against
him, if anything happened to the young king, that he had plotted the

child's death. Rumors of this sort were spread abroad by the queen-mother also. Troubled by all this, and not knowing what it might lead to, Lycurgus thought his wisest course was to escape suspicion by going abroad and traveling about until his nephew came of age, and had a son to succeed him in the kingdom.

4. With this intention, he set sail first for Crete, where he studied the several forms of government, and became acquainted with the leading men. Some things he approved of, and adopted some of their laws with the intention of taking them home and applying them there. Other things he rejected as useless. One of the persons most renowned in Crete for wisdom and statesmanship was Thales,[7] whom Lycurgus persuaded out of courtesy and friendship to go to Sparta. Thales was by profession a lyric poet, but he made a screen of his art, and in reality served as a very able lawgiver. Even his odes were exhortations to obedience and harmony, and the cadence of his verses conveyed a spirit of order and tranquillity, so that those who listened were unconsciously softened and civilized to the point of renouncing the feuds, which were prevalent at that time, and living together in love of the high and the beautiful. Thus in his fashion Thales prepared the way in Sparta for the discipline of Lycurgus.

From Crete Lycurgus sailed to Asia,[8] with the aim, it is said, of studying the differences between the customs of the Cretans, who were sober and temperate, and those of the Ionians, who loved ease and luxury, just as a physician compares healthy with unsound or diseased bodies. He would then note down the differences in their ways of living and their governments. In Asia he had apparently his first sight of Homer's poems, in the keeping of the descendants of Creophylus;[9] and on discovering that the few licentious expressions or examples they contained were far outweighed by lessons of state and rules of morality, he eagerly collected and copied them, to take back to his own country. The epics had already been heard of in Greece, and scattered portions were owned by a few individuals, but Lycurgus first made them really known.

---

[7] This Thales was not the famous philosopher of Miletus of the same name, who lived between 640 and 540 B.C.

[8] Asia, as the word was used by the Greeks, meant western Asia Minor.

[9] Creophylus, an epic poet from Chios, was said to have been a friend or son-in-law of Homer.

The Egyptians say that Lycurgus visited them also, and was so much taken with their way of separating the soldiery from the rest of the population that he adopted it for Sparta, and also removed all working men and artisans from a voice in the government, so as to keep the state pure and refined. Some Greek writers corroborate the Egyptians' assertions, but as for the story that Lycurgus visited Libya and Iberia, or journeyed on to India and met the Gymnosophists,[10] as far as I can find out, it all rests solely on the word of the Spartan Aristocrates, son of Hipparchus.

5. Lycurgus was much missed at Sparta, and often sent for. They had kings,[11] they said, who had the name and insignia of royalty, but otherwise nothing to distinguish them from the common people, adding that he alone possessed the spirit of a ruler and the power to hold men's obedience. Nor were even the kings averse to seeing him back, for they hoped that with him there the people would behave less insolently.

Things being in this state at his return, he promptly set about working a change and revolutionizing the system of government, since a partial reform of the law would be of no avail. Like a physician trying to cure a feeble and thoroughly diseased body, so he would use drugs and purges to reduce and change the constitution, then set it on a totally new regimen. With this resolution he first went to Delphi, and having sacrificed to the god and consulted the oracle,[12] returned with the famous response in which the priestess called him "beloved of the gods," and "a god rather than a man." He was told also that the god had heard his prayer for good laws and that his constitution would be the best in the world.

Thus encouraged, he labored to win to his side the leading men of Sparta, asking them to help him in his undertaking. First he talked privately to his friends, then gradually enlisted more men and banded them together for the task. When the time was ripe for action, he ordered thirty of the leaders to go armed into the market place at dawn, to strike surprise and terror into his opponents. Hermippus has recorded the names

---

10 Gymnosophists was a name given by the Greeks to the philosophers of India. See below, *Alexander,* ch. 65, n. 98.

11 The early Spartan constitution provided for two kings. This provision was said to have originated when the succession once fell to twin brothers, and their mother refused to say which was the older.

12 The god was, of course, Apollo, whose famous oracle at Delphi delivered responses through the mouth of an inspired priestess to those who sought its guidance.

of twenty of the most eminent of these men. The one who was the most useful to Lycurgus in his whole enterprise and in putting his laws into effect, was Arthmiades. When the disturbance began, King Charilaus was afraid that it was a conspiracy against himself and fled to the Brazen House;[13] but he soon learned his mistake, and on receiving oaths of assurance, left his refuge and entered into the project with the others. He was of so gentle a disposition that Archelaus, his brother-king, is said to have remarked to some who were praising him, "How can Charilaus be a good man? He is never severe, even to the bad."

Among the many changes which Lycurgus made, the first and most important was the establishment of a senate or council of elders, which, Plato says,[14] on being added to the feverish rulership of the kings, and granted an equal vote with them on vital issues, gave stability and prudence to the commonwealth. Before this the state had no firm basis to stand on, but leaned first towards the kingship and tyranny, and then towards the people and democracy. But by the establishment of the senate, it acquired a central ballast for the ship, which kept it in safe and steady equilibrium. The twenty-eight senators always stood by the kings in resisting a drift towards democracy, and supported the people against the establishment of a tyranny. As for the number twenty-eight, Aristotle tells us that two of Lycurgus' original thirty comrades dropped out for lack of courage; but Sphaerus says there were at first only twenty-eight with him. Perhaps there is some virtue in the number formed of seven multiplied by four, and the first perfect number after six, for like six it is equal to the sum of all its parts.[15] But I believe that Lycurgus fixed on the number twenty-eight for the senators so that, with the two kings, they might be thirty in all.

6. So eager was he to bring about the establishment of this government that he procured an oracle from Delphi about it, called a *rhetra*,[16] which runs thus: "After you have built a temple to Zeus Syllanius, and to Athene Syllania, and have divided the people into *phylae* and into *obae*, and

---

[13] The Spartan Brazen House was a temple to Athene.

[14] *Laws*, 691 e.

[15] Twenty-eight was called by the Pythagoreans one of the mystic numbers, because the sum of all its factors—1, 2, 4, 7, 14—equals the number itself, as 1, 2, and 3 add up to six.

[16] Therefore Lycurgus' own body of laws was later called the *rhetra*.

established a senate of thirty including the *archagetai,* you shall, from time to time, *apellazein* the people between Babyca and Cnacion,[17] and there propose or revoke your laws. The people shall have the final voice and the power." By *phylae* and *obae* the oracle [18] meant divisions of the people into clans and brotherhoods; by the *archagetai,* the two kings; *apellazein* means assemble, with an allusion to Apollo, the source and author of the new constitution. Babyca and Cnacion they now call Cheimarrus and Oenus. Aristotle says Cnacion is a river and Babyca a bridge. Between this Babyca and Cnacion they held their assemblies, for they had no hall or any other house to meet in. Lycurgus believed that architecture, far from helping, actually hindered men in their deliberations, by diverting their attention from business to idle reveries, as they gazed on statues and pictures, or mural decorations, or elaborately fretted roofs.

When the people assembled, they were not allowed to propose a motion, but merely accepted or rejected proposals laid before them by king or senate. In later times, when the people, by omissions or additions to the proposals laid before them, changed and distorted their meaning, the kings Polydorus and Theopompus added these words to the *rhetra,* "But if the people vote for a distorted motion, the senators and kings shall have power to adjourn"—that is, they shall not approve the vote but dismiss and close the assembly on the ground that it was perversely altering their proposals. The same kings persuaded the city that this addition too came from the god, as appears from these verses of Tyrtaeus: [19]

> "They heard the god, and brought from Delphi home
> Apollo's oracle, words to be fulfilled,
> That over all within fair Sparta's realm
> The honored kings in council should bear sway,
> The elders next to them, the people last,
> Accepting straightway all that was decreed."

7. Although Lycurgus had thus modified the nature of the state, yet those who came after him found the oligarchical element still too solid

---

17 Babyca and Cnacion were apparently streams running into the river Eurotas, on which the city of Sparta stood.
18 The wording of the oracle was in an old and, to Plutarch, obscure Greek dialect.
19 Tyrtaeus (7th century B.C.) was a celebrated Spartan poet; only a few fragments of his verses have survived.

and strong, and to curb its swelling and its foaming put, as Plato says, a bit in its mouth, namely, the power of the ephors.[20] About a hundred and thirty years after Lycurgus, the first ephors, Elatus and his colleagues, were elected in the reign of King Theopompus, who, when his queen one day reproached him with leaving to his sons less authority than he had received, answered, "No, greater; for it will last longer." For by reducing their prerogatives, the Spartan kings freed themselves of jealousies and the danger of suffering what the kings of Argos and Messene did, who refused to give up anything or yield a little power to the people.

Indeed, whoever considers the seditions and the misgovernment of the peoples of Messene and Argos, the Spartans' kinsmen and neighbors, will find great reason to admire Lycurgus' wisdom and foresight. The three states started on equal terms; indeed, in the land they obtained, the other two seemed to have the advantage. Yet their prosperity was of short duration, for by the arrogance of their kings and the unruliness of their people their institutions were upset, showing clearly that the man who framed and adjusted the Spartan system had been in truth a divine blessing. But these events came later.

8. Lycurgus' second task, and indeed the boldest he ever undertook, was the redistribution of the land. There was extreme inequality here, the city overburdened with poor and needy people, while all the wealth was concentrated in the hands of a few. To make an end of arrogance and envy, crime and luxury, and of the still older and more serious diseases of poverty and riches, he persuaded the citizens to put all their land together and divide it anew, and live together as equals in means of livelihood, striving to surpass each other only in virtue. Disgrace for evil doing and credit for noble acts would be the one mark of distinction or inequality among them.

Following the word with the deed, he proceeded to divide the land of Laconia into thirty thousand lots, distributed among the country people, and the city of Sparta's land into nine thousand lots, for that was the number of its inhabitants. Some writers say he assigned only six thou-

---

[20] The ephors were five men invested with special powers as guardians of the constitution, whose authority was often superior to that of the kings. They acted particularly as judges and supervisors of education. They were elected annually by the citizens' assembly. Plato, *Laws,* 692 a.

sand lots to the Spartans, and King Polydorus later added three thousand more; others say that Polydorus doubled the number created by Lycurgus, which was only four thousand five hundred. Each lot was sufficient to supply a man with seventy bushels of barley a year, and twelve for his wife, with oil and wine in proportion. This amount Lycurgus thought enough to keep them in health and vigor, and they needed no more. It is said that some time later, on his return from a journey, he was crossing the country just after harvest, and seeing the sheaves of grain standing in equal rows, he smiled and said to his companions, "All Laconia looks like one family estate divided among a number of brothers."

9. Next, he resolved to divide their movable goods, so as to destroy every trace of property distinction and inequality, but when he saw they would resent his taking their possessions away directly, he went about it another way, and met their avarice by a stratagem. First, he called in all the gold and silver currency and ordered the use of iron money only. This he made of such great size and weight and small value, that to lay by ten minae [21] a large storeroom was required, and to move it a yoke of oxen. With the circulation of this money, many kinds of crime were banished from Lacedaemon. For who would steal or take a bribe or grab something he could neither conceal nor possess with any pleasure, or even cut in pieces for use? For the iron had first been heated red hot, we are told, then quenched in vinegar to spoil its temper and usefulness and make it brittle and hard to work.

Thereafter, he ordered a general expulsion of useless and superfluous crafts. Even without his order, most of them would have vanished with the gold and silver, since there was no market for them. For the iron money could not be transported to other parts of Greece and it had no value there, being regarded as ridiculous. So there was now no currency to purchase foreign goods and trinkets, and no cargo came into Laconian ports. No teacher of rhetoric landed there, no wandering fortune teller, no keeper of harlots, no gold or silver smith, since there was no money. Thus luxury, deprived little by little of what fed it, gradually disappeared of itself; and the well-to-do were on the same footing as other people, since their wealth had no opportunity of displaying itself, but must be

---

21 A mina was worth about $20.

kept at home idle. For this reason, common and necessary things, such
as beds, tables, and chairs, were made better there than anywhere; and
the Laconian cup, we are told by Critias, was especially liked by soldiers
in the field. For its color was such that they did not see the dirtiness of
the water they sometimes had to drink, and its curving caught the mud
and held it inside, so that the mouth got a purer drink. For this, too,
they had their lawgiver to thank, because their artisans, being relieved of
making useless things, showed their fine workmanship in necessary
articles.

10.   The third and most admirable of his reforms to put down luxury
and the thirst for riches, was his institution of common meals, so that all
should eat together of the same prescribed bread and meat, and not dine
at home, lying on costly couches at splendid tables, given over to cooks
and servants, to be fattened in the dark like greedy animals, to the ruin
of both mind and body. For bodies, enfeebled by indulgence and over-
eating, require long hours of sleep, warm baths, much rest, and some kind
of attention daily. It was certainly an extraordinary achievement, to take
away from wealth its desirability, as Theophrastus says,[22] and by the
plain, common meals make it no better than poverty. For the rich, who
went to the same table as the poor, could neither use, nor enjoy, nor see,
nor display their abundance. In Sparta only, of all cities under the sun,
could Plutus [23] be seen lying blind and still and lifeless, like a picture.
Men were not even allowed to eat at home first, and then go to the public
tables, for the others watched one who did not eat and drink with them,
and derided him for being dainty and effeminate.

11.   The rich were particularly exasperated by this last ordinance. They
collected in a body to denounce Lycurgus, shouting angry insults. Finally
some threw stones, so that he ran out of the market place to take sanctuary.
Lycurgus outran them all except one energetic and passionate youth
named Alcander, who overtook him and struck him with his stick, as
he looked back, and put out an eye. Lycurgus paid no attention to the
pain, but stopped short and showed his blood-stained face, with the eye

---

[22] Theophrastus (c.372–288 B.C.) was the scientist and philosopher who succeeded
Aristotle as the head of the school of Athens.
[23] Plutus was the blind Greek god of wealth.

out, to his countrymen. They were so dismayed and ashamed at the sight that they turned Alcander over to him, and escorted him home in sympathy and remorse. Lycurgus thanked and dismissed them, and keeping Alcander with him took him into his house. He did not hurt or reproach him, but sent away his previous servants and bade Alcander wait on him. The young man, who was of a generous nature, silently did as he was bid, and living thus day by day with Lycurgus watched his gentleness, his simple way of life, his unruffled temper, and his unwearied labors. Thereby he became Lycurgus' devoted admirer, and told his relatives and friends that he was not the morose, ill-natured person they thought, but the kindest and gentlest of men. This then was Alcander's punishment, to be changed from a fierce and impetuous youth to a wise and well-behaved citizen.

In memory of this injury, Lycurgus built a temple to Athene Optilitis, for the Dorians there call the eye *optilus*. Some writers, however, including Dioscorides, who wrote a treatise on the constitution of Sparta, say that though he was wounded, he did not lose his eye and that he built the temple in gratitude for its healing. At any rate, after this mishap the Spartans gave up their habit of carrying sticks into their assemblies.

12. To return to the public meals, the Cretans called them *andreia*, the Spartans *phiditia*, which may be another form of *philitia*, friends' banquets, because they furnished opportunities for making friends; or the name may come from *phido*, parsimony, because they teach men simplicity and frugality; or perhaps the first letter is an addition, and the word was *editia*, that is, merely, food. They ate in groups of fifteen, more or less, and each member contributed monthly a bushel of barley flour, eight gallons of wine, five pounds of cheese, two and a half pounds of figs, and a small amount of money to buy meat or fish as a relish. And whenever a man offered a sacrifice of first fruits, or had been away hunting, he sent a portion to his table; for if he was kept out late by a sacrifice or on a hunt, he was allowed to eat at home, though the others had to be at the table. The custom of common meals was strictly observed for a long time. When King Agis [24] returned from his victorious campaign against the Athenians and wished to dine at home with his wife, he sent

---

[24] Agis II, king of Sparta from about 426 to 399 B.C., defeated the Athenians in the long-fought Peloponnesian War for supremacy in Greece.

for his common rations, but the polemarchs [25] refused to let him have them. And when the next day, out of resentment, he did not offer the customary sacrifice, they fined him.

Boys were taken to the public tables as schools of good manners and temperance. There they listened to political debates and so were instructed in statecraft. There they learned to talk easily, to joke without vulgarity, and to take jokes without loss of temper. Indeed it was considered a Spartan trait to be able to stand joking, but if a boy could not, he had only to ask and the joker stopped. As each one came in, the eldest present said to him, pointing to the door, "Through that door no tale goes out."

New members, they say, were voted in to a table in the following way. Each man took in his hand a bit of soft bread and threw it like a ballot, without speaking, into a bowl which a servant carried around on his head. Those who voted for the candidate threw their bit in unaltered; those who disliked him, pressed it hard between their fingers. If one such flattened bit was found in the bowl, the man was rejected, so anxious were they that all should be friendly. A rejected candidate was said to be "caddiched," for *caddichus* is their name for the bowl into which they threw the bread.

Their most famous dish was the black broth. The older men did not even ask for a piece of meat, but dined on the broth, leaving the meat for the young. They say that a king of Pontus, wanting some of this broth, bought a Laconian cook, but on tasting it found it unpalatable. Whereat his cook said, "O king, to enjoy this broth you must first bathe in the river Eurotas."

After drinking in moderation, they all went home without a torch. The use of torches on any occasion was forbidden, so that they might accustom themselves to walking fearlessly at night, in the dark. Such was the style of their common meals.[26]

13. Lycurgus did not put his laws into writing. Indeed one of his *rhetras* expressly forbade it. He thought that the most important principles, on which the city's welfare and health depended, if imprinted on the hearts of the citizens by training and habit, would remain more firmly fixed

[25] The polemarchs were military commanders, supposedly under the kings.
[26] The Utopian system of Thomas More resembled the Spartan in some of its most striking features, viz. its discipline, communal meals, disdain for gold and silver, etc.

than by compulsion; and that this education of the young would turn each of them into a lawmaker himself. As for things of less importance, such as business contracts, and other rules that change from time to time, they were better left unprescribed by written laws or rigid custom, but adaptable to circumstances and the judgment of educated men. The whole duty of lawmaking Lycurgus assigned to the educated.

One *rhetra,* as I have said, forbade written laws. Another was directed against ostentation, and ordered that the roof of every house should be hewed out with an ax only, and its doors smoothed by a saw and no other tool. Epaminondas,[27] we hear, said later at his own table, "Treason and a meal like this do not go together," but Lycurgus was the first to realize that luxury and a house like that did not go together. For no man is so foolish and tasteless as to furnish a plain and common house with silver-footed couches, purple coverlets, goblets of gold, and the lavishness that accompanies such things, but he perforce makes his bed to match his house, his coverlet to match his bed, and his other furniture accordingly. The elder Leotychides, it is said, was so used to simplicity that when, at a dinner in Corinth, he saw a costly paneled ceiling, he asked the host if trees grew square in his country.

A third recorded *rhetra* of Lycurgus forbade making war often against the same enemies, lest, by having to defend themselves frequently, they might become good warriors. This was the accusation brought against King Agesilaus [28] long after, that by his frequent raids into Boeotia he had made the Thebans a match for the Spartans. So when Antalcidas saw him wounded, he said, "This is fine payment you are getting from the Thebans for teaching them to fight, when they neither wanted nor knew how to fight before."

Rules like these Lycurgus called *rhetras,* to suggest that they were divine oracles.

14. But in his opinion the most important and noblest task of a law-giver was education, and he began at the very beginning, with strict regu-

---

27 Epaminondas (c.418–362 B.C.) was the most famous statesman as well as general of Thebes.
28 Agesilaus II, king of Sparta from 399 to 366 B.C., and successor to Agis II, fought many wars for Sparta in the period after the Peloponnesian War, but was finally beaten by the Thebans under Epaminondas.

lation of marriages and births. It is not true, as Aristotle says,[29] that he tried to bring the women under control and gave it up, being foiled by the too great liberty and power they had acquired in the frequent absence of their husbands at the wars. Their husbands were indeed obliged to leave them in charge at home, and they treated them with over-much respect, giving them the title of mistress.

But for them too Lycurgus made what regulations were necessary. He had the girls strengthen their muscles by exercise in wrestling, running, hurling quoits and javelins, so that their children might have strong roots in strong bodies, and blossom well, and that they themselves might come with vigor to childbirth, and bravely and easily undergo its pains. To overcome their delicacy and effeminacy, he had the maidens as well as the young men go naked in the processions, and at certain solemn festivals dance and sing so, while the young men stood about and looked on. On these occasions the girls would make jokes mocking any young man whose conduct in war had been poor. Or else they would sing songs in praise of those who had done something gallant, inspiring the youths to keen ambition. For those who had been praised for their valor went away proud and elated, and those who had been lightly mocked felt it as sharply as if they had been formally reprimanded—all the more, because the kings, the senators, and all the citizens were there too.

There was nothing shameful in the nakedness of the girls. The proceedings were marked by modesty, with no trace of sensuality, and taught them simplicity of manners and love of bodily health and beauty. It gave the women also a sense of high-mindedness, as if they, as well as the men, might be brave and ambitious. So they could think and speak as did Gorgo, the wife of Leonidas,[30] who, when some foreign woman remarked to her, "You Spartan women are the only ones who rule your men," replied, "We are the only ones who bear men."

15. These appearances of the girls naked in the processions and their athletic games in the presence of the young men were incentives to marriage, operating on the young, as Plato says [31] with the necessities of love

---

[29] Aristotle, *Politics*, II, 6, 8.
[30] This Leonidas was the hero king of Sparta, who died in 480 B.C., defending the pass of Thermopylae against the Persian hosts.
[31] Plato, *Republic*, 458 d.

if not of geometry. Furthermore, Lycurgus put a penalty on old bachelors, and they were excluded from the sight of young men and maidens exercising. In winter, the magistrates forced them to march naked around the market place, singing a song about themselves, how they were justly punished for disregarding the laws. They were also denied the honor and respect which the young men paid their elders. Thus no one found fault with what was said to Dercyllidas, fine commander as he was, when once at his approach a young man, instead of offering him his seat, simply remarked, "No child of yours will ever get up for me."

The marriage custom was for the husband to carry off his bride by force. She was not a little, immature girl, but a well-grown woman, fully ripe. After she had been taken to his house, the bridesmaid, so called, received her, cut short her hair, dressed her in a man's cloak and sandals, and then left her alone on a mattress in the dark. The bridegroom then came, not flushed with wine but sober and composed, after eating as always at the common table. He slipped into the room, loosed the bride's virgin zone, and passed a short time with her. Then he left her, and went back as usual to spend the night with the young men. This he would continue to do, spending the days with his comrades and sleeping with them at night, visiting his wife stealthily, afraid that someone in the house might hear him. The bride on her part would contrive secret meetings as chance offered. In this manner they would go on for a long time, so that some men even had children before seeing the faces of their wives by daylight. Such meetings not only called for continual exercise of self-control, but brought the two together with their bodies vigorous and their love young and fresh, not blunted by unchecked intercourse; while their partings left in each of them some unextinguished longing and tenderness.

After guarding marriage with this modesty and reserve, Lycurgus banished the vain and womanish passion of jealousy. While avoiding all wantonness, he made it honorable for men to share their wives with others who were worthy in the begetting of children, ridiculing those who thought such things should not be shared, and who would fight and shed blood over it. If, for instance, an old man had a young wife, and if he liked and approved of some fair and upright young man, he might introduce him to her, and adopt her child by this noble father as his own.

Also, if an honorable man admired a married woman on account of her modesty and the beauty of her children, he might persuade her husband to let him plant, so to speak, in this plot of good ground, and produce fine children for himself, with noble blood in their veins.[32] In the first place, Lycurgus did not think that children belonged to their parents as much as to the state; therefore he did not want his citizens born haphazardly but of the best parents there were. Secondly, the laws of other nations on these subjects seemed to him stupid and absurd. They took great care that their dogs and horses should have the best sires that favor or money could buy, yet they kept their wives shut up, to have children only by themselves, even though they might be dull, old, or diseased, and in spite of the fact that worthless children of worthless parents show their bad qualities first to those who rear them, and well-born children show their goodness in the same way.

This freedom in marriage for physical and political reasons was far from being the immorality with which their women were later charged, and adultery was unknown among them. They say that Geradas, an ancient Spartan, when asked by a stranger how they punished adulterers, answered, "Stranger, there are no adulterers in our country." "But," said the stranger, "suppose there were?" "The offender," replied Geradas, "would have to pay with a bull so big that he could stand on Mount Taygetus and drink from the Eurotas river below." Amazed at this, the man said, "How could there be so big a bull?" "But how could there be an adulterer in Sparta?" said Geradas, laughing. Such are the reports of their marriage customs.

16.   A father did not have the right to rear his offspring, but had to carry it to a place called Lesche, where the elders of the tribes sat in judgment upon it. If the child was well-built and strong, they ordered the father to rear it, and assigned it one of the nine thousand plots of land. But if it was puny and ill-shaped, they ordered it taken to the so-called Apothetae, a chasm below Taygetus, thinking it good neither for the child nor for the state that one who had not from the start been well formed for health and vigor should be brought up. So, too, the women used to wash the newborn infants with wine instead of water, to test their strength; for

---

[32] Kings were excused from the obligation to lend their wives.

they said that epileptic and weakly children were poisoned by the wine and fell into convulsions, whereas healthy children were strengthened by it and given firmness of body. The nurses, too, used great care and skill, putting no swaddling bands on the infants, and leaving their limbs and bodies free. They taught them to be contented and easily satisfied as to food, not afraid of the dark or of being left alone, and not disagreeably peevish and fretful. For this reason foreigners sometimes bought Spartan nurses for their children. It is said that Amycla, the nurse of the Athenian, Alcibiades, was a Spartan, although Plato says [33] that Pericles put him in the care of a tutor named Zopyrus, who was no different from other slaves.

Lycurgus would not entrust the sons of Spartans to bought or hired tutors, nor was each man allowed to bring up and educate his son as he chose, but as soon as the boys reached the age of seven, he took and enrolled them in companies, in which they lived and ate and grew used to playing and working together. The boy who showed the most judgment and courage in a fight was made captain of his company, and the rest looked to him for orders, obeyed his commands, accepted his punishments. Thus their whole education was a training in obedience. The older men used to watch their games, and often set them to battling and contending among themselves, so as to find out which was the boldest and most undaunted in their struggles. The boys learned reading and writing, as much as they needed, but the rest of their training was to make them take orders well, endure pain, and be victors in battle. To this end, as they grew older, their discipline was increased. Their heads were close-cropped, they went barefoot, and played, for the most part, naked.

At the age of twelve, they no longer had tunics to wear, and were given one cloak a year. Their bodies were hard and they seldom bathed or anointed themselves with unguents. On only a few days of the year did they enjoy such comforts. They slept together in their troops and companies, on beds made of the rushes that grew by the river Eurotas, which they had to gather and break off with their hands, not being allowed to use knives. In winter they mixed thistledown with the rushes for greater warmth.

---

33 Plato, *Alcibiades,* I, 122 b.

17. When the boys reached this age they had lovers from among the more promising young men to keep them company. The old men, too, kept an eye on them, coming more often to the exercise grounds to hear and see their battles of wit or strength, not casually but with the thought that they all were in a sense the fathers, tutors, and governors of all the boys. Thus every hour and at every place there was always someone present to reprove or punish a boy who did wrong. In addition to this, one of the noblest and best men of the city was appointed superintendent over them, and each company chose as its own chief one of the cleverest and most warlike of the Irens. The Irens were those who had been graduated a year or two from the number of the boys. The oldest of the boys were called Mell-Irens, in other words, those who would soon be Irens.

An Iren, a young man of twenty, was the captain when they fought their battles and they waited on him at meals. He had the bigger boys fetch wood, while the smaller ones gathered salads and herbs. This they did by stealing, creeping cautiously and slyly into gardens and into the men's dining rooms. If one of them was caught in the act, he was thoroughly whipped for being a careless and clumsy thief. They stole whatever food they could and learned to be sharp at catching people asleep or off guard. Their meals were meager, so they were forced to depend on themselves and use all the skill and boldness they could command to cure their hunger. This was the object of their scanty fare. It helped them too to grow tall, for men develop height of frame when the spirit is not held down by too much food and forced to produce thickness and breadth, but rises lightly and the body grows up unchecked and free. The same treatment seems to make beautiful men. We see this, too, in the case of women who take purgatives during pregnancy; they bear slender but well-shaped and comely children, for the lightness of the material makes them more pliable for molding. However, the reason for this I leave for others to determine.

18. So seriously did the boys take their stealing that once, it is said, a youth who had stolen a young fox, and was carrying it hidden under his cloak, allowed the animal to tear out his bowels with its teeth and claws, and died rather than let it be detected. This story becomes credible

when we see what their young men now endure. I myself have seen many of them dying under scourging at the altar of Artemis Orthia.[34]

After dinner the Iren would recline and bid one of the boys sing, and ask another some question which required a thoughtful answer, such as, "Which citizen is the best man?" or "What do you think of this man's behavior?" The boys were thus accustomed early to form judgments and take an interest in politics. And not to be able to distinguish a good citizen from a bad was thought the sign of a dull and indolent mind. Moreover, they had to give sensible reasons and proof for their opinions in brief and concise language. Anyone who answered badly was punished by having his thumb bitten by the Iren. Often, too, the Iren would punish the boys when elders and magistrates were present, that they might see whether or not his punishments were reasonable and just. While punishing them he was never checked, but after the boys had left, he was called to account if he had gone too far in cruelty or in leniency and gentleness.

The lovers of the boys shared in their honor and disgrace. It is said that when once in a fight a boy let fall an unmanly word, his lover was fined by the magistrates. This kind of love was understood among them, and fair and honorable matrons loved young girls. But there was no jealousy in it; instead, those who loved the same boys made it a reason for friendship with each other, and vied with one another in trying to make the boys as accomplished as possible.

19. The boys were taught to use a terse but courteous way of speaking, and to compress much meaning into a few words.[35] For Lycurgus, who, as we have seen, made iron money of great weight and little value, thought contrarywise that speech should be simple and scanty but full of sound sense. So he had the boys trained to be silent much of the time, but able to answer concisely and to the point. Just as loose and incontinent men are seldom the fathers of many children, so chatterers seldom say anything important or memorable. King Agis, when an Athenian laughed

---

[34] Human sacrifices were offered to Artemis Orthia in very early times, as illustrated by the tale of the offering of Iphigenia at Aulis, at the outset of the Trojan War. Lycurgus was supposed to have abolished this custom and substituted the flogging of victims to placate the fierce goddess.

[35] The adjective laconic derives, of course, from these Laconian habits of speech.

at the Spartan short swords and said they could easily be swallowed by jugglers on the stage, retorted, "And yet with these little daggers we can generally reach our enemies." And I notice that though Laconian speech seems curt, it seldom misses the point, and it has great influence on listeners.

Lycurgus himself apparently was brief and sententious in his talk, to judge from what has been preserved of his sayings; as, for instance, his answer to someone who proposed to establish a democracy in the state, "First, establish a democracy in your own household." When another asked him why he had prescribed such small and cheap sacrifices to the gods, he replied, "So that we may never leave off honoring them." And at athletic contests he allowed only those sports in which the citizens did not stretch out their hands.[36] Similar sayings are ascribed to him in letters to his people. When asked how they might best prevent an invasion by their enemies, he said, "By remaining poor, and by not each trying to be a greater man than another." Again, when asked about walls for the city, he replied, "A city is fortified by a wall of men, not by one of bricks." But the authenticity of these and similar letters it is not easy either to accept or to deny.

20. Their dislike of long speeches is illustrated by the following anecdotes. To a man who talked to him on business but at the wrong time, King Leonidas said, "Sir, this is wanted, but this is not when it is wanted." Charilaus, the nephew of Lycurgus, when asked why his uncle had made so few laws, answered, "Men of few words need few laws." When Hecataeus the Sophist,[37] was invited to the public table, and spoke not one word during the meal, Archidamidas said to his critics, "A man who knows how to speak knows also when." Other instances of sharp but witty retorts are the following. Demaratus,[38] when pestered by a troublesome fellow with unsuitable questions, in particular with one as to who was the best man in Sparta, finally answered, "He who is least like your-

---

[36] Stretching out their hands was a gesture made by men begging their vanquishers to spare their lives.

[37] Hecataeus of Abdera was a fourth century Skeptic philosopher and historian, said to have gone with Alexander the Great on his expedition into Asia.

[38] Demaratus was king of Sparta from about 510 to 491 B.C. He was then deposed by his colleague and eventually found refuge in Persia at the court of Darius, the great enemy of Greece. He accompanied Xerxes on his invasion of Greece.

self." And when some people were praising the Eleans for their just and honorable management of the Olympic games, Agis said, "How big a thing it is for Eleans to act fairly one day in five years!" When a foreigner, to whom he had showed friendliness, said to Theopompus that his own countrymen called him a Sparta-lover, Theopompus answered, "Stranger, it would be better for you to be called a lover of your own city." Pleistonax, son of Pausanias,[39] when an Athenian orator reproached the Spartans for their lack of learning, retorted, "True; we are the only Greeks who have not learned some mischief from you." And when someone asked Archidamidas how many Spartans there were, he replied, "Enough, sir, to keep out bad men."

We may see their character even in their jokes; for they are taught never to talk at random or utter a word that does not contain some thought worth hearing. When one of them was invited to hear a man imitate a nightingale, he said, "I have heard the nightingale itself." Another, who read the epitaph,

"They thought to quench a cruel tyranny, but bronze-clad Ares
Slew them. Selinus [40] from her gates beheld their death,"

said, "It served them right; for they should have let the tyranny burn itself out." A young fellow who was promised some gamecocks that would die fighting, said, "No, give me some that kill fighting." Another, seeing people taking their ease on seats, said, "May I never sit where I cannot get up to make way for an elder!" Their remarks were so caustic that it has been said with some justice that philosophy rather than love of exercise is the characteristic of a Laconian.

21. Instruction in music and poetry was no less carefully supervised than the precision and purity of their speech. Their very songs were such as to rouse men's blood and stir them to enthusiastic action. They were plain and unaffected in style, and in subject serious and moral, usually praises of men who had died for Sparta, calling them blessed and glorious, or denunciations of those who had been cowardly, and of their abject and miserable lives. There were also boastings and promises of great deeds,

---

[39] Pausanias was the Spartan general who commanded at the battle of Plataea against the Persians, in 479 B.C.

[40] Selinus was a Greek city in southwest Sicily.

as befitted the various ages. As an example of this last, at festivals they
had three choruses of the three ages, and the chorus of old men would
begin by singing:

> "Once we were young and valiant and strong."

The chorus of young men would answer them:

> "And we are so now; if you wish, come and see."

Then the third chorus, composed of boys, would chime in:

> "But we shall be stronger by far than you are."

Indeed, if one examines the poetry of Sparta, some of which is still
extant in our day, and learns the marches which they played on flutes as
they charged into battle, he will find that Terpander and Pindar [41] were
right when they said that there was a connection between music and
valor. The former wrote of the Spartans:

> "The spear and song in her do meet,
> And Justice walks about her street."

And Pindar says:

> "Councils of wise elders here,
> And the young man's conquering spear,
> And dance, and song, and joy appear."

They thus represent the Spartans as both extremely musical and extremely
warlike. In the words of one of their own poets:

> "With the iron stern and sharp,
> Comes sweet playing on the harp."

For before their battles, the king would first sacrifice to the Muses, to remind his men, it would appear, of their training and of the judgments
that would be passed on them, so that they would be bold in danger and
perform martial deeds worthy of record.

---

[41] Terpander (7th century B.C.), was a celebrated poet and musician from Lesbos, who
settled in Sparta. Pindar (c.522–443 B.C.), a Theban, was the greatest of all Greek
lyric poets.

22. In time of war they relaxed somewhat the severity of the young men's regimen, allowing them to beautify their hair and wear handsome arms and clothing; they took pride in them as if they were high-spirited horses, whinnying for the race. So as soon as they were out of boyhood, they let their hair grow long, and especially in times of danger kept it shining and well-combed, remembering a saying of Lycurgus that a fine head of hair made a good-looking man more handsome and an ugly one more ferocious. Their exercises too were less severe on campaigns, and in other ways their life was less strenuous and strict, so that they were the only people in the world to whom war brought relief from training for war. When the army was drawn up in battle array and the enemy near, the king sacrificed a she-goat, commanded the soldiers all to put garlands on their heads, and the pipers to play the hymn to Castor,[42] and then he himself began the paean of advance. It was a magnificent and terrible sight to see them marching to the tune of the flutes, with no gap in their lines and no terror in their souls, but calmly and gaily led by music into the perilous fight. Such men were not likely to be either panic-stricken or over-reckless, but steady and assured, as if the gods were with them.

Close to the king marched some man who had been crowned victor in the Olympic games. A Spartan, it is said, was once offered a large bribe at Olympia, but refused it and by a great effort threw his adversary in the wrestling match. When someone said to him, "What more, Spartan, have you won by your victory?" he smiling, answered, "I shall have the place in front of the king when we fight our enemies." After defeating and routing an enemy, they pursued him in his flight far enough to confirm their victory, but then promptly withdrew, thinking it base and unworthy of Greeks to cut down and slaughter men who could fight no longer. This was not only a noble and magnanimous custom, but practically useful, for since their enemies knew that they killed only those who resisted them and gave quarter to the rest, they often thought it better to flee than to stand their ground.

23. Hippias the Sophist says that Lycurgus himself was a great soldier and engaged in many campaigns. Philostephanus attributes to him the

---

[42] The twins Castor and Pollux were legendary heroes, brothers of Helen of Troy, who received divine honors at Sparta and at Rome. The hymn was a marching song celebrating their exploits.

division of the cavalry into troops of fifty drawn up in a square. But Demetrius the Phalerian says he took no part in matters of war and set up his constitution in a time of peace. Indeed, the idea of the Olympic truce makes me think he was a man of gentle and peaceful temperament. However, Hermippus reminds us that some say that at first Lycurgus had nothing to do with Iphitus and his company, but that he chanced once to come by Olympia and was watching the games, when he heard what seemed a man's voice behind him, reproving him and asking why he did not urge his fellow citizens to take part in the great festival. On turning around he saw no speaker anywhere, and was sure a god had spoken; he hastened to Iphitus and assisted him in regulating the festival so as to make it more glorious and more firmly established.

24. The training of the Spartan youth continued up into manhood. No one was permitted to live as he chose, but all lived in the city as in a soldiers' camp. They had a fixed schedule and fixed public duties, and thought of themselves as belonging to their country and not to themselves. When they had no other assignment, they looked after the boys and taught them useful things, or else learned something themselves from the old. Indeed one of the greatest blessings procured by Lycurgus for his fellow citizens was ample leisure, since he forbade them to practice any mechanical art. And as for business and the toil of money-making, they were unnecessary, because wealth aroused no envy and was despised. The helots tilled the ground for them and paid them the produce already mentioned. Hence when a Spartan, once visiting in Athens while the courts were in session, heard that a man had been fined for idleness and was going home much depressed, accompanied by condoling friends, he asked the bystanders to show him the man who had been punished for acting like a freeman. So servile a thing did they regard all labor in crafts and money making.

With the disappearance of gold and silver money, lawsuits also disappeared, for there was no more avarice or poverty but all were equally well off. And life was easy, for their habits were simple. Their entire time was spent in dancing, feasting, hunting, gymnastic exercises, and conversation, when they were not at war.

25. Those under thirty never went to the market place, making their necessary purchases through kinsfolk and friends. And it was thought

discreditable to the older men to be seen lingering there long and not to be spending the greater part of the day at the exercise grounds or the places of conversation, where they passed their time rationally, talking not of money-making or of trade but praising some honorable action or censuring something degrading, with jokes and laughter which made their instruction and correction easy to bear. For Lycurgus himself was not unduly austere. It was he, says Sosibius, who dedicated a little statue to Laughter and introduced seasonable mirth at supper, to sweeten, as it were, their hard way of life.

In short, he trained the citizens to have neither the desire nor the capacity to live by themselves, but like bees to make themselves always one with the community, clustering around their leader, forgetting themselves in their enthusiasm and ambition and devotion to their city. One can see this too in some of their sayings. Paedaratus, when not elected to the top three hundred, went away quite radiant, as if rejoicing that the city had three hundred better men than he. And Polycratidas, who went with an embassy to the generals of the king of Persia, when asked if they came on a private or a public mission, said, "Public if we succeed, private if we fail." When some citizens of Amphipolis came to Sparta, and called on Argileonis, the mother of Brasidas,[43] she asked them if her son had died bravely as became a Spartan. They praised him highly, declaring that Sparta had no one else so brave as he. "Say not so, strangers," she replied, "Brasidas was a brave and gallant man, but Sparta has many better than he."

26. The senate was at first appointed, as I have said, by Lycurgus, from those who participated in his scheme, but later he ordained that when a senator died his place should be filled by the citizen elected as the very best of those past sixty years of age. Of all the contests in the world this seemed the greatest, and the rivalry the keenest. For it was not the swiftest among the swift or the strongest among the strong, but the wisest and best among the wise and good who, as a reward of merit, was to be chosen and entrusted for the rest of his life with supreme authority in the state, with power for death and dishonor and all great decisions. The method of election was as follows. The citizens were all assembled, and certain

---

[43] Brasidas, a distinguished Spartan general, was killed in 422 B.C. at Amphipolis in Macedonia, during the Peloponnesian War.

selected men were shut up in a building close by, where they could neither see nor be seen, but could merely hear the shouts of the assembly. For, as in other cases, the people's voice decided between the candidates. These did not appear as a body, but each one came forward and silently walked through the assembly as his name was drawn. The men in the building had writing materials and wrote down in each instance the amount of the cheering, not knowing who was cheered but only that he came first, second, or third, and so on. They then announced who had received the most and loudest cheers, and he was declared elected. A garland was placed on his head and he went around to the temples of the gods, followed by a crowd of young men hailing and celebrating him, and by many of the women, who sang verses in his honor, extolling his life. Each of his relations and friends set a banquet before him, saying, "The city honors you with this table." But on finishing his round, he went to the common table where he was served as before, except that he was given two portions, the second of which he put by. After supper, his women relatives came to the door of the dining hall, and he beckoned to the one he wished to honor and gave her the portion, saying he had received it as a prize and gave it to her as such. Whereupon she, too, was hailed by the other women and escorted home.

27. As to burials, Lycurgus made very wise regulations. First of all, he abolished superstitious terrors by persuading them to bury their dead within the city, and place their tombs near the temples, thus accustoming the young to such sights, so that they might not be upset by them or feel a horror of death as if it defiled one to touch a corpse or to walk among graves. Next, he ordered them to bury nothing with the body, but to wrap it in a purple cloth with olive leaves when they laid it out. They could not inscribe the name of the dead upon his tomb, except when a man had fallen in battle, or a woman had died as a priestess. A short period of eleven days was fixed for mourning. On the twelfth, they were to sacrifice to Demeter [44] and cease grieving.

Thus nothing was left neglected, and with every necessary act of life something was mingled to encourage virtue and discourage vice. He filled the city with examples of good conduct, by which the citizens were im-

---

[44] Demeter was the earth goddess and protectress of vegetation, whose daughter Persephone spent half of every year beneath the earth, in dark Hades.

pelled towards paths of honor. For this reason he forbade them to live and travel abroad, where they might acquire strange habits and imitate the lives of untrained people with different kinds of government. He even expelled the foreigners who came in throngs to the city on no useful errand, not, as Thucydides says,[45] because he feared they would copy his form of government and learn something for their own improvement, but in order that they might not become teachers of evil in Sparta. With strange men strange doctrines must enter; new doctrines lead to new opinions, and from them come thoughts and feelings out of harmony with the established order. Hence he thought it more important to keep out bad customs than to keep out plagues from the city.

28. In all this there is no trace of the injustice or harshness which some people ascribe to the laws of Lycurgus, calling them effective in making good soldiers but a failure in making good men. The so-called Secret Service of Sparta, if it was one of Lycurgus' institutions, as Aristotle says it was, may indeed have given Plato that impression of the man and his constitution.[46] In this service the magistrates now and again sent some of the ablest young men out through the country, equipped only with daggers and the necessary food. By day they lay quietly hidden and dispersed in remote places, but at night they came down into the highways and killed all the helots they found. Often, too, they ranged the fields and killed the stoutest and best of the helots as they worked. Once also, as Thucydides tells us in his history of the Peloponnesian War,[47] more than two thousand helots who had been singled out by the Spartans for their valor, were crowned with garlands and conducted, like men set free, to all the temples, but soon afterward they all disappeared; and no man, either then or later, could give an account of how they died. Aristotle, in particular, adds that the ephors, when first they took office, declared war on the helots, so as to make it right to kill them.

In other ways, too, the helots were harshly and cruelly treated. They were sometimes forced to drink too much strong wine and then brought into the public dining halls to show the young what drunkenness was. They were ordered to sing songs and dance dances that were low and

---

[45] Thucydides, *History of the Peloponnesian War,* II, vi, 39.

[46] Plato, *Laws,* 630 d.

[47] *History of the Peloponnesian War,* IV, xii, 80.

absurd, and forbidden the nobler kinds. Accordingly, when later the Thebans invaded Laconia [48] and captured a number of helots, they could not make them sing the songs of Terpander, Alcman, or Spendon, the Spartan, for, they said, their masters did not allow it. So the saying seems to have been true that "In Sparta the free are more free and the slaves more slaves than anywhere." For my part, however, I believe that it was later that these cruelties were practiced, especially after the great earthquake,[49] when the helots rose up and joined the Messenians in laying the country waste, and gravely imperiled the city. I cannot myself ascribe to Lycurgus such a brutal institution as the Secret Service, when I remember the humaneness and justice of his character, as shown in other ways. To this the oracle, too, bore witness.

29. When the foremost of his institutions had been firmly planted in the lives of the people and his system had developed so that it could support and defend itself, then, as Plato says of God [50] that he rejoiced to see his universe beginning to live and move, so Lycurgus felt joy and satisfaction at the beauty and grandeur of his legislation, now at work and proceeding on its course. He longed, insofar as human foresight could do it, to make his structure immortal and send it down unchanged to posterity. So assembling all the citizens he told them that the city was now well organized and sufficiently equipped with means for happiness and virtue, but that the most important and valuable gift of all he would not bestow on them until he had consulted the oracle. They must therefore keep to the laws he had established with no alteration until his return from Delphi; after that, he would do what the god commanded. They all agreed to this and bade him hasten on his journey. He then made the kings and the elders, and after them the rest of the citizens, swear that they would abide by his constitution until his return, and then set out for Delphi. On reaching the oracle, he sacrificed to the god and asked whether the laws he had set up were good and adequate for a city's welfare and virtue. The god replied that his laws were good, and that the city would continue to be illustrious as long as it was faithful to his system. He wrote the oracle down and sent it to Sparta, then sacrificed again to

---

[48] The invasion took place under Epaminondas, in 369 B.C.
[49] The "great earthquake" occurred in 464 B.C.
[50] Plato, *Timaeus*, 37 c.

the god and bade affectionate farewell to his friends and his son, resolved never to release the Spartans from their oath and to end his life by his own act.

He was at an age when either to live or to die is not difficult and when his friends seemed on their way to a comfortable prosperity. He therefore made an end of himself by refusing to take food, thinking that a statesman should serve his country even in his death, which should be not fruitless but productive of some good effect. For himself, who had accomplished tremendous tasks, death would come as the consummation of good fortune, and for his people it would ensure the continuance of the excellent things he had done for them in his lifetime, since they had sworn to maintain his constitution until his return. Nor was he deceived in his expectations; his city remained the first city of Greece for wise laws and lofty reputation for five hundred years, and it obeyed the ordinances of Lycurgus. None of the fourteen kings who followed him, down to Agis, son of Archidamas, made any change in them. For the institution of ephors, though they thought it would favor the people, really strengthened the aristocracy.

30. But in the reign of Agis [51] gold and silver money first flowed into Sparta, and with it came selfishness and a greed for wealth. Lysander promoted the change, for though incorruptible himself, he brought gold and silver home from the wars, and filled the country with love of riches and luxury, thus disregarding the laws of Lycurgus. While they were enforced, Sparta lived like a wise and disciplined man, rather than like a city under a government. As the poets tell of Heracles, who went over the world with his lion's skin and club, punishing lawless and cruel tyrants, so we may tell of the Spartans, that with only the common staff and coarse coat of her rulers, they had won the willing obedience of all Greece, unseating ruthless oligarchies and kings, arbitrating wars, and suppressing revolts. And this often without taking down a single shield, but by merely sending a commissioner to whom all at once submitted, as bees, when their queen appears, swarm in order around her. Such an abundance of good law and justice there was in that city.

---

[51] This is the Agis II whom Plutarch mentioned earlier. Lysander was the Spartan commander who won the last victories over Athens and destroyed the city's walls at the end of the Peloponnesian War. He was killed in 395. See below, *Alcibiades*, ch. 34.

I cannot therefore understand those who say that the Lacedaemonians knew how to obey but not how to command, and who cite the saying attributed to King Theopompus. When someone remarked to him that Sparta was safe because her kings knew how to rule, he answered, "No, rather because her citizens know how to obey." But people do not obey rulers who do not know how to command. Obedience is a lesson taught by the ruler, and a good leader makes good followers. Just as it is the aim of a horse-trainer to make a horse gentle and tractable, so it is the task of a royal statesman to teach men to obey him. And the Spartans inspired in other people not only a willingness but a desire to be ruled and led by them. Other Greeks sent to ask them not for ships or money or troops, but for one Spartan commander. And when they got him, they respected and revered him, as the Sicilians revered Gylippus, the Chalcidians Brasidas, and all the Greeks in Asia, Lysander, Callicratidas, and Agesilaus. Everywhere these men were called Regulators, Censors of Peoples and Governors, and the city of Sparta was regarded as a school of orderly life and wise institutions. To this fact Stratonicus seems to have alluded when he jestingly proposed a rule that the Athenians should have charge of mysteries and processions, the Eleans should manage games, since they did that best, but the Spartans should be thrashed if the others did poorly. It was said as a joke, but Antisthenes the Socratic was quite serious when he said of the Thebans, whom he saw so puffed up after the battle of Leuctra,[52] that they were like little boys strutting around because they had beaten their teacher.

31. It was not, however, Lycurgus' chief aim to leave his city ruling over many others. He thought that the happiness of a city as of an individual depended on virtue and harmony within itself. All his efforts and provisions, therefore, were directed towards making the people free-spirited and independent, and keeping them so for a long time. And all those who are praised for their writings on politics, such as Plato, Diogenes, and Zeno, have made use of Lycurgus' design for a state. They left behind them only written words, whereas Lycurgus left no written words but a government which no one could copy. To those who deny

---

[52] At the battle of Leuctra in 371 B.C., the Spartan supremacy in Greece, which the city had held since her defeat of Athens in the Peloponnesian War, was broken by the Theban victory under Epaminondas.

the existence of a so-called natural disposition towards wisdom, he displayed the spectacle of a whole city devoted to wisdom. Thus his fame has risen high above all other Greek lawgivers. Accordingly, Aristotle says, the Spartans did him less honor than he deserved, although they honored him highly and he has a temple there and they offer him yearly sacrifices as a god.

It is said that his remains were carried home, and that his tomb was struck by lightning. Such a thing has happened to no other eminent person since, except Euripides, who at his death was buried at Arethusa in Macedonia. Euripides' admirers consider it a proof of his greatness that what happened to this most holy man and favorite of the gods happened later to him. Some say that Lycurgus died at Cirrha. Apollothemis thinks he was brought to Elis and died there, Timaeus and Aristoxenus that he ended his days in Crete. Aristoxenus adds that the Cretans show you his tomb in the district of Pergamus, near the public road. He is said to have left an only son, Antiorus, who died childless, and so the family became extinct. His friends and relatives, however, started an annual commemoration of him, which went on for a long time. The days when they met were called the Lycurgidae. Aristocrates, son of Hipparchus, says that Lycurgus died in Crete, and that his friends there burned his body and scattered the ashes on the sea, as he had requested, fearing lest his remains might some day be carried back to Sparta, and the people, on the ground that he had come back and they were absolved from their oath, might change his constitution.[53] This is the tale of Lycurgus.

---

[53] Plutarch gives an account of the slackness and corruption which invaded Sparta when she abandoned the stern rules of Lycurgus and became rich and mighty in the third century B.C., in his *Life of Agis IV*, not included in this selection.

Numa Pompilius

7 1 5 – 6 7 2 B.C. ?

1. THERE is great diversity of opinion as to the time of Numa's reign, although from the beginning down to him the genealogies seem to be traced accurately. A certain Clodius, in a book on the verification of chronology, states that the ancient records disappeared in the sack of the city by the Gauls,[1] and that the records now shown as ancient are forgeries, composed to flatter certain persons by introducing their names into the first families and most distinguished houses, to which they do not belong. Some have said that Numa was a close friend of Pythagoras; this statement is emphatically contradicted by others who say that he had no trace of Greek culture, but was a person of great natural capacity for learning; or else that he had been taught by a barbarian[2] better than Pythagoras. Others assert that the philosopher Pythagoras came later, some five generations after Numa, but that another Pythagoras, a Spartan, who won the Olympic footrace in the sixteenth Olympiad,[3] in the third year of which Numa became king, on his travels through Italy met Numa and helped him frame his government. For this reason, they say, many Spartan customs were mixed with Roman, under Pythagoras' instruction. In any case, Numa was a Sabine by birth,[4] and the Sabines believe

---

[1] Rome was destroyed by invading Gauls in 390 B.C. and on their departure was hastily rebuilt.

[2] The Greeks habitually called all other nations barbarians.

[3] 390 B.C.

[4] The Sabines were one of the ancient peoples of central Italy. They had a settlement on the Palatine Hill and were the first to be accepted by the Romans as partners and fellow citizens in their new city.

themselves to be a Lacedaemonian colony. But chronologies are hard to settle, especially when based on lists of winners in the Olympic games, the table of which is said to have been made out much later by Hippias of Elis, on no trustworthy authority. Beginning, however, at a convenient point, I shall relate the noteworthy events of Numa's life.

2. Rome had been founded and Romulus [5] had reigned for thirty-seven years, when on the fifth day of July, called now the Capratine Nones,[6] he was offering a public sacrifice outside the city at the so-called Goat's Marsh, in the presence of the senate and most of the people. Suddenly the sky was darkened and a cloud swept down to earth in a storm of wind and rain. The people fled fearfully in all directions, and Romulus disappeared, never to be seen again alive or dead. Suspicion fell on the patricians, and a story went around among the people that they resented the kingship and were determined to get the power into their own hands, and so had made away with him. For some time, apparently, he had been harsher and more autocratic with them. The patricians, anxious to remove this suspicion, decreed divine honors to Romulus, as to one not dead but translated to a higher sphere. And Proculus, a man of excellent reputation, swore that he had seen Romulus caught up to heaven in his armor, and had heard his voice bidding them thenceforth call him Quirinus.[7]

The city was involved in much disturbance and friction over the election of a new king, for the new citizens were not yet completely merged with the old, the people were split by factions, and the patricians suspected each other because of the differences between them. They all agreed that they wanted a king, but they wrangled over both who it should be and from which race he should come. Those who had first helped Romulus build the city thought it monstrous that the Sabines, who had already

---

[5] The life of Romulus, legendary founder and first king of Rome, precedes this life of Numa in the complete text of Plutarch's *Lives*. The reputed date of the founding of the city was 753 B.C.

[6] *Capra*, in Latin, is goat. *Nones*, in the Roman calendar, was the name given to the fifth day of every month in the year except March, May, July, and October, when the *Nones* were the seventh day. Plutarch seems to have made a slip in setting the *Nones* of July on the fifth.

[7] Quirinus was a Sabine word, derived from Quiris, or Cures, the name of a Sabine town. See below, ch. 3.

received a share in the city and the lands, should propose to rule over them. And the Sabines maintained with reason that, since on the death of their king Tatius they had submitted peaceably to the single rule of Romulus, it was now their turn to have a ruler of their race. They had not, they felt, been adopted as inferiors by a more powerful race, but their coming had both increased the Romans' numbers and contributed to the city's renown, to the benefit of the Romans as well as of themselves.

The patricians then, fearing that discord and confusion would reign in the absence of all command, arranged that one of them should in turn wear the emblems of royalty, perform the usual sacrifices to the gods, and transact public business for six hours by day and six by night. This division of time was to preserve equality among the patricians, and the shifting of power was to dispel the jealousy of the people, when they saw the same man in the space of one day and night raised to the kingship and brought down again to plain citizen. This form of government the Romans call an interregnum.

3. But even by this statesmanlike and moderate way of ruling, the patricians could not escape suspicion and loud charges that to keep the power in their own hands they had changed the form of government to an oligarchy and were refusing to be ruled by a king. At length, the two races agreed that one should choose a king out of the ranks of the other. This, they thought, would put an end to their rivalry for the time being, and also ensure the king's impartiality. He would be friendly to one race as his electors and to the other as his kinsmen. The Sabines first gave the Romans their choice, and the Romans preferred a Sabine king selected by themselves to a Roman chosen by the Sabines. After some consultation they named Numa Pompilius, a Sabine who had not moved his home to Rome, but who was so widely known for his virtue that the Sabines, as soon as they heard his name, acclaimed him as eagerly as the Romans. The choice was then announced to the people, and the leading men of both races were sent as ambassadors to Numa to request him to come and assume the throne.

Numa was a resident of a famous Sabine city, Cures, whence the Romans and the Sabines who had joined them called themselves together Quirites. He was son of an eminent citizen, Pompon, and the youngest of four brothers. By a miraculous coincidence, he was born on the very day, April 21, when Romulus founded Rome. His naturally excellent disposition he had trained by discipline, endurance of hardship, and study of philosophy, and thus had overcome the baser passions of his soul, and also the violence and greediness so common among barbarians. True courage, he thought, consisted in the conquest of one's passions by reason. Accordingly, he had banished all luxury and extravagance from his house; citizens and strangers alike found him an incorruptible counselor and judge. His leisure he devoted not to pleasure or money-making, but to the service of the gods and to rational reflections on their power and nature. Thus he had gained such celebrity that Tatius, the kingly colleague of Romulus at Rome, had chosen him for the husband of his only daughter, Tatia. Numa was not so puffed up by this marriage as to go to live at Rome with his father-in-law, but stayed with the Sabines, caring for his own aged father. Tatia, too, preferred the quiet life of her husband as a private citizen to the honor and pomp she might have had at Rome with her father. She is said to have died in the thirteenth year of her marriage.

4. Numa then left the bustle of the town and passed his time mostly in the country, wandering there alone in the groves of the gods, their sacred meadows and desert places. These habits gave rise to the story of the goddess. Numa, it was said, had forsaken the life of men, not out of melancholy or any disorder of mind, but because he had tasted the joys of a holier companionship and been honored by a heavenly marriage through the love of the nymph Egeria,[8] who dwelt with him and blessed him with divine wisdom. The story is similar to many an ancient fable, such as those the Phrygians liked to tell of Attis, the Bithynians of Herodotus, the Arcadians of Endymion,[9] and other peoples of other mortals thought to have been beloved of the gods. Nor is it unreasonable to imagine that a god, who is not a lover of birds or horses but a lover of man, may take pleasure in the company of men of extraordinary virtue and not despise one who is wise and holy.

---

[8] Egeria, in Roman mythology, was a wood nymph whose home was near a spring that flowed into Lake Nemi, in the heart of the beautiful Alban Hills. See Fraser's *Golden Bough,* one-volume edition, Ch. I.

[9] Attis was a handsome youth, beloved and mourned by the Phrygian goddess Cybele. The Greek Endymion was watched and kissed in his sleep by the Moon. The Bithynian tale of Herodotus must have been something similar.

It is hard, however, to believe that a divine spirit can find enjoyment in intercourse with a young human body. The Egyptians maintain with some show of plausibility that a woman may possibly be made pregnant by the spirit of a god but that a man can have no carnal union with a deity. Yet they ignore the fact that both parties in intercourse have an equal share. But it is right and fitting that the gods should feel kindliness towards men, and thence a love which takes the form of solicitude for their character and virtue. There is some truth in the myths of the poets who tell how Phorbas, Hyacinthus, and Admetus [10] were beloved by Apollo, as was Hippolytus the Sicyonian. Of him they said that every time he set sail from Sicyon to Cirrha [11] the Pythian priestess chanted the verse,

"Now doth our Hippolytus return again,"

as though the god saw him coming and was glad.

There is a legend too that Pan loved Pindar for his verses. And divinity paid honor to Hesiod and Archilochus [12] for the Muses' sake after their death. It is said also that Aesculapius [13] was a friend of Sophocles during his lifetime, and that on his death another god saw to his funeral rites. And if we accept these instances, why should we find it incredible that a spirit from heaven visited Zaleucus, Minos, Zoroaster, Lycurgus, and Numa,[14] pilots of kingdoms and organizers of states? Is it not, indeed, likely that the gods hold earnest converse with men such as these, to counsel and advise them on the highest matters, and visit poets and lyric singers for pleasure, if at all? Yet if anyone has a different idea, as Bacchylides said,

---

10 Phorbas, Hyacinthus, and Admetus were all successful young heroes or kings who excited the admiration and jealousy of Apollo. The first two were slain by him. Admetus would have died if his life had not been saved by the sacrifice of his wife, Alcestis.

11 That is, from Sicyon, in the southeast corner of the Gulf of Corinth, northwest across it to a landing-place at Cirrha, near Delphi.

12 Archilochus (c. 700 B.C.) was renowned as the first great satiric poet of Greece. The Delphic oracle proclaimed a curse on the man who "slew a servant of the Muses." The same oracle told the countrymen of the still more famous poet, Hesiod (c.735 B.C.), to bring his bones home for burial, if they hoped to be delivered from a pestilence.

13 Aesculapius was the Greek god of healing. Sophocles (c.496–406 B.C.) was one of the great Attic tragedians.

14 Zaleucus was the traditional lawgiver of some Greeks from Locris who settled in Italy around the seventh century B.C. Minos of Crete and Zoroaster of Persia had wide fame as founders of the legal systems of their respective countries.

"The road is broad." [15] Another not impossible view is that Lycurgus and Numa and men like them, who had to deal with obstinate and unruly people and were instituting great political changes, pretended they had divine sanction, as a way of ensuring security for the people for whom they were planning.

5. Numa was forty years of age when the ambassadors came from Rome to ask him to be their king. Their spokesmen were Proculus and Velesus. One of them the people at first had thought would be elected their second king, for the race of Romulus favored Proculus and that of Tatius, Velesus. These men spoke to Numa briefly, imagining that he would be delighted at his good fortune. It was, however, no easy task but one calling for much hard pleading to induce the man who had spent his life in peace and quiet to assume command of a city which owed its origin and its growth to war. In the presence of his father and of his kinsman Marcius, he said:

"Every change in a man's life is dangerous; and when a man needs nothing, and is content with his present lot, it is sheer madness for him to alter his habits and familiar way of living, which, whatever it may lack, has the advantage of security, and is therefore better than the unknown. And the troubles to be faced as your king are not unknown to one who watched Romulus' experience, who first fell under suspicion of having plotted against his colleague Tatius, and then got the patricians suspected of wickedly assassinating him. Yet they celebrate Romulus as a son of the gods and say he was cared for and wonderfully preserved as an infant by the gods.

"My birth was mortal and I was reared and taught by men well known to you. The very traits of my character which you praise are not those which should mark a man about to be king, my great love of retirement and impractical studies, my deep devotion to peace and unwarlike occupations, and to men who meet together solely to honor the gods and enjoy friendly conversation, whose lives are otherwise spent in private, feeding their cattle and plowing their fields. But to you, O Romans, Romulus has left many, even unwanted wars, and to lead them the citizens need a king of experience and valor. They have become used to war and like it

---

[15] Bacchylides was a Greek lyric poet of the fifth century, an unsuccessful rival of the greater poet Pindar. The quotation is found in the so-called Fragment 29 of his work

because of their success in it, and everyone knows their desire for expansion and conquest. I should be a laughing stock trying to serve the
gods and teach men to honor justice and hate violence and war, when
what the city demands is a general rather than a king."

6. With these words Numa refused the kingdom. But the Romans became more insistent with him, using every kind of persuasion, begging
him not to plunge them back into civil war and discord, since there was
no other person on whom both parties could agree. His father too and
Marcius, when the others had gone, argued with him to accept so great
a gift of the gods. "If," they said, "you do not want more wealth, having
enough already, nor care for the glory of rulership and power, because
you have the better glory of virtue, yet remember that kingly government
is in itself a service to God, who now calls the strength and uprightness
in you into action, and will not allow them to lie idle and unemployed. So
do not shrink, and refuse this office, which offers to a wise man a field
for great and splendid action, for magnificent worship of the gods, and
for softening a people to reverence, as a ruler can do more easily than anyone else.

"Tatius, though a foreigner, was beloved, and the memory of Romulus
is given divine honors. Who knows but that this people, though victorious, may be satiated with war, and may content themselves now with
their spoils and trophies, and welcome a gentle and just leader, who will
bring them order and peace? And if, on the contrary, they are untamable
and madly bent on war, would it not be better for you to hold the reins
and turn their aggressiveness in new directions? In that way, at least,
your native town and the whole Sabine people would have in you a bond
of good will and friendship with this energetic and powerful city." On top
of these arguments, they say, the omens were favorable, and Numa's own
fellow citizens, when they heard of the embassy, came and ardently besought him to take the kingship and so unite and bring concord to the
two nations.

7. At length Numa, yielding to these inducements, sacrificed to the gods
and set out for Rome. The senate and the people met him on the way,
impatient to welcome him. The women also greeted him with happy
cries; there were sacrifices in the temples, and everyone was as joyous as
if the city were receiving not a king but a kingdom. When they reached

the forum,[16] Spurius Vettius, whose turn it was to be temporary king at that hour, took the vote of the citizens and all voted for Numa. But when they brought him the insignia of royalty, he bade them wait until his authority had been confirmed by God. So taking with him the priests and the augurs, he ascended the Capitol, which the Romans called the Tarpeian Hill. Here the chief augur covered Numa's head, turned his face towards the south, and, standing behind him, laid his right hand on his head and prayed, looking to all quarters of the heavens to see what birds or omens might appear from the gods. A marvelous silence fell on the multitude in the forum, as they eagerly watched and waited until finally auspicious birds appeared and passed on the right. Then Numa put on the royal robes and came down the hill to the people, by whom he was received with welcoming cheers as the most holy of men and most beloved by the gods.

His first act was to disband Romulus' bodyguard of three hundred men, called *Celeres,* that is, Fast Ones, whom he had always kept close to him. Numa said he would not distrust those who were trusting him, nor reign over a people who distrusted him. Next, he added to the existing priests of Jupiter and Mars a third priest, and called him *Flamen Quirinalis.* The Romans called their elder priests *flamines,* from the skull-caps they wore, called *piloi,* or by a longer name, *pilaminae.*[17] For there were more Greek words mixed with Latin then than now. Thus too the name *laena,* which they gave to the priestly robes, Juba says is the same as the Greek *chlaina;* and the name *camillus,* given to a boy who serves the priest of Jupiter—both of whose parents must be alive—some Greeks give to Hermes, because he acts as a servant.

8. When Numa, by such measures, had won the good will and affection of the people, he set himself without more delay to softening the city, as iron is softened by fire, and converting it from its rough and warlike ways to more gentleness and justice. Certainly Rome at that time

---

[16] The famous Forum Romanum lay in a valley between the Capitoline and the Palatine Hills. Once a marsh, the land, according to legend, was filled in and leveled during the rule of Romulus and Tatius. At first intended simply as a market and meeting-ground for Romans from one hill and Sabines from the other, it became later the stately place for public assemblies and the conduct of judicial and other important business.

[17] These are very dubious derivations from the Greek.

was in what Plato calls a "feverish" state.[18] It owed its existence to the amazing daring of utterly reckless and warlike men, who had made their way there from everywhere. By perpetual wars and campaigns it had supported itself and extended its power. It seemed to gain strength from its perils, like a thing set in the ground which stands firmer for being shaken. Numa knew it was no slight undertaking to bend so stubborn a people and direct them towards peace, and he looked to the gods for help. Mainly by sacrifices and processions and religious dances, which he himself organized and led, and which combined solemnity with charming activities and profitable pleasures, he interested the people and tamed their restive, pugnacious spirit. At times, also, he spoke to them of omens from God, strange apparitions of divinities and warning voices, in order to sway and humble them through superstitious fear.

From these measures in particular grew the story that he had learned wisdom and methods from Pythagoras, for in the philosophy of one and in the state policy of the other, religious ritual and services played a large part. His outward dignity and stateliness, it was also said, he derived from Pythagoras. The latter, we hear, tamed an eagle to come down at his call from its lofty height, and when he walked through the crowd at Olympia, he displayed his golden thigh. They tell too of other wonderful devices and acts of his, of which Timon of Phlius wrote:[19]

> "Pythagoras drops to a juggler's tricks,
> Lays traps for men with his solemn talk."

Similarly, Numa had his tale of a goddess or nymph who was in love with him and whom he met in secret, as we mentioned earlier, and of hours which he spent with the Muses, to whose teachings he ascribed most of his oracular utterances. He taught special veneration for a Muse called Tacita, the Silent One, in commemoration perhaps of the Pythagorean law of silence. His rules on images were also in conformity with the doctrine of Pythagoras, who taught that the First Principle cannot be perceived or touched, but is invisible and uncreated and known only by the mind. So Numa forbade the Romans to worship an image of God shaped like a man or a beast. There was then no painted or carved image

---

[18] Plato, *Laws*, III, 691 e.
[19] Timon of Phlius (third century B.C.) was a skeptic who wrote verses ridiculing all other schools of philosophy.

of God, although for the first hundred and seventy years they were building temples and setting up shrines. But they made no statues for them, believing it an impiety to liken higher things to lower, and that God could not be reached except by the mind. Their sacrifices also were similar to those of the Pythagorean rite, for most of them were bloodless and consisted of meal, wine, and things of smallest cost.

Besides these, other arguments are produced to show that the two men knew each other. One is that the Romans enrolled Pythagoras as a citizen, as we are told by Epicharmus, the comic poet,[20] in a letter to Antenor. He lived in the old times and underwent Pythagorean training. Another argument is that Numa named one of his four sons Mamercus, after the son of Pythagoras. From him, they say, sprang the ancient patrician house of the Aemilii, for Numa fondly called the boy Aemilius for his cleverness, aemylia, and grace of speech. I myself have heard many citizens at Rome tell how when an oracle once directed them to erect two monuments, one to the wisest Greek and another to the most valiant, they set up two bronze statues in the forum,[21] one to Pythagoras and the other to Alcibiades. But let us pass from these assertions, which are not well authenticated and not worth discussing more fully.

9. To Numa also is attributed the institution of the *Pontifices,* or high priests, and he himself is said to have been the first. Some say the *Pontifices* were so called from the Roman word, *potens,* powerful, because they serve the gods who are powerful and lords over all. Others say the name meant that the priests were to perform only the duties within their power, and that the lawgiver imposed on them only sacred offices that were possible, and did not blame them if they were prevented. But most authors give an absurd explanation, that the priests were called bridge-builders from the Latin word *pons,* or bridge, because they offered sacrifices on the Tiber bridge which were among the most ancient and sacred. They say too that the keeping and repairing of the bridge, like other unchanging ancestral customs, was the duty of the priests, for the Romans thought it not merely unlawful but even sacrilegious not to pre-

---

20 Epicharmus, a Greek comic poet, lived about 500 B.C.
21 Pliny, in his *Natural History* (XXIV, 12), says that these statues stood where they were erected, from the time of the Samnite Wars (343–290 B.C.) to that of Sulla (138–78 B.C.).

serve the wooden bridge. It is said to have been built without any iron whatever, by command of an oracle,[22] and fastened with wooden pins. The stone bridge was built a long time after, when Aemilius was quaestor.[23] It is also said that the wooden bridge came later than the time of Numa, and was finished by Ancus Marcius, grandson of Numa, when he became king.

The chief priest, or Pontifex Maximus, was the interpreter and mouthpiece of divinity, presiding over sacred rites both in public and in private, making them conform to established custom. He taught the people how to honor the gods and how to pray to them. He was guardian also of the holy Vestal Virgins.

The institution of the Vestal Virgins and their care of the perpetual fire [24] in their charge are attributed to Numa, who may have believed that pure and uncorrupted flame should be entrusted to chaste and unpolluted persons, or else that what is barren and without fruit belongs with virginity. In Greece, wherever an eternal flame is kept burning, as at Delphi and Athens, it is not maidens but widows who attend it. If one of these fires chances to go out, as it did at Athens, when during the tyranny of Aristion [25] the holy lamp is said to have been put out, and at Delphi, when the temple was burned by the Persians, and at Rome, during the Mithridatic and Civil Wars, when not only the fire but the altar was swept away, they say that it must not be relighted from another fire but started afresh, pure and undefiled, from the rays of the sun. This they have done with metal mirrors, made by hollowing the surface of an isosceles right-angled triangle, which conducts all the rays of light to one central point. When these mirrors are placed facing the sun, so that the rays coming from all quarters are collected at the center, the air there becomes rarefied

---

[22] The wooden bridge mentioned here was the first bridge to span the Tiber. It was apparently so constructed that the planks of which it was built could be removed at will.
[23] 179 B.C.
[24] According to legend, this perpetual fire was brought to Latium from Troy by Aeneas, ancestral hero of the Romans, along with his images of the household gods. The worship of Vesta, goddess of the family hearth, was in all probability well established before Numa's time. It lasted until the last days of paganism, her shrine being the most sacred object of Roman religious life. Numa may have built a temple to Vesta and elaborated the services in her honor.
[25] 88–86 B.C.

and light materials placed there, even though resistant, flame up quickly, for the sun's ray has the strength and force of fire.[26]

Some say that the only duty of the Vestal Virgins is to watch this eternal fire, but others say they keep hidden certain sacred objects which no one else may see. But about this I have written as much as it is lawful to divulge in my *Life of Camillus*.[27]

10.   The first maidens consecrated by Numa, they say, were Gegania and Verenia; later, Canuleia and Tarpeia. Servius afterwards added two more and the number has remained at six ever since. Numa ordained that the Vestals should keep their chastity for thirty years. During the first ten they were to learn their duties, during the next ten to perform them, and during the last ten to teach others. After that, any who wished might marry and choose a different form of life. But few, it is said, have availed themselves of this privilege, and those who did so were not happy, and by their unceasing regrets and despondency have made others so afraid that they continue steadily to old age and death as virgins.

Numa gave the Vestals great privileges. They have the power to make wills during the lifetime of their fathers and, like women who have borne three children, they have the administration of their own affairs. When they go out, the *fasces*[28] are carried before them. If they happen to meet a criminal on his way to execution, his life is spared, provided the virgin can swear that the meeting was not planned but accidental. A man who presses on the litter on which they are carried is put to death.

Vestals who commit minor faults are punishable by the high priest, who may scourge the offender, unclothed, in a dark place, with a curtain between them. She who breaks her vow of chastity is buried alive near the Colline Gate, where a low ridge of earth runs along inside the wall. In Latin it is called an *agger*. In this ridge a small underground chamber is constructed, with an entrance from above. In that they place a bed with covers, a lamp burning, and a small quantity of food—bread, water in a bowl, milk, and oil—as though they would clear themselves of the guilt

---

[26] The burning glass which Plutarch here describes was more probably invented by the mathematician, Archimedes, who lived long after Numa.

[27] See below, *Camillus,* ch. 20.

[28] Officials called lictors carried the *fasces,* which were bundles of rods, each containing an ax in the middle, a symbol of the strength of Rome.

of destroying by hunger a body which has been consecrated to the most sacred service of religion. The culprit is put on a litter, which they then cover and tie down so that no sound from her can be heard. They carry her through the forum, and the people make way in silence and deep melancholy, for no spectacle is more appalling, nor does the city know any day sadder than that. When the litter reaches the appointed spot, the attendants loose the bonds, and the chief priest, after uttering cryptic prayers and stretching out his hands to the gods, brings forth the prisoner, closely veiled, and places her on the ladder leading down to the subterranean chamber. Then he and the other priests turn away. When she has descended, the ladder is drawn up, and the site obliterated by masses of earth, so that the spot is level with the rest of the ridge. Thus Vestals are punished who break their vow of chastity.[29]

11.   They say too that Numa built the temple of Vesta that contained the sacred fire in a circular form to imitate not the shape of the earth—as if Vesta were the earth—but that of the whole universe, in the center of which the Pythagoreans place the element fire, which they call Vesta and Monad.[30] The earth, they say, is not motionless, and not in the center of the general orbit, but revolves in a circle about a central fire and occupies by no means the chief or most elemental place in the universe. In this view they agree with Plato, who in his old age, they say, thought that the earth filled a secondary place, and that the central and sovereign space was reserved for some nobler body.

12.   The *Pontifices* explain also to those who ask them the ancestral usages at funerals. Numa taught them not to regard these services as pollution, but to pay their reverence to the gods below, who take what is best in us into their keeping. Especially they were to worship the goddess Libitina, who presides over funeral rites, whether she is Proserpina, or, as the most learned Romans surmise, Venus. For they attribute not unnaturally the beginning and end of man's life to the power of the same goddess.

Numa prescribed also periods of mourning according to the age of the deceased. For a child under three, he allowed none; for older children,

---

[29] The lover of the sinful Vestal was scourged to death.
[30] The Pythagoreans taught that the ultimate reality was a sacred One, or Monad.

one month for every year of the child's life up to ten. For no age was mourning to last longer than ten months. For the same length of time widows were not permitted to marry again. If one did marry before the time was up, the law of Numa obliged her to sacrifice a cow with calf.

Of the many other priesthoods established by Numa I shall mention only two, the *Salii* and the *Fetiales,* which are special evidence of the man's piety. The *Fetiales* were guardians of the peace, and seem to have taken their name from their office,[31] which was to stop armed conflict by conference. They would not allow a resort to arms until all hope of getting justice otherwise had failed. The Greeks, too, call it peace when disputes are settled by words and not by violence. The Roman *Fetiales* often went to people who had injured the Romans, requesting satisfaction. If they were refused, they called the gods to witness, invoking many terrible curses on themselves and their country if they fought without justification; and then they declared war. But against the will of the *Fetiales* neither soldier nor king of Rome could lawfully take up arms. The war must start with their decision that it was just. On hearing their decision, the ruler had to consider ways of waging the war successfully.

It is said that the capture of the city by the Gauls was the result of Roman neglect of this procedure. For when these barbarians were besieging Clusium, Fabius Ambustus was despatched to their camp to negotiate a peace for the besieged. On receiving a rude answer, he imagined that his office as ambassador was over, and, like a youth, took up arms for the Clusians and challenged the bravest of the barbarians to a duel. Fabius won the fight, slew his opponent, and stripped off his armor. But when the Gauls recognized him, they sent a herald to Rome to denounce him for wantonly breaking the truce and fighting against them. At Rome the *Fetiales* tried to persuade the senate to surrender Fabius to the Gauls; but he fled to the people, and by their support escaped punishment. Soon after, the Gauls marched on Rome, and except for the Capitol, sacked the city. More about this is told in my *Life of Camillus.*[32]

13. The priests called *Salii* are said to owe their origin to the following circumstance. In the eighth year of Numa's reign a pestilence ravaged all Italy, and afflicted Rome also. In the midst of the general distress, a

---

[31] Plutarch seems to derive the name *Fetiales* from the Latin verb, *fateri,* to speak.

[32] See below, *Camillus,* chs. 16 ff.

bronze shield, they say, fell from heaven and came into Numa's hands. He gave the people a marvelous account of it, which he had from Egeria and the Muses. The shield was sent for the salvation of the city. To preserve it, they must make eleven others so like it in size and shape that no thief would be able to tell which was the one that had fallen from heaven. He declared further that the place where it fell and the surrounding meadows where he was accustomed to meet the Muses must be consecrated to them; and that the spring by which the land was watered must be pronounced hallowed to the use of the Vestal Virgins, who should take and use the water daily to sprinkle and cleanse their temple. The truth of what he said was verified speedily by the cessation of the pestilence. Numa then showed the shield to the workmen and bade them compete in imitating it, but they all refused to attempt it except one, Veturius Mamurius, an excellent craftsman, who produced such admirable imitations that even Numa himself could not tell which was the original.

He next appointed the *Salii* to guard and keep the shields. These priests were called *Salii* not, as some say, after a man of Samothrace or Mantinea called Salius, who first taught dancing in armor, but rather from their own leaping in their dance.[33] For in the month of March they carry the sacred shields through the city, dancing, dressed in tunics of purple, girt with broad belts of bronze, wearing bronze helmets and carrying short daggers, which they clash against the shields. The dance is mainly a performance of the feet. They move with much grace, carrying out various intricate figures in quick rhythm and with great strength and agility.

The shields are called *ancilia,* from their shape, for they are not round or oval like ordinary shields, but cut in a curving line, with arms that bend back and meet, so that the shape is curvilinear, or, in Greek, *ancylon.* Or the name may come from the *ancon,* or elbow, on which they are carried. At least this is what Juba thinks, trying to make it Greek. But the name may come from *anekathen,* that is, from above, or from *akesis,* healing, because the plague-stricken were healed, or from *auchmon lysis,* because the shield put an end to the drought, or from *anaschesis,* because it meant relief from calamities. The Athenians called Castor and Pollux *Anakes.* All this if we must find a Greek root for the name.

To reward Mamurius for his workmanship, we are told, his name is

---

[33] *Salire* is the Latin verb meaning to leap.

mentioned in a song the Salii sing during their dance; though some say the words are not Veturius Mamurius, but *veterem memoriam,* that is, ancient remembrance.

14.   After Numa had set up the several orders of priests, he built near the temple of Vesta the so-called Regia, or king's house. Here he spent most of his time, engaged in religious duties, or instructing the priests, or reflecting alone on divine things. He had also another house on the Quirinal Mount, the site of which they still point out.

At all ceremonies and processions of priests through the city, heralds went first to bid the people stop their work and rest. The Pythagoreans, they say, do not allow people to worship and pray to the gods casually, but have them go straight from their homes to the temples, prepared in mind for prayer. So Numa too thought his citizens should not see or hear any religious ceremony in a careless, half-hearted manner, but should lay aside everything else and center their thoughts on worship as a most serious business. The streets should be free of noise and shouts and the din that goes with common manual labor, and be cleared for the holy ceremony. Some trace of this custom still survives. When a magistrate is consulting the auspices or sacrificing, the people cry out, *"Hoc age,"* which means "Attend to this," and is an admonition to bystanders to be quiet and orderly.

Many of Numa's other precepts are like those of the Pythagoreans. For instance, they said: "Do not sit on a quart measure," "Do not stir the fire with a sword," "Do not start on a journey and then turn back," "Sacrifice odd numbers to the gods above, even to the gods below." These all had a meaning, hidden from common men.[34] So some of Numa's rules had secret meanings, as, for instance, "Pour no libations to the gods from unpruned vines," "Offer no sacrifices without meal," "Turn around when you worship," "Sit down after worshiping." The first two rules seem to teach that cultivation of the earth is a part of religion; and the turning around of worshipers is said to represent the rotary motion of the universe. It seems more likely that, since the temples face the east, and the wor-

---

[34] The sayings were probably simple folk maxims, obscurely phrased. Not to sit on a quart measure might mean not to yield to idleness; not to stir a fire with a sword, not to irritate one who is angry already; and not to turn back from a journey, not to try to be young again.

shiper at entrance has his back to the rising sun, he turns around to honor
the sun-god, then completes the circle and again faces the temple god, thus
linking both gods together for the granting of his prayer. Or else, by Zeus,
his turning, as the Egyptian wheels do, may signify dimly the instability
of human fortune, and show that, however God may twist and turn our
lives about, we must cheerfully accept it. The sitting down after worship,
they say, is a sign that the prayers are accepted and that the benefits will
be lasting. Or else, since we are accustomed to separating our acts by
periods of rest, we may, after one act of worship, sit down in the presence
of the gods in order to begin the next act with them. This all bears out
what I have just said, that the lawgiver was training them not to approach
divinity hurriedly and with a distracted mind, but only when they had
time and leisure.

15.   By such education in religion, the city became so submissive in spirit
and stood in such awe of Numa's power that it accepted anything he told
them, however fabulously strange, and thought nothing incredible or impossible which he wished it to believe. For instance, they say, he once
invited a large group of citizens to dine with him. The dishes set before
them were plain and the food itself most ordinary. As they began to eat,
he suddenly said that the goddess who was his friend had come to visit
him; whereupon the room was instantly furnished with costly drinking
cups, and the tables loaded with all kinds of meats and dishes.

But the strangest story of all is that of his conversation with Jupiter.
Mount Aventine, says the legend, was not yet an inhabited part of the
city, but was full of springs and shady glens, and haunted by two divinities, Picus and Faunus. These may have been similar to Pan or satyrs,
but they had a knowledge of drugs and a skill in sorcery like that of the
so-called Dactyli [35] of Mount Ida. They went about Italy playing their
tricks, and one day Numa caught them by filling the spring at which they
usually drank with wine and honey. On being seized, they transformed
themselves into many different shapes, assuming strange and terrible
forms; but when they found they could not escape, they revealed to Numa
many future events, and also a charm against thunder and lightning,
made of onions, hair, and sprats, which is used to this day. Some, however, say it was not they who gave them this charm, but that by their

---

[35] The Dactyli were gnome-like creatures believed to dwell on Mount Ida, near Troy

magic they brought Jupiter down from heaven, and that he told Numa angrily that he might charm thunder and lightning with "heads." "With onion heads?" asked Numa. "Heads of men," replied Jupiter. Trying again to soften the cruelty of this dictum, Numa said, "With hairs?" And as Jupiter answered, "With living—" Numa interrupted with "Sprats!" He had learned these answers from Egeria. Jupiter returned to heaven amused, and the place accordingly was called Ilicius.[36] This was the origin of the charm.

These stories, absurd as they are, show us the feeling of the people towards the gods, as expressed in their customs. Numa himself, they say, had such firm confidence in the gods that when someone brought him a message that enemies were approaching, he smiled and said, "And I am sacrificing."

16. He was the first, they tell us, to erect temples to Good Faith and to Terminus. And he gave the Romans the greatest of all oaths, "by Good Faith," which they use to this day. And to Terminus, god of boundaries, they offer both public and private sacrifices at the boundary lines of estates. In the old days, it was a bloodless sacrifice, but now they perform it with living victims. Numa argued that the god of boundaries, who was a lover of peace and a witness to fair dealing, must not be polluted by bloodshed.

Apparently Numa was the first to define the boundaries of the Roman territory, for Romulus was unwilling to admit by measuring off his lands how much he had encroached upon his neighbors. For a boundary, if maintained, is a check on the spread of power, and if not maintained, is evidence of wrongdoing. And the city had at first only a small territory of its own until Romulus enlarged it greatly by his spear.

The new land Numa divided among the needy citizens, thereby relieving the poverty which breeds violence, and turning the people's thoughts to agriculture, so that they grew more civilized as their land was more cultivated. No other calling makes men such keen and quick lovers of peace. The man who lives on his own land has enough martial spirit to fight in defense of it, but loses the warrior's desire to rob and hurt his neighbors. For this reason Numa encouraged agriculture among the

---

[36] Plutarch assumes that Ilicius is derived from the Greek adjective, *hileos*, meaning cheerful or propitious.

Romans, as a charm to bring them peace. He loved it more as a builder of character than as a source of wealth. He divided the whole country into districts, which he called *pagi,* and appointed for each overseers and patrols. Sometimes he inspected their settlements in person, and formed an opinion of a citizen's character from the condition of his farm. Some men then he would raise to positions of honor and trust, while he chided others for their laziness and negligence, trying to teach them to do better.

17.   Of all his other measures, the one most admired was his division of the populace according to their crafts and trades. For, as we have said, the city was at first intended to consist of two races, and they stood aloof from each other and refused to unite. Their differences were endlessly breaking out into conflicts and rivalries. So Numa, reflecting that hard substances which do not readily mix combine easily when beaten first into small particles, resolved to separate the whole population into a great number of sub-divisions and thus obliterate the original major division of race by merging it into the smaller divisions of trade. Accordingly he formed companies of the people by their crafts—musicians, goldsmiths, carpenters, dyers, shoemakers, skinners, blacksmiths, potters. All other craftsmen he gathered into a single company, and each company had its own proper assemblies, meetings, and religious rites. Thus he put an end to speaking or thinking of some citizens as Sabines and of others as Romans, or of some as Tatius' men and of others as belonging to Romulus. So the new division made for harmony and a blending of all together. Commendable also is Numa's amendment to the law which gave fathers the power to sell their sons; he made an exception of married sons, if they had married with their fathers' consent, for it seemed a hard thing for a woman who had married a free man to find herself living with a slave.

18.   Numa solved also an astronomical problem, not with perfect accuracy, yet not without observation and reflection. During the reign of Romulus they had been careless and unsystematic in their reckoning of months, assigning less than twenty days to some months, to others thirty-five, and to some even more. They had no idea of the difference between the motions of the sun and the moon, and insisted on only one thing, that the year should consist of three hundred and sixty days, since the lunar year was three hundred and fifty-four days, and the solar year was three hundred and sixty-five. Instead, he doubled the eleven days, and every

other year introduced, after February, an intercalary month of twenty-two days, which the Romans called Mercedinus. This correction, however, in course of time came to need other and greater corrections.[37]

He altered also the order of the months. March, which had been the first, he put into third place, making January the first, which in the time of Romulus had been the eleventh, and February the second, which had been the twelfth and last. But many writers say that Numa added the months of January and February to the calendar, and that originally the Romans had only ten months in their year, just as some barbarians now have three, and as in Greece the Arcadians have four and the Arcarnanians six. The Egyptians at first had but one month in their year, and afterwards, they say, only four; so, though they live in a very new country,[38] they appear to be very ancient, piling up an enormous number of years in their genealogies by counting their months as years.

19. One proof that the Romans counted at first ten and not twelve months in a year is the name of their last month, which even now they call December, or the tenth month. And the order of their months shows that March was once the first, for the fifth month after March they called Quintilis, the fifth, and the sixth month they called Sextilis, the sixth, and so on for the rest, although when they placed January and February before March, the month they had called the fifth became the seventh. It is natural, too, that the month of March, which is dedicated to Mars, should be put by Romulus first, and April second, as named for Aphrodite. In that month they sacrifice to the goddess, and on the first day the women bathe with myrtle garlands on their heads. Others, however, maintain that since April does not contain the *ph* of Aphrodite, it more likely comes from *aperire,* to open, because it is the month of spring which opens the buds of flowers and plants. As to the following months, May is named for Maia, the mother of Mercury, to whom it is sacred, and June for Juno. But some say that these two months are named for times of life, since old men are called *majores,* and young men, *juniores.*

The remaining months were named according to their numerical or-

---

[37] On the Julian reform of the calendar, see below, *Caesar,* ch. 59.

[38] Egypt might have been called a new country, being shaped anew every year by the deposits of the River Nile. For another Greek view of it, see Herodotus, *History,* II, 5 and 10.

der, Quintilis, Sextilis, and so on for September, October, November, and December. Later, Quintilis became July, after Julius Caesar, the conqueror of Pompey, and Sextilis became August, after the second emperor. The names of the next two months were changed by Domitian to Germanicus and Domitianus, but after his murder they were given their old names again, September and October. Only the last two months have preserved their original names without change.

As for the months which were added or transposed by Numa, February must be an expiation month, for the word nearest to the name means purifying. During it they make offerings to the dead, and hold the festival of the Lupercalia, which in many respects resembles a purification rite.[39] The first month, January, is named for Janus, and Numa, in my opinion, put it before March to show that civilian government should always be honored before military force. For Janus in very ancient times, whether as a deity or a king, was a protector of civil society and is said to have lifted men out of a life of brutality and savagery. For this reason he is represented with two faces, to show that he brought men out of one condition of life into another.

20. There is a temple to Janus in Rome, which has two doors, called the gates of war. In time of war they keep the temple open but close it when peace comes. The latter has rarely happened, for the empire, as it expanded, was always at war with someone, or in collision with the barbarous races around it. In the time of Caesar Augustus, after he had conquered Antony, this temple was closed; and before that, for a short time, in the consulship of Marcus Atilius and Titus Manlius. Then a new war broke out and it was reopened. In Numa's reign it was not seen open for one day, but remained continuously shut for forty-three years.

For not only were the Roman people soothed and pacified by the gentle and just nature of their king, but the neighboring cities too, as if some fresh and healthful air had blown upon them from Rome, began to change, and all longed for good government, so as to live in peace, cultivate the earth, quietly bring up their children, and worship the gods. Gay festivals and feasts, hospitality and friendliness, when people mingled

---

[39] *Februare* means to purify, and *Februa* was a name given to the religious festival of purification in the middle of February, during which occurred the rites of the Lupercalia. See below, *Caesar*, ch. 61.

together fearlessly, became common throughout Italy. From Numa's wisdom, as from a fountain, a spirit of nobility and goodness flowed into everyone, and his serenity diffused itself everywhere. Even the hyperboles of the poets, they say, were inadequate to describe that time.

"Over the iron shield the spiders hang their threads,"

and,

"Rust eats the pointed spear and the double-edged sword.
No more is heard the trumpet's brazen roar,
Sweet sleep is banished from our eyes no more." [40]

No war, uprising, or political revolution is recorded during Numa's reign, nor was there any hatred or jealousy of him, or plot by others to seize the throne. Either fear of the gods, who were thought to watch over him, or reverence for his virtue, or an especially felicitous fortune, kept life in his time innocent and pure and made his reign a living example and proof of Plato's saying,[41] long afterward, that men's only rest and escape from evil would come when by divine providence the power of a king was held by someone with the wisdom of a philosopher, so that virtue had control over vice. "Blessed in himself truly is such a wise man, and blessed are those who hear the words of his wise mouth." [42] They need no coercion or threats, for the sight of such a conspicuous and shining example of goodness in their ruler makes them choose wisdom of their own accord and join him in following the blameless and blessed rule of friendship and harmony, righteousness and temperance, which it is the highest aim of all government to establish. He is most truly a king who can teach these lessons to his subjects, and Numa, beyond all others, seems to have understood this truth.

21. Historians differ in their accounts of Numa's wives and children. Some say that Tatia was his only wife and his only child was a daughter, Pompilia. Others say that he left four sons, Pompon, Pinus, Calpus, and Mamercus, from each of whom descended an illustrious family. From Pompon came the Pomponii, from Pinus the Pinarii, from Calpus the Cal-

---

[40] A free quotation, taken apparently from a memory of lines by the poet Bacchylides. Fragment 13.
[41] Plato, *Republic,* V, 473.
[42] Plato, *Laws,* IV, 711 e.

purnii, from Mamercus the Mamercii, who took also the surname of
Reges, Kings. But a third group of writers accuse the others of inventing
these pedigrees to gain favor with the great families. They say too that
Pompilia was not the daughter of Tatia, but of Lucretia, whom Numa
married after he became king. All agree, however, that Pompilia married
Marcius, a son of that Marcius who persuaded Numa to accept the kingship and accompanied him to Rome, and was later elected senator. After
Numa's death he was Hostilius' rival for the throne, and on being defeated
he starved himself to death. His son Marcius, who married Pompilia, lived
on in Rome and was the father of Ancus Marcius, who became king after
Tullus Hostilius. He was only five years old when Numa died. Piso tells
us that Numa died no quick or sudden death but failed gradually from old
age. He was something over eighty at his death.

22.   His funeral was as enviable as his life, for all the friendly and allied
nations assembled for the rites, with public offerings and garlands. Patricians carried the bier, escorted by the priests of the gods, and a crowd of
men, women, and children followed, weeping and wailing, as if they
mourned the loss not of an old king but of a dearly loved friend, who
had died in the prime of life. At his own wish, they say, his body was not
burned, but placed in one of two stone coffins which were buried below
the Janiculum. The other coffin contained the sacred books [43] which he
himself had written, as the Greek lawgivers wrote their tablets of laws.
During his life he had taught the priests the contents of these books and
implanted in their minds the spirit and purpose of them, and then had
ordered them to be buried with him, since it was not right that holy
mysteries should be left to the keeping of lifeless scripts. For the same
reason, they say, the Pythagoreans never commit their precepts to writing
but impart the memory and discipline of them to men worthy to receive
them. And when once some of their abstruse and mysterious processes in
geometry were divulged to an unworthy person, they said that the gods
were threatening to punish this wickedness by a great public calamity.
After these many instances of similarity in teaching we find it natural to
sympathize with the writers who trace a connection between Numa and
Pythagoras.

---

[43] By "books" is meant no doubt rolls of papyrus, the writing material which was
introduced into Rome from Egypt at a very early date.

Antias, however, says that the books which were buried were twelve priestly books and twelve of Greek philosophy, and that about four hundred years afterwards, when Publius Cornelius and Marcus Maebius were consuls, a torrent of heavy rain washed away the earth and exposed the coffins. The lids had fallen off and one was seen to be quite empty, with no trace of a body; in the other the books were found. The praetor Petilius, it is said, read them and then carried them to the senate, saying that in his opinion it would not be lawful or reverent to make known their contents to the people. They were therefore taken to the *comitium* [44] and burned.

All good and just men receive more praise after their death than before, because envy does not long outlive them and in some cases dies before them. But Numa's glory was even more enhanced by the unhappy reigns of his successors. For of the five who came after him, the last ended his days in banishment; of the other four, not one died a natural death. Three were murdered by conspirators, and Tullus Hostilius, who followed Numa and who derided most of his virtues, especially his devotion to religion, as making him lazy and effeminate, and who turned the people back to warmaking, did not abide long in his folly but was smitten by a terrible disease and fell a victim to superstitions that in no way resembled Numa's piety. Others, too, shared his terrors when he died by a stroke of lightning.

---

[44] The *comitium* was the space used for popular assemblies, later incorporated in the forum.

Comparison of Lycurgus
and Numa Pompilius

1. NOW that we have covered the lives of Lycurgus and Numa and have them both before us, we must attempt the difficult task of comparing their points of difference. They appear to have had much in common: their sagacity, their piety, their capacity for government and education, and their way of deriving their laws from the gods. Yet each had noble traits of his own. In the first place, Numa accepted a kingdom and Lycurgus gave one up. Numa received it without asking for it; Lycurgus had it and renounced it. Numa, though a private citizen and a foreigner, was chosen by the Romans as their lord; Lycurgus, though a king, made himself a private citizen. It was a fine thing to win a kingdom by goodness, but a fine thing too to prefer goodness to a kingdom. For it was virtue that made Numa so famous that he was judged worthy of a kingdom and that made Lycurgus so great that he disdained a kingdom.

Again, like musicians who tune their lyres, Lycurgus drew tighter the relaxed and luxurious Sparta, while Numa slackened the tense and high-strung Rome. The harder task was that of Lycurgus, for he had to persuade the citizens not to take off their breastplates and lay aside their swords but to give up their gold and silver and throw out their costly couches and tables; not to stop their wars and prepare festivals and sacrifices but to cease their banquets and drinking parties, and train themselves to toil at arms and exercise. So Numa was surrounded by good will and honors and effected his aims by persuasion, whereas Lycurgus was always in danger and at times attacked, and carried out his aims with difficulty.

Numa's genius was gentle and kindly and it so softened the violent and fiery temper of the Romans that they became peaceful, well-behaved citizens.

If we must charge to Lycurgus' legislation the cruel and iniquitous treatment of helots, we must admit that Numa was a great deal more Greek and humane as a lawgiver, since he allowed even to actual slaves some taste of liberty, by establishing the custom that they should feast with their masters during the Saturnalia.[1] For that, they say, was one of Numa's institutions, admitting the toilers to the enjoyment of the season's fruits. Some, however, tell us that it was a memorial of the equality which existed in the Saturnian age,[2] when there was neither master nor slave, and all were considered kindred and equal.

2. In general, it seems that both men alike worked to lead their people to independence and self-control. Of the other virtues, Lycurgus valued bravery most, and Numa righteousness, unless indeed it was the different natures and habits of the two states that compelled a difference in treatment. For it was not from cowardice but to stop crime and injustice that Numa forbade war, while Lycurgus made his people warlike not that they might do wrongs but that they might not suffer from them. Each was obliged to make great changes to check the excesses and remedy the defects of their citizens.

As regards divisions and classes in the state, Numa's reform strongly favored the masses—the goldsmiths, flute players, and shoemakers—who made up his motley, democratic populace. Lycurgus' system was rigid and aristocratic, putting all crafts into the hands of slaves and strangers, and confining the citizens to the use of shield and spear, like servants of Mars, whose trade was war and who knew and cared for nothing but how to obey their leaders and conquer their enemies. All business transactions were forbidden to freemen, so that they might be wholly free, and every material concern, such as the cooking and serving of meals, was handed over to slaves and helots. Numa made no such regulations, but while he put an end to military plundering, he permitted every other method of money-getting, and paid no attention to the resulting inequalities or to

---

1 The Saturnalia was a harvest festival in the early winter, in honor of the god Saturn. See below, *Cicero*, n. 28.

2 According to the Romans, the age when Saturn ruled the world, before he was unseated by his son, Jupiter, was a golden time of perfect tranquillity and justice.

the great increase of poverty and the influx of poor men into the city. Yet it was his duty to check greed at the outset, as Lycurgus did, while there was still no wide disparity of fortune and the people still lived much alike. Thus he might have prevented the mischief avarice does, which is no small matter but the seed and beginning of many terrible evils.

As for redistributing the land, Lycurgus, in my opinion, cannot be blamed for doing it, or Numa for not doing it. The equality thus created was the cornerstone and basis of Lycurgus' constitution; but Numa was not impelled to make any new division or to disturb previous arrangements, since the land had lately been divided up by Romulus and his system was probably still in force.

3. As to community of wives and children, each took a wise course to prevent jealousy in husbands, although their methods were somewhat different. A Roman who had a sufficient family of his own might be prevailed upon by a friend who had no children to transfer his wife to him. He had full authority to give her away, permanently or for a time. A Spartan, on the other hand, kept his wife living in his house and retained his original marriage rights, even while he might share her with one who persuaded him to let him have children by her. Many husbands, as we said, even invited and brought home men who they thought would beget fine and goodly children. What is the difference between the two practices? The Spartan shows entire unconcern about the wife and about the passion of jealousy which consumes most men's hearts. The Roman, as if in modesty, veiled the transfer of wives with a new betrothal ceremony, an admission that simple community of wives was intolerable.

Numa's regulations for young girls were designed more for feminine decorum, while those of Lycurgus were altogether unfeminine and set no limits. Indeed, they have been a subject for the poets, who call Spartan girls *phainomerides,* that is, bare-thighed, as Ibycus says, and accuse them all of being mad after men. So Euripides says: [3]

> "With the young men they go out from their homes,
>   Their thighs uncovered and robes flying free."

In fact. the skirts of the girls' tunics were not sewn together and so flew back and exposed the whole thigh as they walked. Sophocles alludes to it clearly in these lines: [4]

---

[3] Euripides, *Andromache,* 587–588.   [4] Sophocles, Fragment 788.

> "She, also, the young maid, whose tunic, open still,
> Hangs round her gleaming thigh
> In folds, Hermione."

Thus Spartan women, it is said, were bold and masculine from the first, even towards their husbands, ruling unchecked over their households, and on important public matters giving their opinions freely.

Under Numa's government, the matrons received from their husbands the respect and honor which Romulus had paid them, as an atonement for the violence done them,[5] but he required great modesty from them, forbade their meddling in business affairs, and preached to them sobriety and silence. They were not to touch wine, or to speak, except in their husbands' company, even on necessary matters. Once, they say, when a woman pleaded her own case in the forum, the senate sent to inquire of an oracle what this might portend for the city. The women's gentleness and submissiveness in general are proved by the notoriety given to the exceptions to the rule. For just as our Greek historians record the names of those who first took the lives of kindred, or fought against their brothers, or murdered their father or mother, so the Romans inform us that the first man to divorce his wife was Spurius Carvilius, and that nothing like that had happened before in the two hundred and thirty years since the founding of the city; also, that one Thalaea, wife of Pinarius, was the first to quarrel with her mother-in-law, Gegania, in the reign of Tarquinius Superbus. So orderly and successful were the lawgiver's rules with regard to marriage.

4. The two men's regulations, also, for marrying young women were consistent with their two methods of education. Lycurgus had them marry only when they were fully mature and eager, so that intercourse with their husbands, when nature called for it, might result in love and tenderness, instead of the hatred and fear that comes with a marriage forced on a girl against nature. Their bodies, too, would then have strength to stand pregnancy and child-bearing, for he thought the sole end of marriage was the production of children. The Romans, on the contrary, gave their

---

[5] The city of Romulus consisted at first largely of runaway slaves, herdsmen and other homeless men, and contained few women. Romulus' remedy for this condition was an expedition against the neighboring Sabines, which ended in every Roman carrying off a Sabine girl to be his wife.

daughters in marriage at the age of twelve, or even younger, thinking that thus they would still be pure and unstained in body and mind when they came to their husbands. Lycurgus' system seems to show more regard for nature and the production of children, and Numa's for character molding and a life together.

The attention which Lycurgus gave to boys, their collection into companies, their discipline and association together, and his careful provisions for their meals, exercises, and sports, prove Numa to be no better than a common lawgiver when he left the rearing of sons to the father's whims or necessities. A Roman father might, if he wished, make his son a farmer, a shipbuilder, a coppersmith, or a musician, as though it were not important for them all to be trained from the beginning to the same common end and to have their characters formed together, but, as though they were like people on a ship, each one there for a different purpose and uniting with the rest for the common good only in time of danger, from fear, and at other times looking out for his own interests. Allowance should be made for ordinary lawgivers, who do no better through want of power or knowledge. But when a wise man has been made king over a new and teachable people, what should have been his first concern but the training of the boys and the discipline of the young men, so that there might be no clashing of dispositions and that, framed and molded together from the very beginning, they might walk in harmony the same way of virtue?

By this and his other measures Lycurgus helped to make his laws permanent. The obligation of oaths to preserve them would have availed little, if the Spartans had not, by their training and education as boys, been imbued with them and with devotion to his constitution. So for more than five hundred years the principal and fundamental features of Lycurgus' legislation, like a deep and penetrating dye, kept fast hold on the nation. But the aim of Numa's policy, that Rome should be at peace with her neighbors, ended with him. No sooner had he died than the gates of Janus' temple, which he had kept closed, flew open, as if war had been caged up there, and Italy was filled with blood and slaughter. Thus his structure of beauty and of justice did not endure even for a little while, because it lacked the binding cement of education.

"What, then," some may say, "has not Rome been advanced and bettered by her wars?" Such a question needs a long answer in an age which values wealth, luxury, and power more than security, peace, and that independence which wrongs no one. However, it is apparently a point for Lycurgus, that as soon as the Spartans fell away from his system, they sank from the highest to the lowest place, and not only lost their supremacy but barely escaped complete destruction, whereas the Romans, after deserting Numa's doctrines, grew and increased in power. This, nevertheless, stands as a remarkable and truly glorious achievement of Numa, that when as an alien, the Romans sent for him to be their king, he changed everything by persuasion, and ruled over a discordant city without need of the armed force which Lycurgus used when he led the nobles against the populace. For Numa won all men and brought them into accord by his wisdom and justice.

Themistocles

C. 514-450 B.C.

1. THEMISTOCLES came of a family too obscure to entitle him to distinction. His father, Neocles, was an ordinary Athenian of the deme of Phrearrhi, of the tribe of Leontis. On his mother's side he was base born, as the verse tells us:

> "I am not of the noble Grecian race,
> I am Abrotonon, born in Thrace;
> Let the Greeks scorn me if they please,
> I was the mother of Themistocles."

Yet Phanias says that the mother of Themistocles was a Carian, not a Thracian, and that her name was not Abrotonon, but Euterpe; and Neanthes gives also the name of her city, Halicarnassus in Caria. The base-born Athenians used to gather at the Cynosarges, a gymnasium outside the gates, dedicated to Heracles, who was himself not a genuine god, having had a mortal for his mother. Themistocles persuaded several young men of pure blood to go with him to the Cynosarges, and join in the wrestling there; by this device he is said to have destroyed the distinction between base-born and full-blood Athenian citizen. However, he certainly had some connection with the family of Lycomidae, for Simonides [1] tells us that he rebuilt the chapel at Phlya, which belonged to that family and had been burned by the Persians, and beautified it with frescoes.

---

[1] On Simonides, see above, *Lycurgus*, n. 4.

2. All agree that he was a child of strong impulses, of quick apprehension, eager to do big things, and with a decided bent towards public life. He did not spend his free time and holidays in play or idleness, as other boys did, but was to be found planning and practicing to himself some speech, often a defense or an accusation of one of his own companions. His teacher then would say to him, "You, my boy, will be nothing small; unquestionably you will be a great man, whether a good one or a bad one." He paid slight and unwilling heed to instruction aimed at forming his character or at teaching him to enjoy some liberal accomplishment, and, strangely for his age, showed little interest in what he heard said on methods of practical efficiency, as though he already had full confidence in his own natural capacity. So later, at gatherings for so-called liberal and elegant amusements, men of culture would jeer at him and he would be compelled to defend himself by saying rather roughly that though he did not know how to tune a lyre and play a harp, he could take a small and obscure city and make it great and glorious.

However, Stesimbrotus says that Themistocles was a disciple of Anaxagoras [2] and studied under the physicist Melissus. But he has his chronology wrong, for it was Pericles,[3] a much younger man than Themistocles, whom Melissus opposed at the siege of Samos, and who was Anaxagoras' friend. One is more inclined to believe those who say that Themistocles was a pupil of Mnesiphilus the Phrearrhian, who was neither a rhetorician nor one of the so-called physical philosophers, but a practitioner of what was then called *sophia* or wisdom, a sort of practical shrewdness and political art, which Mnesiphilus preached as a doctrine handed down from Solon. Later men mixed with it the art of pleading and turned it from the field of public affairs to a mere training in speaking. Those who practiced it then were called Sophists. To this man Themistocles resorted after beginning his political career.

In his first youthful adventures he was not steady or well balanced, but followed his natural impulses, which, when uncontrolled by reason or edu-

---

[2] The historian Stesimbrotus was a contemporary of Themistocles. Anaxagoras (500–428 B.C.), one of the so-called physicist philosophers, famous especially for his original observations in astronomy, was a friend and teacher of Pericles and other notable Athenians. Melissus (middle fifth century), the physicist, spent his life on the island of Samos. The siege of Samos occurred in 440 B.C. By that time Themistocles was dead.
[3] For Pericles, see his *Life,* below.

cation, sweep one into violent extremes and often end in disaster. This he afterwards admitted, but said that the wildest colts made the best horses, if only they were properly trained. As for the stories that his father disinherited him and that his mother killed herself for grief at her son's bad reputation, they seem to be fabrications. On the other hand, some writers say that his father tried to turn him away from public life, and once pointed out to him some old triremes wrecked and abandoned on the beach, saying that that was the way the people treated their leaders when they had no further use for them.

3.   But very early in life politics laid hold of Themistocles and ambition for fame took possession of him. Determined from the outset to be first in the state, he boldly challenged the enmity of those already in power and at the head of the city, especially that of Aristides,[4] who opposed him on every occasion. Yet their hostility seems to have had a very childish beginning. They both became lovers of the beautiful Stesilaus of Cos, as we are told by the philosopher Ariston, and from then on took contrary sides on all public matters. Their different lives and characters probably widened the breach between them. Aristides was gentle and idealistic by nature, and went into politics not to win glory or popularity, but to work for what was best, consistently with safety and fair dealing. He was therefore often driven to oppose Themistocles and resist his growing influence, for the latter was given to stirring the people up and proposing startling novelties.

Themistocles is said to have been so excessively ambitious for fame and so eager to perform great deeds that, though he was very young at the time of the battle with the barbarians at Marathon,[5] when the skillful strategy of the general Miltiades was everywhere talked about, he was observed to be often thoughtful and reserved and sleepless at night, and he refused to join the usual wine parties. When asked the reason for his surprising change of behavior, he replied that the trophy of Miltiades would not let him sleep. But though the others thought that the barbarian

---

[4] Aristides (d.c. 468 B.C.), surnamed "the Just." Plutarch wrote a *Life of Aristides*, not included in this selection.

[5] Marathon, a village on the shore of Attica, was the scene of the celebrated battle in September, 490 B.C., between the Athenians and the Persians, which ended King Darius' attempt to conquer Greece.

defeat at Marathon was the end of war, Themistocles saw that it was but the prelude to greater contests, for which he would prepare himself to be the defender of all Greece, and which he would train his city to meet. He looked far ahead to what was to come.

4. First of all, he, standing alone, had the courage to propose to the people that the Athenians, instead of dividing among themselves the revenue from the silver mines at Laurium,[6] as they were used to doing, should build triremes with the money for the war against Aegina.[7] This war was then the bitterest in Greece, and the Aeginetans controlled the sea through their large fleet. So Themistocles won his point, not by threatening the Athenians with Darius and the Persians, who were too far away and of whose return there was little fear, but by appealing to their pride and their envy of the Aeginetans to get them to arm. With this money a hundred triremes were built, with which afterward they fought against Xerxes.

From this time on he gradually turned the citizens more and more towards the sea, telling them that with their infantry they were no match even for their neighbors, but that with the strength of their ships they could both repel the Persians and make themselves masters of Greece. Thus, as Plato says,[8] from "immovable foot-soldiers" he converted them into seafaring sailors, and brought on himself the reproach that "Themistocles took away from the Athenians the citizen's spear and shield and bound them to the rower's bench and oar." And this, Stesimbrotus says, he accomplished in the face of Miltiades' opposition.

Whether or no he injured thereby the fairness and honesty of the administration, let a philosopher determine. But thereafter salvation came to Greece from the sea, and those triremes rescued the city of Athens after it had fallen, as is proved by the testimony of King Xerxes himself, among others. For though after his naval defeat his infantry force was still intact, he fled from Greece, as if he no longer felt equal to the struggle. And he

---

[6] Laurium, a mountain in southern Attica, was known for its silver mines, which Athens controlled.

[7] Aegina, an island to the south of Athens in the Saronic Gulf, had been in the previous century a prosperous and independent state and a center of Greek art. It was at war with Athens during 484 and 483 B.C.

[8] Plato. *Laws*. IV. 706.

left Mardonius behind more to prevent pursuit, it seems to me, than with any hope of further conquests.

5. Some think that Themistocles was a keen money-maker because he was so free handed; he made costly sacrifices and was lavish in his entertainment of guests, and hence required a large income. Yet others accuse him of great stinginess and parsimony, even of selling eatables which were sent him as gifts. When Philides, the horse breeder, refused to give him a colt he asked for, he threatened to turn his house soon into a wooden horse, meaning that he would stir up trouble and litigation between him and his own household.

In ambition he outdid everyone. While still young and unknown, he prevailed on Epicles of Hermione, a harp player who was much sought after by the Athenians, to come and practice at his house, hoping thereby to attract many people there to see him. At the Olympic games he strove to surpass Cimon [9] in his banquets and tents and splendid equipage. By this ostentation he displeased the Greeks, for they thought such extravagance might be allowed Cimon as a young man of a great family, but was sheer braggadocio on the part of Themistocles, who was as yet undistinguished, and apparently trying to get renown without earning it and without the means to support it. But as *choregus,* or dramatic producer, his tragedies won a prize in a contest which excited great rivalry. He set up a tablet in honor of his victory, with the inscription: "Themistocles of Phrearrhi was the choregus; Phrynichus the author; Adeimantus the archon." [10]

He was, however, well liked by the common people, for he called every citizen by name, and would act as a safe and a fair judge in private disputes between citizens. Once when he was serving as archon and Simonides

---

[9] Cimon (d. 449 B.C.), the subject of another of Plutarch's *Lives,* was the son of Miltiades and scion of a distinguished Athenian family. He was later to become commander of the Athenian fleet, and years after the battle of Salamis was still defying and defeating the Persians on land and sea. He was finally ostracized in 459 B.C.

[10] Phrynichus (512–476 B.C.) was a tragic playwright, who won many victories in the dramatic contests at Athens. The *choregus,* in this case Themistocles, was the man who acted as sponsor and financed the performance of a play. The archons, of whom there were nine, were the chief elected magistrates of the city, and the head archon gave his name to the year in which he served. The year when Adeimantus was archon was 476 B.C.

of Ceos [11] asked an unreasonable favor of him, he replied, "Simonides, you would be a bad poet if your song clashed with the tune, and I should be a poor magistrate if I granted a favor that clashed with the law." Another time, laughing at Simonides, he said he was silly to abuse the Corinthians, who lived in such a fine city, and to have his own statue carved so often, when he was so ugly of face. He continued to grow in influence and popularity with the people, and finally led a party that procured Aristides' banishment by ostracism.[12]

6. When at length the Persians were advancing against Greece [13] and the Athenians were deliberating as to who should be their general, they all are said to have refused the post, terrified of the danger that confronted them, except for Epicydes, son of Euphemides, a popular leader, clever with his tongue, though weak in spirit and open to bribery. He tried to secure the appointment, and seemed likely to win the election. But Themistocles, fearing that all would be lost if the command fell into such hands, bribed him to renounce his ambition.

When envoys came with an interpreter from the king of Persia, to demand earth and water, as a sign of submission, Themistocles seized the interpreter, and had him put to death by a decree of the people for presuming to translate the barbarian's demands into the language of Hellas. He was praised for this act, and also for what he did to Arthmias of Zeleia, who brought in Persian gold to corrupt the Greeks, and was, at Themistocles' suggestion, put on the list of the disfranchised, with his children and his family. But the greatest thing he did was to bring to an end the fighting between Greeks and reconcile the Greek cities with one another, inducing them to forget their mutual enmities during the foreign war. In this work he is said to have received much assistance from Cheileus, the Arcadian.

---

11 Simonides of Ceos (556–468 B.C.), a composer of epigrams, lyrics and other light verse, is not to be confused with the more famous poet, Simonides of Samos, who lived a century earlier.

12 Aristides was ostracized in the year 483–482 B.C.

13 In 480 B.C., the Persians, led by their king, Xerxes, son of Darius, were advancing in a vast host overland through Thrace, having crossed the Hellespont into Europe by a bridge of boats. At the same time the Persian fleet was crossing the Aegean Sea and invading Greek waters.

7. On his appointment as chief commander, he tried at once to persuade
the citizens to embark in their triremes, abandon the city, get well away
from Greece, and meet the Persians out at sea. Since many opposed this
plan, he led a large force of Athenians and Spartans to the Vale of
Tempe,[14] to set up a line of defense for Thessaly, which had not yet declared for the Persians. However, the force retired without achieving
anything, the Thessalians went over to Xerxes, and all the Greeks as far
as Boeotia followed. The Athenians were then more willing to listen to
Themistocles' advice to fight by sea, and sent him with a fleet to guard
the straits of Artemisium.[15]

There the assembled Greeks chose Eurybiades and his Spartans to take
command; but the Athenians refused to follow other leaders, since they
had furnished more ships than all the rest put together. Themistocles,
realizing the danger, gave up his post to Eurybiades and persuaded the
Athenians to submit, promising them that if they behaved well in the war,
he would see to it that afterwards all the Greeks cheerfully paid them
obedience. By this act he seems, more than anyone else, to have deserved
the credit for saving Greece, and especially to have won for the Athenians
the glory of surpassing their foes in valor, and their allies in magnanimity.

Now when the Persian fleet reached Aphetae, Eurybiades was alarmed
at the number of ships that faced him, and on learning that two hundred
more were sailing around above the island of Sciathus, he resolved to retire farther back into Greek waters, to make contact with the Peloponnesus
and base his fleet on the infantry there, for he believed the Persian king
would be invincible by sea. The Euboeans, fearing the Greeks would forsake them, held a secret conference with Themistocles, and sent him
Pelagon, with a large sum of money. He took this money, Herodotus tells
us,[16] and gave it to Eurybiades. Then the man most opposed to Themistocles' policy was Architeles, captain of the sacred galley,[17] who had no
money to pay his crew and was eager to go home. But Themistocles

---

[14] Tempe was a valley in Thessaly, famous for its beauty and for being the haunt of
Apollo and the Muses.
[15] For the location of this and other places named in the following account, see the
map of Greece.
[16] Herodotus, *History*, VIII, 5.
[17] The Greeks had two sacred galleys, used for religious purposes. In times of war they
frequently carried the commanding admirals.

stirred up his seamen against him so that they set on him and took away his dinner. Then while Architeles was still gloomy and angry at their behavior, Themistocles sent him a chestful of bread and meat, at the bottom of which he had hidden a talent of silver, with a message bidding him eat his dinner at once, and pay his crew the next day; if he did not, Themistocles would denounce him to all present as a man who took bribes from the enemy. At least this is what Phanias of Lesbos says.

8. The battles fought at that time with the Persian ships in the straits were not very decisive, but the experience gained there was of the greatest value to the Greeks. They learned from their own exploits in the face of danger that neither number of ships, nor richly decorated figureheads, nor boasts nor shouts, nor barbarian chants of battle, held any terrors for men who knew how to fight hand to hand; and that they must despise such things, charge on the enemy, grapple with them and see it through. Pindar seems to have understood this when he says of the battle of Artemisium:

> " 'Twas there the sons of Athens set
> The shining stone that freedom stands on yet."

For truly the beginning of victory is courage.

Artemisium is a place in Euboea, above the town of Hestiaea, a beach stretching to the north. Nearly opposite to it lies Olizon, once a part of the domain of Philoctetes.[18] There stands a small temple to Artemis, called the Proseoea or Eastward Temple. Around it are trees, and an enclosure of upright slabs of white marble. If you rub the stone with your hand, it gives off the color and smell of saffron. On one of the slabs is engraved this elegy:

> "With numerous tribes from Asia's region brought
> The sons of Athens on these waters fought.
> Erecting, after they destroyed the Mede,
> To Artemis this record of their deed."

They still show you on this shore a spot among great heaps of sand, under which lies a deep bed of black ashes, where they tell you the wrecks and dead bodies were burned.

---

[18] Philoctetes was a celebrated archer, a friend and comrade of Heracles, who figures in tales of the Trojan War.

9. When the news came from Thermopylae to Artemisium that King Leonidas was slain,[19] and that Xerxes was master of all the passes, the Greek ships withdrew farther in towards Greece, the Athenians bringing up the rear because of their bravery, and overflowing with pride at their achievements. Meanwhile, Themistocles sailed along the coast, and wherever he saw useful harbors and places of refuge for enemy ships, he cut conspicuous inscriptions on such stones as he happened to find, or had stones set up near these possible anchorages and watering places, calling on the Ionians, to come over if possible to the Athenians, who were their ancestors, and who were risking everything for their liberty; and if they could not do that, to impede the barbarian army in battle and throw it into confusion. He hoped by this method either to bring the Ionians over to his side, or to distress them by making them suspect to the barbarians.

Meanwhile Xerxes was invading Phocis through Doris, and burning the towns of Phocis, but the other Greeks sent them no help. The Athenians begged all the Greeks to meet the Persians in Boeotia, and make a stand there in defense of Attica, as they themselves had fought by sea in defense of them all at Artemisium. However, no one would listen to their appeals. The others all clung close to the Peloponnesus, determined to collect their forces below the Isthmus of Corinth and build a wall running across the Isthmus from sea to sea. The Athenians were enraged to see themselves betrayed, and disheartened and downcast at being thus forsaken. To fight alone against so vast a host was not to be thought of; so the only thing left to do in the emergency was to abandon their city and trust to their ships. But this the populace were very unwilling to do, saying that they did not ask for victory, and safety would mean little, if they had to desert the temples of their gods and the tombs of their fathers.

10. At this crisis, Themistocles, despairing of winning them over by human arguments, set supernatural devices to work, as the dramatist does in his tragedy, and produced signs and oracles from heaven. As a sign he

[19] Leonidas, king of Sparta, had been sent to hold the pass at Thermopylae against the oncoming Persians, with a force of only five thousand men, three hundred of whom were Spartans. Plutarch, who is telling just the story of Themistocles, passes over this renowned action with a bare mention. Our chief authority on the Persian Wars is, of course, Herodotus.

took the disappearance of the serpent of Athene from the enclosure on the Acropolis. The priests found the daily offerings set out for it untouched, and announced to the people, at Themistocles' suggestion, that the goddess had left the city and was leading the way to the sea. He worked on them again with an oracle which had bidden them trust to a wall of wood, telling them that the wooden wall could mean nothing but their ships, and that because Apollo in this oracle spoke of Salamis as "holy," not as "terrible" or "sad," the island would one day give its name to a great and happy event for the Greeks.

At last his opinion prevailed, and he proposed a decree that the city should be left in the care of Athene, the guardian of Athens, and that all able-bodied men should go aboard the triremes, after providing as best they could for the safety of their children, wives, and slaves. On the voting of this decree, most Athenians sent their wives and children to Troezen, where the Troezenians received them most hospitably and voted to maintain them at public expense, allowing them two obols apiece daily, and permitting the children to pick fruit anywhere, and paying, too, for teachers for them. This action was proposed by Nicagoras.

There were no public funds at this time in Athens; so, Aristotle says, the Council of the Areopagus [20] gave eight drachmas to each man who went to the ships, and thus helped to man the fleet. But Cleidemus tells us that this too was a device of Themistocles. When the Athenians were on their way, he says, down to the harbor of the Piraeus, the Gorgon's head was found missing from the shield of the goddess. Under pretext of hunting for it, Themistocles ransacked everyone's luggage, and found great sums of money concealed. The money was confiscated, and with it the crews of the ships were well equipped with necessaries.

The spectacle of the whole city putting out to sea called forth pity in some beholders and wonder in others at the men's courage, for they were sending their families away in one direction, and, unshaken by their tears and lamentations, moving over to the island to meet the enemy. The many aged citizens who were left behind were also a piteous sight, and the devotion of the domestic animals, who ran howling and crying in entreaty beside the men headed for the ships, was touching. They tell that

[20] The Council of the Areopagus, the highest court of Athens, was composed of ex-archons, and had special jurisdiction over questions involving religion.

one of them, a dog belonging to Xanthippus, father of Pericles, would not be left behind, but leapt into the sea and swam along by the side of his master's trireme as far as Salamis, where he came ashore, but at once collapsed and died. The place where this dog is buried, they say, is what is still shown as "Dog's Grave."

11. Among the great deeds of Themistocles at this time was the recall of Aristides, who had been ostracized when Themistocles came to power. He saw that the citizens wanted Aristides back, for fear that out of resentment he might join the Persians and work for the ruin of Greece. He therefore proposed a bill to the effect that citizens who had been banished for a while might return again and give Athens their best assistance by word and deed, along with the rest of the people.

Eurybiades was now in command of the Greek fleet, because of the prestige of Sparta, but in the face of the danger he was fainthearted and anxious to weigh anchor and sail for the Isthmus of Corinth, where the Peloponnesian infantry lay encamped. Themistocles argued against the move, and uttered then, they say, his long remembered words. Eurybiades had said to him, "Themistocles, in the Olympic games those who start before the rest get a whipping." "Yes," replied Themistocles, "but those who hang back get no crown." And when Eurybiades lifted his staff as if to strike him, Themistocles said, "Strike me, but listen!" Amazed at his calmness, Eurybiades then told him to speak, and Themistocles again urged him to abide by their plan.

Someone else said that a man who had no city had no right to tell those who still possessed one to abandon and betray it. Themistocles turned on him and said: "Wretch, we have indeed left our houses and our city walls, for we do not think fit to become slaves for the sake of lifeless things; but we have a city, the greatest in Greece, our two hundred triremes, which are here to defend you, if you choose to be saved by them. And even if you desert and betray us a second time, all Greece will soon hear that the Athenians still own a free city and a country that is fairer than the one they abandoned!" When Themistocles said this, Eurybiades began to think, and to fear that the Athenians might leave him and depart. When an Eretrian tried to argue against him, Themistocles said, "Ah, have you too a speech to make about war, you, who like a cuttlefish have a sword but no heart?"

12. It is said that while Themistocles was thus speaking on the deck of his ship, an owl [21] was seen flying over the ships from the right and perching on his mast. The Greeks were swayed by that sight to take his advice, and made ready to fight in their ships. But the Persian fleet swept down along the coast of Attica as far as Phalerum and with its numbers blotted out the shore thereabout. And the king in person came down with his infantry to the sea, and could be seen amid his hosts. And with all this power gathering against them, the Greeks forgot the counsel of Themistocles, and the Peloponnesians cast eager glances again towards the Isthmus and resented anyone's mentioning anything else. In fact, they determined to slip away that night, and their pilots had orders what course to steer.

Themistocles, frantic at the thought of the Greeks losing the advantage of the narrow straits and breaking up into small groups by cities, planned a stratagem which was carried out by Sicinnus. This Sicinnus was a Persian by birth, a war captive but much attached to Themistocles and the tutor of his children. Themistocles sent him secretly to Xerxes, with orders to tell him that Themistocles, the Athenian general, had resolved to desert to his side, and, first, would inform him that the Greeks were in process of withdrawing, and urge him to prevent their escape. While the fleet was still in confusion and at a distance from the land army, he should attack it and destroy the whole force. Xerxes was joyful at this message, receiving it as sent from a well-wisher, and at once he issued orders to his captains to put out immediately with two hundred ships and encircle the strait, taking in all the islands, so that not one of the Greeks might escape. The rest of the fleet they should man at their leisure.

While this was being done, Aristides, son of Lysimachus, who was the first to perceive the movement, went to the tent of Themistocles, though Themistocles was no friend of his and had had him ostracized, as we have said. When Themistocles came out, Aristides told him that they were being surrounded. Themistocles, knowing the noble nature of Aristides, and moved by his coming at that time, told him then of the plot with Sicinnus, and begged him, as one in whom the Greeks had most confidence, to assist in the attempt to hold them there and persuade them

---

[21] The owl was the bird of the goddess Athene, protectress of Athens. Flying from the right, it came as an auspicious omen.

to fight in the narrows. Aristides praised Themistocles for what he had done, and went around to the other generals and captains heartening them to fight. And while they were still doubtful, a trireme from Tenos appeared, commanded by Panaetius, a deserter from the Persians, and announced that they were surrounded. Thereupon, with the courage of necessity, the Greeks prepared to face their peril.

13. As soon as it was day, Xerxes took his seat on a high spot, overlooking the array of his host. Phanodemus says that the spot was just above the temple of Heracles, where the island is separated from Attica by only a narrow channel, but Acestodorus says it was close to the border of Megara, on the so-called Horns. A golden throne was set up for the king and a crowd of scribes stood near, whose duty it was to write down everything done in the battle.

Themistocles was sacrificing beside the commander's trireme when three prisoners were brought to him, beautiful of face and richly dressed with splendid gold ornaments. They were said to be the sons of Sandauce, Xerxes' sister, and Artayctus. At the moment when Euphrantides the prophet saw them, a great and brilliant flame blazed up from the consecrated offerings, and a man sneezed on the right, which was a good omen. So seizing Themistocles by the hand, he bade him consecrate the three young men and sacrifice them all with prayers to Dionysus the Devourer.[22] So should the Greeks obtain safety and victory. Themistocles was horror-struck at the prophet's monstrous and terrible proposal; but the people, who in any great crisis are more apt to look for deliverance to irrational than to rational methods, called with one voice on Dionysus, dragged the captives to the altar, and compelled the performance of the sacrifice as the prophet had commanded. At least, this is what Phanias of Lesbos says, who was a philosopher and well read in history.

14. As for the number of the barbarian ships, the poet Aeschylus, in his tragedy of *The Persians*,[23] as if of his own certain knowledge, says:

---

[22] Dionysus was the god of wine and passion and song and the cultivation of the grape. He was becoming also the god of drama and tragedy, Greek tragedy having already begun to develop out of the ritual dances and songs at the Dionysiac festival in Athens.

[23] Aeschylus, *The Persians*, 341–343.

> "Xerxes—and this I know—a thousand ships
> Had under him; and seven and two hundred
> Of more than common speed.
> That was the count."

The Attic ships were a hundred and eighty. In each ship eighteen men fought on the deck, four of whom were archers and the rest men-at-arms.

Themistocles chose the best time for fighting as cleverly as he chose the best place. He waited to send his triremes prow on against the barbarians until that hour of day which always brings a fresh breeze from the open sea and a strong swell through the straits. This did no harm to the Greek ships, which were low-built and comparatively small; but it was calamitous for the barbarian ships, which had high sterns and lofty decks and were slow and cumbrous in their movements. It struck and swung them around broadside to the Greeks. The Greeks attacked fiercely, keeping watch on Themistocles, because he saw best what needed doing and because in front of him was Xerxes' admiral, Ariamenes, in a big ship. He was a brave man and by far the strongest and best of the king's brothers, and was pouring down arrows and darts, as if from a city wall. But Aminias the Decelean and Socles the Paeaenian, who were on one ship, made for him, and the two vessels met prow on, crashed into each other and were caught by their bronze beaks. Then as Ariamenes attempted to board the Greek trireme, they fought him off, struck him with their spears and pitched him into the sea. His body was recognized by Queen Artemisia,[24] floating amid the wreckage, and she had it carried to Xerxes.

15. At this point in the struggle, it is said, a great light shone out from Eleusis,[25] and an echoing shout filled the Thriasian plain down to the sea, as though a multitude of men were escorting the mystic Iacchus [26] in procession. Then out from the shouting throng a mist seemed to rise slowly from the earth, move forward and envelop the ships. Others

---

[24] Artemisia, queen of Halicarnassus in Caria, Asia Minor, had accompanied Xerxes on this expedition.

[25] Eleusis, where were the shrines of the great earth goddess Demeter and of the famous Eleusinian mysteries, lay on the coast a little northwest of Athens, across from Salamis.

[26] Iacchus was another form of the name Bacchus, given to the god Dionysus.

seemed to see apparitions and shapes of armed men coming up from Aegina with arms outstretched to shield the Greek triremes. These, they supposed were the Aeacidae,[27] to whom before the battle they had appealed in prayer for aid.

The first man to capture a Persian ship was Lycomedes, an Athenian captain. He chopped off its figurehead and dedicated it to Apollo, the Laurel-crowned, at Phlya. And since the barbarians had to fight by sections in the narrow channel, and so fell foul of one another, the Greeks were equal to them and overcame them, though they held out until evening. Thus, as Simonides says, was won "that splendid and famous victory, than which no more glorious sea exploit was ever performed by Greek or by barbarian. The valor and zeal of all who fought and the shrewdness of Themistocles brought it to pass."

16.   After the sea-fight, Xerxes, enraged at his failure, tried to extend breakwaters out from the shore to dam up the strait between, and so make a passage for his infantry over to Salamis to attack the Greeks. Then Themistocles, in order to test Aristides, told him that he proposed sailing to the Hellespont, to break the bridge of ships there,[28] "and so," he said, "conquer Asia inside Europe." But Aristides did not like the plan, and said: "Up to now we have fought the barbarian while he sat at ease. If we shut him up in Greece, and put the compulsion of fear on a man who is master of forces so immense, he will no longer sit under a golden umbrella to look on comfortably at his battles, but because of his danger, will dare everything and superintend everything himself in person, and thus correct his past negligences and make wiser plans for the future. So, Themistocles, we must not destroy the bridge that is already there, but rather, if possible, build another and drive him fast out of Europe." "Well, then," answered Themistocles, "if you think that the better plan, it is time we were all considering and devising a way to rid Europe of him as soon as possible."

This being decided, Themistocles sent a royal eunuch, named Arnaces,

[27] The Aeacidae were members of a Greek family of great fame and antiquity. Its founder was Aeacus, a son of Zeus, who for his justice on earth was appointed judge of souls in Hades. Other members were the Homeric heroes, Peleus, Achilles, Telamon, and Ajax. See Herodotus, *History*, VIII, 64–65.
[28] This was the bridge of boats across the Hellespont, already mentioned, by which Xerxes' armies had entered Europe.

whom he had discovered among the prisoners, with orders to inform the king that the Greeks, being now supreme by sea, had resolved to sail up the Hellespont to where the boats were linked together, and destroy the bridge; and that Themistocles, who felt for the king, strongly advised him to hasten back to his own waters and take his army across. Meanwhile he, Themistocles, would contrive delays to hinder his allies and postpone their expedition. On hearing this, the barbarian was terrified and started retreating in haste. The sagacity of Aristides and Themistocles was later proved again during the struggle with Mardonius at the battle of Plataea,[29] where the Greeks fought a small fraction of the forces of Xerxes, but came near losing everything.

17. Herodotus says [30] that of all the cities of Greece Aegina was the bravest. But everyone gave, though jealously and reluctantly, first rank as a man to Themistocles. For after their return to the Isthmus the generals voted, taking their ballots from the altar there; and each voted for himself as the most valorous, and for Themistocles as the second. The Lacedaemonians carried him with them to Sparta, and there awarded an olive crown as a prize for courage to Eurybiades, and another for wisdom to Themistocles. They presented him too with the finest chariot in the city, and sent three hundred young men to escort him as far as their border. And at the next Olympic games, they say, when Themistocles entered the stadium, the spectators took no further interest in the contests, but all day long looked at him, admiring and applauding, and pointing him out to strangers, so that, much gratified, he told his friends that he was now reaping the fruit of all his labors for the Greeks.

18. By nature he was indeed extremely fond of admiration, if we may judge from the stories told of him. After the Athenians chose him as admiral, he would conclude no business, public or private, at the time appointed, but would defer a settlement until a day on which he was to sail, so that he would be seen despatching a great deal all at once, and having meetings with all kinds of people, and thus make an appearance of importance and power. On surveying the dead bodies of the barbarians

29 The battle of Plataea was fought in 479 B.C., between the Greeks and the land army under Mardonius, whom Xerxes had left behind him when he retreated into Asia, after Salamis.

30 Herodotus, *History*, VIII, 93.

cast up by the sea, he noticed the gold bracelets and collars they wore. He himself did not touch them, but pointing them out to a friend who was following him, he said, "You may take these for yourself; you are not Themistocles." To Antiphates, who had once been a handsome youth and had then treated him scornfully, but who now courted him for his fame, he said, "Time, young man, though late, has taught us both a lesson."

He used to say that the Athenians did not really honor or admire him but used him as a sort of plane tree, under which they took shelter in bad weather. As soon as it was fair again, they lopped off its leaves and branches. And when a citizen of Seriphos remarked to him that it was not for his own merits that he was famous but for the greatness of his city, he replied, "Very true; I should not have been famous had I been a Seriphian, nor you, had you been an Athenian."

When another general, who thought he had performed a considerable service for the city, once boasted to Themistocles, comparing his feats with what Themistocles had done, the latter said to him: "Once upon a time the Day after the Festival found fault with the Festival, saying: 'On you there is nothing but work and fatigue, but when I come, everybody sits down and enjoys what they find prepared.' 'That is true,' the Festival admitted, 'but if I had not come first, you would not have come at all.' So," went on Themistocles, "if I had not come that day, where would you all be now?"

Of his son, who cajoled his mother and through her himself, he said jokingly that he was the most powerful person in Greece; for the Athenians commanded the rest of Greece, he himself commanded the Athenians, the boy's mother commanded him, and the boy commanded his mother. He liked being peculiar in everything, and when he had a piece of property to sell, he ordered notice given that it had good neighbors. When two men were paying suit to his daughter, he chose the more promising rather than the one who was rich, saying he preferred a man without money to money without a man. He would make sage remarks, such as these.

19. After the events described he began promptly to rebuild and fortify the city. Theopompus says that he bribed the Spartan ephors not to oppose it, but most writers say he outwitted them. For he went to Sparta

on the pretext of conducting an embassy. Then when the Spartans complained that the Athenians were rebuilding their walls, and Polyarchus was sent down from Aegina especially to denounce them, he denied the charge and bade them send men to Athens to see if it were true, with the idea both of gaining time for the walls to be built and of having the Athenians hold the men as hostages for himself. And it turned out as he planned. When the Lacedaemonians learned the facts, they did him no harm but suppressed their anger and sent him away.

Next he built the port of the Piraeus, for he had observed the excellent shape of the harbor and wanted to tie the whole city to the sea. Therein he was reversing the policy of the old Athenian kings, who are said to have tried to keep the citizens away from the sea and accustom them to live by tilling the ground, not by sailing about. They spread the story of Athene and her contest with Poseidon for control of the region, and how she won the judges' decision by producing the sacred olive trees. However, Themistocles did not so much "stick the Piraeus on to Athens," as Aristophanes, the comic poet, said,[31] as fasten the city on to the Piraeus, and the land to the sea. By this step he increased the power of the people as against the nobility, and made them bolder, because authority came now into the hands of sailors, boatswains, and pilots. So the Thirty Tyrants later ordered that the rostrum in the Pnyx,[32] which had faced towards the sea, should be turned around to face inland, because they thought the maritime empire was the source of democracy and an oligarchy would be less resented by cultivators of the soil.

20. Themistocles had an even more ambitious scheme for making Athens a sea power. After the departure of Xerxes, when the Greek fleet had put in at Pagasae and was wintering there, he made a speech to the Athenian people, telling them that he had a plan for their safety and prosperity which he could not divulge in public. The assembly then ordered him to impart it to Aristides alone, and if he approved of it to put it into effect. Thereupon Themistocles told Aristides that his plan was to burn the whole Greek fleet as it lay beached. Aristides reported back

---

[31] Aristophanes, *The Knights,* 815.

[32] The Thirty Tyrants were an obligarchic clique set up by Sparta to govern Athens after her defeat in the Peloponnesian War. The Pnyx was a hill overlooking the agora at Athens, on one of whose slopes public assemblies were held.

to the people that nothing could be more advantageous or more dishonorable than the scheme Themistocles proposed. The Athenians accordingly ordered Themistocles to drop it.

At a meeting of the Amphictyonic Council [33] the Spartans proposed that all cities which had not fought with them against the Persians should be excluded from the Council. But Themistocles was afraid that if they shut out the Thessalians and Argives and Thebans, the Spartans would have complete control over the voting and put through whatever they wished. So he spoke on behalf of those cities and changed the minds of the delegates, pointing out that only thirty-one cities, most of them very small, had taken part in the war; and that it would be intolerable if all the rest of Greece were excluded, and the Council came to be ruled by the two or three biggest cities. By this move especially he incurred the displeasure of the Spartans, who now set about promoting the popularity of Cimon and establishing him as a political rival to Themistocles.

21. He made himself obnoxious to the allies also by sailing around the islands to get money from them. Herodotus [34] says that when he asked for money from the people of Andros, he told them he had brought with him two gods, Persuasion and Force. They replied that they also had two great gods, Poverty and Helplessness, who kept them from giving him money. Timocreon, the poet of Rhodes, in one of his songs upbraids Themistocles bitterly for taking bribes to let some exiles return, and for money abandoning him who was his host and his friend. The song runs thus: [35]

"Though ye may sing Pausanias or Xanthippus in your lays,
Or Leotychidas, 'tis Aristides whom I praise,
The best of men as yet produced by holy Athens' state,
Since now upon Themistocles has fallen Leto's hate,
That liar, knave, and traitor base, who for a bribe unclean,

---

[33] The Amphictyonic Council or League was a loose confederation of Greek states, pledged to enforce certain principles of inter-state right. Its purpose in the beginning had been solely to regulate the observance of religious festivals, provide for the upkeep of shrines, etc. It later came to exercise political power as well.

[34] Herodotus, *History,* VIII, 111.

[35] The following translation in rhyme, based on the version by Aubrey Stewart in the Bohn edition of Plutarch, does not, of course, represent in the least Timocreon's free, unrhymed verse form.

Refused to reinstate a man who his own friend and host had been,
Or bring him back again to Ialysus, but who took
Three silver talents offered, and Timocreon forsook.
Let him sail to perdition! He unjustly some restores
From exile, while some others he keeps banished from our shores,
And some he puts to death; and sits among us gorged with pelf.
He kept an absurd table at the Isthmian games himself,
And gave to every guest that came a plenty of cold meat,
The which they with a prayer did each and every of them eat,
Their prayer was not again to have Themistocles to meet."

After the banishment and condemnation of Themistocles, Timocreon denounced him much more immoderately and extravagantly in a song which begins thus:

"Muse, let this song
Resound through all Hellas
Since it is meet and right."

It is said that Timocreon was exiled for having dealings with the Persians, and that Themistocles voted for his sentence. So when Themistocles was accused of intriguing with the Persians, Timocreon wrote these lines about him:

"Timocreon is not the only Greek to treat with Persians
But there are others traitorous as well.
I'm not the only fox without a tail."

22. At length Themistocles' fellow citizens began out of jealousy to listen more willingly to the slanders against him, and he was obliged to weary them with constant reminders in the assembly of the services he had performed. To those who were critical of him, he once said, "Why do you grumble at receiving benefits often from the same hands?" But he irritated the people, too, by building a temple to Artemis, to whom he gave the title, Best Counselor, intimating thereby that he had given the best counsel both to the city and to all the Greeks. He built this temple near his own house, in the district of Melite, where at present public officials throw out the bodies of persons executed and the clothing and ropes of those who have hanged themselves. A statue of Themistocles stood in this temple of Artemis, the Best Counselor, down to my own time. It looks like a person heroic both in spirit and in appearance.

The Athenians finally ostracized him,[36] thus humbling his pride and dignity, as they used to do everyone's they thought too oppressively powerful, unfitted for living in a state of democratic equality. For ostracism was not a punishment but an outlet for the jealousy which enjoys humbling the great and expressing its resentment by depriving them of their honors.

23. After Themistocles' banishment from Athens, and while he was staying at Argos, some events connected with Pausanias [37] gave his enemies ground for further action against him. Leobotes, of the deme of Agraule, son of Alcmaeon, brought an indictment for treason, and the Spartans supported him in his accusation. Pausanias had at first concealed his treacherous schemes from Themistocles, friends though they were. But when he saw Themistocles banished from his country and chafing at this treatment, he had been emboldened to invite him to take part in his own activities. He had showed Themistocles a letter he had received from the Persian king, and had tried to inflame his bitterness against the Greeks, as a worthless, ungrateful people. Themistocles had rejected Pausanias' invitation and refused utterly to join him, but he had revealed their conversation to no one and warned no one of the conspiracy, expecting either that Pausanias would let it drop, or else that his visionary and fantastic enterprise would be discovered in some other way.

Thus it happened that after Pausanias was put to death, certain letters and documents on the subject were found, which threw suspicion on Themistocles. The Spartans were vehement against him and his jealous countrymen accused him, absent though he was from Athens. He defended himself, however, in writing, referring especially to earlier charges. And as long as his enemies, he wrote, accused him to his fellow citizens of being ambitious to rule, and of having no disposition or willingness to obey, he could never sell himself and Greece to the barbarians or to their foes. But his enemies prevailed on the Athenians to send men with orders to arrest him and bring him up to be tried by a court of Greeks.

---

[36] Themistocles' ostracism came in 471 B.C., nine years after Salamis.

[37] Pausanias was the Spartan general who had commanded at the victory of Plataea and continued for some time afterward to direct the war against Persia. Later he secretly entered into a treasonable correspondence with Xerxes, and was finally detected and put to death in Sparta, about 466 B.C.

24. He learned of this in time to cross over to Corcyra, a state which was under obligation to him. For once, when Corcyra was in a dispute with Corinth, he had acted as arbiter and ended the quarrel by ordering the Corinthians to pay twenty talents and treat Leucas as a joint colony of both cities. From Corcyra he fled to Epirus, but as he was still pursued by the Athenians and Spartans, he made a hard and desperate resolve, namely, to take refuge with Admetus, king of the Molossians. Admetus had once, when Themistocles was at the height of his power, made some request of the Athenians, and been insultingly refused by him. He had ever since remained incensed at him, and palpably ready for vengeance, if he caught him. But as things then stood, Themistocles feared the fresh anger of his countrymen more than an old grudge of a king.

So he threw himself on Admetus' mercy and became his suppliant in a strange and novel fashion. He took the king's young son in his arms and sat himself down at Admetus' hearth, for the Molossians considered this the most sacred form of supplication, and one that could scarcely be refused. Some say that Phthia, the king's wife, suggested to Themistocles this form of entreaty, and placed her child beside him on the hearth; while others say that Admetus himself arranged the scene and rehearsed it beforehand with Themistocles, in order to have religious reasons to allege to Themistocles' pursuers for his inability to give him up. Epicrates the Acharnian managed to convey Themistocles' wife and children stealthily out of Athens and send them to him, for which act, we are told by Stesimbrotus, Cimon later had him condemned and executed. But somehow or other Stesimbrotus either forgets this incident, or makes Themistocles forget it, for later he tells us that Themistocles sailed to Sicily and asked from Hiero the tyrant [38] the hand of his daughter in marriage, promising to bring the Greeks under his sway. Hiero rejected his proposals, and so Themistocles went to Asia.

25. However, this is not a likely story. Theophrastus,[39] in his treatise *On Monarchy,* tells us that Hiero once sent race horses to the Olympic games, and put up a pavilion there with costly decorations, but that Themistocles made a speech to the Greeks, urging them to pull down the tyrant's

---

[38] Hiero was the tyrant ruler of Syracuse in Sicily, from about 478 to 472 B.C.
[39] See above, *Lycurgus,* n. 22. Theophrastus was the author of works in many fields. His treatise *On Monarchy* is lost.

pavilion and not allow his horses to run. Also, Thucydides says [40] that Themistocles crossed to the other coast and sailed to Asia from Pydna, none of his fellow voyagers knowing who he was until the ship was driven by a storm to Naxos, which was then under siege by the Athenians. Alarmed, he told the master and the captain who he was, and partly by entreaty and partly by a threat that he would denounce and incriminate them with the Athenians and say that they had known his identity from the first, but had taken him with them for a bribe, he forced them to sail on by and make for the coast of Asia.

A great part of his property was secretly secured by his friends and sent after him to Asia. But a total of a hundred talents was discovered and confiscated by the state, according to Theopompus; Theophrastus says eighty, though Themistocles was never worth three talents before he entered public life.

26.   On landing at Cyme, he learned that all along the coast people were on the watch to capture him, particularly Ergoteles and Pythodorus. For the hunt was a profitable one for men who were out to get money from any source, since the King of Persia had proclaimed a reward of two hundred talents for his arrest. He fled then to Aegae, a small Aeolian city, where no one knew him save his host Nicogenes, the richest man in Aeolia, well known to the magnates of the interior. In his house Themistocles lay hidden for some days. One day, after sacrifice and the dinner which followed, Olbius, the tutor of Nicogenes' children, fell into an inspired trance and uttered this verse:

> "Night shall speak, night give its counsel,
> Night shall bring thee victory."

That night in bed, Themistocles dreamed that a snake coiled itself around his body and crept up to his neck; then as soon as it touched his face, it turned into an eagle, which spread its wings over him, lifted him up and flew away with him a long distance. At length there appeared a herald's golden staff, on which the eagle set him securely down, free from his helpless terror and perplexity.

Then Nicogenes managed through the following device to send him on. Most barbarian nations, and especially the Persians, are jealous and

---

[40] Thucydides, *Peloponnesian War,* I, 137.

suspicious of their women. Both their wives and their bought slaves and concubines are kept in the most strict seclusion, so as not to be seen by any outsider. At home they are kept locked up and when they travel they are carried on wagons, in tents hung around with curtains. Such an equipage was prepared for Themistocles, and hidden inside it he was conveyed away. Those who were met on the journey and who asked questions were told by his escort that they were bringing a Greek girl from Ionia to a courtier of the king.

27. Thucydides [41] and Charon of Lampsacus say that by this time Xerxes was dead, and that Themistocles' interview was with his son. But Ephorus, Dinon, Clitarchus, Heraclides, and many others say that it was to Xerxes himself that he came. Thucydides' account seems to agree better with the chronological tables, although they are not reliably worked out.

At any rate, Themistocles at this critical point saw first Artabanus, the chiliarch, or high commander, and told him he was a Greek who desired an audience with the king on highly important matters, in which the king was much interested. Artabanus replied: "Stranger, the customs of men differ, and different races have different standards of right. But all think it right to honor and preserve their own customs. We are told that you Greeks prize freedom and equality above all else; we, on the other hand, think the best of all our good laws is that which commands honor and worship paid to the king, as the image of the god who preserves the universe. If you, then, will accept our customs, and do obeisance to the king, you may both see and speak to him. But if you refuse, you must use messengers to communicate with him, for it is not the custom here for the king to give a hearing to anyone who has not done obeisance."

To which Themistocles replied: "But, Artabanus, I have come to increase the power and glory of the king, and will myself both obey your customs, since that is the will of the god who exalts the Persians, and add to the number of those who do him obeisance. So let this question be no obstacle to the interview I desire." "And what Greek," said Artabanus, "shall we tell him has come? For you seem to be a man of no ordinary intelligence." "That, Artabanus," answered Themistocles, "must no man hear before the king himself." Such is the story told by Phanias. Eratosthenes, in his treatise *On Wealth*, tells us also that it was through a woman

---

[41] Thucydides, *Peloponnesian War*, I, 137.

from Eretria, the chiliarch's wife, that Themistocles got his interview with him.

28. When then he was brought into the king's presence and had done obeisance and was standing silent, the king told his interpreter to ask who he was. And when the interpreter asked him, he replied: "I who have come to you, O King, am Themistocles the Athenian, an exile pursued by the Greeks, to whom the Persians owe many calamities, but even more good fortune. For I stopped the Greek pursuit as soon as Greece was safe, and when my own home was secure, was able to do you a favor. In my present fallen state, anything may happen to me, and I come prepared either to accept the kindness of one who is graciously willing to be reconciled or to deprecate the anger of one who cherishes his grievances. Take my adversaries in Greece as witnesses to the service I did the Persians, and use my misfortunes now to show your magnanimity, not to vent your wrath. For you will be saving one who is your suppliant, or else destroying one who is now, too, an enemy of the Greeks."

Themistocles next mentioned certain divine omens, relating the dream he had at the house of Nicogenes, and the oracle of Zeus at Dodona,[42] which had bidden him go to the namesake of the god, whereat he had concluded that he was being sent to the king, because they were both Great Kings and were so called. To this speech Artaxerxes made no answer at the time, although he was full of admiration at such boldness of spirit. In conversation with his friends he is said to have congratulated himself on his great good fortune, and in his prayers to have begged Arimanius[43] always to influence his enemies to drive out their ablest men. He then sacrificed to the gods and presently fell to drinking. In the night he cried out three times joyously, in his sleep, "I have Themistocles the Athenian!"

29. In the morning, he called his friends together and had Themistocles brought in. Themistocles anticipated nothing pleasant, for he had seen the men at the gates, as soon as they heard the name of the newcomer, turn hostile and mutter ugly words. And Roxanes, the chiliarch, as Themistocles came forward and passed him—the king being seated and

---

[42] The oracle of Zeus in the oak groves of Dodona, in Epirus, was more ancient than that of Apollo at Delphi, and equally revered.

[43] Arimanius, in Persian Ahriman, was the evil deity of the Persian religion of Zoroaster.

everyone else silent—whispered softly, "You subtle Greek serpent, the king's good genius brought you here!" But when he came before the king and had again done him obeisance, the king greeted him cordially, saying that he already owed him two hundred talents. For since Themistocles had brought himself there, he should receive the reward offered for his capture. And he promised him much more than this, and encouraged him to speak freely on affairs in Greece.

Themistocles replied that a man's talk was like rich embroidered rugs, for like them it showed its patterns only when spread out; when folded up, it hid and distorted them. Wherefore he asked for time. The king was pleased with this comparison, and bade him take what time he needed. Themistocles then asked for a year. In that time he learned the Persian language sufficiently well to talk to the king without an interpreter. Those outside supposed that their talks concerned the state of affairs in Greece, but many changes were made by the king about this time in the court and among his friends, and it was borne in on the resentful nobles that Themistocles was daring to advise him freely, and not to their advantage. In fact, he was honored as no other foreigner ever was, took part in the king's hunting and in the life of the palace. He even came to the notice of the king's mother, and became well acquainted with her. By the king's command also he was instructed in the learning of the Magi.

Once when Demaratus the Spartan [44] was told to ask for a boon, he requested permission to ride through Sardis wearing his tiara upright as the Persian kings did. Mithropaustes, the king's cousin, laid his hand on Demaratus' tiara and said, "But this tiara covers no brains! You will not become Zeus simply by grasping the thunderbolt." The king was irate at Demaratus' request, and seemed implacable in his attitude toward him, but Themistocles by entreaty persuaded him to relent.

It is said that later Persian kings, in whose reigns Persia was more and more involved in Greek affairs, whenever they invited a Greek into their service, would promise him in their letter that he would be an even greater man at court than Themistocles. They tell also how Themistocles, then so prosperous and courted, when once a magnificent banquet was set before him, said to his children: "My children, we should be ruined

---

[44] On Demaratus, see above, *Lycurgus,* n. 38.

if we had not been ruined before." Three cities, most writers say, Magnesia, Lampsacus, and Myus, were allotted him to supply him with bread, meat, and wine. Neanthes of Cyzicus and Phanias add two more, Percote and Palaescepsis, which provided bedding and clothing.

30. On one occasion, when Themistocles went down to the coast on business connected with Greece, a Persian named Epixyes, satrap of Upper Phrygia, plotted against his life. For a long time he had kept a number of Pisidians in readiness to kill him when he came to a village called Lion's Head to spend the night. But Themistocles, in sleep at mid-day, saw, it is said, the Mother of the Gods [45] in a vision, who said to him: "Themistocles, be slow to go to a lion's head lest you fall in with a lion. And for this advice I ask your daughter Mnesiptolema as my handmaid."

Themistocles, much astonished, prayed to the goddess, and then left the highway and made a detour to avoid the place, and as night came on pitched his camp. Now one of the beasts of burden, which carried the furnishings for his tent, had fallen into the river; so his servants hung up the wet curtains to dry. Meanwhile the Pisidians were creeping towards them with swords drawn, but not being able to see clearly in the moonlight, they thought the drying curtains were Themistocles' tent and they would find him resting within. When they came close and lifted up a curtain, the guards fell on them and seized them. Thus Themistocles escaped this danger, and in gratitude for the appearance of the goddess built a temple to Dindymene at Magnesia, and appointed his daughter Mnesiptolema as its priestess.

31. On a trip to Sardis he was visiting at his leisure the temples of the gods and observing the immense number of offerings, when he saw in the temple of the Mother of the Gods the bronze statue of a maiden, two cubits high, called the Water Carrier. As overseer of the water supply at Athens, Themistocles had had this very statue made, after collecting the money for it out of fines imposed on those who diverted and drew off the water illegally. Whether he was saddened at seeing it a captive or whether he wished to show the Athenians how much honor and influence

---

[45] In Asia Minor, the so-called Mother of the Gods, or Magna Mater, was variously known as Cybele or Dindymene. She was identified also with the Greek goddess Rhea, wife of Cronos and mother of Zeus, Poseidon, and Hera. The worship of this ancient female deity was universal throughout Western Asia.

he possessed in the royal circle, he proposed to the satrap of Lydia to send it back to Athens. But the barbarian was angered and threatened to write the king about it. Alarmed by this, Themistocles got access to the women's quarters and won over the satrap's concubines by presents of money, and in this way pacified him. In the future he was more cautious in his dealings with the barbarians, for he perceived now that he had their jealousy to fear. He stopped traveling about Asia, Theopompus tells us, and made his home at Magnesia, receiving rich presents and being held in as much honor as the high Persian nobility. He lived there a long time in tranquillity, for the king's attention was absorbed by the situation in the interior, and he gave little thought to what was going on in Greece.

But when Egypt revolted, with Athenian aid, and Greek triremes roved about as far as Cyprus and Cilicia, and Cimon made himself master of the sea, the king was compelled to resist the Greeks and check the growth of their hostile power. At once forces were set in motion, generals dispatched hither and yon, and messages came to Themistocles ordering him to grapple with the Greek situation and make good his past promises. Themistocles felt no resentment against his countrymen, and was wholly indifferent to the prospect of more honor and authority in war. Perhaps also he thought his task an impossible one, for Greece then had many great generals, and Cimon was extraordinarily successful in his tactics. Most of all, Themistocles was ashamed to sully the glory of his own past deeds and the trophies he had won. So he decided that his best course would be to put a fitting end to his life. He offered sacrifices to the gods, called his friends together, and after grasping their hands, drank bull's blood. This is the usual story, though some say he drank a quick poison. Thus he died in Magnesia, at the age of sixty-five years, most of which he had spent as a leader in political life. The king, they say, when he heard of the cause and manner of his death, admired him more than ever, and continued to treat his friends and kinsfolk with kindness.

32. Themistocles left three sons, Archeptolis, Polyeuctus, and Cleophantus, by Archippe, daughter of Lysander of the deme Alopece. Cleophantus is mentioned by Plato, the philosopher,[46] as being an excellent horseman but otherwise worthless. Of the older sons, Neocles as a child was bitten by a horse and died, and Diocles was adopted by his

---

[46] Plato. Meno, 93.

grandfather Lysander. He also had several daughters, of whom Mnesiptolema, born of his second wife, married Archeptolis, her half-brother,
Italia married Panthoides from Chios, and Sybaris married Nicomedes,
an Athenian. After Themistocles' death, his nephew Phrasicles went to
Magnesia, and, with her brother's consent, married Nicomache, another
daughter. He also took charge of Asia, the youngest of all the children.

The people of Magnesia have a splendid tomb of Themistocles in the
market place. And Andocides is not worth believing when he states in
his address to his associates that the Athenians stole his remains and
scattered them far and wide, for Andocides would tell any falsehood to
incite the oligarchy against the people. Phylarchus, too, creates the ma-
chinery of a near tragedy for his story, bringing in a Neocles and a
Demopolis, as sons of Themistocles, to make a touching scene that anyone
would know was fiction. Diodorus, the cosmographer, in his treatise on
Tombs, states—though more as a conjecture than as a matter of certain
knowledge—that near the great harbor of the Piraeus, where a kind of
elbow juts out from the promontory opposite Alcimus, if you sail around
this and get inside, where the sea is always calm, you see a large foundation of masonry. The structure on it, shaped like an altar, is Themistocles'
tomb. He thinks that Plato, the comic poet, confirms this idea in the
following lines:

> "Thy tomb stands high in a fair place.
> Its name shall be ever on merchants' lips.
> It shall watch the sailors outbound and returning home,
> And look down on the racing of their ships."

For the descendants of Themistocles certain privileges have been preserved
in Magnesia even to my day. Themistocles, an Athenian, my friend and
fellow-student in the school of Ammonius the philosopher, enjoyed them.

Camillus

C. 445–365 B.C.

1. MANY remarkable things are told of Furius Camillus,[1] the strangest of which is that, although he had many great successes as a commander, was five times chosen dictator, four times held a triumph, and was called the second founder of Rome, he was never once a consul. The reason for that was the political situation at the time. The people were at loggerheads with the senate and opposed the election of consuls,[2] choosing military tribunes instead. These acted with full consular authority and power, but because of their numbers their rule was less offensive to the people. To have six men instead of two in charge of affairs was some consolation to those who bitterly resented being ruled by a few. It was during this period that Camillus reached the height of his fame and achievements, and he would not become consul against the popular will, although during that time the city on several occasions agreed to the election of consuls. Whatever other and varied offices he filled, he always contrived, even when the authority was his only, to share it with others, yet the glory always redounded to him, although others had shared in the command. In the first instance, his moderation kept his position from arousing envy, and in the second, everyone knew that his intelligence made him the real leader.

---

[1] Camillus was originally a special name given temporarily to patrician boys who were serving in the temples of the gods. This Camillus was the first to adopt the appellation as a surname. See above, *Numa*, ch. 7.

[2] Up to this time the consulate had been solely a patrician office, from which plebeians were excluded.

2. The house of the Furii was not as yet especially notable, and he was
the first to win distinction by his achievements. He did this in the great
battle with the Aequians and the Volscians,[3] where he served under the
dictator Postumius Tubertus. When riding out ahead of the army, he
was struck in the thigh by a dart, but did not stop. Carrying the weapon
in its wound along with him, he attacked the bravest of the enemy and
put them to flight. For this feat he received various honors, and was appointed censor,[4] an office of great dignity at that time. One admirable
measure is recorded of his censorship; by persuasion and by threat of fines,
he got the unmarried men to take as wives the widows, of whom there
were many as a result of the wars. Another necessary measure of his was
the taxing of orphans, who before had been exempt from taxation. The
reason for this act was the heavy expenditures made obligatory by the
unremitting wars.

Especially costly was the siege of Veii.[5] Some call the inhabitants of
this city Veientani. It was the bulwark of Etruria, and had as many soldiers under arms as Rome itself. It was proud of its wealth, and of the
luxury, refinement, and lavishness of its way of life, and had fought honorably with the Romans in their wars for prestige and mastery. By now
it had been defeated in several great battles and had abandoned its former
ambitious schemes; but the people had built strong high walls, provided
the city with food, armor, missile weapons, and every other equipment,
and boldly defended it.

The siege they endured was long, and was no less toilsome and difficult
for the besiegers. For the Romans had been accustomed to short campaigns
abroad in early summer, and to winters at home. Now, for the first time,

---

[3] During most of the fifth and early fourth centuries B.C., the Romans were struggling to gain control over their Latin neighbors on the plains close around them, to
drive back the Aequians and the Volscians, fierce marauders from the mountains to
the east and south, and to hold their own against the more powerful and more civilized
Etruscans to the north.

[4] Plutarch is at fault in his timing here. The office of censor came to Camillus many
years later. It was never given to a young man.

[5] The Etruscan city of Veii, north of the Tiber, about eleven miles from Rome, was
Rome's most formidable opponent all through the fifth century. The momentous
question at issue was which should control the Tiber's mouth and the access to the
sea. By a desperate effort the Romans, about 396 B.C., took the city, as described below,
and soon afterward destroyed it.

they were compelled by their tribunes to build forts, entrench themselves, and spend both summer and winter in the enemy's country, until almost seven years of conflict had passed. Their leaders began then to be blamed and criticized as slack in their conduct of the siege. So they were removed from office, and others appointed, among whom was Camillus, then a tribune for the second time. For a while he had nothing to do with the siege, for it fell to his lot to carry on the war with the Falerians and the Capenates,[6] who during the Romans' preoccupation with Veii, had cruelly ravaged their territory, and all through the Tuscan war been very troublesome. They were now beaten and driven back by Camillus, with great losses, to the shelter of their city walls.

3. Then, when the war was at its height, great alarm was caused by the breaking out of the Alban Lake,[7] which seemed a most unbelievable prodigy and not to be accounted for by natural, familiar causes. For it was the beginning of autumn and the summer just ended had not been especially rainy or damp with south winds. In fact, many of the lakes, streams, and springs in Italy were quite dried up, and others barely moist, and all the rivers, as always in summer, were running low and sunk deep in their beds. But the Alban Lake, which has its source and outlet in itself and lies surrounded by fertile mountains, was seen for no reason, unless it were the will of heaven, to rise and swell until it touched the lower slopes and from there mounted to the topmost heights, all without surge or billow. At first, the sight was only an amazement to the shepherds and herdsmen; but when the volume and weight of water broke through the earth, which like an isthmus held the lake back from the land below, and a huge torrent poured down over the fields and orchards to the sea, not only were the Romans thunderstruck but the people of all Italy took it as a portent of some great evil to come. There was much talk of it in the camp before Veii, so that even the city population learned of the disaster of the lake.

4. As often happens during a long siege, when many meetings and conferences with the enemy are held, it chanced that a certain Roman had

---

6 Capena and Falerii, in the territory of the Faliscans, north of Veii, were two more cities of the Etruscans.

7 The Alban Lake, in the crater of an extinct volcano, is a small, deep and picturesque body of water in the Alban Hills, about fourteen miles southeast of Rome.

become intimate and free with a citizen of Veii who was deeply versed
in ancient lore and as a soothsayer was supposed to be exceptionally wise.
When this man heard of the overflowing of the lake, the Roman observed
that he was overjoyed, and began to speak in a jeering tone of the siege.
He then told him that that was not the only wonder taking place, but
that other signs even stranger were appearing to the Romans, about which
he would like to consult him, so as, if possible, to get help for himself
amid all the general calamities. The man listened eagerly and agreed to
a talk, expecting to hear some marvelous stories, and thus conversing was
gradually drawn some distance outside the city gate. Then suddenly, the
Roman, who was the sturdier of the two, seized and overpowered him,
with the aid of others who came running up from the camp, and turned
him over to the generals. Under compulsion and seeing there was no
escape from fate's decrees, the man revealed a secret oracle concerning his
city, that it could not be taken until the Alban Lake had overflowed,
and then been driven back by the Romans, turned in the other direction,
and prevented from flowing to the sea.

On hearing this, the senate was at a loss what to do, and decided to
send an embassy to Delphi, to ask counsel of the god. The envoys were
men of high repute and standing—Licinius Cossus, Valerius Potitus, and
Fabius Ambustus. They crossed the sea and came back with several responses from Apollo. One was that certain ancestral rites connected with
the Latin festivals had been neglected; [8] another that the water of the
Alban Lake must be kept away from the sea and shut up within its
ancient bounds, or, if that could not be done, it must be diverted into
canals and ditches and thus spread over the plain. On receiving this message, the priests performed the neglected sacrifices, while the people went
out into the fields and turned the course of the water.[9]

5.   In the tenth year of the war, the senate suspended all the other offices
and made Camillus dictator. He chose Cornelius Scipio to be master of
the horse, and vowed to the gods that if the war ended successfully he

---

[8] These were festivals of the allied Latin peoples, which had come down from the
times of the Roman kings. The Romans presided over them but the peoples of all the
allied tribes attended.

[9] The tunnel which the Romans bored through the rocky shore of the lake to carry
off surplus water is still to be seen, with the water running through it.

would celebrate great games in their honor, and dedicate a shrine to the goddess whom the Romans call Mater Matuta.[10] This goddess, according to the ceremonies by which she is worshiped, is much the same as the Greek Leucothea. For the women take a maidservant into the temple and beat her, then drive her out; they embrace their brothers' children instead of their own, and behave at the sacrifice like the nurses of Dionysus, and like Ino in her misery over her husband's concubine.

After making his vow, Camillus invaded the territory of the Falerians, and in a great battle overthrew them and the Capenates, who came to their assistance. Next he turned to the siege of Veii, and seeing that it would be difficult and hazardous to take the city by assault, he had tunnels dug, for the soil around the city was easily worked and the tunnels could be dug deep without the enemy's knowledge. While this work was going forward as he had hoped, he kept attacking the city from outside to call the enemy to the walls. Thus the other Romans made their way unperceived through the tunnels inside the citadel to the temple of Juno, the largest temple in the city and the most revered. There, it is said, at that very crisis, the Etruscan commander happened to be sacrificing, and his diviner, on inspecting the entrails of the victim, exclaimed in a loud voice that the goddess would give victory to those who completed that offering. The Romans underneath in the tunnel heard these words, and quickly broke up through the temple pavement and burst out with shouts and clashing of arms. The enemy fled in terror, while the Romans seized the entrails and carried them to Camillus. This story, however, sounds perhaps rather like fiction.

But the city was stormed and the Romans seized and carried off an enormous amount of plunder. Camillus, watching from the citadel what was taking place, at first stood and wept. Then while those around him were offering their congratulations, he raised his hands to the gods and uttered this prayer: "O Jupiter, most mighty, and all ye gods who look down on men's good and evil deeds, ye know that it is not unrighteously but of necessity and in self-defense that we Romans have taken vengeance on this city of our lawless enemies! If in retribution for what we have done, some punishment is due to fall on us, may it fall, I pray, not on

---

[10] Mater Matuta was the name of a Latin divinity who was early identified with the Greek Ino, daughter of Cadmus, known also as Leucothea.

the city or on the army of Rome, but on my head, with the least possible hurt." With these words, he faced around to the right, as is the Roman habit after prayer and worship, and while turning stumbled and fell. All present were startled, but he got up from his fall and said that he had received now what he had prayed for, a trifling mishap to atone for a great good fortune.

6. Having sacked the city, he determined to carry the statue of Juno to Rome, to fulfill his vow. And when the workmen had come together for the task, he offered sacrifice, and begged the goddess to accept their devotion and graciously to take up her abode among the gods of Rome. And the statue, they say, answered in a low voice that she was ready and willing to go. But Livy tells us [11] that though Camillus indeed offered this prayer and touched the statue in his entreaties, it was some of the bystanders who replied that she was ready and willing and glad to go with him.

However, those who insist on and maintain the truth of the miracle have a great argument in their favor in the marvelous fortune of the city, which from its small and mean beginning could never have reached such glory and power without God and the many signal manifestations of his presence every now and again. Other prodigies of the same kind are recorded by many ancient historians, statues often dripping with sweat or groaning audibly, or turning away and closing their eyes. We too might tell of the many extraordinary things we have heard from men of our own day, not lightly to be impugned. But it is equally dangerous to be too credulous about such stories and to disbelieve them utterly. Human weakness knows no limits and no control over itself and swings from blind superstition to contempt and neglect of the gods. Caution is best and avoidance of extremes.

7. But now Camillus, either because of the magnificence of his achievement in taking a city as great as Rome after ten years of siege, or because of all the congratulations he received, became vain and had thoughts unworthy of a law-abiding magistrate. He conducted his triumph with great ostentation. He drove through Rome in a chariot drawn by four white horses, a thing no commander had ever done before or has done since, for such an equipage was held sacred and set apart for Jupiter,

---

[11] Livy, *History,* V. 22.

king and father of the gods. The citizens, unaccustomed to such splendor, were displeased with him for this.

They had a second ground for displeasure in his opposition to a law for dividing the city. The tribunes had proposed a measure for dividing the senate and the people into two equal parts, one of which should stay at home, and the other, on which the lot fell, should move to the captured city. Thus they all would be better off, and with two fine, great cities, they could guard more safely their lands and their security. The people, who had now become numerous and poor, took the scheme up eagerly, and were constantly crowding around the rostrum with demands that it be put to a vote. But the senate and the most powerful citizens thought that the tribunes were proposing not the division but the destruction of Rome, and in their indignation rallied round Camillus. He, fearing a struggle, kept suggesting schemes to keep the people occupied, and thus he postponed the voting. On this account too he fell out of favor.

The greatest and most obvious reason for the popular resentment against him was the matter of the tenth of the spoils of Veii. In this they had a plausible grievance, though one not altogether fair. On his way to Veii, it seems, he had made a vow that if he took the city he would dedicate a tenth part of the loot to the god. But when the city was taken and sacked, he either dreaded interfering with the soldiers, or in the pressure of his duties, he forgot his vow. Afterwards, when he had resigned his command, he brought the matter before the senate; and the diviners announced that the sacrifices showed that the gods were angry and must be propitiated with offerings.

8. The senate voted not that the booty should be redistributed, for that would have been difficult, but that those who had taken any of it should themselves under oath bring a tenth part to the treasury. The vote bore very harshly and arbitrarily on the soldiers, poor men who had endured much, and who now were forced to bring in a large part of what they had earned and what they might have already spent. Assailed by them, and having no better excuse to put forward, Camillus made the fantastic apology that he had forgotten his vow. The soldiers angrily said he had vowed a tenth of the enemy's property, but that he was taking the tenth from his fellow citizens. Nevertheless, everyone brought in his due share, and it was decided to make a golden bowl and send it to Delphi.

There was a scarcity of gold in the city, but while the magistrates were considering where to procure it, the women held a meeting among themselves, and offered the golden ornaments which they were wearing on their persons and which came to eight talents' weight of gold. As a fit reward for their action, the senate voted that thenceforth a suitable funeral oration should be pronounced over a woman's grave, as it was over a man's.[12] Hitherto it had not been customary to bestow a public eulogy on a dead woman. They then chose three of the noblest citizens as envoys, and gave them a ship of war, fully manned with good seamen and splendidly equipped, and sent them off. But both storms and calms are dangerous at sea, and it happened to these envoys to come close to destruction and unexpectedly escape. Becalmed off the Aeolian Islands, they were attacked by some Liparian triremes that mistook them for pirates. Moved by their prayers and beseechings, the Liparians did not run them down, but took their ship in tow and brought it to harbor. There they put up the Romans' goods and persons for sale, treating them as pirates. At last and with difficulty, through the courage and efforts of one man, Timesitheus, their own general, the Liparians were persuaded to let them go. Timesitheus then launched ships of his own, accompanied the Romans the rest of the way, and took part in the ceremony of dedication. In return for this service, he received proper honors at Rome.

9. Again the tribunes of the people agitated for the law to divide the city, but the war with the Faliscans broke out opportunely, giving the patricians a chance to hold what elections they pleased. As a commander of ability, reputation, and experience seemed to be needed, they chose Camillus military tribune, with five colleagues. When the people had confirmed the election, Camillus took the army, marched into Faliscan territory and besieged Falerii, a strongly-fortified city, plentifully stored with all the essentials for war. He thought it would be a long and difficult task to take the city, but he was anxious to distract the people's at-

12 Plutarch's chronology is again mistaken. It was not at this time but later, when the Gauls were demanding gold for leaving Rome, that the women contributed their ornaments and were rewarded by being given the right to public funeral orations. See below, ch. 28. On this earlier occasion they received the right to appear in chariots at the public games and to ride through the streets in open carriages. Roman women were still much circumscribed in their activities and kept ordinarily in a state of almost oriental seclusion.

tention and keep them busy, so that they would not sit around idly at home and be swayed by demagogues and factious groups. This was always the effective policy which the Romans, like doctors, used as medicine to cure the state of troublesome disorders.

10. The Falerians had such confidence in all their defenses that they thought little of the siege. Except for the guards on the walls, the inhabitants walked about the city in the dress of peace; the boys went to school as usual and were taken by their teacher beyond the walls for exercise and play. For the Falerians, like the Greeks,[13] had a single teacher for all their boys, wishing their sons from the start to grow up in a herd together. Now this teacher had determined to betray Falerii through its boys, and kept leading them outside the walls every day, at first but a little way, bringing them back inside after their exercise. Then little by little he led them farther and accustomed them to being fearless, as if there were no danger. At last, one day he brought them all as far as the Roman pickets, delivered them up, and demanded to be taken to Camillus. On being taken before Camillus, he said he was the boys' instructor and teacher, but that he preferred Camillus' favor to doing his duty, and so had come to hand over the city to him, in the persons of its boys.

On hearing this, Camillus thought the man had done a terrible thing, and turning to the others present he said: "War is, indeed, a cruel thing, waged with much injustice and violence. Nevertheless, for good men even war has its laws, and we must not be so hot after victory as to accept the aid of base and ungodly crimes. A great general relies on his valor in the fight, not on the scoundrelly deeds of other men." Thereupon he commanded his attendants to tear off the man's clothes, tie his hands behind his back, and give the boys sticks and scourges with which to beat the traitor and drive him back to the city.

The Falerians had just at that moment discovered the schoolmaster's treachery, and, as might be expected, the city was filled with lamentation at the dreadful calamity. Men and women together were rushing distractedly to the walls and gates, when, lo, there came the boys, whipping their teacher back, stripped and bound, and singing the praises of Camillus as their savior, father, and god! Not only the parents of the boys but

---

[13] The Greeks of whom Plutarch is thinking are of course the Spartans. On their method of training their sons in bands together, see above, *Lycurgus,* chs. 16–19.

all the citizens who saw it were struck with admiration and a desire for Camillus' justice. They quickly assembled and sent ambassadors to him, placing themselves and their possessions in his hands. Camillus sent the men on to Rome. There they stood before the senate and said that the Romans, by prizing justice more than victory, had taught them to prefer defeat to freedom, not that they thought themselves outdone in strength so much as that they acknowledged themselves inferior in virtue. The senate referred the matter back to Camillus to judge as he thought right. He took some money from the Faliscans, made a treaty of alliance with them, and departed.

11. But the soldiers had looked forward to looting Falerii, and when they came home empty-handed, they railed to the other citizens against Camillus, as a hater of the people, who begrudged the poor what belonged to them. And when the tribunes again introduced the proposal for dividing the city, and summoned the people to vote, Camillus openly opposed it, caring nothing for the people's outspoken hatred. So the measure was voted down against the people's will, and they were so furious with Camillus that even when he met with domestic affliction and lost one of his two sons by illness their anger was not softened by pity. He was prostrated by this sorrow, being a man of loving and kindly disposition, and even after the publication of his indictment he stayed grieving at home, secluded with the women of his family.

12. His accuser was Lucius Apuleius, and the charge was theft of the spoils from Etruria. It was said that some bronze doors, which were part of the booty, had been seen in his house. And the people were so enraged that it was clear they would use any pretext to condemn him. So eventually he gathered together his friends and comrades, a considerable number in all, and begged them not to allow him to be convicted on false accusations and made the mock and scorn of his enemies. But his friends, after consulting together, replied that they did not think they could help him in his trial, but that if he were fined, they would help him pay. This he would not endure, so in anger he determined to quit the city and go into exile. Taking leave of his wife and son, he walked silently from his house to the city gate. There he halted and turned around and stretching out his arms to the Capitol prayed the gods that if he were besmirched and driven out unjustly through the insolence and jealousy of the people,

the Romans might soon have to repent and show all men that they needed Camillus and wanted him back.[14]

13. Like Achilles then,[15] he cursed his countrymen and left them. His case was undefended, and he was fined fifteen thousand *ases*,[16] which in Greek money amounts to fifteen hundred *drachmas*. The *as* was the common coin at that time, and the coin worth ten copper *ases*, called a *denarius*, was the same as our *drachma*.

Every Roman believes that the prayers of Camillus were quickly heard by Justice, and that bitter punishment followed to avenge his wrongs. Indeed all men's mouths were full of it. For a fearful retribution fell on Rome, and a season of catastrophe, peril, and disgrace, whether chance had ordained it, or whether it was the work of some god who looks out for virtue which has met with ingratitude.

14. The first omen of an impending great evil was the death of Julius the censor. The Romans particularly revere this office and consider it sacred. The second omen appeared a short time before Camillus went into exile. One Marcus Caedicius, a man of no special importance, not even a senator, but considered respectable and honest, reported to the military tribunes something that deserved attention. He said that the night before he had been walking along what is called New Street when someone called him clearly by name. Turning around, he saw no one but heard a voice louder than any man's voice, saying, "Go, Marcus Caedicius, early in the morning and tell the government that they may shortly expect the Gauls." On hearing the story the tribunes laughed it to scorn. And shortly afterward Camillus had his troubles.

15. Now the Gauls are a people of the Celtic [17] race who are said to have become too numerous to be sustained by their own country, and consequently left it to search for other lands. There were many thousands of young warriors, and they brought with them a still greater number

---

14 Camillus went into exile at Ardea, a Latin town a few miles south of Rome.

15 See Homer, *Iliad*, Classics Club edition, p. 18.

16 Approximately $2,500. On the value of *as*, *denarius* and *drachma* in ancient times, see Glossary.

17 The Romans gave the name of Celts to all the inhabitants of northern Italy, Gaul, Spain, and Britain.

of women and children. One body of them crossed the Rhipaean Mountains [18] and went towards the northern ocean, settling in the most distant part of Europe. Another body found homes between the Pyrenees and the Alps, near the Senones and the Celtorii, and dwelt there for a long time. At length they tasted wine, which was then for the first time brought out of Italy, and were all so enchanted with the drink and in such ecstasy over the new pleasure that they snatched up their arms and, taking their families with them, marched directly to the Alps to find the land which produced such fruits, regarding all other countries now as barren and savage.

The man who introduced wine among them and did most to make them eager to go to Italy is said to have been one Arron, an Etruscan. He was a man of some note and naturally well-intentioned, but he had met with the following misfortune. He was guardian to an orphan named Lucumo, the wealthiest person in his city and extraordinarily handsome. The boy had lived with Arron from childhood and even when he grew up did not leave his house, but pretended to enjoy his company. Then for a long time he secretly corrupted Arron's wife, and was corrupted by her. Finally they were both so carried away by passion, and so powerless either to suppress their desires or to conceal them, that the youth openly attempted to elope with the woman and have her to wife. Arron thereupon took his case to court, but was defeated because of the influence and lavish expenditures of Lucumo. He then left the city, and hearing of the Gauls, went up to them, and became the leader of their expedition into Italy.

16.   They came in throngs and at once made themselves masters of all the country that the Etruscans inhabited of old, extending from the Alps down to both seas. The names thereabout are evidence of their occupation, for the northern sea is called the Adriatic, from the Etruscan city Adria, and the southern is called the Etruscan Sea. That whole country is well-wooded, with plenty of pasturage for flocks and abundant rivers. It had also eighteen large and fine cities, well fitted for trade and for festive living. The Gauls then took these cities from the Etruscans, and settled in them themselves. But all this had taken place a long time before Camillus' day.

---

[18] Rhipaean Mountains was a name given vaguely to a range of mountains supposed to lie somewhere in the extreme north of Europe.

17. In his time the Gauls had made an attack on the Etruscan city of Clusium,[19] and were besieging it. The Clusians appealed to the Romans to send ambassadors for them with a letter to the barbarians. So they sent three men of the Fabian gens, of high standing and distinction in the city. The Gauls received them with courtesy because of the fame of Rome, halted the assault on the city walls, and gathered for a conference. The Romans inquired what wrong the people of Clusium had done them that they should come down against the city. At this, Brennus, king of the Gauls, laughed and replied: "The people of Clusium wrong us by claiming a right to possess a large share of the earth, though they can cultivate only a small part of it, and refusing to share it with us, who are strangers, numerous, and poor. You were wronged in the same way, O Romans, in the past by the people of Alba and Fidenae and Ardea, and more recently by the Veientines and Capenates, and many of the Faliscans and Volscians. And you make war on these people if they refuse to share their possessions with you; you make slaves of them, plunder their lands, and destroy their cities. In this you do nothing shocking or wrong, but simply obey that most ancient of all laws, which gives the property of the weak to the strong, a law which begins with God and ends with the beasts of prey. For in them too is the instinct of nature that makes the stronger fight to have more than the weaker. So now leave off pitying these besieged Clusians, lest you teach us Gauls to be kind and compassionate towards people maltreated by Romans."

This speech showed the Roman ambassadors that Brennus had no thought of coming to terms. They therefore went on into Clusium and heartened and encouraged the inhabitants to sally out with them against the barbarians, whether they did this because they wished to test the valor of the Gauls, or to display their own. The Clusians then sallied out and a battle began along the walls, during which one of the Fabii, Quintus Ambustus, spurred his horse at a tall and handsome Gaul who was riding well out in advance of the rest. At first no one recognized the Roman, because the clash came quickly and his glittering armor hid his face. But when he had conquered and overthrown the Gaul, and was stripping

---

19 Clusium, now called Chiusi, not far from Perugia, was one of the largest and most important Etruscan cities. Many remains of Etruscan architecture, sculpture, and painting have been excavated there.

him of his arms, Brennus recognized him and called the gods to witness
that, contrary to the just and holy laws of all men, one who had come
as an ambassador was behaving as an enemy. He immediately stopped
the battle, left the Clusians in peace, and led his army on against Rome.
He did not, however, wish it to be thought that the Gauls were glad of
the incident and only wanted a pretext for a quarrel with the Romans.
He therefore sent ahead to demand the surrender of Fabius for punishment, and meanwhile led his army slowly forward.

18. At Rome the senate was convened, and many blamed Fabius. The
priests who go by the name of *Fetiales* called urgently on the senate in
the name of the gods to turn the curse for the offense upon the sinful
head, and thus cleanse the rest of the city from guilt. The *Fetiales* had
been instituted by Numa Pompilius, mildest and justest of kings, to be
guardians of peace, and judges and confirmers of just reasons for declaring a war. But the senate referred the matter to the people, and although the priests repeated their charges against Fabius, the people, with
only scorn and ridicule for religious scruples, appointed Fabius and his
brothers military tribunes.

The Gauls heard of this and were enraged; they held back no longer,
hastening on at top speed. The people of the regions through which they
passed were terrified at their numbers, the splendor of their arms, their
energy and strength. They thought the whole land was already lost and
the cities would soon be taken. Contrary to their expectations, the Gauls
did them no injury and took nothing from their fields, but called out, as
they passed close by the cities, that they were marching against Rome
and only Romans were their enemies; all other men they considered their
friends.

To meet this onrush of the barbarians the military tribunes led the
Romans out to battle. In numbers they were not inferior, for they had
no less than forty thousand heavy-armed men, but the majority were
untrained and were handling weapons for the first time. Besides, they had
neglected the rites of the gods and sacrifices under good omens, and had
not consulted the diviners, as was the custom before risking battle. And
dire confusion was created by the number of commanders. Previously,
before far less important engagements, they had often chosen a single
commander, whom they called a dictator, knowing how important it is

in a dangerous crisis that all should unite in obedience to one supreme authority, who holds justice in his hands. The unfair treatment, too, which Camillus had received now bore disastrous fruit, for it was terrifying to be a commander if one did not ingratiate oneself with the people.

However, they proceeded about eleven miles from the city and encamped beside the river Allia, not far from where it joins the Tiber. There the barbarians came upon them, and after a disgraceful and disorderly struggle they turned and fled. Their left wing was at once driven by the Gauls into the river and destroyed. Their right wing, which retreated before the enemy's charge from the plain to the hills, was less cut up, and from the hills most of the soldiers got back to the city. The rest, as many as survived after the enemy wearied of slaughter, fled by night to Veii, supposing that Rome was lost and her inhabitants all slain.

19. This battle was fought soon after the summer solstice,[20] with the moon almost full, on the very day of a former great disaster to the Fabii, when three hundred men of that clan were killed by the Etruscans. This second great defeat so far outdid the earlier one that the day is still known as the Allia Day, from the river where it took place.

As to unlucky days, whether we should consider some days unlucky, or whether Heraclitus was right in rebuking Hesiod for calling some days good and others bad, as though he were ignorant that the nature of every day is the same, I have discussed the question thoroughly elsewhere.[21] But even in this present essay the mention of a few coincidences may not be out of place. On the fifth day of the month Hippodromios, which the Athenians call Hecatombaeon,[22] two signal victories were won by the Boeotians, which restored liberty to Greece. One was at Leuctra, when they conquered the Spartans[23] and the other at Ceressus, over two hundred years earlier, when they conquered Lattamyas and the Thessalians.

[20] The year was probably 390 B.C.

[21] In Plutarch's *Essays*.

[22] Hecatombaeon included the period from July 15 to August 15; Boedromion from September 15 to October 15; Thargelion from April 15 to May 15; Metageitnion from August 15 to September 15. The Attic calendar year began on July 15.

[23] This was the famous victory of 371 B.C., when the Thebans under Epaminondas broke the power of Sparta over Greece.

Again, on the sixth of Boedromion, the Persians were beaten by the Greeks at Marathon; [24] on the third, both at Plataea and at Mycale; and on the twenty-sixth, at Arbela. Near the full moon of Boedromion too the Athenians won their naval victory off Naxos, under Chabrias, and about the twentieth of the month, that of Salamis, as I have stated in my treatise *On Days*. The month of Thargelion evidently brings misfortune to the barbarians, for Alexander defeated the Persian king's generals on the Granicus [25] in Thargelion, and the Carthaginians were worsted by Timoleon in Sicily on the twenty-fourth of that month. On that day too, apparently, Troy was taken, according to Ephorus, Callisthenes, Damastes, and Phylarchus.

On the other hand, the month of Metageitnion, which the Boeotians call Panemos, has not been favorable to the Greeks. On the seventh of that month, they were defeated by Antipater [26] at Crannon and utterly overwhelmed, and before that, in the same month, they were routed by Philip at Chaeronea. And in that same year, on the same day of the month, Archidamus and his troops, who had crossed into Italy, were cut to pieces by the barbarians there. The Carthaginians also beware of the twenty-second of that month, because it has always been the day that brought the biggest and heaviest misfortunes to them.

I recall, too, that Thebes was destroyed for the second time by Alexander

---

[24] At Marathon, in 490 b.c., the Persians on their first invasion of central Greece were beaten by the Athenians; at Plataea, in 479, on their second invasion, by the combined Greek army led by Sparta; at Mycale, on the same day, by the Greek fleet; at Arbela in Assyria, in 331, by the army of Alexander the Great. Near Naxos, in 376, the Athenian fleet defeated the Spartan under Chabrias, and at Salamis, in 480, the Greeks won their resounding victory over the Persian ships, as described in *Themistocles*, above, chs. 12–16.

[25] The first victory of Alexander over the Persians was won on the Granicus River in Asia Minor, in 334 b.c. See below, *Alexander,* ch. 16. Timoleon, a Corinthian, about 339, reestablished Greek power in Sicily and defeated the Carthaginians, whom he met there. The capture of Troy was also of course a victory of Greeks over so-called barbarians.

[26] On Alexander's death in 323 b.c., Antipater, a Macedonian general, succeeded him as ruler of Macedonia and Greece, and completely defeated the revolting Athenians and their allies at Crannon, in 322. Philip, Alexander's father, had conquered the Athenians at Chaeronea in 338. Archidamus III was a king of Sparta who, in that same year. was killed battling in Italy.

at the time of the celebration of the mysteries.[27] Later, Athens was garrisoned by Macedonian soldiers on the twentieth of Boedromion, the day on which they bring out the mystic Iacchus in procession. Also the Romans, on that same day, lost their army under Caepio to the Cimbrians, but still later, when Lucullus was in command, defeated Tigranes and the Armenians. King Attalus and Pompey the Great both died on their own birthdays. However, one could mention many instances when the same days have produced both good and evil for the same people. But the Romans regard the day of Allia as one of the most unlucky, and because of it two other days in every month. For dread and superstition grow worse with misfortune. This subject I have treated more fully in my *Roman Questions*.

20. If, after this battle, the Gauls had at once followed up the fugitives, nothing could have prevented their destroying Rome and killing everyone left in it, such terror did the beaten troops create when they reached home, and such confusion and panic filled them all again. Actually the barbarians did not realize the extent of their victory, and in their glee turned to merry making and to dividing the spoils they had taken in the Roman camp. This gave the crowds who wanted to leave Rome full time to escape, and those who were for remaining time to pick up hope and make some preparations for defense. They abandoned all but the Capitol, and fortified that with ramparts and stores of missiles. One of their first acts was the conveyance of all sacred objects to the Capitol. The fire of Vesta, however, the virgins took with their other sacred possessions on their flight.

Some authors say that nothing is entrusted to their keeping but the sacred fire, which King Numa ordained should be worshiped as the source of all life.[28] For fire has the liveliest motion of anything in nature, and everything that comes alive is motion or is accompanied by motion. All parts of matter without heat lie inert and apparently dead, waiting for the power of fire as the breath of life. And when it comes, in whatever way, it makes it possible for them to act and to feel.

[27] During the month of Boedromion, 335 B.C., Alexander destroyed Thebes for its rebellion against him. The Cimbrians, a people from central Europe, pushed down into northern Italy at the end of the second century; in 105, they beat the Roman army under Caepio. Lucullus defeated Tigranes and his Armenians in the year 69.

[28] On Numa and his institution of the Vestal Virgins, see above, *Numa,* chs. 9–10.

Wherefore, Numa, a remarkable man, who because of his wisdom was thought to hold communion with the Muses, is said to have consecrated a fire, and ordered it to be kept sleepless forever as an emblem of the eternal power that orders all things. Others say that the fire burns before Vesta's temple simply for purification, as it does with the Greeks, but that inside are other objects which no one may see except these virgins who are called Vestals. There is a widespread notion that the famous Trojan Palladium,[29] brought to Italy by Aeneas, is stored there. Others maintain that the Samothracian gods are there, and they tell the legend of Dardanus,[30] how after founding Troy, he brought them to that city and consecrated them with their rites, and how Aeneas at the fall of Troy, carried them away and kept them until he settled in Italy.

Those who profess to know more about these things say that two small jars are preserved there, one open and empty and the other full and sealed, and that both may be seen only by the holy virgins. Whereas others call this an error, which arose from the fact that in the crisis of which we are speaking the virgins placed most of their sacred things in two jars and buried them in the earth under the temple of Quirinus. The place is called Doliola, or Jars, even at the present day.

21.   However this may be, the virgins took the chiefest and most important of their holy things and fled along the Tiber. There it happened that Lucius Albinius, a man of the people, was traveling with the other fugitives, conveying his wife and small children and their necessary goods in a wagon. When he saw the virgins carrying in their bosoms the sacred tokens of the gods and hastening along on foot unattended and in great distress, he immediately removed his wife, children, and belongings from the wagon, and gave it to the virgins to ride in, so that they might escape to a Greek city.[31] The piety of Albinius and the high honor he paid the gods in a time of such terrible peril deserve not to be forgotten.

The rest of the priests and the old men who had been consuls and had been honored with triumphs could not bear to leave the city. At the sug-

[29] The Palladium was a sacred statue of Pallas Athene, which Aeneas was said to have rescued from burning Troy and brought with him to Italy.

[30] According to the legend, Dardanus came to Troy from Arcadia, in Greece. The gods referred to here were what the Romans called their Penates, or household deities.

[31] They went, the story goes, to Caere, an Etruscan city, from whose name their rites came to be called *caerimonia,* in English, ceremonies.

gestion of Fabius, the Pontifex Maximus, they put on their sacred robes of splendor, and after offering prayers to the gods, like persons dedicating themselves to death for their country, they sat down thus arrayed in their ivory chairs in the forum to await their fate.

22. On the third day after the battle Brennus arrived, leading his army to attack the city. Finding the gates open and no guards on the walls he at first feared treachery and an ambuscade, for he could not believe that the Romans had so utterly given up hope. But when he discovered the truth, he marched in through the Colline Gate and took possession of Rome. This was a little more than three hundred and sixty years after her founding, if indeed we can believe that any exact chronology of events at that time has been preserved, when the order of later events is so doubtful as a result of the confusion created by the catastrophe. However, some vague rumor of the disaster and fall of the city seems to have reached Greece very soon, for Heraclides of Pontus, who lived not long after that time, speaks in his book *On the Soul,* of a report from the West that an army had come from the Hyperboreans [32] and captured a Greek city called Rome, which stood somewhere on the Great Sea.[33] Now since Heraclides was given to fanciful tales, I should not be surprised if he had adorned the original report with his Hyperboreans and his Great Sea. But Aristotle the philosopher had evidently heard a correct account of the taking of the city by the Gauls, though he says it was saved by one Lucius. Now Camillus' name was Marcus, not Lucius. But that was only Aristotle's conjecture.

Brennus, then, after occupying Rome, posted guards around the Capitol and himself went into the forum, and was astonished to see the old men sitting there in state and silent. They neither rose from their seats before the approaching enemy nor changed expression or color, but sat still, at ease and fearless, leaning on their staffs, facing one another. The Gauls were so amazed and puzzled by the strange sight that for a long while they were too awed to draw near them, as though they took them for superior beings. But at length one of them ventured to go up to Marcus

---

[32] In Greek mythology, the Hyperboreans were a people who lived an ideal life in eternal sunshine, beyond the North Wind. Later the name was applied to any of the tribes of northern Europe.

[33] The Great Sea was of course the Mediterranean.

Papirius and, stretching out his hand gently, touch his chin and stroke his long beard. At that Papirius struck him a smashing blow on the head with his staff, whereat the barbarian drew his sword and killed him. Thereupon the Gauls fell on the rest and killed them, and slew every other Roman they found. They then spent many days stripping and plundering the houses, finally burning them down and pulling them to the ground in their rage at the men who were still holding the Capitol. For when summoned they refused to surrender but drove back with loss the Gauls' assaults on the ramparts. So the Gauls wreaked their vengeance on the city, and put to death all their captives, men and women, old and young alike.

23.   As the siege was a long one, the Gauls began to want for provisions. They therefore divided their forces. Some stayed with the king to keep watch on the Capitol, while others went out to forage the country, attacking and plundering the villages, not keeping all in one body, but splitting up into small commands and detachments. Their successes had filled them with great confidence and they had no fear of thus dispersing their forces. The largest and best disciplined band went towards the city of Ardea, where Camillus had been living since his banishment, quietly, like a private person. But he had the hopes and plans not of one who is anxious to evade or escape from his enemy but of one who intends to avenge himself, if an opportunity offers. So, seeing that the people of Ardea were numerous enough but lacked confidence because of the inexperience and timidity of their commanders, he began to suggest to the young men, first, that they should not attribute the misfortune of the Romans to the valor of the Gauls, nor the sufferings of a misguided people to the prowess of men who did nothing to win the victory, but that they should look on the event as merely a stroke of fate. It would, he urged, be a glorious thing now to risk some danger to drive back the foreign and barbarous invader, whose purpose in conquering was like that of a fire, to destroy what it won. And if they were brave and in earnest, he would give them a chance to gain a victory with no risk at all.

When the young men had accepted his proposals, Camillus went to the magistrates and council of Ardea, and when he had persuaded them too, he armed all of age to bear arms, but kept them inside the walls that they might not be seen by the enemy, who had now drawn near. The Gauls had been scouring the country and were now returning laden down with masses of booty, and had encamped without heed or caution in the plain. Then when night had fallen on their revels, and silence enveloped the camp, Camillus, who was kept informed by his spies of the situation, led out the men of Ardea. Moving stealthily over the ground between, they charged the camp about midnight, and with loud shouts and blasts of trumpets from every direction, by their din threw the Gauls, half-drunk and heavy with sleep as they were, into complete confusion. A few in their fright recovered their senses, seized their arms and put up some resistance to Camillus and his men, and so fell defending themselves. The greater part, still overpowered by sleep and wine, were surprised without arms and slain. A few fled from the camp in the dark, but when day came they were wandering scattered over the country and were chased by horsemen and killed.

24. Rumor soon carried reports of this event to the neighboring cities, and stirred up many other men of fighting age, especially the Romans who had escaped to Veii from the battle of Allia. These men were mourning to one another: "What a leader Providence took from Rome, when it sent Camillus to glorify Ardea with his victories, leaving the city which bore and reared the hero to perish and die! And we, with no commander, sit shut up in strange walls and see Italy forsaken! Come, let us send to Ardea and beg our general of them, or else take up arms ourselves and go to him. He is no longer an exile, nor are we citizens, since we have no country but what is in the possession of the enemy."

To this all agreed, and they sent and asked Camillus to take command of them. But he refused to do so until the citizens on the Capitol had lawfully elected him. For in his opinion they were saving the country, and if they gave him orders, he would gladly obey them; but without their consent he would take no action. The soldiers admired these honorable scruples of Camillus, but there was the difficulty of making the situation known to the Capitol. Indeed, it seemed quite impossible for any messenger to reach the citadel, as long as the enemy held the city.

25. Among the young men was a Pontius Cominius, who, though of ordinary birth, had a passion for glory and honor, and he undertook the exploit. He carried no letter with him to the men on the Capitol, for fear that if he were captured, the enemy might by it discover Camillus' plans.

He dressed himself in poor clothing, beneath which he concealed pieces of cork. Most of the journey he made boldly by daylight, approaching the city as it grew dark. He could not cross the river by the bridge, for it was guarded by the enemy, but he wrapped his clothes, which were scanty and light, around his head, fastened the corks to his body, and with their help swam across, and came out on the side towards the city. Avoiding always those quarters where the enemy was on watch, as shown by their lights and noise, he went on to the Carmental Gate, where it was quietest, and where the Capitoline Hill rises steepest, bordered by a tall, rocky cliff. Up this he climbed unseen, and with great labor and pains reached the sentries on guard where the rampart was lowest. Hailing them he told them his name, and was drawn up over the rampart and taken to the Roman magistrates. The senate met at once, and he reported Camillus' victory, which they had not heard of before, and told them of the soldiers' decision. He then urged them to confirm Camillus' appointment as general, since he was the only man the citizens outside would obey. On hearing this, the senate deliberated and appointed Camillus dictator. It then sent Pontius back by the way he had come, and he had the same good fortune. For he got through unobserved by the enemy and carried the senate's messages to the Romans outside the city.

26. They heard the news with enthusiasm, and when Camillus came, he found twenty thousand men already armed. He collected more troops from the allies, and prepared to attack.[34] Thus was Camillus appointed dictator a second time, and proceeding to Veii, he joined the soldiers there and collected more from the allies to attack the enemy. But meanwhile at Rome some barbarians, who happened to be passing the place where Pontius had climbed at night up to the Capitol, noticed the marks of hands and feet made as he scrambled up, and indications of plants and vines having been uprooted. They told the king, who came and inspected the place. He said nothing at the time, but in the evening he called together the Gauls who were lightest in weight and most used to mountain climbing, and said to them: "Our enemies have shown us the road up to them, which we had not discovered, and have proved it passable for a man. It would be disgraceful if we, after our good beginning, should

---

[34] The following sentence, "Thus was Camillus . . . attack the enemy," is omitted by some editors of the text. It is clearly a superfluous repetition.

not go on to the end, but give the place up as impregnable, when the enemy himself has taught us how it may be taken. For where it was easy for one man to get up, it cannot be hard for many to climb, one by one. In fact they will be a great support and help to each other in the ascent. Rewards and honors worthy of their valor will be given to everyone."

27. This speech from the king made the Gauls eager for the enterprise, and about midnight a large company of them climbed the rock, mounting in silence and clinging close to the crags that were rough and precipitous, but easier to tackle than they had expected. The first men to reach the summit made ready and were on the point of seizing the outworks and falling on the sleeping garrison. They had been heard by neither man nor dog. But there were sacred geese kept in the temple of Juno, which at other times were plentifully fed, but which, since there was scarcely enough food for the men, were neglected and hungry. These creatures are naturally keen of hearing and afraid of noise, and they now were wakeful and restless through hunger. They heard the Gauls advancing and rushed squawking at them, and so waked the whole garrison. Whereat the barbarians, knowing themselves discovered, no longer tried to be quiet but violently began the assault.

The Romans hastily snatched up whatever arms came to hand, and met the crisis as they could. First of all, Manlius, a man of consular rank, powerful in body and mighty in spirit, engaged two of the enemy at once. As one of them lifted up his battle-ax, Manlius cut off his right hand with his sword, and dashing his shield into the other's face, pushed him backwards over the cliff. Then he took his stand on the wall and with the help of those who ran up to join him beat off the rest of the enemy, for not many had reached the top and completed their daring feat. So the Romans escaped this danger, but at dawn they threw the captain of their sentinels down the rock to the enemy. On Manlius they voted to confer a reward of victory which was more honorable than serviceable. They collected for him from everyone a day's ration, consisting of half a pound of the local meal, by Roman measure, and one-eighth of a Greek pint of wine.

28. This failure disheartened the Gauls. They were short of provisions and could not forage as before, for fear of Camillus. Disease also crept

among them, encamped as they were amid ruins, with piles of corpses scattered about. The clouds of ashes blown about by the hot winds made the air dry and stinging and injurious to breathe. Most of all they were upset by the change in their mode of life. For they had come abruptly from a shady country, where there are plenty of retreats from the summer heat, to a flat land, abnormally hot in autumn. Added to these trials were the tediousness and inactivity of the siege of the Capitol, which was now in its seventh month. There was much mortality, therefore, in the camp and so many died that the dead were no longer buried.

Things were no better with the besieged, for they were growing hungrier, and their ignorance of what Camillus was doing made them despondent. No one could reach them with news from him, because the city was now guarded closely by the barbarians. Since both sides were in such dire straits, proposals for a compromise were made, first, by the sentries as they came in contact with each other; then the leaders took it up. Brennus and Sulpicius, the Roman tribune, met for a conference, and it was agreed that the Romans should pay a thousand pounds of gold and the Gauls, on receipt of it, should at once withdraw from the city and the country. Oaths were sworn to these terms, and the gold was brought to be weighed. But the Gauls tampered with the scales, stealthily at first, and then openly pulling on and upsetting the weights, so that the Romans became angry. Brennus, with a scornful laugh, pulled off his sword and belt and threw them both onto the weights. "What does this mean?" cried Sulpicius, and Brennus replied, "What should it mean, but woe to the vanquished!" Indignant at this behavior, some of the Romans thought they should take their gold back again and go on enduring the siege. Others said they must put up with petty injustices, and remember that the disgrace lay not in paying more but in paying at all. So in the emergency they submitted, not nobly but of necessity.

29. While the Romans were thus disputing with the Gauls and among themselves, Camillus was at the gates with his army. Learning what was going on, he ordered the main body of his soldiers to follow him in order, close behind, while he himself pushed ahead with picked troops and soon reached the Romans. They all made way for him in silence and respect, accepting him as their dictator. He then lifted the gold from the scales and gave it to his attendants, and ordered the Gauls to take their

scales and weights and depart, saying that it was the custom of Romans to save their country with iron and not with gold.[35] When Brennus in anger said they were wronging him by breaking their agreement, Camillus answered that the agreement was not legal or binding, because when they made it, he had already been elected dictator and there was no other lawful ruler. The compact had therefore been made with men who had no authority. Now they might say what they wanted, for he had come with full legal power to pardon those who asked for it and to punish the guilty, unless they repented.

At this, Brennus raised a shout and started a fight; but both sides got no further than drawing their swords and shoving each other about, for the meeting had taken place among the houses and narrow lanes of the city where no military formation was possible. Brennus soon realized this and led his men off to their camp, with the loss of only a few. Then in the night, with all his forces, he left the city, and after a march of about eight miles, encamped along the Gabinian Way.[36] At daybreak Camillus and his troops, in glittering array and full of confidence, were upon him. After a long and fiercely contested battle, they routed the Gauls with great slaughter and took their camp. Some of the fugitives were pursued and slain immediately, but most of them straggled off and were caught and killed by the people of the neighboring towns and villages.

30. Thus was Rome strangely taken, and yet more strangely delivered, after having been for seven months in the possession of the Gauls. They entered it a few days after the Ides of July [37] and were expelled about the Ides of February. Camillus held a well-deserved triumph, for he had saved a country that was lost and brought the city back to itself. The citizens who had left it, with their wives and children, accompanied him, while those who had been besieged on the Capitol and all but starved

---

35 But according to Polybius, Suetonius, Justin, and other historians, the Gauls did take the gold with them when they went back to their own country.
36 The Gabinian Way was the road from Rome to the Latin town of Gabii, twelve miles to the east, now called Castiglione. The road is more commonly known as the Praenestian Way, or Via Praenestina, from the larger town of Praeneste beyond Gabii.
37 The Ides of July would be the fifteenth, the Ides of February the thirteenth of the month. See Glossary.

there came down to meet him, all embracing one another and weeping for the joy of that day. The priests and servants of the gods also appeared, with such of the sacred things as they had saved by either burying them on the spot or carrying them away. They displayed these longed-for sights to the citizens, who greeted them as gladly as if the gods themselves were now coming back with them to Rome. And after Camillus had sacrificed to the gods and purified the city according to the instructions of those who were wise in such matters, he proceeded to restore the existing temples, and erected a new one to Rumor, or Voice, having carefully sought out the place where the voice from God in the night, warning of the approach of the barbarian armies, had come to Marcus Caedicius.

31. With great toil and difficulty the sites of the temples were cleared of rubble by the zeal of Camillus and the hard labor of the priests. When it came to the necessary rebuilding of the city, which had been totally destroyed, the people were disheartened at the vast undertaking, and put it off. Thy lacked everything, and at the moment needed rest and respite from troubles instead of more struggling and straining after something for which they had neither the materials nor the strength. So again their thoughts turned easily towards Veii, a city which still stood intact and filled with all they wanted. Thus an opportunity was presented to the demagogues who usually played for popularity, and who now spoke seditiously of Camillus. For his own private ambition and glory, they said, he would deprive them of a city that was waiting to receive them, and compel them to stay there among the ruins and rebuild that enormous funeral pyre, so that he might not only have the title of dictator and general of Rome, but might usurp the place of Romulus and be called its founder as well.

Frightened by the uproar, the senate would not allow Camillus to do as he wished and lay down the dictatorship within a year, although no previous dictator had served for more than six months. Meanwhile, the senators themselves were meeting and trying to steady the people with encouraging and persuasive words. They pointed out the monuments and tombs of their fathers, reminded them of the shrines and holy places which Romulus and Numa and other kings had consecrated and left in their keeping. Among the great omens from the gods was a newly severed head, which was found when they laid the foundations of the Capitol, and which showed that the spot was destined to be the head of Italy.[38] They mentioned too the sacred fire of Vesta, which had been rekindled by the virgins after the war. To extinguish or let it go out and abandon the city would be a disgrace, whether they saw it reinhabited by strangers or left deserted as grazing ground for cattle. But while the senators persisted in urging these considerations on the people, both individually, in private, and in the public assemblies, they were deeply moved by the lamentations of the masses over their forlorn condition. They were, they declared, like men saved from a shipwreck, naked and destitute, and they begged not to be forced to patch together the remains of a ruined city, while another was standing all prepared to receive them.

32. Camillus then thought it wise to have the question debated in council. He himself made a long appeal on behalf of their native country, and everyone else spoke who wished to. Finally, he rose and bade Lucius Lucretius, who habitually voted first, state his opinion, and then the other senators in order. In the silence that followed, just as Lucretius was about to begin, it happened that a centurion, leading a detachment of the guard for the day, went by outside and in a loud voice called to the standard bearer to stop and pitch the standard there, for it was the best place to fix the post. The voice came at that crisis, in the midst of all their thought and perplexity as to the future, and Lucretius, with an obeisance, said that he cast his vote with the god. And all the others followed his example. Among the people there was a wonderful change of feeling, and they urged and encouraged one another to begin the work. Since it was begun without any concerted plan, and each man took for his site whatever was available or attractive, the result was a hastily-built city with intricate narrow lanes and a confusion of houses. But within a year, they say, a new city with its walls and private dwellings had arisen.

Those whom Camillus had ordered to take the sacred places in charge and mark out their sites found them all in total ruin. And when, in their circuit of the Palatine, they came to the shrine of Mars, they found it, too, like the rest, wrecked and burned by the Gauls. But as they were

[38] According to the more usual legend, this marvel occurred much earlier, at the time of the building of the Capitoline temple to Jupiter, under King Tarquin the Elder, whose reign traditionally covered the years from 616 to 578 B.C.

searching through and cleaning up the spot, they came on the augur's staff of Romulus buried under a deep heap of ashes. This staff is curved at one end and is called a *lituus*. It is used to divide off the separate quarters of the heavens when taking auspices by the flight of birds, as Romulus himself, who was a great augur, used it. When he vanished from the sight of men, the priests took his staff and kept it untouched, like any other holy object. That this staff, when all the other holy things had perished, should be found unhurt, gave them fresh hope for Rome, for it seemed a sign assuring her of safety.

33.   However, they were not yet rested from their tasks when war again fell on them. The Aequians, Volscians, and Latins together invaded their territory, while the Etruscans besieged Sutrium, a city allied with Rome. The tribunes in command of the army encamped near Mount Marcius, and were there besieged by the Latins and in danger of being driven from their camp. They sent to Rome for help, and the Romans appointed Camillus dictator for the third time.

Two stories are told of this war; I shall repeat the more legendary first. It is said that the Latins, either as a pretext for a war, or because they really wished to mix the two races together again, sent a request to Rome for free maidens to be sent them as wives. The Romans were at a loss what to do, for they dreaded war, while still so unsettled and so far from recovery, and they suspected that the request for wives was actually a demand for hostages, under the specious title of marriage. Then a slave girl named Tutula, or, as some say, Philotis, proposed to the magistrates to send her and some of the most attractive female slaves, most like free women in appearance, all of them decked out like freeborn brides, saying she would manage the rest. Persuaded by her, the magistrates chose as many slave girls as she thought were needed, dressed them in fine clothes and gold and handed them over to the Latins, who were encamped not far from the city. At night the girls got possession of the enemy's swords, and Tutula, or Philotis, climbed up a tall, wild fig tree, and spreading out her cloak behind her, brandished a torch in the direction of Rome. This signal had been agreed on between her and the magistrates, though no other citizen knew of it. The Roman soldiers in a mob hurried out of the gates, as their leaders called them to arms, shouting to one another and with difficulty getting into their places in the lines. When they reached the enemy's trenches, they found them asleep, expecting nothing, so they took the camp and slew most of them.

This battle occurred on the Nones of the month then called Quintilis, now called July, and the festival now held at that time is in memory of that victory. On that day the men flock out of the city in crowds, shouting out familiar and common first names, Gaius, Marcus, Lucius, and names like those, in imitation of the soldiers' calls to each other in their haste. Next, slave girls, brilliantly dressed, walk around joking and romping with everyone they meet. They also skirmish among themselves, as though they had helped in the fight with the Latins. Afterwards they sit down to a feast in the shade of fig-tree boughs. The day is called Capratine Nones [39] from the wild fig tree, they think, from which the girl waved her torch. For the name of the tree is *caprificus.* Others think that most of what is said and done at this festival refers to the disappearance of Romulus, for on this same day he vanished from sight outside the gates, in a sudden darkness and storm, caused, some suppose, by an eclipse of the sun. And the day is called Capratine Nones from the spot where Romulus disappeared. For a name for a she-goat is *capra,* and Romulus vanished while addressing the people near the Goat's Marsh, as we have related in his *Life.*

34. The other story, which most writers prefer, is as follows. After Camillus had been appointed dictator for the third time, and had learned that the army under the military tribunes was besieged by the Latins and the Volscians, he felt obliged to arm even those citizens who were past the age for military service and already well on in years. Marching in a long circuit around Mount Marcius, unobserved by the enemy, he established his army in their rear; then by lighting many fires he gave notice of his arrival. The besieged Romans took courage and started to sally out and take part in the fight, but the Latins and Volscians drew back inside their trenches, fenced themselves in behind a great palisade, and barricaded their camp on all sides. For they were now caught between two hostile armies, and their plan was to wait for reinforcements from home. They expected aid also from the Etruscans.

[39] For other mention of the Capratine Nones and the end of Romulus, see above, *Numa,* n. 6.

Camillus perceived their plan, and fearing he might be surrounded in his turn hurriedly seized his opportunity. The enemy's barricade was of wood, and a strong wind blew down from the mountains at dawn. He made his preparations accordingly and at daybreak led out his forces. One division he ordered to start attacking the camp at one point with missile weapons and loud shouts, while he himself, with those assigned to hurl fire, waited for the right moment on the opposite side, where the wind blew hardest on the enemy's defenses. As the fighting began, the sun rose and the wind swept blustering down. At this Camillus gave the signal for the assault, and blazing darts flew scattering along the trenches. The flames quickly found their fuel in the thick-set timber of the wooden palisades, and spread in every direction. The Latins, having nothing wherewith to keep them off or extinguish them, and their camp in flames, drew together in a small space, but finally were forced to charge out against an enemy well armed and drawn up beyond the entrench-ment. Few of them escaped, and all who remained in the camp perished in the fire, until the Romans extinguished it and took the plunder.

35. Camillus then left his son Lucius in charge of the camp to guard the prisoners and the booty, and himself went on to invade the enemy's country. He captured the Aequians' city, reduced the Volscians to sub-jection, and then led his army towards Sutrium. He had not yet heard of what had happened to the Sutrians, but supposing they were still in the perils of siege by the Etruscans hurried to their aid. But the Sutrians had already surrendered their city to the enemy, and had been turned out of it with nothing save the clothes they were wearing. Camillus met them on the road with their wives and children, bewailing their mis-fortunes. Moved to compassion at the piteous sight, and seeing that his Roman soldiers too, as the Sutrians clung to them in entreaty, were in tears and rage at their plight, he determined to avenge their wrongs at once and to march on Sutrium that very day.

He assumed that men who had just captured a prosperous and wealthy city and left no enemy in it, and were expecting none from outside, would be found completely relaxed and off guard. In this he was right. He not only passed unperceived through the country, but was actually before the city gates and taking over the walls before the enemy was aware of him. There was no one on guard, for they were all carousing and drinking, scattered through the private houses. Even when they learned that their enemy already had them in his power, they were so stupefied with over-eating and drunkenness that many did not even try to escape, but waited shamefully inside the houses and were killed or surrendered. Thus was the city of Sutrium taken twice in one day, and thus did its captors lose it again and those who had lost it regain it, thanks to Camillus.

36. The triumph he received for these victories brought him as much popularity and honor as his first two had done. Even those citizens who were most disparaging of him, and who had chosen to attribute all his successes to his good fortune rather than to his ability, were forced by these new exploits to give the man's brilliancy and vigor credit for his renown. His chief opponent and detractor at that time was Marcus Manlius, the man who had been first to throw the Gauls down the cliff during their night attack on the Capitol, and who for that feat had been surnamed Capitolinus. This man wanted to make himself first in the city, and not being able to outrival Camillus by fair means, he employed the method commonly used by a would-be tyrant. He ingratiated himself with the people, especially with those who were in debt. Some of these he defended and helped in their suits with their creditors, while others he rescued by force and saved from any trial by law. For this reason a large party of the impoverished quickly gathered around him and became the terror of the more respectable citizens by their riotous disturbances in the forum. To put an end to these disorders, Quintus Capitolinus was made dictator, and he sent Manlius to prison.

At this the people put on mourning, a thing done only in times of great public disaster, and the senate, intimidated by the uproar, ordered Manlius to be released. But when set at liberty, he was no better, indeed rather more insolent, filling the whole city with a spirit of faction and turbulence. Camillus was therefore again chosen military tribune. The case of Manlius was tried, but the location told greatly against his accusers; for the spot on the Capitoline Hill where Manlius had stood when he fought off the Gauls that night could be seen from the forum and stirred the onlookers to pity. Manlius, too, stretching out his hands towards that spot and weeping, reminded them of how he had struggled, so that the judges did not know what to do and several times adjourned the trial. They would not acquit him of a crime which had been clearly proved against him, and yet they could not execute the law, when the place where they sat was bringing his great exploit before their eyes again.

Realizing this, Camillus had the court removed to the Peteline Grove outside the city gates, from which the Capitol is not visible. There the prosecutor pressed the accusation, and the judges' memories of Manlius' past heroism gave way to righteous indignation at his recent crimes. So he was convicted, taken to the Capitol, and thrown over the cliff, which was thus a monument to his greatest achievement and his most miserable fate. The Romans tore down his house and built on the site a temple to the goddess they call Moneta.[40] They decreed also that in future no patrician should have a house on the Capitoline Hill.

37. When Camillus was appointed military tribune for the sixth time, he begged to be excused, as he was by now growing old and feared perhaps the envy and resentment of the gods at his undimmed glory and brilliant successes. The most obvious reason for his refusal, however, was his physical weakness, for he happened to be ailing at the time. But the people would not relieve him of his command. They clamored that they did not want him to ride with the cavalry or to fight in the ranks but merely to counsel and give orders. Thus they compelled him to keep his office, and with one of his colleagues, Lucius Furius, straightway to lead an army against the enemy. These were the Praenestians and the Volscians, who with a large force were ravaging the territory of Roman allies. Accordingly he left the city and encamped near the enemy, but thought it wise to go slowly with the war, so that if a battle should later become inevitable, he would be sound of body for the fight. His colleague, Lucius, was so eager for glory that he could not be restrained from running into danger, and he kindled the same ambition in the subordinate officers.

Accordingly Camillus, fearing that someone would think that out of jealousy he was depriving the younger men of the successes for which they were yearning, agreed against his judgment to allow his colleague to lead the army out to battle, while he, because of his illness, with a few troops was left behind in the camp. But Lucius was rash in his conduct

---

[40] The temple of Juno Moneta on the Capitoline Hill, near the great temple of Jupiter Capitolinus, was early used as the national mint, and one of Juno's functions, therefore, came to be guardianship of Roman finance.

of the fight and was defeated. And when Camillus heard that the Romans were in flight, he could not restrain himself. Springing from his couch, he ran with his attendants to the gates of the camp. There he pushed his way through the fugitives towards their pursuers. The Romans he passed turned around at once and followed him, while those beyond, who were fleeing towards him, halted and formed ranks ahead of him, calling to one another not to desert their general. For the moment, then, the enemy's pursuit was checked. The next day Camillus led out his forces, fought a battle, and utterly routed them. He took their camp, too, falling on it at the same time that their fugitives were escaping to it, and killing most of them. Next, hearing that the city of Satricum had been captured by the Etruscans, and its inhabitants, who were all Romans, put to death, he sent the greater part of his army, the heavy infantry, back to Rome, and with the youngest and most vigorous of his men suddenly attacked the Etruscans who held the city, and vanquished them, driving some of them out and killing the rest.

38. His return to Rome with immense spoils proved that the men of most sagacity had been those who had not feared the weakness or old age of a commander of such courage and experience, but had chosen him, ill and unwilling, over more youthful men who were begging hard for the post. So again, when the Tusculans [41] were reported to be in revolt, Camillus was ordered to select one of the other five tribunes as his aide, and march against them. All five were eager and asked to be chosen, but Camillus, to everyone's surprise, passed over the others and chose Lucius Furius, the very man who shortly before, against Camillus' judgment, had recklessly hazarded and lost a battle. Camillus, it would appear, wished to obliterate that misfortune and wipe out that disgrace, and so took Lucius in preference to all the rest.

The people of Tusculum, as soon as Camillus set out against them, started very cleverly to correct their misbehavior. They filled their fields with men cultivating the soil and tending cattle, as in times of peace; their city gates stood open, and their boys were at school, learning their lessons. As for the rest, the artisan was to be seen plying his trade, and

---

41 Tusculum, a Latin city beautifully situated in the Alban Hills, southeast of Rome, was at this time supposedly an obedient ally of Rome.

the man-about-town strolling in the forum in his toga. The magistrates were bustling about the city arranging quarters for the Roman soldiers, as if they feared no danger and were conscious of no shortcomings. Although this artfulness did not shake Camillus' belief in their guilt, he had compassion for the repentance that had come after it. So he ordered them to go to the wrathful senate and plead for forgiveness. He himself joined in their pleas, and so Tusculum was acquitted of all guilt and admitted to Roman citizenship. These then were the outstanding events of Camillus' sixth term as tribune.

39. Later, Licinius Stolo stirred up a great commotion in the city, through which the people came again into conflict with the senate. For the people demanded that when the dual consulate was reestablished, one consul should always be a plebeian and not both patricians. Tribunes of the people were elected, but the election of consuls was prevented by the populace. As the situation was growing more and more chaotic, the senate, much against the people's will, made Camillus dictator for the fourth time. He himself did not want the office, and was loath to oppose men who had fought with him through many hard campaigns and who could say to him that his achievements had been more in battles with them than in politics with the patricians, and that it was out of envy that they had made him dictator. If successful, he would crush the people; if he failed, he would be crushed himself.

However, he made an effort to meet the current emergency. Having heard the day on which the tribunes intended to bring forward their law, he proclaimed it the day for a general muster, summoning the people from the forum to the Campus Martius, and threatening those who disobeyed with a heavy fine. The tribunes, on the other hand, responded by vowing solemnly that they would fine him fifty thousand drachmas if he did not stop trying to deprive the people of their law and their vote. Thereupon he retired to his house, either because he feared a second sentence of banishment, a disgrace to an old man who had achieved so much, or because he neither would nor could resist the power of the people, who were now too strong to be suppressed. And after professing for some days to be ill, he resigned his office.

The senate then appointed another dictator; he made the same Licinius Stolo, leader of the revolutionary party, his master of horse, and thus enabled him to get his law passed.[42] It was a law very distasteful to the patricians, for it forbade anyone to own more than five hundred acres of land. At the time of his victory at the polls, Stolo was a distinguished personage, but shortly afterward he was convicted of possessing more land than he allowed others to have, and was punished as his law provided.

40. There was still dissension over the election of consuls, this being the most difficult point at issue, as it had been the starting point of trouble and the senate's chief problem in its differences with the people. Then came definite news that the Gauls had again set out from the Adriatic Sea, and were marching in countless thousands against Rome. And with the news came reports of their acts of war. The country was being plundered, and the inhabitants who could not readily escape to Rome were scattering into the mountains.

This terror put an end to internal disputes. The rich and the poor, the senate and the people, met together and with one voice chose Camillus dictator for the fifth time. He was now a very old man, close to eighty. Realizing the peril and the necessity they were under, he made none of his former excuses or pretenses, but at once took over command and began levying men to fight. He knew that the strength of the Gauls lay chiefly in their swords, which they used like barbarians, with more strength than skill, dealing heavy blows on the heads and shoulders of their opponents. He therefore had helmets forged for most of his soldiers of smooth iron, so that the swords would either break or glance off them. He also had their shields rimmed with bronze, because the wood alone was not strong enough to withstand heavy blows. And he taught his soldiers how to use their long pikes and thrust them under the enemy's swords to receive their down strokes.

41. When the Gauls were near by, encamped on the river Anio and laden down with masses of loot, Camillus led out his troops and posted them in a sloping glen with many little depressions in it, so that the greater part of his men were hidden, and those that were visible appeared to be crowding up the hillside in terror. This impression Camillus was

42 This was the beginning of the famous Licinian legislation of 367–366 B.C., which marked an important victory for the plebeians in their struggle to democratize the Roman state. A limit was put on the amount of land a patrician could own as his private estate, and a little later the consulship was thrown open to the plebeians.

anxious to confirm, so he did not go to the defense of the people who were being plundered at his very feet, but fenced in his trenches and lay quiet until he saw a part of the enemy straggling off on foraging parties, while those in their camp did nothing but eat and drink. Then, in the night, he sent forward his light-armed troops to prevent the Gauls from forming their ranks properly and to harass them as they emerged from their camp; and as dawn was breaking, he led down his men-at-arms and drew them up in the plain, manifestly a numerous and confident army, and not, as the Gauls had imagined, a few disheartened men.

The fact that the Romans had started the battle first dashed the courage of the Gauls, who thought it dishonorable not to be the attackers. Next, the onset of the light troops, which forced them into action before they had got themselves into their usual formation and divided into companies, compelled them to fight haphazardly and in disorder. And when at last Camillus led on his heavy-armed troops, and the Gauls, brandishing their swords, ran to meet them, the Romans thrust their pikes at them and received the sword cuts on shields which were bound with iron. So the Gauls' swords, which were made of soft iron, poorly tempered, turned and bent double, while their shields were pierced and weighed down by the pikes which stuck in them. Accordingly, they dropped their own weapons and tried to take hold of those of the Romans, and to push aside the pikes by seizing them with their hands. But the Romans, seeing them now defenseless, began to use their own swords and slew many in the front lines, while the rest fled every way over the flat plain. For Camillus had previously taken possession of the hills and high places, and the Gauls knew that their camp could be easily taken, for they had been so sure of themselves that they had not fortified it.

This battle is said to have been fought thirteen years after the capture of Rome,[43] and it gave the Romans a confident attitude towards the Gauls, of whom they had earlier been profoundly afraid. For at the outset they had been defeated by them, although their defeat had been due to disease and exceptional circumstances, rather than to the Gauls' valor. None the less, their fear had been so great that they had passed a law exempting priests from service in the army, except during a Gallic war.

---

[43] This important victory over the Gauls took place not thirteen but twenty-three years after their capture of Rome.

42. This was the last of Camillus' military exploits, for his taking of the city of Velitrae was a result of this campaign, and it yielded to him without a battle. His greatest political struggle was still to come, and it was harder to resist the people now that they were returning elated with victory, and insisting on choosing a plebeian consul, contrary to the estab-lished law. The senate opposed them and would not permit Camillus to lay down his office, for they thought that with the help of his firmness and immense authority they could put up a better fight for the aristocracy. One day, however, when Camillus had taken his seat and was attending to public business in the forum, an official sent by the tribunes ordered him to come with him, and even laid hands on him, as if to drag him away. At this such an outcry and tumult filled the forum as had never been known before. Some of Camillus' party pushed the plebeian official down from the tribunal, while the people below called on him to take Camillus away. Camillus himself, not knowing what to do, did not resign his office, but with the senators went to the senate-house. There, before entering, he turned towards the Capitol and prayed the gods to bring their troubles to a happy ending, vowing to build a temple to Concord [44] when the disturbance was over.

In the senate there was a violent contest of opposing judgments, but the more conciliatory prevailed and the concession was made that the people might elect one of the consuls from their own number. When the dictator announced this to the people as the senate's decision, they were at once delighted to be reconciled with the senate, as was to be expected, and accompanied Camillus home with vociferous applause. The next day they met and voted to build a temple of Concord, as Camillus had vowed, facing the forum and the assembly place, in memory of these events. They voted too to add a day to the so-called Latin festival, and celebrate it for four days, and ordered all Romans immediately to put on garlands and sacrifice. At the election of consuls, presided over by Camillus, Marcus Aemilius, a patrician, and Lucius Sextus, the first plebeian to hold the office, were elected. This was the last of Camillus' public acts.

---

[44] The temple to the Goddess of Concord was built in 367 B.C. on the edge of the forum. In 9 A.D., it was restored by the Emperor Tiberius and Livia. Two other temples, in course of time, were dedicated to the same goddess, each after a period of strife and disorder.

43. In the following year a pestilence broke out in Rome which killed enormous numbers of the common people and most of the magistrates. Camillus, too, died at that time. He was as ripe for death as any man ever was, in view of his age and the completeness of his life, yet he was more mourned by the Romans than all the others who died of the plague.

Pericles

C. 495-429 B.C.

1. CAESAR,[1] we hear, on seeing one day some wealthy foreigners at Rome carrying puppies and young monkeys around in their arms and petting them, asked if in the country they came from women did not bear children. By that royal reprimand he showed his disapproval of persons who lavish on brute beasts the natural love and tenderness we ought to bestow on human beings. In like fashion, we may reasonably criticize those who waste the instinct for learning and the love of seeing, which nature has implanted in our souls, by spending them on worthless sounds and sights instead of on things beautiful and useful. It is, probably, unavoidable that every external object we meet, whether good or bad, should by its mere impact, produce some effect on our senses; but we can all of us, if we choose, concentrate our minds on, or turn away from any object, and shift easily to something we like better. We should, therefore, look for the best, not merely to contemplate it, but to be benefited by the contemplation. Just as those colors are healthful whose fresh and pleasant hues strengthen and stimulate our eyes; so with our mental vision we should fix our sight on things which by the joy they give it attract it to its own proper good. Such things are acts of virtue, which create in the minds of those who study them a strong desire and eagerness to imitate them.

In other fields, admiration of a deed is not instantly followed by an impulse to perform it. On the contrary, we are often charmed with a piece

---

[1] The story was told of Caesar Augustus, the first Roman emperor.

of work but look down on the workman. In the case of dyes and perfumes, for instance, we enjoy them but think of dyers and perfumers as servile and vulgar people. Antisthenes, when he heard that Ismenias was a fine flute-player, said a clever thing, "But he is a worthless man or else he would not be so fine a flute-player." And Philip of Macedon once said to his son, when over the wine he was playing charmingly and skillfully on the harp, "Are you not ashamed to play so well?" For it is enough for a king to spend some of his leisure listening to harpists, and he does the Muses great honor when he looks on at other men's musical contests.

2. To work hard over petty things shows, by the effort spent on trifles, that one is indifferent to nobler things. No well bred youth, on seeing the Zeus at Pisa or the Hera at Argos, yearns to be a Phidias, or a Polycletus;[2] nor, though he takes pleasure in their poems, would he wish to be an Anacreon, a Philetas, or an Archilochus.[3] For it does not necessarily follow that when a work charms us with its grace, its maker is worth our admiration. So men are not benefited by things the sight of which does not quicken in them any ardor for imitation, or any inspiration stirring them to an ambition to do likewise. But virtuous deeds have a swift influence on us, so that as soon as we admire them we long to emulate those who did them. The good things of fortune we love to possess and enjoy; the good deeds of virtue we love to perform. The former we like to receive from others; the latter we prefer to have others take from us. For nobility of itself moves us to action and creates a lively impulse within us. Not through imitating only does it mold the beholder's character but through a study of great deeds he arrives at a purpose in life.

For this reason I have decided to go on writing *Lives,* and have composed this tenth book to include the life of Pericles and of Fabius Maximus,

---

[2] Phidias (c. 500–432 B.C.) was the great Athenian sculptor and architect whose work with Pericles in designing and carrying out the beautifying of the Acropolis is described below. His most famous single statue, done in ivory and gold, was that of Olympian Zeus seated on his throne, which he made for the temple at Pisa, a small town at the site of the Olympian games. Polycletus of Argos, a younger contemporary, was celebrated for his ivory and gold statue of the goddess Hera.

[3] Anacreon (c. 563–478 B.C.), a courtier poet, wrote charming lyrics in praise of love and wine. Philetas (c. 318–275 B.C.) was a scholarly poet of the later Alexandrian school. Archilochus (early seventh century) led a wandering soldier's life and was famed for his terse and bitter satirical verses.

who fought the long war against Hannibal. The two men were like each other in their virtues, especially in their gentleness and uprightness and in their ability to endure with patience the follies of their fellow citizens and their colleagues. Their qualities made them greatly serviceable to their countries. Whether I succeed in my aim may be judged from what I write.

3. Pericles was of the tribe Acamantis, and the deme Cholargus, of eminent family and lineage on both sides. Xanthippus, his father, defeated the Persian generals at Mycale.[4] His mother, Agariste, was the granddaughter of Clisthenes,[5] who fearlessly drove out the sons of Pisistratus, put an end to the tyranny, enacted laws and established a new constitution excellently designed to bring about harmony and security. She dreamed once that she had brought forth a lion, and a few days later gave birth to Pericles. In bodily appearance he was faultless, save that his head was disproportionately long. For this reason nearly all the images of him wear a helmet, the artists being apparently unwilling to expose his blemish.

The Attic poets called him Squill-head, and the comic poet, Cratinus,[6] in his *Chirons,* says:

"Old Chronos once took Queen Sedition to wife:
Which two brought to life
That great tyrant far famed,
Whom the gods the supreme Head-assembler have named";

and in his *Nemesis,* addresses him:

"Come, Zeus, thou guest and head!"

---

[4] At the naval battle of Mycale, off the Ionian coast, in 479 B.C., Xerxes' invading fleet was put to rout by the Greeks.

[5] Actually Pericles' mother was the niece, not the granddaughter, of Clisthenes, the popular reformer of Athens, who in 510 B.C., on the expulsion of the two sons of the tyrant Pisistratus, brought about the democratization of the old constitution of Solon, broke the power of the landed aristocracy, and centered authority in the citizen assembly.

[6] The comic poets, Cratinus, Teleclides, and Eupolis, as well as most of the other writers to whom Plutarch alludes in his biographies are unknown to us except for such chance mention of their names and occasional quotations from their works as he gives us here.

And Teleclides speaks of him as sitting in the city, perplexed by his problems, "now heavy-headed, and now, still alone, creating loud turmoil out of the eleven chambers of his head." And Eupolis, in his *Demes,* when he inquires about each of the demagogues as they come up from Hades, exclaims, as Pericles gets the last summons:

> "The head indeed of those below hast thou now brought."

4.   Most writers agree that Damon (whose name, they say, should be pronounced with the first syllable short) was his teacher in music, but Aristotle [7] tells us that he worked at music under Pythoclides. This Damon, it seems, was an expert Sophist, who covered his real profession under a cloak of music in order to conceal his powers from the populace. He was a companion of Pericles as trainer and tutor for a young athlete in politics. His lyre, however, did not prove successful as a blind, for eventually he was ostracized as a dangerous meddler and supporter of tyranny, and was ridiculed by the comic poets. The poet Plato [8] represents someone as addressing him thus:

> "First of all, you tell me, if you please,
>   Since you're, they say, the Chiron who taught Pericles."

Pericles was a pupil too of Zeno of Elea,[9] who lectured on nature like Parmenides. He developed too a method of reducing any opponent to silence by catching him in a refutation. Timon of Phlius alludes to his skill in the verse:

> "Mighty and great was the power of the tongue of Zeno, which argued
>   both ways,
> And attacked all that is."

But the man who was closest to Pericles and had most to do with giving him the dignity of manner that appealed more than the insolence of the demagogues, and with strengthening and elevating his character, was

---

[7] Plato, not Aristotle, makes this statement in his *Alcibiades,* I, 118.

[8] There was a comic poet named Plato, whom we know only by such casual references as this.

[9] Zeno of Elea in southern Italy (fifth century B.C.) was a follower of Parmenides, the founder of the so-called Eleatic school of philosophy, who taught the oneness and the permanence of all nature and the inconceivability of movement or change.

Anaxagoras of Clazomenae.[10] The men of that time called him *Nous,* or Mind, either because they admired his intellect, which was showing itself so wonderful, or because he was the first to call the cause behind the order of the universe, not Chance and not Necessity, but Mind, pure and simple, which, when all things were mixed and chaotic, separated out those which had elements alike.

5. Pericles had great esteem for this man, and became deeply absorbed in his so-called higher philosophy and profound speculations. Thus he acquired both solemnity of spirit and a lofty style of speech, free from vulgarity and spiteful buffoonery; also a gravity of countenance that did not break out into laughter, a gentleness of demeanor and a quietness of tone that no emotion disturbed while he was speaking, as well as other qualities that impressed and astonished his hearers. Once he sat silently in the agora all day, working at some important business, while a low, worthless fellow was reviling and abusing him. Towards evening he went calmly home, with the man following and heaping every kind of insult on him. When about to enter his own door, he ordered one of his servants, since it was dark, to take a torch and escort the man to his house.

The poet Ion, however, says that Pericles was overbearing and arrogant in conversation, and that with his pride was mixed considerable disdain and scorn of others. As a contrast he praises Cimon for his tact, ease, and grace in company. But we may disregard Ion, who thought that virtue, like a tragic trilogy,[11] should have a satirical appendage to it. Zeno used to tell those who called Pericles' austerity a bid for glory and sheer conceit, to make some such bid for glory themselves, as if a pretense of nobility might produce in them, without their being aware, a desire to practice it.

6. And this was not all that Pericles gained from his intimacy with Anaxagoras. He seems to have been lifted by him above that superstition which is created by amazement at the heavenly bodies in persons who know nothing of their causes, and are foolish about supernatural things

---

10 Anaxagoras (500–428 B.C.), the famed Ionian scientist and philosopher, came to Athens in his youth and stayed for thirty years. He created a sensation by his astronomical observations.

11 The prescribed form for the great dramatic sequences presented at Athens during the Dionysiac festival was a trilogy of three connected tragedies, followed by a satirical farce on a different theme.

and easily terrified by their ignorance of such phenomena. Natural philosophy delivers one from such ignorance and replaces fearful and feverish superstition with sound piety and good hopes. We are told that the head of a one-horned ram was once brought to Pericles from the country, and that Lampon, the diviner, when he saw how the horn grew strong and solid out of the middle of the forehead, said that although there were then two parties in the city, that of Thucydides [12] and that of Pericles, the leadership would eventually come to one man, the one who possessed this emblem. But Anaxagoras cut open the beast's skull, and showed that its brain did not fill the whole space but had shrunk together to a tip, like an egg, at the spot where the root of the horn began. At that time it was Anaxagoras whom everyone admired, but soon afterwards it was Lampon. For Thucydides met disaster, and Pericles won complete control of the government of the state.

Yet there was, I think, no reason why both the natural philosopher and the diviner should not have been right, the one discovering the cause of the phenomenon, the other its meaning. It was the business of one to find out why the thing happened and how it came about, and of the other to tell for what purpose it happened and what it betokened. Those who say that when the cause of a sign is found the sign is disposed of do not realize that they are denying the value not only of heavenly signs but also of human signs, such as the ringing of gongs, the blaze of beacon fires, and the shadows on sun-dials. Each of these, besides being caused and prepared, is made as a sign of something. But this subject belongs probably in another treatise.

7. As a young man, Pericles shrank very much from facing the people, for in appearance he was thought to resemble the tyrant Pisistratus.[13] His voice, too, was sweet and his tongue fluent and quick in conversation, so that older men were struck by the likeness. Also, he was wealthy, of distinguished lineage and had extremely powerful friends, so that he was afraid of being ostracized and kept out of politics, even though in military service he proved himself brave and daring. Accordingly, after Aris-

---

[12] This is the same Thucydides (c. 471–c. 401 B.C.), mentioned again later, who after his failure as a general and subsequent banishment wrote the objective and priceless *History of the Peloponnesian War*.

[13] Pisistratus, though twice expelled, had continued as tyrant of Athens until his death in 527 B.C. His name remained afterwards a symbol of despotism for Athenians.

tides'[14] death and Themistocles' banishment, with Cimon generally absent from Greece on his campaigns, Pericles devoted himself to the people, taking the side of the poor and the many against the rich and the few, contrary to his own natural bent, which was far from democratic. He apparently dreaded incurring the suspicion of playing tyrant, so when he saw that Cimon took the aristocratic side and was very popular with the Noble and the Good,[15] he began making overtures to the people, thereby obtaining safety for himself and power to oppose Cimon.

Soon afterward he changed his way of life and was never seen on any street in the city but that which led to the agora and the council hall. Invitations to dinner and all such friendly social gatherings he refused. During the whole course of his long political life he never went to a friend's house to dine, except when his cousin Euryptolemus was married. Then he sat at the table until the libations were poured, and immediately rose and departed.[16] For at convivial gatherings even the proudest are likely to unbend, and an impressive demeanor is hard to maintain in familiar talk. True virtue, indeed, appears the fairer the more it is seen, and nothing in a good man's life is so much admired by the world as his day-by-day treatment of his friends. But Pericles tried to avoid making himself too familiar and common with the people by frequent appearances. He did not address them on every subject, nor always attend the assembly, but, as Critolaus says, kept himself, like the trireme at Salamis, for the great crises. He had his friends and other speakers manage affairs of less importance. One of these friends, they say, was Ephialtes, who broke the power of the Council of the Areopagus, pouring out, as Plato described it,[17] "a full and unmixed draught of liberty" for the citizens, which made them as unruly as a horse. As the comic poets said then, they "would stand no rein, but grabbed at Euboea and trampled on the islands.[18]

---

14 Aristides died soon after 468 B.C., and Themistocles was banished after 472.

15 The Noble and the Good was a name applied ironically to the party of aristocratic conservatives in Athens.

16 After the libations had been poured to the gods, the festive drinking began.

17 Plato, *Republic,* VIII, 562.

18 A reference to the change of policy during the period between the Persian and the Peloponnesian Wars, by which Athens transformed the free league of islands and coastal cities, supported by voluntary contributions, of which she was the accepted head, to a maritime empire under her rule, compelled to pay her tribute.

8. Pericles was anxious to acquire a style of speaking which, like a musical instrument, would harmonize with his manner of life and lofty spirit, and he often made use of Anaxagoras, as another string, mingling with his own rhetoric touches of Anaxagoras' natural science. For, as the divine Plato says,[19] it was from natural science that he acquired that loftiness of soul and perfect competence which he added to his native powers, and by applying this knowledge to the art of speaking, he far outstripped everyone else. By this means, they say, he got his name of Olympian; though some think it came from the buildings with which he beautified the city, and others from his skill in politics and war. It is likely that his fame was the result of the blending of many great abilities in him. However, the comic writers of that day, who aimed many a shaft at him, both in jest and in earnest, always imply that the name was given him because of his way of speaking. They describe him as "thundering and lightning," when he addressed the people,[20] and as "carrying awful thunders on his tongue."

A jest of Thucydides, son of Melesias, has been preserved, one that testifies to Pericles' cleverness. Thucydides was one of the Noble and the Good, and for a long time a political opponent of Pericles. One day Archidamas, king of the Lacedaemonians, asked him whether he or Pericles was the better wrestler. "When I throw him in wrestling," Thucydides answered, "he insists that he did not fall, and he beats me by making the very spectators believe him."

For all this, Pericles was careful about his words, and always when he ascended the tribune to speak, he prayed to the gods that nothing unfit for the occasion might fall unintentionally from his lips. He left no writings behind him except the laws he sponsored, and very few of his sayings are recorded, such as, for example, his urging the suppression of Aegina as "the eyesore of the Piraeus," and his statement that he "already saw war descending upon them from the Peloponnesus." And once when Sophocles, who was commanding with him on a naval expedition, said something in praise of a handsome boy, he replied, "Not only his hands, Sophocles, must a commander keep clean but his eyes as well." And Stesimbrotus tells us that in his funeral oration over those who fell at Samos,

---

[19] Plato, *Phaedrus,* 270.
[20] See Aristophanes, *Acharnians,* 528–531.

he declared that they had become immortal, even as the gods. The gods themselves we do not see, but by the honors they receive and the blessings they confer we are assured they are immortal. The same is true of those who die for their country.

9. Thucydides [21] represents the government of Pericles as actually an aristocracy, "in name a democracy, but in fact a rule of the foremost citizens." But many other writers tell us that the people were first introduced by him to grants of public land, funds for spectacles, and payments for public services, and that they thereby learned bad habits and became extravagant and licentious instead of sober and hard-working. Let us then, in the light of the facts, consider the reason for the change in him. From the beginning, as we have said, measured as he was against the famous Cimon, Pericles set about winning the people's affection. He had not the wealth and resources of Cimon by which to attract the poor, offering a dinner every day to any Athenian who needed one, clothing aged persons, and taking down fences from his estates so that anyone who wished might pick the fruit. So, unable to compete on these popular lines, Pericles turned to distributing the people's own property, at the suggestion, Aristotle [22] tells us, of Damonides of the deme Oa. And soon by his funds for spectacles, jurors' fees, and other large payments and expenditures, he had bribed the whole population, and was able to use them against the council of the Areopagus. He himself was not a member of that body, never having been chosen archon, thesmothete, king archon, or polemarch.[23] Those offices had from ancient times been filled by lot, and from their ranks those who had discharged them acceptably were advanced to the Areopagus. For this reason, Pericles, when he had gained strength with the people, organized a party against the council. Through Ephialtes [24] it was deprived of most of its judicial powers, while Cimon, on a charge of being a friend of Sparta and a hater of the people, was banished by ostracism. Cimon, as will be related later in his *Life,* was second to none in birth and fortune, had won brilliant victories over the

---

[21] Thucydides, *Peloponnesian War,* II, vii, 65.

[22] Aristotle, *Constitution of Athens,* XXVII, 4.

[23] For the meaning of these terms, see Glossary.

[24] Pericles was unable to protect Ephialtes from the aristocratic party. Within a year he was murdered by one of them.

Persians, and had filled the city with rich spoils of war. So great was the power of Pericles with the people!

10. By law the duration of exile by ostracism was set at ten years. But in the middle of Cimon's term the Spartans with a great force invaded the territory of Tanagra,[25] and the Athenians at once marched out against them. Whereupon Cimon came back from exile and took his place in the ranks with his tribe, hoping by his deeds and by sharing the danger of his fellow citizens to clear himself of the accusation of favoring the Spartans. But Pericles' friends gathered around and forced him, as a banished man, to leave. On that account, probably, Pericles fought his hardest in that battle, and was more conspicuous than anyone in his reckless daring. The friends of Cimon, whom Pericles had accused of Spartan leanings, were every one of them killed. Then the Athenians were overcome by remorse and wanted Cimon back, seeing that they had been defeated on the very frontier of Attica and anticipated a serious war in the spring. Pericles perceived their feeling and did not hesitate to give the people what they wanted, and himself wrote the decree for Cimon's recall. On his return Cimon made peace between the two cities,[26] for the Spartans were as amiably disposed towards him as they were hostile to Pericles and the other popular leaders.

Some say, however, that Pericles did not write the decree for Cimon's recall until a secret compact was made between them, through Elpinice, Cimon's sister, to the effect that Cimon was to sail out with two hundred ships and take command abroad in a campaign against the territory of the Persian king, while Pericles kept the chief power in the city. Earlier too, it seems, Elpinice had influenced Pericles to be more lenient to Cimon when he was being tried for his life,[27] for Pericles was then one of the prosecutors appointed by the people. When Elpinice came and pled with him, he said with a smile, "Elpinice, you are an old woman, an old woman to be doing this!" For all that, he spoke only once in carrying out his commission, and ended by pressing Cimon less hard than the other prosecutors did.

---

[25] Cimon was ostracized in 461 B.C. The Spartans attacked the Boeotian town of Tanagra four years later.

[26] The peace was concluded in 450 B.C.

[27] Cimon had been tried for treason in 463 B.C.

How, then, can one believe Idomeneus, when he accuses Pericles of murdering his friend and partner in political policy, the popular leader Ephialtes, out of jealousy and envy of his high reputation? This calumny Idomeneus has dug up somewhere and venomously hurled against a man who, though perhaps not faultless, still had too noble a mind and aspiring a spirit to harbor so savage and brutal an idea. Ephialtes was feared by the oligarchs, and was relentless in demanding accounts and prosecuting all who had wronged the people. Consequently his enemies laid a plot and had him secretly assassinated by Aristodicus of Tanagra, as Aristotle tells us.[28] Cimon died on a campaign in Cyprus.

11. The aristocrats had for some time been noting that Pericles was now the most important man in the state, but they hoped to find someone in the city to stand up against him and dull the edge of his authority, lest it turn into an outright monarchy. Accordingly they set up Thucydides of Alopeke as his rival. He was a man of good sense, a relative of Cimon, but less of a warrior and more of a public speaker and politician. By watching opportunities in the city and opposing Pericles on the platform, he soon brought about a more balanced administration. He did not allow the so-called Noble and Good to move about and mix with the people in the assembly, as they had done hitherto, so that their dignity was lost among the masses, but singled them out and collected them in a separate body; thus their aggregate influence counted more heavily as a counter-balance in the scale. From the beginning there had been a kind of split under the surface, as in an iron bar, marking the difference between the popular and the aristocratic party policies, but now the struggle for power between Pericles and Thucydides was cutting a deep line of severance across the state, as a result of which one party was called the People and the other the Few.

Pericles, now particularly, surrendered the reins to the people and planned his policy to please them, constantly arranging some kind of pageant or festival or procession in the city, thus entertaining them with refined amusements. Every year, too, he sent sixty triremes out on a cruise, and many citizens sailed around on them for eight months with pay, at the same time learning and practicing the art of seamanship. Besides

---

[28] Aristotle, *Constitution of Athens*, XXV, 4.

this, he sent a thousand settlers to the Chersonese,[29] five hundred to Naxos, half as many to Andros, a thousand to Thrace, among the Bisaltae, and others to Italy, when Sybaris, which they called Thurii, was being rebuilt.[30] All these things he did in order to relieve the city of a mob of lazy and idle agitators, provide for the wants of the needy, and establish formidable garrisons near the allies of Athens to prevent revolt.

12. But what brought the greatest pleasure and beauty to Athens and the most astonishment to the rest of the world, and now alone bears witness for Hellas that the tales of her ancient power and glory were not fables, was Pericles' building of shrines. Yet for that, more than for all his other public enterprises, his enemies slandered and impugned him. They shouted in the assemblies that the Athenians had lost their good name and disgraced themselves by moving the common treasury of the Greeks from Delos to their own custody.[31] And the most plausible excuse which they could make to their accusers, that out of fear of the barbarians they had moved the treasury from Delos to keep it safe in a fortress, Pericles had taken from them. "So Greece feels herself terribly outraged," they said, "and subjected to a flagrant tyranny, when she sees us spending the funds we extorted from her for war on gilding and adorning our city like a wanton woman, bedecking her with precious stones and statues and temples costing thousands of talents!"

But Pericles told the people that they owed no account of the money to their allies, so long as they carried on the war for them and defended them from the Persians. Not a horse, nor a ship, nor a soldier, he said, were the others contributing, but merely money, which belonged then not to the givers but to the receivers, provided they furnished the things for which they were paid. It was right, he argued, that, after the city had supplied itself with all that was necessary for war, it should devote its surplus to works which, when finished, would be its glory forever, and

29 Settlers were sent to the Chersonese, the peninsula that forms part of the northern coast of the Hellespont, in the year 447 B.C. For more details of this settlement, see below, ch. 19.

30 This was in 444 B.C. Sybaris had been destroyed in 510.

31 The annual contributions of the league of Greek states for carrying on the war with Persia were kept at first in the temple of Apollo on the sacred island of Delos, the legendary birthplace of Apollo and his sister Artemis. These hoards Pericles now took and transferred to what he called safer custody at Athens.

while in process of construction, would put its wealth to good use. For they would create all sorts of activity and manifold demands, calling on every art and setting every hand to work, so that almost the whole city would be earning wages, and thus while it beautified itself, would be supporting itself.

Those who were of the right age and vigorous were already receiving good pay in military service from the public treasury. Then, since he did not wish the unwarlike mass of common workmen to go without a share in the city's revenues, nor yet to be paid for idleness, he proposed to the people plans for great edifices and designs for elaborate works, which would take a long time to complete. Thereby, those who stayed at home would have as good a claim to a share of the public funds as the sailors, garrison troops, and active soldiers. The materials to be used were stone, when they had it, bronze, ivory, gold, ebony, and cypress wood. The craftsmen who would execute and finish off the works were carpenters, molders, smiths, stonecutters, dyers, artists in gold and ivory, painters, embroiderers, embossers, together with carriers and supply men, merchants, sailors and pilots on the sea, wagon makers, team owners and drivers on land; also rope makers, weavers, leather workers, road builders, and miners. And as each craft, like a commander at the head of an army, employed a number of unskilled and ignorant laborers, like tools or bodies for subordinate service, the city's wealth would be divided and dispersed to meet the needs of people of every age and ability.

13. The buildings rose, towering in size and matchless in contour and grace, for the workmen strove to outdo themselves in the perfection of their handiwork. Most remarkable was the speed with which they were built. Each one of them, men thought, would take many succeeding generations to complete, but all were finished during the climax of one man's administration. They say that Zeuxis,[32] once hearing the painter Agatharchus boasting how easily and rapidly he could produce a picture, said, "I take a long time." Certainly ease and speed of execution do not usually produce a work of permanent value or faultless beauty, whereas time spent in painstaking labor makes for lasting quality. For this reason

[32] Zeuxis of Heraclea in southern Italy (fifth-fourth centuries B.C.), was the most celebrated painter of ancient times. Agatharcus of Samos, a contemporary, was a popular scene painter for the theater. Unhappily, no work of the Greek painters has survived.

the works of Pericles are all the more wonderful; they were quickly created, and they have lasted for ages. In beauty each one appeared venerable as soon as it was finished, but in freshness and vigor it looks even now new and lately built. They bloom with an eternal freshness that seems untouched by time, as though they had been inspired by an unfading spirit of youth.

Pericles' general overseer and manager was Phidias, although the separate works had excellent architects and artists besides. Callicrates and Ictinus built the hundred-foot-long Parthenon.[33] Coroebus began to build the sanctuary at Eleusis, erecting the columns and tying them together with architraves. On his death, Metagenes of the deme Xypete put up the frieze and the upper row of columns, and Xenocles of the deme Cholargos set the skylight over the shrine. As to the Long Wall,[34] for which Socrates says that he heard Pericles introduce a motion, Callicrates undertook to build it. Cratinus made fun of the job for going so slowly:

> " 'Tis long since Pericles, if words would do it,
>   Shored up the thing, but actually does not move it."

The Odeum, whose interior consisted of many rows of seats and many columns, and whose roof was made sloping down all around from a central peak, was said to have been copied from the king of Persia's tent. It was constructed under Pericles' own direction. So Cratinus, in his *Thracian Woman,* laughs at him:

> "Here comes the Squill-head Zeus,
>   Wearing the Odeum on his cranium,
>   Now that ostracism's gone."

At this same time, Pericles, eager for honors, had his first decree passed for a musical competition to be held at the Panatheniac festival. He was himself chosen judge and laid down the rules as to how the candidates were to blow their flutes or sing, or play their lyres. Both then and afterwards, these musical contests took place in the Odeum.

---

[33] The Parthenon, the matchless Doric temple crowning the Acropolis, was said to have cost a thousand talents. It was built on the site of an older temple, destroyed by the Persians during their occupation of Athens in 480 B.C., and was dedicated in 438.
[34] The Long Wall connected Athens with the sea at the Piraeus and so provided the city with its own safe harbor. It was five miles long and wide enough on top for two chariots to drive abreast. For Socrates' words, see Plato, *Gorgias,* 455.

The Propylaea [35] of the Acropolis was finished in five years, by the architect Mnesicles. An extraordinary thing happened while it was building, which seemed to show that the goddess did not disapprove of it, but was helping both at its start and at its completion. The most energetic and enthusiastic of the workmen slipped and fell from a great height, and lay in a grave condition, given up for dead by the physicians. Pericles was much distressed, but the goddess appeared to him in a dream and prescribed a course of treatment for him to use, whereby he quickly and easily cured the man. In memory of her aid, he set up the bronze statue of Athene the Healer on the Acropolis, near the altar that stood there before, they say. But it was Phidias who made the golden statue of the goddess [36] and his name is inscribed on its base as the maker. Almost everything was under his supervision, and all the artists, as we have said, took orders from him, because of his friendship with Pericles.

Their association, however, brought down envy on him and slander on Pericles. It was said that Phidias made appointments for Pericles with freeborn ladies, who came ostensibly to see the works of art. The comic poets caught up the story and besmirched Pericles with tales of utter profligacy, also slandering the wife of his friend Menippus, who had been his colleague in war, as well as Pyrilampes, a bird collector and comrade of Pericles, whom they charged with giving peacocks to the women Pericles was meeting. But why should one be surprised that men of lascivious lives themselves bring foul accusations against their betters, offering them up as victims to the evil demon of popular envy, when even Stesimbrotus of Thasos dared to bring the monstrous and preposterous charge against Pericles of an intrigue with his own son's wife? It is a hard and baffling thing to discover even by search the truth of any such report, since those who come after the event find that the passage of time debars them from true knowledge of the facts, and contemporary accounts of men's acts and careers, whether through hatred and envy, or a desire to curry favor, are often twisted and distorted from the reality.

---

[35] The word means gateway or portico, especially one leading to a temple. This most stately approach to the Acropolis consisted of a broad, marble passage way and doors, with a columned wing on either side. It was completed in 442 B.C.

[36] This was the splendid statue of ivory and gold, thirty-eight feet high, which stood inside the Parthenon. At that time it was a capital offense for an artist to inscribe his name on such a work.

14. The speakers of Thucydides' party denounced Pericles for squandering the public funds and exhausting the revenues. He then asked the people in the assembly whether they thought he had spent too much. On their answering, "Altogether too much," he said, "Very well; put it down as spent not for you but for me, and I will insert my name in all the inscriptions." At these words from Pericles, the people, whether in admiration of his magnificence, or because they wanted a share of the glory of his works, cried out to him loudly to take the money from the treasury for his building and spend it without stint. At last he underwent with Thucydides the test of ostracism, and by taking that risk succeeded in getting Thucydides banished [37] and so broke up the faction that had been organized against himself.

15. Then, as the opposition had been entirely overcome and the city was smoothed over and thoroughly united, he brought under his own control both Athens and everything connected with Athens—her tribute, armies, triremes, islands, the sea, the huge strength she derived from the Greeks and also from the barbarians, and her empire, based on subject peoples, royal friendships, and dynastic alliances. From that time on he was no longer the same man, not so submissive to the people nor so ready to yield and give way to their wishes, as a steersman yields to the winds. He left off his previous lenient and rather womanish democratic rule, as though it had been a flowery, tender tune he had been playing, and turned to a firm and monarchical form of government, though using it honorably and unwaveringly for the public good, and leading the people, as a rule willingly, by persuasion and education. However, there were times when they were much irritated with him, and when he held them tight, and forced them masterfully to do something expedient. He was like a wise physician dealing with a complicated and long standing disorder, who at one time cheers his patient with harmless comforts, and at another prescribes bitter salutary medicines.

Every kind of disorder, naturally, was to be found in a crowd of men who possessed so large an empire, and only Pericles had the ability to handle each efficiently, working particularly on the people's hopes and fears, checking them when over-confident, and raising their spirits when dis-

---

[37] Thucydides was banished in 442 B.C.

heartened. Thus he proved that, as Plato says,[38] the art of rhetoric is "a bewitchment of the soul," and its highest aim is to move sentiments and passions, which are, as it were, the strings and stops of the soul, and require skillful fingering and touch. The secret of his power was not merely his gifts as a speaker, but, as Thucydides says,[39] the renown of his life, and the confidence the people had in him as one palpably incorruptible and above bribery. For though he had made the city, which was already great, the greatest and richest in Greece, and though he himself became more powerful than many kings and tyrants, some of whom chose him to be guardian of their sons, he did not enrich by one drachma the estate his father left him.

16. Of his power Thucydides gives a clear picture, and the comic poets testify to it even in their spite, when they call him and his friends "the new sons of Pisistratus," and demand that he swear never to make himself a tyrant, since his ascendancy was not compatible with a democracy and was felt as too heavy a load on those about him. Teleclides says that the Athenians had surrendered to him:

"Their tribute from the cities, the cities themselves, some to bind, some
    to loose,
  Their stone walls to build up or destroy,
  Their treaties, resources, strength, peace, and rich treasures,
  And whatever kind fortune may bring."

And all this was not just on a special occasion, nor at some momentary blooming time of popularity for his administration, but for forty years [40] he held first place among such men as Ephialtes, Leocrates, Myronides, Cimon, Tolmides, and Thucydides; and, after the fall and ostracism of Thucydides, for no less than fifteen years he possessed a continuous and unified authority, holding the office of general every year. During all that time he proved himself incorruptible by bribes, although he was not quite without interest in money matters. He was loath to have the estate he inherited lawfully from his father slip away from neglect, and loath too to have

---

[38] Plato, *Phaedrus*, 271.
[39] Thucydides, *Peloponnesian War*, II, vii, 65.
[40] The forty years, calculated roughly, cover the period from 469 to 429 B.C.

it cause him much trouble and waste of time, when he was busy with other things. Consequently he adopted what seemed to him the simplest and most accurate method of managing it. Each year's produce he sold all together as a whole, and then bought one by one in the market the articles he needed, thus carrying on his mode of life a day at a time. He was not, therefore, beloved by his grown sons, nor was he a generous provider for their wives, who complained of his purchases day by day and his requirement of careful spending, and the lack of the abundance that was common in great and wealthy households. Every outgo and every intake went by count and measure. One servant, Evangelus, was responsible for the whole exact system. Whether naturally able or trained by Pericles, he knew more than anyone else of the household economy.

This way of living had little in common with that of the wise Anaxagoras, who left home and let his land lie idle for sheepgrazing, while he pursued his lofty speculations. But the life of a speculative philosopher and that of a statesman are not, I think, the same. The one exerts his intelligence to noble ends without need of instruments, and independent of outside things. The other devotes his genius to human wants, and accordingly may find wealth both a necessity and a good, as was true in Pericles' case, for he helped many poor people.

There is a story, too, that at a time when Pericles was absorbed in his work, Anaxagoras, by then grown old, was lying neglected on his bed, starving himself to death, his head already covered. When Pericles heard of it, he was horrified, and at once hurried to him and besought him earnestly to live, grieving not so much at Anaxagoras' fate as at his own, if he should lose so valuable an advisor for his government. Thereupon Anaxagoras uncovered his head and said to him, "Pericles, even those who need a lamp pour oil into it."

17. As the Spartans began to be worried by the growing prosperity of the Athenians, Pericles, in an effort to stir the people to still grander ideas and to make them feel capable of greater achievements, sponsored a resolution to invite all Greeks, wherever they lived, in Europe or in Asia, in large cities or in small, to send delegates to a meeting at Athens. There they would consult about restoring the Greek temples which the Persians had burned down, and about paying the sacrifices they owed to the gods on behalf of Greece and the vows they had made when they were fighting

the Persians, and about the sea, how all men might sail on it peaceably and without fear. To carry the invitation, twenty men, selected from citizens over fifty years of age,[41] were sent out, five to the Ionians and Dorians in Asia Minor and on the islands as far as Lesbos and Rhodes, five to the regions of the Hellespont and Thrace as far as Byzantium, five to Boeotia, Phocis, and the Peloponnesus, and from there through Locris to the neighboring country as far as Acarnania and Ambracia, while the remaining five went through Euboea, to the Oetaeans and the Malian Gulf, and to the Achaeans of Phthia and the Thessalians. They urged all these Greeks to come and take part in discussions for the peace and general welfare of Greece. But nothing came of all this, and the cities never assembled, because, it is said, of Spartan opposition, since the experiment met with its first resistance in the Peloponnesus. I have mentioned it, however, as an indication of Pericles' spirit and the greatness of his conceptions.

18. As a general, he was remarkable chiefly for caution. He would not willingly begin a dangerous battle whose outcome was doubtful, nor did he admire or imitate those who took chances and had good luck, and so were hailed as great commanders. He was always saying to his fellow citizens that as far as it depended on him they would live like immortals forever.

When, then, he saw that Tolmides, son of Tolmaeus, elated by his previous successes and the distinguished honors which had been given him for his campaigns, was preparing a raid into Boeotia for no reason at all, and had persuaded a thousand of the bravest and most ardent men of military age to volunteer for the expedition, along with the rest of the army he tried to stop and dissuade him. He used in the assembly those memorable words that if Tolmides would not take his advice, he would do well to wait for that wisest of counselors, Time. The speech made little impression at the moment, but a few days later, when news came that Tolmides himself was dead after a defeat in battle near Coronea, and that many brave citizens had died with him, Pericles was famous and highly regarded as a sage and a patriot.

---

41 At fifty, Athenian men were presumed to have arrived at ripe wisdom; only those who had reached this age were called upon to give their opinions in the public assembly.

19. Of all Pericles' expeditions the people approved most warmly the one to the Chersonese,[42] which turned out to be the salvation of the Greeks living there. Not only did he bring in a thousand Athenian colonists, and thus strengthen the cities afresh with a sound body of men, but he built a line of fortifications reaching across the isthmus from sea to sea. Thereby he shut off the raiding Thracians, who had spread all over the Chersonese, and put an end to the constant and harassing border warfare in which the country was always being involved, situated as it was among barbarian neighbors and swarming with brigands from outside and within its borders.

Foreigners too applauded and admired him, when, starting from Pegae, the port of Megara, he sailed around the Peloponnesus with a hundred triremes.[43] Not only did he lay waste a long stretch of the coast, as Tolmides had done before him, but with the soldiers from his ships he pushed far inland, and drove the inhabitants within their walls in fright at his approach. At Nemea, however, the men of Sicyon stood their ground and engaged him in battle, but by sheer force he put them to flight and erected a trophy of victory. He then took more troops on board his triremes from the friendly district of Achaia, and crossing to the opposite side of the Corinthian Gulf, sailed up the river Acheloüs, overran Acarnania, drove the people of Oeneadae inside their city walls, and ravaged and pillaged the country before turning back. He had proved himself a terror to his enemies but a safe and competent leader of his fellow citizens, for there was not even one unlucky accident to the men under his command.

20. He went also on a voyage to the Black Sea [44] with a large and splendidly equipped fleet, and did what they wanted for the Greek cities there, treating them with generosity, while to the barbarian tribes nearby and their kings and chiefs he displayed the size of his forces and the fearless confidence with which they sailed wherever they pleased, and brought the whole sea under their control. He left thirteen ships at Sinope [45] under

---

[42] The other Greek states were with some reason suspicious of a project which would have served to confirm Athenian political hegemony, already partly established by the size of her contributions to Greek victory in the Persian wars.

[43] In 453 B.C.

[44] Probably about 436 B.C.

[45] Sinope, at this time the largest city on the Black Sea, had been founded by colonists from Miletus

Lamachus, and soldiers to assist the people against Timesileus. After that tyrant and his party were driven out, Pericles had a decree passed that six hundred Athenian volunteers should sail to Sinope, to settle among the Sinopians and divide up the houses and lands which had previously belonged to the tyrants.

But at other times he would not assent to the impulsive proposals of the Athenians, nor go along with them in their excitement over their power and good fortune, as when they were eager to recover their hold on Egypt [46] and to stir up the seaboard of the Persian empire. Many, too, were already obsessed by that ill-starred passion for Sicily, which was afterwards blown into a flame by Alcibiades [47] and other orators. Some even cherished sanguine dreams of Etruria and Carthage, in view of the extent of their own supremacy and the sweeping success of all their undertakings.

21. Pericles, however, kept restraining these outbursts, and put a stop to meddling with foreign states. He used the largest part of their resources to guard and consolidate what Athens already had, and thought it achievement enough to hold the Spartans in check. He did everything to oppose them, as is proved by many of his acts, above all by what he did in the Sacred War. [48] The Spartans had sent a force to Delphi and made the Phocians, who held the shrine, give it back to the people of Delphi. But as soon as they were gone, Pericles led a counter excursion and restored the Phocians. Since the Spartans had engraved the special right of consulting the oracle, which the Delphians had given them, on the forehead of the bronze wolf which stands there, Pericles got from the Phocians the same right for the Athenians, and had it engraved on the right side of the same wolf.

22. Events proved that Pericles was right in trying to confine the Athenian empire to Greece. For, first of all, Euboea revolted, [49] and he crossed over with an army to subdue that island. Then, immediately afterward,

---

46 The Athenians had held a position of over-lords in Egypt and had only a short time before been driven out by the Persians.

47 See below, *Alcibiades,* ch. 17, n. 34.

48 The Sacred War was so called because of its connection with the shrine of Apollo at Delphi.

49 In 446 B.C.

news came that the Megarians [50] had joined the enemy, and that a hostile army under command of Plistoanax, king of the Spartans, was at the Attic frontier. So Pericles promptly withdrew his troops from Euboea to fight in Attica. He did not venture to try a battle with the enemy's numerous brave and well-trained infantry, but on discovering that Plistoanax was a very young man, and more under the influence of Cleandridas than of any of the other advisers whom the ephors had sent along to act as his guardians and assistants because of his youth, Pericles made secret approaches to Cleandridas. He soon succeeded in bribing and persuading him to withdraw all the Peloponnesians from Attica.

On the return and dispersal of their army among the cities, the Spartans were so incensed that they imposed a fine on their king, which he was unable to pay in full and so left the country, while Cleandridas, who fled, was condemned to death. This Cleandridas was the father of the Gylippus who achieved the ruin of the Athenians in Sicily.[51] Nature seems to have implanted avarice in Gylippus too, as if it were a hereditary disease, for after some brilliant exploits, he was caught in a disgraceful transaction and banished from Sparta. All this, however, I have told fully in my *Life of Lysander.*

23. When Pericles submitted his accounts for this campaign, there was an item of ten talents spent "for a necessary purpose." The people accepted it without meddlesome questioning or inquiries into the mystery. But some historians, among whom is Theophrastus, the philosopher, say that every year ten talents made their way to Sparta from Pericles, by means of which he placated all the chief magistrates there and so postponed the war, buying not peace but time to make leisurely preparations for a better struggle. He then turned his attention back to the insurgents in Euboea, and crossing over with fifty ships and five thousand heavy-armed troops, he reduced their cities to submission. He banished from Chalcis the so-called "knights," prominent for wealth and station, and he drove all the inhabitants of Hestiaea from their country, replacing them by Athenian

---

[50] Megara, Athens' near neighbor on the Isthmus of Corinth, had, like Corinth, for a long time resented and feared the growing expansion of Athenian control over the routes to the west, and the imports of grain, cattle, and metals from Italy and Sicily. Megara had seized the chance to attack Athens while Pericles was occupied in Euboea.
[51] See below, *Alcibiades*, ch. 20.

settlers. These were the only people he treated with pitiless cruelty, because on capturing an Athenian ship, they had killed the crew.

24. After this, when the Athenians and the Spartans had made the truce for thirty years,[52] Pericles got a resolution passed for an expedition against Samos, on the charge that, though ordered to stop their war on the Milesians, they were not obeying. And as it was thought that he began this attack on the Samians to please Aspasia, here may be a good place to speculate about that woman, and the extraordinary skill and power she had, to wind around her finger the first statesman of the day and set the philosophers to discussing her in lofty terms and at great length. That she was a Milesian by birth, daughter of Axiochus, is generally agreed. They say also that she copied Thargelia, an Ionian lady of ancient times, in setting out to allure men of power. This Thargelia had great beauty, grace, and cleverness. She had many lovers among the Greeks, and brought all who had to do with her over to the Persian side, sowing the seeds of Persianism in the Greek cities through her high-placed, influential friends.

As for Aspasia, some say that Pericles prized her for her political wisdom. Socrates himself came sometimes with his friends to her house, and those who knew her well on occasion brought their wives to hear her, even though she conducted a business which was far from respectable or decent, for she kept young girls as courtesans in her house. Aeschines tells us that Lysicles, a sheep-dealer, a man of low birth and character, became the first man of Athens, because he lived with Aspasia after Pericles' death. In Plato's dialogue, *Menexenus,* though the first part is written in a humorous vein, there is this much of truth, that she had the reputation of meeting with many Athenians to discuss rhetoric. But the feeling that Pericles had for her seems to have been love. His own wife was closely related to him, and had previously been married to Hipponicus, by whom she became the mother of Callias, surnamed the Rich. By Pericles she had two sons, Xanthippus and Paralus. But afterwards, as they did not live

---

[52] The Thirty Years' Truce between Athens and Sparta was concluded in 446 B.C. Samos was an important island city off the coast of Ionia. It had joined the Athenian confederacy as a free ally, but later Pericles decided to seize its fleet and set up a democratic government there, of whose loyalty he could feel better assured. See Thucydides, *Peloponnesian War.* IV, 114–118.

happily together, he, with her consent, gave her to another man, and himself took Aspasia and loved her intensely. Every day, it is said, when he went out or came in from the agora he greeted her with a kiss.

In the comedies she is spoken of as the new Omphale and as Deianira, [53] and again as Hera. Cratinus bluntly calls her a prostitute in the following lines:

> "To him Vice bore a Hera new,
> Aspasia, shameless harlot."

Pericles appears to have had a bastard son by her, for whom Eupolis, in his play *The Demes,* makes him inquire: "And is my bastard living?" To which Myronides answers:

> "Yes, and long ago had been a man,
> Had he no dread of harm from the prostitute."

Yet so renowned and illustrious, they say, was Aspasia, that the Cyrus [54] who fought with the king for the empire of Persia gave the name of Aspasia to his favorite concubine, who previously had been called Milto. She was a Phocaean by birth, daughter of Hermotimus. After Cyrus fell in battle, she was taken to the king and acquired great influence over him. These things came to my memory as I wrote, and it seems unnatural to omit them or pass them by.

25. As for the war against Samos, they accused Pericles of getting it voted to help the Milesians, at Aspasia's request. The two cities were fighting for possession of Priene,[55] and the Samians were winning, and when the Athenians ordered them to take the dispute to Athens for arbitration, they would not obey. So Pericles went by ship to Samos, put an end to the oligarchical government there and took fifty of their leading men as hostages, and fifty children, and sent them to Lemnos. It is said that each of these hostages offered him a talent for his freedom, and that the party

---

[53] Omphale, in the legend was the Lydian queen and mistress of Heracles, who kept him in bondage for three years, Deianira was Heracles' wife.

[54] This was Cyrus the Younger, with whom Xenophon and ten thousand Greeks made the expedition into Persia to depose King Artaxerxes, and who was killed there in battle, in 401 B.C.

[55] The town of Priene lay between Samos and Miletus on the Ionian coast.

which opposed democracy in the city offered him many more. Besides all this, Pissouthnes the Persian, who had a kindly feeling for the Samians, sent him ten thousand pieces of gold and interceded for the city. But Pericles refused all these bribes and dealt with Samos as he had previously determined to do, set up a democracy, and returned to Athens. The Samians at once revolted, for Pissouthnes had stolen back their hostages for them and in other ways helped them prepare for war. Again, therefore, Pericles sailed against them, and found them neither supine nor terrified, but all eager to challenge his control of the sea. In a fierce naval battle off an island called Tragia, Pericles won a remarkable victory, with only forty-four ships defeating seventy, twenty of which were transports.

26. Immediately on his victory and the enemy's flight, he seized the harbor of Samos, and besieged the Samians, who somehow still had courage enough to sally forth and fight under their walls. Soon a larger force arrived from Athens, and the Samians were completely blockaded. Pericles now took sixty triremes and sailed out into the open sea with the intention, most writers say, of meeting a Phoenician fleet which was coming to help the Samians, and having the fight as far as he could from Samos. Stesimbrotus thinks he meant to attack Cyprus, which seems improbable.

But whatever his intention, he appears to have blundered. For as soon as he had sailed, Melissus, son of Ithagenes, a philosopher, who was then in command at Samos, contemptuous of the small number of ships Pericles had left behind and of their commanders' inexperience, persuaded his fellow citizens to attack them. In that battle, the Samians were victorious, taking many Athenian prisoners and sinking many of their ships. Thus they got control of the sea, and supplied themselves with more necessities for war than they had before. Aristotle says that Pericles himself had been beaten earlier by Melissus in a sea fight. Out of vengeance the Samians branded the figure of an owl [56] on the foreheads of their Athenian prisoners, because the Athenians had branded them with the *samaena*. The *samaena* is a ship with a prow shaped like a boar's head, and a roomy hull like a paunch, so as both to carry a large cargo and to sail fast. It got its name because it was first seen at Samos, where the tyrant Polycrates had

---

[56] The owl was the sacred bird of Athene, the tutelary goddess of Athens.

several built. To that branding, it is said, the enigmatic line of Aristophanes [57] refers:

"How lettered are the people of Samos!"

27. When Pericles heard of the disaster that had befallen his fleet, he
returned in haste to assist it. He beat Melissus, who came out to meet
him, and after routing the enemy, promptly built a wall around the city,
preferring to take and conquer it at a cost of money and time rather than
of wounds and lives of men. And when the Athenians grew impatient
at the delay and were burning to fight and it was hard to keep them in
check, he divided the whole force into eight divisions, and made them
draw lots. The division which drew the white bean he permitted to feast
and take its ease, while the rest did the fighting. For this reason, they
say, persons who have had a good time call it a "white day," alluding to
the white bean.

Ephorus tells us that Pericles, attracted by the novelty, made use of
battering engines in this siege and that Artemon the engineer was there
with him. Artemon was called Perephoretus, Lugged-About, because he
was lame and had to be carried in a litter to works which required his
quick attention. But Heraclides of Pontus disproves this tale by quoting
Anacreon's poems, in which Artemon Perephoretus is mentioned many
generations before the war and siege of Samos. He says that Artemon was
a man who led a luxurious life and was cowardly in the face of danger.
Most of the time he sat at home, with two servants holding a bronze shield
over his head so that nothing might fall on it. If obliged to go out, he had
himself carried in a hammock so low as almost to touch the ground. From
that he got the name of Perephoretus.

28. In the ninth month of the siege, the Samians surrendered. Pericles
demolished their walls, confiscated their fleet, and imposed a heavy fine
on them. A part of this the Samians paid at once, and the rest they promised to pay at a set time, giving hostages as security. Douris of Samos
makes a tragic tale of the event and accuses the Athenians and Pericles
of great cruelty, no mention of which is found in either Thucydides, or
Ephorus, or Aristotle. He probably is not telling the truth when he says
that Pericles took the captains and sailors of each Samian trireme to

---

[57] The line is from Aristophanes' comedy, *Babylonians*, now lost.

the market place at Miletus, crucified them there, and after they had
suffered for ten days, had them knocked on the head with clubs and
killed, then cast out their bodies unburied. Even in cases where he had
no personal bias, Douris was not accustomed to hold his story down to
the exact truth. All the more likely, then, that in this instance he exaggerated the afflictions of his country in order to blacken the Athenians.

After the reduction of Samos, Pericles returned to Athens and gave
those who had died in the war a splendid burial. He was much admired
for the oration which, in accordance with custom, he spoke over their
graves. As he descended from the rostrum the women grasped his hands
and crowned him with garlands and ribbons, like a victorious athlete.
But Elpinice came up to him and said: "A fine exploit, Pericles, and
well worthy of garlands! You have lost us many of our brave citizens,
not fighting Phoenicians or Persians, as my brother Cimon did, but
crushing a city of allies and men of our own blood." But at her words,
it is said, Pericles merely smiled quickly and repeated Archilochus' line:

"Old woman, thou shouldst not perfume thyself." [58]

Ion says that he was very proud of himself for his conquest of the
Samians. Agamemnon had taken ten years to capture a barbarian city,
but he in nine months had subdued the greatest and most powerful people of Ionia. And this judgment of himself was not unfair, for the struggle had been precarious and full of dangers, if, as Thucydides says, the
city of Samos came exceedingly close to wresting from the Athenians
their dominion over the sea.

29. After these events, as the Peloponnesian War began to loom ever
nearer, Pericles persuaded the Athenians to send assistance to the people
of Corcyra,[59] who were at war with the Corinthians, and thus gain for
their side an island with a powerful fleet at a moment when the Pelopon-

---

[58] Another way of saying, "You are too old to meddle in these matters."
[59] Corcyra, now known as Corfu, lying off the west coast of Greece and a natural way
station for traders between Greece and Italy, had been colonized by Corinthians. But
as Athens more and more got into her hands the rich trade with the west, Corcyra
broke her ties with Corinth, proposing to enter into a more profitable alliance with
Athens. Corinth, unwilling to see herself crowded out of the western market, declared
war on Corcyra in 433 B.C., to compel her to remain faithful to her mother city and
to continue as a member of the Peloponnesian bloc.

nesians were all but at war with them already. When the people had voted this assistance, Pericles sent Lacedaemonius, son of Cimon, with only ten ships, as if meaning to insult him. Now the house of Cimon was on very friendly terms with the Spartans. In order, therefore, that no great or distinguished success should be achieved under Lacedaemonius' leadership and that he might be accused even more than he was already of Spartan leanings, Pericles gave him only a small number of ships and sent him off against his will. Indeed, Pericles was constantly throwing obstacles in the way of Cimon's sons, maintaining that not even in their names were they true Athenians, one being called Lacedaemonius,[60] another Thessalus, and another Eleius. They were all supposed to be sons of an Arcadian woman.

Pericles was severely criticized for sending only these ten ships, which were of very little help to the needy Corcyreans and yet gave his enemies excellent grounds for their accusations.[61] So he soon sent another and larger force to Corcyra, though it arrived after the battle. However, the Corinthians were enraged and denounced the Athenians at Sparta, as did also the Megarians, who complained that they were excluded and driven from every market and every harbor under Athenian control, contrary to the common laws and the oaths which all Greeks had taken. The people of Aegina also considered themselves ill-treated and oppressed, and secretly poured their grievances into the ears of the Spartans, not daring to bring charges openly against the Athenians. And at this crisis Potidaea,[62] a city subject to Athens, but a colony of Corinth, revolted, and its siege by Athens further hastened the outbreak of war.

In spite of all this, deputations were being sent to Athens, and Archidamus, king of the Spartans, was finding a peaceful solution for many of the complaints against Athens and was calming down his allies. In fact, it does not seem as if the other reasons would have brought the war down

---

[60] Lacedaemon, Thessaly and Elis are, of course, all non-Attic place names; Arcadia is a province of the Peloponnesus.

[61] By aiding the Corcyreans against the Corinthians, Athens gave grounds for a charge of breaking the Thirty Years Truce which she had made thirteen years earlier with Sparta, and which had included Corinth and other leading cities of the Peloponnesus.

[62] Potidaea, a Corinthian colony on the peninsula of Chalcidice, north of the Aegean Sea, had been for some time a tributary ally of Athens, but was now revolting against orders from Athens which would deprive her of all political independence.

on the Athenians, if only they could have been persuaded to revoke their edict against Megara and make peace with her. But Pericles led the opposition to such a course and stiffened the people to maintain their resentment against the Megarians. On this score he alone was to blame for the war.

30. It is said that once, when an embassy came to Athens from Sparta to discuss these questions, Pericles put forward as excuse a law which forbade him to take down the tablet on which the edict against Megara was written. "Then," said Polyalces, one of the ambassadors, "do not take the tablet down, but turn it to the wall. There is certainly no law against that!" Clever as this retort was, it had no effect on Pericles. He had, it seems, a secret grudge against the Megarians, though the reason he put forth publicly was that they had appropriated for their own use the sacred ground of Eleusis. He proposed that a herald be sent to the Megarians, the same to proceed afterward to the Spartans to complain of them; a decree that seems to justify him as a reasonable and humane man.

But the herald who was sent, Anthemocritus, was killed at the instigation, it was thought, of the Megarians, whereupon Charinus introduced a resolution to the effect that there should be deadly and implacable hatred between Athens and Megara, that any Megarian entering Attica should be punished with death, that Athenian generals, when they took the traditional oath, should swear in addition to invade Megarian territory twice every year, and that Anthemocritus should be buried at the Thriasian Gates, now called the Dipylum, or Double Gate. But the Megarians denied any guilt for the murder of Anthemocritus, and blamed Pericles and Aspasia for Athenian hatred, quoting the famous and hackneyed lines from the *Acharnians:* [63]

"Some young Athenians, drunk and full of play, to Megara went
And stole away the tart, Simaetha.
The men of Megara next, inflamed with wrath,
Stole in return two of Aspasia's girls."

31. The true origin of the quarrel it is not easy to ascertain, but all writers agree in calling Pericles responsible for the fact that Charinus' resolution was not revoked. However, some attribute his firmness to greatness of

---

[63] Aristophanes, *Acharnians*, 524–528.

spirit and judgment as to what was best, and say that the protest was made in order to try him, and that any concession would have been taken as an admission of weakness. Others say that he treated the Spartans disdainfully out of arrogance and combativeness, and in order to display his own strength.

But the worst charge of all, and the one supported by most witnesses, runs as follows. Phidias, the sculptor, was contractor for the great statue, as I have said. His intimacy with Pericles and strong influence over him got him many jealous enemies. And others tried to use him to test the temper of the people and to see what sort of judges they would be in a case involving Pericles. These men persuaded Menon, one of Phidias' workmen, to sit in the agora as a suppliant and ask for protection while he was giving testimony and accusing Phidias. The people took the man under protection, and a suit against Phidias was brought in the assembly. Theft indeed was never proven, for on the advice of Pericles, Phidias had, at the very beginning, wrought and fastened the gold around the statue in such a way that it could all be taken off and weighed, which is what Pericles ordered the prosecutors to do on this occasion.

The fame of Phidias' works imposed a crushing burden of jealousy on him, especially since, when carving the battle of the Amazons on the shield of the goddess, he had introduced a figure like himself as a bald-headed old man lifting up a stone with both hands; also, a very fine portrait of Pericles fighting an Amazon. The position of Pericles' hand, holding out a spear in front of his face, is cleverly devised to conceal the likeness, but it is plainly to be seen from the sides. So Phidias was put in prison, where he fell ill and died; though some say he was poisoned by Pericles' enemies in order to blacken his reputation. As for Menon, the informer, at Glycon's proposal the people voted him relief from all taxation, and instructed the generals to see to his safety.

32. At about the same time Aspasia was indicted for impiety, on the charge of Hermippus, the comedy writer. He accused her, too, of harboring freeborn Athenian ladies, with whom Pericles had assignations. And Diopithes proposed a decree that public action should be taken against all persons who did not believe in the gods, or who taught new doctrines about the heavens. He was aiming at Pericles through Anaxagoras. The people adopted this decree and eagerly listened to the slanders. Accord-

ingly, a motion was made by Dracontides, and carried, ordering Pericles to lay his accounts for public moneys expended before the *prytanes,* and the judges to take ballots which had lain on the goddess' altar on the Acropolis to use in the city when they decided the case. But Hagnon got them to strike out that clause of the bill, proposing instead that the case be tried by fifteen hundred jurors.[64] It might be called either a prosecution for theft and bribery, or one for misconduct.

Pericles got Aspasia acquitted by shedding many tears at the trial, Aeschines says, and appealing to the jurors. In fear for Anaxagoras he sent him out of the city. And now, through the Phidias affair, he had clashed with the people and was afraid of a jury. He therefore fanned the oncoming smoldering war into a flame, for he hoped through it to dispel the accusations against himself and allay the popular jealousy, since in other serious and dangerous crises, the city had entrusted herself only to him, because of his high character and ability. These, then, are reasons for his refusal to allow the people to make concessions to the Spartans, but the real truth cannot be known.

33. The Spartans knew that if he could be removed from power, they would find the Athenians much easier to deal with. So they sent them word that they should get rid of the pollution of Cylon, in which the family of Pericles on his mother's side was implicated, as Thucydides tells us.[65] But their effort had an effect just opposite to what they intended. Instead of suspicion and dislike, Pericles won more confidence and respect from the citizens than he had ever had before, because they saw how much more their enemies hated and feared him than they did anyone else. With this situation in mind, before the Peloponnesians under Archidamus invaded Attica, Pericles notified the Athenians that if Archidamus, while devastating other places, spared his estates because of some friendly relation between them, or to give his enemies ground for scandal, he himself would present his lands and the houses on them to the city.

The Spartans and their allies now invaded Attica with a great host led

---

[64] The usual size of a citizen jury was five hundred.

[65] Pericles' mother came from the family of the Alcmaeonidae, a member of which, the archon Megacles, about 636 B.C., had killed the followers of a political conspirator, named Cylon, who had taken refuge at the sanctuary of Athene; the family was thenceforth regarded as tainted with the guilt of sacrilege. Thucydides, *Peloponnesian War,* I, iv, 126, 127.

by their king, Archidamus. Ravaging the country as they advanced, they got as far as Acharnae,[66] where they were encamped, thinking the Athenians would not endure seeing them there but would be driven by their proud spirit to come out to battle. Pericles, however, thought it too perilous to fight for the fate of Athens against sixty thousand Peloponnesian and Boeotian heavy-armed troops, for those who took part in this first invasion were as many as that. So he tried to pacify those who were eager to fight and were upset by what was going on by telling them that trees, when lopped or cut down, grow again quickly, but when men are lost it is not easy to find them again.

He would not call an assembly of the people because he feared they might force him to act against his better judgment, but like the pilot of a ship, who, when a gale blows up at sea, makes everything tight, trims his sails, and exerts his seaman's arts to the utmost, disregarding the tears and entreaties of the seasick and terrified passengers, so Pericles shut the city gates, posted guards for safety at all points, and carried out his own policy, ignoring the grumblers and the dissatisfied. Many of his friends waylaid him with entreaties, many of his enemies threatened and abused him. Choruses sang jeering songs to shame him, deriding his generalship as a cowardly abandonment of everything to the enemy. Cleon,[67] too, was already at his heels, using the people's resentment against him to further his own advance to leadership, as we see from the following lines of Hermippus:

> "O king of the Satyrs, why ever dost thou
> Refuse to grasp boldly the spear, and use only
> Fierce words for thy weapons in war?
> Is the soul of a Teles within thee?
> If a man takes his knife or his billhook to whet
> On a stone hard for sharpening, thou grindest thy teeth,
> As though stung by furious Cleon."

34. Pericles was unmoved by these attacks, but quietly and silently endured the storm of obloquy. He sent out a fleet of a hundred ships against

---

[66] Acharnae was a town about seven miles north of Athens. Aristophanes wrote a play called *The Acharnians*.

[67] Cleon was the demagogic leader of the popular party who came into power on the death of Pericles and stood always for a strong, aggressive policy toward Sparta. He was defeated and killed in a battle with Spartans, in 422 B.C.

the Peloponnesus but did not himself sail with it, staying at home to keep
a tight hand over the city until the Peloponnesians withdrew. Then, to
cheer the common people, who were still suffering from the war, he provided distributions of money and proposed grants of land. He drove out
the whole population of Aegina, and divided their island by lot among
the Athenians. They got some consolation, too, from what their enemies
had to endure. For their fleet, as it sailed around the Peloponnesus laid
waste much country and plundered many villages and small towns, while
Pericles himself invaded by land the territory of Megara and ravaged it.
Thus it was clear that, although the enemy had done damage to the
Athenians by land, they had suffered severely from the Athenians by sea.
Nor would they have protracted the war for so long a time, but would
soon have put an end to it, as Pericles had foretold from the first, had not
an act of heaven confounded human counsels.

For now a deadly pestilence [68] fell upon the Athenians and cut off the
flower of their youth and strength. Suffering in both body and mind they
raged wildly against Pericles, and as people in delirium attack their physicians or their fathers, so they tried to strike at him. They were urged
on by his enemies, who declared that the cause of the plague was the
crowding of the country population into the city, where, during the summer heat, many were herded together in small huts and stifling barracks,
compelled to live a confined and idle life, instead of being out in the pure
and open air to which they were accustomed. And the author of all this
trouble, they said, was the man who, when the war began, had brought
the mob of people from the country into the walled city, and then had
found no uses for all those men, but allowed them to be penned up like
cattle and spread contagion from one to another, giving them no change
or chance to recover.

35.   Hoping to relieve the situation, and also to harass the enemy, Pericles
manned a hundred and fifty ships, sending many brave infantry and cavalry soldiers on board, and was about to put out to sea. The Athenians
had high hopes of the enterprise, and the enemy was terrified at the size
of the fleet. But when all were on board and Pericles himself had embarked in his own trireme, an eclipse of the sun happened to take place.

---

[68] The plague struck Athens in 430 B.C. For a vivid account of its ravages, see Thucydides, *Peloponnesian War,* II, vii, 47–54.

darkness fell, and everyone was panic-stricken at the sinister portent. Pericles saw that his helmsman was frightened and bewildered, and held his cloak in front of the man's eyes, covering them; he then asked him if he thought that was anything terrible or a sign of anything terrible. The man said, "No." "But what is the difference," asked Pericles, "between it and that up there, except that that which made the darkness is something bigger than my cloak?" This, at least, is a story told in the philosophers' schools.

Pericles then sailed off, but apparently accomplished nothing worthy of all his preparations. He besieged the sacred city of Epidaurus and had high hopes of taking it, but failed on account of the plague. For the disease attacked and killed not only his men but those who in any way came in contact with his army. After this, the Athenians again turned against him, though he tried to appease and encourage them. But he did not succeed in pacifying them or in winning them back before they got their ballots into their hands to vote against him. Then they became his masters, stripping him of his command and punishing him with a fine, which by the lowest estimate is set at fifteen talents and by the highest at fifty. The record of the trial named Cleon as the prosecutor, according to Idomeneus, though according to Theophrastus it was Simmias; Heraclides of Pontus says it was Lacratides.

36. However, Pericles' public troubles were likely to be soon over, now that the people had stung him and vented their wrath in the stinging. But his private affairs were in a sad way, as he had lost many of his best friends by the plague and his life was distracted by a family feud. Xanthippus, the eldest of his legitimate sons, a spendthrift by nature, had married a young woman of expensive habits, a daughter of Tisander, son of Epilycus, and was much offended by his father's thrift, because he made him so scanty an allowance and paid it a little at a time. So he sent to one of his father's friends and borrowed money from him, pretending that Pericles had told him to do it. Then when the friend later asked Pericles for his money back, Pericles brought the case to court, at which young Xanthippus was so infuriated that he began speaking abusively of his father in public, describing, to make men laugh, how he spent his time at home, and his conversations with the Sophists.

He told how, when some athlete accidentally hit Epitimus of Pharsalus with his javelin and killed him, Pericles wasted a whole day arguing with Protagoras [69] whether the javelin, or the man who threw it, or the directors of the games, ought strictly speaking to be held responsible for the mishap. Besides all this, Stesimbrotus tells us, Xanthippus spread the scandal about Pericles and his own wife. The young man's quarrel with his father remained irreconcilable until his death, for Xanthippus fell ill and died of the plague.

At that time, too, Pericles lost his sister and most of his relatives and friends and those who had been most useful to him in his conduct of the government. Yet he did not succumb or lose his nobility and grandeur of spirit under his misfortunes. No one saw him weep even at the funeral or at the grave of any of his kinsfolk, until he lost Paralus, the last of his legitimate sons. He was crushed by this blow, though he tried to preserve his customary composure and keep his greatness of spirit; but when he came to lay a garland on the corpse, he was so overcome by grief at the sight that he broke into a wail and storm of tears, which he had never done before in all his life.

37.   The city experimented with its other generals and public speakers as leaders in the war, but none seemed to have sufficient weight or adequate authority for so critical a post. Then they wanted Pericles again, and invited him back to the rostrum and the army command. Disheartened by his sorrow, he was sitting at home. But Alcibiades and his other friends prevailed on him to appear once more. The people apologized for their ungrateful treatment of him, and he resumed his office and was elected general again. He then asked that the law for bastards, which he himself had originally introduced, be suspended, so that the name and lineage of his house might not become totally extinct for lack of an heir.

The history of the law was as follows. Many years before, when Pericles was at the height of his political power and had sons born in wedlock, as I have said, he had proposed a law that only the offspring of Athenians on both sides should be counted Athenians. And when the king of Egypt sent to the people a present of forty thousand measures [70] of wheat,

[69] Protagoras (c.481–c.411 B.C.), a Thracian, came to Athens to teach philosophy, and was the first to call himself a Sophist and to teach his subject for pay. He was expelled from Athens for atheism about 411, and died shortly after.

[70] The measure used was the *medimnus,* equivalent to 1.47 bushels.

which was to be divided among the citizens, a crowd of lawsuits sprang up over men who were illegitimate by Pericles' law, but who up to that time had escaped notice and been overlooked. Many were betrayed by informers. Nearly five thousand were convicted of illegitimacy and sold as slaves, while those who retained their citizenship and were pronounced true Athenians numbered only fourteen thousand and forty. It was, therefore, a serious matter to have the law, which had been enforced against so many, suspended now for the sake of the very man who had proposed it, but the calamities Pericles was suffering at home seemed like penalties he was paying for his former haughtiness and arrogance, and an answer to Athenian objections. They felt that his misfortunes were a retribution, and that his request was natural and human. So they let him enroll his illegitimate son in the ward lists and give him his own name. This son subsequently fought in the naval battle with the Peloponnesians at Arginusae [71] and then was put to death by the people, together with his fellow commanders.

38. It was now, apparently, that Pericles was first attacked by the plague, not a sharp or violent attack, like those which others had had, but a slow illness that went on for a long time with varying symptoms, gradually sapping his strength and undermining his lofty spirit. At least Theophrastus, in his *Ethics,* when discussing the question whether a man's character changes with his fortunes and is affected by bodily pain so as to lose its goodness, says that when Pericles was sick he showed a friend who came to see him an amulet which the women had hung around his neck, as though to say that he was in a very bad way when he submitted to such a piece of folly.

As he was nearing his end, the best of the citizens and the friends who still survived were seated around him, recalling how great had been his virtue and power, and enumerating his achievements and his many trophies. There were nine of them, which he had set up as a general winning victories for the city. They were chatting thus together, imagining that he had lost consciousness and no longer understood them. But he

---

71 406 B.C. The battle of Arginusae, to keep open Athenian traffic routes to the Black Sea, was won by the Athenian fleet, but it was fought during a storm and the victorious commanders were afterwards executed by order of the Athenian assembly for failing to rescue their drowning men.

was following the whole conversation and suddenly spoke out in the middle of it, saying that he was surprised at their remembering and praising him for deeds which were matters of luck, and exploits in which many other generals had had a part, while never mentioning his finest and greatest claim to fame. "No Athenian," he said, "ever put on mourning because of me."

39. Pericles, then, is to be admired not only for his reasonableness and gentleness, which he preserved in the midst of heavy pressures of business and outbreaks of bitter hatred, but for his loftiness of soul. He counted it the best of his own accomplishments that with all his immense power he had never given way to anger or envy, and had never regarded any enemy as one with whom he could not be reconciled. It even seems to me that the childish and high-sounding nickname for him is made unobjectionable and suitable by the fact that it was a character so gracious, a life of power so pure and unstained, that was called Olympian. For we believe that the gods, who are the rulers and kings of the universe, are the authors of good, and not of evil, and are not as the poets describe them, for they perplex us with their ignorant imaginings and contradict themselves by their own tales. They picture the place where the gods dwell as a safe and serene abode, without wind or cloud, but shining evenly and forever with a soft radiance, since such an existence best beseems the blessed and the immortal. Yet the gods themselves they represent as full of spite and resentment and anger and other passions, which are unseemly even for men of intelligence. But these reflections will probably be thought to belong elsewhere.

The course of events after his death soon made the Athenians appreciate Pericles, and long to have him back. Those who during his lifetime had felt oppressed by his power, which, they thought, threw them in the shade, as soon as he was out of the way, tried other orators and leaders and eventually were obliged to admit that a nature more moderate in its stately dignity and more august in its gentleness had never existed. The power which had been so envied and which had once been called a monarchy and a tyranny was now seen to have been the saving bulwark of the state. For now great corruption and wickedness, which he had kept powerless and abject and under cover, and had thus prevented from becoming incurable, took possession of the scene.

Fabius Maximus

C. 270–203 B.C.

1. THE FOREGOING were the memorable deeds of Pericles, as we
have learned them. Let us now turn the course of our narrative to Fabius.
It was a nymph, they say, or a woman of the district, who met Hercules
by the Tiber River and bore him a son, Fabius, from whom descended
the large family of the Fabii, so renowned at Rome. But some historians
say that the first men of this family were called Fodii, from their use in
olden times of pits to trap wild animals, for to the present day ditches,
in Latin, are known as *fossae,* and to dig is *fodere*. Thence, in time, by a
change of two letters, the name became Fabii.[1]

The family produced many great men, the greatest of whom was Rullus,
who for that reason the Romans called Maximus. Fourth in descent from
him was the Fabius Maximus of whom we are now writing. He had a
personal nickname, Verrucosus,[2] from a small wart that grew above his
lip. In childhood, however, he was called Ovicula, which means Lambkin,
because of his mild and serious disposition. He was so quiet and silent,
so very cautious about taking up childish games, so slow and laborious
about learning, and so yielding and submissive to his companions, that
those who knew him but slightly considered him rather dull and stupid.
Only a few said that this slowness came from depth of character, and
recognized the greatness and lionlike quality of his nature. Before long,
however, as time went on and he was stirred by public events, it became
plain, even to the public, that his seeming want of energy was actually

---

[1] A more plausible derivation is that Fabius came from *faba*, bean.
[2] From the Latin noun *verruca*, meaning a protuberance or wart.

freedom from passion, his caution was prudence, and that while he was never quick or easy to move, he was always steady and sure.

Seeing as he did the size of the Roman state and the number of its enemies, he trained his body, nature's own armor, for warfare, and his speech to be an instrument for moving the people, and adapted it very suitably to his own character. There was not much artifice to it, or empty oratorical grace, but there was his own individual point of view, made more weighty by quotation of old maxims. His maxims, they say, were much like those Thucydides used. One of Fabius' speeches is still extant, a funeral oration which he delivered in the assembly over his son who died after being consul.

2. He himself was consul five times. In his first consulship he won the honor of a triumph over the Ligurians. They were defeated by him in battle with heavy losses and driven back into the Alps, after which they stopped ravaging and troubling their neighbors in Italy. Later, Hannibal invaded Italy [3] and won at the outset a victory near the river Trebia. He then marched down through Etruria, laying everything waste as he went, and filling Rome itself with terror and panic. Signs and portents appeared, some, such as thunderbolts, familiar to the Romans, others entirely different and strange. It was said, for instance, that shields were discovered drenched with blood, that ears of corn at Antium were found bloody at harvest time, that flaming, fiery stones fell from heaven, and that the sky above Falerii was seen to open and drop down a rain of tablets, on one of which was written, plain to read: "Mars is brandishing his spear." [4]

However, none of these omens daunted Gaius Flaminius, the consul, [5]

---

[3] Fabius' first consulship, during which he defeated the Ligurians in northwest Italy, was in 233 B.C. Plutarch leaves a gap here of about fifteen years in the life of Fabius. Hannibal did not invade Italy until the spring of 218 B.C., when he began the Second Punic War with an attack on Rome in Spain, then crossed the Pyrenees and marched through southern Gaul and over the Alps, by way, probably, of the Little St. Bernard Pass, and down into Italy. There he was met by a Roman army under the young Publius Scipio, and defeated it in the battles of the Ticino and the Trebia rivers.

[4] Plutarch took this story and most of those that follow from Livy.

[5] Gaius Flaminius, both a statesman and a general, as most of Rome's eminent men were at this period, had already won distinction, not only by his victory over the Gauls in the north, but by his civic measures as tribune, consul, and censor, and by two famous public works, the Circus Flaminius and the Via Flaminia, a new highway leading from Rome directly north.

for he was a man of spirited and ambitious nature, and elated by the great successes he had already won, contrary to all calculations. For in spite of the senate's disapproval and the violent opposition of his own colleague, he had fought the Gauls and beaten them. And while many others were alarmed by the omens, Fabius too was but little disturbed by them, for he thought it foolish to mind them. And when he heard how few the enemy were in numbers, and how deficient they were in supplies, he called on the Romans to have patience, not to start fighting a man who had an army trained in many encounters for just such occasions, but instead to send aid to their allies, keep a tight hold over their subject cities, and allow Hannibal's brilliant force to waste and die of itself, like a flame which flares up brightly for a moment from a little light kindling.

3.   But this reasoning had no effect on Flaminius, who said he would not endure having the war draw close to Rome, and would not, like Camillus of old, fight inside the city to save her. He ordered the tribunes to lead the army out, and leapt himself on his horse. As he did so, the horse, for no visible reason, began to tremble, and Flaminius was thrown headlong to the ground. He was not, however, turned from his purpose, but did what he had from the first set out to do, marched to meet Hannibal, and drew up his forces for battle near the lake called Thrasymene,[6] in Etruria.

The soldiers of the two armies had met and the battle was at its height, when there took place an earthquake which overturned cities, changed the courses of rivers, and broke off pieces of cliffs. Yet with all that violent destruction, not one of the fighters noticed it. Flaminius himself, after many feats of valor and strength, fell dead, and around him lay the bravest of the Romans. The rest were routed with great slaughter. Fifteen thousand were cut to pieces and another fifteen thousand taken prisoner.[7] The body of Flaminius, which Hannibal was anxious to bury with honors for his bravery, could not be found among the slain and no one knew how it had disappeared.

Now the previous defeat on the Trebia had not been truly reported either by the general who wrote the dispatch or by the messenger who brought it, as it had been falsely represented as drawn and doubtful. As soon as the praetor Pomponius heard of this later disaster, he called the

---

[6] Livy calls this lake Trasimenus. It lies near Perugia, in modern Umbria.

[7] Hannibal lost only fifteen hundred men.

people to an assembly and with no roundabout or dissembling phrases said to them straight out: "Men of Rome, we have lost a great battle! The army is destroyed, and the consul Flaminius is dead. So take measures for your own deliverance and safety." His words fell on the sea of people before him like a blast of wind, and threw the city into consternation. No cool reasoning could stand or hold its own against such a shock. But all were finally brought to one opinion, namely, that the situation required a one-man, absolute authority—which they call a dictatorship—and a man who would wield it energetically and fearlessly, and that Fabius Maximus was the only one with a mind and dignity of character adequate to so important an office. He was, moreover, at the time of life when bodily strength is still capable of carrying out the designs of the mind, but when courage is tempered by reflection.

4. The people, then, passed the decree, Fabius was appointed dictator,[8] and he in turn appointed Marcus Minucius master of horse. He next asked leave of the senate to use a horse during the campaign; for he was forbidden to do so by an ancient law against it, either because the chief strength of the army was thought to lie in the infantry and for that reason the commander should stay with the phalanx and not leave it, or else because in all other cases the dictator's power was as absolute as a tyrant's, and in this one instance they wished to have him plainly bound fast to the people. But Fabius was anxious to display immediately the greatness and majesty of his office, and so make the citizens more submissive and ready to obey him. Accordingly, he appeared in public with an escort of twenty-four lictors carrying fasces,[9] though when the surviving consul came to meet him, he sent an officer to order him to dismiss his lictors, leave off his insignia of office and meet him as a private citizen.

Next he made a proper approach to the gods. He explained to the people that their defeat was due to their commander's neglect and disdain of divine things, not to any fault in those who fought. Thus he encouraged them not to fear their enemies, and to honor and propitiate the gods. He implanted no superstitious terrors in them, but increased their valor by

---

[8] A dictator could not be legally appointed by anyone but a consul, and the sole surviving consul at this crisis, Servilius, was absent with the army. Fabius was therefore named pro-consul by the people.

[9] A consul was allowed only twelve lictors.

piety and diminished their dread of the enemy with hopes of divine assistance. Then many of the precious and mysterious books, called the Sibylline Books,[10] were consulted, and some of the sayings preserved in them are said to have had bearing on the fortunes and events of the day. What was learned from them could not be divulged, but the dictator appeared before the people and publicly vowed to sacrifice to the gods all the young of the year from the goats, swine, sheep, and cattle, whatever were born in the coming spring on the mountains, plains, rivers, and pastures of Italy. He swore also to hold musical and dramatic festivals, and to expend on them three hundred and thirty-three sestertii, three hundred and thirty-three denarii, and one-third of a denarius. In Greek money the sum is equal to eighty-three thousand, five hundred and eighty-three drachmas and two obols. What was the virtue of setting this precise figure is hard to say, unless it was to exalt the power of the number three, which is by nature perfect, being the first of the odd numbers, the starting point of magnitude, and containing within itself the first differences, and the elements of every number, mixed and blended together.[11]

5. By thus teaching the people to put their minds on divine things, Fabius made them more cheerful and more hopeful with regard to the future. For his own part, he trusted entirely to himself for victory, believing that God grants success to bravery and prudence. He turned then against Hannibal, not with any plan of fighting it out with him, but intending to use his own abundance of time, funds, and men to wear out and exhaust the other's high-pitched valor, scanty resources, and small army. With this design he always camped high up in the hilly country, where he was secure from the enemy's cavalry, but hung menacingly over them. When they were still, he was quiet, but when they moved, he circled around them, coming down from the heights and showing himself far enough off so that he could not be compelled to fight against his will, yet near enough to keep them afraid that after all his delay he was about to do battle at last.

---

10 The Sibyls were women prophets and seers. One of them, who, according to legend, came to Italy from the East, is reported to have sold to King Tarquinius the collection known as the Sibylline Books, which were consulted as oracles. They were preserved in the Capitol until 405 A.D.

11 The virtues of the number three were part of the mystic doctrine of numbers taught by the Greek philosopher and mathematician, Pythagoras.

By spending his time in this fashion he incurred general contempt, and was scornfully spoken of in his own camp. The enemy thought him a worthless coward. Only one man, Hannibal, did not. He alone recognized the shrewdness of Fabius' tactics and the type of war he was waging, and knew that by some artifice or compulsion he must draw him into battle, or all was over with the Carthaginians. For they could not make use of the weapons in which they were superior, but were losing and expending to no end the men and money in which they were weak. He tried, accordingly, every strategic device and scheme, seeking like a crafty wrestler to get a hold on his antagonist. Now he attacked Fabius directly, again he attempted to confuse him, and led him hither and yon in an endeavor to tempt him from his policy of safety. But Fabius had faith in the success of his method and remained firm and unmovable.

He was vexed, however, by his master of horse, Minucius, who was eager for action at the wrong times and recklessly bold, and who intrigued for leadership of the army, which he filled with crazy excitement and empty hopes. The soldiers jeered at Fabius and called him Hannibal's lackey, while Minucius they considered a great man and a general worthy of the name of Roman. So Minucius became more free with his arrogant boasts, and began ridiculing their way of camping on the heights, saying that the dictator always provided them with beautiful theaters from which to look down on the burning and plundering of Italy.

And he used to ask the friends of Fabius whether he took his army up to heaven because he had lost all interest in earth, or whether he shrouded himself in clouds and mist to escape from the enemy. When his friends reported these things to the dictator and begged him to wipe away these calumnies by risking battle, he answered: "If I did that, I should be more of a coward than I now seem to be, abandoning the policy I have determined on for fear of sneers and slanders. It is no shame to be afraid for one's country; but to be terrified of men's opinions and their abuse and censure is unworthy of a man who holds this high office. It would make him a slave of the rascals he ought to be controlling and governing."

6. Eventually Hannibal blundered. Wishing to move his army farther away from Fabius and to get hold of some level ground for pasture, he ordered his guides one night after supper to lead the way directly to Casinum. But they did not hear the name correctly because of his foreign

pronunciation, and led the way straight to the borders of Campania, to the district of the city of Casilinum, through the midst of which flows the river Lothronus, which the Romans call Vulturnus.[12] Otherwise the region is surrounded by mountains, except for one ravine which opens out towards the sea, where the river overflows into marshes and deep beds of sand and then empties onto a beach, lashed by waves and impracticable for ships.

As Hannibal was moving down into this ravine, Fabius, with his superior knowledge of the roads, went around him, placed four thousand infantrymen to block the narrow outlet, stationed the rest of his troops in good positions on the heights, and then with the lightest and most agile of his men fell on the enemy's rear, throwing the whole army into disorder and killing about eight hundred men. At this, Hannibal determined to retrace his steps, and perceiving the mistake he had made in the place and the danger he was in, he crucified his guides, but was at a loss how to drive his enemies away from the passes which were in their possession. All his men, too, were terrified and disheartened, believing themselves surrounded on all sides by perils from which there was no escape. He therefore resolved to deceive his foes by a trick, as follows.

He ordered his soldiers to take about two thousand of the captured cattle and fasten to each of their horns a torch made of a bundle of twigs or faggots; then at night, at a given signal, to set the torches on fire and drive the animals towards the passes, along the narrow paths guarded by the Romans. While they were carrying out his orders, he got the remainder of his troops under arms in the darkness and led them slowly forward. While the flames were small and burned only the wood, the cattle walked peacefully on as they were driven, towards the hillsides, astonishing the shepherds and herdsmen up there, who looked down from the hilltops and saw the fires shining on the tips of the horns. They thought it must be an army marching in one great column, with masses of torches.

When the beasts' horns had burned down to the roots, and the flesh felt

---

12 Actually Casinum and Casilinum are not very far apart, Casinum being farther to the northwest and nearer Rome; but Casilinum on the Volturno River, where it flows through mountainous country, was a more dangerous place in which to be caught. In that same region a fierce campaign was fought in World War II.

the heat, they shook and tossed their heads wildly with pain. They kept no order then in their march but in their terror and suffering set off in a wild stampede through the mountains, with their foreheads and tails blazing, setting fire to much of the woods through which they fled. To the Romans guarding the passes the sight was terrible, for the flames looked like torches carried by men running; they fell into dire confusion and fright, sure that the enemy had surrounded them and were closing in on them from every direction. So they did not dare to wait but abandoned the passes and made for the main body of their troops. At once Hannibal's light troops came up and took possession of the passes, and his main army passed fearlessly through, though heavily loaded with plunder.

7. Before the night was over Fabius recognized the trick, for some of the oxen in their wild flight had fallen into the hands of his men. But he feared an ambuscade in the dark and so stayed quiet, with his soldiers under arms. When day broke he pursued and harried Hannibal's rearguard, and there was skirmishing over the rough ground and much confusion. Finally Hannibal sent back from his van his practiced Spanish mountaineers, swift, nimbled-footed men, who attacked the heavy-armed Roman infantry, killed many of them, and forced Fabius to withdraw. And now the scorn and contempt for Fabius reached their highest point. He had refrained from pitched battles, expecting to overcome Hannibal by superior strategy and foresight, but he had been conspicuously defeated and outgeneraled in his own methods.

Hannibal, proposing to inflame still more the anger of the Romans against Fabius, when he came to lands belonging to him, ordered burned and ravaged everything around them, but forbade his men to touch them. He even placed a guard to see that no damage was done and nothing stolen from them. When this was reported at Rome, it added to the bitterness against Fabius. The tribunes of the people brought all kinds of public charges against him. These were instigated and pushed chiefly by Metellus, not for any personal enmity to Fabius, but because he was a relative of Minucius, the master of horse, and thought that by depreciating one man he would increase the other's honor and renown.

The senate also angrily blamed Fabius, particularly for the terms he had arranged with Hannibal for the exchange of prisoners. They two had agreed that the prisoners should be exchanged man for man, and if one party had more prisoners than the other, the latter should redeem the rest of his men for two hundred and fifty drachmas apiece. When the man-for-man exchange was over, it was found that two hundred and forty Romans still remained in Hannibal's hands. The senate refused to send the money to recover men whose cowardice had delivered them to the enemy. Fabius heard of all this, and bore his countrymen's indignation calmly, but he could not endure breaking his word to Hannibal and deserting his captive fellow citizens. Since he had no money, he despatched his son to Rome with orders to sell his lands and bring the money back at once to camp. The young man sold the lands and returned with speed, and Fabius sent the ransom to Hannibal and got back the prisoners. Many of them offered afterward to repay him, but he would take nothing from anyone and forgave all the debts.

8.   Later on Fabius was recalled by the priests to Rome to perform certain sacrifices. He then transferred the command to Minucius, with strict orders from himself as dictator to fight no battle nor engage the enemy in any way. Repeatedly too he advised and requested him not to attempt it. To all this, however, Minucius paid little attention, but started immediately harassing the enemy. Observing once that Hannibal had sent the greater part of his army out foraging, he attacked those left behind and drove them into their trenches, killing many and terrifying them all with a threat of encircling them. Then when Hannibal's forces collected again in the camp, Minucius managed a safe retreat. This filled him with presumption and his soldiers with reckless daring. An exaggerated report of the incident spread quickly to Rome, where Fabius, when he heard of it, said he was more afraid of Minucius' success than he was of his failure. But the populace were delighted, and hurried rejoicing to the forum, where Metilius the tribune mounted the rostrum and made a speech glorifying Minucius and accusing Fabius not merely of weakness and cowardice but of actual treachery. He included also in his charges the most influential and eminent men of the city, as having brought on the war from the very beginning in order to crush the people, and having promptly turned the city over to a single man with absolute powers. This man was to give Hannibal time to establish himself firmly and obtain reinforcements from Libya for the conquest of all Italy.

9. Then Fabius came forward but with no intention of defending himself against the tribune. He said only that he was performing his sacrifices and sacred duties as quickly as possible, so that he might return to the army and punish Minucius for having fought a battle against his orders. At this the people were intensely excited, since they knew the danger threatening Minucius. For a dictator has the power to imprison and put to death without trial, and they imagined that Fabius, a singularly mild man, when stirred to wrath would be harsh and implacable. So they all stood in silent dread. But Metilius, having as a tribune nothing to fear (for that is the one office which does not lose its prerogatives at the election of a dictator, but remains unaltered while the rest are suspended) made a violent appeal to the people not to desert Minucius, nor allow him to suffer the penalty Manlius Torquatus imposed on his son,[13] whom he had beheaded, although he had fought brilliantly and been crowned with laurel for his victory. He then told them to strip Fabius of his tyrannical power and entrust the state to one who was able and willing to save it.

Stirred as they were by these words, the crowd did not dare to compel Fabius to resign his dictatorship, in spite of their indignation. They voted that Minucius should assume an equal share of the command and conduct the war with powers the same as the dictator's. It was a thing never done before in Rome, but it happened again shortly afterwards, following the disaster at Cannae. Marcus Junius, the dictator, was then away at camp, and at Rome it was necessary to fill up the senate, since many of its members had died in battle. So they chose a second dictator, Fabius Buteo. He, however, after coming forward and selecting the men to fill up the senate, that same day dismissed his lictors, evaded his escort, mixed with the crowd, and went about the forum transacting business of his own and attending to his affairs like any private citizen.

10. Now that they had placed Minucius on the same footing as the dictator, the Romans thought that Fabius would feel his power curtailed and be generally humiliated; but they had estimated their man wrongly. For he did not consider their error a blow to him, but was like the wise

---

[13] This occurred after the son had disobeyed his father, who was then consul, by fighting and killing a Latin champion in single combat.

Diogenes,[14] who, when someone said, "They are mocking you," answered, "But I am not mocked," meaning that those only are mocked who are affected or upset by mockery. So Fabius coolly and quietly endured all that happened to him, thereby demonstrating the truth of the philosophic maxim that a good and honest man cannot be insulted or disgraced. Yet for his country's sake he grieved over the folly of the people, who had given means for war to a man crazy with ambition, and in fear that he would be so dazzled by empty glory and dignity that he would rush headlong into disaster, Fabius left Rome without anyone's knowledge. On reaching the camp he found Minucius no longer endurable. He was insolent and overbearing and demanded sole control of the army every other day. To this Fabius would not consent, but divided the forces with him, thinking it better to have complete command of a part than part command of the whole. The first and fourth legions he took for himself, and left the second and third to Minucius, dividing the troops of the allies, too, equally with him.

When Minucius put on haughty airs and bragged that he had brought about the humbling and abasement of the highest and greatest office in the state, Fabius reminded him that he was there to fight not Fabius but Hannibal, if he had the sense to realize it. If, however, he persisted in this rivalry with his own colleague, he should see to it that he, the honored victor, should not be proved more careless of the safety and well-being of his fellow citizens than the man who had been abused and ill-treated by them.

11.   But Minucius thought this was merely an old man's hypocrisy, and taking the force assigned to him he set up a camp of his own. [15] Meanwhile Hannibal, far from being ignorant of what was going on, kept watch on everything. There was a hill between the two armies, not difficult to capture, which if taken would be a strong place for a camp and in every way well adapted for one. The plain which surrounded it, seen from a distance, looked flat and bare and smooth, but actually had small ditches and other depressions in it. For this reason Hannibal had not

---

14 Diogenes (c.412–323 B.C.) was the celebrated Cynic philosopher, whose pithy expressions of scorn for the world's standards of success and greatness were often quoted by later Greek and Latin writers.
15 A mile and a half from Fabius, according to Polybius. *History of Rome,* III, 103.

chosen to take the hill, although he could easily have done so by stealth, but had left it untouched between the armies, to furnish an object for a fight. When he saw Minucius separated from Fabius, he distributed some of his troops by night through the ditches and hollows, and at daybreak sent a few men conspicuously out to take the hill, so as to draw Minucius into fighting for it.

And that was what happened. Minucius first sent out his light troops, then his cavalry, and finally, as he saw Hannibal advancing to the aid of his men on the hill, came down himself into the plain with his whole army in array. He fought stoutly, and held his own against the missiles shot from the hill, meeting the enemy in a close and even struggle, until Hannibal, seeing that he was well deceived and was exposing an unprotected rear to the soldiers he had placed in ambush, raised the signal. At that they rose up from many sides and sprang forward with a shout, and cut down the men in the rear. Thereat indescribable confusion and panic seized the Romans. Minucius himself had his courage shattered, and looked around terrified for one after another of his generals, not one of whom dared to stand his ground but rushed to escape, though there was no safety in that. For the Numidians, now the conquerors, scoured the plain in circles, cutting off the fugitives as they scattered.

12. The Romans were thus in a bad plight, but Fabius had observed their danger. Apparently he had foreseen what would happen, for he had his soldiers drawn up under arms, while he gathered his information not from messengers' reports but from what he himself beheld, standing in front of his camp. When he saw Minucius' army surrounded and thrown into confusion, and heard their cries as they yielded ground and panic-stricken turned to flight, he smote his thigh and with a heavy groan said to his companions, "Hercules! How much faster than I expected Minucius has ruined himself, though it is later than he tried to do it!" He then gave orders to bring the standards forward as quickly as possible and the army to follow, and shouted loudly: "Now, men, you must everyone think of Marcus Minucius and hurry to help him, for he is a brave man who loves his country. If he has made a mistake in his eagerness to beat the enemy, we will blame him for that later."

As soon as Fabius appeared, he chased away and dispersed the Numidians, who were galloping around the plain. Next he moved against those who were attacking the Roman rear, and killed everyone he met. The rest, for fear they would be cut off and surrounded as the Romans had been by them, turned and fled. Hannibal, seeing that his fortune had changed, and that Fabius himself, with an energy beyond his years, was pushing his way through the fighters up the hill to Minucius, gave up the battle and trumpeted a retreat, leading his Carthaginians back to their entrenchments. The Romans too were glad of the relief. They say that as Hannibal was withdrawing, he remarked lightly to his friends, "Did I not often tell you that the cloud which has been brooding on the heights would some day drown us in a downpour of storm and tempest?"

13.   After the battle, Fabius stripped the enemy he had killed, and then retired to his camp, letting fall not a single boastful or offensive word about his colleague. But Minucius called his men together and said to them: "Fellow soldiers, to live without making a mistake in matters of grave importance is beyond human power, but when one has made a mistake, a man of courage and sense will use his failure as a lesson for the future. For myself I confess that I have little fault to find with Fortune, and great reason to thank her. For in the short space of a day she has taught me something that in all this time I had never learned. I realize now that I am not able to command others, but need someone to command me. I have been ambitious to outdo men by whom it is more glorious to be outdone. Your leader in everything now is the dictator, except that I will lead you to express our thankfulness to him, and will be first to follow his counsel and obey his orders."

Thereupon he ordered the eagles to be raised aloft and everyone to follow them, and led the way to Fabius' camp. On entering it, he walked to the general's tent, while everyone wondered and did not know what to expect. As Fabius came out, Minucius had the standards planted before him, and in a loud voice called him "Father," while his soldiers hailed Fabius' soldiers as "patrons," a name given by freemen to those who have set them free. When silence was obtained, Minucius said: "Dictator, today you have won two victories. By your valor you have conquered Hannibal, by your sagacity and kindness, your colleague. By one victory you have saved our lives, by the other you have taught us a lesson. Our defeat by him was disgraceful; our defeat by you meant honor and safety. I call you by the good name of father, since I have no more honorable name to give you, though your kindness to me is greater than the kindness of the father who begot me. From him I received merely existence; from you I and all these with me obtained deliverance." With these words he embraced and kissed Fabius, and the soldiers followed his example, embracing and kissing one another, so that the camp was full of joy and happy tears.

14. After this, Fabius resigned his office, and consuls were elected again. The first of these continued the type of war which Fabius had initiated, avoiding pitched battles with Hannibal but sending help to the allies and preventing defections. But when Terentius Varro, a man of low birth,[16] notorious for his hasty temper and his pandering to the people, was promoted to the consulate, it was plain at once that with his inexperience and his audacity he would stake all on a single throw. He was always shouting in the assemblies that the war would last as long as the city employed generals like Fabius, but that he would smash the enemy the day he caught sight of him. With these boastful speeches he collected and enrolled as soldiers a larger army than the Romans had ever raised before against any enemy. Eighty-eight thousand men were organized for battle, to the great anxiety of Fabius and all sensible Romans; for they did not believe the city would recover if she were to lose so many of her youth.

The colleague of Terentius was Paulus Aemilius, a man of experience in many wars but not popular with the people and afraid of them, because of a fine they had once imposed on him. Fabius now tried to arouse and encourage him to put some check on Terentius' folly, pointing out that his struggle for his country's safety would be as much against Terentius as against Hannibal. "One," he said, "is eager to fight because he does not know what his strength is; the other, because he knows his own weakness. It is right, Paulus, for you to trust me more than Terentius, when it comes to dealing with Hannibal, and I assure you that if no one attempts a battle with him this year, the man will either be ruined, staying in Italy, or will quit the country as a fugitive. For even now, when he seems to be victorious and to have everything in his power, not one of his enemies has come over to his side, and his army is now less than a third of what he brought from home." To this Paulus is said to have replied: "For my part, Fabius, I think it better to fall by the spears of the

16 Terentius Varro was the son of a butcher.

enemy than by the votes of my countrymen again. But if that is how it
stands with the state, I shall try to be a good general, more for you than
for all the rest who are trying to thwart you." With this determination
Paulus went out to the war.

15. But Terentius insisted on taking command on alternate days.[17] H'
proceeded to encamp near Hannibal by the river Aufidus, near the town
of Cannae,[18] and at daybreak he displayed the signal for battle, a scarlet
tunic flying over the general's tent. At first the Carthaginians were dismayed at the sight of the Roman general's boldness and at the size of
his forces, for they had not half the number. But Hannibal ordered them
to arm, and himself rode with a few others to the top of a sloping hill,
from which he watched the Romans forming in line. When one of his
companions named Gisco, a man of the same rank as himself, said that
the numbers of the enemy were astonishing, Hannibal replied, with a
serious air, "Something else still more astonishing, Gisco, you did not
notice." And when Gisco asked what that might be, Hannibal answered,
"It is that in all those numbers there is not a man named Gisco." At this
unexpected jest, they all began to laugh, and as they came down the hill
they told it to everyone they met, so that the laughter became general
and Hannibal's staff was overcome with merriment. Seeing this, the
Carthaginians took courage, for they reasoned that their commander must
hold the enemy in great contempt to laugh and joke so in the presence of
danger.

16. In the battle Hannibal used more than one stratagem. First, he took
advantage of his position to get the wind at his back. For it was blowing
a fiery hurricane, which lifted a huge cloud of dust from the sandy plains,
and drove it over the Carthaginian phalanx straight at the Romans, who
turned their faces away and fell into disorder. Secondly, in the disposition of his forces, he placed his strongest and best fighters on each side
of the center and filled the center up with the poorest, so as to use it as a
wedge, having it project far beyond the rest of the line. And the best men
on the wings were told that when the Romans had driven in this center

17 The Romans had a rule that consuls, when on the same service, should take command of the army by turns.
18 The ruins of Cannae by the river Aufidus, northwest of Bari, are still to be seen
near the Apulian coast.

and were pursuing it excitedly, it would retreat and make a deep hollow, and so let the Romans inside the phalanx. Then each wing must turn sharply inward and fall on the flanks and encircle them by closing in on their rear. The scheme seems to have produced terrible slaughter. For when the center gave way and took in the pursuing Romans, Hannibal's line changed its shape to a crescent form, and the captains of the picked troops, wheeling them quickly to the left and the right, attacked the Romans' unguarded flanks, overpowering and killing all save the few who escaped before they were quite surrounded.

An extraordinary disaster, too, they say, befell the Roman cavalry. Paulus' horse, apparently, was wounded and threw him, and one after another of his staff dismounted and went to defend him on foot. The cavalrymen, seeing this, took it for a general order, and all dismounted and met the enemy on foot. Whereupon, Hannibal said: "I like this better than if they had handed them over bound hand and foot." But these are anecdotes related by the writers of more detailed histories.

As for the consuls, Varro rode off with a few followers to the city of Venusia, but Paulus was caught in the whirling eddies of the rout, and covered with wounds in which the darts were still sticking. Overwhelmed in body and spirit by the catastrophe, he sat down on a stone waiting for an enemy to finish him. His head and face were so smeared with blood that few recognized him, and even his friends and attendants passed by him without knowing it was he. Only Cornelius Lentulus, a young patrician, saw who he was, and sprang from his horse and led it up to him, begging him to mount and save himself for his fellow citizens, who now more than ever needed a brave commander. But Paulus refused his entreaty and forced the youth in tears to remount. He then rose and took him by the hand, saying: "Tell Fabius Maximus, Lentulus, and bear witness yourself, that Paulus Aemilius was faithful to his instructions to the end and broke not one of his promises; but he was vanquished first by Varro and then by Hannibal." With this message he sent Lentulus off, and throwing himself into the thick of the melée was slain. They say that fifty thousand Romans fell in that battle and four thousand were captured alive, and that after the battle no less than ten thousand more were taken in the camps of the two consuls.[19]

---

[19] Less than six thousand Carthaginians were killed.

17.   After this tremendous success, Hannibal's friends urged him to follow up his good fortune and descend on Rome along with the fugitives,
declaring that in five days after his victory he would be supping on the
Capitol. It is not easy to say what reasoning turned him against the proposal. It seems rather like the work of some evil genius or divinity, which
made him hesitate and choose a timid policy. So, they say, the Carthaginian, Barca, told him angrily, "You know how to win a victory but
not how to use one." Yet a great change in his situation was effected by
his victory. Before the battle he had not a city or a market or a harbor in
Italy, and with the utmost difficulty obtained scanty provisions for his
army by plunder. Having no strong base of operations for war, he wan-
dered about with his army like a huge band of brigands. Now he had
nearly the whole of Italy in his hands. Most of the largest and most
powerful tribes came over to him of their own accord, and Capua,
reckoned the most important city next to Rome,[20] became his submissive
ally.

   Not only is it a very bad thing, as Euripides says, to put our friends to
the test, but the same is true of confident generals. However, what the
Romans had called Fabius' cowardice and lack of spirit before the battle
they now considered superhuman sagacity, even divine and inspired intelligence, since he saw so long beforehand the disaster that would happen,
which still seemed well-nigh incredible even to those who had suffered
from it. On him, then, Rome placed her last hopes. To his wisdom she
fled for refuge as to a temple altar, convinced that it was his prudence,
more than anything else, that had kept her standing, instead of lying
wrecked as she was at the time of the invasion of the Gauls. And he who
had seemed cautious and pessimistic in days when there was no apparent
danger, now, when everyone was giving way to unbridled grief and
futile lamentation, was the only man to walk through the city with a
calm step, serene countenance, and kindly voice, checking womanish
wailings and forbidding gatherings of people to lament publicly their
common distress. He persuaded the senate to meet, put fresh courage into
the magistrates, and was himself the strength and power of every office, for
they all looked up to him.

---

[20] Capua, an Etruscan city, in the district of Campania, a few miles north of Naples,
was celebrated for its wealth and luxury. In 343 B.C. it had come under Roman rule.

18. He placed guards at the gates to stop the frightened mob from deserting the city. He set limits of time and place for mourning the dead, ordering whoever wished to mourn to do so for thirty days at home. After that, all mourning must cease and the city be cleansed of such rites. The festival of Ceres fell during those days, but it was thought better to omit altogether the sacrifices and the procession than to proclaim the extent of their misfortunes by the fewness and despondency of the persons who took part.[21] For the gods find pleasure only in honors paid them by happy people. But everything the soothsayers advised to appease the anger of the gods and avert bad omens was performed, and Pictor, a relative of Fabius, was sent to Delphi to consult the oracle. When two of the Vestal Virgins were found to have been seduced, one was buried alive, according to custom,[22] and the other died by her own hand.

Remarkable was the spirit of quiet composure in the city when the consul Varro returned after his flight. He came humbled and speechless, as a man would after bringing about so disgraceful a disaster, but at the gates the senate and the whole people met and welcomed him. The magistrates and the chief men of the senate, among whom was Fabius, when silence had been obtained, spoke their praises of him, because after such a calamity he had not despaired of the city but had come back to take control of affairs and put the laws and his countrymen to work at saving themselves, as they could.

19. When they learned that Hannibal after the battle had turned away to other parts of Italy, the Romans again took heart and sent out more armies and commanders. Of these the most distinguished were Fabius Maximus and Claudius Marcellus,[23] men equally respected, for almost opposite characteristics. Marcellus, as I have related in his *Life,* was a man of brilliant and impetuous energy, quick with his hands, and by

---

[21] The feast of the earth goddess Ceres was one of the most important in the Roman calendar. No one in mourning was ever allowed to participate in it. Since every family in Rome had suffered bereavement at Cannae, its omission in the year of that disaster, 216 B.C., was natural.   [22] See above *Numa,* ch. 10.

[23] Marcus Claudius Marcellus, Fabius' colleague in office and in the field for over twelve years, first defeated the Gauls in northern Italy, and then moved south to take part in the struggle with Hannibal. In 212 B.C. he captured the rich city of Syracuse in Sicily, then an ally of Carthage. His generous treatment of the conquered people was praised by Cicero in 70 B.C. in his speeches against the plunderer Verres.

nature like the warriors whom Homer calls "lovers of war" and "stern in fight." His first battles he fought in the venturesome and headlong style of warfare which met the daring Hannibal with equal daring. Fabius, on the contrary, was convinced that his previous reasoning was correct, and was sure that Hannibal, if only no one fought him or attempted a struggle, would wear himself out and suddenly lose his high-pitched vigor, like an athlete whose body has been overtrained and its strength exhausted. For this reason, Posidonius says, the Romans called Fabius their shield, and Marcellus their sword, and the combination of the steadiness and firmness of Fabius with the high spirit of Marcellus was the saving of Rome. In his frequent bouts with Marcellus, who was like a raging torrent, Hannibal saw his forces shaken and shattered, while Fabius, like a slow quiet river, kept constantly and imperceptibly at work undermining them and wearing them away. He was at length reduced to such a pass that he was exhausted with fighting Marcellus, and afraid of Fabius when he was not fighting.

They were the men with whom he fought most of the time, for they were the appointed praetors or else consuls or pro-consuls. Each of them was consul five times. During Marcellus' fifth consulship, Hannibal lured him into an ambush and killed him; but with Fabius he got nowhere, though he tried every ruse and stratagem on him again and again. Just once did he deceive him and nearly destroy him. He composed and sent to Fabius letters from the leading citizens of Metapontum, telling him that the city would surrender to him if he appeared before it, and that those who were making the arrangements were only waiting for him to come and show himself near by. Fabius was moved by these letters and was planning to take a part of his army and start off at night. But the auspices were unfavorable and he changed his mind, and soon afterwards learned that the letters were crafty forgeries by Hannibal, who was preparing an ambush for him near the city. This escape may be attributed to the favor of the gods.

20. The revolt of cities and the turbulence of allies Fabius thought should be restrained and checked by pacific and gentle methods, without investigating every suspicion and treating harshly every person suspected. They say, for instance, that he heard once that a Marsian soldier, a leader among the allies for his bravery and noble birth, had been talking with

some of the soldiers about deserting. Fabius showed no anger, but admitted that the man had been unfairly neglected. Up until now, he said to him, his commanders had been to blame for distributing their honors by favor rather than by merit; but in future it would be his own fault if he did not come to Fabius and tell him whenever he wanted something. So saying, he presented the man with a war horse and other rewards of valor, and thenceforth there was no one more loyal or zealous. Fabius thought it shocking that while trainers of horses and dogs used care and friendliness and good food, instead of whips and heavy collars, to tame their animals' obstinacy and rage and moroseness, commanders of men did not base most of their training on kindness and gentleness, but treated their men more roughly and severely than gardeners do the wild fig trees, pear trees, and olives which they reclaim and domesticate and turn into trees bearing good fruit.

So when his captains informed him that another soldier, a Lucanian by birth, was frequently roving away from camp and absent from his post, Fabius asked what kind of man he was in other ways. All agreed that it would be hard to find another soldier so good, and mentioned some of his exploits conspicuous for gallantry. Seeking then for the cause of the man's irregular behavior, Fabius found he was possessed by love for a girl, and took the risk of a long journey from camp each time he went to see her. Without the soldier's knowledge, he sent for the girl and hid her in his own tent. He then summoned the Lucanian to him privately and said: "We know you are often away from camp over night, contrary to Roman custom and law, but we know also that you have been a good soldier. Your offenses, therefore, you have atoned for by your valiant deeds, but for the future I shall hand the custody of you over to someone else." Then to the soldier's astonishment he led out the girl, put her hand in his, and said, "This lady pledges her word that you will remain in camp with us. You will show by your conduct whether it was for some other, vicious reason you left us, making a pretext of her and your love." These are stories told on the subject.

21. The city of Tarentum,[24] which the Romans had lost by treachery, Fabius retook in the following way. In his army was a young man of

---

[24] Tarentum, originally a Spartan colony, was an important seaport on the western side of the Italian "heel." Hannibal had taken it in 212 B.C. Fabius got it back three years later.

Tarentum, whose sister was faithfully and devotedly attached to him. In love with her was a Bruttian, the commander of Hannibal's garrison there. This fact made the Tarentine hope he might do something, and with Fabius' consent he made his way into the city, giving out that he had deserted from the Romans in order to be with his sister in Tarentum. For the first few days thereafter the Bruttian remained in his quarters, for the girl thought her affair with him was not known to her brother. But then he said to her: "There was a rumor going around widely in the Roman army that you were intimate with a man of great authority here. Who is he? For if, as they say, he is a man of high courage and distinction, it does not matter what his race is, for war mixes up everything. Nothing done under compulsion is disgraceful, and at a time when justice is weak, it is a lucky man who finds the mighty ones propitious to him." At this, the woman sent for her Bruttian and introduced him to her brother, who, by encouraging him in his passion and by making his sister appear more friendly and submissive to him, got the barbarian's confidence. So it was not hard, since the man was only a mercenary and in love, to get him to change sides, in view, too, of the large gifts he was assured Fabius would give him.

This is the account given by most writers, though some say the lady by whom the Bruttian was brought over was not a Tarentine but herself a Bruttian by race and a concubine of Fabius, and that when she discovered that the commander of the Bruttian garrison was a fellow countryman and an acquaintance of hers, she told Fabius of it and had an interview with him under the city walls, and so worked on him as to win him over.

22. While this enterprise was on foot, Fabius was scheming to draw Hannibal away from the scene and sent orders to his garrison at Rhegium to overrun Bruttium and take Caulonia by storm. This garrison consisted of eight thousand men, mostly deserters, in fact, the poorest of the disgraced soldiers sent back from Sicily by Marcellus, whose loss would cause the least grief and harm to Rome. He hoped that by throwing them out as a bait to Hannibal he might entice him away from Tarentum, as actually he did. For Hannibal at once hurried off with his troops in pursuit. And on the sixth day, Fabius began a siege of Tarentum, and the young man who had previously made arrangements with the Bruttian

through his sister came to him at night. He had observed the precise place where the Bruttian was on guard, ready to admit and surrender the city to the besiegers. However, Fabius would not let his enterprise depend entirely on one man's treachery. So while he himself went stealthily to the appointed place, the rest of his army attacked the walls by land and sea, with loud clamor and din, until most of the Tarentines had rushed to the aid of their defenders. Then the Bruttian gave the signal to Fabius, who mounted by ladder and took possession of the city.

On this occasion, however, Fabius seems to have been overcome by his ambition, for he ordered his men to put the Bruttians to death first of all, that it might not be known that he had taken the city by treachery. Yet he did not succeed in suppressing this knowledge, but merely got a reputation for cruelty and perfidy as well. Many of the Tarentines, too, he had killed, thirty thousand sold as slaves, and the city was sacked by his army. Three thousand talents were brought into the public treasury.

While everything else was being carried off, it is said that the record-keeper asked Fabius what his orders were with regard to the gods, meaning thereby their statues and pictures. Fabius replied, "Let us leave the Tarentines their angry gods!" But he took the colossal statue of Hercules from Tarentum and set it up on the Capitol, and near it erected a bronze statue of himself on horseback. In this instance his behavior seems much stranger than that of Marcellus. Indeed it made Marcellus seem admirably lenient and humane, as I have described in his *Life*.

23. Hannibal is said to have been hastening to Tarentum, and to have been within five miles of it when he heard it was taken, and to have remarked aloud only, "So, then, the Romans also have a Hannibal, for we have lost Tarentum in just the way we took it." But in private he for the first time acknowledged to his friends that he had long been aware of the difficulty of conquering Italy, and he now saw that, with things as they were, it was impossible.

For this success Fabius enjoyed a second triumph more glorious than his first, for he was contending with Hannibal like a competent athlete, easily baffling all his thrusts, as though his holds and grips no longer had the same strength. And Hannibal's army was growing weaker, in part corrupted by luxury and wealth,[25] and in part dulled and exhausted by the unceasing struggle.

There was a Marcus Livius who had commanded the Roman garrison in Tarentum when Hannibal induced the city to revolt. He had continued to hold the citadel and could not be dislodged, but kept it until the Romans recaptured the town. This man was vexed at the honors paid to Fabius, and was once so overcome by jealousy and ambition as to say to the senate that it was not Fabius but himself who should be thanked for the taking of Tarentum. Whereat Fabius laughed and said, "Very true; for if you had not lost the city, I could not have taken it."

24.   Among other marks of distinction which the Romans bestowed on Fabius, they elected his son Fabius consul.[26] After he had entered on his office and was making some arrangements for the conduct of the war, his father, either because of his age and infirmities or else in order to test his son, once mounted his horse and rode towards him through a crowd of bystanders. The young man saw him approaching from some distance off and would not permit it, but sent a lictor to tell his father to dismount and come forward on foot, if by chance he wanted anything of the consul. All the rest present were offended at this order and regarded Fabius in silence, as if they felt he was being unworthily treated, in view of his great eminence. But he instantly alighted, almost ran to his son, embraced and kissed him, saying: "You are right, my son, in your thought and your act. You understand what kind of people you command, and how solemn an office you have received. By this method we and our ancestors have made Rome great, by always thinking less of our parents and children than of our country's good."

As a matter of fact, it is said that the great-grandfather of Fabius,[27] who in his day was the most famous and powerful man in Rome, and was five times consul and celebrated splendid triumphs for great wars, when his son was made consul, accompanied him to battle as his lieutenant, and in the subsequent triumph, when his son entered the city in

---

[25] In the winter of 216–215 B.C. Hannibal had made Capua his headquarters. His soldiers are said to have become demoralized by the voluptuous life they led there.

[26] Plutarch's chronology is slightly at fault here. Fabius' son was consul in 213 B.C.

[27] He was Fabius Maximus, surnamed Rullianus, who distinguished himself in the final war with the Samnites, the most powerful tribe to the south of Rome. By his victory he opened the way for Roman expansion southward. He was made dictator in 315 B.C.

a four-horse chariot, followed on horseback in his train. For, though he was master of his son and the greatest of Rome's citizens in fact and in name, he exulted in submitting himself to the law and to the chief magistrate. But our Fabius was remarkable on other counts as well. His son died later, and this sorrow he bore with fortitude, as became a wise man and an upright father. The oration, which at the funeral of a public figure is delivered by some relative, he spoke himself, standing in the forum. Afterwards, he wrote down the speech and had it given out.

25. Cornelius Scipio [28] meanwhile had been sent to Spain, where he defeated the Carthaginians in many battles, drove them out of the country, and won over to Rome a great many tribes and large cities glittering with spoils. So, on his return to Rome, he was received with such favor and honor as no other man ever had, and was elected consul. He knew that the people demanded and expected extraordinary things of him, and he regarded the close-knit tussle with Hannibal on Italian soil as an antiquated, old man's method. He therefore proposed at once to flood Carthage and Libya with Roman arms and troops and devastation, and thus move the war away from Italy to Africa. He bent all his energies to winning the people for this project.

But Fabius spread alarm all through the city, pointing out that this reckless young man was trying to hurry them into extremely grave danger; and he spared neither words nor acts that he thought would turn the citizens against it. He persuaded the senate, but the people thought he was opposing Scipio because he was jealous of his success and afraid that if by some great and brilliant feat Scipio did finish the war or move it out of Italy, he himself would be considered dilatory and cowardly, since in all those years the war had not been ended.

When Fabius began to oppose Scipio, he was probably influenced by his own great caution and prudence and by fear of the danger, which was formidable. But as he grew more heated, he was carried further by ambition and obstinacy in an effort to hinder the rise of Scipio. He even tried to induce Crassus, Scipio's colleague as consul, not to relinquish command of the army and not to give way to Scipio, but if the expedition to Carthage were determined on, to lead it himself. Fabius also prevented

[28] This was Publius Cornelius Scipio, surnamed Africanus, who was finally to defeat Hannibal in Africa in 202. Fabius died in 203.

the granting of funds for the campaign. So Scipio was obliged to raise
money for himself, and he obtained it privately from the cities of Etruria,
which felt warmly to him. As for Crassus, it was partly his nature, which
was not quarrelsome, that kept him at home, and partly a religious rule,
for he was also Pontifex Maximus.

26. Fabius now tried another method of opposing Scipio, by restraining
and holding back the young men who were keen to take service with
him. In meetings of the senate and the assembly he would call out that
not only was Scipio himself running away from Hannibal but that he was
taking with him all of Italy's remaining strength, deluding her young
men with hopes, and inducing them to desert their parents, their wives,
and their city, at whose gates the enemy still sat, powerful and undefeated.
Indeed he so worried the Romans with his talk that they voted to allow
Scipio only the troops then in Sicily and three hundred of the men who
had been with him in Spain. In this instance certainly Fabius' policy
seems to have matched his own cautious nature.

But after Scipio had crossed over into Africa, news at once began coming to Rome of wonderful deeds and achievements, magnificent in extent
and splendor. In proof of the reports there followed vast quantities of
booty. The king of Numidia was taken captive. Two enemy camps were
destroyed at one time by fire, with great loss of men, horses, and arms.
Delegations were sent to Hannibal from Carthage, summoning and beseeching him to abandon his fruitless hopes for Italy and come back to
succor his home.

When at Rome the name of Scipio was in every man's mouth for his
victories, Fabius asked to have a successor sent out to take his place. He
gave no other reason, but quoted the familiar proverb that it was not safe
to trust undertakings of such vast importance to one man's luck, for it
was hard for the same man to be lucky always. Therewith he offended
many of his countrymen, who thought him a peevish and ill-tempered
fellow, or one whom old age had made thoroughly timid and pessimistic,
and who had an exaggerated fear of Hannibal. For not even when Hannibal had sailed from Italy with his army, would Fabius allow his countrymen's joy and fresh spirits to be unmixed with alarm and suspense, for
he told them that now Rome's fortunes were indeed in a bad way and
the city was headed for more peril than ever, since Hannibal would fall

on their men all the more crushingly in Libya, before the walls of Carthage, and Scipio would meet an army still warm with the blood of many rulers, dictators, and consuls. Accordingly, the city was once again perturbed by his talk, and though the war had been taken to Libya, they thought of its terror as being nearer than before.

27. But shortly afterward Scipio defeated Hannibal himself in a pitched battle, and humbled and trampled underfoot the pride of fallen Carthage, and restored to his fellow citizens a joy beyond even their highest hopes. Truly "he did steady" their power, "shaken by the stormy billow." [29]

Fabius Maximus did not live to the end of the war, or hear of Hannibal's defeat, or see the immense and secure prosperity that followed for his country, for about the time that Hannibal left Italy, he fell sick and died. The Thebans buried Epaminondas [30] at public expense, because he died in such poverty that nothing, they say, was found in his house after his death but one small iron coin. The Romans did not give Fabius that kind of burial, but every private citizen contributed the smallest coin he had towards the cost. It was not that they needed to help out his poverty, but that they felt they were burying the father of his people. And so in death he had the honor and renown he deserved in life.

---

[29] The words in quotation marks seem to be an adaptation of a line in Sophocles' *Antigone*, 163.

[30] For Epaminondas, the hero of Theban history, see above, *Lycurgus,* n. 27.

Comparison of Pericles and Fabius Maximus

1. SUCH is the story of the lives of these two men. And as they both left behind them many fine examples of political and military ability, let us take up first their success in war. Pericles was leader of his people during the height of their prosperity, when their own strength was greatest and their empire at its peak. The general good fortune and energy then seem to have made his enterprises secure from failure, whereas Fabius took over his city in a time of utter disgrace and calamity, and his achievements did not merely keep her safe and prosperous but raised her out of miseries to a far higher position. Moreover, the victories of Cimon, the trophies of Myronides and Leocrates, and the many exploits of Tolmides, made it Pericles' duty, as civil head of the city, to provide it with holidays and festivals rather than to expand and defend its domain by war.

Fabius, on the other hand, saw many routs and defeats, and much dying and slaughtering of generals and commanders. He saw lakes, plains, and forests littered with soldiers' bodies, and rivers flowing with blood and corpses to the sea. Yet with firm resolution he grasped and supported his city and kept her from being overwhelmed by the misfortunes other men brought on her. However, it would seem to be less difficult to control a city in adversity, when she is humbled and compelled by necessity to listen to wisdom, than to bridle a bold and arrogant people, puffed up by prosperity, as the Athenians were when Pericles governed them. On the other hand, the magnitude and number of the troubles which fell on the Romans testified to the steadfastness and greatness of the man who was unbroken by them and held to the policy on which he had determined.

2. The capture of Samos by Pericles we may set against the retaking of Tarentum by Fabius, and the conquest of Euboea against that of the Campanian cities. Capua itself fell to the consuls Fulvius and Appius. In formal, regular warfare, Fabius seems never to have won a battle, except the one for which he celebrated his first triumph, whereas Pericles set up nine trophies for victories by land and sea. But again there is no deed recorded of Pericles equal to Fabius' act when he snatched Minucius from defeat at the hands of Hannibal, and saved an entire Roman army from destruction. That was a noble act, combining courage, sagacity, and goodness of heart. On the other hand, there is no report of Pericles making such a blunder as Fabius did when out-maneuvered by Hannibal with his flaming cattle. Fabius had Hannibal caught in a narrow valley, which he had entered, by chance, of his own accord, yet he allowed him to escape unwatched by night, and at daybreak to take advantage of his own slowness, and so to get away from his captor.

And if it is the part of a good general not merely to deal with present problems but to have sound judgment of what is to come, we may note that the Athenians' war ended as Pericles had foreseen and foretold, for they grasped at too much and lost their empire. Whereas it was contrary to Fabius' advice that the Romans sent Scipio to attack Carthage, and thus won their sweeping victory, not by luck but by the skill and valor of their general, who thoroughly crushed the enemy. So the mistakes that Pericles' country made show that he was a good prophet, and the Romans' successes prove that Fabius was entirely wrong. And it is as much a fault in a general to let slip an opportunity for victory for want of confidence as it is to run into trouble for want of foresight. Inexperience, in my opinion, is a thing that both produces recklessness and also robs one of courage. So much for their military records.

3. In the political field, the Peloponnesian War is a great blot on the name of Pericles, for it is said to have been caused by his refusal to yield a point to the Spartans. I imagine, however, that Fabius Maximus would have conceded nothing to the Carthaginians, but would valiantly have risked any danger to defend the power of Rome. His kind and lenient treatment of Minucius contrasts with Pericles' bitter feud with Cimon and Thucydides, good men of the aristocratic party, whom he forced into exile by ostracism.

But the influence and power of Pericles were greater than those of Fabius. So Pericles did not permit any other general to bring disaster on the city by bad strategy, except Tolmides, who broke away from his control and fell in his attack on the Boeotians. All the others, because of Pericles' great authority, submitted to his judgment and shaped their plans accordingly. But Fabius, though he could manage his own army surely and unerringly, was obviously hampered by his inability to prevent others from making mistakes. Certainly the Romans would not have suffered so many defeats if Fabius had had as much authority at Rome as Pericles had at Athens.

As for high-mindedness in money matters, one showed it by never touching a bribe, the other by generosity to men in need, for he ransomed his captured soldiers at his own expense, even though the sum of his property was not large, only about six talents. I cannot say what valuable gifts Pericles, with all his influence, might have received from deferential allies and kings, yet he kept himself completely above bribes and his hands always clean. As for the great public works, the temples and buildings with which Pericles adorned Athens, all the ambitious edifices in Rome taken together, down to the time of the Caesars, are not worthy to be compared to them, for both in splendor of design and splendor of workmanship the Greek achievement far surpassed the Roman and is indeed beyond comparison.

Alcibiades

C. 450–404 B.C.

1. THE FAMILY of Alcibiades [1] is said to begin with Eurysaces, son of Ajax, who was its founder. On his mother's side Alcibiades belonged to the Alcmaeonidae,[2] being the son of Dinomache, the daughter of Megacles. Clinias, his father, fought gallantly at Artemisium [3] in a trireme fitted out at his own expense, and subsequently fell fighting the Boeotians in the battle of Coronea.[4] Alcibiades after this was entrusted to Pericles and Ariphon, the two sons of Xanthippus, who acted as his guardians because they were next of kin. It is said with some likelihood that the friendship and affection of Socrates for him did much to win him a reputation. Nicias, Demosthenes, Lamachus, Phormio, Thrasybulus, and Theramenes were all famous men in his lifetime; yet we do not even know the name of the mother of any of them, while in Alcibiades' case we know that he had a nurse, a Spartan woman, named Amycla, and a tutor called Zopyrus. Antisthenes gives us the first item, and Plato the second.[5]

Of Alcibiades' beauty I probably do not need to speak, except to say that it bloomed out in childhood, youth, and manhood, at every age and season

---

1 Alcibiades is one of the participants in Plato's dialogue, the *Symposium*. He is also the subject of two other dialogues, *Alcibiades I* and *II*, ascribed to Plato but probably not his.
2 Pericles, who was Alcibiades' cousin, belonged to this family. See above, *Pericles*, n. 65.
3 See above, *Themistocles*, chs. 7–9.
4 This was the first battle of Coronea, 447 B.C., in which the Athenians were defeated by the Boeotians in an attempt to extend their power over their neighbors. Alcibiades was left fatherless at the age of three.
5 *Alcibiades, I,* 122.

of his life, making him lovable and charming. The saying of Euripides, "All beautiful things have a beautiful autumn too," is not universally true, but it was so in the case of Alcibiades, and of a few others, because of the natural comeliness and perfection of his body. Even his lisp is said to have added distinction to his speech and made his talk winning and attractive. Aristophanes mentions the lisp in the lines in which he makes fun of Theorus: [6]

> "Sosias: Then Alcibiades said to me, with his lisp:
>   'Do you thee Theolus? He hath the head of a *kolax*.'
> Xanthias: This time Alcibiades lisped right."

And Archippus, when he is ridiculing the son of Alcibiades, says, "He swaggers in his walk, trailing his cloak behind him, to look the very image of his father, and bends his affected neck, talks with a lisp."

2.   His character, in time, showed inconsistencies and contradictions, as was natural in a career of such great undertakings and changeable fortunes. By nature he was a man of many strong passions, the strongest of which were combativeness and ambition, as is clear from the anecdotes told of his boyhood. Once, when he was hard pressed in a wrestling match, rather than take a fall he began to bite his opponent's arm, and might have bitten through it, but the other boy let go his hold, and cried, "You are biting, Alcibiades, like a woman!" "Not I," said he, "but like a lion!" While still small, he was playing at dice in a narrow street, and as his turn came to throw, a loaded wagon appeared. He first ordered the driver to stop, since his throw lay directly in the path of the wagon. The man, however, was a boor and paid no attention. As he drove straight on, the other boys got out of the way, but Alcibiades flung himself on his face in front of the team, stretched himself out and bade the fellow drive on if he chose. Alarmed, the man now stopped his team, and the frightened spectators ran shouting to rescue Alcibiades.

In his studies he was properly obedient to all his teachers, except that he refused to play the flute, declaring that it was not a fitting instrument for a gentleman and a free citizen. Playing the lyre with a plectrum did

---

[6] Aristophanes, *Wasps*, 44–46. Alcibiades' lisp apparently turned his r's into l's. The point here seems to be that instead of saying "Theolus" is wearing the head of a *korax*, or raven, as he does in Aristophanes' comedy, Alcibiades says he has the head of a *kolax*, or flatterer.

not spoil the look and appearance of a gentleman, he said, but when a man was puffing on a flute, his own family could scarcely recognize him. Moreover, the lyre was an accompaniment to a man's voice and speech. "Let Theban boys," he used to say, "play their flutes, for they do not know how to talk. But we Athenians, as our fathers tell us, have Athene as our foundress and Apollo as our protector. One of them threw the flute away in disgust, and the other flayed a flute-player." [7] With such talk as this, half in jest and half in earnest, Alcibiades kept both himself from learning the flute and other boys as well. For the word quickly went around among them that Alcibiades despised flute-playing and jeered at those who were studying it, and that he was right. In consequence, the flute was dropped altogether from liberal studies and regarded with utter scorn.

3. Among the scandals Antiphon [8] reports of Alcibiades, we read that as a boy he once ran away from home to Democrates, one of his admirers. His guardian Ariphon proposed having a public proclamation made of his disappearance, but Pericles would not permit it, saying, "If he is dead we shall learn of it by the proclamation one day sooner; and if he is safe, he will be injured for the rest of his life." Antiphon says too that he killed one of his servants with a blow of his stick, at Sibyrtius' wrestling field. Perhaps we should not believe these stories, told by a man who admits that he hated Alcibiades and so was vilifying him.

4. Already many men of noble birth were gathering around and paying him attention, most of them charmed by his youthful brilliance, and heaping flattery on him. But the love Socrates had for him is a strong proof of the boy's natural soundness and good disposition, which the philosopher discerned embodied in this radiant form, and which he feared would be corrupted by wealth and position, and by the throng of citizens, foreigners, and allies who tried to get a hold on him by adulation and favors.

---

[7] Athene in the story threw her flute away on seeing her distorted face reflected in a spring. Apollo outplayed the braggart satyr Marsyas in a musical contest and then flayed him alive for his presumption.

[8] Antiphon (c. 480–411 B.C.), an Attic orator, lawyer, and politician, was an influential member of the Athenian aristocratic party that opposed Pericles. After the failure of his party to make a success of the oligarchic government of the Four Hundred, in 411, he was put to death by the people's order. The attack on Alcibiades which Plutarch here attributes to him is not extant and may not have been his.

Socrates was anxious to protect him and not allow so fair a blossoming plant to shed its natural fruit and die. And no one is ever so enclosed and wrapped around by fortune in the so-called good things of life that he cannot be pricked by philosophy and stung by her bold and caustic words. So Alcibiades, spoiled as he was from the very first and hindered ¹ʸ his companions in pleasure from listening to one who would advise and instruct him, still was led by his own goodness of heart to appreciate Socrates and attach himself to him, discarding his rich and fashionable suitors.

Soon afterward he made Socrates his comrade and began listening to the words of a lover who pursued him for no unmanly entertainment and asked for no caresses or embraces, but aimed at exposing the disease in his soul, and bringing down his vain and foolish pride.

"Though a cock, he crouched like a slave, with drooping wing,"

for he thought the work of Socrates was really an instrument of the gods for the guardianship and salvation of youth. So learning to despise himself and to admire Socrates, loving his kindliness and revering his virtue, he insensibly acquired an "image of love, in response to love," as Plato says.[9] And all were astonished to see him dining, exercising, and sharing a tent with Socrates, while treating his other admirers with coldness and reserve. To some of them he was extremely insolent, as he was to Anytus, son of Anthemion.

This man was in love with Alcibiades, and when he was entertaining his friends at dinner, asked him to come. Alcibiades refused the invitation, but that night after drinking at home with some companions, he went with his revelers to the house of Anytus and took his stand at the door of the men's hall. Looking in and seeing the tables covered with gold and silver drinking cups, he ordered his slaves to pick up half of them and carry them home. He did not deign to go in, but after playing that trick he departed. When Anytus' guests in indignation complained of his being so arrogantly and outrageously treated by Alcibiades, "No," he said, "he was reasonable and considerate. He might have taken them all, and he has left us half."

---

9 Plato, *Phaedrus*, 255.

5. He treated his other lovers in the same way, except, they say, one of the resident aliens, who was not rich but who sold all he had and brought the hundred staters he received to Alcibiades, entreating him to accept them. Alcibiades laughed with amusement and invited him to dinner. After feasting him well, as a friend, he gave him back his gold and told him to go the next day and bid against the farmers of the public taxes and bid higher than all of them.[10] The man begged to be excused, because the contract would cost many talents; but Alcibiades, who then had some private grudge against the collectors, threatened to have him thrashed if he did not do it. Accordingly, the next morning the alien went to the agora and bid a talent more than the customary amount. The tax collectors angrily clustered around him and bade him name his surety, confident he would not be able to name one. The man was frightened and about to withdraw, when Alcibiades, who was standing at a distance, called out to the magistrate, "Write down my name! He is a friend of mine. I will be surety for him." On hearing this, the tax collectors were greatly embarrassed, for it was their habit to pay what they owed on one year's contract out of the proceeds of the next, and they saw no way now of doing this. So they begged the man to retract his bid, and offered him money if he would. Alcibiades would not let him accept less than a talent, but when they offered him that amount, he told him to take it and retire. This is the way he did the man a kindness.

6. Alcibiades' love for Socrates, though it had many powerful rivals, took a great hold on him, for he had a noble disposition, and his teacher's words touched him and wrung his heart and moved him to tears. Yet sometimes he would yield to the flatterers who enticed him with many pleasures, and would slip away from Socrates and let himself be hunted down by him, as if he were a runaway slave. He revered and feared Socrates, and only him, and was scornful of everyone else. Cleanthes [11] used to say that his only hold on the one he loved was by the ears, though many other holds, which he would not touch, presented themselves to his rivals, meaning by them the other bodily senses. Alcibiades was of course

---

10 Farming the public taxes was the method used for securing tax-gatherers. The office was let each year to the highest bidders, who paid the state the sum stipulated in their contracts and kept for themselves what they collected over and above that amount.
11 Cleanthes (c.300–c.220 B.C.) was an early Stoic philosopher.

easily led away to pleasure. What Thucydides calls "the lawlessness of his life and habits" [12] makes one realize that. But the men who really corrupted him made their special appeal to his ambition and thirst for glory. They pushed him too early into planning great projects, persuading him that as soon as he entered public life he would instantly outshine all the generals and politicians, and would even surpass Pericles in influence and renown among the Greeks. But just as iron which has been softened in the fire grows hard again when dipped in cold water, so Alcibiades, whenever Socrates found him puffed up by vanity and folly, collapsed at his master's words and became humble and modest. He learned from him how great were his own deficiencies and how far he was from perfection in virtue.

7.   When he was growing out of boyhood, he stopped one day a teacher of grammar, and asked him for a book by Homer. The teacher said he had nothing of Homer's, whereat Alcibiades struck him with his fist, and went on. Another teacher told him he had a Homer corrected by himself. "What!" said Alcibiades. "Are you teaching children to read, when you are able to correct Homer? You should be teaching men!" He once wished to speak to Pericles and went to his house, but was told that Pericles was busy planning how to present his accounts to the Athenians.[13] "Would it not be better," Alcibiades remarked, as he turned away, "for him to plan how not to present his accounts to the Athenians?"

While still a youth, he served as a soldier in the expedition against Potidaea,[14] and had Socrates as his tent-mate and stood next to him in battle. In a sharp fight they both won distinction, and when Alcibiades fell wounded, Socrates stood in front of him, protecting him, and so saved his life and his armor. Properly, therefore, the prize for valor belonged to Socrates, but when the generals appeared anxious to bestow the honor on Alcibiades, because of his rank, Socrates, who wished to encourage his ambition for noble things, was the first to testify to his courage, and to demand that they crown him and give him the suit of armor. Another

---

12 Thucydides, *Peloponnesian War*, VI, xviii, 15.

13 See above, *Pericles*, ch. 23.

14 Potidaea, port on the peninsula of Chalcidice, and a tributary ally of Athens, revolted in 432 B.C. The Athenians blockaded the city and finally forced it to submit, in 430. See above, *Pericles*, ch. 29.

time, during the rout of the Athenians at the battle of Delium,[15] Alcibiades was on horseback when he saw Socrates retreating with a few others on foot. He would not pass by him, but rode beside him and defended him, although the enemy was pressing them hard and cutting off many. This happened some time later.

8. He once struck Hipponicus, father of Callias, a man whose birth and wealth made him a person of great influence and repute. He did it not in anger nor as part of a quarrel, but simply for a joke, because he had made a wager with his friends. The brutal act was reported all over the city and everyone was naturally indignant. The next morning Alcibiades went to the house of Hipponicus, knocked on the door and was admitted to Hipponicus' presence. Here he threw off his cloak and offered his body to be flogged in punishment. At this Hipponicus forgot his anger and pardoned him, and later chose him as a husband for his daughter Hipparete. Some say, however, that it was not Hipponicus but Callias, his son, who gave Hipparete to Alcibiades, with a dowry of ten talents; and that when her child was born, Alcibiades demanded and received ten more talents, claiming that that had been the arrangement, if there were children. And Callias was so afraid of Alcibiades' scheming that he made a public offer of his wealth and house to the people, in case he chanced to die childless.

Hipparete was a dutiful and affectionate wife, but much distressed by her husband's love affairs with foreign and Athenian courtesans, so that in time she left his house and went to her brother's. As Alcibiades was not at all disturbed and continued his wanton ways, she was obliged to lodge a petition for divorce with the magistrate, and not by proxy but in person. When, in obedience to the law, she presented herself to do this, Alcibiades came forward and seized her and carried her off home with him through the agora, no one daring to oppose or to take her from him. She lived with him then until her death, but she died not long afterward, when Alcibiades was on a trip to Ephesus. This show of force, however, was not considered illegal or inhumane at all, for the object of the law in

---

15 Near the town of Delium in Boeotia, in 424 B.C., the Athenians were defeated in another attempt to get possession of the country. For a description by Alcibiades of Socrates' behavior on this campaign, see Plato, *Symposium,* Classics Club edition, p. 213.

making a wife who leaves her husband present herself in court is apparently to give the husband an opportunity to get hold of her again.

9.   Alcibiades had a remarkably large and handsome dog which had cost him seventy minas. He had its tail, which was a very beautiful one, cut off, and when his friends scolded him and said that everybody was vexed for the dog and blaming him, he said, laughing, "But that is what I want. I want the Athenians to chatter about this, so that they may say nothing worse about me."

10.   His first entrance into public life was, they say, in connection with a subscription of money for the state, and happened accidentally. He was passing by the assembly when he heard shouting and asked the reason for it. He was told that contributions were being taken for the state, whereupon he came forward and contributed something. The people clapped and cheered him, at which he quite forgot a quail he was carrying under his cloak, and the bird flew out and escaped. The Athenians applauded all the more, and many jumped up to help him chase it. Antiochus, a pilot, caught it and gave it back to him, and thenceforward became one of his favorites.

Wide doors to public life were opened to Alcibiades by his birth, his riches, his personal courage in battle, and his crowd of friends and connections, but he relied on nothing so much as his own charm of speech to give him influence with the people. The comic poets bear witness to his powers as a talker, and the greatest of orators, in his speech against Midias, says that Alcibiades, among other things, was a most gifted speaker.[16] And if we are to believe Theophrastus, an interested and learned philosopher, Alcibiades was the quickest of everyone to discover and understand what was needed, and he aimed not only at saying the right thing, but at saying it in the right words and phrases. Yet he was not fluent, and would often stumble in the middle of a speech and stop and wait while the words eluded him. Then he would pick up and go carefully on.

11.   His breeds of horses were famous and so was the number of his racing chariots. No other person, whether king or commoner, ever entered seven chariots at the Olympic games. And to have won the first, second,

---

[16] Demosthenes, *Against Midias,* 145.

and fourth places, as Thucydides says he did, or the third, as Euripides tells us, is a glory that exceeds all that any man can aspire to in these contests. The ode of Euripides runs as follows: [17]

> "Thee will I sing, O Clinias' son.
> Victory is fair, but fairest what no other Greek has done,
> To run first, second, and third in the chariot race,
> And go off unwearied, crowned with the olive of Zeus,
> A theme for the herald's proclamation."

12. His splendor was made all the more conspicuous at Olympia by the manner in which the cities vied with each other to celebrate him. The Ephesians pitched a magnificent tent for him; Chios furnished provender for his horses and plenty of animals for sacrifice; Lesbos supplied him with wine and other provisions for unlimited entertainment of the multitudes. Yet even more talk was caused by a scandal or misdeed of his own, connected with this rivalry. It is said that there was at Athens one Diomedes, a man of standing and a friend of Alcibiades, who was eager to win a victory at Olympia. Hearing that there was a racing chariot at Argos belonging to the city, and knowing that Alcibiades had great influence and many friends there, he persuaded him to buy the chariot for him. But Alcibiades, after buying the chariot, entered it in the lists as his own, letting Diomedes whistle for it. The latter was outraged and called on gods and men to witness Alcibiades' behavior. It seems too that there was a lawsuit over this affair, and Isocrates [18] wrote a speech for Alcibiades' son on the *Team of Horses*. In the speech, however, Tisias, not Diomedes, is the plaintiff.

13. When, as a mere youth, Alcibiades plunged into politics, he at once outshone all the other popular leaders, but had to struggle against Phaeax, son of Erasistratus, and Nicias, son of Niceratus.[19] The latter was a man

---

17 This is an ode for victory at the Olympic games, like the odes of Pindar.

18 Isocrates (436–338 B.C.) was a much admired Athenian orator and teacher of eloquence. The reference here is to his *Oration XVI, On the Team*.

19 Nicias (c.470–413 B.C.), a wealthy and conscientious Athenian general, was the leader of a moderate democratic party, which stood for a conservative policy and economy and peace with Sparta, as soon as favorable terms could be obtained. For some years after Pericles' death, his words carried much weight in Athens.

already advanced in life, with the reputation of being a most excellent general. Phaeax, like himself, was starting his career, and though of distinguished ancestry, was inferior to Alcibiades in other respects, particularly as a speaker. He was apparently affable and persuasive in private conversation but not so well able to take part in public argument. For he was, as Eupolis says,

"The best of talkers, but the feeblest speaker."

There is extant a speech written by Phaeax, *Against Alcibiades*,[20] in which, among other things, he is charged with using all the city's abundant gold and silver ceremonial plate in his daily life, as if it were his own.

There was a certain Hyperbolus, of the deme Perithois, mentioned by Thucydides as a rascal,[21] who was a general butt for the jokes of all the comic dramatists. His utter disregard of the harsh things said of him and indifference to them were due to his contempt for popular opinion, which was nothing but impudence and stupidity, though there were some who called it courage and intrepidity. Nobody liked him, yet the people often made use of him when they wished to have scurrilous abuse leveled at someone in high position. At this time they were persuaded by him to vote for an ostracism, the means by which from time to time they cut short by banishment the career of a citizen who was outstanding in reputation and power. They did it to assuage their envy of him rather than because they feared him. But when it became clear that one of the three, Nicias, Phaeax, or Alcibiades, would be the man ostracized, Alcibiades arranged matters with Nicias, combined their two parties into one, and turned the vote of ostracism against Hyperbolus. Some say that it was not Nicias but Phaeax with whom Alcibiades had his conference and whose party he annexed to his own, thus managing to exile Hyperbolus, who had not expected such a result. For hitherto no lowborn or disreputable person had ever been punished in this way. So Plato, the comic poet, says somewhere in speaking of Hyperbolus:

---

[20] This speech has by chance come down to us among several by the orator Andocides. *Oration IV.* It is obviously a fictitious speech, put by its unknown author into the mouth of Phaeax.

[21] Thucydides, *Peloponnesian War*, VIII, xxv, 73.

"Men before him were worthy of what he suffered,
But he and his band were not worthy of it,
For ostracism was not designed for such as he."

We have given elsewhere more fully what the writers tell us of this incident.[22]

14. But Alcibiades was irritated at the respect shown for Nicias by his enemies, as well as at the honor he was receiving from his fellow citizens. For Alcibiades was then the agent for the Spartans at Athens, and had been of service to their men who were captured at Pylos.[23] Yet it was mainly by Nicias' efforts that the Spartans obtained a peace treaty and the return of their prisoners, and so they were lavish in their attentions to him. Among all the Greeks the saying ran that Pericles had brought on the war and Nicias had finished it. And the peace that followed most men called the Peace of Nicias. Thereat Alcibiades was irked beyond measure, and out of jealousy planned a violation of the treaty. In the first place he saw that the Argives hated and feared the Spartans and were looking for a way to break with them. Accordingly, he held out hopes to them in secret of an Athenian alliance, and both in person and through his agents encouraged the leading men of their popular party not to fear or give way to the Spartans but to turn to the Athenians and await their cooperation, for, he said, they had already begun to regret what they had done and would soon break the peace.

And when the Spartans made an alliance with the Boeotians and delivered up Panactum to the Athenians,[24] not intact, as it should have been, but in a dismantled condition, Alcibiades whipped up the Athenians' irritation to still greater wrath. He raised a clamor against Nicias, and brought false but plausible charges against him in the assembly. As a

---

22 The reference is to Plutarch's *Life of Nicias*. The above is the last recorded instance of ostracism at Athens. As a procedure intended to be used only against men of great prominence and dignity, it was considered debased by its application to a commoner like Hyperbolus.

23 In 425 B.C., an Athenian fleet took Pylos on the west coast of the Peloponnesus, and with it a considerable Spartan garrison. As a result Sparta sued for an armistice.

24 The Boeotians had refused to sign the Peace of Nicias and so were still at war with Athens. One clause of the treaty had required the return to Athens of Panactum, a town on the northern border of Attica, which had been seized and used by the Spartans as a center for raids on Athenian territory.

general, he said, Nicias had refused to make prisoners of the enemy's
forces who were cut off on the island of Sphacteria,[25] and when others had
captured them, he set them free and sent them home, to please the Spartans. Then, though Nicias was their friend, he failed to dissuade the
Spartans from making an alliance with the Boeotians and the Corinthians.
Yet when any Greek state wished to become a friend and ally of Athens,
he tried to stop it, unless the Spartans signified their approval.

But while Nicias was suffering under these accusations, by good luck
ambassadors arrived from Sparta to propose from the outset reasonable
terms, with assurances that they had full authority to accept any further
terms that were conciliatory and fair. The council received them cordially,
and the next day the people were to hold an assembly to hear them.
Alcibiades, afraid that they would succeed, contrived to get a private interview with them, and at their meeting said to them: "What is wrong
with you, men of Sparta? How have you failed to note that the council
is always moderate and considerate of those who appear before it, but that
the people's assembly is arrogant and full of ambitious notions? If you
tell it you have come with unlimited authority, it will make unreasonable
demands and force great concessions from you. So listen, and stop being
so simple! If you wish to find the Athenians reasonable and not be forced
into submission against your will, then discuss what would be a just arrangement, but say you have not full power to decide. I will stand by you,
out of friendship to Sparta."

With these words he gave them his oath, and thus enticed them away
from Nicias and made them put all their trust in him. They were impressed by his acuteness and intelligence, and thought him an extraordinary man. On the following day the people assembled, and the ambassadors
appeared before them. They were then politely asked by Alcibiades in
what capacity they had come, and they replied that they did not have full
power. Instantly, Alcibiades assailed them loud and furiously, as though
he, not they, were being mistreated, calling them untrustworthy, shifty
men, who had not come to do or say anything honest. The council was
indignant at them, the assembly in a rage, and Nicias was shocked and

---

[25] Sphacteria, now called Sphagia, is a small island near the entrance to the harbor of
Pylos. A Spartan garrison had been blockaded there in the course of the Athenian
attack on Pylos. Nicias' rival, Cleon, compelled them to surrender.

distressed at the men's change of tune. He knew nothing of Alcibiades' deceit and trickery.

15. Thus the negotiations with Sparta came to nothing, and Alcibiades was elected general and promptly organized an alliance between Athens and Argos, Elis, and Mantinea.[26] No one approved of the way he did this, but much was accomplished by it, since it split and upset almost all the Peloponnesus, and in one day secured many men to fight the Spartans at Mantinea.[27] It removed, too, the scene of struggle and its dangers far from Athens, so that, although the Spartans won, they got no great advantage from their victory, whereas if they had been defeated, they would have been put to it to survive.

After the battle of Mantinea the oligarchs in Argos, called the Thousand, tried at once to overthrow the popular government and make themselves masters of the city; and the Spartans came and abolished the democracy. But the people took up arms again and got back control, and Alcibiades came to their aid and made their victory secure. He also persuaded the people to build long walls and carry them down to the sea, so to connect their city on every hand with the Athenian empire. He even brought carpenters and stone masons from Athens, and showed himself full of zeal, thus winning popularity and influence for himself as much as for Athens. He induced the people of Patrae [28] also to join their city by long walls to the sea. And when someone said to them, "Athens will swallow you up!" Alcibiades answered, "Perhaps it may, but it will be a little at a time, beginning with your feet; whereas Sparta will catch you by the head and swallow you all at once."

However, he advised the Athenians to establish their power on land as well as on sea, and to fulfill in action the oath which is always administered to their young men in the shrine of Agraulos.[29] They swear that they will

26 By this alliance much of the northern half of the Peloponnesus was engaged on the side of Athens.
27 The battle of Mantinea, in central Peloponnesus, between Sparta and Athens with her new allies, was fought in 418 B.C. The Athenian side was not thoroughly united or in earnest, so that the Spartans won an important victory.
28 The town of Patrae, on the Peloponnesian side of the entry to the Corinthian Gulf, built its long walls in 419 B.C.
29 Agraulos, the wife or daughter of Cecrops, the legendary first king of Athens, figured in many Attic traditions.

regard wheat, barley, the vine, and the olive as the boundaries of Attica, and are taught thus to consider all the cultivated and fruitful earth as their own.

16. But with all these displays of political ability, eloquence, sagacity, and astuteness, Alcibiades now lived a life of luxury, drinking, and debauchery. He was effeminate in dress, trailing long purple mantles through the agora, and recklessly extravagant. He had the decks of his triremes cut away, so that he might sleep more comfortably with his mattresses laid on bedsteads instead of on planks. He had a gold shield made for himself, emblazoned with Eros wielding a thunderbolt, instead of with his ancestral arms. The respectable men of Athens beheld his conduct with disgust and indignation, and feared his insolent and lawless spirit, as tending in the direction of tyranny and a revolution. But Aristophanes has well expressed the feeling of the people about him in the line: [30]

"They love him, they hate him, they would not give him up."

He alludes to him again, more sternly, in a figure:

" 'Tis best to rear no lion in your city,
But if he's reared, submit to all his whims."

His lavish contributions of money, his support of public exhibitions, his unequaled displays of munificence towards the city, his noble birth, his power of eloquence, his bodily strength and beauty, his prowess and bravery in war, made the Athenians tolerant and patient with him in other things. They always gave his misbehavior the mildest names, calling it youthful escapades and bids for fame. For example, he once locked up Agatharchus, the painter, until he had painted his house, and then set him free with a present. He boxed Taureas' ears because he was paying for a show in competition with one of his own, so ambitious was he for the prize. And he took one of the captive Melian women [31] for his mistress, and

---

[30] Aristophanes, *Frogs*, 1425; 1431–1432.

[31] The small island of Melos in the southern Aegean had remained neutral through the long war between the powerful states of Greece until the summer of 416 B.C., when the Athenians demanded that it should become their tributary ally. On its refusal, the Athenians took the island, put all the grown males to death, and sold the women and children as slaves.

brought up a son he had by her. That was what they called his kindness. Yet it was he who was chiefly responsible for the slaughter of all the adult men of Melos, since he sponsored the motion for it.

When Aristophon painted Nemea [32] holding Alcibiades seated in her arms, everybody flocked to see the picture. But the older men were displeased at this, too, thinking it suggested lawless tyranny. So it seemed that Archestratus was correct when he said that Greece could not stand two of Alcibiades. Once when Alcibiades had spent a successful day and was being conspicuously escorted home from the assembly, Timon the misanthrope met him.[33] He did not go on by or avoid Alcibiades, as he did others, but went up and took him by the hand, and said: "You are growing well, my boy; you will grow to be a big calamity for all your crowd." Some laughed, some scolded, and some took the words to heart. So uncertain was the people's opinion about Alcibiades, because of the inconsistency of his character.

17. Even during the lifetime of Pericles the Athenians had cast longing eyes on Sicily, and after his death they endeavored to get hold of it.[34] From time to time they sent out expeditions, ostensibly to succor their allies who were being oppressed by the Syracusans but actually paving the way for something greater. The man who eventually fanned their desires into flame and persuaded them not to keep up their half-hearted, dilatory attempts, but to sail to the island with a great fleet and subdue it, was Alcibiades. He raised grand expectations among the people, and his own hopes were grander still. He looked on Sicily as only a starting

---

[32] Nemea was the name of a valley in northern Peloponnesus, not far from Argos, where games in honor of Zeus were held every second year. Because of Alcibiades' victories in those games Aristophon seems to have painted Nemea personified as a woman, holding him in her lap.

[33] Timon (later half of the fifth century B.C.), the Athenian, was notorious as a man-hating solitary. For more about him, see below, *Antony,* chs. 69-70. He is the subject of Shakespeare's play, *Timon of Athens.*

[34] The rich island of Sicily, colonized largely by Greek settlers, and a center of trade for Greeks, Phoenicians, Carthaginans, and Italians, its cities homes of Greek civilization and art, was a prize which, if won, would go far to give Athens supremacy over the western Mediterranean. The fatal expedition against Syracuse, a Corinthian colony, on which the Athenians expended the best of their ships and the flower of their young men, took place in the summer of 415 B.C. For the whole story see Thucydides, *Peloponnesian War,* VI and VII.

point for what he aspired to do, not as the end of the expedition, as other people did. So while Nicias was trying to dissuade the people from attacking Syracuse as too difficult an undertaking, Alcibiades was dreaming of Carthage and Libya, and after acquiring them, of adding soon Italy and the Peloponnesus. Sicily he thought of as little more than a means to the greater conquest.

He quickly carried away the young men by these visions, and they listened to their elders telling of the many wonders of the country. Groups sat about in the wrestling grounds and open places, tracing on the ground the shape of Sicily and the position of Libya and Carthage. They say, however, that the philosopher Socrates and the astronomer Meton [35] expected no good to come to the city from the expedition. Socrates, probably, received a presentiment from his familiar spirit. Meton either was frightened of the future by the calculations he had made, or else he resorted to some kind of soothsaying. He feigned madness, seized a blazing torch, and attempted to set his house on fire. Others say that he made no pretense of madness but did burn his house down one night, and in the morning came and begged the people, in view of his misfortune, to exempt his son from serving on the expedition. In either case he deluded his fellow citizens and got what he wanted.

18.   Much against his will, Nicias was chosen a general. His unwillingness to take the command was due in large part to the fact that Alcibiades was to be his colleague. For the Athenians thought that the war would go better if they did not send out Alcibiades unchecked, but tempered his rashness with the prudence of Nicias. For the third general, Lamachus, though advanced in years, seemed still to be no less fiery than Alcibiades and as prone to take risks in battle. While the people were debating about the size and character of the equipment, Nicias tried again to block the measure and stop the war. But Alcibiades opposed him and swept all along with him, and the orator Demostratus moved that the generals should have full power over the preparations and over the whole campaign.

The people approved this motion, and everything was made ready for

---

[35] Meton (latter half of the fifth century B.C.) was an Athenian mathematician and astronomer, famous for having worked out a calendar with a nineteen-year cycle through which he correlated the lunar and the solar years.

the sailing of the fleet. Then some unlucky omens appeared, connected especially with the festival of Adonis.[36] The festival took place at that time, and the women were displaying in many places images like corpses on their way to burial, imitating funeral rites, beating their breasts, and chanting dirges. The mutilation, too, and disfigurement in one night of the faces of most of the Hermae [37] disturbed many persons, even those who as a rule made light of such things. A story was spread that the Corinthians, who colonized Syracuse, had committed the sacrilege, hoping that such a portent would either delay or put an end to the war. The people, however, paid no heed to this story, nor to those who thought there was no terrible omen in the affair at all, but merely the effect of strong wine on undisciplined youth, carried away by sport to utter recklessness. The people regarded the incident with rage and fear, taking it as a proof of a dangerous conspiracy against them. They kept a keen watch on everything suspicious, and the council and the assembly met many times for the purpose within the next few days.

19. During this time, Androcles, a popular leader, brought forward a number of slaves and aliens, who accused Alcibiades and his friends of mutilating other images and also of parodying the mysteries of Eleusis during a carouse. The part of the Herald, they said, had been taken by one Theodorus, that of the Torch-Bearer by Polytion, and that of the High Priest by Alcibiades, while the rest of the company were the initiates, and were addressed as Mystae. These charges were specified in an indictment brought by Thessalus, son of Cimon, in which he accused Alcibiades of sacrilege against the two goddesses.[38]

The people were indignant at this and bitter against Alcibiades. Androcles, his most determined enemy, made the most of the charge. Alcibiades and his friends were at first alarmed. But then they learned that

---

36 Adonis, in Greek mythology, was a beautiful youth, beloved by Aphrodite, who was killed while hunting a boar, but was allowed by Zeus to spend a half of each year on earth with the goddess. His festival, marked by the mourning of women for his untimely end, came in the spring.

37 Hermes, the messenger god, was the guardian of those who used roads. Busts of Hermes on the tops of stone or bronze pillars stood in large numbers about the streets of Athens and other Greek cities.

38 The two goddesses worshiped in the sacred mysteries of Eleusis were Demeter and her daughter Persephone.

all the sailors and soldiers about to sail to Sicily were on his side, and heard that the Argive and Mantinean infantry, a thousand of them, were saying openly that it was all for Alcibiades that they were going on that long voyage across the seas, and that if he were being ill-used, they would go directly home. So they were encouraged and demanded an opportunity to defend themselves. His enemies now lost heart, for they feared that at the trial the people would be too lenient because of their need of him.

This being the situation, they arranged that certain orators, who were not known to be enemies of Alcibiades but who nevertheless hated him as much as his outspoken foes, should rise in the assembly and declare it absurd, when a general had been appointed to full command over so large a force, and the host and their allies had assembled, to waste time over drawing lots for a jury and measuring out water for the clocks.[39] "Let him sail now," they said, "and good luck go with him! Then when the war is over, let him come back and make his defense, for the laws will be the same then as now." Alcibiades saw clearly the malice in this postponement, and protested in the assembly that it was a terrible thing to be sent off as head of a great force, leaving behind him such accusations and slanders. If he could not disprove them, he ought to be put to death. If he could disprove them and clear himself, he could then turn on the enemy without having to fear informers at home.

20. However, he did not convince the people, and they ordered him to sail. He then set out with his colleagues and one hundred and forty triremes, fifty-one hundred men at arms, about thirty-one hundred archers, slingers, and light-armed troops, and the rest of his equipment in proportion. After reaching Italy and capturing Rhegium,[40] he proposed a plan for the further conduct of the war. Nicias opposed it, but Lamachus favored it. So Alcibiades sailed over to Sicily and secured Catana, but was able to do nothing more, for the Athenians now sent for him to return and stand his trial.

At first, as I have said, there had been only vague suspicions and scandals brought against Alcibiades by slaves and aliens. But during his absence his enemies had pushed their attack on him hard, and had connected the

---

[39] The water clock was a common device of antiquity for measuring time.
[40] Rhegium, now Reggio di Calabria, was a Greek city, on the straits separating Italy from Sicily.

insults to the Hermae with the parody of the mysteries. Both, they insisted, were the work of one group of conspirators, bent on a revolution. So all who were in any way implicated were thrown into prison without a trial, and the people regretted that they had not tried and judged Alcibiades on these grave charges. And any relative or friend or comrade of his who angered them found them very stern.

Thucydides omits the names of the informers,[41] but others say they were Dioclides and Teucer. Phrynichus, the comic poet, gives them as follows:

> "O dearest Hermes, look out lest you fall,
>   Do yourself damage, furnish grounds for slander
>   To a new Dioclides, with a mind to mischief."

And Hermes says:

> "I will look out. I do not wish to give
>   Informers' pay to Teucer, that guilt-stained foreigner."

However, the informers produced no sure or trustworthy evidence for anything. One of them, when asked how he recognized the faces of the mutilators of the Hermae, answered, "By the light of the moon," a reply which discredited his whole tale, because there was no moon when the crime was committed. Thoughtful men were disturbed by this, but the people were still no less eager to believe the slanders. They went on, as they had begun, arresting and throwing into prison whomever anyone denounced.

21. One of those detained and held in prison for trial was the orator Andocides,[42] whom Hellanicus, the historian, counts among the descendants of Odysseus. Andocides was considered a foe of popular government and an oligarch, but what made him particularly suspected of defacing the Hermae was the fact that a large Hermes, which stood near his house, a votive offering of the tribe Aegeis, was almost the only one of the few conspicuous statues to remain unbroken. For this reason, it is called, even

---

[41] Thucydides, *Peloponnesian War*, VI, xviii, 53.

[42] Andocides was banished from Athens before the year 415 B.C. was over and not permitted to return until 402. In 399, the old charge of sacrilege with the Hermae was revived, and he defended himself in a speech *On the Mysteries*, which is still extant. He was then acquitted.

to this day the Hermes of Andocides, and everyone gives it that name, in spite of the inscription.

Now it happened that Andocides became intimate and friendly with a man named Timaeus, more than with any of the others who were imprisoned on the same charge. He was a man of inferior rank, but cleverer and more daring. He persuaded Andocides to turn accuser against himself and a few others, for if he confessed, the people would vote to pardon him, whereas the outcome of a trial, uncertain enough for everyone, was especially to be dreaded by influential men like him. It was better to save his life by a lie than to be put to a shameful death for the same amount of guilt. It was right, too, if one looked to the common good, to sacrifice a few persons of doubtful character and thereby save many good men from the people's wrath. Andocides was convinced by Timaeus' arguments and turned informer against himself and some others. So he obtained a pardon by popular vote, but all whose names he gave, except those who fled, were executed. To get more credit, Andocides added to his list some of his own servants.

However, the people were still not entirely pacified, and having got rid of the statue mutilators, with energy refreshed they concentrated on attacking Alcibiades. At length they sent the Salaminian galley after him, sagely commanding its officers not to use violence or seize his person, but in mild terms to bid him come back with them and stand trial and set himself right with the people. For they were afraid of an outbreak or a mutiny in the army on enemy territory, which Alcibiades could easily have brought about had he wished it. In fact, the soldiers did lose heart at his departure, expecting that under Nicias the war would be long drawn out with delays, now that the spur to action was taken away. Lamachus was a brave and competent soldier, but his poverty kept him from having much prestige or dignity.

22. At the outset of his return voyage Alcibiades took Messana from the Athenians. For a group in that city was about to deliver it over to the Athenians, but he knew them and supplied the Syracusan party with exact information and so ruined the plot. On reaching Thurii,[43] he left

---

[43] Thurii, on the instep of the Italian "boot," would be a stopping-point on the route to Greece, if one were keeping near the shore and crossing the Adriatic at its narrowest width.

the trireme and hid so that searchers could not find him. When someone recognized him and said, "Do you not trust your own country, Alcibiades?" he answered, "In everything else, yes, but when my life is at stake, I would not trust my own mother not to mistake a black bean for a white one when she cast her vote." [44] Later, when he heard that the city had condemned him to death, he said, "I will show them that I am alive."

The indictment against him ran thus: "Thessalus, son of Cimon, of the deme Lacia, has accused Alcibiades, son of Clinias, of the deme Scambonium, of sacrilege against the two goddesses, Demeter and the Maiden,[45] by parodying their mysteries and revealing them to his comrades in his private house, himself wearing a robe such as the High Priest wears when he shows the sacred things, and calling himself High Priest, Polytion Torchbearer, Theodorus, of the deme Phegaea, Herald, and addressing the rest of the company as initiates and novices, contrary to the rules and institutions of the Eumolpidae,[46] and the heralds and priests of Eleusis." In Alcibiades' absence, then, they condemned him, confiscated his property, and in addition decreed that all priests and priestesses should publicly pronounce him accursed. They say that Theano, the daughter of Menon, of the temple of Agraulos, was the only one who refused to carry out this decree. She said she was a priestess to pray and not to curse.

23. While these severe decrees and sentences were being passed against Alcibiades, he was stopping in Argos, for as soon as he left Thurii, he made his way to the Peloponnesus. But fearing his enemies there and renouncing his country altogether, he sent a message to Sparta and asked them to pardon and trust him, for he would give them service and aid in the future greater than all the damage he had done them in the warfare of the past. The Spartans granted his request and accepted him as one of them. On his arrival, he at once by his zeal accomplished one thing. They had been postponing and delaying sending succor to Syracuse. He roused and stirred them up to despatch Gylippus as commander

---

[44] A black ballot in such a case would be a vote for condemnation or death, a white one for acquittal.

[45] Persephone was often called simply the Maiden.

[46] The Eumolpidae called themselves descendants of Eumolpus, the mythical founder of the mysteries at Eleusis. They were hereditary priests in the cult of Demeter and Persephone.

to smash the Athenian forces there. Next, he had them push on the war in Greece against the Athenians. The third and most important of his achievements was persuading them to seize and fortify Decelea.[47] Nothing did more to bring ruin and destruction to his city.

In Sparta, then, he became publicly renowned and was no less admired privately. He was a favorite with the people, whom he charmed by his adoption of Spartan habits. When they saw him with his hair left long, bathing in cold water, living on barley and black broth, they could hardly believe it and began to wonder whether such a fellow had ever had a cook in his house, or set eyes on a perfume, or felt the soft touch of a Milesian cloak. For Alcibiades had, they say, one outstanding gift among his many others, an unfailing device for catching men. He could adapt himself and take on the ways and habits of others, going through changes more violent than those of a chameleon. The chameleon, indeed, cannot, by report, make itself one color, white, but Alcibiades could go among good and bad alike and never find any custom he could not imitate and make his own.

Thus at Sparta he loved exercise, simplicity, and seriousness; in Ionia, luxury, gaiety, and frivolity; in Thrace, hard drinking; in Thessaly, horsemanship. And when he was consorting with the satrap Tissaphernes, he outdid even the magnificent Persian in pomp and splendor. He did not actually pass so easily from one kind of man to another or accomplish a complete change of character, but when he knew that his natural behavior would offend the persons he was with, he was always ready to put on and pretend to a manner and deportment which would please them. In Sparta, certainly, you would say, judging by his outward appearance, " 'Tis not Achilles' son, but he himself," just such a man as Lycurgus trained. But if you judged by what he really felt and did, you would say, " 'Tis the same woman still." [48]

For while King Agis [49] was away at the wars, Alcibiades seduced his wife Timaea, so that she was with child by him and did not deny it.

---

[47] Decelea was a walled town on one of the hills of Attica, about fourteen miles from Athens, commanding the shortest routes to Boeotia and Euboea. The Spartans occupied it in the spring of 413 B.C. and made it a thorn in the side of Athens for the remainder of the war.

[48] Electra says this of Helen in Euripides' play, Orestes, 129.

[49] This was Agis II, king of Sparta from about 426 to 399 B.C.

When the boy was born, he was called Leotychides in public, but in her own house the mother whispered to her friends and attendants that his name was Alcibiades; so passionately was the woman enamoured of him. Alcibiades said jestingly that he had not acted thus out of wantonness, or under the spell of pleasure, but so that his posterity might some day reign over Sparta. King Agis heard it all from many sources and believed it, especially when he took count of the time. For during an earthquake he had rushed in fright out of his wife's chamber, and for ten months afterward had had no further intercourse with her. Leotychides was born at the end of those ten months. So Agis declared the child was not his, and for that reason he later failed to succeed to the throne.

24. After the Athenian disaster in Sicily, ambassadors came to Sparta from Chios, Lesbos, and Cyzicus to discuss rebellion against Athens. The Lesbians were supported by the Boeotians, and the Cyzicenes by Pharnabazus.[50] But at Alcibiades' recommendation, the Spartans decided to help the Chians first of all. He himself sailed off and got almost all Ionia to revolt from Athens, and acting with the Spartan generals did much injury to the Athenians. Agis was, however, his enemy because of the wrong he had done him through his wife, and he resented the fame Alcibiades was winning, since rumor was ascribing most of the Spartan successes to him. The most powerful and ambitious men of Sparta were already intensely jealous of him, and they had influence enough with the archons at home to induce them to send orders to Ionia for his execution.

But Alcibiades had secret warning of this, and though he went on fearfully cooperating with the Spartans in all their enterprises, he avoided falling in any way into their hands. For safety he now betook himself to Tissaphernes,[51] the king's satrap, and soon was first and foremost at his court. For the barbarian, who was himself no simple person but malicious and fond of rogues, admired Alcibiades' versatility and exceeding clever-

---

[50] Pharnabazus was the Persian governor of northwestern Asia Minor, the district around the Hellespont. For some years he sided with Sparta against Athens, but when Sparta seemed too successful, he encouraged the Athenians to hope for favor from his king, Darius II. In 404 B.C., as related here, the Spartans got the ear of Darius and Pharnabazus ordered Alcibiades assassinated.

[51] Tissaphernes, governor of the southwestern coastal provinces of Asia Minor, was as a rule the declared enemy of all Greeks. In 412, however, he was inveigled by Alcibiades into supporting the Spartans for a time.

ness. Indeed no character could withstand and no nature fail to be captivated by the charms of Alcibiades' day-by-day society and conversation. Even those who feared and hated him found a kind of enchantment in being with him and watching him. And so Tissaphernes, though otherwise the worst hater of the Greeks among the Persians, was so won by the flatteries of Alcibiades that he repaid him by flattery even more extravagant. The most beautiful of his parks, a place of refreshing streams and meadows, with delightful walks and retreats laid out in regally lavish fashion, he called the Alcibiades, and from that time everyone called it that.

25.   Alcibiades now deserted the side of the Spartans, since he no longer trusted them and was afraid of Agis. So he began to malign and talk against him to Tissaphernes, preventing him from helping them effectually, as also from decisively defeating the Athenians, advising him rather to send out only scanty aid, and so gradually to pinch and wear them both down and make them easy prey for the king, when they had subdued and exhausted one another. Tissaphernes was easily convinced and made no secret of his affection and admiration for Alcibiades, who was now looked up to by the Greeks on both sides. The Athenians regretted their decrees against him, which were bringing them such suffering. And he, on his part, began to be anxious and to fear that if Athens were completely ruined, he would fall into the hands of the Spartans, who hated him.

At this time [52] almost all the forces of Athens were at Samos. With that island as their naval base they were trying to regain some of the Ionian cities which had revolted, and were keeping watch on others, for they still, in one way or another, could hold their own by sea against the Spartans. But they were afraid of Tissaphernes and of the fleet of one hundred and fifty Phoenician triremes, which was said to be on the point of arriving; for once it appeared, no hope would be left of saving Athens. Alcibiades knew this and sent a secret message to the Athenian leaders at Samos, in which he held out hopes that he might bring Tissaphernes over to their side. He was not, he said, aiming to win favor with the Athenian populace, whom he did not trust, but with the aristo-

---

[52] That is, the winter of 412–411 B.C. The Sicilian expedition had come to its disastrous end in 413. Nicias had been one of those who died.

crats, in case they had the courage to act like brave men, put a stop to the people's presumptuous behavior, and themselves undertake by their own exertions to save the state and the city.

All the aristocrats were eager to adopt Alcibiades' proposals, except one of the generals, Phrynichus [53] of the deme Deirades, who suspected the truth, that Alcibiades cared no more for an oligarchy than for a democracy, but was merely seeking some method of getting back to his own city, and attempting to pay court to and ingratiate himself with the nobles by speaking harshly of the people. Accordingly he opposed them, but he was overruled. So now, since he stood out as a foe of Alcibiades, he sent a secret message to Astyochus, head of the Spartan fleet, bidding him beware of Alcibiades and seize him, for he was playing a double game. But without his knowledge, this was a case of traitor dealing with traitor. Astyochus stood in great dread of Tissaphernes, and seeing that Alcibiades had much influence with him, he informed them both of Phrynichus' message. Alcibiades at once sent men to Samos to charge Phrynichus with treason, and the Athenians were all indignant and joined together against him. He, seeing no other way of escape from his situation, tried to blot out one crime by another and a greater one. He sent again to Astyochus, reproaching him for his betrayal of confidence, but telling him that he would deliver up to him the fleet and army of the Athenians.

However, Phrynichus' treachery did no harm to the Athenians, because of the counter-treachery of Astyochus, who gave this message also to Alcibiades. But Phrynichus had expected that he would, and looked for a second charge of treason from Alcibiades. He therefore got ahead of him by telling the Athenians himself that the Spartans were about to attack them and advising them to keep by their ships and fortify their camp. This the Athenians were doing when there came another letter from Alcibiades, warning them to beware of Phrynichus, since he was about to betray their fleet to the Spartans. This letter, however, they did not believe at the time, for they thought that Alcibiades, who knew perfectly all the equipment and intentions of the enemy, was making use of his knowledge to cast false aspersions on Phrynichus. Yet afterwards,

---

[53] This Phrynichus is not to be confused with the playwright of the same name, mentioned above in *Themistocles,* ch. 5.

when Hermon, one of the Athenian frontier guards, stabbed Phrynichus with a dagger and killed him in the agora, the Athenians tried the case and found him after his death guilty of treachery, and voted crowns to Hermon and his companions.

26.   Meanwhile, at Samos, the friends of Alcibiades got their way, and sent Pisander to Athens to alter the form of government, encourage the nobles to seize control of affairs, and put an end to the democracy. If this were done, Pisander said, Alcibiades would make Tissaphernes their friend and ally. On this pretext and excuse they set up an oligarchy. But as soon as the so-called Five Thousand, who were actually only Four Hundred,[54] got the government into their hands, they paid no more attention to Alcibiades, and showed little vigor in carrying on the war, partly because they distrusted the citizens, who still held aloof from their new rulers, and partly because they thought that the Spartans, who always favored an oligarchy, would give them better terms. The populace in the city was compelled by fear to remain quiet, for many who openly resisted the Four Hundred were put to death. But when the soldiers at Samos heard of all this, they were furious, and wanted to sail for the Piraeus at once. They sent for Alcibiades, and appointed him general, and bade him lead them in putting down the tyrants.

Many a man raised suddenly to high position by the grace of the people would have set about petting them, and would have thought he must instantly humor their every whim and thwart them in nothing, since they had taken him, a wanderer and a fugitive, and made him commanding general of so good an army and so large a fleet. But Alcibiades, as befitted a great leader, realized that he must oppose their storms of wrath, and keep them from making a dire mistake. That time, at least, he was undeniably the savior of Athens. For if they had sailed off home, all Ionia, the Hellespont, and the islands might have fallen immediately into the enemy's hands without a battle, while Athenians were fighting Athe-

[54] The revolution of May, 411 B.C., at Athens, which overthrew the democracy and set up an oligarchic government under a picked assembly of five thousand men of wealth, with an inner council of four hundred, was the result of the failure of the democracy to retrieve the losses of the Sicilian catastrophe. The fleet at Samos refused to recognize the authority of the Four Hundred, and the ships they sent to fight the Spartans at Euboea were beaten. A rising of moderates against them put an end to their rule after four months, and the following year the democracy was restored.

nians, bringing the war into their own city. This disaster was prevented by Alcibiades more than by anyone else. He not only warned and lectured the men as a body, but took them one at a time and entreated some and put pressure on others. He was assisted, too, by Thrasybulus of Stiria, who went about with him and did the shouting, for he had, they said, the loudest voice of any Athenian.

A second fine act of Alcibiades was his assurance that he would either bring over to the Athenian side the Phoenician fleet which the Persian king had sent and the Spartans were expecting, or at least see that it did not reach the Spartans. He then put off in great haste, and though the Phoenician ships were seen off Aspendus, Tissaphernes did not bring them farther and thus cheated the Spartans. Both sides believed that Alcibiades had brought this change about, especially the Spartans, who thought he was teaching the barbarian how to let the Greeks destroy one another. For it was clear that such a force added to either party would rob the other completely of its power on the sea.

27. Later on the Four Hundred were overthrown and the friends of Alcibiades collaborated zealously with the democratic party. The Athenians now wished and ordered Alcibiades to come home, but he felt he must not come back empty-handed through the people's grace and pity, without doing anything, but as a conquering hero. So first he sailed from Samos with a few ships, and cruised around Cnidos and Cos. There he heard that Mindarus, the Spartan admiral, had moved up the Hellespont with his whole fleet, and that the Athenians were following him. So he hurried to the assistance of their commanders.

Sailing northwards with eighteen triremes, he chanced to arrive on a critical day, when both sides had been fighting with all their ships off Abydos until evening, victory swinging sometimes to one and sometimes to the other, and they were still locked in a desperate struggle. The appearance of Alcibiades produced an opposite effect on the two parties. It alarmed the Athenians and emboldened the enemy. But he suddenly raised the Athenian banner on his admiral's ship, and bore down straight on the victoriously pursuing Peloponnesians. He routed them and drove them towards the shore, pushing after them and ramming and breaking up their ships. Their crews escaped by swimming, and Pharnabazus came to their rescue with infantry and fought for their ships along the water's edge. In the end the Athenians captured thirty ships, recovered their own, and erected a trophy.

After so splendid a success, Alcibiades was ambitious to show himself at once to Tissaphernes, and providing himself with the gifts of a guest, he set off with a general's retinue to visit him; but he did not have the reception he expected. For Tissaphernes had for a long time been complained of by the Spartans to the king, and he was now afraid that the king was displeased with him. So he thought Alcibiades had come very opportunely, and had him seized and imprisoned in Sardis. This piece of violence, he thought, would prove that the Spartans' insinuations were unfounded.

28.   However, after thirty days Alcibiades somehow obtained a horse, slipped away from his guards, and escaped to Clazomenae. As a revenge on Tissaphernes, he gave out that he had privately released him, and so brought more opprobrium on the Persian. Then he sailed to the Athenian camp and learned there that Mindarus, together with Pharnabazus, was in Cyzicus.[55] He made a rousing speech to the soldiers, telling them that they must now do sea-fighting, land-fighting, and, by Zeus, wall-fighting, too, against their enemies, for unless they were victorious everywhere, there would be no pay. Thereupon he manned the ships and proceeded to Proconnesus, giving orders to seize all the small vessels they met and hold them under guard so that the Spartans might get no warning of their approach from anyone. It happened then that a heavy storm of rain fell suddenly, and thunder and darkness helped to keep his project hidden. Not only did he take the enemy unawares, but the Athenians themselves had no idea of anything more afoot, when suddenly he ordered them again on board, and put out to sea. After a little the darkness broke and the Peloponnesian fleet came in sight, hanging about the harbor of

---

[55] The Athenian camp was then at Cardia, on the northern side of the entrance to the Hellespont. Since Athens had failed so ignominiously in her effort to expand to the west, she was turning to the northeast, hoping to build up her empire and commerce in the undeveloped countries around the Propontis, now called the Sea of Marmora, and the Black Sea. The town of Cyzicus lay inside the Hellespont, on the southern shore of the Propontis, and the island of Proconnesus a little way to the north. Chalcedon, which Alcibiades besieged later, was at the east end of the Propontis, at the entrance to the Bosporus, Abydos at the west end, on the Hellespont, and Selymbria on the northeast coast.

Cyzicus. Fearing that if the enemy saw how numerous his ships were, they would take refuge on shore, Alcibiades ordered the other commanders to sail slowly along behind him, while he with forty ships showed himself and challenged the enemy to an engagement. The Peloponnesians were entirely deceived, and despising what seemed only a few vessels, at once sailed out to meet them and grappled with them in a close fight. Then, in the midst of the battle, the rest of the Athenian ships came up and fell on the enemy, and they fled in panic.

Thereat Alcibiades, with twenty of his best ships, put in to shore, landed his crews, and attacked the fugitives from the enemy's ships with terrible slaughter. Mindarus and Pharnabazus came to the rescue only to be beaten back. Mindarus was killed while fighting bravely, but Pharnabazus escaped. The Athenians got possession of many corpses and their arms, and took all the enemy's ships. They then stormed Cyzicus itself, which Pharnabazus had abandoned, and put the Peloponnesians there to the sword. Thus they not only obtained a firm hold on the Hellespont but forcibly drove the Spartans from the rest of the sea. A despatch was seized, reporting the disaster to the Spartan ephors in true Laconic style: "Our ships are gone; Mindarus is dead; the men are starving; we do not know what to do."

29. The soldiers of Alcibiades were now so elated and proud of themselves that they thought it beneath them to mix with the other soldiers, who had often been defeated, while they were invincible. In fact, not long before this, Thrasyllus had been beaten near Ephesus, and the Ephesians had put up a bronze trophy to the disgrace of the Athenians. This was the reproach Alcibiades' men flung at Thrasyllus' soldiers, bragging of themselves and their commander, and refusing to share with the others either their exercise grounds or their quarters in camp. But then Pharnabazus, with a great force of horse and foot, fell on Thrasyllus and his men while they were raiding the territory of Abydos, and Alcibiades came to their aid, routed Pharnabazus, and together with Thrasyllus, pursued him till nightfall. Thus the two armies mingled and returned to their camp in mutual friendliness and rejoicing.

The next day Alcibiades erected a trophy and ravaged the territory of Pharnabazus, no one daring to defend it. He even took captive some priests and priestesses, but let them go without ransom. He then set out

to attack Chalcedon, which had revolted from Athens and accepted a
Spartan governor and garrison On hearing that the inhabitants had collected all their belongings from the country and were putting them in the
care of the Bithynians, who were their friends, he led his army to the
Bithynian frontier and sent a herald to confront them with his demands.
In terror, the Bithynians gave up the property and swore a friendship
with him.

30.   He was building a wall to shut in Chalcedon from sea to sea, when
Pharnabazus came up to raise the siege, and at the same time Hippocrates,
governor of the city, led out his forces and attacked the Athenians. Alcibiades arranged his army so as to face them both at once. He then put
Pharnabazus to flight in disgrace, and killed Hippocrates and many of
his defeated men. He next went on a cruise through the Hellespont, to
take contributions from that region.

He also captured Selymbria, after exposing himself to a quite improper
risk. The party which was letting him into that city had agreed to raise
a lighted torch as a signal at midnight. But they were compelled to do it
before the appointed time, out of fear of one of the conspirators, who
had suddenly changed his mind. So when the torch was raised, the army
was not yet ready. Alcibiades, with some thirty soldiers, rushed up to the
walls, leaving word for the rest to follow at full speed. The gate was
opened to him, he hurried into the city, twenty targeteers having joined
his thirty. And at once he saw the Selymbrians under arms advancing
to meet him. To await their onset did not seem safe, and he was too
spirited to retreat, undefeated as he had been in all his campaigns down
to that day. Instead, he had the trumpet sound for silence, and then
ordered one of his men to announce to the Selymbrians that they must
not take arms against Athenians.

This proclamation made some of the townspeople less anxious to fight,
imagining, as they did, that their enemies were now all inside the walls;
in others it raised cheering hopes of a truce. While they were thus standing and parleying together, Alcibiades' army came up. But judging now
correctly that the Selymbrians wanted peace, he became alarmed that his
Thracian troops might pillage the city. For there were many of these
barbarians serving zealously in his army out of good will and liking
for him. He therefore sent them all out of the city and at the Selymbrians'

entreaty did them no harm, but merely exacted a payment of money, left
a garrison in the town, and departed.

31. Meanwhile the Athenian generals who were besieging Chalcedon
made peace with Pharnabazus on the understanding that they should
receive a sum of money, that the Chalcedonians should become again
subjects of Athens, that the territory of Pharnabazus should not be injured, and that Pharnabazus should provide a safe escort for Athenian
ambassadors to the Persian king. On Alcibiades' return from Selymbria,
Pharnabazus asked him to swear to observe these terms, but Alcibiades
refused to do so until Pharnabazus had sworn.

When both oaths had been taken, Alcibiades went next to Byzantium,
which had revolted from Athens, and built a wall around that city.
Anaxilaus and Lycurgus, with some others, now agreed to betray the
city to him on condition that it be left unhurt. So Alcibiades put out a
report that uprisings occurring in Ionia called for his presence, and sailed
away in broad daylight with all his fleet. But that same night he returned
and landed with his men-at-arms and advanced stealthily up to the city
walls, while his ships sailed back to the harbor and with great clamor
and uproar and din forced their way in. The noise and unexpectedness
of this naval attack terrified the Byzantians, and gave the Athenian party
an opportunity to admit Alcibiades safely into the city, while everybody
was hurrying down to the harbor and the ships. They did not, however,
get through without a fight. For the Peloponnesians, Megarians, and
Boeotians who were there in Byzantium beat back the men from the ships
and drove them down on board again, and then, seeing that there were
Athenians inside the city, they formed and went to engage them. The
battle was sharp, but Alcibiades on the right wing and Theramenes on
the left were victorious and took some three hundred of the enemy alive
as prisoners. No Byzantian was put to death or banished after this battle,
for it was on those terms that the conspirators had delivered up the city,
namely, that they should suffer no loss of life or property.

Anaxilaus was afterwards tried at Sparta for treason, but explained in
defense that his act was not shameful. For he said he was not a Spartan
but a Byzantian, and that Sparta was not in danger. But he saw Byzantium
encircled so that nothing could be brought in, and what food was in the
city was being eaten by the Peloponnesians and the Boeotians, while the

Byzantians starved with their wives and children. He did not, he said, betray the city to its enemies, but rescued it from war and its horrors, imitating thereby the noblest Spartans, for whom the one entirely right and noble deed was to serve their country. On hearing this speech, the Spartans respected the men and let them go.

32. Now at last Alcibiades longed to see his home again, and still more wished to be seen by his countrymen, since he had vanquished their enemies so many times. He set sail [56] with his Attic triremes decorated all around with countless shields and spoils of war, towing behind him many more ships that he had captured, and bringing in them still more prows of vessels he had taken and destroyed. All of them together amounted to as much as two hundred.

Douris, the Samian, who declared he was a descendant of Alcibiades, adds some details. He says that Chrysogonus, a victor at the Pythian games, with his flute marked time for the oarsmen, while Callipides, the tragic actor, gave them their commands. Both wore buskins, trailing robes, and other artistic garments. The admiral's ship came in to harbor with purple sails, as if he had been having a drinking party out on a pleasure trip. But neither Theopompus, nor Ephorus, nor Xenophon mentions these things, nor is it likely that Alcibiades assumed such splendor for the Athenians on his return from exile and many calamities. On the contrary, he was afraid when he came into harbor, and on anchoring would not leave his trireme until from the deck he saw Euryptolemus, his cousin, at the landing place with many other friends and relatives there to welcome him and calling to him.

But when he landed, the people seemed to have no eyes for the other generals they were meeting and all rushed shouting towards him, cheering him and escorting him on his way, and as they got near to him crowning him with flowers. Those who could not get near gazed at him from a distance, the older men pointing him out to the younger. Yet the joy of the city was mingled with regret, as they remembered their past misfortunes and compared them with their present prosperity. They reckoned that they would not have failed in Sicily, nor would any other project of theirs have been defeated if they had kept Alcibiades at the head of their enterprises and their armies. For now he had taken the city

[56] Alcibiades sailed from Samos to Athens in the spring of 408 B.C.

when she was almost driven from the sea, on land mistress of little more than her own environs and torn apart by faction, and had raised her up from that miserable and wretched condition, not only restoring to her her dominion over the sea but making her again victorious on land everywhere against her enemies.

33. The decree for his recall had been passed beforehand, on the motion of Critias, son of Callaeschrus, as Critias himself has recorded in his elegies, reminding Alcibiades of his service:

"The motion that brought you back I made before everyone. I wrote it
     and did the deed,
And the seal of my words is here."

Then the people met in the assembly and Alcibiades addressed them, rehearsing and lamenting his own sufferings, but laying little and moderate blame for them on his countrymen, and attributing his misfortunes all to bad luck and a spirit that was working him evil. He spoke at length of the enemy's intentions and roused them to courage. So they crowned him with golden crowns and elected him general with absolute power on land and sea. They voted also to restore his property to him, and ordered the Eumolpidae and the heralds to retract the curses they had pronounced on him at the people's command. They all retracted them except Theodorus the High Priest, who said, "I have laid no curse on him so long as he does the city no wrong."

34. While Alcibiades was enjoying this heyday of glory, some persons were disturbed by the time of his return. For he had arrived in harbor on the day when the Cleansing Festival of the goddess was being celebrated.[57] The Praxiergidae perform the ceremony secretly on the twenty-fifth day of Thargelion, stripping the goddess of her robe and covering up her statue. The Athenians, therefore, consider the day the most to be avoided of all inauspicious days. So they felt that the goddess was not receiving Alcibiades graciously or with favor, but was veiling herself and shutting him away from her presence. Everything else, however, turned out as

---

[57] Once a year, in the month of Thargelion, between the middle of our May and the middle of our June, the golden robes of the statue of Athene in the Parthenon were removed and washed. During the process the statue was kept covered from human eyes. Phidias had had her robes made so that they were removable. See above, *Pericles*, n. 36.

Alcibiades had hoped. A hundred triremes were manned, with which he was to go to sea again, but first he was seized with a noble ambition which kept him there until the Eleusinian mysteries.

Ever since Decelea had been fortified and the enemy stationed there had commanded the roads to Eleusis, the festive procession had lost its splendor, having to be brought by sea. The sacrifices, dances, and many of the sacred rites, habitually performed on the road, when they bring Iacchus [58] to Eleusis, had necessarily been omitted. It seemed to Alcibiades, therefore, that it would be a fine thing, an act of piety towards the gods which would increase his reputation among men, if he restored the ceremony to its ancient form, escorting the procession on land with his troops and protecting it past the enemy. For if Agis made no move to attack, he would lose prestige. And if there was a battle, Alcibiades would be fighting in a holy cause, approved by the gods, in defense of things most sacred and most great, in the sight of his native city and with all his fellow citizens witnesses of his valor.

On determining to do this, he informed the Eumolpidae and the heralds, posted sentinels on the hilltops, and sent off an advance guard at daybreak. Then taking with him the priests, initiates, and initiators, and surrounding them with his men-at-arms, he led them to Eleusis in proper order and perfect silence. This one of his exploits he made so august and solemn a spectacle that all who were not envying him called it a priestly and mystic ritual. No enemy ventured to attack, and he brought the procession safely back to Athens. He was exalted in spirit himself, and he made his army exalted, regarding itself as invincible as long as he was its commander. He won such ascendancy over the common people and the poor that it was astonishing how ardently they desired to have him as a tyrant. Some even talked of it and came to him to urge it. He should rise superior to jealousy, sweep away decrees and laws and the fools who were ruining the city, so that he might conduct the government himself, with no fear of informers.

35. What his own views were about a tyranny we do not know. But the leading citizens were afraid of one and eager to have him go off to sea as quickly as possible, so along with everything else they now voted him colleagues of his own choosing. He set sail then with the hundred ships

[58] See above, *Themistocles*, n. 26.

and attacked Andros. He defeated the inhabitants in battle, and the Spartans who were there. He did not, however, capture the city, and this was the first of the new charges urged against him by his enemies. For if ever a man was ruined apparently by his own glory, it was Alcibiades. His successes had given him a reputation for such boundless daring and intelligence that any failure of his made men suspect he had not been in earnest. They refused to believe that he could not; if he were in earnest, they thought, nothing would be too much for him. Thus they were expecting to hear of the capture of Chios and all the rest of Ionia, and were vexed when news came that he had not done everything as quickly and as promptly as they wished. They did not stop to consider his need of money, which compelled him, while he was fighting men who had the great king of Persia as their paymaster, frequently to leave his camp and sail off to get pay and supplies for his soldiers.

The final charge against him was occasioned by this necessity. Lysander [59] had been sent by the Spartans to take command of their fleet. On his arrival, by means of money received from Cyrus, he increased the pay of his sailors from three obols a day to four. Alcibiades, who could pay three obols only with difficulty, had to sail to Caria to levy contributions. The man he left behind in command of his fleet, Antiochus, was a brave pilot but in other ways a foolish and vulgar fellow. He had precise orders from Alcibiades not to attempt a battle, even if the enemy sailed towards him. But he was high-handed and conceited, so manning his own trireme and one other, he set sail for Ephesus, doing and calling out many rude and ribald things as he went past the enemy's prows. With a few ships, Lysander at once weighed anchor and chased him. When the Athenians came to Antiochus' assistance, Lysander brought out all his ships and men as well, and set up a trophy. As soon as Alcibiades heard of this, he came back to Samos, put to sea with his whole fleet, and challenged Lysander to battle. But Lysander was satisfied with the victory he had and would not meet him.

36.   There were persons in the Athenian camp who hated Alcibiades, and one of them, Thrasybulus, son of Thrason, a bitter enemy, now went back

59 Lysander, an able Spartan general, contrived to get the good will of Cyrus, a younger son of the Persian king. With his support he gradually won back for Sparta all the ground in the north and east she had lost to Alcibiades. Plutarch has a *Life of Lysander.*

to Athens to accuse him. He stirred up the city against him, telling the
assembly that Alcibiades had wrecked their empire and lost their ships
by his irresponsibility in office. He had entrusted his command, Thrasybulus said, to men who had won great influence over him, by drinking
with him and exchanging sailors' yarns, so that he himself could be free
to sail around raising money and indulging in drunken orgies with the
courtesans of Abydos and Ionia. Meanwhile he had left the enemy's fleet
lying close to his own. He was blamed, too, for having built a fortress
near Bisanthe, in Thrace, as a retreat for himself, in case he could not or
would not live in his own country.

The Athenians were convinced he was guilty and elected other generals
to take his place, showing thus their anger and displeasure with him.
On hearing of it, Alcibiades was alarmed and left the Athenian camp
altogether. He collected a body of mercenary soldiers and made war on
his own account against the Thracians, who have no king. He raised a
good deal of money from his captives, and at the same time gave the
Greeks who lived in that vicinity security from the barbarians.

Then [60] the generals Tydeus, Menander, and Adimantus collected all
the ships that remained to the Athenians together at Aegospotami. They
would put out with them early in the morning against Lysander, who
was lying at Lampsacus, and challenge him to a fight, after which they
would sail back and spend the rest of the day in careless indolence, contemptuous of their enemy. Alcibiades, who was not far away, was neither
blind nor indifferent to their danger, but rode over on horseback and
pointed out to them that they were badly anchored, in a place with no
harbor and no city, where they had to get their provisions from Sestos, a
long way off. They allowed their crews, too, when they were on shore,
to wander and scatter wherever they pleased, while there lay close to them
a fleet trained to do everything silently, at a single man's command.

37.   But though Alcibiades told them this, and advised them to move
their fleet to Sestos, the generals would not listen to him. Tydeus indeed
insultingly ordered him to leave, saying that others, not he, were in com-

---

[60] Plutarch here skips over an interval of some two and a half years. Lysander's victory over the Athenian ships under Antiochus was in the spring of 407 B.C. His greater
victory at Aegospotami was not until the autumn of 405.

mand now. So Alcibiades left, suspecting some treachery among them. He told his acquaintances who escorted him out of the camp that if the generals had not treated him so rudely he would have compelled the Spartans either to fight against their will or else to lose their ships. Some considered this mere empty boasting, but others thought it likely he could do what he said, by bringing up his host of light-armed Thracian troops and cavalry to assault and derange the Spartan camp by land.

In any case, the outcome soon proved that he had estimated correctly the Athenians' mistakes. Lysander suddenly and unexpectedly fell upon them and only eight of their triremes escaped, with Conon.[61] The rest, nearly two hundred, were captured and carried off. Three thousand of the men aboard Lysander took alive and put to death. Shortly afterward [62] he also took Athens, burned her ships, and pulled down her Long Walls.

Alcibiades was now terrified of the Spartans, who were masters on both land and sea. So he shifted his headquarters to Bithynia, taking with him a great amount of treasure, but leaving still more behind in the fortress where he had been living. But in Bithynia he lost a large part of his wealth, being robbed by the Thracians there. He therefore determined to go to the court of Artaxerxes, believing that if the Persian king would give him a trial, he would find him as useful as Themistocles had been,[63] and his reason for coming to him a better one. For it was not to harm his fellow countrymen, as Themistocles did, but to assist them against the enemy that he would serve the king and solicit his aid. He thought that Pharnabazus could best provide him with a safe passage to the Persian court, so he went to him in Phrygia and remained there for a time, paying him court and being honorably treated.

38. The Athenians were much grieved at the loss of their supremacy. But when Lysander robbed them of their liberty as well and turned the

---

[61] Conon, an Athenian soldier, made his name later, when in 394 B.C. he led the Athenian fleet in a decisive defeat of the Spartans, and in 393 rebuilt the Long Walls and fortifications of Athens and the Piraeus.

[62] Actually, it was eight months later, in the spring of 404 B.C., that Lysander took Athens and pulled down her Long Walls, to the strains of flute music.

[63] Themistocles had taken refuge with a Persian king some sixty years earlier. See above, *Themistocles*, ch. 27.

city over to the Thirty,[64] and their cause was completely lost, they began
to use their reason as they had not done when they might have saved
themselves from disaster. They sorrowfully reviewed their past blunders,
the worst of which they considered to be their second fit of anger against
Alcibiades. They had thrown him aside for no fault of his, but because
they were vexed with his subordinate for having disgracefully lost a few
ships. They had disgraced themselves much more by depriving their city
of its ablest and bravest general. And even in their desperate situation a
faint hope prevailed that Athens was not utterly lost so long as Alcibiades
was alive; for he had not during his former exile been satisfied with an
idle life, and surely now, if he had the means, he would not sit by and
look on at the Spartans' arrogance and the outrages of the Thirty.

It was not strange that the people had such dreams, when even the
Thirty were wondering and inquiring and anxiously speculating as to
what Alcibiades was doing and planning. At last, Critias [65] informed
Lysander that so long as the Athenians had a democracy, the Spartans
could not rule Greece in safety and that though now they were accepting
the oligarchy very quietly and well, yet while Alcibiades lived, he would
not allow them to remain undisturbed in that state. However, Lysander
was not moved by these arguments until a despatch came from the magistrates in Sparta, bidding him get rid of Alcibiades, either because they
too feared his great ability and enterprise, or because they wished to please
King Agis.

39.   Lysander then sent orders for his death to Pharnabazus, who directed
his brother Magaeus and his uncle Susamithras to do the deed. Alcibiades
at that time was living in a village in Phrygia, with Timandra, the courtesan, and in his sleep he had the following vision. He saw himself dressed
in his mistress' clothes, while she was holding his head in her arms, and
adorning his face with paint and pigment like a woman's. Others say that

---

[64] In June, 404 B.C., Lysander vested the government of Athens in an oligarchical
clique of her own citizens, known as the Thirty, supported by a Spartan garrison on
the Acropolis. The reign of terror that followed, however, lasted for only about six
months, when the Thirty were overthrown and their leaders put to death by the revolting populace. The Spartans were expelled and the democracy once more restored
by June, 403.
[65] Critias was a leader of the Athenian oligarchs and the most implacable of the Thirty.

he saw in a dream Magaeus cutting off his head, and his body on fire. All, however, agree that he had a vision shortly before his death.

The men sent to kill him did not venture to enter his house, but surrounded it and set it on fire. When Alcibiades realized what was happening, he collected a great quantity of garments and bedding and threw them on the blaze. Then wrapping his cloak around his left arm and drawing his dagger with his right, he dashed out unhurt by the flames, before his clothing caught fire. At sight of him the barbarians scattered. Not one faced him or came near him, but from a distance they slew him with darts and arrows. Thus he fell, and when the barbarians had gone, Timandra took up his dead body and wrapped it in her own robes, and as best she could gave it a handsome and honorable burial. This Timandra is said to have been the mother of Lais, commonly called the Corinthian, though she was really a prisoner of war from Hyccara, a small town in Sicily.

Some writers, though agreeing in other respects with this account of Alcibiades' death, say it was neither Pharnabazus, nor Lysander, nor the Spartans who were the cause of it, but Alcibiades himself. He had seduced a girl of a well-known family and had her with him. Her brothers, enraged by his insolence, set fire by night to the house where he was living, and, as has been related, shot him down as he came leaping through the flames.

Gaius Marcius Coriolanus[1]

FIRST HALF OF THE FIFTH CENTURY B.C.

1. THE PATRICIAN family of the Marcii at Rome produced many men of distinction. Among them was Ancus Marcius, Numa's grandson by his daughter, who became king after the death of Tullus Hostilius. To this family also belonged Publius and Quintus Marcius, who brought into Rome its most abundant and excellent water supply[2] and Censorinus, twice appointed censor by the Roman people, who thereupon persuaded them to pass a law that no one should hold that office twice.

Gaius Marcius, of whom 1 am writing, lost his father early and was brought up by his widowed mother. He proved, however, that though the lot of an orphan may be hard, it does not prevent him from becoming an upright and distinguished man, and that bad men have no right to lay the blame for their misbehavior on it, on the ground that they were ruined by neglect. At the same time, he furnished an argument to those who believe that a generous and noble nature, if not properly disciplined, will produce much that is poor along with the good, like a rich field without a farmer's cultivation. For though his strong energy and vigorous intelligence in every line made him undertake enterprises which were highly fruitful,

---

[1] Plutarch gives here his version of what modern historians consider a legendary story of an early Latin hero who lived in a time of poverty, famine, and internal dissension at Rome and of war with the Volscians to the south. Plutarch's material comes mainly from the historians Livy and Dionysius of Halicarnassus.

[2] This was the aqueduct known as Aqua Marcia, built in 144 B.C., the first to bring water from hills at a distance through a stone conduit, supported by arches over stretches of low ground and across ravines.

on the other hand, his harsh temper and stubborn combativeness made him a difficult and unadaptable associate for other men. They would admire his indifference to pleasure, pain, and wealth, and speak of his self-control, justice, and courage, but in intercourse with him on public affairs they were offended by his haughty and ungracious and morose manner. The greatest benefit indeed which men gain from the friendship of the Muses is that softening of the nature which comes from their teaching and training, as we learn from them to prefer moderation and reject extremes. It is, however, true that in Rome at that period the virtue which expresses itself in warlike and soldierly exploits was valued above all others. Evidence for this is the fact that the Romans had only one word for virtue, that which means manly bravery;[3] they make the name of the particular virtue, valor, serve also as the name for virtue in general.

2.   Marcius was born more keen than other boys for warlike activities, and from childhood was used to handling arms. He realized too that artificial weapons were of no value to men who had not their natural, native armor made ready and prepared to serve them. So he exercised his body in every kind of contest, until he was both fleet as a runner and stout in grappling and wrestling, and hard for an enemy to escape from. Those who now and again contended with him in feats of prowess and courage and were beaten would blame their defeat on his invincible bodily strength, which no effort could exhaust.

3.   He went on his first campaign while still a youth, when Tarquin,[4] who had been king of Rome and then expelled, after many unsuccessful battles was staking everything on one last throw. Most of the Latins and many of the other Italian peoples took his part and marched with him against Rome, not from any attachment to him, but from fear and envy, which made them attack the growing power of Rome. In this battle,[5] which took many turns, first towards one side and then towards the other,

---

[3] The Latin word *virtus,* often translated "virtue," does by derivation mean manliness, i.e. courage.

[4] By tradition the last king of Rome was the Etruscan Tarquinius Superbus, said to have reigned from about 534 to 510 B.C. The tale of his violation of the Roman matron Lucretia was probably a later invention to explain his expulsion. The campaign mentioned here is said to have taken place in 493.

[5] This is known as the battle of Lake Regillus.

Marcius was fighting bravely under the eye of the dictator, when he saw
a Roman soldier fallen nearby. He at once made for the man, stood in
front of him, defended him, and killed his assailant. So when the Roman
general was victorious, he crowned Marcius among the first with a garland of oak leaves.[6] This is the crown which the law confers on one who
has saved the life of a citizen in battle, whether the Romans honored the
oak for the sake of the Arcadians,[7] who, in an oracle of Apollo, were called
"acorn-eaters," or because there were plenty of oaks to be found quickly
wherever they were fighting, or because the crown of oak leaves, sacred
to Jupiter, the city's protector, was fittingly awarded to one who had saved
a citizen's life. The oak too has the most beautiful fruit of all wild trees,
and is the sturdiest of those under cultivation. Its acorn once provided
food, and the honey in it drink, and through it men obtained the flesh
of many animals and birds, for it bears the mistletoe which is used in
snares.

In this battle, they say, the Dioscuri,[8] Castor and Pollux, appeared, and
immediately after the battle were seen, their horses dripping with sweat,
in the forum by the fountain where their temple now stands, announcing
the victory. Hence the day of the victory, the Ides of July, was kept sacred
to the Dioscuri.

4.   Sometimes, when young men win distinction and honor very early in
life and their natural ambitions are not keen, it seems as if their fastidious
thirst for glory was soon quenched. But serious and steadfast spirits are
strengthened by honors, and glow more brightly, as if fanned by a wind
to reach out towards what more promises to be good. They feel not that
they are receiving pay for a thing they have done, but that they are giving
pledges for something they will do, and are ashamed to fall below the
reputation they have, but must surpass it by new achievements. Marcius
felt this and was ever trying to outdo himself in valor, and reaching after
something new. He piled exploit on exploit and heaped up spoils upon

---

[6] The crown gave certain prerogatives through life, among which was the right to
have senators rise when he came into their presence. Compare the oak-leaf cluster
awarded by the United States Army for acts of special worth and valor.

[7] The Arcadians were early colonists at Rome, according to tradition.

[8] See above, *Lycurgus,* n. 42. The cult of the Dioscuri, sons of Zeus, was introduced into
Rome at about this time, and fragments of their temple are still to be seen in the forum.
A parade of Roman knights in their honor took place on July 15.

spoils, so that the later generals under whom he served were always vying with his earlier commanders in showing their esteem for him, and rivaling one another in testifying to his merits. Many were the struggles and the wars in which the Romans were then engaged, but from none of them did Marcius return without a crown or a prize for gallantry.

For other men glory was the aim of their acts of courage, but Marcius strove for glory to give his mother pleasure. That she should hear him praised, see him crowned, and embrace him with tears of joy, was, he thought, his highest honor and happiness. Epaminondas [9] undoubtedly felt the same when, as they say, he called it his greatest good fortune that his father and mother were both alive to hear of his generalship and victory at Leuctra. But he had the satisfaction of having both his parents share his joy and success. Marcius thought he owed his mother, Volumnia, all the loving consideration he would have given his father, and could not do enough to gratify and honor her. He even married the woman she chose and asked him to marry, and went on living in the house with his mother after his children were born.

5. His reputation and influence due to his gallant achievements were already considerable in the city, when the senate, which stood for the wealthy class, took sides against the people, who felt they were suffering many terrible wrongs at the hands of the money-lenders. Those who possessed a small property were being stripped of it all by mortgage or sale, while those who were absolutely destitute were being seized and imprisoned, even though their bodies were scarred with the marks of many wounds received and hardships borne in campaigns for the defense of their country. The last campaign had been against the Sabines, when their richest creditors had promised to give them fair treatment, and the senate had voted that Marcus Valerius, the consul, should guarantee the promise.

But though they served loyally in that campaign and defeated the enemy, they met with no consideration from their creditors, and the senate made no pretense of remembering its engagement, but allowed them again to be taken and dragged off to prison. So there were tumults and violent riots in the city, and the enemy learned of this popular disturbance, and invaded and ravaged the country. And when the consuls called all men of

---

[9] On Epaminondas, see above, *Lycurgus,* n 27.

military age to arms, no one obeyed. In this situation, the men in office
were of different minds. Some thought that concessions should be made to
the lower classes and the excessive severity of the laws softened, while
others, among whom was Marcius, opposed the idea. He did not regard
the money troubles as most important, but urged the magistrates to show
their wisdom in checking and suppressing this first attempt at insolent
effrontery on the part of the mob in revolt against the laws.

6.   The senate met many times within a few days to discuss the matter
but came to no decision. The plebians then suddenly assembled in a body,
and cheering one another on marched out of the city and took possession
of what is now called the Sacred Mount, near the river Anio. [10] They committed no act of violence or sedition, but called out, as they went along,
that they had for a long time been excluded from their city by the rich.
Air and water, they said, and a place to be buried they could find anywhere in Italy, but that was all they had when they lived in Rome, except
the privilege of being wounded and killed, fighting battles for the wealthy.

The senate was frightened by this behavior, and sent the most fair-
minded and popularly inclined of its older members to treat with the
people. Its spokesman was Menenius Agrippa, who, after much pleading
with them, and much frank speaking on behalf of the senate, concluded
his speech with a well-known fable: "Once on a time all the other members
of man's body revolted against the stomach, accusing it of being the only
member to sit idle in the body, contributing nothing, while the rest endured great hardships and labor to satisfy its appetites. But the stomach
laughed at their folly in not knowing that it received into itself all the
body's nourishment only to send it back again and distribute it fairly among
the other members. This," he concluded, "is the function of the senate
for you. The discussions and actions which there are given the proper attention and regulation, provide for you all and individually what is helpful
and beneficial."

---

[10] A withdrawal of the Roman plebeians *en masse* from the city, an act which had
much the effect of a modern general strike, took place more than once during their
later struggles against domination and exploitation by the patricians. The secession
here described, dated in 494 B.C., may be only part of the legend of that early period.
Menenius Agrippa is quite probably a fictitious character. The fable attributed to him
was one common among many ancient peoples. The Sacred Mount was about three
miles from Rome.

7. On this, a reconciliation followed, the senate acceding to the people's request for the right to elect men to be protectors of those who needed help, officials now called tribunes of the people. As their first tribunes they chose men who had led the secession, Junius Brutus and Sicinius Vellutus. Then as soon as the city was united again, the people were ready with their arms, and offered themselves to the consuls, eager to serve in the war. But Marcius was not pleased to have the people growing stronger at the aristocracy's expense, and he saw that many other patricians were feeling as he did. However, he told them they must not be outdone in patriotism by the plebeians, but must prove themselves superior in courage, if not in political power.

8. In the Volscian nation,[11] with which Rome was then at war, the most important city was Corioli. The consul Cominius was besieging it and the rest of the Volscians, fearing it might be taken, were coming to its aid against the Romans from all directions. Their plan was to fight a battle under the city walls, and thus attack the Romans on two fronts. But Cominius divided his forces and himself led one part of them to meet the Volscians who were coming up from outside, leaving Titus Lartius, one of the best of the Romans, in charge of the siege. The men of Corioli, scorning the Romans who were left behind, sallied out to do battle, and at first beat them and chased them back to their camp. There Marcius with a few followers sprang out on the pursuers, cut down the foremost, brought the rest to a standstill and called on the Romans with a great shout to turn around and fight. For he had, as Cato [12] thought a soldier should have, not merely an arm to strike, but a tone of voice and an expression of face which made him terrifying for an enemy to meet and difficult to stand against. Many soldiers rallied around him and the enemy retreated in panic. Not satisfied with this, Marcius pressed hard after them and soon was driving them in headlong flight up to the city gates.

On his arrival there, he saw that the Romans were falling back from the pursuit as a cloud of missiles from the walls began raining down on them, and that none of them had the daring to think of breaking into the city

---

11 The Volscians, the warlike inhabitants of the hilly region southeast of Rome, were still a threat to Roman peace as late as the time of Camillus, in the early fourth century, B.C. See above, *Camillus,* n. 3.

12 The reference is to Cato the Elder.

along with the fugitives, filled as it was with armed enemies. Yet he stood
there and called to them and tried to put heart into them, shouting that fortune had opened the city for the pursuers rather than for the pursued. Only
a few were ready to follow him, but he pushed his way through the fleeing
enemy, charged the gate, and burst into the city with them, no man venturing at first to oppose or withstand him. But then when the enemy saw
how few Romans altogether there were inside the gates, they rallied and attacked. In the midst of this mass of friends and foes within the city, Marcius
fought, they say, with incredible feats of strength, swiftness of foot, and
boldness of spirit. He vanquished everyone he attacked, driving some to
the farthest quarters of the town, and compelling others to stop fighting
and throw down their arms. So he made it quite safe for Lartius to bring
in the Romans who were outside.

9. When the city had thus been taken, most of the soldiers there fell
straight to plundering and looting it, at which Marcius was much displeased. He told them loudly that he thought it a disgrace, when the
consul and the citizens with him had perhaps just encountered the enemy
and were still in the midst of battle, that they should be running around
after booty, or, on a pretense of finding booty, keeping safely away from
danger. Few paid any attention to him, but with those who were willing
to go he set out on the road which he heard the consul's army had taken,
often urging his followers on, begging them not to give way to fatigue,
and praying the gods that he might not come too late for the battle, but in
time to share the labors and perils of his countrymen.

It was customary with the Romans of that time, when they were forming in battle array, and preparing to gird up their tunics and take their
shields in their hands, to make at the same time an unwritten will, naming
their heirs, in the hearing of three or four witnesses. Marcius found the
Roman soldiers doing that, with the enemy in sight. At first some were
alarmed at seeing him appear with only a few men, and covered with
blood and sweat. But when he ran joyfully up to the consul, seized his
hand, and announced his capture of Corioli, Cominius embraced and
kissed him; and then those who heard of his victory and even those who
only guessed at it cried out to be led into battle.

Marcius next asked Cominius how the enemy's line was arranged, and
where the toughest fighters were stationed. And when the consul answered

that he thought the troops in the center were made up of men from Antium, who were the bravest and most high-spirited, Marcius said, "I ask and demand of you, then, to put us opposite those men." Amazed at his order, the consul granted his request.

As soon as the spears were flying, Marcius charged out ahead, and the Volscians who faced him gave way, and at the point of his attack their phalanx was soon split apart. However, the ranks on either side turned towards him and hemmed him in with their weapons, so that the consul feared for his safety and sent the choicest men he had with him to his aid. Then the battle raged hotly around Marcius and in a short time many had fallen, but the Romans pressed hard and forcefully on their enemies and drove them back. And as they started to pursue them, they begged Marcius, who was now weighed down with fatigue and wounds to retire to the camp. But he replied that fatigue was not for victors, and set out after the flying foe. The rest of the Volscian army too was defeated, many were slain, and many made prisoners.

10. On the following day when Lartius had arrived and the rest of the troops were assembled before Cominius, he ascended the rostrum and rendered due thanks to the gods for their great victories. He then turned to Marcius, and first described and praised his astounding exploits, some of which he had himself seen in battle, while Lartius bore witness to the rest. He then bade Marcius choose for himself a tenth part of the multitude of treasures and horses and captives that had been taken, before they were distributed to the soldiers. Besides all this, he presented him with a horse and trappings as a reward of valor. When the Romans had applauded his speech, Marcius came forward. He said that he gladly accepted the horse, and was happy at the praises he had received from the consul. But the other gifts looked to him like pay, not honor, and he refused them and was satisfied with his single share of the allotment. "But one special favor," he said, "I do ask you to grant me, and I beg I may receive it. I had a guest-friend among the Volscians, a kindly and just man. He is now a captive, and after being rich and prosperous has become a slave. Seeing that so many miseries have befallen him, I should be glad to save him from one more—from being put up for sale."

At these words Marcius was cheered even more than before, for there were more men who admired his superiority to greed than applauded his bravery in war. Even those who secretly were jealous of his extraordinary honors now thought he deserved to receive great rewards, because he would not receive them, and liked better the manliness that led him to disdain such prizes than the deeds by which he had won the right to them. For to make a right use of riches is a nobler thing than to perform feats of arms, and not to want riches is a holier thing even than using them rightly.

11. When the shouting and applause of the crowd had ceased, Cominius continued: "You cannot, fellow soldiers, force the man to receive these presents against his will; but let us give him a gift which, once given, he cannot reject. Let us vote to call him Coriolanus, unless, indeed, his acts have already bestowed that title on him before we do so." Thus it was that he won his third name of Coriolanus.

So it was quite clear that Gaius was his personal name, and his second name, Marcius, was the common name of his family or clan, and his third name was a later addition, given because of some particular exploit, or accident, or peculiar feature in the man. Thus the Greeks gave a surname to a man for an exploit, as they did to Soter [13] and Callinicus, or, for a peculiar feature, as they did to Physcon and Grypus; or for virtue, as they did to Euergetes and Philadelphus; or, for his good luck, as they did to Eudaemon, the second Battus.[14] Some of their kings had surnames given them in jest, as Antigonus was called Doson, and Ptolemy Lathyrus.

Surnames of this sort were given still more commonly by the Romans. For instance, one of the Metelli was called Diadematus, because for a long time he suffered from an ulcer and went around with his forehead bound up. Another member of the family was called Celer, because of the speed with which he provided funeral games of gladiators only a few days after

---

[13] The following are the meanings of the surnames cited in this and the next paragraph: Soter, Savior; Callinicus, Noble Victor; Physcon, Fat-Belly; Grypus, Hook-Nose; Euergetes, Benefactor; Philadelphus, Brother-Lover; Eudaemon, Fortunate; Doson, Promiser; Lathyrus, Vetch; Diadematus, Fillet-Wearer; Celer, Swift; Proculus, Far-Away; Postumus, Late-Born; Vopiscus and Sulla, meanings unknown; Niger, Black; Rufus, Red; Caecus, Blind; Claudius, Lame. Many of these surnames, Soter, Physcon, Euergetes, Philadelphus, Lathyrus, were given to kings of the Ptolemaic line in Egypt, 306–47 B.C.

[14] Battus II was king of Cyrene on the coast of northeast Africa, from about 575 to 555 B.C.

his father's death. People marveled at the swiftness and promptness of his arrangements. Some even today get their names from an incident of their birth. A child is named Proculus if his father is abroad when he is born, and Postumus if his father is dead. If one of twins survive while the other dies, he is called Vopiscus. Of names derived from bodily features, there are not only Sulla, Niger, and Rufus, but also Caecus and Claudius. So the Romans wisely accustom men to consider neither blindness nor any other bodily mishap a disgrace or matter for reproach, but to answer to these names as if they were really their own. However, this subject would be more suitably discussed in another kind of treatise.

12. But when the war was over, the popular leaders renewed the party dissensions. They had no new cause of complaint or just grievance, but they made the evils which necessarily followed their previous wranglings and disturbances a ground for more attacks on the patricians. For the greater part of the land had been left unsown and uncultivated, and the war had allowed no opportunity to provide for importation of supplies. There was, therefore, a serious shortage of food, and when the popular leaders saw that the people had no provisions, and that even if there had been any, the people had no money to buy them, they falsely accused the rich of having purposely brought the famine on them as a malicious revenge.

At this point an embassy arrived from the people of Velitrae,[15] offering to give up their city to the Romans, and asking them to send over colonists to people it, since pestilence had attacked them and made such havoc among the citizens that scarcely a tenth of them were still alive. The more intelligent Romans thought that this request from Velitrae had come at a useful and opportune moment, for the scarcity of food in Rome required some decrease in population. At the same time they hoped to dissipate the seditious element by purging the city of its most turbulent members and those most affected by the popular leaders, like unwholesome and troublesome refuse. Such men the consuls selected to be the colonists, and ordered to resettle Velitrae. Others they enlisted for another campaign against the Volscians, so that they would have no leisure for plotting uprisings at home. When they were all once more gathered together under

---

15 Velitrae, now Velletri, was an important Latin town, situated on a spur of the Alban Hills, twenty-one miles southeast of Rome. See above, *Camillus*, ch. 42.

arms in camp for a common struggle, rich and poor, patrician and plebeian alike, they thought they might regard one another with more kindliness and good will.

13. But the popular leaders, Sicinnius and Brutus, now interposed, crying
out that the consuls were veiling a cruel act under the specious name of
colonizing. They were shoving poor men into a deadly pit, as it were,
sending them off to a city filled with pestilential air and unburied corpses,
to live under a foreign and bloodthirsty deity. And then, as if it were not
enough that some of their fellow citizens were dying of famine and others
were exposed to a plague, the consuls must likewise be bringing on a war
of their own choosing, so that the city might suffer every misery, because
it refused to remain enslaved to the rich. With their ears filled with such
speeches, the people would not come to the consuls to be enlisted, and believed only ill of the new colony.

The senate was perplexed, but Marcius, now a person of great importance, having grown lofty-spirited and admired by all the influential of
the city, openly headed the resistance to the popular leaders. The colony
was sent out, and those whose names were drawn by lot were compelled to
go or pay severe penalties. And when people utterly refused to serve in
the Volscian campaign, Marcius himself made up troops of his clients and
as many others as he could persuade, and led a raid into the territory of
Antium.[16] There he found a great quantity of corn, and took a rich booty
of prisoners and cattle. The other citizens, accordingly, regretted their decision and envied those who had done so well for themselves, but they
were bitter against Marcius and resented his fame and his power, which
was increasing, they thought, to the detriment of the people.

14. Shortly after this, however, Marcius stood for the consulship,[17] and
the people relented and felt ashamed to affront and humiliate a man who
was first in lineage and in daring and had accomplished so many and such
fine achievements. It was the custom at Rome for those who were candidates for the office to greet and solicit the favor of their fellow citizens,
going down into the forum in a toga, without a tunic underneath, either

---

16 Antium is the modern Anzio.
17 The date given for his election is 488 B.C.

to forward their candidacy by the humility of their dress, or to display any wounds they had as tokens of their prowess. There was certainly at that period no suspicion of money being distributed as bribes, and so it was not for that reason that they had the candidates for the people's votes come before them ungirt and without tunics. For it was much later that the buying and selling of votes crept in, and elections in the assembly were swayed by money.

Thereafter, indeed, bribery spread to the courts and the camps, and ended by transforming the city to a monarchy by reducing its armies to slaves of money. It was well said that he first ruins a people who first feasts and bribes them. But the evil seems to have crept secretly and gradually into Rome, and not to have been discovered at once. We do not know who was the first to bribe the people or the courts of law. At Athens the first to give money to his jurors, they say, was Anytus, son of Anthemion, when he was tried for treachery in failing to relieve Pylos, towards the end of the Peloponnesian War. But in Marcius' time a pure race of the golden age still had possession of the forum at Rome.

15. Marcius displayed many scars, gained in many battles, in which for seventeen years he had constantly taken a leader's part. The people were abashed at this record of valor, and agreed among themselves to elect him. But when, on the day set for the voting, he appeared ostentatiously in the forum, escorted by the senate, and all the patricians collected around him, evidently more set on victory than ever before, the people lost their good will towards him in a rush of indignation and animosity. Their emotions were heightened by their fear that if an aristocrat with such influence over the patricians should get control of the government, he might deprive the people entirely of their liberty.

Such being their state of mind, they voted against Marcius. When the other candidates were declared elected, the senate was angry, feeling that an indignity had been inflicted on it more than on Marcius, and he himself did not take what had happened reasonably or with good grace. He had made a practice of indulging the passionate and combative elements in his nature, under the impression that they were the great and lofty parts, and had not learned from reason and training the gravity and considerateness which are the chief virtues of a statesman. He did not know that one who is undertaking public office must, above all, avoid self-will, which

Plato calls [18] "the housemate of solitude," and must mingle with men and enjoy taking their buffeting, even though to some that attitude seems undignified. But Marcius, always a straightforward and stubborn man, believed that the task of bravery was to conquer and ride down completely all opposition, and not to show pliancy and yielding, which mostly appear like sores to a straining and suffering spirit. He therefore went off full of resentment and bitterness towards the people.

The young patricians too, the element in the city which prided itself most on noble birth and made a great show, and which had ever been his fast friend, now served him ill by keeping close to him and sharpening his anger with their sympathetic indignation and disappointment. For he had been their leader and generous instructor in the arts of war on their campaigns, and had exulted over their victories with a zeal for valor that knew no jealousy of another man's achievement.

16.   Meanwhile, grain was coming to Rome, much of it bought in Italy, but as much more sent as a present from Syracuse by the tyrant Gelon.[19] So most men were very hopeful, anticipating that the famine would end and the city be freed of discord. The senate was promptly convened, and the people swarmed about outside, awaiting its decision. They looked forward to easier prices and a free distribution of what had come as a gift. There were some too in the senate who advised such a course. But Marcius arose and violently attacked those who were for favoring the people, calling them demagogues and traitors to the aristocracy, and insisting that they were nourishing to their own hurt the wicked seeds of audacity and insolence which had been sown among the rabble, and which they would have done well to destroy on their first appearance. Instead, they had strengthened the plebeians by granting them such powerful magistrates as the tribunes. They had now grown formidable, since everything they wanted was given them and nothing was forced upon them against their wishes. They were refusing to obey the consuls and had their own leaders in anarchy, whom they called their rulers. To sit there voting them gifts and provisions, like Greeks, who were entirely democracy-ridden,

---

[18] In a letter to Dion; Plato, *Letters*, IV.
[19] Shortly before this time, Gelon (c.540–478 B.C.) had made himself tyrant of Syracuse and master of much of Sicily. Under him Syracuse had fended off the Carthaginians and become the richest and most powerful Greek city then existing.

was, he said, supporting them in disobedience, to everyone's total destruction.

"Certainly they will not look on your gifts as rewards for the military
services they refused to render, the secession in which they deserted their
country, and the slanders they permitted against the senate! Instead, they
will fancy you are offering them gifts and concessions because your fears
compel you to flatter and submit to them. So they will set no limit to their
disobedience, and never stop quarreling and rioting. To make them such a
gift is therefore absolute madness. If we are sensible, we will take the
tribunate away from them, for it nullifies the consul's authority, and creates dissension in the city. Romans are now no longer one, as before, but
have been cut apart, never to grow together again, or to think as one, or
to cease afflicting and tormenting one another."

17. With much more to the same effect, Marcius had the younger senators and almost all the wealthy ones filled with his proud enthusiasm,
and shouting that he was the only man in the city who would not flatter
or submit. Some of the older senators, however, opposed him, foreseeing
the result. And indeed the outcome was bad, for the tribunes were present,
and when they saw that Marcius' proposals were winning, they ran out
among the crowd and called loudly on the people to unite and stand by
them. There was a tumultuous meeting of the assembly, and when Marcius' speech was reported to them, the people were aroused to such a fury
that they almost broke in on the senate. But the tribunes put all the blame
on Marcius himself, and sent for him to come and make his defense. And
when he contemptuously drove away the officials they sent, the tribunes
themselves, with the aediles, went to bring him by force, and were trying
to lay hands on him. The patricians in a band pushed away the tribunes,
and actually struck the aediles.

Nightfall put an end to the disorder, but at daybreak the consuls saw
the excited people streaming into the forum from all quarters and were
alarmed for the city. They convened the senators and urged them to try
to quiet and pacify the masses by reasonable arguments and helpful resolutions, since it was no time for wise men to stand on their dignity or
fight for a big name. The crisis was acute and dangerous and required a
patriotic and humane policy. The majority of the senators agreeing, the
consuls went out and proceeded to reason with and soothe the people as

well as they could, answering their charges fairly, and only in moderation reproving and warning them. As for the price of market wares and provisions, they said they would not quarrel with them over that.

18. The people then for the most part began to cool down, and it was plain from their orderly and serious way of listening that they were being influenced and appeased. The tribunes stood up and declared that since the senate was now acting reasonably, the people in turn would make whatever concessions were right. They insisted, however, that Marcius should answer the following questions. Could he deny that he had urged the senate to violate the constitution and annul the rights of the people? When summoned to appear before them, had he not refused to come? And lastly, by beating and affronting the aediles in the forum, had he not done all he could to start a civil war and incite the citizens to arms? They said this either to humble Marcius, by compelling him against his nature to control his haughty spirit and beg for the clemency of the people, or else, if he followed his own disposition, to drive him to do something that would make the people's wrath implacable. The latter was what they rather expected, and they were correct in their estimate of his character.

For Marcius came forward as if to speak in his own defense, and the people stood silent and quiet listening to him. But instead of the apologetic language they expected, he began not only to speak with a freedom which was offensive and more like vituperation than mere candor, but to show by the tone of his voice and the expression of his face that his fearlessness came close to contempt and scorn. Then the people grew angry again and expressed plainly their disapproval and indignation. Thereat Sicinnius, the boldest of the tribunes, after a short consultation with his colleagues, announced publicly that the tribunes had condemned Marcius to death, and ordered the aediles to take him up to the Tarpeian rock at once, and cast him down the cliff. But when the aediles laid hold of him, it seemed even to many of the plebeians a terrible and inhuman sentence, and the patricians, wildly excited and horror-struck, rushed shouting to his rescue. Some by main force shoved away the men who were seizing Marcius, and got him into their midst. Some held out their hands in entreaty to the people, as no words or voice could be heard in such confusion and uproar.

At last the friends and relatives of the tribunes, seeing that it was impossible without killing many patricians to carry off Marcius and punish him, persuaded them to withdraw what was cruel and unprecedented in their sentence, and not to put him to a violent death without a trial, but let him go and refer the case to the people. Then Sicinnius, who had grown calm, asked the patricians what they meant by taking Marcius away from the people when they wished to punish him. The patricians retorted: "What do you mean and what is your plan, when you drag one of the best men of Rome, without a trial, to a cruel and illegal punishment?" "Very well," said Sicinnius, "you shall not make that an excuse for partisan quarrels with the people, for they grant what you ask—a trial for the man. And we summon you, Marcius, to appear on the third market day ensuing and convince the citizens of your innocence, and they will decide your case by vote."

19. For the moment the patricians were satisfied with that truce, and went off, glad to have Marcius with them. And during the time which elapsed before the third market day (for the Romans hold their markets every ninth day, and so call them *nundinae*), a campaign was started against the city of Antium, which gave rise to a hope that the issue might be entirely evaded. The campaign would last long enough, it was thought, for the people to become manageable and their anger to abate or vanish altogether in their preoccupation with war. But then they came quickly to terms with Antium, the people were home again, and the patricians held frequent meetings, for they were full of anxiety, wondering how they might avoid surrendering Marcius and still not give the popular leaders cause to stir the people up again. Appius Claudius, who had the reputation of being the bitterest enemy of the people, gave as his solemn opinion that the senate would destroy itself and completely betray the state, if it permitted the people through their votes to assume power over the patricians. The oldest senators and those most sympathetic with the people asserted, on the contrary, that this power would make them not harsh or oppressive but considerate and humane. For they were not contemptuous of the senate, but they felt that the senate was contemptuous of them. So the right to try a senator would seem an honor and a consolation, and once they took their ballots in hand, they would forget their bitterness.

20. Marcius saw that the senate was in a dilemma, torn between its regard for him and its fear of the people, and he asked the tribunes what were the accusations against him, and on what charge he would be tried,

if they brought him before the people. They answered that the charge against him was that of setting up a tyranny, and that they would prove that he had planned to make himself a tyrant. On this he rose and said he was going immediately before the people to defend himself and would make no protest against any form of trial, nor, if convicted, against any punishment. "Only," he said, "keep to this one accusation, and do not play false with the senate." The tribunes agreed, and on these terms the trial went forward.

But when the people had assembled, the tribunes first insisted that the voting should be by tribes, and not by centuries.[20] By this device they made the poor and meddlesome rabble, who had no idea of nobility, superior by their votes to the rich and respectable military class. Then they dropped the charge of tyranny, as being impossible to prove, and recalled the speech Marcius had made earlier before the senate, when he tried to prevent their lowering the price of grain and urged them to deprive the people of the tribunate. They brought also a fresh charge against him in connection with his distribution of the spoils he had taken from the territory of Antium. Those, they said, he had not turned over to the public treasury, but had divided among his companions on the campaign.

This last accusation is said to have disturbed Marcius more than all the rest, for it was unexpected and he was not ready at once with a satisfactory answer to the mob. But he began to praise those who had gone on the campaign with him, at which the far greater number who had not gone raised a loud clamor against him. At last the vote was taken by tribes and a majority of three [21] condemned him. The penalty fixed was perpetual banishment. Upon the announcement the people departed in greater elation and glee than they had ever shown for any victory in battle over their enemies. But the senate was distressed and steeped in gloom, re-

---

[20] The tribes were ancient divisions of the Roman populace on a territorial basis, and included from the first, apparently, plebeians on an equal footing with the patricians. When the assembly voted by tribes, the plebeian votes outnumbered the patrician. This form of assembly was therefore as a rule called only by the plebeians to transact business of their own. The centuries were divisions based on wealth. There were one hundred and ninety-three of them, and the wealthiest class and the mounted knights alone made up the first ninety-eight. The centuriate assembly, therefore, was controlled by the senatorial party and the aristocracy.

[21] That is, nine of the twenty-one tribes were for acquittal.

gretful and vexed that they had not done and suffered everything, rather than allow the people to be so insolent and to grasp at so much power. There was no need then for any distinction of dress or other mark to tell one class from the other, for a plebeian was conspicuous by his joyousness and a patrician by his dejection.

21. Marcius himself was not daunted or humbled, but in manner, bearing, and countenance remained unmoved. Among all the woeful patricians he seemed the only one who was not sorry for himself. This apparent calmness, however, was not due to reasoning or gentleness of temper, or patient endurance of fate, for he was consumed by rage and a deep bitterness of spirit, which many do not realize is pain. And when pain changes to anger, it is set, as it were, on fire, and casts off all meekness and submissiveness. Hence an angry man seems full of energy, as a feverish man is hot, because his spirit feels the throbbing and the straining and the burden.

And Marcius soon showed by his acts that this was his condition. He went home, and embraced his weeping and wailing wife and mother, and bade them bear the calamity with patience; then immediately left them and went on to the city gates. Thither all the patricians in a body escorted him, but taking nothing with him and asking nothing of anyone, he departed, accompanied by only three or four of his clients. For a few days he stayed by himself in some place in the country, torn by many conflicting considerations. His anger made him want to do nothing good or useful at all, but only to avenge himself on the Romans. At last he resolved to stir up some neighbor to a destructive war against them, and started first to try out the Volscians, who he knew were still well provided with men and money, and, he thought, had suffered in their late defeat only so much loss of power as to fill them with pugnacity and wrath.

22. There was a man of Antium named Tullus Aufidius, who, by reason of his wealth, courage, and illustrious birth, held the position of king among all the Volscians. Marcius knew that this man hated him more than any other Roman, for they had often in battle challenged and defied one another, and with their rival boasts, such as young warriors in their ambitious ardor are given to making, they had added to their national antipathy a personal hatred of each other. Nevertheless Marcius knew that Tullus had a certain grandeur of nature, and that more than any

other Volscian he was longing to retaliate on the Romans, once they furnished him an opportunity. He testified then to the truth of the words,[22] "With anger it is hard to fight, for what it wants it buys, even with its life." For he put on clothes and a disguise in which he would look to any observer quite different from the man he was, and, like Ulysses,

"Entered the city of his deadly foes." [23]

23.   It was evening, and though many met him, no one recognized him. He went to the house of Tullus, and entering unnoticed, sat down by the hearth in silence,[24] his head covered over. The people in the house were surprised, but did not dare to tell him to move, for there was a certain dignity in his demeanor and his silence. So they told Tullus, who was at supper, of the strange incident. Tullus rose and went to Marcius, and asked him who he was and what he wanted. Thereupon Marcius uncovered his face, paused a moment, and said: "If you do not yet recognize me, Tullus, or do not believe your eyes, I must become my own accuser. I am Gaius Marcius, who has done you and the Volscians more harm than anyone else, and who bears the title of Coriolanus which prevents me from denying it. No other prize have I won for my many labors and perils but this name, which is a mark of animosity towards you. This name cannot be taken from me. Of everything else have I been stripped by the spite and insolence of the Roman people, and the cowardice and treachery of the magistrates and my own class.

"I have been driven too into exile and am now a suppliant at your hearth, not begging you for safety and protection—for why should I have come here if I were afraid to die?—but craving vengeance on those who drove me forth, which I am already taking by putting myself in your hands. If then, brave Tullus, you have a mind to attack your foes, come, take advantage of my trouble, and let my ill fortune bring good fortune to the Volscians. I shall fight for you better than I have fought against you, because men who know the secrets of their enemies fight better than those who do not. But if you are through with war, I do not wish to live, nor is it right that you should spare the life of one who has long

---

[22] Heraclitus, Fragment 105.

[23] Homer, *Odyssey*, IV, 246.

[24] As we have noted earlier, the hearth, which housed the domestic gods, was a sacred refuge for a suppliant. See above, *Themistocles*, ch. 24.

been your adversary and enemy, and who now is worn out and useless."
But when Tullus heard this he was immensely pleased, and gave him
his hand, saying: "Rise, Marcius, and be of good heart! In coming and
delivering yourself to us you have brought us a great gift. Expect greater
gifts from the Volscians." He then entertained Marcius with lavish hospitality, and in the days that followed they conferred together about the
war.

24. Rome meanwhile was disturbed by the resentment of the patricians
against the plebeians, provoked especially by their condemnation of Marcius, and many portents were announced by diviners and priests and
private persons. One of these, they say, was the following. Titus Latinus,
a man of no great note but a quiet and respectable person in general and
not given to superstitious alarms, had a dream. He dreamed that Jupiter
appeared to him and bade him tell the senate that they had sent a bad
dancer to lead his procession, and one very displeasing to him. On seeing
this vision for the first time, he said, he thought nothing of it; but after
he had seen it a second and a third time and still was disregarding it, he
witnessed the death of his own good son, and himself suddenly became
paralyzed. He was carried on a litter to the senate, to whom he told this
story, and as soon as he had told it, they say, he felt strength returning to
his body, and arose and walked home by himself.

The senators, astonished, made a thorough inquiry into the matter. And
what had happened was this. Some man had handed over one of his slaves
to other slaves, with orders to flog him through the forum and then put
him to death. While they were doing this and torturing the wretch, who
was twisting and writhing pitifully in his suffering and pain, it happened
that the procession in honor of Jupiter came up behind. Many of those
who were in it were horrified by the unhappy spectacle and the man's
frantic contortions, but no one tried to stop it. They only denounced and
swore at the man who was inflicting so cruel a punishment. For the Romans at that period treated their slaves with great kindness. They worked
and ate with them and were therefore more intimate and mild with them.
A severe punishment for a slave who had done wrong was to be obliged
to pick up the block of wood with which they support the pole of a wagon
and carry it around the neighborhood. A slave who had been seen doing
this no longer had any credit in his own household or among the neigh-

bors. He was called a *furcifer*, or *furca*, carrier, for what the Greeks call a prop or support, the Romans call a *furca*.

25.   When then Latinus told his dream to the senators, and they were wondering who the bad and unacceptable dancer could have been who led the procession, some of them recalled the unusual punishment of the slave who had been flogged through the forum and then put to death. With the consent of the priests, the slave's master was punished, and the procession and ceremonies in honor of the god were performed anew. Thus we may see how sage was Numa, a most wise director of religious rites, with his rule to ensure popular reverence.[25] Whenever magistrates or priests are engaged in any religious ceremony, a herald walks before them crying in a loud voice, *"Hoc age,"* meaning "See to this." It is a command to pay full attention to the sacred rite, and allow no task or business activity to distract one, since as a rule men stop what they are doing only when they are somehow compelled to do so.

So it is the custom in Rome to repeat sacrifices and processions and spectacles not only for such a cause as that just mentioned, but also for more trivial reasons. Thus, if one of the horses drawing the sacred chariots, called *tensae,* seems languid, or again, if the charioteer takes the reins in his left hand, the citizens have decreed that the procession must start afresh. In later years they have even performed one sacrifice thirty times, because each time some slip or mishap occurred.

26.   Meanwhile Marcius and Tullus were holding secret conferences with the chief men at Antium, and urging them to start the war while the Romans were divided by domestic quarrels. But they were ashamed to do this, because they had made a two-year truce and treaty with them. However, the Romans themselves gave them an excuse for breaking the truce by making a proclamation at some public games, because of a suspicion or ugly rumor that all Volscians must leave the city before sunset. Some say this was the result of a crafty stratagem of Marcius, who sent a man to the consuls at Rome with a false accusation against the Volscians, to the effect that they were planning to attack the Romans during the games and set fire to the city. This proclamation inflamed the Volscians' hostility to the Romans, and Tullus magnified the incident and worked

---

[25] See above, *Numa*, ch. 14.

on his countrymen until he persuaded them to send ambassadors to Rome to demand back the territory and the cities which the Romans had taken from the Volscians in war. On hearing the ambassadors, the Romans were highly indignant, and replied that the Volscians might be the first to take up arms but that the Romans would be the last to lay them down. At this, Tullus called an assembly of all his people, and after they had voted for war, suggested that they call in Marcius, remembering no evil against him, but expecting that he would be more helpful as an ally than he had been hurtful as an enemy.

27.   Marcius was then summoned, and having addressed the people, they saw that he was as skillful a fighter with words as he was with arms, and extraordinarily keen and daring. So they appointed him general with Tullus, and put him in full charge of the war. But he feared the Volscians would take so long to prepare for battle that meanwhile the opportunity for action would be gone. He therefore ordered the leading men and magistrates in the city to be collecting and procuring whatever they needed, and he himself, after persuading the most ardent spirits to go ahead with him as volunteers, without waiting for enrolment, made a sudden inroad into Roman territory when no one expected it. There he took so much plunder that the Volscians had more than they could either carry away or use in camp.

But to him the winning of booty and the ravaging of the country were the smallest achievement of the raid. His great motive in making it was to give the Roman people new grievances against the patricians. So while he wrecked and destroyed everything else, he carefully protected the patricians' farms, and allowed no one to damage them or take anything away. This led to more scandals and disorders at Rome, the patricians accusing the people of having unjustly banished so able a man, and the plebeians charging the patricians with inviting Marcius to attack them out of malice, and then sitting by as spectators while others fought and the war itself kept guard over their wealth and estates outside the walls. Having then accomplished this and done much to inspire the Volscians with courage and scorn for their enemies, Marcius led his men safely back.

28.   The whole Volscian army was quickly and eagerly got together and was then seen to be very large. They decided therefore to leave a part behind to protect their cities, and with the other part to proceed against

Rome. Marcius left it to Tullus to choose which part he would command, and Tullus said that he knew Marcius to be as brave a man as himself, and to have had better fortune in all his battles. So he should command the army that would take the field while he himself would remain behind to guard the cities and get supplies to the fighting troops.

Thus Marcius, stronger than he was before, set out first against Circeii,[26] a Roman colony. It surrendered of its own accord and he did it no injury. Next he laid waste the Latins' territory. There he expected the Romans would fight to defend it, for the Latins were their allies and had sent them many appeals for help. But the people of Rome were uninterested, and the consuls were approaching the end of their term of office, and unwilling to take risks. They therefore sent the Latin envoys away. Marcius then led his army against the Latin cities of Tolerium, Lavicum, and Pedum, and then Bola, taking by storm those which resisted him, making slaves of the inhabitants, and looting their property. But the cities which surrendered voluntarily he treated with great consideration, even pitching his camp at a distance for fear the people might suffer some injury against his will, and keeping his men away from their lands.

29.   And when he had taken Bola, a city not more than twelve miles from Rome, and had captured huge spoils and put nearly all the grown inhabitants to the sword, then the Volscians who had been detailed to garrison the cities became impatient and came flocking to Marcius with their arms, saying that he was the one and only general and leader they would recognize. His renown was great all over Italy, and everyone was astonished to see how one valiant man by changing sides had so remarkably transformed the situation.

But in Rome everything was confusion. The people refused to fight and spent their days in wrangling and partisan disputes until news came that the enemy was besieging Lavinium, the town where the sacred objects and images of the Romans' ancestral gods were kept, and the birthplace of their nation, since it was the first city founded by Aeneas. At this news a singular change of opinion took place in every plebeian; also one quite strange and unpredictable in the patricians. The people now wanted to

---

[26] Circeii lay on the coast, south of Antium, in the direction of Naples. The four Latin towns were hill towns north of Antium, within a radius of fifteen or twenty miles from Rome.

revoke their sentence against Marcius and call him back to Rome, but the senate, after meeting and considering this proposal, rejected and forbade it, either because they were resentfully bent on opposing whatever the people wanted, or because they did not wish him to come back by grace of the people, or because they were now angry with Marcius himself for having harmed all classes alike, though not all had injured him, and for having become the enemy of his whole people, though he knew that the noblest and most influential citizens had sympathized with him and felt his wrongs. When the senate's decision was made public, the people were left powerless, for they could not vote to enact a law without a previous decree of the senate.

30. When Marcius heard this, he was more exasperated than ever, and lifting the siege of Lavinium, marched furiously towards Rome. He pitched his camp near the so-called Cluilan Ditches, only five miles from the city. The appearance of his army caused great terror and consternation, but it put a stop to dissensions for the time being, since no one now, whether consul or senator, dared any longer oppose the people's desire to recall him. Indeed when they saw the women running distractedly about the city, and the old men weeping and praying in supplication at the altars, and nowhere any courage or planning for defense, they agreed that the people were right in wanting a reconciliation with Marcius, and that the senate was entirely wrong when it began exhibiting anger and hostility at just the time when all ill feeling should have been buried. It was decided, therefore, by everyone that an embassy should be sent to Marcius, to offer him a recall to his country and to entreat him to stop his war against it. The senate's envoys were close friends of Marcius, who expected to be treated with kindness and warmth as soon as they met the man who had been their familiar companion.

But nothing of the sort happened, for after being led through the enemy's camp, they found him seated in state, wearing a look of intolerable severity. With the Volscian chiefs standing around him, he bade the Romans say what they wanted. They spoke in a reasonable and courteous way, a style suitable to the occasion. But when they finished he answered them in bitterness and anger, first, on his own account, for what they had done to him. Then, speaking for the Volscians, as their general, he commanded the Romans to restore the cities and the territory they had torn from them in war, and to vote a decree granting the Volscians equality in civil rights, such as they had granted the Latins.[27] For no other peace, he said, would be lasting but one based on fair and equal rights. He gave them a period of thirty days for deliberation, and on the departure of the ambassadors immediately withdrew his forces from that region.

31. This movement provided those Volscians who had long resented and been jealous of Marcius' influence and power with their first ground of complaint. Among them was Tullus himself, who, though he had not been personally wronged by Marcius, felt a human vexation at having his own reputation all overshadowed and himself ignored. For the Volscians now thought of Marcius by himself as everything to them, and expected their other leaders to be thankful for whatever power and authority he would share with them. Hence the first hints of dissatisfaction were already secretly going about, and now his enemies joined together and gave voice to their displeasure. They called Marcius' withdrawal from Rome a betrayal, not of cities or of armies, but of opportunities, through which all things may be won and lost again. He had given the enemy thirty days of war time, though in war the greatest of changes may happen in less time than that.

Yet Marcius was not spending this time in idleness, but was attacking the enemy's allies, wasting and ravaging their lands and capturing seven large and populous cities. The Romans did not dare to come to their assistance, but were intimidated in spirit, behaving towards the war like men benumbed or paralyzed. When the time had elapsed, and Marcius presented himself again before Rome with his whole army, they sent a second embassy to implore him to forget his anger, withdraw the Volscians from the country, and then take such steps and make such proposals as he thought would be advantageous to both nations. The Romans, they said, would make no concessions to fear, but if he thought that some mark of friendship was due the Volscians, they would do anything for them, provided they laid down their arms. To this Marcius answered that, as

---

[27] In 493 B.C., a Roman consul had made a treaty with the Latin peoples around Rome, providing for mutual military assistance on equal terms whenever needed. Roman pride in after years represented that treaty as a grant by Rome of privileges to her neighbors of inferior status.

a general of the Volscians, he could give them no answer, but that as one who was still a citizen of Rome he would advise and urge them to adopt a more modest view of what was justice in their case, and come to him in three days with an acceptance of his demands. If they decided otherwise, they must understand that it would not be safe for them to visit his camp again with only empty words.

32. When the ambassadors returned, and the senate had heard their report, they felt as if the city were tossing in the waves of a terrible tempest and they let down their most sacred anchor. They voted that all the priests of the gods, all the celebrants and guardians of the mysteries, and all who practiced the ancient, ancestral art of divination from the flight of birds, all these should go to Marcius, each man clad as he was accustomed to be at religious services, and speaking as before, should beg him to end the war and then discuss with his fellow citizens the matter of the Volscians. Marcius received these men in his camp, but made no other concession and relaxed none of his harshness, bidding them either to make peace on the terms already stated or else accept the war. So when the priests came back, it was resolved to do nothing more, but guard the city walls and repulse any assault the enemy might make, and put their hopes mainly in time and the unpredictable changes of fortune. For they knew that nothing they did themselves could save them.

Panic and terror and rumors of evil possessed the city until something happened that resembled many of the stories in Homer, which as a rule men do not altogether believe. For when great and extraordinary deeds were to be done, Homer says:

"And this the goddess, gray-eyed Athene, put in his mind," [28]

and again:

"But some immortal changed his mind, and put in his heart
A thought of what men would say," [29]

and again:

"Either it was that he thought it, or else a god
Commanded him so to do." [30]

---

[28] Homer, *Odyssey*, XVIII, 158.

[29] These lines are not to be found in any extant text of Homer.

[30] *Odyssey*, IX, 339.

But men look down on the poet, because, they say, with his impossible doings and incredible tales he teaches us not to believe that a man's reason controls his choices. Now this Homer does not do, but actions which are natural and habitual and dictated by reason he ascribes to our own initiative. Certainly he says often:

> "But I took counsel in my mighty soul"; [31]

and:

> "Thus spoke he, and sorely distressed was Peleus' son,
> And divided his soul within his shaggy breast"; [32]

and again:

> "But she persuaded not
> The wise Bellerophon, the fiery-hearted." [33]

And even in accounts of strange and extraordinary deeds, which called for some burst of inspiration and desperate strength, he speaks of the god not as obliterating the man's will, but as stimulating it, and as the source not of his impulses, but of the imaginings which led to his impulses. So the deed is not done without the man's willing, but his will receives a prompting; and courage and hope are given him as well. And either we must deny all influence and intervention of the gods in our affairs or say in what ways they assist and work with us. Certainly they do not directly mold our bodies, or move about, as needed, our hands and feet, but with motives, thoughts, and ideas they rouse the active and willing powers of our souls, or, on the contrary, divert and restrain them.

33. In Rome at this time the women were praying in supplication at various temples, most of them and those of the highest rank at the altar of Jupiter on the Capitol. Among them was Valeria, a sister of the great Poplicola,[34] who served the Romans well and often, in war and in government. Poplicola had died some time before, as I have related in my

---

[31] *Odyssey,* IX, 299.

[32] *Iliad,* I, 188, 189.

[33] *Iliad,* VI, 161, 162.

[34] Valerius Poplicola, according to tradition, was one of the first consuls chosen to govern Rome after the expulsion of the kings, in 509 B.C. He was said to have been the author of important legislation and to have led the Romans to victory over their neighbors. Plutarch wrote a *Life of Poplicola.*

account of him, but Valeria was held in great honor and esteem at Rome, where her life did credit to her noble birth. She suddenly was taken with one of the promptings of which I have spoken, and seized on it as an inspired aim. She rose and called on all the other women to rise and go with her to the house of Volumnia, the mother of Marcius. On entering she found her sitting with her daughter-in-law, and holding Marcius' children on her lap. Valeria with her companions surrounded her and said: "Volumnia, and you, Virgilia, we have come here as women to women, at no senate's decree or consul's order. But our God, we believe, has had pity on our prayers, and put into our minds an impulse to turn to you and implore you to save both us and all our countrymen. If you consent, you will win a glory more splendid than that of the Sabine daughters,[35] who brought their husbands and fathers from war to friendship and peace. Come, go with us to Marcius, join in our entreaties, and bear just and true witness for your country, that though she has suffered much from him, she has done you no harm and never thought of harming you in her indignation, but is restoring you to him, even though she receives no fair treatment from him in return."

When Valeria had spoken, the other women cried out their appeals, and Volumnia answered: "We too, O women, share as much as you in the general suffering, and have besides, our special misery. We have lost the glory and valor of Marcius, and now behold him guarded by an enemy's arms but still in no safety. And the greatest of our misfortunes is that our country has grown so weak as to have to rest its hopes on us. For I cannot tell whether he will pay any heed to us, seeing that he pays none to his country, which he used to honor above his mother, wife, and children. However, take us and use us and bring us to him, and if we can do nothing more, we can die breathing out prayers for our country."

34. Thereupon, she took Virgilia and the children, and went with the other women to the Volscian camp. Their piteous appearance produced, even among their enemies, a respectful silence. Marcius, as it happened, was sitting on a tribunal with his chief officers and when he saw the women advancing he was struck with surprise. When he recognized his mother walking at their head, he tried to maintain his usual inflexible and implacable attitude, but was overcome by emotion and shaken at the

[35] On the Sabine women, see above, *Comparison of Lycurgus and Numa*, n. 5.

sight. He could not endure to remain seated while they approached him, but stepped quickly down from the tribunal and ran to meet them. He embraced first his mother, holding her a long time, and then his wife and children, no longer restraining his tears and caresses, but giving himself up, as it were, to a torrent of feeling.

35. When he had had his fill of emotion, he perceived that his mother wished to speak, and calling the Volscian councilors together, he listened as Volumnia said: "You see and may judge, my son, by our wretched dress and appearance, even without our speaking, to what desolation your exile has reduced us. And think now how unhappy we who have come here must be, beyond all other women, since fortune has made what was our dearest sight the most terrible, when I see my son, and your wife here sees her husband, besieging the walls of his own city. That which for others is a consolation in every misfortune and calamity—prayer to the gods—is become for us utterly impossible, for we cannot ask the gods at the same time to give our country victory and to preserve you, and what we pray for is the same as what our enemies would bring down on us as a curse. For your wife and children must lose either you or their native country. For my part, I will not live and wait for war to decide my lot. If I cannot now persuade you to bring friendship and concord to the two nations instead of strife and woe, and thus become a benefactor of both instead of the bane of one, then consider and be assured that you cannot invade your country without first trampling on the corpse of her who gave you life. I need not wait for the day when I behold my son either led in triumph by his countrymen or triumphing over his country.

"If I were asking you to save your country by destroying the Volscians, the question would be a hard one, my son, and grievous to answer, for it is neither honorable to be the ruin of your fellow citizens, nor right to betray those who have trusted you. But we are asking merely for release from sufferings and deliverance for both nations alike—more glorious and happy for the Volscians, because their superiority in the field will make it seem that they are granting us the great blessings of peace and friendship, even though they will obtain as much themselves. If this comes to pass, it will be chiefly through you. If it does not, you alone will bear the blame in both nations. For though the issue of the war is doubtful, this much is clear, that if you succeed, you will be your own country's evil genius, and if you fail, you will have the name of one who out of spite inflicted great calamities on men who have been your friends and bene-factors."

36. While Volumnia spoke, Marcius listened to her and made no reply. And after she ceased, he stood mute for a long time. She then went on: "Why, my son, are you silent? Is it right to give way completely to your anger and sense of grievance, and not right to satisfy your mother, when she pleads with you thus? Or does it become a great man to cherish the memory of his injuries? Is it not the duty of a good and great man to remember in reverence and honor the benefits which his parents bestowed on their children? And surely, no one ought to show his gratitude more than you, who attack ingratitude so bitterly. Yet though you have already punished your country terribly for its ingratitude, you have made your mother no return for her kindness. A truly pious act it would be for you to grant me freely my fair and just petition. But if I cannot persuade you, why not try my last resource?" Whereupon she, his wife, and children all threw themselves at his feet.

At that Marcius cried out, "What have you done to me, mother?" and lifted her up from the ground, and pressing her hand, said, "You have conquered, and your victory is a boon for my country but destruction for me. I will retreat, defeated by you, though by no other." He then con-ferred a short while in private with his mother and his wife, and after-wards at their request sent them back to Rome. The next morning he led the Volscians away. They did not all feel the same way or with the same intensity about what had happened. Some denounced both him and what he had done, while others, who wanted an end of the war, approved. Others disliked what he had done, but still did not condemn him as a renegade, and thought it pardonable that he should have broken down under such pressure. No one refused to obey him, but all followed him in his retreat, though more out of admiration for his courage than respect for his authority.

37. Now that the war was over, the Roman people showed more plainly than before to what terrifying straits they had been reduced. As soon as the guards on the walls saw the Volscians moving off, every temple was immediately opened, the people crowned themselves with garlands, and offered sacrifices as though for a victory. The city's joy was especially

shown in the affectionate honor paid to the women by the senate and the whole people, everyone declaring and believing that their deliverance was unquestionably due to them. The senate decreed that whatever they asked for themselves in the way of glorification or favor, the magistrates should do or provide for them. But they asked for nothing but the building of a temple to Women's Fortune, the cost of which they would contribute, if the city would undertake to maintain at the public charge the sacred services and honors which belong to gods. The senate praised their nobility of spirit and erected the temple and the image at public expense.[36] But the women also subscribed money and set up a second image of the goddess, which, the Romans declare, spoke, as it was being placed in the temple, and said something like, "The gods are pleased, O women, with your gift of me."

38. The legend says that this voice was heard twice, a tale hard for us to believe of a thing not likely ever to have happened at all. That statues have seemed to sweat, shed tears, or exude bloody drops is not impossible, because wood and stone often collect a mold that oozes moisture, and by themselves produce a variety of colors and take on tints from the air. And there is nothing to prevent our believing that the Deity sometimes uses these appearances as signs. It is possible too that statues may make a sound like a moan or a groan in the breaking or tearing apart of their particles, which is more violent when it occurs inside them. But that articulate voice and speech, so clear and fluent and expressive, should come from a lifeless thing is absolutely impossible, when not even a human spirit or a god has ever uttered words or conversed without a body organized and equipped with means to speak. And when historians with numerous trustworthy witnesses force us to accept some story of this kind, we must suppose that a sensation different from actual perception was felt in the imaginative region of the soul, which persuaded the man to think it perception, just as in sleep we think we hear when we are not hearing, and to see when we are not seeing.

Nevertheless, those who have intense feelings of religious fervor and

---

36 The temple was erected on the Via Latina, about four miles from Rome, near the spot where Volumnia was said to have met her son. Virgilia, Coriolanus' wife, was, according to the story, the first priestess of the temple. It became very popular with Roman women.

love of God, and cannot disregard or reject any of these wonders, find great support for their faith in the marvelous power of God, which is more than ours. For in nothing does he resemble man, neither in nature, nor motion, nor skill, nor strength; nor is it strange if he does what we cannot do, or achieves what we cannot achieve. Indeed, though he differs widely from us in every respect, it is in his works that he is most unlike us and most surpasses us. But, as Heraclitus says,[37] most of the works of God "escape our knowledge through our unbelief."

39. When Marcius then came back to Antium from his campaign, Tullus, who had long hated him and been tormented by jealousy of him, plotted to get rid of him at once, thinking that if Marcius eluded him now, he would never have another chance. So he marshaled and prepared a considerable party against him, and then called on him to lay down his command and render an account of his generalship to the Volscians. But Marcius was afraid of being reduced to a private station, when Tullus was still in office and the most powerful citizen in the country, and said he would resign his command to the Volscian people, if they demanded it, for it was at the people's order that he had assumed it. As to rendering an account and report of his generalship to the people of Antium, he was ready to do that at once, if they wished it. Accordingly, the people assembled and the popular leaders, who had been prepared for this, rose and tried to excite the masses against him. When, however, Marcius rose to speak, the uproarious mob was awed to silence and gave him a chance to talk fearlessly, while the nobility of Antium and those who were especially happy for the peace, made it plain that they would listen favorably to him and judge him fairly. But Tullus was afraid to have him defend himself, since Marcius was a most brilliant speaker, and his previous services had earned him a gratitude which far outweighed his recent offense. Indeed, the very charge against him was proof of the great gratitude they owed him. For they would not have thought themselves wronged by his failure to take Rome, if he had not brought them so near to taking it.

The conspirators, therefore, thought it best not to wait and not to see what the majority wanted, and the boldest of them shouted that the Volscians should not listen to the traitor, nor permit him to play the tyrant

---

[37] Heraclitus, Fragment 116.

and refuse to lay down his command. With this they fell on him in a body and killed him,[38] and no one attempted to protect him. But the majority of the Volscians were displeased by the act, as they quickly showed by streaming in crowds out of their cities to gather around his body and give it an honorable burial, decorating his tomb with arms and trophies, like that of a prince and a general.

When the Romans heard of Marcius' death they made no expression of either honor or resentment towards him, except that they granted the women's request that they might mourn for him ten months, as was the custom when one of them lost her father, her son, or her brother. This was the period of the longest mourning decreed by Numa Pompilius, as I have related in his *Life*.[39]

The loss of Marcius was felt at once by the Volscian state. First of all, they had a quarrel over supremacy with the Aequians, their friends and allies, and went to the length of bloodshed and slaughter. Next, they were defeated by the Romans in a battle in which Tullus was killed and the finest flower of their army perished. Thereafter they were glad to accept peace on quite dishonorable terms and become subjects of Rome, promising to obey her commands.

---

[38] Dionysius of Halicarnassus says he was stoned to death. *Roman Antiquities*, VIII, 59. The date commonly given for his death is 475 B.C.

[39] See above, *Numa*, ch. 12.

Comparison of Alcibiades
and Coriolanus

1. WITH all the acts of these men now set before us, so far as we regard them worthy of record and remembrance, we can see that their military exploits do not tip the scales much either way. Both alike performed many feats of daring and valor as soldiers, and of skill and acumen as generals, though some might choose to call Alcibiades the more perfect general, because he was continually victorious and successful in many struggles both on land and on sea. Both certainly, when at home and in command, always maintained their country's cause with conspicuous success, and, on the other hand, did it even more conspicuous injury when they went over to the opposite side. As for statesmanship, the unbridled wantonness of Alcibiades, and the taint of lawlessness and buffoonery in all his associations with the people, in order to win their favor, made him detested by the sober citizens. But Marcius' ungraciousness, pride, and oligarchical methods on all occasions made him hated by the people of Rome. For his political methods, neither man can be praised; but one who caters to the people to get himself liked is less to be criticized than one who insults them for fear he should be thought to cater to them. It is base to flatter the people to buy power, yet to make oneself powerful by terror, crime, and oppression is wicked as well as base.

2. We know that Marcius is considered to have been rather simple and straightforward in disposition, while Alcibiades was unscrupulous and dishonest as a politician. The latter is blamed especially for the crafty trick by which he outwitted the Lacedaemonian ambassadors, as Thu-

cydides tells us,[1] and broke the peace. Yet that stroke of policy, though it involved Athens again in war, made her strong and formidable, through the alliance with Argos and Mantinea which Alcibiades procured for her. And Marcius too, Dionysius says,[2] brought on war between the Romans and the Volscians by falsehood, when he circulated fictitious slanders against the Volscians who came to see the festival. And the reason for his action makes it the more reprehensible of the two, for he was not moved by ambition or by political rivalry, as was Alcibiades, but simply yielded to anger, from which, Dion says, no one has ever profited.

And he threw many regions of Italy into confusion, and destroyed many innocent cities in his rage against his country. On the other hand, though Alcibiades too out of anger brought great misfortunes on his countrymen, as soon as he found that the city had relented towards him, he took her part again; and even when he had been banished a second time, he felt no glee at the mistakes of her generals, and could not sit by and see them employing poor tactics and exposing themselves to danger. He did what Aristides is so warmly praised for doing to Themistocles;[3] he went to the men then in command, though they were not his friends, and pointed out to them what they ought to do. But Marcius, to begin with, made the whole of Rome suffer, though not all the people had injured him, for the best and most important citizens had been wronged and aggrieved with him. Then when his countrymen were sending many embassies to entreat him and try to heal his solitary wrath and blindness, he made it plain to them that he was waging a stern and implacable war to wreck and destroy his country, not to be reinstated and return to it.

In this other respect, too, they are said to differ. Alcibiades went back to the Athenian side in fear and hatred of the Spartans because they had begun to plot against him; but Marcius was in every way well treated by the Volscians and acted dishonorably in deserting them. He had been elected their commander and along with his power had enjoyed their full confidence; not like Alcibiades, whom the Spartans abused more than they used, and who drifted around their city and was bandied back and forth in their camps until finally he threw himself into the arms of Tis-

---

[1] Thucydides, *Peloponnesian War*, V, xvi, 43–45.

[2] Dionysius of Halicarnassus, *Roman Antiquities*, VIII, 2.

[3] See above, *Themistocles*, ch. 12.

saphernes—unless, by Zeus, he was courting him just in order to save Athens from complete destruction, and was still hoping to return to her.

3. As for money, we are told that Alcibiades often got it discreditably from bribes, and spent it wrongly on luxury and dissipation; whereas Marcius could not be persuaded to accept what the generals offered him with honor. And this was actually a reason why he seemed so hateful to the people during the disputes over debts, because they said it was not to enrich himself that he was so hard on the poor, but out of sheer arrogance and scorn.

Antipater, writing in a letter about the death of Aristotle the philosopher, observes, "Besides all his other gifts, the man had the art of persuasion." The lack of this art in Marcius made all his achievements and virtues irksome, even to those who benefited from them, for they could not endure his pride and self-will, "the housemate," as Plato says, "of solitude." Alcibiades, on the contrary, knew how to make a friend of everyone he met, so it is no wonder that the fame of his successes brought a flowering out of pleasant good will and honor, and even some of his errors often seemed charming and natural for his age. Hence it was that, after he had done so much terrible damage to his city, he was nevertheless many times appointed her commander and general, whereas Marcius, when he tried for the consulship, which he deserved for his valiant services, failed to obtain it. So the one could not be hated by his countrymen, even when they were suffering from the harm he did them, while the other, even when admired, was never loved.

4. Marcius, in fact, as a general accomplished nothing remarkable for his city, but only for his enemies against his country, whereas Alcibiades frequently served the Athenians well, both as soldier and as commander. Whenever he was in Athens, he managed his enemies as he chose, and their calumnies succeeded only in his absence. But Marcius was in Rome when the Romans condemned him, and with the Volscians when they plotted to kill him. And though his killing was an unjust and unrighteous act, he furnished his enemies with an excuse for it, since after refusing the Romans' public offers of peace, and then yielding to the women's private entreaties, he yet failed to put an end to hostilities and left the two nations still at war, utterly wasting the favorable opportunity that was his.

If he had had a real regard for what he owed the Volscians, who had
trusted him, he would have obtained their consent before withdrawing
from Rome. But if he cared nothing for them and was conducting the war
merely to satisfy his own anger, and his anger was then satisfied, he
should rightly not have spared his country for his mother's sake, but have
spared his country and his mother together, for his mother and wife
were a part of the city he was besieging. But after his rough treatment
of the Roman people's supplications, the pleas of their ambassadors, and
the prayers of their priests, then to retire as a favor to his mother was not
so much an honor to her as a dishonor to his country, which was saved
by the pitiful entreaty of a single woman, as though it did not deserve to
be saved for its own sake. The mercy he showed the Romans was grudg-
ing and harsh, and really no mercy at all, and it pleased neither side. He
withdrew without accepting the reasoning of his foes or giving his own
reasons to his friends. All this was due to his unsocial, haughty, and un-
bending temper, which in itself is odious to the people, and when coupled
with ambition makes a man savage and ruthless. Such men do not court
popularity but profess a disdain of honor, and then are irritated when
they do not get it.

Men like Metellus and Aristides and Epaminondas[4] had no taste for
importuning or courting popular favor, and were genuinely contemptuous of what the people could give or take away, and so were often ostracized, defeated in elections, and condemned in court. Yet they were not
angry with their unappreciative countrymen, but were their friends again
as soon as they changed their minds, and reconciled to them as soon as
they asked for reconciliation. Certainly the man who makes up least to
the people ought to feel least vengeful towards them for what they do;
his anger at not receiving honor is likely to spring from too much ambition
for it.

5. Now Alcibiades made no secret of his delight in being honored and
his vexation at being slighted; in consequence he endeavored to make
himself agreeable and attractive to all comers. But the pride of Marcius
would not permit him to pay court to persons who had the power to

[4] Quintus Metellus, surnamed Numidicus for his conquest of Numidia in North Africa,
in 106 B.C., was banished for a year in 100. On Aristides, see above, *Themistocles*, ch.
11 ff. and on Epaminondas, see above, *Lycurgus*, n. 27.

honor and promote him, while his ambition made him angry and hurt with anyone who overlooked him. The above are the traits one would find blameworthy in him. All others are splendid. For his sobriety and his superiority to riches he deserves to be compared with the best and most upright of the Greeks—not, by Zeus, with Alcibiades, who in these respects was the most ungoverned of men and the most indifferent to rules of honor

Demosthenes

3 8 4 – 3 2 2 B . C .

1.   THE AUTHOR, friend Sosius,[1] of the ode to Alcibiades, at the time
he won the chariot race at Olympia,[2] whether it was Euripides, as common report has it, or some other poet, tells us that the first essential for a
happy man is birth in "a famous city." But for my part, I believe that for
the enjoyment of true happiness, which depends chiefly on a man's character and disposition, it is all the same if one comes of a poor and obscure
country, just as it is if one is born of a small and uncomely mother. It
would be absurd to imagine that Iulis, a tiny spot in the little island of
Ceos, and Aegina, which some Athenian wanted to have removed because it was an eyesore to the Piraeus, can breed good actors and poets,[3]
and yet cannot possibly produce a just and independent man, wise and
great of soul. The arts which men cultivate for the sake of glory or profit
are indeed apt to fall into decay in poor and obscure towns; but virtue,
like a stout and hardy plant, takes root in any place where it finds a
noble nature and a spirit willing to put forth effort. Hence, if we fail to
think and to live as we ought, we cannot in justice blame the smallness
of our native city for it, but ourselves.

2.   However, for one who is engaged in compiling a history from materials which are not ready to hand or to be found at home, but are for the
most part scattered abroad among different owners, it is really most im-

---

[1] This *Life* was dedicated by Plutarch to one of his Roman friends, Sosius.
[2] See above, *Alcibiades,* ch. 11.
[3] The famous poet, Simonides, came from Ceos, and a popular actor, Polus, from
Aegina.

portant to live in some well-known, cultivated, and populous city, where he can have plenty of books of all kinds, and where by listening and asking questions he can learn of many things which escape the recorders, but are preserved with luminous exactitude in the memories of men. He may thus be saved from publishing a work defective in many, even essential, details.

For myself, I live in a small city,[4] and choose to live there to keep it from growing still smaller. And during my stays in Rome and in various parts of Italy, what with my public duties and the instruction of my pupils in philosophy I had no leisure to practice the Latin language. It was therefore late and I was far on in years when I first began the study of Roman literature. And what happened to me then was a surprising thing but true. For it was not so much that through words I arrived at an understanding and knowledge of things, as that from things I had somehow obtained an experience by which to grasp the meaning of words. A full appreciation of the beauty and swiftness of the Roman tongue, its figures of speech, its music, and other adornments, is, I think, a graceful and pleasant accomplishment. But the study and practice which it requires are not easy for any but those who have more leisure and years yet to spend on such ambitious occupations.

3. Wherefore, in this the fifth book of my *Parallel Lives,* which tells of Demosthenes and Cicero, I shall examine their acts and their political principles in order to compare their natures and dispositions, but shall make no close comparison of their speeches, nor decide which of the two was the more winning or the more brilliant orator. "For a dolphin's strength," as Ion remarks, "is powerless on dry ground," a saying which Caecilius, who goes too far in everything, quite forgot when he made his brash comparison of Demosthenes and Cicero. Perhaps, however, if the command, "Know thyself," [5] were an easy thing for us all to obey, we might not take it as the word of the god.

As to Demosthenes and Cicero, it would seem that heaven originally shaped them on the same model, implanting in them many of the same

---

4 Plutarch was a native of Chaeronea, a small town in rural northern Boeotia, famous chiefly for having been the scene of the momentous defeat in 338 B.C. of the Athenian and Theban armies by Philip of Macedon.

5 The famous motto engraved on stone at the temple of Delphi.

qualities, such as ambition and love of freedom in government, but small courage in war and danger, adding also many chance similarities of fortune. I think it would be hard to find another pair of orators who rose from such obscure and small beginnings to such power and greatness, resisted kings and tyrants, lost each a daughter, were banished from their countries and brought back with honor, were forced again to flee, were captured by their enemies, and perished as the liberties of their countrymen came to an end. So that, if it were a question of deciding between nature and fate as the artists who created them, it would be hard to say whether the two men's resemblance was due more to the characters which nature gave them, or to the circumstances in which fate placed them. First, I must speak of the older of the two.

4. Demosthenes, the father of Demosthenes, belonged, Theopompus [6] tells us, to the Noble and the Good [7] class of Athenian citizens. He was commonly called the Cutler, because he had a large workshop and slaves skilled in that craft. As for what the orator Aeschines said about his mother,[8] that she was the daughter of one Gylon, who was banished from the city for treason, and of a barbarian woman, I cannot tell whether he was speaking the truth or only slander and lies. Demosthenes was left by his father an orphan at the age of seven, but well off, since the total value of his property came to almost fifteen talents. But he was wronged by his guardians, who appropriated some of his estate and neglected the rest and robbed even his teachers of their pay. As a consequence, apparently, he grew up untrained in the subjects that are suitable and right for a free-born boy. His poor bodily health and delicacy also kept his mother from allowing him to work hard and his tutors from pressing him. From the first he was a thin and sickly child, and the opprobrious nickname of Batalus was given him, they say, by his mates, who jeered at his physique. For Batalus, some writers tell us, was an effeminate flute-player, who was ridiculed in a comic play written by Antiphanes. Others recall Batalus as a poet who wrote licentious verses and drinking songs. It seems also that one of the unmentionable parts of the body was called

---

[6] Theopompus of Chios, a historian, was a contemporary of Demosthenes.

[7] That is, the well-to-do, conservative class.

[8] Aeschines, *On the Crown*, 152. For Demosthenes' rival, Aeschines (c.390–c.315 B.C.), see later in this *Life*.

batalus by the Athenians of that time. Demosthenes' other nickname, Argas, was given him either because of his temper, which was fierce and hot, for some poets call a snake *argas;* or else because of his way of speaking, which grated on his hearers, for Argas was the name of a poet who wrote bad and unpleasant songs. And so much for that.

5. We are told that he first became interested in oratory through the following incident. Callistratus the orator was about to present an argument in court in the case of Oropus,[9] and the trial was keenly anticipated, both because of the ability of the orator, who was then at the height of his reputation, and also because of the action involved, which was notorious. Demosthenes heard the teachers and tutors making arrangements to attend the trial, and by eager pleading persuaded his own tutor to take him to the hearing. This tutor was a friend of the doorkeepers of the court, and he managed to obtain a place where the boy could sit unseen and hear all that was said. Callistratus won the case and was immensely admired. Demosthenes saw him being escorted home by a great crowd and receiving congratulations, and envied him his glory. He was even more amazed and impressed by the power of his oratory, which seemed able to win over and convert everyone.

Accordingly, he left off studying other subjects and taking part in boyish sports, and laboriously practiced exercises in speaking, with the intention of becoming an orator himself. He studied rhetoric under Isaeus,[10] although Isocrates was giving lessons at the same time. He did this, some say, because as an orphan he was unable to pay the sum of ten minae which was Isocrates' fee, or because he preferred the style of Isaeus for its vigor and general effectiveness in ordinary use. But Hermippus informs us that he once found some anonymous memoirs which contained the statement that Demosthenes was a pupil of Plato, and owed most of all to his training in the art of speaking. He also mentions having heard from Ctesibius that Demosthenes secretly obtained the textbooks of Isocrates

9 Oropus was a town on the frontier between Attica and Boeotia, which in 366 B.C. was seized by Thebes. As a consequence, a trial for treason was held at Athens, but the details are obscure.

10 Isaeus (c.420–350 B.C.) was a lawyer and teacher of rhetoric, noted for his lucidity, and for his knowledge of law. Isocrates (436–338 B.C.) was an orator and head of a school of rhetoric at Athens, but not a legal pleader. His style was more elaborate and polished than that of Isaeus.

and Alcidamas from Callias, the Syracusan, and others, and then learned them by heart.

6.   In any event, when he came of age he began bringing suits against his guardians and composing speeches against them. They contrived many times to evade him and procure new trials, but Demosthenes got practice through these exercises in danger and toil, as Thucydides [11] says, and eventually proved his case, though he was unable to recover a scrap of his inheritance. But he gained considerable confidence and experience as a speaker, and had a taste of the distinction and power which come of such contests and thereafter attempted to step out and take a hand in public affairs. We are told that Laomedon of Orchomenus, on his physicians' advice, used to run long distances as a remedy for a disease of the spleen, and then, after reestablishing his health, entered the great games and became one of their best long distance runners. And so it happened with Demosthenes, who first started to practice oratory in order to recover his personal property, and thereby acquired such skill and power as a speaker that he soon, in public debates as though in the great games, stood first among the citizens who argued on the rostrum.

Yet when he first addressed the people he was noisily interrupted and ridiculed for his inexperience, for they found his speech confused with long sentences and tortured with over-elaborate rhetorical devices. It appears too that his voice was weak, his enunciation indistinct, and a shortness of breath made him pause in his sentences, so that it was difficult to follow the meaning of what he was saying. He finally left the assembly and was wandering despondently about the Piraeus when Eunomus of Thriasia, a very old man, saw him and scolded him because, although he had a manner of speech very much like that of Pericles, out of cowardice and weakness he was being false to himself, not facing the crowd boldly, or training his body to meet the strain of such contests, but letting it grow feebler in idleness.

7.   Another time, they say, when he had failed to hold the people's attention and was going home upset and miserable, Satyrus the actor, a good friend of his, followed and walked along with him. Demosthenes told

---

[11] Speaking of Athenians and Spartans, Thucydides says: "They grew more experienced as they practiced amid dangers." *Peloponnesian War*, I, xviii, 3.

him mournfully that he worked harder than any other speaker and had come closer to exhausting his physical energy in his efforts, and yet the people did not like him and would listen to drunken sots, sailors,[12] and illiterate fellows who took the platform, while he went unnoticed. "That is true, Demosthenes," Satyrus answered, "but I will soon cure your trouble, if you will recite for me offhand some speech from Euripides or Sophocles." Demosthenes repeated one, whereat Satyrus took the same speech after him and so altered it in his delivery, giving it appropriate feeling and character, that it seemed to Demosthenes a different thing altogether. Thus he learned how much any speech gains in style and charm by proper delivery, and realized his labor was of little or no use, so long as he went on paying no attention to his enunciation and his manner of presenting what he said. He then had built for himself an underground study, which was preserved down to our time, and into which he descended every single day to practice declamation and develop his voice. He often spent two or three months at a time there, with half of his head shaved, so that even if he wished to go out, shame would keep him indoors.

8. In addition, he would make his meetings, conversations, and business with persons outside his study the starting point and subject of his speeches. For as soon as they left him, he would return to his study, and go over in order the incidents and the arguments about them. Whatever speeches, too, he happened to hear, he would review by himself and break up into propositions and periods, and insert all kinds of corrections and new modes of expressing either what some other man had said against him, or what he had retorted in answer. All this gave rise to the impression that he was not a man of natural ability, but one who earned his skill and power by hard work. A proof of this idea seemed to be the fact that Demosthenes was seldom heard speaking on the spur of the moment. Though the people frequently called on him by name as he sat in the assembly, he would not come forward unless he happened to have thought over the subject and had prepared to speak.

Many of the popular leaders ridiculed him for this, and Pytheas once scoffingly said that his arguments smelt of lamp wicks. To which De-

12 Possibly a reference to Demosthenes' later antagonist, the orator Demades, who had risen from a common sailor.

mosthenes made the sharp reply, "My lamp, Pytheas, does not see the same things as yours." To others, however, he never denied it, but declared that his speeches were neither all written out nor all unwritten. He also maintained that a democratic man would prepare his speeches carefully, for such preparation showed respect for the people, whereas carelessness as to what the multitudes thought of his speech was a mark of a man with oligarchic leanings, who counted more on force than on persuasion. But that he lacked courage for ex tempore speaking is, they say, shown by the fact that when at times he was rowdily interrupted, Demades [13] often rose and spoke for him offhand, but he never did the same for Demades.

9.   How then, one might ask, was it that Aeschines [14] spoke of Demosthenes as a man of amazing boldness in his speeches? And how was it that when Python of Byzantium [15] was pouring out a flood of rude invective against Athens, Demosthenes alone stood up and answered him? Or how was it that when Lamachus the Myrinaean had written a panegyric on the kings Philip and Alexander, full of abuse of the Thebans and the Olynthians, and was reading it aloud at Olympia,[16] Demosthenes came forward and recounted with historical proofs all the fine services the Thebans and the Chalcidians had performed for Greece, and, on the other hand, all the evils which the toadies to the Macedonians had brought about, and so swayed the audience that the Sophist was frightened by the clamor against him and sneaked away from the festival?

Demosthenes did not apparently think that all the characteristics of Pericles were suited to himself, though he admired and imitated his car-

---

[13] Demades (c.375–319 B.C.) was early convinced that Greece must somehow come to terms with Macedonia and strove to induce Athens to accept what he thought was inevitable. He acted as mediator between Athens and Philip, first, and Athens and Alexander afterward. No fragment of any of his speeches has been kept.

[14] On the Crown, 152.

[15] Python was an envoy sent by Philip to raise difficulties between the Greeks at the Athenian assembly in 343 B.C. See Demosthenes, On the Crown, 136.

[16] These were the Olympic games of 324 B.C. The kings, Philip (382–336 B.C.) and his son Alexander (356–323 B.C.), were, of course, the two great kings of Macedonia who between them made of their country for a short time the strongest power in the Near East and reduced Greece to a subject province. The cities of Thebes in Boeotia and of Olynthus on the peninsula of Chalcidice had both joined with Athens to defy Philip. Olynthus was destroyed by Philip in 348, Thebes by Alexander in 335.

riage and his dignity of manner, and his refusal to speak at a moment's notice on every occasion—as if he had become great by such things. He was not anxious for fame won in a quick crisis, nor did he often by choice risk his power on a chance. However, the impromptu speeches he made had more fire and daring than those he wrote out, if we may trust Eratosthenes, Demetrius of Phalerum, and the comic poets. Eratosthenes tells us that in his speeches Demosthenes was often like a man in a frenzy, and Demetrius says that once, as if inspired, he swore to the people the famous metrical oath:

"By earth, by springs, by rivers, and by floods."

One of the comic poets calls him a "rodomontader" and another makes fun of his bent for antithesis in the verse:

"A. And what he took, he retook.
B. Demosthenes would have been glad to take over those words."

Unless, by Zeus, Antiphanes meant this as a joke on Demosthenes' speech on Halonnesus,[17] in which he advised the Athenians not to take that island from Philip, but to retake it.

10.   Everyone, however, agreed that Demades, when relying on his own natural wit, was invincible, and that speaking on the spur of the moment he would demolish the carefully studied orations of Demosthenes. Ariston of Chios has preserved an opinion, shared too by Theophrastus, of the two orators. When asked how good an orator he thought Demosthenes was, the man replied, "Worthy of the city"; and how good Demades, he said, "Too great for the city." The same philosopher relates that Polyeuctus of Sphettus, one of the Athenian statesmen of the time, used to say that Demosthenes was the best orator, but that Phocion [18] was the most power-

---

[17] This speech, though listed among his works as Oration VII, is now known to have been wrongly attributed to Demosthenes.

[18] Phocion (4th century B.C.), an Athenian statesman and general, though an aristocrat in politics, was highly respected both for his military ability and for his honesty and patriotism. He sided with Demades and Aeschines against Demosthenes in urging Athens to treat for terms with Philip, and later to keep the peace with Alexander and Alexander's successor in Macedonia, Antipater. But with Demades he also advocated a narrowing of the Athenian franchise, and in 318 he was sentenced to death. Plutarch has a *Life of Phocion*.

ful speaker, for he conveyed the most ideas in the fewest words. They say, indeed, that Demosthenes himself, whenever Phocion mounted the platform to answer him, would murmur to his friends, "Here comes the knife to my speech!" It is not clear whether Demosthenes felt that way because of Phocion's oratorical skill, or because of his blameless life and reputation, thinking that one word or nod from a man whom the people trusted had more weight than a multitude of long periods.

11. Demetrius of Phalerum describes the devices by which Demosthenes worked to overcome his physical defects, of which he says he heard from Demosthenes himself in his old age. The indistinctness of his wording and tendency to lisp he corrected by taking pebbles in his mouth and then declaiming orations. His voice he strengthened by talking while running or walking up hill, and by repeating speeches or lines of poetry all in one breath. And he had a large mirror in his house, and used to stand before it practicing his exercises.

They say that a man once came to him and asked him to act as his counsel, reporting at length how someone else had caught and beat him. "But," said Demosthenes, "you have certainly not been hurt as you say." At this, the man raised his voice and shouted, "What, Demosthenes, was I not hurt?" "By Zeus," answered Demosthenes, "now I hear the voice of a man who has really been injured." So important did he think the tone and manner of the speaker were in carrying conviction. His own way of speaking was marvelously pleasing to most people, though fastidious persons, such as Demetrius of Phalerum, thought it low and vulgar and sentimental. Hermippus informs us that Aesion, when asked to compare the ancient orators with those of his own day, said that a listener to the ancient orators would have admired their decorous and stately way of talking to the people, but that the speeches of Demosthenes, as read aloud, seemed much more carefully constructed and more effective.

Needless to say, his written speeches have much in them that is bitter and harsh, but in his impromptu retorts he was often amusing. As, for example, when Demades exclaimed, "Demosthenes teach me! A sow teach Athene!" Demosthenes' reply was, "But this Athene was caught in adultery in Collytus the other day." And when the thief nicknamed the Brazen started to ridicule him for sitting up late and writing at night, Demosthenes answered, "I know that I irritate you with my lamp. But, men of Athens, you should not wonder that thefts are committed, when our thieves are brazen and our walls are clay." I could tell several more anecdotes of this sort, but I shall stop here. Other traits of Demosthenes' character and way of life may be gathered from his acts and public policies.

12. He began to play a part in public affairs during the Phocian War,[19] as he himself says, and as we may gather also from his Philippics. Some of these were delivered after the war was over, but the earliest of them touch on matters closely connected with it. When he made his preparations to speak in his suit against Midias [20] he was thirty-two years old, but evidently had at that time no influence or reputation in politics. His timidity seems to me the chief reason why he made up that quarrel with a person he hated for a sum of money. "For he was no sweet-tempered man nor mild in his nature," [21] but vehement and violent in his reprisals. But he must have seen it would be a difficult task, and one beyond his power, to defeat a man like Midias, so well hedged about with wealth and rhetoric and friends, and therefore he yielded to those who asked him to let the case drop. For I do not believe that the three thousand drachmas by themselves would have blunted Demosthenes' vindictiveness, if he had hoped or had the power to win his suit.

But when he took as a noble purpose for his political career the defense of the Greeks against Philip, and was fighting worthily for that cause, he soon acquired renown, and by his fearless speeches rose to so conspicuous a position that Greece was thrilled by him, and he was courted by the great King of Persia himself. At Philip's court, too, he was more talked about than any other popular leader. Even those who hated him had to admit that their antagonist was a man of distinction, for both Aeschines and Hyperides acknowledged that much even while they denounced him.

---

[19] The Phocian War was fought in 357–346 B.C. It was also called the Sacred War. See below, n. 28. Demosthenes speaks of his activities in his speech *On the Crown*, 18. His celebrated *Philippics* were a series of four scathing attacks on Philip, delivered by him in his endeavors to kindle Athenian courage to the point of resisting the invader by force.

[20] The suit was started about 350 B.C., but Demosthenes' speech against Midias, Oration XXI, was never delivered.

[21] Homer, *Iliad*, XX, 467. The words are there spoken of Achilles.

13. I cannot, therefore, understand how Theopompus came to say that Demosthenes was inconstant by disposition, and could never remain long loyal to the same policies or the same men. For we know that after he had once ranged himself with a certain party and line of action in city politics, he upheld them to the end, and not only never changed his position while he lived, but even sacrificed his life because he would not change. He was not like Demades, who excused himself for his change of sides by saying that he had often spoken against himself but never against the city. Nor was he like Melanopus, who was politically opposed to Callistratus but was often bribed by him, and then would say to the people, "The man is my enemy, but let the good of the city come first!" And Nicodemus the Messenian, who was first on Cassander's side [22] and afterwards joined Demetrius' party, used to insist he was not being inconsistent, for it was always well to listen to the strongest.

Of Demosthenes we can say that he was not one to deviate or swerve from his course in word or in deed but that he followed always, as it were, one unchangeable public policy and sounded one note in all he did. The philosopher Panaetius declares that most of his speeches were written on the principle that the good is the one thing to choose for its own sake. Such were his speech *On the Crown*, the speech *Against Aristocrates*, the speech *For the Immunities*, and the *Philippics*, for in all these he is not inviting his countrymen to adopt the pleasantest or the easiest or the most profitable course, but is again and again declaring they must make safety and security secondary to honor and obligation. So if to his lofty principles and noble speeches he had added the courage of a warrior and hands clean of corruption, he would have deserved to rank, not with such orators as Moerocles, Polyeuctus, and Hyperides, and their companions, but higher, with Cimon, Thucydides, and Pericles.[23]

14. Among his contemporaries, there was Phocion, who though he was leader in a regrettable policy and apparently favored Macedon, still because of his bravery and honesty was considered quite the equal of Ephi-

---

[22] Cassander was the son of Antipater, whom Alexander appointed regent of Macedonia in his absence. After Alexander's death, Cassander made himself master of Athens from 318 to 307 B.C. Demetrius then took possession of the city.

[23] Cimon, Thucydides, and Pericles were all distinguished not only for their exceptional abilities but also for their fortitude and incorruptibility.

altes,[24] Aristides, and Cimon. But Demosthenes, Demetrius says, was not trustworthy in a battle, nor altogether proof against a bribe, for although he was never to be bought by money from Philip and Macedon, he was reached and swept off his feet by the torrent of gold which poured from Susa and Ecbatana. So while he was better able than anyone else to praise the splendid deeds of his ancestors, he was not so strong in imitating them. However, even in his life he behaved better than the other orators of his time, leaving out Phocion.

He evidently used bolder language than anyone else when talking to the people, opposed their wishes, and persistently pointed out their faults, as we may see in his speeches. Even Theopompus [25] says that once when the Athenians elected him to impeach a man, and on his refusal raised a disturbance, he rose and said, "Men of Athens, I will serve you as adviser, even though you dislike it; but not as false accuser, even though you ask it." His method of dealing with Antiphon was markedly aristocratic, for the assembly had acquitted him, but Demosthenes had him arrested and brought before the court of the Areopagus, and regardless of the offense he was giving the people, proved him guilty of having promised Philip to set fire to the docks. So the court turned Antiphon over for punishment and he was executed. Demosthenes also charged the priestess Theoris with various wicked practices, especially with teaching slaves to be deceitful. He had the penalty fixed at death, and so got her also executed.

15. It is said that the speech by which Apollodorus obtained a sentence for debt against the general Timotheus was written for him by Demosthenes; also Apollodorus' speeches against Phormio and Stephanus. But those speeches did not redound to his credit, for Phormio answered Apollodorus with a speech which Demosthenes had written for him. He simply sold to the contestants, as though out of one armorer's shop, daggers to stab each other.

---

[24] Ephialtes (5th century B.C.) was a radical leader of the Athenian democracy, of stainless character, who with the help of the youthful Pericles, in 456 B.C., put through measures stripping the aristocratic court of the Areopagus of much of its authority. He was murdered that same year.

[25] The historian Theopompus had Spartan sympathies and became later a supporter of Alexander. He tends to be very harsh in his judgments of Athens and her democratic leaders. A few fragments of his work remain.

Of his public speeches, those against Androtion, Timocrates, and Aristocrates were written for other persons to deliver, since he had not at that time entered public life, for apparently he composed them at the age of twenty-seven or eight. But the speech against Aristogeiton he spoke himself, as he did the one *On the Immunities,* out of regard, he says, for Ctesippus, son of Chabrias, though some say it was because he was courting the young man's mother. He did not, however, marry her but took a woman of Samos as his wife, as Demetrius of Magnesia tells us in his book *On Synonyms.* Whether his speech against Aeschines for treachery on the embassy [26] was delivered we do not know, but Idomeneus tells us that Aeschines was acquitted by only thirty votes. Yet this seems unlikely, if we are to judge from the speeches of both Demosthenes and Aeschines *On the Crown,* for they neither of them say plainly or distinctly that the earlier case came as far as a trial. This question, however, others will settle better than I.

16. Even during the peace, the policy for which Demosthenes stood was clear, for he allowed no act of the Macedonian to pass uncriticized and seized every opportunity to arouse and inflame the Athenians against him. Consequently there was much talk of him at Philip's court, and when he came with nine others on an embassy to Macedon, Philip listened to them all, but replied to Demosthenes' speech with the greatest care. Yet in the bestowal of other honors and marks of friendliness he did not treat Demosthenes so well as the rest, making his overtures rather to Aeschines and Philocrates. And when these men praised Philip as a powerful speaker, most handsome to behold, and, by Zeus, a most proficient drinking companion, Demosthenes must sneeringly reply that their eulogies were appropriate for a Sophist, for a woman, and for a sponge, but none of them for a king.

---

26 On the first Athenian embassy to Philip, in 348 B.C., Aeschines had gone determined to resist Philip's designs to the utmost, and returned to urge compliance and compromise. In 346, he was again a member of an embassy to Macedonia, which, in spite of Demosthenes' fierce opposition, concluded the so-called Peace of Philocrates or treaty of alliance with Philip. In 343, Demosthenes charged Aeschines with accepting bribes from Philip and acting as his tool in Greek affairs. We have the speeches of both men, *On the Embassy.*

17. When events were moving finally towards war, since Philip could not live in peace, and the Athenians were being stirred up by Demosthenes, the latter first of all prevailed on the Athenians to invade Euboea, which its own tyrants had reduced to bondage to Philip. On Demosthenes' motion, the Athenians crossed over to the island and drove out the Macedonians. Next, he had aid sent to the populations of Byzantium and Perinthus,[27] on whom the Macedonian was making war. He persuaded the Athenians to forget their anger and the sins of each city in the Social War, and to send them reinforcements, which actually saved them. After this he went on an embassy to the other Greeks, and by reasoning with them and spurring them on, he gathered nearly all of them into a league against Philip. So they raised a trained army of fifteen thousand infantry and two thousand cavalry, in addition to the citizen troops, and willingly subscribed money to pay the mercenaries. It was then, Theophrastus says, when the allies were demanding that their contributions should be fixed at a definite sum, that Creobylus, the popular leader, answered, "War does not live on fixed rations."

Greece was now in a state of strained expectation, and its peoples and cities, Euboea, Achaia, Corinth, Megara, Leucas, and Corcyra, were agreeing on a league. But the most important task of all remained for Demosthenes, to induce the Thebans to join the alliance. Their territory bordered on Attica, they had a fighting army, and they were at that time reckoned the best soldiers in Greece. But it was not easy to get them to change sides in view of the favors by which Philip had recently ingratiated himself with them during the Phocian War.[28] Above all, the petty skirmishing occasioned by their nearness to Athens was constantly aggravating afresh the differences between the two cities, which made for war.

---

[27] At the outbreak of the Social War, 357–355 B.C., these allied cities had revolted against Athenian control.

[28] The full story of the Phocian or Sacred War is too complicated to tell here. Suffice it to say that the first steps were taken by Thebes to punish some Phocians who had cultivated a plain adjacent to Delphi, sacred to Apollo. In the lineup of cities that followed, Athens acted as a non-belligerent ally of Phocis. Philip was an interested onlooker, and after some exhausting years of struggle was invited by Thebes to intervene. Eventually Athens joined with Philip, and the defeated Phocians were penalized by the loss of their seats in the all-Greek Amphictyonic Council, which were then, in 346, awarded to Philip.

18. But when Philip, excited by his success at Amphissa,[29] suddenly marched on Elatea [30] and made himself master of Phocis, the Athenians were panic-stricken, and no one dared to mount the rostrum or knew what to say. When all were dumb with bewilderment, Demosthenes came forward alone and advised them to stand by the Thebans. Then, having encouraged and buoyed up the people, as was his custom, he was sent with others as an ambassador to Thebes. Philip, on his side, as Marsyas tells us, sent the Macedonians, Amyntas and Clearchus, the Thessalian Daochus, and Thrasydaeus to Thebes to argue against Athens.

The Thebans, regarding the situation, did not fail to consider their own interests, for each man had before his eyes the terrors of war, and their wounds in the Phocian War were still fresh. But the power of the orator, Theopompus says, awakened their courage and fired their ambition and cast all other considerations into the shade, so that they repudiated fear and cool calculation and partisan favoritism, and were inspired by his words to choose the side of honor. So great and so brilliant was Demosthenes' achievement that Philip at once sent an embassy to ask for peace, while Greece stood erect and ranged itself beside Athens for the future. Not only the Athenian generals, but the Boeotian commanders too served under and took orders from Demosthenes, and he directed at that time all the assemblies of the Thebans as well as those at Athens. He was beloved by both peoples and was supreme in both cities, not unlawfully nor undeservedly, Theopompus declares, but as it was quite fitting he should be.

19. But some fatal destiny in the course of events was, it seems, at that crisis bringing to a close the freedom of the Greeks, counteracting their efforts, and giving many indications of what was to come. Among these last were the dire predictions of the Pythian priestess and an ancient oracle which was cited from the Sibylline Books:

> "Far from the battle on Thermodon may I be,
> Beholding it as an eagle from the clouds and high air.
> The vanquished weeps and the victor has perished."

---

[29] In 339, Philip was deputed by the Amphictyonic Council to punish the city of Amphissa in Locris for sacrilege.

[30] That is, from Amphissa Philip marched northeast to the town of Elatea in Phocis, which commanded several important routes to the east and south. From there he threatened the security both of Thebes and of Athens, barely three days' march away.

Now the Thermodon, they say, is in my country of Chaeronea, a little river which runs into the Cephisus. I know of no river by that name now, though I imagine that the stream we call Haemon may then have been called Thermodon; for it flows past the Heracleum, where the Greeks were encamped, and I judge that after the battle it was filled with blood and corpses and so became known by its present name.[31] According to Douris, however, the Thermodon was not a river at all, but some men who were pitching a tent and digging a trench around it found a small stone image with an inscription saying that it was Thermodon carrying a wounded Amazon in his arms.[32] But on this same topic they repeat another oracle, as follows:

> "For the battle on Thermodon, wait, thou bird of blackness;
> There thou shalt find a plenty of human flesh."

20. What the facts are it is not easy to decide. But Demosthenes, they say, was so tremendously encouraged by the arming of the Greeks, and raised to such a pitch of elation by the strength and ardor of so great a host eager for battle, that he would not allow them to pay any heed to oracles or listen to prophecies. He even hinted that the Pythian priestess was an agent of Philip, and reminded the Thebans of Epaminondas, and the Athenians of Pericles, telling them that those great men regarded tales of that sort as mere pretexts for cowardice, and relied on their reason.

Up to this point Demosthenes was a valiant man, but in the battle itself[33] he did nothing brave or worthy of his speeches. He abandoned his post, threw away his arms, and took to his heels in a most disgraceful manner, not shamed by the motto on his shield, which, Pytheas tells us, was engraved in gold letters, "For good fortune." Immediately after his victory, Philip, in the insolence of his delight, held a drunken revel over the dead bodies, and chanted the opening words of the decree proposed by Demosthenes, dividing it by feet and beating time:[34]

> "Demosthenes Paeanian, son of Demosthenes, so moved."

---

[31] The Greek word for blood was *haema*.

[32] Such a statue would have been a figure of the god of some river Thermodon, quite probably of the river Thermodon in Asia Minor, on whose banks the Amazons were said to have lived.

[33] This was the fateful battle of Chaeronea, 338 B.C.

[34] The Greek words may be read as a line of iambic verse.

But when he grew sober again and realized the gravity of the struggle in which he was involved, he trembled at the skill and power of the orator who had forced him to risk his empire and his life in the short space of a single day. The fame of Demosthenes reached the king of Persia, and he sent letters to his satraps on the seacoast, bidding them offer money to Demosthenes and pay him more attention than any other Greek, since he could distract and hold up the Macedonian by making trouble in Greece.[35] Alexander discovered all this later, for he found at Sardis letters of Demosthenes and papers of the king's generals, revealing the sums of money they had given him.

21. In the interval after this catastrophe to the Greeks, the spokesmen of the party opposed to Demosthenes attacked him and had audits and indictments drawn up against him. But the people not only acquitted him of their charges but continued to treat him with honor and to invite him, as their friend, to participate in affairs of state. So when the bones of those who had fallen at Chaeronea were brought home for burial, they chose him to pronounce the eulogy over them. They bore all their disaster in no mean or ignoble spirit, as Theopompus writes in his dramatic style, and by showing special honor and esteem for their counselor they signified that they did not regret the counsels he had given them. Demosthenes then delivered the funeral oration; but he would not propose a decree in the assembly in his own name, but always in the name of one of his friends, avoiding his name as inauspicious and unlucky, until he again took courage at Philip's death.[36] He was killed only a short time after his victory at Chaeronea, and it was his death, apparently, which was prophesied in the last line of the oracle:

"The vanquished weeps and the victor has perished."

22. Demosthenes had secret information of Philip's death and used it to put heart into the Athenians for the future. He went with a radiant face to the council and declared that he had had a dream which betokened some great good for Athens. And not long after, messengers arrived with the news of Philip's death. At once the Athenians made

---

[35] Philip seemed to the Persians at that time to be threatening an invasion of Asia.

[36] In 336 B.C. Philip was assassinated by Pausanias, one of his bodyguard. See below, *Alexander*, ch. 10.

sacrifices of thanksgiving to the gods and voted a crown to Pausanias. Demosthenes came wearing a gorgeous robe, with a garland on his head, although his daughter had died, Aeschines says,[37] only six days before. Aeschines berates him for this, denouncing him as an unnatural father. But Aeschines himself was both vulgar and sentimental if he made wailings and lamentations the signs of a grieving and loving heart, and saw nothing in bearing sorrows patiently and without complaint.

Yet I would not say that the Athenians behaved well in putting on garlands and offering sacrifices at the death of a king who, in the midst of his victories, had dealt so leniently and humanely with them in their defeat. It was an ignoble thing, meriting the anger of the gods, to honor a man while he lived and make him a citizen of Athens, and then when he fell by a foreigner's hand to abandon themselves to joy, dance, as it were, over his body, and sing paeans of victory, as if they had been the valorous ones themselves. On the other hand, I praise Demosthenes for leaving his domestic afflictions and tears and mourning to the women, and himself doing what he thought was for the city's good.

I consider it a manly and patriotic spirit which looks always towards the welfare of the community and finds support in its personal griefs and cares in the people's service, and thus maintains its dignity far better than those actors who play the parts of kings and tyrants in the theater, and whom we see wailing and laughing, not as their own feelings prompt them but as the subject of the play requires. Besides, it is our duty not to allow an unfortunate man to lie uncheered in sorrow, but to speak comforting words and lead his thoughts to happier things, as people do who tell sufferers with sore eyes to turn them from bright and glaring colors and fix them on what is green and soothing. And how could a man find better consolation, when his country has a piece of good fortune, than by sinking his private distress in the public joy, thus covering evil things over with good. I am led to make these remarks by observing how Aeschines, through this speech of his, has swayed many people to a sentimental kind of pathos.

23. The cities of Greece under Demosthenes' provocation now once more combined in a league. The Thebans attacked their Macedonian garrison and killed many of them, with arms furnished partly by De-

[37] Aeschines, *On the Crown,* 77. See n. 40.

mosthenes, and the Athenians prepared to fight as their allies. In the assembly Demosthenes again ruled supreme. He wrote letters, too, to the king's generals in Asia, urging them to start a war from there on Alexander, whom he dubbed a boy and a Margites.[38] But when Alexander, after settling the affairs of his kingdom, marched with his army into Boeotia, the Athenians' courage collapsed, and Demosthenes himself was silenced. The Thebans, deserted by their allies, fought on by themselves, and lost their city. At this, great confusion prevailed at Athens, and Demosthenes was chosen and sent with others on an embassy to Alexander. But he dreaded Alexander's anger and turned back at Mount Cithaeron, deserting the embassy.

Alexander then sent at once to Athens to demand the surrender of ten of her popular leaders, according to Idomeneus and Douris, though most of the more trustworthy writers say that he asked for only eight: Demosthenes, Polyeuctus, Ephialtes, Lycurgus, Moerocles, Demon, Callisthenes, and Charidemus. It was then that Demosthenes told the people the fable of the sheep who gave up their watch-dogs to the wolves, and compared himself and his friends to dogs fighting for the people, calling Alexander the "great wolf of Macedon." "And just like the grain merchants we see," he went on, "who sell their whole crop by means of a few grains of wheat which they carry around as samples in a bowl, so by letting us go, you unknowingly give up yourselves, too, every one of you." This story is told by Aristobulus of Cassandrea.

But while the Athenians were debating their answer and not knowing what to do, Demades agreed with the leaders whom Alexander was demanding to go, for the sum of five talents, as their deputy to Alexander and intercede for them. He may have been relying on the friendship between himself and Alexander or expecting to find him sated, like a lion gorged with slaughter. And he actually succeeded in persuading the king to let the men go, and made peace with him for the city.

24.   So after Alexander left Greece, Demades and his party were the great men at Athens, and Demosthenes played a humble role. When the Spartan Agis attempted a revolt,[39] Demosthenes again gave him a brief assistance,

---

[38] Margites was the hero of a mock heroic poem, anciently ascribed to Homer.

[39] Agis III, king of Sparta, with help from the Persians, fought the Macedonians from 333 to 330 B.C. He was defeated and killed by Antipater.

but as the Athenians refused to join in the insurrection, he again retired, and Agis was killed and the Lacedaemonians crushed. At this time also the indictment against Ctesiphon in the case of the crown came up for trial.[40] The suit had been started when Chaerondas was archon, a little before the battle of Chaeronea, but the trial took place ten years later, when Aristophon was archon. It became the most celebrated of all public cases, both on account of the renown of the orators and because of the spirited behavior of the jurors, who, though the prosecutors of Demosthenes were then at the peak of their power and catering to Macedonia, would not vote against him, but acquitted him so splendidly that Aeschines did not receive a fifth of the ballots.[41] In consequence, he left the city immediately and spent the rest of his life at Rhodes and in Ionia as a teacher of rhetoric.

25. Shortly afterwards, Harpalus [42] arrived in Athens from Asia, in flight from Alexander, because he knew he had committed crimes out of sheer prodigality and was afraid of the king, who was hard now even on his friends. On his taking refuge with the Athenian people and placing himself, his ships, and his riches in their hands, the other orators immediately cast longing glances at his wealth and set about helping him and trying to persuade the Athenians to receive and protect the suppliant. Demosthenes, however, at first advised them to send Harpalus away and

---

[40] The case of the Crown was one of the most famous trials of history. In 337 B.C., shortly before the battle of Chaeronea, which decided Greek destiny for the time being, Ctesiphon, an admirer of Demosthenes, moved publicly at Athens that a decoration in the form of a crown—a garland of olive interwoven with gold—be bestowed on Demosthenes for his patriotic labors for the state. Aeschines, who had long favored coming to a compromise with the threatening power of Philip and was bent on preventing such a demonstration of approval of Philip's enemy, thereupon brought suit against Ctesiphon on the score of certain technical illegalities. Chaeronea and the events which followed caused the whole matter to be dropped, but seven years later, when Alexander had completed the conquest of Greece, the suit was revived. Aeschines, the prosecutor, made his speech against Ctesiphon the occasion for a scorching attack on Demosthenes' character and career, especially his struggle with Macedon. Demosthenes' answer was a defense of his long fight for Greek liberty and a crushing denunciation of Aeschines' policy of opportunism.

[41] Aeschines' failure to get as much as a fifth of the jurors' ballots made him liable to a fine of a thousand drachmas and loss of the right to bring suit again in an Athenian court.

[42] Harpalus had served as Alexander's treasurer. See below, *Alexander*, ch. 8 and n. 22.

beware of dragging the city into war on wrong and unnecessary grounds. Yet a few days later, when they were making an inventory of Harpalus' property, the man saw that Demosthenes was taken with a cup of barbarian workmanship and was studying its form and the reliefs on it. He therefore bade him weigh it in his hands and note the heft of the gold. And when Demosthenes, surprised at its weight, asked how much it would bring, Harpalus answered smilingly, "For you it will bring twenty talents." Then as soon as it was night, he sent Demosthenes the cup and twenty talents.

For Harpalus was quick to recognize the character of a person with a passion for gold, by the softening of his look and the glances of his eyes. And Demosthenes could not resist but succumbed to the bribe, and having admitted, as it were, the garrison into his fortress, went over entirely to the side of Harpalus. The next day he carefully wound his throat in woolen bandages and went out to the assembly, and when he was called on to rise and speak, made signs that he had lost his voice. The wits, however, mockingly proclaimed that their leader had caught overnight not a plain quinsy, but a silver quinsy. Later the whole populace learned that he had been bribed and would not listen to him when he tried to defend himself and convince them, but angrily shouted him down. Someone then rose and said jestingly, "Men of Athens, will you not listen to the man who holds the cup?" [43] The people thereupon sent Harpalus away from the city and in fear that they might be called to account for the money of which the orators had robbed him, they made a vigorous search for it and went around examining their houses, all but the house of Callicles, son of Arrhenides. His house was the only one they did not allow to be searched, because he was newly married and his bride was indoors. So Theopompus tells us.

26. But Demosthenes put a bold face on the affair and introduced a motion to the effect that the matter should be referred to the council of the Areopagus, and that those whom it found guilty should stand trial. However, he was one of the first whom the council found guilty and who appeared before a court of justice. There he was condemned to pay a fine of fifty talents, and since he could not pay, was sentenced to prison,

---

[43] At a banquet, the wine cup was passed from hand to hand, and at any time the man who held it had the right to speak and be heard.

ashamed now of his misbehavior. But unable to bear the confinement because of his physical weakness, he escaped by duping some of his jailers and getting the help of others. According to the story, he had gone only a short distance from the city when he learned that some of his political opponents were on his track, and tried to hide himself. But shouting his name they caught up with him and asked him to accept funds from them for his journey, telling him they had brought money from home for that purpose and had been pursuing him simply to give it to him. At the same time, they bade him take heart and not be too depressed at what had happened. At this Demosthenes broke down still more and exclaimed: "How can I not be unhappy to leave a city where my enemies are more generous than any friends I am likely to find elsewhere?"

He bore his banishment in a poor spirit, spending most of his time in Aegina and Troezen, gazing towards Attica with tears in his eyes. Sayings of his are recorded that are unfair and inconsistent with his courageous career in Athenian politics. They say that as he was leaving the city he stretched out his hands towards the Acropolis and exclaimed, "O guardian mistress of our city, why dost thou delight in those three most savage beasts, the owl, the snake, and the people?" And when young men came to see him and talk with him, he would try to dissuade them from entering public life, and would say that if two roads had lain before him in the beginning, one to the rostrum and the assembly, and the other straight to destruction, and if he could have foreseen the evils of public life, the fears and jealousies and backbitings and struggles, he would have chosen the road that led directly to death.

27. While he was still in exile, as I have said, Alexander died,[44] and the Greek states leagued together again. Leosthenes,[45] their valiant leader, shut Antipater up in Lamia and besieged him there. Pytheas the orator and Callimedon the Crab fled from Athens and joined Antipater's party, and traveled about Greece in company with his friends and ambassadors,

---

[44] Alexander died in Babylon, in 323 B.C.

[45] Leosthenes was an Athenian general, who even before Alexander's death had secretly made preparations for another anti-Macedonian war. He commanded the Greek army when it laid siege to the town of Lamia, a key point on the road north from central Greece into Thessaly, and shut up Antipater there from 323 to 322 B.C. Leosthenes' death during the siege was a fatal blow to Greek hopes.

trying to keep the other Greeks from revolting and joining the Athenians. But Demosthenes took the part of the ambassadors from Athens and did his best to help them persuade the cities to rise all together against the Macedonians and drive them out of Greece.

In Arcadia, Phylarchus says, a wordy battle took place between Pytheas and Demosthenes in a public meeting, Pytheas speaking for Macedonia and Demosthenes for Greece. The story is that Pytheas said that we are used to presuming that a house has sickness in it when asses' milk is carried into it; so too a city must be in a bad way when an Athenian embassy appears there. But Demosthenes turned his illustration around by saying that asses' milk was brought into a house to cure the sick, and the Athenians came to save them.

The Athenians then were pleased with Demosthenes' conduct and voted his release from exile. The resolution was proposed by Demon of Paeania, a cousin of Demosthenes, and a trireme was sent to Aegina to bring him home. As he came up from the Piraeus to the city, all the citizens met him in a body and greeted him with enthusiasm. Not an archon nor a priest was missing. And Demetrius of Magnesia says that he stretched out his hands to heaven and called himself blessed that day, for he was returning from exile more gloriously than did Alcibiades,[46] since he had persuaded, not compelled, his countrymen to receive him back. The fine imposed on him still remained in force, for it was not permissible to remove a fine by special favor, but they devised a scheme to circumvent the law. It was their custom at a sacrifice to Zeus the Savior to pay a sum of money to those who prepared and decorated the altar. They now appointed Demosthenes to see to all this and supply what was wanted for a payment of fifty talents, the amount of his fine.

28.   But he did not long enjoy his home after his return, for the Greek rising was rapidly crushed. In the month of Metageitnion the battle of Crannon [47] took place, in Boedromion a Macedonian garrison occupied

---

[46] See above, under *Alcibiades*, ch. 32.

[47] The battle at Crannon, in Thessaly, was fought on August 6, 322 B.C. In it, Antipater and Craterus, another of Alexander's generals, smashed the combined forces of the Greek cities. Munychia was a harbor situated immediately to the east of the Piraeus. For the months of Metageitnion and Boedromion see above, *Camillus*, n. 22. Pyanepsion, the fourth month of the Attic year, extended from the middle of our October to the middle of our November.

Munychia, and in Pyanepsion Demosthenes died, as follows. As soon as it became known that Antipater and Craterus were marching on Athens, Demosthenes and his friends stealthily left the city, and the people, on Demades' motion, sentenced them to death. As they scattered in various directions, Antipater sent men around to arrest them, under Archias, whom they called the Exile-hunter. This man, a native of Thurii, is said to have once been a tragic actor. In fact, Polus of Aegina, the finest artist of them all, is reported to have been his pupil. Hermippus puts him among the pupils of the rhetorician Lacritus, while Demetrius tells us that he was a student of Anaximenes. This Archias now tore the orator Hyperides, Aristonicus of Marathon, and Himeraeus, the brother of Demetrius of Phalerum, away from the shrine of Aeacus at Aegina, where they had taken sanctuary, and sent them to Antipater at Cleonae. There they were put to death, and Hyperides, they say, also had his tongue cut out.

29. Hearing then that Demosthenes had gone for shelter to the temple of Poseidon at Calauria,[48] Archias crossed over there with some Thracian spearmen in small boats, and on landing tried to persuade him to leave the temple and go with him to Antipater, promising that he should not be harmed. But Demosthenes happened to have had a strange dream the night before. He dreamed that he was acting in a tragedy, competing with Archias for the prize, and that although he acted well and enchanted the audience, he was beaten by Archias for want of stage properties and means to pay a chorus. So now, after Archias had tried long to cajole him, he simply sat and looked him in the face, and said, "Archias, your acting never convinced me, and no more do your promises now." And when Archias began angrily to threaten him, "Now," said Demosthenes, "you speak like the Macedonian oracle; until now you were acting a part. But wait a moment, while I write a word to my people at home."

So saying, he retired into the temple and took a scroll, as though he were going to write. He then put his pen [49] to his mouth and bit it, as he often did while pondering what to write. He held it there for some

---

48 Calauria was a small island off the coast of Argolis. Poseidon's temple was one of the most inviolable of sanctuaries.

49 The Greek pen was a reed; in the hollow upper part a dose of poison might be hidden.

time, then wrapped himself in his robe and bowed his head. The spear-man standing at the door jeered at him for being a coward, and called him weak and unmanly, and Archias stepped forward and urged him to rise, repeating his previous arguments and promising to make his peace with Antipater. At last Demosthenes, aware that the poison was working and mastering him, uncovered his head and looking straight at Archias, said: "There is a chance for you now to play the part of Creon in the tragedy, and throw this body out without burial.[50] But I, O beloved Poseidon, while still alive, will leave thy shrine, though Antipater and his Mace-donians have not let even thy temple go unprofaned." On this, he bade them support him, for he was already shaking and staggering, and as soon as he came out and had passed the altar, he fell and with a groan breathed his last.

30. As for the poison, Ariston says he got it from his pen, as I have de-scribed. One Pappas, from whom Hermippus borrowed his account, says that after Demosthenes fell beside the altar, they found written in the scroll the opening words of a letter, "Demosthenes to Antipater," though nothing more. But while they all were standing surprised at the sudden-ness of his death, the Thracians at the door said that they saw him take the drug in his hand out of a bit of cloth, and put it in his mouth and swallow it. They themselves imagined that what he had swallowed was gold. A little maid who waited on him told Archias' men, who ques-tioned her, that Demosthenes had for a long time carried the packet as a safeguard. Eratosthenes says that he kept poison in a hollow bracelet which he wore as an ornament. Numerous other persons have written on this subject and it is unnecessary to rehearse all their differences, except to say that Demochares, a relative of Demosthenes, gives as his opinion that Demosthenes did not die of poison but was honored by a providence of the gods, who rescued him from Macedonian cruelty by the grant of a swift and painless death.

He died on the sixteenth of the month Pyanepsion, the most solemn day of the Thesmophoria,[51] which the women spend fasting at the temple

---

[50] In Sophocles' tragedy of *Antigone,* the ruler Creon orders the body of his nephew Polynices left exposed and unburied.

[51] The Thesmophoria was the three-day women's festival, held late in October, to procure the blessing of fertility for the grain about to be sown.

of the goddess. And soon afterwards the people of Athens bestowed on him the honor he deserved by erecting a bronze statue of him [52] and decreeing that the eldest member of his family should have public maintenance in the Prytaneum.[53] On the base of the statue were inscribed the celebrated lines:

"If only thou had hadst strength, Demosthenes, equal to thy understanding,
Never would an Ares from Macedon have ruled over Greeks."

As for those who say that Demosthenes himself composed the couplet in Calauria, as he was on the verge of taking poison, they are talking mere nonsense.

31. A short time before my own first visit to Athens, the following incident is said to have occurred. A soldier, summoned for trial by his commanding officer, put the little gold he possessed into the hands of the statue, which stood with its fingers laced together. Beside it grew a small plane tree and many leaves from this tree were either blown accidentally by the wind over the gold, or else were laid over it by the soldier to hide it, so that they kept the gold concealed for a long while. And when the soldier returned, he found it again. This story went the rounds, and many of the wits took it as an illustration of Demosthenes' incorruptible honesty and rivaled each other with their epigrams.

Demades did not long enjoy the prestige he had won, for the case of Demosthenes took him to Macedonia, where the men he had basely courted justly put him to death. They had detested him even before this, and now an uncontestable charge was brought against him. A letter of his came to light, in which he urged Perdiccas [54] to seize Macedonia and rescue the Greeks, who, he said, were tied to it only by an old and rotten

[52] The statue was erected in 280–279 B.C. The marble figure of Demosthenes in the Vatican is thought to be a copy of that original.

[53] The right to dine regularly in the circular building where the *prytanis,* or committee in charge of preparing business for the council and the assembly, met and ate daily, was an honor bestowed on persons or descendants of persons who had done notable service for Athens.

[54] Perdiccas, a Macedonian noble and general, accompanied Alexander into Asia and on Alexander's death attempted to assume the position of regent of the whole empire. His own Macedonians, however, mutinied and killed him in 321 B.C.

thread (meaning Antipater). Dinarchus of Corinth acted as accuser, and Cassander was so outraged that he stabbed Demades' son at his father's side, and then ordered Demades killed in the same way. Thus Demades learned in terrible calamity the truth of a saying which Demosthenes had often repeated to him and which he had never before believed, that traitors first of all betray themselves.

And so, friend Sosius, you have the life of Demosthenes, according to all that I have read or heard of him.

Cicero

106–43 B.C.

1. CICERO'S mother Helvia came, they say, of a good family and lived accordingly,[1] but everything one hears of his father is an extreme. For some say he was born and brought up in a fuller's workshop, and others trace his ancestry back to Tullus Attius, a distinguished Volscian king who fought hard against the Romans. Certainly the first of the family to be called Cicero must have been a man of note, and for that reason his descendants did not repudiate the name but liked it, though many people thought it ridiculous. For *cicer* is the Latin word for chick pea,[2] and the first Cicero probably had a dent at the end of his nose like the cleft in a chick pea, from which he got his surname. Cicero himself, of whom I am writing, when he first entered public life and tried for office, was advised by his friends to drop the name or change it, but he replied proudly, they say, that he would endeavor to make the name of Cicero more glorious than that of Scaurus or of Catulus.[3] When as quaestor in Sicily he was offering a piece of silver plate to the gods, he had inscribed on it his first two names, Marcus and Tullius, but next to them, in place of a third name, he jestingly told the artisan to engrave a chick pea. These are stories told about his name.

---

1 Plutarch was misinformed; Cicero's mother was a plebeian.
2 The famous family names of Fabius, Lentulus, and Piso were also derived from Latin names for vegetables—bean, lentil, and pea. The founders of these families were probably simply farmers.
3 The Scauri and Catuli were aristocratic families whose members had attained honors in literature or in public service.

2.   He was born, they say, without travail or suffering to his mother, on
the third day of the new Calends,[4] the day on which the magistrates now
offer up prayers and sacrifices for the emperor. It seems too that an apparition appeared to his nurse and predicted that the child she was nursing would be a great blessing to all Romans. These omens were dubbed
mere dreams and nonsense, but as soon as he reached school age, Cicero
proved them to be true prophecy. For then his natural ability shone out
and he got a great name and reputation among his fellows, so that their
fathers used to visit the schools to have a sight of Cicero and witness the
quickness and intelligence in learning which their sons talked about. The
cruder among them would be angry with their own sons, when they
saw them on their walks giving Cicero the central place as a sign of
honor.

He showed a capacity for enjoying all kinds of learning and for ap-
preciating every kind of literature and discipline, as Plato says [5] a natural
lover of knowledge and wisdom does, but he had a rather special propensity for poetry. There is a little poem in tetrameter verse now extant,
which he wrote as a boy, called Pontius Glaucus. And as he grew older
and with increasing versatility courted the Muse of poetic art, he acquired
the reputation of being not only the best orator but also the best poet
among the Romans. His fame as an orator has lasted to the present day,
even though there have been great innovations in the style of speech-
making. But since many poets of genius have risen since his time, his
poetry has sunk altogether into obscurity and neglect.

3.   After finishing his youthful studies, he attended the lectures of Philon [6]
of the Academy, whom, of all of the disciples of Clitomachus, the Romans
most admired for his eloquence and loved for his disposition. At the
same time, through his friendship with Mucius Scaevola, a statesman and

---

[4] January 3. Strictly speaking, only the first day of a month was the Calends, but here
the several opening days of a new year are called the "new Calends."

[5] Plato, *Republic,* V, 475.

[6] Philon of Larissa in Thessaly (c.160–80 B.C.) was a Greek philosopher, who, when
war broke out in Greece in 88 B.C., fled to Rome and settled as a teacher of philosophy
there. He taught a form of more or less sweeping Skepticism. Cicero studied also under
an Epicurean and under a Stoic. His own ethical code later was that of a Stoic, but
in philosophy he kept the skeptical attitude he had learned from Philon.

leader of the senate, Cicero got some knowledge of the law. For a time too he served under Sulla in the Marsian War.[7] But seeing that events were leading to civil war, and from civil war to despotism,[8] he retired to a life of quiet and contemplation, keeping company with learned Greeks and devoting himself to study until Sulla got the mastery and the government appeared somewhat stabilized.

At that time, Chrysogonus, a freedman of Sulla, reported an estate which he said had belonged to a man put to death during the proscriptions, and then bought it himself for two thousand drachmas.[9] Roscius, son and heir of the dead man, in indignation produced evidence to show that the property was worth two hundred and fifty talents. Sulla, angry at having the transaction questioned, with assistance from Chrysogonus then had Roscius tried for murdering his father. No one would help Roscius, and everyone avoided him in dread of Sulla's vengeance. Being thus forsaken, the young man sought out Cicero, and Cicero's friends urged him to take the case, telling him he would never again have a more splendid or honorable opportunity to win a reputation. Accordingly, he undertook the defense of Roscius and won the case and great admiration thereby. But he was afraid of Sulla and went off to Greece, giving out that he needed treatment for his health. Actually he was a very thin man, afflicted with a stomach weakness, so that he ate only a little light food late in the day. His voice was full and powerful but harsh and unmodulated, and in the vehemence and heat of his oratory it constantly rose to so high a pitch that it made people alarmed for his health.

---

7 The Marsi, a people of central Italy, had been loyal to Rome through the Carthaginian wars, but afterward led the Socii, or Italian allies, in an uprising against Rome, 90–88 B.C., the object of which was to obtain the rights of Roman citizenship. This conflict, known as the Marsian or Social War, was ended when Sulla granted the demand for citizenship. Cicero's service in the war was under the young commander, Pompey.

8 The events referred to here were, of course, the struggle between Lucius Sulla, the rising leader of the aristocratic party, and Gaius Marius, the veteran soldier and head of the popular movement in the army and the state. In 87 B.C. Marius seized Rome and massacred many of his opponents; he died the following year, whereupon Sulla marched into Rome, reversed Marius' popular legislation, tightened the power of the senate over the government, and issued the first "proscription," or public list of enemies declared outlaws, outside the protection of the state.

9 Plutarch here makes a slip, counting his Roman money in denarii instead of in sestertii. The sum Chrysogonus paid was only five hundred Greek drachmas.

4. On his arrival at Athens he attended the lectures of Antiochus of Ascalon [10] and was fascinated by his fluency and grace of speech, though he disliked his innovations in doctrine. For Antiochus had already seceded from the so-called New Academy and deserted the sect of Carneades, whether influenced by the plain evidence of his senses, or, as some say, by an ambition to differ from the disciples of Clitomachus and Philon, which led him to change and adopt the Stoic position on many points. But Cicero was devoted to the doctrines of Philon and became all the more attached to them, and was planning, if he were excluded altogether from public life, to move to Athens and live out his life away from the forum and politics, in the tranquil study of philosophy.

But by the time the news came that Sulla was dead,[11] his body had been strengthened by exercise and grown more vigorous, his voice had become modulated and pleasant to hear and controlled to accord with his physical condition; and his friends at Rome were writing long letters begging him to return. Antiochus too was urging him strongly to take up a public career. So he began again to prepare to use oratory as his instrument and revive his gift for politics, practicing exercises by himself and going as pupil to famous rhetoricians. Thus he went to Asia and to Rhodes. In Asia he studied under the orators Xenocles of Adramyttium, Dionysius of Magnesia, and Menippus of Caria; in Rhodes, under the orator Apollonius, son of Molon, and the philosopher Posidonius. Apollonius, they say, did not understand the Roman tongue and asked Cicero to do his exercises in Greek, to which Cicero readily agreed, thinking that in this way his faults would be better corrected. When he spoke his exercise, his other hearers were amazed and vied with each other in complimenting him. But Apollonius listened and expressed no approbation, and when Cicero had finished, sat a long time in thought. Then as Cicero showed his disappointment, he said, "Indeed, Cicero, I do compliment and admire you, but Greece I pity for her fate, seeing that the only glories that were left us—learning and eloquence—even these are now through you passing to the Romans."

---

10 Antiochus of Ascalon (c.125–c.68 B.C.), who had been a pupil of Philon, later led a movement away from his teachings. His system was an eclectic one, with features from Aristotelianism and Stoicism. Cicero often alludes to him.
11 Sulla died suddenly in 78 B.C.

5. However, as Cicero, full of hopeful expectations, turned again towards a political career, his ardor was dampened by an oracle. For on consulting the god at Delphi as to how he might win the most fame, the Pythia told him to make his own nature, not the judgment of the crowd, his guide in life. So at first he lived discreetly at Rome,[12] and was slow about standing for public office. Consequently he was slighted, and called a "Greek" and a "scholar," epithets readily and familiarly applied by the vulgar classes at Rome. But he was naturally ambitious and was urged on by his father and his friends, and when once he undertook the profession of an advocate he advanced rapidly to the top, acquiring immediately a reputation for brilliance and far outshining his competitors in the forum.

Still he too, they say, no less than Demosthenes, was poor in his delivery; so he studied closely the methods of Roscius the comedian and, again, of Aesopus the tragedian. This Aesopus, the story goes, was once playing in a theater the part of Atreus planning how to avenge himself on Thyestes,[13] when one of the attendants suddenly ran past him, and carried away by his passion he struck the man with his scepter and killed him. Much of Cicero's power of persuasion came, in time, from his delivery. He used to ridicule orators given to loud shouting, saying that they depended on yelling because they were weak, like lame men who climb on horses. His humor and quickness to joke were considered clever and well adapted to courts of law, though by over-use of such things he offended many persons and got the reputation of being spiteful.

6. He was elected quaestor [14] at a time of food scarcity, and had Sicily assigned to him as his province. At first he irritated the people there by compelling them to send their grain to Rome. But later, when they had proof of his carefulness and justice and clemency, they respected him as they had never respected any other governor. When a number of young Romans of good repute and noble birth were accused of lack of discipline

---

12 In 77 B.C. Cicero returned to Rome, at the age of twenty-nine.
13 Atreus and Thyestes, in Greek mythology, were brothers who fought each other for possession of the kingdom of their father Pelops. Thyestes seized it, but was ousted by Atreus, who then in revenge invited Thyestes to a banquet at which he was given the flesh of his own murdered sons to eat.
14 He was quaestor for the year 75 B.C.

and misconduct in war and sent up for trial to the praetor of Sicily, Cicero pleaded for them admirably and got them acquitted. Highly elated at all this, he was on his way back to Rome, as he tells us,[15] when a ludicrous thing happened to him. In Campania he met a prominent man whom he considered his friend, and asked him what the Romans were saying and thinking about his achievements, supposing the city would be full of his name and the fame of his works. But the man said, "Why, where have you been all this time, Cicero?" For the moment he was completely disheartened, feeling that the report of what he had done had sunk into the city as into a bottomless sea, without making any perceptible addition to his renown. Afterwards he reasoned with himself and set much narrower limits to his ambition, realizing that the fame he was striving for was an indefinite thing, with no precise goal. However, an extreme pleasure in the praise of other men and a too passionate yearning for fame stayed with him through all his life, and often interfered with his correcter judgment.

7. As he was now beginning to engage more actively in public life, he thought it a shame that while artisans, who use lifeless implements and tools, know the name and place and strength of each one, a statesman, who carries on the work of the state by means of other men, should be uninterested and careless about knowing his fellow citizens. Accordingly, he not only trained himself to remember persons' names but learned the district where every man of note lived, where his country place was, who his friends and neighbors were. On whatever road he was traveling in Italy, he could readily name and point out the lands and abodes of his friends.

He himself had only a small property, though sufficient for his expenses, and men were surprised that he accepted neither pay nor gifts for his services as an advocate, particularly when he undertook the case against Verres. This man [16] had been praetor of Sicily and was being prosecuted

---

[15] See Cicero, *In Defense of Plancius*, 26.

[16] The case of the notorious Verres, who used his office openly to terrorize and plunder the Sicilians, was a scandal even in a Rome accustomed to senatorial maltreatment of the provinces. Cicero brought eyewitnesses from Sicily to Rome to testify, and built up such an overwhelming case that Verres gave up all notion of defending himself and went into exile at Marseilles. It was essential to get the verdict against him by the last day of the year 70 B.C., for the new praetor, or chief judge, who would assume office on

by the Sicilians for many flagrant crimes in office. Cicero brought about his conviction, not by speaking, but, in a way, by not speaking. For the praetors who favored Verres, by numberless obstructions and delays, had put off the case to the last day of the year, for it was obvious that the space of a day would not give sufficient time for the advocates' speeches and so the trial would be unfinished. But Cicero rose and said that the speeches were not necessary. He then brought forward his witnesses, took their evidence, and bade the jurors cast their votes.

Yet many lively remarks of his at this trial have been preserved. The Romans call a castrated pig a *verres*. So when a freedman named Caecilius, suspected of an inclination towards Judaism, would have brushed aside the Sicilians and himself undertaken to prosecute Verres, Cicero said: "What has a Jew to do with a pig?" Verres had a young son who was supposed to have fallen into low habits. Hence, when Verres reproached Cicero with voluptuous living, "You would better," said Cicero, "reproach your sons at home." The orator Hortensius did not venture to defend Verres directly but was induced to speak for him when the fine was being assessed, in payment for which service he received an ivory sphinx. When Cicero made some indirect reference to him, Hortensius remarked that he had no skill in solving riddles. "And yet," said Cicero, "you have the sphinx at your house!"

8. Verres being thus convicted, Cicero set his fine at seven hundred and fifty thousand denarii,[17] and then was accused of having taken a bribe to keep the fine low. However, the Sicilians were grateful, and during his aedileship they came up to Rome bringing quantities of livestock and provisions from their island. He made no profit from this himself but used their generosity to reduce the market price of food.

He owned an attractive villa at Arpinum, a farm near Naples, and another near Pompeii; none of them were large. He had also the dowry of his wife Terentia, a hundred thousand denarii, and he received a legacy

---

January 1, belonged to Verres' party, and the lawyer, Hortensius, who was speaking for Verres, would become consul. Cicero had so much evidence that he composed seven speeches *Against Verres,* only two of which he delivered. See Classics Club's *Selected Works of Cicero,* pp. 13 ff.

[17] Plutarch makes the same error here as above. See n. 9. The fine was one hundred and eighty-eight thousand.

which came to ninety thousand. On these he lived in a liberal but modest style, with the Greek and Roman scholars who were his friends. He rarely if ever dined before sunset, not so much because he was busy but because his stomach made him delicate. He was precise and careful too in other matters concerned with the care of his body and took a set number of walks and rubbings. By thus regulating his physical habits, he kept himself free from illness and equal to facing heavy strains and labors.

His father's house he gave up to his brother, and lived himself near the Palatine Hill, so that those who paid their respects to him might not have the trouble of walking far. And people came daily to his doors to pay him respect, quite as many as came to Crassus [18] because of his wealth, or to Pompey because of his authority over the soldiers. Those two were then the greatest Romans and the most admired. Even Pompey courted Cicero, and Cicero's political policy contributed greatly to Pompey's power and fame.

9. There were many influential competitors with him for the praetorship, but he was appointed first of all [19] and got the name of handling his cases with integrity and skill. They say that once when Licinius Macer,[20] a man of considerable influence of his own in the city, who had Crassus' support as well, was being tried before Cicero for fraud, he was so sure of his own power and of the efforts of his friends for him that while the jurors were still voting, he went home, hurriedly clipped his hair, and put on a fresh toga, as if he had been acquitted. He was setting out again for the forum when Crassus met him at his door and told him he had been unanimously convicted. Whereat he turned back, lay down on his bed, and died. His case gave Cicero a name for strict conduct of the court. Another time, Vatinius, a rude man and insolent to the magistrates before whom he argued, was standing before Cicero to make some request.

---

[18] Marcus Crassus (c.112–53 B.C.) and Gnaeus Pompey (106–48 B.C.) had both won glory as military commanders under Sulla. Crassus was the wealthier of the two, having amassed a fortune in Roman real estate. He was now jealous of Pompey's success in the Near East. Plutarch has lives of both Crassus and Pompey.

[19] There were eight praetors at this time, the one who received the most votes being appointed city praetor or chief judge. Cicero became praetor in 66 B.C.

[20] As a tribune in the year 73 B.C. Licinius Macer had stood for the protection of popular rights, but after serving as praetor in 68 or 67, he was convicted in Cicero's court of extortion. He is said to have committed suicide.

He had a neck covered with swellings. Cicero did not grant his request forthwith but considered it a long while, whereat Vatinius said that he himself would not hesitate if he were the praetor. Cicero turned and said, "But I have not your kind of neck." [21]

Two or three days before the expiration of his term of office Manilius [22] was brought before Cicero on a charge of fraud in his accounts. This Manilius had the good will and warm support of the people, for they thought he was being prosecuted because of Pompey, whose friend he was. So when he asked for several days to present his defense and Cicero gave him only the following day, the people were indignant, since the praetors were accustomed to allow the defendants ten days at least. The tribunes brought Cicero down to the rostrum and denounced him. But he asked to be heard and said that he had always treated accused persons, as far as the laws permitted, with consideration and kindness, and had thought it would be very wrong not to do the same for Manilius. But there was only one day left in which he would have authority as praetor; so he had purposely fixed that day for the trial, for to put it off to another man's praetorship was not what one would do who wished to be of help. These words made a wonderful change in the people's attitude. With hearty approval they begged him to undertake the defense of Manilius. Cicero readily assented, principally for the sake of Pompey, who was absent. He returned to the speaker's stand and harangued the assembly in bold terms, assailing the oligarchical faction and those who were jealous of Pompey.

10. Yet Cicero was elected consul by the aristocrats as much as by the people, both parties supporting him for the good of the city. The reason was as follows. The changes which Sulla had made in the constitution had at first seemed preposterous, but now by time and use they had come to seem to most people a not unsatisfactory arrangement. Yet there were

---

[21] A thick neck was sometimes considered a sign of low character.

[22] Manilius as tribune had conferred on Pompey the supreme command of the war in Asia Minor, and at the end of his tribunate was prosecuted by Pompey's enemy, Piso, on a charge of corruption in office. Cicero hoped to get the case tried while he still held the office of praetor, but shortness of time compelled its postponement. When it came up in January, 65 B.C., he agreed to act as Manilius' advocate, but the suit was soon afterward dropped.

some who were out to make trouble and get things changed again for their own profit, not for the public interest, while Pompey was still fighting the kings of Pontus and Armenia and there was no power in Rome able to resist the innovators. They had as their leader a bold and resourceful visionary, one Lucius Catiline,[23] who, among his other great crimes, had once been accused of violating his virgin daughter and of killing his own brother. Fearing prosecution for the latter crime, he had persuaded Sulla to put his brother's name, as though he were still alive, on the list of those who were sentenced to death by proscription. This man the desperadoes now chose as their captain. They gave various pledges to one another, among which they sacrificed a man and tasted his flesh. And Catiline corrupted a large number of the city's youth by constantly providing them all with entertainments, feasts, and harlots, himself paying lavishly for these debauches.

Etruria too was all roused to revolt, and the greater part of Cisalpine Gaul. And Rome was most dangerously exposed to a threat of change because of the inequality in the distribution of property. The men of highest reputation and character had beggared themselves on shows, banquets, expenses of office, and houses. So the wealth had flowed into the hands of lowborn and vulgar men, and it needed but a slight push to upset everything. Any reckless fellow might overthrow the government, which itself was in a diseased condition.

11. Catiline, however, wished first to procure a strong base for his operations, and therefore ran for the consulship. He had bright hopes of being

---

[23] Lucius Catiline had been one of Sulla's lieutenants. Now he represented the jobless, discontented, returned soldiers, for whom the government had made no adequate provision. He attempted to get himself elected consul for the year 63 B.C. but was defeated by Cicero, though both Crassus and the rising young Julius Caesar favored his candidacy as against Cicero, who stood for the more conservative, law-abiding elements in the senatorial party. He then proposed a measure for the abolition of debts and other radical reforms, and when it failed, along with his effort to win the election for consul in 62, he organized an armed conspiracy and uprising of landless veterans and proletariat to take over the government. Neither Crassus nor Caesar seems to have been involved in the later phase of the conspiracy. Plutarch's account is based largely on Cicero's exaggerated denunciations of Catiline. Neither he nor Cicero mentions the real and deep social grievances which underlay the movement.

elected with Gaius Antonius as his colleague,[24] a man who by himself would not take the lead either for good or for bad, but would add strength to another who was a leader. Realizing the situation, most of the good and honest citizens backed Cicero for the consulship, and the people willingly accepted him. Catiline was defeated, and Cicero and Gaius Antonius were elected. Yet Cicero was the only one of the candidates who was the son of a knight [25] and not of a senator.

12. The designs of Catiline still remained unknown to most people, but serious preliminary troubles broke out as soon as Cicero became consul. In the first place, those who were excluded from holding office by the laws of Sulla, and they were neither weak nor few in number, applied for appointments and worked for popular favor. They made many accusations against Sulla's tyranny which were true and just, but nevertheless harassing to the government at this inconvenient time. In the second place, the tribunes proposed measures looking towards a similar end, by which they would set up a board of ten men with autocratic power, to whom would be committed the rulership of all Italy, the whole of Syria and all Pompey's new conquests, the right to sell the public lands, to try whomever they chose, to banish into exile, to maintain as many soldiers as they wanted. Many men of prominence favored this law, in particular Antonius, Cicero's fellow consul, who expected to be one of the ten. It looked too as if he knew of Catiline's conspiracy, and in view of his heavy debts was not opposed to it, an idea most alarming to the aristocracy.

Cicero first tried to assuage this alarm by having the province of Macedonia voted to Antonius, though he himself refused an offer of Gaul. By this favor he so won over Antonius that, like a hired actor, he was willing to play second to Cicero in saving the country. Having thus secured Antonius and made him tractable, Cicero was emboldened to resist the revolutionaries openly. Accordingly he attacked their measure in the senate and so frightened its proponents that they had nothing to say in its

[24] Gaius Antonius, uncle of Mark Antony, was a dubious character who had also seen service under Sulla. In 70 B.C. he had been expelled from the senate for robbery committed on the allies of Rome. At the close of his consulship with Cicero, he went to Macedonia as governor, and in 59 was convicted of extortion there.

[25] The knights at Rome formed at this time a second rank of nobility, with some of the rights and privileges of the senatorial class. They acted often as rivals or even as enemies of the senate.

defense. When they made a second attempt, and after much preparation summoned the consuls to appear before the assembly, Cicero was not the least dismayed, but bidding the senate follow him, led the way, and not only got that law rejected but forced the tribunes to drop their other proposed measures, so subdued were they by his eloquence.

13. For this man more than anyone showed the Romans what grace eloquence lends to goodness, and how invincible justice is when fairly expressed in words, and how always a prudent statesman must not only in his action choose what is right instead of what is flattering but by his speech remove the sting from what is sound policy. An illustration of his charm as a speaker is an incident which occurred during his consulship in connection with the public spectacles. In former times men of the knights' class had mingled with the crowd in the theaters and watched the show along with the people, as chance offered, but Marcus Otho, when he was praetor, had separated the knights, as a mark of honor, from the rest of the citizens and assigned them a particular place at the spectacles, which they still retain.[26] The people regarded this move as an insult to themselves, and when Otho appeared in the theater, they hissed him spitefully, while the knights hailed him with vigorous applause. The people then hissed louder, and the knights did the same with their clapping. Later on, they turned to shouting abuse at one another, and the theater was in an uproar. When Cicero heard of it, he came and summoned the people to the temple of Bellona, where he reproved and admonished them. They then returned to the theater and applauded Otho loudly and rivaled the knights in showing him honor and respect.

14. But Catiline and his conspirators, who at first had been awed and frightened, soon began to take heart again. They met together and urged one another audaciously to start their project before Pompey's return, for he was said to be now on his way home with his army. The old soldiers who had served under Sulla were Catiline's chief inciters to action. They were distributed all over Italy, but the greatest number and the most aggressive of them were scattered through the cities of Etruria, where they were dreaming again of plunder and of seizure of the wealth that lay close around them. They had as their leader one Manlius, who had

---

[26] The law gave the knights the fourteen rows of seats next to those of the senators.

served with distinction under Sulla, and they now joined forces with Catiline and came to Rome to vote in the consular election. For Catiline was again running for the consulship and had a plan to assassinate Cicero during the excitement of the election.

The very heavens seemed to forecast what was coming by earthquakes, thunderbolts, and strange apparitions. There was evidence too from human testimony, which was correct but not sufficient for the conviction of a man of Catiline's eminence and power. Accordingly Cicero put off the day for the election, summoned Catiline into the senate, and questioned him as to the rumors that were going on about him. Catiline, supposing there were many in the senate who wanted a change and at the same time showing himself off to the other conspirators, gave Cicero a crazy answer. "What crime," he said, "am I committing, if, when I see two bodies, one thin and wasted but with a head, the other headless but big and stalwart, I constitute myself a head for that one?" This riddling allusion to the senate and the people alarmed Cicero still more. He put on his breastplate, and all the influential citizens and many of the young men formed an escort for him from his house to the Campus Martius. Here he intentionally displayed a piece of his breastplate, letting his tunic slip off his shoulders, and thus indicated to the onlookers the peril he was in. The people in indignation gathered around him, and eventually by their votes rejected Catiline again and elected Silenus and Murena consuls.

15. But soon after this, the conspirators in Etruria gathered to support Catiline and formed themselves into companies. The day fixed for their uprising was approaching when, at midnight, the most powerful of the leading citizens of Rome, Marcus Crassus, Marcus Marcellus, and Scipio Metellus, came to Cicero's house, knocked at the door, and calling the porter ordered him to wake Cicero and tell him they were there. Their story was as follows. Crassus' porter, after dinner, had brought him some letters which an unknown man had delivered to him. They were addressed to various persons; one, without a signature was for Crassus himself. This one only Crassus had read, and it informed him that through Catiline much blood was about to be shed and advised him quickly to leave the city. The other letters he had not opened but had come straight to Cicero, appalled at the danger and also to clear himself of any charge there was against him on the score of his past friendship with Catiline.

Upon deliberation, Cicero called a meeting of the senate at daybreak, and bringing the letters with him he handed them to the persons to whom they had been addressed and commanded them to read them aloud. They all alike spoke of a plot, and Quintus Arrius, a man of praetorian rank, reported the companies which were being formed in Etruria. News came too of Manlius hovering about the cities there, with a large force, expecting momentarily some word from Rome. The senate thereupon decreed to put the whole situation in the hands of the consuls. They were to accept their duty and contrive as best they knew how to save the city. The senate does not customarily take this action, but only when it is in dread of some grave danger.

16. On receiving this authority Cicero entrusted everything outside Rome to Quintus Metellus and himself took the city in hand. He went forth daily, escorted by so large a bodyguard that when he entered the forum his guard filled up much of the space. Thereat Catiline, impatient of further delay, resolved to escape to the army of Manlius. He also commissioned Marcius and Cethegus to take their swords and go to Cicero's door in the early morning, on pretense of paying him their respects, and fall on him and kill him. But Fulvia, [27] a woman of rank, came to Cicero at night and reported the plot to him and warned him to be on guard against Cethegus and his band. The men came at daybreak, and were not permitted to enter. At this they clamored angrily at the door, and so made themselves more suspect.

But Cicero, going forth, called the senate to meet in the temple of Jupiter Stesius,[28] whom the Romans call Stator, which stands at the head of the Sacred Way as you go up to the Palatine. Catiline came there too with the rest to speak in his own defense, but none of the senators would sit beside him. Everyone moved away from his bench and when he began to speak there was a commotion. Finally Cicero rose and ordered him to leave the city. His own government, he said, was one of words, but Catiline's of arms, and there must be a wall between them. Thereupon Catiline immediately left the city with three hundred armed men, sur-

---

[27] Fulvia was the mistress of Gaius Curio, who was implicated in some of the mysterious plotting of the time.

[28] The Greek *Stesius* has the same meaning as the Latin *Stator*, that is, Establisher.

rounding himself with fasces and axes as though he were a magistrate, and, standards upraised, marched to join Manlius. About twenty thousand men in all had now been collected, and he made a round of the cities, trying to persuade them all to revolt. The war had now become open, and Antonius was sent out to fight them.

17. Those of Catiline's minions who had been left behind in Rome were assembled and encouraged by Lentulus Sura, a man of distinguished lineage, who had led a dissipated life and had once been expelled from the senate for debauchery. He was holding the office of praetor for the second time, as men usually do when they are trying to regain the dignity of senator. His surname, Sura, he is said to have got in the following way. As a quaestor in Sulla's time, he had lost and squandered a great quantity of the public money and Sulla had indignantly demanded an account from him in the senate. Lentulus had come forward wearing a very cool and scornful air, and said he had no account to give but would offer his leg, as boys used to do at ball-playing, when they missed a throw. Thereafter he was called Sura, *sura* being the Roman word for leg.

Another time, when a suit was brought against him, he bribed some of the jurors and was acquitted by just two votes. But he complained that what he had given to the second juror was a waste, for one vote would have been enough to acquit him. This was the type of man who had been inflamed by Catiline and further demoralized by the fortune-tellers and sorcerers who had held out false hopes and repeated fictitious oracles, taken, they said, from the Sibylline Books, to the effect that three of the name of Cornelius had been destined to be monarchs of Rome. Two of them had already fulfilled their destiny, Cinna and Sulla, and divinity was now come to the third and last Cornelius, bearing the gift of monarchy, which he ought certainly to accept and not spoil his opportunities by delay, as Catiline had done.

18. So Lentulus hatched a scheme neither small nor trivial. His plan was to kill all the senators and as many other citizens as they could, and burn down the city, sparing nobody but Pompey's children. These they would seize, and hold as hostages for making peace with Pompey. For by now widespread and reliable reports were going about that he was on his way back from his great campaigns. A night was fixed for the rising, one of

the Saturnalia.[29] Swords, tow, and brimstone had been brought and
hidden in Cethegus' house, and a hundred men were appointed and assigned by lot to the same number of sections of Rome, one to each. With
so many setting off fires the city might burst into flames everywhere in a
moment. Others were to stop up the aqueducts and cut down whoever
tried to get water.

But while all this was going on, it happened that two ambassadors from
the Allobroges, a nation which was then in a very unhappy situation and
restive under Roman rule, were staying at Rome. These men Lentulus
and his followers thought would be helpful in rousing Gaul to revolt,
and consequently they admitted them into the conspiracy. They gave them
letters, too, to their own senate and letters to Catiline, promising the
senate liberty and urging Catiline to set free the slaves and march on
Rome. They sent a man, Titus of Croton, to go with them to Catiline
and carry the letters. But the conspirators were unsteady men, who met
each other for the most part over wine and in the company of women,
and Cicero was diligently keeping track of their plans with sober judgment and exceptional intelligence. He had many men outside the conspiracy who spied on what was being done and aided him to keep watch
of it; and many too who were ostensibly members of the conspiracy but
with whom he held stealthy and confidential conferences. He thus learned
of the negotiations with the men from Gaul, and laying an ambuscade at
night, he caught Titus of Croton and the letters, with the secret connivance
of the Allobroges.

19.   Then at daybreak Cicero convened the senate at the temple of Concord, read the letters aloud and examined his informers. Silanus Junius
reported that Cethegus had been heard to say that three consuls and four
praetors were marked for murder. Piso, a man of consular rank, had other
similar tales to tell. Caius Sulpicius, one of the praetors, was dispatched
to Cethegus' house, and found there a quantity of missiles and other
weapons, in particular, a great quantity of swords and sabers, all freshly

---

[29] The Saturnalia was an ancient Roman festival in honor of Saturnus, the mythical
father of Jupiter, Juno, Neptune, and Pluto. In Cicero's time the rites were celebrated
on December 19. Later, in Plutarch's day, the festival lasted for several days. It was
marked by riotous gaiety, and since slaves were given exceptional freedom, it would
be difficult to suppress disorder.

sharpened. The senate voted to pardon the man from Croton on condition he told all he knew. So finally Lentulus was convicted and resigned
his office of praetor, taking off in the senate house his purple-edged robe
and putting on a garment suitable to his situation. He and his companions
were then turned over to the praetors to be kept in custody, but not in
chains.[30]

It was now evening and crowds of people were waiting around the
temple when Cicero came out and announced to his fellow citizens what
had happened. He was then escorted to the house of a neighboring friend,
for his own house was occupied by the women who were celebrating the
mysteries of the goddess the Romans call Bona Dea, and the Greeks call
Gynaeceia. A sacrifice is performed to her every year in the consul's house
by his wife or his mother in the presence of the Vestal Virgins.

On arrival at his friend's house Cicero debated with himself and a very
few companions what he should do with the prisoners, for he was reluctant to inflict the extreme penalty which such shocking crimes demanded.
He hesitated both because of the gentleness of his own disposition, and
because he thought he might seem to be over-straining his authority and
crushing too mercilessly men of the noblest birth, with powerful friends
in the city. Yet if he treated them more leniently, he was afraid of the
danger they might create, for if they received any punishment milder
than death, he believed they would not be placated but would break out
again in more daring attempts, with fresh fury added to their previous
villainy, while he himself, who did not now stand very high for courage
with the masses, would be thought feeble and cowardly.

20. While Cicero was pondering over this dilemma, a sign came to the
women who were sacrificing. After the fire on the altar seemed to have
gone out, there shot up from the ashes and charred pieces of bark a high
and brilliant flame. The other women were frightened by it, but the
sacred virgins bade Cicero's wife, Terentia, go quickly to her husband and
tell him to perform what he had been contemplating for his country's
sake, since the goddess was sending him a great light to guide him to
safety and glory. Terentia was in general not a meek woman nor timid
by nature, but ambitious and, as Cicero himself says, more interested in

---

[30] The term meant confinement in their own houses, under guard.

sharing with him his political problems than in confiding to him her domestic worries. She now delivered the message, and tried to incite him to act against the conspirators. So also did Quintus his brother, and Publius Nigidius, one of his comrades in philosophy, whose advice he often took seriously in affairs of state.

On the following day the senate discussed the punishment of the conspirators. Silanus, who was first asked his opinion, said they ought to be taken to prison and there suffer the extreme penalty. All who followed agreed with him, until it came the turn of Gaius Caesar [31] who later became dictator. Caesar was then a young man and at the outset of his rise to fame, but already in his policy and his hopes he had entered on that course by which he transformed the Roman state into a monarchy. Of his aims other men saw nothing, but to Cicero he had given many grounds for suspicion, though nothing to lay hold of for a trial. There were men, however, who said audibly that he had come near to being caught, though he had so far escaped. Others were saying that Cicero had purposely overlooked and ignored the information given him against Caesar, for fear of his friends and his influence. For it was evident to everyone that if Caesar were accused, the other conspirators would be more likely to be acquitted with him than he to be punished with them.

21.   When, then, it came Caesar's turn in the senate to state his opinion, he rose and declared that he was against putting the conspirators to death, but proposed that their property be confiscated and they be removed to whatever cities of Italy Cicero selected, and kept there under guard and in chains until Catiline was defeated. Caesar's proposal was moderate, and as a speaker he was extremely able. Cicero himself added considerable weight to what he said, for when he rose to speak, he argued the question from both standpoints, speaking now in favor of the first suggestion and now of Caesar's. All Cicero's friends thought that Caesar's proposal would be better for Cicero, since he would come in for less criticism if he did not have the men killed. So they advocated the second sentence. Silanus himself changed his mind and begged to say that he had not

---

[31] Gaius Julius Caesar had served as a soldier in Asia, held offices in Spain and Rome, and had allied himself with Crassus against the increasing power of Pompey, showing sympathy with the popular party.

meant a death sentence, since "the extreme penalty" for a Roman senator was imprisonment.

The first man to speak against Caesar's proposal was Lutatius Catulus.[32] Cato [33] followed him, and with his vehement speech contrived to turn suspicion against Caesar, so that the senate, again full of indignation, voted to have the men executed. But Caesar now opposed confiscation of their property, thinking it unfair to reject the humane part of his proposal and adopt the severest part. When many insisted on it, he appealed to the tribunes, but they would not listen to him. However, Cicero himself gave way and remitted the part of the sentence that imposed confiscation.

22. He then went with the senate to get the conspirators. They were not all in the same place, but one praetor had one in custody and another another. Cicero first took Lentulus from the Palatine and led him along the Sacred Way and through the middle of the forum, with men of the highest rank in a body around him as guards. The people, shuddering at what was taking place, passed him in silence, especially the young men, as though they felt they were being initiated in fear and trembling into some ancient mysteries of aristocratic rule. Thus traversing the forum, Cicero arrived at the prison and delivered Lentulus to the executioner with orders to put him to death. He next took Cethegus and the rest in turn, conducted them to the prison, and had them executed. He then saw that there were still many of the conspirators collected in the forum, who did not know what had been done and were waiting for the night, supposing their leaders were still alive and might possibly be rescued. So he shouted to them in a loud voice, "They were alive!" That is the way in which Romans, who do not wish to use words of bad omen, signify that someone has died.

It was now evening, and Cicero went back through the forum to his house, with the citizens accompanying him, no longer in silence or in proper order, but all whom he met greeting him with shouts and clapping of hands, and calling him "savior" and "establisher of his country."

[32] Lutatius Catulus, a man of great integrity, was the head of the conservative party in the senate and one of those who felt that Caesar was dangerous.

[33] Marcus Cato the Younger, great grandson of Cato the Censor, was at this time a young but prominent member of the conservative aristocracy, already conspicuous for his Stoic rectitude. See below, *Cato the Younger*, chs. 22–23.

Everywhere lights shone in the streets, for the people set lamps and torches
at their doors and the women placed lights on the house roofs as marks
of honor; so too that they might see him coming back to his home in great
state, with his escort of the highest nobility. Among them were many
who had fought through heavy wars and driven into the city in triumph
and who had won for Rome vast stretches of land and sea. Now they
walked along admitting to one another that though the Roman people
were indebted to many a commander and general for their wealth, their
booty and their power, they owed their security and safety to Cicero
alone, who had preserved them from so special and terrible a danger. To
prevent crimes and punish the criminals did not seem so wonderful, but
to suppress the most serious of all revolutions with but slight disturbance
and no tumult or civil conflict was an extraordinary feat. For most of
those who had flocked to Catiline, as soon as they heard the fate of Lentulus and Cethegus, deserted him and left. Catiline, with the troops who
stayed by him, fought it out with Antonius, and was killed himself and
his army annihilated.

23.   However, there were some who were prepared to blame and make
trouble for Cicero for doing what he did, and they had for their leaders
some of the magistrates of the coming year—Caesar as praetor, and Metellus and Bestia as tribunes. The latter took office while Cicero had still a
few days as consul,[34] and they would not allow him to address the people,
but set up their benches before the rostrum and did not permit him to
speak. They said, if he wished, he might just take the oath of retirement
from office.[35] But when he had got silence, he swore instead of the traditional oath a new one of his own, to the effect that he had truly saved his
country and secured her supremacy. And all the people swore to the truth
of his oath.

At this Caesar and the tribunes were much irritated and schemed to
create more difficulties for him. They proposed a resolution calling Pompey home with his army, that he might put an end to Cicero's authority.
But Cato, who was then a tribune, was a great aid to Cicero and to the

---

[34] Consuls and praetors took office on January 1, but the tribunes began their terms a
month earlier.
[35] The consuls took two oaths, one on entering office and the other on retiring. In the
latter they swore that they had done nothing unlawful during their year of service.

whole city, for his power was equal to that of the other tribunes and his reputation was greater, and he opposed their measures. In fact, he easily defeated their other projects and in a speech to the people lauded Cicero's consulship so highly that they voted him the greatest honors ever bestowed, and called him the "father of his country." Apparently Cicero was the first to bear this title, Cato having bestowed it on him in the assembly.[36]

24.   Cicero was now the most powerful man in the state. Yet he made himself generally disliked not by doing anything wrong but by perpetually praising and glorifying himself, to many people's annoyance. For neither senate, nor assembly, nor court could meet without having to hear his interminable talk of Catiline and Lentulus. He even filled his books and writings with praises of himself and made his oratory, which had been delightful and full of charm, distasteful and tiresome to his hearers, for this unpleasant habit clung to him like a disease. Nevertheless, greedy as he was for fame for himself, he was free of envy of other men and most liberal in his praises of his predecessors and contemporaries, as we may observe in his writings.

Many of these sayings of his are remembered. Speaking of Aristotle, for instance, he called him a river of flowing gold, and of Plato's dialogues he said that if it were Jupiter's nature to use human speech, his language would be like theirs. Theophrastus he called his own special treasure. And when he was asked which of Demosthenes' orations he thought the finest, he answered, "The longest." Yet some who profess to be followers of Demosthenes make much of an expression Cicero used in a letter to one of his friends, to the effect that in some passages in his speeches Demosthenes nodded. They overlook the extraordinary words of praise with which he often referred to Demosthenes and the fact that the title he chose for his own speeches on which he worked the hardest, that is, the speeches against Antony, was the *Philippics*.[37]

As for his contemporaries who were celebrated for eloquence or learning, not one did he fail to make more celebrated by writing or speaking

---

[36] Cicero says that it was Quintus Catulus who gave him the title in the senate. *Against Piso*, III, 6.

[37] The word Philippics came from Demosthenes' famous invectives against Philip of Macedon, whose rising power threatened the liberties of the Greeks.

favorably of him. For Cratippus the Peripatetic he got the Roman citizenship from Caesar, who was then in power, and he prevailed on the Council of the Areopagus to pass a motion requesting him to stay in Athens as an instructor of the young and an ornament to the city. There are letters, too, extant from Cicero to Herodes, and others to his son, urging them to study philosophy under Cratippus. But Gorgias, the rhetorician, he blamed for leading his boy into frivolity and drinking, and forbade him his company. That letter and one to Pelops the Byzantine are about the only two of Cicero's Greek letters which were written in temper. He was justified in upbraiding Gorgias, if he was as unscrupulous and intemperate as he was said to be; but to Pelops he wrote in a petty complaining tone, charging him with having neglected to procure for him certain honors to be voted by the Byzantines.

25. These things were a part of his love of fame, as was also the fact that in his exhibitions of cleverness as a speaker he was often led on to forget propriety. He once acted as advocate for Munatius, who immediately on being acquitted brought suit against Sabinus, a friend of Cicero, whereat Cicero was so infuriated that he exclaimed, "Was it on your own merits, Munatius, that you were acquitted, and not because I plunged the court into deep darkness where it had been light?" He was once applauded for eulogizing Marcus Crassus from the rostrum, and then, a few days later, he publicly berated him. When Crassus said to him, "Were you not praising me the other day on that same spot?" Cicero replied, "Yes, for the sake of practice, exercising my eloquence on a poor subject." Another time Crassus remarked that no Crassus at Rome had ever lived beyond the age of sixty. Later he denied that, and said, "Whatever was the matter with me to say such a thing?" "You knew," said Cicero, "that the Romans would be pleased to hear it; so you were making yourself popular." And when Crassus once expressed his approval of the Stoics for their doctrine that the good man is a rich man, Cicero said, "Do you mean their saying that all things belong to the wise?" For Crassus was charged with being avaricious. One of Crassus' sons was thought to look so much like a man named Axius as to implicate his mother in a scandal with Axius. He once made a successful speech in the senate, and on being asked what he thought of it, Cicero said in Greek, "*Axios Krassou.*" [38]

---

[38] This is one of Cicero's ill-natured puns. The Greek words mean "worthy of Crassus."

26. When Crassus was preparing to start for Syria, he was anxious to leave Cicero behind him as a friend instead of as an enemy. So he said to him in a pleasant way that he would like to take dinner with him, and Cicero cordially received him at his house. But a few days later some of Cicero's friends were interceding with him for Vatinius, who had been his enemy but who, they said, was suing for reconciliation and friendship. "Surely," said Cicero, "Vatinius too does not want to take dinner with me!" Such was his attitude to Crassus. Vatinius had swellings on his neck, and once when he was arguing a case, Cicero called him a "tumid orator." Again, he heard that Vatinius was dead and soon after was reliably informed that he was alive. "I hope the wretch perishes," he said, "who lied so wretchedly."

When Caesar put through a measure for dividing the land in the Campania among his soldiers, many of the senators were displeased, and Lucius Gellius, one of the oldest of them, declared that the division should never take place while he lived. "Let us wait," said Cicero. "Gellius is not asking for a long delay." There was a man named Octavius, reported to have come from Libya, who at some trial remarked that he could not hear Cicero. "And yet," retorted Cicero, "your ear is pierced!" [39] Metellus Nepos declared that Cicero had destroyed more persons by testifying against them than he had saved by defending them. "Yes," said Cicero, "I admit that I am more honest than eloquent." A young man who had been accused of giving his father poison in a cake was talking impudently of how he was going to insult Cicero. "I would rather take that from you," said Cicero, "than a cake." Publius Sextius engaged Cicero, with some others, as his advocate in a lawsuit, but then wanted to do all the talking himself and permit no one else to say a word. When it was plain that the jurors would acquit him and they were already casting their votes, Cicero remarked, "Make the most of your chance today, Sextius, for tomorrow you will be nobody."

Publius Consta, a dull and ignorant fellow, wished to be a lawyer. He was called once by Cicero as a witness in a trial, but kept repeating that he knew nothing. "Perhaps," said Cicero, "you imagine you are being asked about a point of law." Metellus Nepos, during a dispute with

---

[39] Pierced ears were one mark of a slave.

Cicero, asked again and again, "Who is your father?" "For you," said Cicero, "your mother has made it rather hard to answer such a question." Nepos' mother had the reputation of being a loose woman, and he himself was a changeable sort of man. On one occasion he abruptly abandoned his post as tribune, sailed off to join Pompey in Syria, and then came back home for still less reason. He buried his teacher Philagrus with great ceremony, and set a stone raven on his tomb. "In this instance," said Cicero, "you have acted more sensibly than usual; for he taught you how to fly rather than how to speak." Marcus Appius at a trial prefaced his speech by saying that his friend had asked him to be careful, eloquent, and honest. "In that case," rejoined Cicero, "are you such a man of iron as not to be any of the things your friend requested you to be?"

27. Now the use of savage taunts against enemies or opponents at law seems characteristic of orators. But this lashing out at anybody for the sake of getting a laugh aroused a great deal of hatred against Cicero. I will give a few examples. Marcus Aquinius, who had two sons-in-law in exile, Cicero used to call Adrastus.[40] Lucius Cotta, a great lover of wine, was censor when Cicero was candidate for the consulship. Cicero was feeling thirsty and his friends were standing around him while he drank. "You are right," he said, "to fear that the censor may be hard on me for drinking water." And once, when he met Voconius with his three very ugly daughters, he called out:

"It was against Phoebus' command that he begat children." [41]

Marcus Gellius, reported to be the son of slaves, once read some letters to the senate in a loud, clear voice. "Do not be surprised," said Cicero. "He too is one of the criers." [42] And when Faustus Sulla, son of Sulla, the Roman dictator, who by his placards had condemned many a citizen to death, got into debt, dissipated much of his property, and placarded the rest for sale, Cicero remarked that he liked his placards better than his father's.

---

40 Adrastus, a legendary king of Argos, married his two daughters to two exiles, Polynices and Tydeus, and thus started a train of wars and bloodshed.

41 A line from some lost play, possibly Euripides' *Oedipus*.

42 A slave who was procuring his freedom, by one form of Roman procedure, entered a fictitious claim or "cry" for his liberty.

28. This habit of his made Cicero dreaded by many people. Clodius' party conspired against him too, for the following reason. Clodius was a man of noble birth, young, bold, and wayward in disposition. He was in love with Pompeia, Caesar's wife, and made his way into his house secretly, wearing the dress and attire of a lute player.[43] The women were celebrating in Caesar's house that mysterious rite which men must not see, and not a man was present. Clodius, still beardless, hoped to slip through the women to Pompeia without being discovered. But it was night when he got in, and the house being large, he lost himself in the corridors. A waiting maid belonging to Caesar's mother, Aurelia, saw him wandering about and inquired his name. Forced to speak, he said he was looking for a servant of Pompeia, named Abra. The maid realizing that it was not a woman's voice, cried out and summoned the women, and they closed the doors and searched everywhere. Thus they found Clodius, who had fled for refuge to the room of the girl with whom he had entered the house. The incident was much talked about, and Caesar divorced Pompeia and had an indictment for sacrilege filed against Clodius.

29. Now Cicero had been a friend of Clodius and during the Catiline affair had found him a most zealous supporter and bodyguard. But in answer to this indictment Clodius asserted that he had not even been in Rome at the time but had been staying in a place very remote. And Cicero testified against him that he had come to his house and talked with him about several matters, which was the truth. However, Cicero, it seems, was not testifying for the truth's sake but as a way of protecting himself against his own wife, Terentia. For she detested Clodius on account of his sister Clodia, whom she suspected of a design to marry Cicero and of working to bring it about with the aid of one Tullus, an intimate friend of Cicero's. Tullus' frequent visits to Clodia, whose house was nearby, and his services to her excited Terentia's suspicions. A hot-tempered woman, she dominated Cicero and insisted now on his taking part in the proceedings against Clodius and giving testimony against him.

Many other men of high standing appeared as witnesses against Clodius on grounds of perjury, lawlessness, bribing the masses, and seducing

---

[43] For more about this episode, see below, *Caesar,* chs. 9–10. See also Cicero's speech, *In Defense of Caelius,* in Classics Club's *Selected Works of Cicero,* pp. 157 ff.

women. Lucullus [44] even produced maids to testify that Clodius had debauched his youngest sister while she was living with Lucullus as his wife.
There was also a widespread report that he had done the same to his
other two sisters, Tertia, wife of Marcius Rex, and Clodia, wife of Metellus
Celer. The latter was called Quadrantia, because one of her lovers had put
copper coins in a purse and sent them to her instead of silver, and the smallest copper coin was called a quadrant. The reports about Clodius with
regard to this sister were the worst.

However, the people at this time ranged themselves against those who
were unitedly testifying against Clodius. The jurors were intimidated and
kept a guard around to protect them, and most of them turned in their
ballots with the writing on them illegible.[45] But it seemed that those for
acquittal were in the majority. Some bribery too was said to have been
employed. So when Catulus met the jurors, he said to them, "You really
were right when you asked for a guard to protect you and were frightened
that someone would steal your money." And when Clodius said to Cicero
that as a witness the jurors had not believed him, Cicero replied, "Ah, but
twenty-five of them believed me, for that many voted against you; and
thirty did not believe you, for they did not acquit you until they had got
your money." Caesar, however, when called upon, would not testify
against Clodius and denied that he was convinced of his wife's adultery.
He had divorced her, he said, because Caesar's wife must not only be above
disgraceful misconduct but also above suspicion.

30.   Clodius then escaped this peril and soon was elected tribune [46] and
at once began an attack on Cicero, collecting and stirring up every thing
and every man against him. He secured the people's favor by generous

44 Lucius Lucullus was another of the generals who learned the art of war under Sulla.
From 74 to 66 B.C. he had been in command of the war in Asia Minor. By his just
and able administration of conquered territories, however, he earned the enmity of men
in Rome who were making huge fortunes out of plundering the provinces. Pompey
was appointed to supersede him, and he returned to Rome, bitterly disillusioned, to
spend the rest of his life as a master of the art of fine living.
45 Plutarch seems to have misunderstood his source here. The jurors did not write on
their ballots. Each man, at the opening of a trial, was given three ballots, one marked
with an A, for "absolve," the second with a C for "condemn," the third with an NL
for "non-proven" (non licet). At the end each juror dropped into an urn the ballot
which expressed his verdict.
46 Clodius was tribune for the year 58 B.C.

laws, got large provinces assigned to each of the consuls—Macedonia to Piso and Syria to Gabinius. He gave many of the poorer citizens places in the government and kept armed slaves around him. Of the three men who were then the most powerful,[47] Crassus was openly Cicero's enemy, Pompey was coquetting with both Clodius and Cicero, and Caesar was on the point of departing with his army for Gaul. To him Cicero now paid court, though Caesar was not his friend but had been an object of his suspicions ever since the Catiline affair. However, Cicero asked to go with him as a legate on his campaign, and Caesar agreed. But when Clodius saw that Cicero was escaping from his tribune's authority, he pretended to want a reconciliation with him. By laying most of the blame on Terentia and always speaking courteously of Cicero, using kindly expressions about him, like a man who harbored no hatred or ill-will, but had merely reasonable and friendly criticism to make of him, he quite removed all Cicero's fears. Accordingly he declined Caesar's offer of a legateship and again immersed himself in city politics.

At this Caesar was annoyed and threw his support to Clodius and completely estranged Pompey from Cicero. He also testified in the assembly that he thought it wrong and unlawful that men should be put to death without a trial, as Lentulus and Cethegus and their gang had been. For this accusation was now brought against Cicero and he was summoned to make an answer. So being under a dangerous indictment, he changed his dress and with disheveled hair went about as a suppliant of the people. But everywhere in the streets Clodius would meet him with an escort of haughty and insolent companions, who jeered freely and insultingly at his change of dress and pelted him with mud and stones, thus interrupting his words of entreaty.

31. At once, however, nearly the whole body of knights also changed their attire, and no less than twenty thousand young men went around after Cicero with hair untrimmed and joined in his pleas. Then the senate met to pass a decree that the people should change their clothes as in a time of public mourning. But the consuls opposed it, and Clodius surrounded the senate house with armed men, and not a few senators ran out crying and tearing their cloaks. But the sight of them aroused neither compassion

---

47 The First Triumvirate, or temporary working alliance of Pompey, Crassus, and Caesar, had been formed in 60 B.C.

nor sense of shame, and Cicero had either to go into banishment or settle his case with Clodius by force and the sword.

He appealed to Pompey to help him, but Pompey had purposely gone away and was staying at his villa in the Alban Hills. As his first step, Cicero sent his son-in-law Piso [48] up there to plead for him, and then went up himself. Pompey, who had heard of his coming, could not bring himself to see him, for he felt a deep shame, remembering the great battles Cicero had fought on his behalf and the many political efforts he had made to please him. For Pompey was now Caesar's son-in-law,[49] and at his request he threw over his old obligations, stole out by another door, and fled from the meeting. Thus deserted by him and abandoned, Cicero turned for refuge to the consuls. Gabinius was harsh with him, as always, but Piso spoke more kindly, advising him to withdraw and retire before Clodius' attack and wait for a change of seasons, and then appear once more as a savior of his country, now so racked with commotions and calamities because of Clodius.

On receiving this response, Cicero consulted with his friends. Lucullus advised him to stay, saying he would be sure to win in the end, but others thought he should go into exile. The people, they said, would soon want him back again, when they grew tired of Clodius' mad folly. And this was Cicero's own judgment. So he carried to the Capitol the statue of Minerva which he had had standing for a long time in his house and for which he felt a special reverence, and dedicated it there with the inscription, "To Minerva, guardian of Rome." Then, with an escort provided by his friends, about midnight he quietly left the city and made his way on foot through Lucania, hoping to reach Sicily.

32. When it was known that he had departed, Clodius put through a vote of banishment against him, and issued an order that no man should give him fire or water or furnish him shelter within five hundred miles of Italy. Most people paid no attention to this order, for they revered Cicero and sent him on his way with every show of friendliness. But at Hipponium, a city of Lucania,[50] now called Vibo, one Vibius, a Sicilian

---

[48] This Piso was, of course, not the consul Lucius Piso, Caesar's father-in-law, mentioned earlier and again immediately below.

[49] Pompey had married Caesar's daughter Julia in 59 B.C., as one more token of their alliance.   [50] The city was in Bruttium, not Lucania.

who had profited a great deal from Cicero's friendship and in particular had been appointed prefect of engineers during Cicero's consulship, refused to receive him in his house, but sent word that he would put his name down for a stay at his country villa. And Gaius Vergilius, praetor of Sicily, who had been one of the closest to Cicero, wrote him to keep away from Sicily. Depressed by this treatment, he made for Brundisium, and from there with a favoring breeze tried to cross to Dyrrachium.[51] But he met a head wind and the next day put back to shore, and thence made a fresh start. On reaching Dyrrachium, they say, as he was about to step ashore, there was an earthquake and a great surge of the sea, which diviners said meant his exile would not last long, for they were signs of change.

But though many men visited him out of good will, and the cities of Greece vied with each other in sending him delegations, still he remained very disconsolate and despondent, gazing off towards Italy like an unhappy lover. And in his mind he grew small and miserable under his misfortune, and pettier than one would have expected a man to be who had devoted his life to such noble studies. He often asked his friends not to call him an orator but a philosopher, for philosophy, he said, he had chosen as his occupation, but oratory he had employed simply as an instrument for gaining his objects in public life. But popular talk has great power to wash reason out of the soul, as if it were merely a dye, and in everyday intercourse it impresses the emotions of the crowd on a man in public life, unless he is strictly on his guard, when taking part in external things, to involve himself only in the things themselves and not in the passions they arouse.

33. Clodius, after driving out Cicero, burned down Cicero's villas and his city house, and on its site built a temple to Liberty. The rest of Cicero's property he put up for sale and had it offered daily, but no one would buy any of it. By his measures he made himself a terror to the aristocracy; the people he carried along with him in an orgy of wanton recklessness. He turned next on Pompey, some of whose arrangements during his campaign he denounced savagely. This ignominy made Pompey reproach himself for having deserted Cicero. He now reversed his attitude, and made every effort along with Cicero's friends to bring about his recall.

---

51 Dyrrachium, is modern Durazzo, on the Adriatic.

Clodius opposed it, but the senate resolved to ratify nothing for the time being and to transact no public business until Cicero was allowed to return. Under Lentulus' consulship [52] the rioting increased until tribunes were wounded in the forum, and Quintus, Cicero's brother, lay unnoticed as dead among the corpses.

The people then began to experience a change of opinion. First, one of the tribunes, Annius Milo, ventured to bring Clodius before a court for violence. Many, too, from the populace and from the neighboring cities sided with Pompey, and in their company Pompey came forward, drove Clodius from the forum, and called the citizens to vote. Never, they say, did the people vote any measure with such unanimity. The senate too, vying with the people, wrote letters of thanks to all the cities which had been helpful to Cicero in his exile, and ordered rebuilt at public expense his city house and the country villas which Clodius had destroyed. In the sixteenth month after his exile Cicero came back, and so joyful were the cities and so eager were men to meet him that what he afterwards said about it was less than the truth. He said that Italy lifted him on her shoulders and carried him into Rome. Even Crassus, who was his enemy before his exile, met him then with cordiality and was reconciled to him, to please, he said, his son Publius, who was an admirer of Cicero.

34. Not much later, after waiting for Clodius to be away from the city, Cicero went with a great crowd up to the Capitol and pulled down and smashed the tribunes' tablets which contained the records of Clodius' administration. When Clodius charged him with this, Cicero declared that it was illegal for Clodius, a patrician, to become a tribune, [53] and hence none of his acts were valid. Cato, however, took offense at this action and protested, not expressing any approval of Clodius, for he condemned his political methods, but explaining that it was an irregular and violent act of the senate to vote the annulment of so many measures and decrees, among which were those for Cato's own administration in Cyprus and Byzantium. His attitude led to a breach between himself and Cicero which, though it came to no open enmity, weakened their friendship.

---

[52] Lentulus was consul for the year 57 B.C.

[53] To get around the law that the office of tribune was reserved for plebeians, Clodius had had himself adopted into a plebeian family before standing for election.

35. Later, Clodius was murdered by Milo,[54] who, on being prosecuted for the murder, got Cicero to be his advocate. But the senate was afraid that the trial would create a disturbance in the city, since Milo was a man of standing and bold spirit. Accordingly it entrusted to Pompey the supervision of this and other trials, and the maintenance of security in the city and the courts of law. So in the night Pompey surrounded the forum with soldiers stationed on the heights, whereat Milo, fearing that Cicero would be upset at the unusual sight and argue his case less effectively, persuaded him to be carried early in his litter to the forum and to wait there until the jurors met and the courthouse was full.

For Cicero, it seems, was not only timid in the use of weapons but nervous at the beginning of a speech, and at many trials had barely ceased shaking and trembling when his eloquence reached its sustained height. As Licinius Murena's advocate once, in a suit brought against him by Cato,[55] he was ambitious to outshine Hortensius, whose speech had been very convincing. So he slept not at all the night before and what with his worry and sleeplessness he seemed feeble and not up to his usual mark. On this occasion, when he stepped out of his litter to go to Milo's trial and saw Pompey planted on the heights as in a camp, and arms gleaming around the forum, he was so appalled that he could hardly begin his speech, while his body trembled and his voice choked. Milo, however, conducted himself at the trial like a brave man. He would not stoop to letting his hair grow long or putting on a dark cloak, though his behavior seems to have been an important cause of his condemnation. Yet in spite of all this, men thought of Cicero as one who cared much for his friends rather than as a coward.

---

[54] Titus Annius Milo was one of those who felt that as force was already being used to overturn the republic, force must be used to defend it. Taking Cicero's side, he had organized a band of gladiators to fight Clodius' ruffians, and a period of rioting, varied by prosecutions for lawlessness, had set in which lasted until Milo murdered Clodius in 52 b.c. The senate then appointed Pompey as sole consul to restore order. He had Milo prosecuted and set such heavy guards around the forum that Cicero had not the courage to deliver his speech in Milo's defense. Milo went into exile at Marseilles.

[55] In 63 b.c. in the midst of the crisis over Catiline, Licinius Murena, consul-elect, was accused of bribery by Cato. It was not politic to find so important an official guilty at such a time, and Cicero defended him and procured his partial acquittal.

36. He was appointed also one of the priests whom the Romans call augurs, replacing the younger Crassus, who was killed in Parthia. Then the province of Cilicia [56] was assigned him by lot, and with an army of twelve thousand men-at-arms and twenty-six hundred horses he set sail, with orders also to keep Cappadocia [57] friendly and obedient to Ariobarzanes, its king. This Cicero accomplished peacefully and satisfactorily without recourse to arms. He saw that the Cilicians were restive because of the Roman defeat in Parthia and the risings in Syria, and quieted them by his mild administration. He would not accept presents, even when kings offered them, and he lifted the burden of entertainment from the people of the province. Daily he himself had men whom he liked at dinners which were not costly though liberal. His house had no doorkeeper, but no one ever saw him lying in bed. At sunrise he would be standing or walking in front of his dwelling, receiving those who came to pay their respects. They say too that not once did he have a man scourged with rods or his clothes torn off, and never did he abuse a man in anger or inflict a humiliating punishment. On ascertaining that much of the public property had been stolen, he restored the wealth of the cities, but allowed thieves who made restitution to retain their civil rights without more penalty.

He undertook a war too and defeated the brigands who were living on Mount Amanus, and for this achievement was saluted by his soldiers as *Imperator*. When Caecilius the orator requested him to send him panthers from Cilicia for a show at Rome,[58] Cicero, pluming himself on his achievements, wrote back to him that there were no panthers in Cilicia, for they had fled to Caria, indignant that they were the only things he made war upon, while everything else was at peace. On his voyage back from his province, he first put in at Rhodes and then paid a happy visit to Athens, in affectionate memory of his former stay there. He met the men who were leaders in learning, greeted his old friends and companions, and

---

[56] Cilicia was a fertile coastal land of southern Asia Minor. It had been conquered by Pompey in the course of his drive against the pirates of the eastern Mediterranean.

[57] Cappadocia was an upland plateau northeast of Cilicia. It had been overrun by Pompey during his wars with King Mithridates, but then restored by him as a Roman protectorate under its native ruler.

[58] Panthers, lions, and other wild beasts were regularly shipped back to Rome for use in shows and gladiatorial games.

received from Greece the honors he deserved. He then returned to Rome, where the state was already breaking apart, as if in flames, on the verge of civil war.[59]

37. In the senate, when they were voting him a triumph, he said he would prefer to follow Caesar in his triumph, if an understanding could be reached. Privately he wrote to Caesar, giving him a great deal of advice, and in person he offered the same to Pompey, doing his best to pacify each of them and make him see reason. But when things were past remedy and Caesar was advancing on Rome, and Pompey would wait no longer but with many good citizens had left the city, Cicero did not join in their flight and it was supposed that he was taking Caesar's side. It is plain that his mind was pulled strongly in both directions and that he was very unhappy. For he writes in his letters that he was perplexed which road to choose, that Pompey had an honorable and righteous cause to fight for, but that Caesar was an abler manager and a safer protector for himself and his friends. So he knew from whom to flee but not to whom to flee.[60] Trebatius, one of Caesar's friends, wrote Cicero a letter to say that Caesar thought he should above everything join his party and share his hopes, but if for reasons of age he was unwilling to do this, he should go to Greece and stay there quietly out of the way of them both. But Cicero, surprised that Caesar had not written himself, replied irritably that he would do nothing unworthy of his political principles. These are things he tells in his letters.

38. When Caesar went off to Spain, Cicero immediately sailed to join Pompey.[61] Most of Pompey's company were pleased to see him, but when Cato met him, he told him privately that he was doing very wrong to choose Pompey. For himself, he said it would not be right to abandon the political course he had chosen from the outset, but Cicero would have been of more use to his country and his friends if he had remained at Rome, taking no sides and shaping his conduct by events. Yet for no reason or necessity he had made himself Caesar's enemy and had come there to involve himself in their grave peril.

These words were upsetting to Cicero's ideas, as was the fact that

---

[59] Cicero arrived in Rome on January 4, 49 B.C.

[60] *Letters to Atticus,* VIII, 7, 2.

[61] In April of 49 B.C. Caesar left for Spain. Two months later Cicero sailed for Greece.

Pompey gave him nothing important to do. He had himself to blame for that, for he did not deny that he regretted coming and spoke scoffingly of Pompey's preparations and with deep-seated dissatisfaction of his plans, and did not hesitate to jibe and jeer at his fellow soldiers. He went about the camp always unsmiling and morose, though he made others laugh even against their will. I would better give a few instances. When Domitius was putting a man who was no soldier in a commander's post, and describing him as kindly in disposition and sagacious, Cicero said, "Then why are you not keeping him to take care of your children?" And when some people were praising Theophanes the Lesbian, prefect of the engineers in the camp, for the admirable way he had consoled the Rhodians on the loss of their fleet, "What a boon it is," he said, "to have a Greek for a prefect!"

When Caesar was winning many victories and blockading Pompey's troops after a fashion,[62] Lentulus said he had heard that Caesar's friends were unhappy. "You mean," said Cicero, "that they do not like Caesar." One Marcius, who had recently arrived from Italy, said that there was a widespread report in Rome that Pompey was besieged. "And then," said Cicero, "did you sail off here so that you might confirm it with your own eyes?" After their defeat,[63] Nonnius said they should still be hopeful, for seven eagles were left in Pompey's camp. "That would be right," said Cicero, "if we were fighting jackdaws." And when Labienus, relying on oracles, said that Pompey must be victorious, "Yes," said Cicero; "under his generalship we have lost our camp."

39. After the battle of Pharsalus, at which Cicero was not present on account of illness, and after Pompey's flight, Cato, who had a large army at Dyrrachium and a big fleet, asked Cicero to take over the command according to custom, since as consul he was the ranking official. But he refused the command and declined utterly to take part in any continuation of the war, and came close thereby to being killed. For the young Pompey and his friends called him a traitor and would have drawn their swords on him if Cato had not intervened and with difficulty got him away and sent him out of the camp.

He then made for Brundisium and stayed there waiting for Caesar,

---

[62] At Dyrrachium. For all these events, see below, *Caesar*, chs. 37–45.
[63] At Pharsalus, in Thessaly, August, 48 B.C.

who was delayed by troubles in Asia and Egypt. And when the news came that Caesar had landed at Tarentum [64] and was coming around by land from there to Brundisium, Cicero hurried to meet him, not altogether hopeless, though embarrassed to be testing before a crowd of people the feeling of a victorious enemy towards himself. However, he did not need to do or say anything undignified, for when Caesar saw Cicero coming to meet him, considerably ahead of the rest, he dismounted and greeted him, and went on for many furlongs, talking with him alone. And afterwards he continued to treat Cicero with honor and friendliness. When Cicero wrote a eulogy of Cato,[65] Caesar in his reply spoke highly of Cicero's eloquence and of his career, as much like that of Pericles or Theramenes. Cicero's eulogy was called *Cato;* Caesar's reply, *Anti-Cato.*

They say too that when Quintus Ligarius was being tried for being one of Caesar's enemies and Cicero was acting as his advocate, Caesar said to his friends, "What is to keep us after all this time from listening to Cicero's speech? It was long ago decided that Ligarius was a scoundrel and our enemy." But when Cicero began to speak, he moved his audience profoundly; and as his speech went on with its varying emotions and extraordinary power to charm, Caesar's face changed color again and again, and it was plain that the depths of his soul were being stirred. When towards the close the orator alluded to the fighting at Pharsalus, Caesar was so moved that his body trembled and he dropped some of the papers that were in his hands. Thus he was compelled to acquit Ligarius of the charge.

40. Later, when the government had been changed to a monarchy,[66] Cicero withdrew from public life, and spent his time with young men who were interested in studying philosophy. And mainly through his close intercourse with them he again acquired great influence in the city, for they were young men of the noblest families and highest position. He occupied himself too with composing and translating philosophical dialogues, and with turning into Latin every term used in logic and natural

---

[64] This was in September of 47 B.C.

[65] Cicero's eulogy was written after Cato's suicide in 46 B.C. See below, *Caesar,* ch. 54. Both the *Cato* and the *Anti-Cato* are lost.

[66] In 46 B.C., Caesar was appointed supreme dictator for ten years. In 45, he was chosen as consul without a colleague. At the beginning of 44, he was made dictator for life.

science. It was he, they tell us, who first and chiefly furnished the Romans with names for *phantasia,*[67] *syncatathesis, epoche,* and *catalepsis;* also for *atomon, ameres, kenon,* and many other such expressions, contriving sometimes with metaphors and sometimes with different familiar words to make them intelligible and bring them into common use. For recreation he exercised his talent for writing verses, and when he was in the mood, they say, would turn out five hundred lines in a single night.

The greater part of his time he now spent at his villa in Tusculum. He wrote to his friends that he was living the life of Laertes,[68] either jesting, as his custom was, or else regretful because his ambition made him still long for a part in politics and grieve at the way things had turned out. He seldom went down to the city, and when he did it was to wait on Caesar. He was foremost among those who spoke for giving him honors and were continually striving to say something new about him and his achievements. Such, for example, was his remark about the statues of Pompey, which Caesar had ordered set up again after they had been pulled down and carried away. They were set up again, and Cicero said that by that act of generosity Caesar had both erected statues to Pompey and made sure of his own.

41.   He was planning, they say, to write a comprehensive history of his country, inserting in it much about Greece and adding all the stories and legends which he had collected.   But he was hindered against his will by many public and private events and by troubles, most of which he seems to have brought on himself. First of all, he divorced his wife, Terentia, because she had shown no concern for him during the war. He had gone into exile without even the necessaries for traveling, and on his return to Italy he had not found her kind to him. She had not come to join him in Brundisium, where he stayed a long time, and when her daughter, a young girl, was making the lengthy journey there, she had not provided her with a suitable escort or with funds. She had stripped Cicero's house bare and empty of everything, besides piling up many

---

[67] In English these terms of Greek natural philosophy are respectively: image, assent, refraining from assent, perception, atom, indivisible, void.
[68] Laertes, the father of Ulysses, is described in the *Odyssey* as living a life of rustic simplicity. During this time Cicero wrote several of his most famous rhetorical and philosophical works.

heavy debts. These were the quite suitable reasons stated for the divorce.

Terentia, however, denied them all, and Cicero himself gave color to her defense by marrying soon afterward a young girl.[69] He did it, Terentia claimed, for love of her beauty, but Tiro, his freedman, writes that it was for her money, that he might pay his debts. The girl was very rich and Cicero had been left her trustee and guardian of her property. He did owe many tens of thousands and his friends and relatives urged him to marry her, notwithstanding his age, and to use her money to satisfy his creditors. Antony,[70] who mentioned this marriage in his answers to the *Philippics,* said that he had turned out of doors the wife with whom he had grown old. At the same time he made some humorous remarks on Cicero's homekeeping ways, calling him fit neither for work nor for soldiering. Not long after this marriage, Cicero's daughter died in childbirth in Lentulus' house, for she had married Lentulus after the death of her former husband, Piso. Cicero's friends came from all directions to console him, but his grief at this loss was very great.[71] He even divorced his newly married wife because he thought she was glad of Tullia's death.

42. Such then was Cicero's domestic situation. In the plot that was forming against Caesar he had no share, though he was one of Brutus' most intimate friends and was thought to regret the current state of affairs and to long for things as they had been more than anyone else. But the conspirators were afraid of his timid disposition, as well as of his age, since at that time of life even the sturdiest natures lose courage. When the deed [72] had been done by Cassius and Brutus and their partisans, and Caesar's friends were uniting against the doers of it, there was fear that the city might once more be plunged into civil wars. So Antony, who was consul, convoked the senate and spoke briefly on the need of harmony, and Cicero, with a long speech appropriate to the crisis, persuaded the senate to imitate the Athenians and vote an amnesty [73] for the crime

---

69 She was a patrician girl, Publilia by name.

70 Mark Antony had served under Caesar in Gaul and again in the war with Pompey. After Pharsalus he had been sent back to Rome as Caesar's representative. In 44 B.C. he was Caesar's colleague in the consulship.

71 Cicero's daughter Tullia seems to have been the person he loved best in life.

72 "The deed" was the murder of Caesar on the Ides of March 44 B.C.

73 After the overthrow in 403 B.C. of the tyranny of the Thirty, set up by Sparta and the aristocracy at Athens, the Athenian people voted a general amnesty.

against Caesar, and assign provinces to Brutus and Cassius. Yet none of those things were done. For when the people, who already were saddened and full of pity, saw Caesar's body carried through the forum, and Antony showed them his clothing soaked with blood and slashed by swords, they went mad with fury. They searched for the murderers in the forum and ran to their houses with firebrands to burn them down. This danger the conspirators avoided by being prepared for it, but expecting many more serious dangers, they left the city.

43. Antony at once took over the leadership and everyone was afraid that he would set up a monarchy, and Cicero feared it more than anyone. And Antony, seeing that Cicero was retaining his influence in the state and knowing that he was on warm terms with Brutus and his party, was uneasy at his presence in the city. Even earlier they had been somewhat suspicious of each other because of the dissimilarity and divergence of their careers. In his alarm, Cicero was first about to sail to Syria with Dolabella [74] as his legate; but the consuls elected to succeed Antony, Hirtius and Pansa, who were good men and devoted to Cicero, begged him not to desert them and promised to get rid of Antony if he would stay. So Cicero, neither entirely trusting nor distrusting them, arranged with Hirtius that he would spend the summer at Athens and come back again after they had taken office. He then sailed off by himself.

There was, however, some delay about the voyage, and, as often happens, new reports reached him from Rome, to the effect that there had been an extraordinary change in Antony, that he was acting and conducting the whole government as the senate wished, and that the situation needed only Cicero's presence to bring things to the happiest conclusion. Accordingly he blamed himself for his over-caution and turned back towards Rome. In his first hopefulness, he was not disappointed; such a throng of people poured out in joy and affection to meet him. Nearly a day was taken up with friendly greetings at the gates and as he entered the city. But on the following day, when Antony called a meeting

---

[74]Publius Dolabella, a profligate and spendthrift, who had been a husband of Cicero's daughter Tullia, at first, attached himself to Caesar's murderers but was bought off by Antony, through whose influence he was assigned the province of Syria for five years. In February, 43 B.C., the senate pronounced him a public enemy for his flagrant misgovernment and he committed suicide to escape arrest.

of the senate and asked Cicero to come, he did not go but stayed in bed, pretending to be suffering from fatigue. Actually he seems to have been in terror of some plot against him, as a result of some suspicion or hint which had reached him on the road. Antony, however, was much offended by the affront and sent out soldiers with orders to bring Cicero or else burn down his house. But as many people opposed him and pled with him to desist, he did so, after merely taking sureties. Thereafter they kept quietly apart, always on their guard, until the young Caesar[75] arrived from Apollonia to take possession of his inheritance from the elder Caesar, and quarreled with Antony over the twenty-five million drachmas which Antony was retaining from the estate.[76]

44. Then Philippus, who was married to young Caesar's mother, and Marcellus, who was married to his sister, came with the young man himself to Cicero and arranged with him that he should give to Caesar, both in the senate and in the assembly, the support of his oratory and his political activity, and that Caesar should give him the security of his wealth and his armed forces. For already the young man had with him many of the soldiers who had fought under the elder Caesar. There appears too to have been an even stronger reason why Cicero accepted Caesar's friendship so eagerly. It seems that while Pompey and Caesar were still alive, Cicero had a dream that someone was summoning the sons of the senators to the Capitol, because Jupiter was about to appoint one of them ruler of Rome. The citizens were hurriedly running up to stand around the temple, while the youths in their purple-bordered robes were silently taking their seats. Suddenly the temple doors were thrown open, and one by one the boys rose and walked around past the god, who looked at them all and sent them disappointed away. But when young Caesar stepped forward towards him, the god stretched out his hand and said, "O Romans, your civil wars will be over when this boy is your ruler."

[75] "The young Caesar" was of course, Octavian, the later Augustus, named in Caesar's will as his chief heir, and at this time nineteen years old. He was in Apollonia, in Illyrium, finishing his education, when he heard of his great uncle's murder, and returned at once determined to avenge it.
[76] Caesar's widow had appointed Antony temporary guardian of the estate, until Octavian took over.

The memory of this dream, they say, imprinted the boy's appearance on Cicero's mind, and he recalled it clearly, although he did not know who the boy was. But the next day, he was going down to the Campus Martius just as the boys who had been exercising there were leaving, and he saw this boy for the first time, exactly as he had seen him in his dream. Astonished, Cicero asked who his parents were. His father was Octavius, a man of no special distinction, but his mother was Attia, a daughter of Caesar's sister. Consequently, Caesar, who had no children of his own, bequeathed to the boy his property and his family name. From that time on, they say, Cicero was careful to notice him when he met him, and the boy was pleased by his friendly attentions. By chance too he was born during Cicero's consulship.

45.   These then were the reasons mentioned, but it was primarily Cicero's hatred of Antony and his natural yearning for glory which led him to Caesar, with the idea of getting Caesar's power to further his own political aims. And the young man went so far in paying homage to Cicero as to call him father. At which Brutus was so displeased that in his letters to Atticus he spoke bitterly of Cicero, because in his courting of Caesar out of fear of Antony, he was manifestly not securing liberty for his country but wooing a kind master for himself. Cicero's son, however, who was studying philosophy at Athens, Brutus took over, gave him a command, and employed him successfully in many enterprises.

Cicero's power in the city was now at its height. Since he could do what he chose, he organized a party against Antony, drove him out of Rome, and sent the two consuls, Hirtius and Pansa, to carry on the war with him. He also prevailed on the senate to vote Caesar the lictors and insignia of a praetor, as though he were fighting to defend the country. But when Antony had been defeated,[77] and both consuls had died after the battle, their armies united under Caesar. The senate then became frightened of a young man of such extraordinary good fortune, and tried by gifts and honors to win his armies away from him and put a limit on his power, seeing that they needed no defenders any longer, with Antony

---

[77] In April of 43 B.C. Antony, who had been attempting to seize Cisalpine Gaul, or northern Italy, as his province, was defeated by Octavian, Hirtius, and Pansa at Mutina (now Modena). Both consuls died of wounds after the battle. Antony fled to southern Gaul, where he had allies.

in flight. Caesar then grew alarmed and secretly sent messengers to Cicero urgently requesting him to get the consulship for them both together. After they took office, he said, Cicero might handle affairs as he thought wise, and give his instructions to his young colleague, who was only out for a name and reputation. Caesar himself acknowledged later that it was his fear of a disbanding of the troops and the danger of his being left alone that made him in his emergency appeal to Cicero's love of office and persuade him to try for the consulship, with his own assistance to win the election.

46. And certainly Cicero, now an old man, was pushed on and cajoled by a young one. He worked with Caesar soliciting votes, and procured the good will of the senate for him. For this his friends at once blamed him, and ere long he too saw that he had ruined himself and betrayed the people's liberty. For when Caesar grew strong again and had secured the consulship, he bade farewell to Cicero, made friends with Antony and Lepidus,[78] joined his forces with theirs, and divided the rule with them, as if it were a piece of property. They also made out a list of more than two hundred men to be put to death.

The worst disagreement in all their discussions was over the proscription of Cicero. Antony would accept nothing if he were not the first to be killed, Lepidus supported Antony, and Caesar stood out against them both. They met by themselves secretly for three days, near the city of Bononia. Their meeting place was a spot away from the camps, encircled by a river. Caesar, they say, fought hard for Cicero through the first two days, but yielded on the third and gave him up. The terms of their compromise were as follows: Caesar was to give up Cicero, Lepidus his brother Paulus, and Antony Lucius Caesar, his uncle on his mother's side. Thus in their anger and vindictiveness they were lost to all human feelings or, rather, proved that no wild beast is more brutal than man, when his wrath is accompanied by power.

---

[78] Marcus Lepidus had been Julius Caesar's master of horse and his colleague as consul in 46 B.C. After Caesar's death he supported Antony, whom he joined in southern Gaul after his defeat at Mutina. A few weeks later he and Antony met the young Caesar near Bologna, and came to an understanding. By a senate decree of November, 43 B.C., they were appointed triumvirs for five years, with almost absolute power. One of their first acts was the publication at Rome of the list of their enemies.

47. Meanwhile, Cicero was with his brother at his private villa in Tusculum. Hearing of the proscriptions, they decided to go to Astura, a villa of Cicero's on the coast, and thence to sail to Macedonia to join Brutus, for now it was rumored that he was in control there. They traveled in litters, overcome with anxiety, stopping at times on the way when, with their litters set side by side, they would condole with one another. Quintus was the more depressed as he began to realize his impecunious state, for he said he had brought nothing from home. Even Cicero had but little for the journey. It would be better, then, Quintus said, for Cicero to push on ahead in his flight and for himself to collect some supplies from home and hurry after him. This they resolved to do, and embracing one another, parted with many tears.

Quintus, a few days later, was betrayed by his slaves to those who were looking for him, and with his son was put to death. Cicero arrived at Astura, and finding a boat there embarked immediately and sailed as far as Circaeum, the wind in his favor. From there the pilots wanted to sail straight on, but Cicero, either afraid of the sea or having not yet lost all faith in Caesar, went ashore, and on foot traveled back towards Rome a hundred furlongs. Then, perplexed and distracted, he once more changed his mind and went down to the sea at Astura. There he spent the night in terrible and desperate thought. He even hatched a plan to make his way secretly into Caesar's house and stab himself on the hearth, and so precipitate on Caesar an avenging deity. But a fear of torture kept him from this course. So turning over many confused and contradictory plans in his mind, he at last let his servants take him by sea to Caieta, where he owned land and a pleasant spot to retire to in the summer when the Etesian winds blow refreshingly. The place has also a temple to Apollo, a little way above the sea. From it a flock of crows came flying and screeching loudly towards the boat as it was being rowed to land, and lighting on each end of the yard-arm, some of them went on cawing, while others pecked at the ends of the ropes. Everyone supposed the omen was bad. However, Cicero landed, went up to his house, and lay down to rest. A flock of the crows then perched at his window, cawing lustily. One of them flew down to the couch where Cicero lay wrapped up and with its beak little by little was pulling his cloak away from his face. At this sight, the slaves reproached themselves for standing idly by to be spectators of their master's murder, doing nothing to protect him, while brute beasts came to assist and care for him in his unmerited plight. Partly then by entreaty and partly by force, they took him up and carried him in his litter towards the sea.

48. But in the meantime the assassins had arrived, Herennius, a centurion, and Popilius, a tribune, who had once been defended by Cicero when under prosecution for parricide. They had helpers with them too. Finding the doors shut, they broke them open, but Cicero was not to be seen and the people indoors declared they did not know where he was. And then, they say, a young man who had been educated by Cicero in liberal letters and mathematics, a freedman of Cicero's brother Quintus, named Philologus, told the tribune that the litter was being carried through the shady paths down to the sea. Thereat the tribune, taking a few men with him, hurried around to the place where it would come out. But Herennius went running through the paths, and Cicero saw him coming and ordered his slaves to set the litter down on the spot. Holding his chin in his left hand, as he had a way of doing, he looked steadily at his murderers, his hair all unkempt and dusty and his face worn by anxiety. Most of those who were there covered their faces while Herennius was killing him. He was stabbed, stretching his neck out from the litter, being then in his sixty-fourth year.[79] Following Antony's orders, Herennius cut off his head and his hands, with which he wrote the *Philippics*. Cicero himself called his speeches against Antony *Philippics*.

49. When the head and hands were brought to Rome, Antony happened to be holding an election, but on hearing they had come and seeing them, he called out that the proscriptions were now finished. The head and hands he ordered fastened up over the ships' prows on the rostrum,[80] a sight to make Romans shudder, for they saw there, they thought, not Cicero's face but an image of Antony's soul. Yet Antony had a sense of fairness about one thing at least in the case. He turned Philologus over to Pomponia, Quintus' wife, who, when she had him in her power, wreaked terrible vengeance on him—even made him cut off his own flesh bit by bit, broil, and eat it. This, at least, is the story some

---

[79] Cicero's murder occurred on December 7, 43 B.C.

[80] From the fourth century B.C. the speaker's platform or rostrum, which looked down on the meeting place of the assembly in the forum, had been adorned with the prows of enemy ships, captured in war.

historians tell, but Cicero's own freedman, Tiro, says nothing at all of Philologus' treachery.

I am told that Caesar a long time afterward went once to see one of his daughter's sons, and the boy had in his hands a book by Cicero. Frightened, he tried to hide it in his cloak. But Caesar spied it, took the book, and, standing there, read a good part of it, then gave it back to the boy, saying, "A learned man, my boy, a learned man and a patriot!"

As soon too as Caesar had finally conquered Antony,[81] as consul he selected Cicero's son to be his colleague. Under him the senate pulled down the statues of Antony, annulled the other honors bestowed on him, and further decreed that no Antony should ever bear the name of Marcus. Thus Heaven granted to the house of Cicero the final punishment of Antony.

---

[81] In the battle at Alexandria, in 30 B.C. See below, *Antony,* chs. 55–6.

Comparison of Demosthenes and Cicero

1. THE FOREGOING are the memorable things recorded of Demosthenes and Cicero which have come to our knowledge. And though I have refrained from comparing their styles of oratory, this much, I think, should be said, namely, that Demosthenes concentrated all his powers of reasoning, natural and acquired by training, on the speaker's art, so that in brilliance and adroitness he outshone his rivals in the law courts and public assemblies, in dignity and grandeur the pure rhetoricians, and in accuracy and skill the Sophists. Cicero, on the other hand, was a man of wide learning and versatile in his literary accomplishments. He left behind him a number of philosophic works of his own on the model of the Academy. In fact, even in the speeches he wrote for the law courts and the assembly, he is obviously trying to show that he is also a man of letters.

In their speeches too we can discern something of the character of each man. Demosthenes' speeches were devoid of any trace of floridness or jesting, concise, and impressive in their earnestness; they did not smell of lamp wicks, as Pytheas sneeringly said, but of water-drinking and hard thinking and of what men called a stern and morose temper. But Cicero was often carried away by his jocoseness into sheer buffoonery, and to win his suits in the courts he would banter laughingly and flippantly about important subjects and show no regard for propriety. Thus in his defense of Caelius he argued that in an age of such luxury and extravagance it was not strange that a man went in for pleasures, since not to help oneself to what was within one's reach was sheer folly, especially as highly distinguished philosophers had declared that happiness was to be found in pleasure.[1]

They say that when Cato prosecuted Murena, Cicero, who was consul at the time, defended him, and to embarrass Cato [2] ridiculed the Stoic school for the absurdities of its so-called paradoxes. Loud laughter spread from the audience to the jurors, but Cato, with a smile, merely remarked to those who sat near him, "What a hilarious man we have as consul, gentlemen!" Evidently Cicero was given to laughter and fond of a joke, and his face was usually smiling and serene. Demosthenes' face always bore a look of anxious gravity, and this air of thoughtfulness and intense meditation he did not easily put aside. In consequence, his enemies, as he tells us himself, called him bad-tempered and sullen.

2.   In their speeches again we may observe that Demosthenes mentions praises of himself cautiously and in an indifferent tone and only when he needs to do it for some important purpose, while usually he is discreet and modest. But Cicero's endless bragging about himself convicts him of an overmastering craving for applause, as when he cries that arms must yield to the toga, and the triumphal laurel give place to the tongue.[3] He took, finally, not only to praising his own acts and achievements but also his own speeches, both spoken and written, as though he were a boy trying to outdo Isocrates [4] and Anaximenes, instead of a man remembering his duty to lead and guide aright the Roman people,

"Massive, stern men-at-arms, on fire 'gainst their foes." [5]

It is, of course, essential for a politician to be a powerful speaker, but ignoble for him to dote on and be greedy for glory for his eloquence. So, in this respect, Demosthenes evidently was the more dignified and high-minded, for he maintained that his eloquence was only a matter of prac-

---

1 An allusion to the teaching of Epicurus. But Plutarch is not being fair either to Epicurus or to Cicero in this description of Cicero's speech.

2 See below, Cato the Younger, ch. 21.

3 Cicero, Against Piso, 29; 72 ff.

4 Isocrates of Athens (436–338 B.C.), orator and teacher of rhetoric, and Anaximenes of Lampsacus (c. 380–320 B.C.), historian and rhetorician, and instructor of Alexander the Great, were famous models of Greek eloquence.

5 The line has been ascribed to Aeschylus.

tice and very dependent on the good will of his audience,[6] and thought it ill-bred and vulgar to be puffed up over such things.

3. In their influence over their people and in politics they were both equally strong, so that even the heads of armies and camps needed their support. Chares, Diopithes, and Leosthenes had need of Demosthenes, Pompey and the young Caesar of Cicero. Caesar himself admits this in his Memoirs addressed to Agrippa and Maecenas. But what is said and thought to be the most revealing test of a man's character, namely, power and high office, which stir up every passion in him and uncover every weakness, Demosthenes never had. Nor did he stand any such test of himself, for he never held a distinguished post and would not even take command of the forces he himself had collected against Philip. But Cicero was sent out as quaestor to Sicily, and as proconsul to Cilicia and Cappadocia, at a time when the craze for wealth was at its height, and when the generals and governors sent to the provinces, though they thought it beneath them to steal, made a practice of wholesale plunder. For it was not then thought shocking to appropriate other men's property, and he who did so only in moderation was beloved by the people. Cicero, however, gave many a proof of his disdain for riches and many of his kindliness and goodness. In Rome itself he was elected consul in name, though in fact he had the power of a dictator to deal with Catiline and his accomplices. He was then an illustration of Plato's dictum [7] that states would find rest from their evils when by some good fortune great power and wisdom were combined in the same man with justice.

Further, Demosthenes is criticized for selling his eloquence for money, writing speeches secretly for men on opposite sides, as he did in the case of Phormio and Apollodorus. He was accused too of taking money from the Great King and convicted of taking bribes from Harpalus. And even if we should say that the reporters of these stories—and they are many—were repeating falsehoods, we cannot deny that Demosthenes had not the heart to look coldly on royal presents, when offered with signs of favor and honor, and that it was not likely that a man who trafficked in shipping ventures would be above taking them. Whereas, speaking of Cicero, we have already told how the Sicilians, when he was quaestor, and the

---

[6] Demosthenes, *On the Crown*, 277.

[7] Plato. *Republic*, V, 473.

Cappadocian king, when he was consul, and his friends in Rome, when he was going into banishment, offered him large sums and pressed him to accept them, and he would not.

4. When it came to banishment, for Demosthenes it was a disgrace, since he was convicted of theft, but for Cicero it was a great honor, for he had freed his country of a set of villains. Accordingly no notice was taken of Demosthenes when he left Athens, but for Cicero the senate changed its robes and put on mourning and could not be persuaded to express an opinion on any subject until it had voted his recall. On the other hand, Cicero spent his exile living idly in Macedonia, while Demosthenes made his exile contribute a great deal to his political aims. He helped the other Greeks in their struggle, as I have said, and brought about the expulsion of the Macedonian ambassadors from the cities he visited, and proved himself a much better citizen than Themistocles or Alcibiades under similar circumstances. Again, after his return, he pursued the same policy and kept up his fight against Antipater and the Macedonians. But Cicero was reproved by Laelius in the senate for sitting silent when young Caesar asked permission to be a candidate for the consulship, contrary to the law, for he was still a beardless youth. And Brutus in a letter accused [8] him of having fostered a tyranny greater and more oppressive than the one Brutus himself had overthrown.

5. On top of all this, Cicero's death was more pitiable—an old man, ignobly carried back and forth by slaves, striving to escape death and hiding from those who were coming after him, though they were not far ahead of nature. And then to have his throat cut! Whereas Demosthenes, even though he attempted a little supplication, was admirable in his provision and safe-keeping of poison, admirable too in his use of it. For when the god no longer granted him sanctuary, he found refuge, as it were, at a greater altar, removed himself out of reach of arms and soldiers, and laughed to scorn the cruelty of Antipater.

---

[8] Cicero, *Letters to Brutus,* I, 17, 2. The letter is from Brutus to Cicero's friend Atticus.

PLUTARCH

SELECTED LIVES
AND ESSAYS

VOLUME TWO

ANCIENT ITALY

GAUL

ALPS MTS.

Scale in Miles
0   50   100   150   200

VENETIA

CISALPINE GAUL

PO RIVER

LIGURIA

Mutina

Luca

ARNUS R.

RUBICON R.

Ariminum

UMBRIA

ETRURIA

APENNINE MTS.

ADRIATIC SEA

ILLYRICUM

LAKE TRASIMENUS

TIBER R.

SABINI

AEQUI

MARSI

Sutrium

Veii

ETRUSCI

Rome

Tusculum

Ostia

ALBAN LAKE

LATIUM

VOLSCI

Arpinum

SAMNIUM

Antium

Circeii

Gaeta

Misenum

Capua

CAMPANIA

APULIA

Cannae

Dyrrachium

Brundisium

Naples

LUCANIA

CALABRIA

Tarentum

CORSICA

TYRRHENIAN
SEA

SARDINIA

BRUTTIUM

Messana

Rhegium

SICILY

Syracuse

IONIAN
SEA

Utica
Carthage

AFRICA

Thapsus

Alexander

356–323 B.C.

1. IN WRITING for this book the lives of Alexander the king, and of
Caesar, the conqueror of Pompey, I have before me such an abundance
of materials that I shall make no other preface but to beg my readers not
to complain of me if I do not relate all their celebrated exploits or even
any one in full detail, but in most instances abridge the story. I am writing
not histories but lives, and a man's most conspicuous achievements do not
always reveal best his strength or his weakness. Often a trifling incident, a
word or a jest, shows more of his character than the battles where he
slays thousands, his grandest mustering of armies, and his sieges of cities.
Therefore as portrait painters work to get their likenesses from the face
and the look of the eyes, in which the character appears, and pay little
attention to other parts of the body, so I must be allowed to dwell especially on things that express the souls of these men, and through them
portray their lives, leaving it to others to describe their mighty deeds and
battles.

2. On his father's side, as everyone believes, Alexander was descended
from Heracles through Caranus, and on his mother's side from Aeacus
through Neoptolemus.[1] His father Philip, they say, was initiated into the

---

[1] Like other great men of the past, Alexander was given superhuman stature by having
his descent traced from gods and legendary heroes. Heracles was the son of Zeus, and
Caranus, the founder of the Macedonian dynasty, his descendant. Aeacus, grandfather
of the hero Achilles, was also a son of Zeus. Neoptolemus was Achilles' son. Alexander's
father, Philip II of Macedon, unified his half-barbaric kingdom, developed its resources,
and created an invincible army. With it he conquered west Thrace and Thessaly, and
defeated the Greeks at Chaeronea.

I

mysteries at Samothrace[2] at the same time as Olympias, and he, still a boy, fell in love with her, an orphan girl, and pledged himself to her in marriage, with the consent of her brother Arymbas. The night before they met in the bridal chamber, the bride dreamed that there came a crash of thunder and a lightning flash fell on her womb, from which a sheet of fire sprang out and spread flaming in every direction and then died away. And Philip, some time after he was married, dreamed that he was sealing up his wife's womb with a seal stamped, he thought, with the image of a lion. Most of the soothsayers interpreted the vision as a warning to Philip to keep more careful watch over his wife; but Aristander of Telmessus[3] said that it meant she was with child, because men do not seal up anything empty; and that she would bear a son of a nature as courageous as a lion. Once, however, Philip saw a snake stretched out by Olympias' side as she slept, and this, it is said, quite cooled the heat of his passion for her, so that he no longer went often to rest beside her, whether he feared she might practice some magic arts or spells on him, or thought himself excluded from intimacy with one who lived close to a greater being.

But there is another story about all this. The women of that country[4] from ancient times have all been addicted to the Orphic rites and the frenzied worship of Bacchus, for which reason they have been called Clodones and Mimallones. They have many practices like those of the Edonian and Thracian women around Mount Haemus, from whom the word *threskeuein* seems to have been derived as a term for excessive and fantastic forms of worship. Olympias, they say, was particularly devoted to these wild rites and expressed her inspirations like a true barbarian, bringing great tame snakes in among the reveling women, which often frightened the men, as they crept out of the ivy and mystic baskets and wound themselves around the women's wands and wreaths.

---

[2] Samothrace, a small island in the northern Aegean, was a center for the worship of certain mystic divinities, called the Cabiri, whose cult was often connected with that of Demeter or of Bacchus.

[3] Aristander became later Alexander's constant companion as priest and chief soothsayer.

[4] That is, Macedonia. Orpheus and Bacchus were both worshiped in mystery cults, especially in northern Greece and Thrace. For a description of wild Bacchic rites, see Euripides' *Bacchae*. Clodones and Mimallones seem to have been Macedonian names for Bacchantes.

3. After his vision, Philip sent Chaeron of Megalopolis to Delphi, and he brought back an oracle from Apollo commanding him to sacrifice to Ammon [5] and to revere him especially above all other gods. He was told, however, that he would lose that eye with which he had peeped through the chink in the door and seen the god, in the form of a serpent, lying beside his wife. Eratosthenes [6] says that Olympias, when she sent Alexander away on his great expedition, told him, and him only, the secret of his birth, and bade him have thoughts worthy of his parentage. But others say that she disclaimed any such pretensions, and would exclaim, "Will Alexander never leave off slandering me to Hera?" [7]

Alexander was born on the sixth of Hecatombaeon,[8] the month the Macedonians call Loüs, and the day of the burning of the temple of Artemis at Ephesus, a coincidence on which Hegesias of Magnesia [9] delivered himself of a joke frigid enough to have put out the conflagration. Naturally, he said, the temple burned down when Artemis was absent, assisting at the birth of Alexander. But all the seers who happened to be in Ephesus at the time took the temple's destruction as a portent of a coming calamity, and ran around beating their faces and crying out that doom and a terrible disaster for Asia had both that day been born.

4. Philip had just taken Potidaea [10] when he received three messages at the same time: first, that Parmenio [11] had overthrown the Illyrians in a great battle, second, that his race horse had been victorious at the Olympic games, and, third, that Alexander was born, whereat he was naturally

---

[5] Ammon was an Egyptian name for the chief of the gods, whom the Greeks identified with their god Zeus. Alexander was later to visit his shrine in the Egyptian desert.

[6] Eratosthenes (c.276–c.196 B.C.) was a famous Alexandrian chronologist, geographer, and astronomer.

[7] In other words, "Will he never stop talking of the affair between me and Zeus?" Hera was, of course, the wife of Zeus.

[8] Hecatombaeon, the first month of the Attic year, covered the time between what is now July 15 and August 15.

[9] Hegesias was one of Alexander's many early biographers known to Plutarch, whose writings have since disappeared.

[10] This Macedonian town had been a possession of Athens. Philip took and destroyed it as one of the first steps in his advance towards the south.

[11] Parmenio was one of the chief generals of both Philip and Alexander. In his old age he and his son Philotas were executed by Alexander on charges of disloyalty. See later in this *Life,* chs. 48, 49.

well pleased. He was still more delighted when the soothsayers told him that the son whose birth was one of three successes would be invincible.

Alexander's personal appearance is best shown in the statues of Lysippus,[12] the only artist he would permit to portray him. The peculiarities which many of his successors and friends later tried to imitate, the droop of the neck a little towards the left and the melting eye, were shown by this artist with great accuracy. Apelles,[13] however, who painted him holding a thunderbolt, did not copy exactly the color of his skin, but made it too dark and swarthy. For he was fair, they say, with a fairness that tended to ruddiness, particularly on his face and chest. In the *Memoirs* of Aristoxenus we read that his skin exhaled a very sweet odor, and that his mouth and flesh all over were so fragrant as to scent his tunics with perfume. The cause of this was perhaps the unusually warm and burning temperature of his body. For fragrance, Theophrastus [14] believes, is produced by heat acting on moisture and for that reason the dry and parched countries of the world produce the most and the finest spices, since the sun draws out the moisture which, as material for putrefaction, rises in bodily substances. And so, probably, the heat of Alexander's body made him fond of drinking, and fiery in temper.[15]

But even as a lad he showed his power of self-control in that, while in most occupations he was hot-headed and vehement, he was hard to interest in bodily pleasures and always took them in great moderation. His ambition kept him serious and high-minded beyond his years. Yet it was not for every kind of glory in every field that he cared, unlike Philip, who prided himself like a Sophist on his eloquence and had the victories of his chariots at Olympia engraved on his coins. But when Alexander

12 Lysippus (c.372–c.316 B.C.) was the famous Greek sculptor who set the pattern for the type of slender beauty most admired in the fourth century B.C.

13 Apelles was the greatest painter of the day, and painted portraits of Philip, Alexander, and their circle. His portrait of Alexander holding the thunderbolt was placed in the restored temple of Artemis at Ephesus.

14 Theophrastus (d.c. 288 B.C.), the successor of Aristotle as head of the Peripatetic school, was an authority on botany.

15 Plutarch is not consistent in his reports of Alexander's personal habits. His later statement that Alexander drank mainly to be sociable is more in agreement with the accounts of other biographers.

was asked by his companions, whether, since he was swift of foot, he would run in the foot race at the Olympic games, he answered, "If I had kings to run against." He seems in general to have been quite indifferent to the whole tribe of athletes, for though he arranged many contests not only for tragedy writers and players on the flute and the lyre, but also for rhapsodists [16] and every sort of hunter and player with sticks, he never was interested in offering a prize for boxing or wrestling.

5. When during Philip's absence ambassadors once came from the king of Persia, Alexander entertained them and went about with them constantly. He charmed them by his friendly ways, and by the questions he asked them, which were never childish or trivial. He inquired the length of the roads and the nature of the traveling from the coast back inland, and about their king, whether he was warlike or not, and what was the strength and power of Persia, so that they were amazed and looked on the far-famed cleverness of Philip as nothing in comparison with the strenuous and soaring disposition of his son. Whenever news came that Philip had taken a famous city, or had won an illustrious victory, he was not overjoyed to hear it, but would say to his comrades, "Boys, my father will get everything before we can and leave nothing big and brilliant for me, to show what we can do!" For he was not eager for pleasure or riches but only for excellence and glory, and thought that the greater his inheritance from his father the less there would be for himself to accomplish. So he felt that with his father's successes all the chances for great deeds were being lavished on him, and he longed to be heir not to a wealthy and luxurious and pleasant kingdom but to one involved in troubles and wars and contentions.

Many persons, naturally, were appointed to watch over him, nurses, tutors, and teachers. Over all of them stood Leonidas, a kinsman of Olympias and a man of austere temper. He did not himself object to the title of tutor, a noble and honorable office, but his dignity and his relationship to Alexander obtained for him from other people the title of Alexander's foster father and director. The man who assumed for himself the manner and name of tutor was Lysimachus, an Acarnanian. He had nothing in the way of urbane cultivation, but because he called himself

---

[16] A rhapsodist was a public singer or reciter of poems.

Phoenix, Alexander Achilles, and Philip Peleus,[17] he was popular and ranked next to Leonidas.

6. Philonicus the Thessalian brought the horse Bucephalus to Philip, offering to sell him for thirteen talents, but when they went down to the plain to try him, they found him vicious and quite unmanageable. He allowed no one to mount him and paid no attention to the voice of any of Philip's attendants, rearing up against everyone. On this Philip grew angry and bade them take the brute away as completely savage and intractable. But Alexander, who stood by, said, "What a horse they are ruining for lack of skill and tact to handle him!" Philip at first made no reply, but when Alexander repeated the remark several times and seemed much distressed, he said, "Are you criticizing your elders, as though you knew more and were better able to manage a horse?" "This horse, anyway," he replied, "I could manage better than anyone has." "And if you do not," said Philip, "what will you pay for your rashness?" "By Zeus," answered Alexander, "I will pay the price of the horse!"

At this there was laughter and then a settling of the terms of the wager. But at once Alexander ran up to the horse and taking him by his bridle turned him around towards the sun, having, it seems, observed that he was worried by the sight of his shadow falling in front of him and dancing before his eyes. After thus calming the horse a little, he stroked him until he saw he was regaining his courage and spirit, and then gently dropped off his cloak and with one leap securely mounted him. Then with a light pressure of the reins on the bit, without a blow or a cut, he drew him in, and when he saw he was no longer frightened but only impatient for a gallop, he let him go, finally urging him on with a confident voice, and a touch of the heel. Philip and his friends were at first silent with dread, but when he wheeled the horse around correctly and rode back to them proud and happy, they all broke into cheers. His father, it is said, shed tears of joy, and on his dismounting kissed him and exclaimed, "O son, look for a kingdom equal to yourself, for Macedonia has not space for you."

---

[17] Phoenix in the *Iliad* is the old family friend of the hero Achilles, who knew him from infancy; Peleus is Achilles' father.

7. Philip saw that his son was by nature hard to move and that he fought against compulsion, but was easily led to his duty by reason. So he himself endeavored to persuade instead of commanding him. Nor would he entrust the guidance and education of the boy entirely to ordinary teachers of poetry and common subjects, since it was too important a matter, and, as Sophocles says,[18]

> "A task for many bridles, and rudders besides."

Accordingly, he sent for Aristotle,[19] the most learned and celebrated philosopher of the time, and paid him a handsome and suitable instruction fee. He rebuilt, too, Aristotle's native city, Stagira, which he had himself demolished, and restored its citizens who were in exile or slavery. As a place for his son's work and study, he assigned the temple of the nymphs, near Mieza, where, to this day, they show you Aristotle's stone seat and shady walks.

It would seem that Alexander learned from him not only his theories of ethics and politics, but also something of those secret and more profound doctrines which philosophers call by special names, the oral teachings for initiates which they divulge only to a few. For after he had crossed into Asia, on hearing that Aristotle had published some treatises on those subjects, he wrote him a blunt letter on philosophy, of which this is a copy: "Alexander to Aristotle, greeting. You have done wrong to publish your books of oral doctrine, for how now do we differ from other men, if the things we have been taught are to become the common property of everyone? I would rather excel others in the knowledge of what is most excellent than in power. Farewell."

So Aristotle, to appease his passion for distinction, wrote in reply that those doctrines were in fact both published and not published. Actually, his book on metaphysics is useless for ordinary study and teaching, and was composed as a memorandum for persons already thoroughly instructed.

---

18 Sophocles, Fragment 785.

19 This was in 343 or 342 B.C., when Alexander was thirteen and Aristotle forty-two. The latter remained in Macedonia for seven years and then returned to Athens to found his Peripatetic school of science and philosophy.

8. It was, I believe, to Aristotle more than to any other that Alexander owed the interest he took in medicine. He was not only fond of discussing the theory but, when any of his friends were sick, he would try to help them and prescribe certain treatments and diets, as we gather from his letters. He was naturally too a lover of literature and of reading. Onesicritus [20] tells us that he thought and spoke of the *Iliad* as a manual of military art and always carried with him a copy corrected by Aristotle, called "the Iliad of the Casket," [21] which he kept with his dagger under his pillow. When he found himself without books in the interior of Asia, he ordered Harpalus [22] to send him some. He sent him Philistus' *History,* a number of the tragedies of Euripides, Sophocles, and Aeschylus, and the dithyrambic odes of Telestus and Philoxenus. He admired and loved Aristotle at first, as he used to say himself, as much as he did his father, since one had given him life and the other had taught him to live nobly. Later he felt a distrust of him, not so far as to do him any harm, but his friendship with him lost its former warmth and affection and showed evidence of an estrangement. In his soul, however, he always kept that eager thirst and passion for philosophy, which was part of his nature and had been nurtured in him from the beginning, as proved by his veneration for Anaxarchus,[23] his present of fifty talents to Xenocrates, and the generous encouragement he gave Dandamis and Calanus.

9. When Philip went on his expedition against the Byzantines, he left Alexander, then sixteen years old, in charge of administration in Mace-

---

[20] Onesicritus was a Greek who went with Alexander on his expedition into Asia and later wrote a history of his campaigns. His book, like those of all Alexander's other companions and contemporaries, on which Plutarch drew, has for centuries been lost.

[21] On Alexander's use of Homer, see below, ch. 26.

[22] Harpalus (c.355–323 B.C.) was Alexander's friend and treasurer during most of his campaigns. He was guilty of waste and mishandling of funds, if not of theft, while Alexander was absent in India, and on his return fled to Athens and tried to buy security there. See above, *Demosthenes,* ch. 25. When the Athenians imprisoned him, he escaped to Crete and was murdered there by one of his men.

[23] Anaxarchus, a materialistic Sophist, was one of several philosophers who accompanied Alexander on his expeditions, but he exerted no restraining influence on the youthful king. See below, ch. 52. Xenocrates was head of the Platonic Academy at Athens. For Dandamis and Calanus, Indian sages, see below, ch. 65.

donia and of his royal seal. The boy put down the rebellious Maedi,[24] took their city, drove out the barbarians, and planted a colony of mixed peoples there, calling it Alexandropolis. He was present at, and took part in, the battle of Chaeronea [25] against the Greeks, and is said to have been first to break into the Thebans' Sacred Band. Even in my time, there was shown an old oak near the river Cephisus, called Alexander's oak, beside which he on that occasion pitched his tent. Not far off are the graves of the Macedonians. This early bravery made Philip naturally so fond of his son that it even pleased him to hear the Macedonians call Alexander their king and Philip simply their general.

But there were disorders in the household, caused by Philip's marriages and amours,[26] which in a way infected the kingdom with the malady of women's quarters, and created many grievances and serious quarrels between Philip and his son. And the violence of Olympias, who was a jealous and sullen woman, made these still worse, for she exasperated Alexander against his father. The most conspicuous outbreak was brought on by Attalus [27] at the wedding of Cleopatra, a girl with whom Philip had fallen in love and was marrying, though she was much too young for him. Attalus was her uncle and while fuddled with drink he told the Macedonians to pray to the gods to give them from the union of Philip and Cleopatra a legitimate heir to the kingdom. At this Alexander was furious, and crying, "You villain, do you call me a bastard?" threw his cup at him. Philip then rose to his feet, drawing his sword against him, but fortunately for them both his anger and his wine made him slip and fall; at which Alexander mockingly said, "This, gentlemen, is a man who was preparing to cross from Europe into Asia but who tumbles down crossing from one couch to another." After this piece of drunken folly he took Olympias and established her in Epirus, and stayed himself for a while in Illyria.

Meanwhile, Demaratus the Corinthian, an old friend of the family and

---

24 The Maedi were a tribe in the mountainous country of eastern Macedonia.

25 This battle, fought in 338 B.C., gave Philip the mastery over northern Greece, including Athens and Thebes, as a result of which he was able to impose a federal constitution on Greece as a whole, under his own leadership.

26 Philip had in all seven wives.

27 Attalus, a Macedonian, was one of Philip's generals. After Philip's death Alexander had him killed.

free to speak his mind, came to visit Philip. After the first cordial greetings, Philip asked him how the Greeks were getting on together. "Indeed, Philip," replied Demaratus, "you would better be solicitous about Greece, when you have filled your own house with such trouble and strife!" Thus brought back to reason, Philip sent to summon Alexander home, and by Demaratus' mediation prevailed on him to return.

10.   But then Pixodarus, satrap of Caria,[28] tried by a marriage connection to procure an alliance with Philip and proposed a match between his eldest daughter and Philip's son Arrhidaeus,[29] sending Aristocritus to Macedonia to make the arrangements. At once Alexander's mother filled his head with false stories, as to how Philip, by a splendid marriage and other great doings, was preparing to settle his kingdom on Arrhidaeus. In alarm at this, Alexander despatched Thessalus, the tragic actor, to Caria to persuade Pixodarus not to take Arrhidaeus, who was both illegitimate and a fool, but to accept himself instead as his son-in-law. This proposition was much more agreeable to Pixodarus than the other. But when Philip heard of it, he went to Alexander's apartment, taking with him Philotas, son of Parmenio, one of Alexander's friends and companions, and reproved him severely, scolding him sharply for being so degenerate and unworthy of his lofty position as to wish to be the son-in-law of a Carian, who was servant of a barbarian king. He wrote too to the Corinthians to send Thessalus back in chains, and he banished from Macedonia Harpalus, Nearchus, Erigyius, and Ptolemy,[30] other comrades of Alexander, whom Alexander afterwards recalled and raised to great honor.

Not long after this, Pausanias [31] was grossly insulted at the instigation

---

[28] Caria was a district in southwestern Asia Minor whose inhabitants were considered an inferior and backward people.

[29] For further mention of Arrhidaeus, see below, ch. 77.

[30] Nearchus of Crete became Alexander's trusted admiral. See below, chs. 66, 68 ff, for his great voyage. Ptolemy I, surnamed Soter or Savior, proved another of Alexander's able officers. At Alexander's death he assumed the administration of Egypt, and in 304 B.C. proclaimed himself king, thus founding the Ptolemaic dynasty which ruled Egypt until its last representative was put to death by Augustus in 30 B.C. He was also the author of a life of Alexander now lost, which was used by the historian Arrian for his *Anabasis of Alexander*.

[31] Pausanias was a Macedonian youth of noble family. He murdered Philip in August, 336 B.C.

of Attalus and Cleopatra, and when he could get no reparation for his disgrace, he murdered Philip. Most men laid the blame for his deed on Olympias, who was said to have encouraged and incited the angry youth to revenge. There was some suspicion too of Alexander, who, it is said, when Pausanias came and complained to him of his injury, repeated the line from the *Medea,*

"The guardian, the bridegroom, and the bride." [32]

However, he certainly took pains to find out and punish all who were involved in the crime, and was indignant at Olympias for her cruelty to Cleopatra in his absence.

11.   Alexander was but twenty years old when he succeeded to a king· dom beset on all sides with bitter jealousies, savage hatreds, and perils. For the neighboring barbarian tribes chafed at being held in bondage and wanted their own ancestral kingdoms, and though Philip had vanquished the Greeks in battle, he had not had time to subdue and accustom them to his yoke. He had simply overthrown and upset their institutions and left things in a state of restlessness and commotion, for all was still strange. The Macedonians were alarmed at the situation and thought Alexander should let Greece go altogether and give up the use of force there, and win back the insurgent barbarians by gentle methods, and so check the beginnings of rebellion. But he took a contrary view of affairs, and set out to win safety and security for his dominions by daring and high ambition, feeling that once he was seen to be slackening in courage, everyone would set on him. So he promptly put an end to barbarian disturbances and wars by a rapid march with an army through their country as far as the Danube, where he defeated Syrmus, king of the Triballians, in a great battle. Then hearing that the Thebans were in revolt and the Athenians were conniving with them, he at once brought his troops down through the pass of Thermopylae, saying that Demosthenes had called him a boy while he was among the Illyrians and the Triballians, and a youth when he reached Thessaly, but he would show him he was a man before the walls of Athens.

---

32 Euripides, *Medea,* 289. Medea, the Scythian princess, when deserted by Jason, sent poisoned gifts which killed Jason, his bride, and the bride's father. The allusion implied here is to Attalus, Philip, and Cleopatra.

On his arrival at Thebes, he gave the citizens a chance to repent of their conduct, demanding of them only the surrender of Phoenix and Prothytes, and proclaiming a general pardon to all who came over to him. But the Thebans retorted by demanding that he turn Philotas and Antipater [33] over to them, and issued a proclamation inviting all who wished to aid in the liberation of Greece to join them. Accordingly, he had his Macedonians prepare for war. The Thebans, though greatly outnumbered by their enemies, fought with a zeal and valor beyond their strength, but when the Macedonian garrison sallied out from the Cadmeia [34] and fell on them from the rear, the majority of them were surrounded and fell in the fray. The city was taken, sacked, and leveled to the ground. Alexander's main reason for this act was his hope that by so severe a punishment the Greeks would be terrified and cowed into submissiveness. He prided himself also on satisfying the grievances of his allies, for the Phocians and Plateans had complained against the Thebans. He separated out the priests, and all the guest-friends of the Macedonians, the descendants of the poet Pindar, and those who had voted against the revolt, and sold the rest of the inhabitants, more than thirty thousand in number, as slaves. More than six thousand were killed in the battle.

12. Amid the many fearful outrages committed in the city, some Thracians broke into the house of one Timoclea, a lady of noble reputation and character. While the men were looting her property, their leader forcibly violated and shamed her, and then asked whether she had gold or silver hidden anywhere. She said that she had, and led him alone into her garden where she showed him a well, into which, she said, on the capture of the city, she had thrown her most precious possessions. Then as the Thracian was stooping over and peering into the depths, she came behind and pushed him in, and hurled large stones down on him and killed him. And when the Thracians brought her bound before Alex-

---

[33] Antipater (397–319 B.C.), one of Philip's best Macedonian generals and diplomatists, was left by Alexander governor of Macedonia and "Europe" during his absence in the East. After Alexander's death, he put down the revolt in Greece, as recounted above, *Demosthenes,* ch. 29. He later was regent of the whole empire, which he held together until his death.

[34] The Cadmeia was the citadel or acropolis of Thebes, standing on a hill above the city, and called after Cadmus, its legendary founder. Philip had placed a Macedonian garrison there. Alexander's capture of Thebes took place in September, 335 B.C.

ander, she showed at once by her look and carriage that she was a person of dignity and lofty mind as calmly and fearlessly she followed her captors. When the king asked her who she was, she replied that she was a sister of Theagenes, who had organized the army that fought against Philip for the liberty of Greece, and who fell commanding at Chaeronea. Impressed both by her answer and by what she had done, Alexander bade her go free, with her children.

13. With the Athenians he made terms, even though they expressed the deepest sympathy for unhappy Thebes. The festival of the mysteries for which they were preparing they omitted altogether out of sorrow, and showered every kindness on the Thebans who took refuge in Athens. Whether he had had his fill of anger, like a sated lion, or wished to counterbalance a most brutal and savage deed by one of mercy, he not only acquitted Athens of every charge against the city, but even advised it to watch its course with care, since, if anything should happen to him, it would become the ruling state of Greece. And later on, they say, he often felt remorse over his destruction of Thebes, and was therefore more lenient to many other people. As for the murder of Clitus,[35] which he committed over his wine, and the refusal of his Macedonians to invade India,[36] by which they left his expedition and its glory incomplete, he ascribed these mishaps always to the wrathful vengeance of Dionysus.[37] And not one Theban survivor who afterward ever asked a favor of him failed to get it from him. So much for the story of Thebes.

14. Soon after, the Greeks assembled at the Isthmus and voted to send an expedition under Alexander against Persia, and proclaimed him their leader. Many officials and philosophers came to congratulate him and he expected that Diogenes of Sinope,[38] who was then living at Corinth, would do the same. But he paid not the least attention to Alexander and went on enjoying his leisure in the suburb of Cranium. So Alexander went to him, and found him lying stretched out in the sun. At the approach of so many people, he sat up a little and turned his gaze on Alex·

---

[35] See below, chs. 50-51.

[36] See below, ch. 62.

[37] The god Dionysus was said to be the son of Zeus and Semele, who was the ʳ ʌughter of Cadmus, the founder of Thebes.

[38] This was Diogenes, the famous Cynic philosopher.

ander. But when Alexander greeted him and asked him if he wanted anything, "Move a little," he said, "out of my sun." At this answer, they say, Alexander was so surprised and admired so much the arrogant greatness of the man who had scorned him, that as they went away, he said to his companions who were laughing at him, "Nevertheless, if I were not Alexander I would be Diogenes."

He wished to consult the god about the expedition to Asia, and so went to Delphi, but he happened to arrive there on one of the inauspicious days when it is not lawful to give out oracles. However, he at once sent for the prophetess, and when she refused to act and pleaded the words of the law, he went up himself to the temple and tried to drag her in. And she, as if giving way to his importunity, said, "You are invincible, my son." On hearing which, Alexander said he wanted no further prophecy but had from her now the oracle for which he was looking. When he started on his expedition [39] it seems there were other signs from heaven. The statue of Orpheus at Libethra, made of cypress wood, shed a quantity of sweat during those days. Everyone was alarmed at that omen, but Aristander told them to take heart, for Alexander would perform deeds so fit for song and story that poets and musicians would sweat and strain heavily to celebrate them.

15.   As for the number of his soldiers, those who give the smallest figure put it at thirty thousand foot and four thousand horse; those who give the largest at forty-three thousand foot and five thousand horse.[40] To provide for the journey, Aristobulus tells us that he had no more than seventy talents, Douris that he had provisions for only thirty days; and Onescritus says he was in debt for two hundred talents besides. Yet though he himself was starting with such slender resources, he would not board ship until he had inquired into the means of his companions and had bestowed on one a farm, on another a village, and on another the income from a rooming house or from a harbor. When at length he had spent or assigned away almost all his royal possessions, Perdiccas [41] asked him,

---

[39] Alexander set out for Asia in the spring of 334 B.C.

[40] The smaller number is probably nearer correct.

[41] Perdiccas, a Macedonian noble, was one of Alexander's most competent generals, who undertook the regency of the empire after his death. See also above, under *Demosthenes*, ch. 31.

'My king, what are you leaving for yourself?" "My hopes," replied Alexander. "Then," said Perdiccas, "we who go with you will share with you." Thereupon he refused to accept the property allotted to him, as did some others of Alexander's friends. Those, however, who accepted his gifts or asked for anything he treated so generously that most of what he owned in Macedonia he distributed and spent in this way. Such was his ardent state of mind when he crossed the Hellespont.

Marching thence to Troy, he offered sacrifice there to Athene, and poured libations to the heroes. The gravestone of Achilles he anointed with oil, and with his company ran a race around it naked, as is the custom, and then laid garlands on it, calling Achilles happy in having a faithful friend while he lived and a glorious herald of his deeds when he was dead. While he was walking through the city, looking about, someone asked him if he would like to see the lyre of Paris. He was not, he said, interested in that lyre but wished he might find Achilles' lyre, to which he once sang the glorious deeds of the heroes.

16. Meanwhile the generals of Darius had collected a large army and posted it at the ford across the river Granicus, so that it seemed necessary for Alexander to fight, as if at the gates of Asia, for entrance and control there. Most of the Macedonians were afraid of the depth of the river and of the rough and broken ground of the farther bank, up which they would have to scramble while fighting. Some also thought they should observe the rule regarding the month, for Macedonian kings did not customarily begin a war during the month of Daesius.[42] But this difficulty Alexander remedied by ordering them to consider the month a second Artemisius. And when Parmenio begged him not to risk a battle because the hour was too late, he said the Hellespont would blush for shame if after crossing it, he was frightened by the Granicus. With that, he plunged into the stream with thirteen squadrons of cavalry.

It seemed the act of a mad and reckless commander rather than of a wise one, to charge against a storm of missiles towards steep banks crowded with armed men and horses, through a river which washed up around his men and swept them away. But he kept on trying to get across

---

[42] Daesius and Artemisius were Macedonian names for months. Daesius began about the middle of our May and extended to about the middle of our June, Artemisius was the month before.

and with struggle and difficulty reached the opposite bank, which was wet and slippery with mud. There at once he had to engage in a confused man-to-man encounter with his attackers before the soldiers who were crossing could form in any order. The enemy fell on them with a shout, and setting horse against horse fought with spears, and with swords when their spears were broken. Many of them pressed up to Alexander himself, for he was conspicuous by his shield and by the crest of his helmet, on either side of which stood up a plume, strikingly white and tall. But though struck by a javelin in the joint of his breastplate, he was not wounded.

Rhoesaces and Spithridates, Persian generals, now attacked him together, but he evaded Spithridates and struck Rhoesaces, who wore a breastplate, with his spear. When his spear snapped he resorted to his sword. But while they closed together, Spithridates rode up beside him and, raising himself on his horse, dealt him such a mighty blow with his barbarian battle-ax as to cut off his crest and one of his plumes. His helmet barely stood the blow and the blade of the battle-ax touched the topmost hair of his head. But as Spithridates was rising for another stroke, Black Clitus caught him and ran him through with his lance, and at the same moment Alexander with his sword laid Rhoesaces dead at his feet. While this perilous and desperate cavalry battle was going on, the Macedonian phalanx was crossing the river and the infantry forces were coming to grips. However, the enemy put up no stout or lengthy resistance but soon turned and fled, all except the Greek mercenary troops, who made a stand on a hill and asked Alexander for quarter. But he, too furious to be reasonable, charged head on at them and lost his horse, which was stabbed through the ribs by a sword thrust. It was not Bucephalus but another horse. Most of the Macedonians who were killed or wounded in that battle suffered and fell there, struggling with men who were desperate and experienced in warfare.

The Persians, they say, lost twenty thousand infantrymen and twenty-five hundred horse. According to Aristobulus, Alexander's losses were but thirty-four men in all, of whom nine were foot soldiers. He ordered bronze statues erected of them, the work of Lysippus, to make the Greeks feel sharers in the victory, and to the Athenians specifically he sent three hundred of the captured shields. Over the other spoils generally he had placed the highly vainglorious inscription: "Alexander, son of Philip, and the Greeks, all but the Lacedaemonians, won these from the barbarians who dwell in Asia." But the drinking-cups and purple robes and other things of the sort, which he took from the Persians, he sent, all save a few to his mother.

17. This victory straightway made a great change in Alexander's position. He was able to occupy Sardis, the outpost nearest the sea of the barbarians' dominion, and then to take over the rest of the country. Only Halicarnassus and Miletus still resisted him, and those cities he stormed, and subdued all the region around them. He was then in two minds as to what to do next. At one moment he would be impatient to attack Darius and risk everything on one blow, and at another he would decide to gain experience and strength first by completing his conquest of the seacoast and its resources, and then to go up against the king. Now there is in Lycia a spring, near the city of Xanthus, which, they say, boiled up and overflowed at this time of its own accord, and threw up from its depths a bronze tablet, on which, carved in ancient letters, was the statement that the Persian empire would be overthrown and ended by the Greeks. Encouraged by this prediction, Alexander hurriedly cleared up the coast as far as Cilicia and Phoenicia.

His rapid progress through Pamphylia has been a subject of amazement and awe for many historians, for they say that by some miracle the sea retired before him, though always, except then, it has rolled dashing in from the deep, barely showing at times the low crags which lie at the foot of the steep cliffs. Menander is evidently alluding to the marvel in a jest in one of his comedies: [43]

"How like this is to Alexander! If I wish to meet someone,
 All of his own accord, he's here; and if I plainly must
 Go through the sea to reach some place, it will lie open to me."

Alexander himself, however, in his letters, speaks of no such miracle, but merely tells us that he started from Phaselis, [44] and went by way of the so-called Ladder, and thus made the journey. He spent some days in Phaselis, during which he saw that a statue of Theodectes, [45] lately dead,

---

[43] A fragment from a lost comedy by Menander.

[44] Phaselis was the main harbor of Lycia, in southernmost Asia Minor.

[45] Theodectes, a rhetorician and poet, had been a pupil of Plato, Isocrates, and Aristotle. He had spent his life mostly at Athens.

a former citizen of Phaselis, had been set up in the market place. After supper, and his wine, he led a gay procession to it and crowned it with many of their wreaths, paying the man thus merrily a graceful honor and testifying to the bond he felt there was between them through Aristotle and philosophy.

18. After this he put down a revolt among the Pisidians and conquered Phrygia. He took the city of Gordium, said to have been the home of the ancient Midas,[46] and saw the celebrated wagon there which he had tied fast with a knot of cornel-tree bark. He heard too the story about it, be- lieved by all the barbarians, that whoever undid the knot was destined to become king of all the world. Most writers say that the cords were twisted together many times over in intricate coils, with their ends hidden, and that Alexander, unable to loosen the knot, cut through it with his sword, and that when cut it showed it had many ends. But Aristobulus says that he undid it quite easily by pulling out what they call the pin of the wagon pole to which the yoke band was fastened, and then drawing off the yoke.

From there he went on to occupy Paphlagonia and Cappadocia, and was encouraged to advance inland by hearing of the death of Memnon,[47] one of Darius' generals on the coast, who had been expected to give him much trouble and create endless obstacles and hindrances. But now Darius himself started down from Susa, confident in the numbers of his host, for he was bringing an army of six hundred thousand men. He was em- boldened too by a dream which his soothsayers were interpreting to please him, instead of as reason dictated. For he dreamed that he saw the Macedonian phalanx all aflame, and Alexander, dressed in a robe such as Darius himself had once worn when he was king's courier, acting as

---

[46] Midas was the legendary king of Phrygia about whom several stories were told, all more or less fanciful. Alexander's cutting of the Gordian knot became itself the theme of another tale.

[47] Memnon (4th century B.C.), a captain from Rhodes, had married Barsine, a daugh- ter of Artabazus (c.387–c.325), son of the satrap Pharnabazus (c.413–370), for whom see above under *Alcibiades,* ch. 24, n. 50. Taking service under Artaxerxes III, as a Persian general in Asia Minor, Memnon had fought ably against both Philip and Alexander. After his death his wife was taken by Alexander as his mistress. See below, ch. 21.

nis servant. And then Alexander went into the temple of Belus,[48] and disappeared. By this dream the god probably was warning Darius that the future of the Macedonians would be brilliant and renowned, that Alexander would conquer Asia, just as Darius had conquered it, rising from a mere courier to be king, and would die soon afterward in glory.

19. Darius was even more encouraged by Alexander's long sojourn in Cilicia, which he took as evidence of cowardice. His delay, however, was caused by an illness, which some say came from exhaustion, and others say from bathing in the icy waters of the Cydnus. No physician dared to prescribe treatment, for they all thought his state was too dangerous for any cure, and were afraid of being blamed by the Macedonians if they failed to save him. But Philip, the Acarnanian, realized his plight and trusted his friendship, and thought it a terrible thing not to take a share of the danger by trying his utmost to cure him, even at considerable risk. So he put together a medicine for him and persuaded him to drink it, if he wanted to get back strength for war.

But at this same time Parmenio sent Alexander a letter from the camp, bidding him beware of Philip, because he had been bribed by Darius with rich presents and a promise of marriage with Darius' daughter to murder him. Alexander read the letter, showed it to none of his friends, but laid it under his pillow. At the hour set, Philip and his companions entered the room, bringing the medicine in a cup. Alexander handed him the letter while he himself took the medicine pleasantly and with no sign of suspicion. It was a strange and dramatic scene, one reading and the other drinking, and then looking into each other's faces, though not in the same way—Alexander with a serene and beaming countenance was showing his friendliness and his trust in Philip, while Philip, horrified at the accusation, was now raising his hands to heaven and calling on the gods, and now casting himself down by the bed and begging Alexander to keep up his courage and follow his directions. The medicine at first overcame Alexander, driving his energy down, as it were, and sinking it deep, so that he became speechless, fell into a swoon, and almost lost consciousness.

---

48 Belus is a Greek form of the Asiatic Bel or Baal, name of an important god of the Babylonian and Phoenician pantheons, and the god of the Canaanites in the Old Testament.

He quickly recovered, however, under Philip's care, and when well again, showed himself to his Macedonians, who would not stop worrying about him until they saw him.

20. Now in Darius' army there was a Macedonian fugitive named Amyntas, who knew a great deal about Alexander's character. This man, on seeing that Darius was preparing to attack Alexander and move on into the mountain passes, urged him to remain where he was on the wide and open plains, where with his enormous army he would overwhelm Alexander's smaller force. Darius answered that he feared the enemy would escape him there by taking to its heels, and that Alexander would get away. "O king," said Amyntas, "have no fears on that score, for he will come straight against you. Even now, in all likelihood, he is on his way." But Amyntas' words went unheeded, and Darius broke camp and advanced into Cilicia, while at the same time Alexander was marching into Syria to meet him. By night they missed one another and both turned back, Alexander delighted at his good fortune and eager to catch Darius in the narrow passes, Darius anxious to regain his former camping ground and disentangle his army from the passes. For already he perceived his mistake in pushing on into regions hard for cavalry and broken into many parts by sea and mountains and the river Pinarus which ran between them, all of which gave great advantages to the smaller number of his enemies.

So fortune made a gift of the place to Alexander, yet he owed his victory even more to his generalship. Since his numbers were so much less than those of the barbarians, he gave them no chance to surround him, but himself with his right wing outflanked their left and put those that were opposite him to flight. He himself fought among the foremost so that he was wounded by a sword in the thigh. According to Chares,[49] he was stabbed by Darius, for the two had a hand-to-hand fight. But Alexander, in a letter he wrote to Antipater about the battle, did not say who the man was who wounded him, but only that he had been wounded in the thigh with a dagger and that the wound had done him no serious injury.

---

[49] Chares of Mitylene, Alexander's chamberlain, was the author of a detailed and anedoctal history of his life, now lost.

He won a brilliant victory,[50] and killed over a hundred and ten thousand of the enemy, but did not capture Darius who with a start of four or five furlongs, escaped by flight. However, Alexander got his chariot and bow, and on his return found his Macedonians carrying off the wealth of the barbarians' camp and seizing a tremendous quantity, although the Persians had come to battle in light marching dress and had left most of their luggage behind in Damascus. But the royal tent of Darius, full of handsome slaves and furniture and riches, he found the soldiers had reserved for himself. At once then he took off his armor and went to bathe, saying, "Let us go and wash off the sweat of the battle in Darius' bath." "No, by Zeus," exclaimed one of his companions, "in Alexander's bath, for the goods of the vanquished, which belong to the victor, must be called his." And when he saw the jars and pitchers and tubs and boxes, all of gold and intricately wrought, and smelled the delicious fragrance of spices and perfumes in the pavilion, and when he passed from it to a tent magnificent in its height and size, and in the splendor of the couches and tables and the banquet set out there, he looked at his friends and said, "This, it seems, is to be a king."

21. Then, as he turned to his banquet, someone told him that among the captives were the mother and wife and two maiden daughters of Darius, and that on seeing his chariot and bow they had beat their breasts and wailed for him as dead. Alexander sat hushed for a long time, more moved by their woes than by his own success. He then sent Leonnatus to inform them that Darius was not dead and they need not fear Alexander, for though he was at war with Darius for supremacy, they would still receive everything they thought was their due when Darius ruled the realm. This message seemed to the women gracious and merciful, and his acts turned out to be still more humane. For he permitted them to bury as many Persians as they wished, and to use for the burial apparel and ornaments taken from the plunder. He deprived them of none of the service and deference they were accustomed to receive, and they enjoyed even larger revenues than before.

The noblest and most kingly favor he showed to these captive gentle

---

[50] This was the battle of Issus, fought at a strategic point on the Cilician coast, near the modern Alexandretta, in November, 333 B.C.

ladies was to prevent their ever hearing or suspecting or anticipating any thing to shame them. They lived sheltered in pure and holy maidens' quarters, away from common talk and sights. Yet the wife of Darius is said to have been much the most beautiful of all royal princesses, just as Darius himself was the tallest and handsomest of men, and their daughters resembled their parents. But Alexander, it appears, thought it more kingly to master himself than to subdue his enemies, and he never touched them, nor indeed did he know any other woman before his marriage except Barsine.

This lady, left a widow by the death of Memnon, was taken captive at Damascus. She had been educated by the Greek method, was naturally attractive, and her father, Artabazus, had been son of a king's daughter. Parmenio, Aristobulus says, advised Alexander to take for himself a woman so beautiful and so high-born. But on seeing other captive ladies of extraordinary beauty and stature, he merely remarked in jest that Persian women were a pain to the eyes. To their charms he opposed the beauty of his strong will and self-control, and passed by them as if they were lifeless images, made for ornament.

22. And when Philoxenus, the commander of his troops on the coast, wrote that there was with him a certain Theodorus of Tarentum, who had two boys of remarkable beauty for sale and wished to know if Alexander would buy them, he was furious and cried out again and again to his friends, asking them what signs of baseness Philoxenus had ever observed in him that he should waste his time making disgraceful proposals. To Philoxenus himself he wrote a letter of severe reprimand, ordering him to send Theodorus and his wares to the devil. He sent a cutting rebuke to Hagnon too for writing to him that he was thinking of buying Crobylus, a famous boy beauty in Corinth, to bring to him.

On hearing that Damon and Timotheus, two Macedonians of Parmenio's command, had outraged the wives of some mercenary soldiers, he wrote to Parmenio, ordering him, if the charges were proved, to punish the men by death, as wild beasts born to prey on mankind. In that letter too he spoke particularly of himself. "For myself you will find that not only have I not seen or desired to see the wife of Darius, but I have not even allowed people who talk of her beauty to speak of it to me." And he used to say that sleep and sexual intercourse, more than anything else, reminded him that he was mortal, since in each case a single natural weakness brought him both pleasure and weariness.

He had great control over his appetite, and showed it on many occasions, especially in what he said to Ada, whom he adopted as his mother and made queen of Caria. Out of affection for him she would send him every day dainty dishes and sweetmeats and at last presented him with pastry cooks and bakers who were considered to be very expert. But he told her he wanted none of them, for he had better cooks provided for him by his tutor Leonidas—for breakfast a night's march, and for dinner a scanty breakfast. "This same tutor," he said, "would come and open my chests of bedding and clothes, to see that my mother had not hidden there some special delicacy for me."

23. He was less given to wine than is commonly supposed. He was thought to be a great drinker because of the time he would spend over each cup, doing more talking than drinking, for he was always talking at great length about something, whenever he had leisure for it. But when there was work to do he never allowed wine or sleep or amusement or wife or spectacle to interfere with it, as other generals did. This fact is evident in his life, which, though cut so short, he crammed full of so many grand achievements. In times of leisure, however, he would sacrifice to the gods immediately on rising, then sit down to breakfast, and pass the day hunting, or judging disputes, or making military arrangements, or reading.

When on a march, if it was not very urgent, he would practice as he went, either archery or jumping on and off a chariot in motion. Often too for entertainment he would hunt foxes and birds, as we may learn from his journals. After halting for the night, while he was bathing or being anointed, he would ask his cooks and bakers if they were well supplied with provisions for dinner. Not until it was late and growing dark, would he lie on his couch and begin his dinner. He was wonderfully careful and watchful at table to see that everything was fairly and generously served. Over his wine, as I have said, he would linger a long time because of his love of conversation. But though at other times he was the most delightful of kings to be with, possessed of every grace, at such a time his bragging would make him disagreeable, too much like an ordinary soldier. He would grow excited and boastful, and also unduly susceptible to persons who flattered him. Such men were an embarrassment to the more sincere members of the company, who wished neither to compete with the flatterers in praising him, nor yet to lag too far behind them. One policy seemed disgraceful, the other was dangerous.

After the drinking, he would take a bath and sleep often until noon. Sometimes he spent a whole day in sleep. But when it came to delicacies he was abstemious and often when the rarest fruits and fish were brought to him from the coast, he would send them around to every one of his friends until there was nothing left for himself. Yet his dinners were always magnificent, and the cost of them rose with his conquests until it reached ten thousand drachmas. But there it remained and at that sum it was fixed for all who would entertain Alexander.

24.   After the battle of Issus, he sent troops to Damascus and captured all the Persians' treasure and baggage, with their women and children. The Thessalian cavalry chiefly benefited, for since they had distinguished themselves in the battle, they were purposely sent by him on this service so that they might enrich themselves. But the rest of the army too was laden with booty. There for the first time the Macedonians got a taste of gold and silver and women and barbaric luxury, and thenceforth, like hounds that have fastened on a scent, they were eager to pursue the track of Persian wealth.

Alexander, however, thought it best, before proceeding farther, to complete his conquest of the seaboard. The kings of Cyprus came at once and surrendered their island to him, as well as Phoenicia, all but Tyre. But for seven months he besieged Tyre,[51] with moles and engines and a fleet of two hundred triremes on the sea. Meanwhile he had a dream that he saw Heracles reaching his hand out to him from the city wall and calling to him. And many of the Tyrians thought in their sleep that they heard Apollo saying to them that he was leaving them for Alexander, because he was displeased with their behavior in the city. After which they treated the god as if he were a man caught in the act of deserting

---

[51] Possession of the supposedly impregnable naval base of Tyre was of such moment to Alexander that he spent the greater part of the year 332 B.C. besieging it, succeeding only after he had built a mole from the mainland out to the island of Tyre over which his troops could advance to batter down the walls. It was one of the famous sieges of antiquity, each side showing great ingenuity in the use of new engines of destruction.

to the enemy, for they bound his colossal statue with cords and nailed it to its base, calling him an "Alexandrist."

Alexander now had another dream. He thought that a satyr appeared to him, mocking him from a distance and slipping away when he endeavored to catch him, but that, at length, after much wheedling and chasing, he gave himself up. The soothsayers divided the word satyr in two and told him, plausibly, "Tyre shall be yours." [52] And today they point out a spring near which Alexander in his sleep dreamed he saw the satyr.

In the middle of the siege, he went off on an expedition against the Arabs who live near the mountain Antilebanus, during which he risked his life for his tutor Lysimachus. For Lysimachus insisted on accompanying him, declaring that he was no feebler or older than Phoenix.[53] But when they approached the mountains, they left their horses and went on foot, and the others got a long way ahead. Though evening was closing in and the enemy was nearby, Alexander would not desert the worn and exhausted Lysimachus, but tried to encourage and help him along. So before he knew it, he was separated from his army, with only a few companions. The night was dark and bitterly cold, the country rugged, and he saw in the distance a line of the enemy's scattered watchfires. Confident of his own physical nimbleness and accustomed always to cheer the Macedonians in a dilemma by some exertion on his own part, he ran over to the nearest fire and struck down with his dagger two barbarians who were sitting beside it. Then seizing a burning firebrand he carried it back to his own men. They now built up an enormous fire which immediately terrified many of the enemy so that they fled. Others who started to attack them they drove back, and passed the night in safety. This, at any rate, is Chares' account.

25. The siege of Tyre came to an end as follows. Alexander was giving the main body of his army a rest from its many previous labors, but in order to keep the enemy occupied he was about to lead a few men up against the walls, while Aristander, the soothsayer, was offering sacrifice. But when Aristander saw the omens, he boldly informed the onlookers that that very month the city would surely be taken. They jeered and

---

[52] The Greek words, "Se Tyr," might be construed to mean "Tyre yours."
[53] See above, ch. 5, and n. 17.

laughed at him, for it was then the last day of the month. But Alexander, seeing his perplexity and always anxious to support the credit of prophecies, ordered that that day should be counted not the thirtieth but the twenty-eighth. Then with his trumpet giving the signal, he attacked the walls more forcefully than he had originally intended. The attack was skillful, and the troops left behind in camp did not stay there but rushed out in crowds to help. So the Tyrians surrendered and Alexander took their city that very day.

Later, while Alexander was besieging Gaza, the largest city of Syria, a clod of earth was dropped on his shoulder from aloft by a bird. The bird then alighted on one of the siege engines, and at once became blindly entangled in the network of sinews which they used when twisting the ropes. And that omen too turned out as Aristander predicted, for Alexander was wounded in his shoulder but he took the city.

A great mass of spoils he now sent home to Olympias and Cleopatra and his friends, and to his tutor Leonidas he sent five hundred talents' weight of frankincense and a hundred talents of myrrh, to remind him of a hope Leonidas had given him as a child. For once, it seems, when Alexander was sacrificing and taking incense with both hands to throw on the sacred fire, Leonidas, said to him, "When you have conquered the country from which the spices come, Alexander, you may then be so free with your incense, but now you must use sparingly what is here." Accordingly, Alexander now wrote him, "We have sent you frankincense and myrrh in plenty, so that you may stop being stingy with the gods."

26. A small casket was brought to him, which the receivers of the wealth and luggage of Darius thought as precious as anything there, and he asked his friends what valuable article they thought he should keep in it. Many of them made various suggestions, but Alexander then said he was putting the *Iliad* in it to keep it safe. This story is told by many reliable historians. And if what the Alexandrians say, on the authority of Heraclides, is true, Homer was apparently no idle or useless companion to him on his expedition. For they say that after conquering Egypt he wished to build a great and populous Greek city, to be called by his own name, and with the advice of his architects he was about to measure off and enclose a site, when one night, in his sleep, he had an extraordinary vision. He

saw a man with very hoary hair and venerable aspect standing beside him, who repeated these verses: [54]

> "Then there is an island in the billowy sea,
> Close in front of Egypt, Pharos is its name."

So he arose quickly and went to Pharos, then still an island a little beyond the Canobic mouth of the Nile, though now connected by a causeway with the mainland. And there he saw a site outstanding in advantages, a strip of land, the width of an isthmus, lying between a large lake and the sea, and ending in a large harbor. Thereat he declared that Homer was certainly not only wonderful in other ways but the wisest of architects, and gave orders that the city should be mapped out to fit that site. They had no chalk with them, but they took barley meal and on the black earth marked out a circular area, with straight streets running up into the center from the border, like the pattern of a military cloak, narrowing evenly the space between the lines. The king was delighted with the plan, but suddenly an innumerable flock of birds of every kind and size from the river and the lake swooped down on the spot in clouds and devoured every morsel of the barley. Even Alexander was disturbed at this omen. But the soothsayers bade him take heart, for the city he was founding would be exceedingly rich in its resources and a nurse and feeder of men of every race. At this, he ordered his overseers to push on with the work, while he himself set off for the shrine of Ammon.[55]

The journey was long and extremely toilsome and painful. There were two dangers, one the lack of water, for there is none to be found for many days, the other, the furious south wind, as it blows on men journeying through vast depths of sand. This, they say, is what happened to Cambyses' army [56] long ago. The wind raised huge waves of sand over the plain,

---

[54] Homer, *Odyssey,* IV, 354–355. The ancient city of Alexandria, as founded by Alexander, lay on a neck of land between Lake Maeotis and the sea. By joining the city with a causeway to the island of Pharos, about three quarters of a mile out, Alexander gave it a second or outer harbor and made it the one port on the Nile Delta which had room for a large fleet. It soon became the center of commerce and industry for the southeastern Mediterranean.

[55] On the Greek identification of their god Zeus with Ammon, see above, n. 5.

[56] Cambyses, king of Persia from 529 to 521 B.C., invaded and conquered Egypt in 525, but in an attempt to push on south to the Siwa Oasis he lost the greater part of his army in the waterless desert.

engulfing and destroying fifty thousand men. All these perils were in men's minds, but Alexander was hard to turn away from any project on which he had started. For Fortune by yielding as she had to his demands was making him stubborn in his determination, and the high spirit with which he faced untoward circumstances was rendering him invincible in his ambition, subduing not only his enemies but even place and time.

27.   On that journey, at any rate, the assistance the god gave him in his difficulties was more impressive than the oracles which he received later, and the impression it created in its way was what made men believe in the oracles. In the first place, a heavy rain from Zeus and abundant showers removed the dread of thirst, moistened the dry sand, which became damp and cohesive, and kept the air cleaner and good to breathe. Then when the landmarks for the guides seemed confused and the troops were scattered and wandering, ignorant of their path, ravens appeared and took over the leadership of the march, flying swiftly before them as long as they followed, and waiting for them when they loitered and fell behind. Most amazing of all is Callisthenes' story,[57] that by their cries at night the birds called back stragglers, screaming until they had brought them again into the line of march.

When then Alexander had crossed the desert and arrived at the temple, the prophet of Ammon greeted him in the name of the god, as though he were his father. Alexander asked whether any of his father's murderers had escaped him, to which the prophet answered that he must be careful how he spoke, for his father was not a mortal. Alexander now altered the form of his inquiry and asked whether he had punished all of Philip's murderers; then, thinking of his own empire, he asked whether the god would grant him lordship over all mankind. And the god replied that he was granting him this, and that Philip was amply avenged; whereupon Alexander made magnificent offerings to the god and gifts of money to the priests.

This is what most historians tell us about the words of the oracle. But

---

[57] Callisthenes, a Greek philosopher and historian, author of an account of Alexander's expedition to Asia, was a member of the king's circle of companions until put to death on a charge of treachery, in 325 B.C. See below, chs. 52–55. His works, like those of Alexander's other companions, are lost.

Alexander himself, in a letter to his mother, says that he received certain secret messages, which on his return he would tell to her alone. Some also relate that the prophet wished to greet him cordially in the Greek tongue and to say, *"O paidion,"* but that in his barbaric way he ended the word with an "s" instead of an "n" and said *"O paidios."* And Alexander was pleased at his slip of the tongue, and the story spread that the god had addressed him as *"O pai Dios."* [58] They say too that while Alexander was in Egypt he heard the lectures of the philosopher Psammon, and found especially acceptable his teaching that all men are ruled by God as king, because in every instance that which leads and governs is divine. Still more profound, however, was what Alexander himself believed and said on the subject, namely, that God is the common father of all men, but makes the best of them peculiarly his own.

28. In general he was haughty with the barbarians, like one convinced of his own divine birth and parentage, but with the Greeks he was unpretentious and cautious in his assumptions of divinity. Yet once, when writing to the Athenians about Samos, he said, "I could not have presented you with that free and glorious city. You received it from the man who was then its ruler and my reputed father," meaning Philip. Later, however, when he had been wounded by an arrow and was in great pain, he said, "This, my friends, is blood that is running here, and not

'Ichor, such as courses through the veins of the blessed gods.' " [59]

Once when it thundered so loudly that everyone was terrified, Anaxarchus the Sophist, who was there, said to him, "Can you, O son of Zeus, thunder so loud?" Alexander laughed and replied, "I do not want to frighten my friends, as you are proposing I should—you, who despise my dinner because you find the tables set 'with fish instead of satraps' heads.' " Actually, they say, Anaxarchus once, when Alexander sent some small fish to Hephaestion, used the above words, as a way of ironically disparaging those who pursue fame at the cost of great labor and danger. and yet get little or no more pleasure and diversion from it than other men have. From what I have said it is plain that Alexander did not him

---

[58] *"O paidion"* means "O little son"; *"O pai Dios,"* "O son of Zeus."
[59] Homer, *Iliad,* V, 340.

DANUBE R.

THRACE

BLACK SEA

CAUCASUS

MACEDONIA

Pella

Byzantium
Chalcedon

Sinope

PAPHLA-
GONIA

Stagira
SAMOTHRACE

HELLESPONT

GRANICUS R.
BITHYNIA

PONTUS

LEMNOS

Troy

MYSIA
PERGAMUM

GALATIA

GREECE

LESBOS

CHIOS

Sardis

PHRYGIA

CAPPADOCIA

ARMENIA

ABAXES R.

Mycale Mt.

Ephesus

SAMOS

Miletus

PELOPONNESUS

CARIA

TAURUS MTS.

MEDI

RHODES

CILICIA

Samosata

CRETE

Xanthus

Tarsus

Issus

Arbela

MESOPOTAMIA

CYPRUS

Antioch

EUPHRATES R.

TIGRIS R.

LIBYA

Sidon

Tyre

PHOENICIA

Damascus

SYRIA

PHAROS

Alexandria
LAKE
MAREOTIS

Pelusium

JUDAEA

Babylon

Ammonium

Memphis

BABYLONIA

ARABIA

EGYPT

Thebes

NILE R.

RED SEA

ALEXANDER'S EMPIRE

| 0 | 100 | 200 | 300 | 400 | 500 | 600 | 700 | 800 |

Scale in Miles

━ ━ ━ Alexander's Route

Alexandria

SOGDIANA

BACTRIA

HINDU-KUSH MTS.

HYRCANIA
PARTHIA

tana

Alexandria

Taxila
Bucephala
Alexan-
dria

INDUS R.
JHELUM R.
HYDASPES R.

INDIA

PERSIA

Persepolis
ARAXES R.

CARMANIA

GEDROSIA

Alexandria

Alexandria

PERSIAN GULF

CUTCH

ARABIAN SEA

AN SEA

S

self become affected or have his head turned by the report of his divinity, but used it as a means of subduing others.[60]

29.   On his return to Phoenicia from Egypt [61] he offered sacrifices and stately processions to the gods and held contests of cyclic choruses and tragedies, made splendid both by their settings and by the men who competed in them. For the kings of Cyprus provided the choruses and staging, just as the men do at Athens who are elected by lot from the tribes, and with immense ambition they tried to outdo each other. Keenest of all was the contest between Nicocreon of Salamis and Pasicrates of Soli, for to them were allotted the two most celebrated actors, Athenodorus to Pasicrates and Thessalus to Nicocreon. Alexander himself favored Thessalus, though he did not reveal his preference until the vote had been taken and Athenodorus proclaimed victor. But then, it seems, as Alexander was leaving the scene, he said that he approved the judges' decision but that he would gladly have given up a part of his kingdom not to have seen Thessalus beaten. When Athenodorus was fined by the Athenians for not appearing at their Dionysiac festival and asked the king to write them a letter in his excuse, Alexander refused to do it, but sent them the fine from his own treasury. Once Lycon of Scarphia was acting a part cleverly in the theater and inserted into the comedy a line in which he begged for ten talents, and Alexander laughed and gave them to him.

Darius now sent him a letter and an embassy of friends, begging him to accept ten thousand talents as ransom for his prisoners and proposing that he keep all the territory west of the Euphrates, marry one of Darius' daughters, and become his friend and ally. Alexander laid the proposal before his friends. Parmenio said, "I should accept it if I were Alexander," and Alexander said, "So, by Zeus, would I if I were Parmenio." To Darius he wrote that if he would come to him, he would receive every consideration; but if not, he himself would at once march against him.

----

[60] It is a moot question how far Alexander believed in his own divinity. Traditionally Persians and Egyptians accepted their monarchs as deities, and Greeks were familiar with the idea of a benefactor to mankind, like Heracles, becoming a god. After Alexander's visit to the desert oracle of Ammon, his propaganda made much of his so-called recognition there as a son of Zeus Ammon. And to a man so interested in gods of all kinds and with so exalted a conception of his own role as world ruler and regulator of nations it would seem natural to regard himself as something rather more than human.   [61] This was early in 331 B.C.

30. Soon after this, however, Alexander regretted his answer, for Darius' wife died in childbirth, and he was obviously vexed that he had missed an opportunity of doing a great kindness. At any rate, he spared no expense for the woman's burial. One of the eunuchs attached to her bedchamber, a man named Teireos, who had been captured with the women, escaped from the camp, rode on horseback to Darius, and told him his wife had died. Thereupon Darius beat his head and broke into lamentations. "Alas," he cried, "for the evil fate over Persia, if the wife and sister of the king is not only taken captive while living but at death must go without royal burial!" "But, O king," replied the eunuch, "you have no cause to blame the evil fate of Persia on grounds of your wife's burial, or of any lack of due honor to her. Not while she lived did our lady Statira, or your mother, or your children want for any of their former comforts and joys, except for the light of your countenance which Lord Oromasdes [62] will kindle again in full luster. Nor after her death did she lie unadorned; she was even honored by the tears of her enemies. For Alexander is as merciful after victory as he is terrible in battle."

But at hearing this, Darius' distress and grief carried him into strange suspicions, and leading the eunuch into an inner part of his tent, he said: "If you too have not gone over to the Macedonians, along with the fortunes of Persia, and if I, Darius, am still your lord, tell me, as you reverence the great light of Mithras [63] and the right hand of your king, am I not bewailing the least of Statira's misfortunes? Did I not suffer something even more grievous during her lifetime? Would not my misfortune have been more honorable if I had found an enemy really savage and inhuman? For what honest communication can a young man have had with his enemy's wife, to lead to his showing her so much honor?" But while Darius was speaking, Teireos fell at his feet and besought him to beware of wronging Alexander and disgracing his dead sister and wife, and not to deprive himself of the greatest consolation in his disaster, the thought that he had been conquered by one who was more than mortal man. He should indeed marvel at Alexander, for he had displayed

[62] Oromasdes is a corrupt form of Ahura-Mazda, the name of the Persian great god of Heaven. See below, *Isis and Osiris,* ch. 46.

[63] Mithras, commonly worshiped as a Persian sun-god, was one of the beneficent powers of light under Ahura-Mazda, who fought an unending battle against the evil powers of darkness.

even more self-control with Persian women than valor with Persian men. With solemn oaths the eunuch assured him that those things were true, and at the same time he spoke of Alexander's self-restraint and high-mindedness in other matters.

So Darius went out to his friends and raising his hands to heaven prayed: "Ye gods of my race and my throne, grant me first of all that i may leave the fortune of Persia established again in the prosperity in which I received it, so that in victory I may return to Alexander the favors I received from him when I lost what was dearest to me. But if this now is the fated hour when we pay our debt to Nemesis and Change, and the empire of Persia is finished, may no other man but Alexander sit on the throne of Cyrus." This account of what took place and.was said is given by most historians.

31. Alexander next overcame all the country west of the Euphrates, and then marched to attack Darius, who was advancing to meet him with an army of a million men.[64] During the march one of his comrades told him that the camp attendants in sport had divided themselves into two sections, each of which had its general and commander. One of these the men called Alexander, and the other Darius. They had begun by throwing clods of earth at each other, then had come to fists, and finally had grown so hot for the fight that they were resorting to clubs and stones. They now had gathered a large crowd and were parted with difficulty. On hearing this, Alexander ordered the two commanders to fight in single combat, and he himself armed the one called Alexander, while Philotas armed the one called Darius. The whole army looked on, thinking the event would be some omen of the future. The battle was a hard one, but the man called Alexander won and received as a reward twelve villages and the right to wear Persian garb. We hear of this incident from Eratosthenes.

The decisive battle with Darius was fought, not at Arbela, as most writers tell us, but at Gaugamela. The name means, they say, "Camel's House," for one of their ancient kings who had escaped from his foes on a swift camel kept the animal there and assigned the revenues from certain villages for its maintenance. Now in the month of Boedromion, at the time the mysteries at Athens begin, there was an eclipse of the moon,[65] and

[64] This figure is undoubtedly greatly exaggerated.
[65] The date was September 20, 331 B.C.

on the eleventh night after the eclipse the two armies were within sight of each other. Darius kept his host under arms and inspected its ranks by torchlight, but Alexander let his Macedonians rest, while he himself, with the soothsayer Aristander, spent the hours in front of his tent, performing some secret ceremonies and sacrificing victims to the god Fear.

Meanwhile, the older of his companions, in particular, Parmenio, were watching the plain between the Niphates and the mountains of Gordyaea, all lit up with the barbarians' fires, and hearing the vague confused roar of voices from their camp, like the roaring of a vast ocean. They were amazed at the size of the host and said to one another that it would be a prodigious and difficult task to attack such an army by daylight and drive it back. So, when the king had finished sacrificing, they went to him and tried to persuade him to fall on the enemy by night and so shroud in darkness the terrifying sight of the struggle ahead of them. But he gave them his famous reply, "I am not stealing my victory." Some thought it a boyish and boastful answer, a jest in the face of gravest danger. Others thought it showed confidence in the situation as it was and a correct judgment of what would happen. For he was not giving Darius, if defeated, an excuse to get up courage again for another battle by attributing this defeat to the darkness of night, as he had attributed his earlier failures to the narrow passes of the mountains and to the sea. Nor was it loss of arms or men that would make Darius give up the fight, with all his resources of power and territory. He would only do it when he lost spirit and hope through a crushing defeat in broad day.

32. When these men left him, Alexander went to bed in his tent and is said to have slept through the rest of the night more soundly than usual, so that his commanders were surprised when they came to him at daybreak and found him still asleep, and themselves gave orders that the soldiers should at once have breakfast. Then, as time pressed, Parmenio entered the tent and standing by Alexander's bed called him two or three times by name. On his awaking, Parmenio asked him how he could sleep the sleep of a victor, as if he were not about to fight the most tremendous battle of his life. Alexander said with a smile, "What, do you not feel that we are already victorious, now that we are through with wandering around and chasing Darius over a vast, devastated country, while he refuses to fight?"

Not only before the battle but in the thick of danger Alexander showed himself great and steady in his judgment and his bravery. For in the struggle his left wing, under Parmenio, was repulsed and shaken when the Bactrian cavalry fell on the Macedonians in force with a great rush, while Mazaeus sent horsemen around outside the Greek phalanx to attack the men guarding the baggage. Parmenio, upset by the two movements, dispatched messengers to Alexander to tell him that his camp and baggage were lost, if he did not quickly send strong reinforcements from the front to the rear. It happened that at that moment Alexander was about to give the signal to his men to advance, and when he heard Parmenio's message he cried that the man was out of his senses and had lost his reason to have forgotten in his excitement that if they were winning, they would have the property of the enemy as well as their own, and that if they were being defeated, they must not think of riches or slaves but of how to fight splendidly and die with honor.

Sending this message to Parmenio, he put on his helmet, but the rest of the armor he had been wearing when he left his tent, an undergirdle of Sicilian make, and over that a corselet of two thicknesses of linen from the spoils taken at Issus. His helmet was of iron, but it shone like polished silver and was made by Theophilus; attached to it was a collar, also of iron, set with precious stones. He carried a light sword, of wonderfully fine temper, a present to him from the king of Citium, and he had practiced making great use of a sword in fighting. He wore a cape too of more elaborate workmanship than the rest of his armor, for it was made by the ancient artist Helicon and had been given to Alexander by the city of Rhodes as a mark of honor. He usually wore it in battle. As long as he was riding around, getting some section of his phalanx into battle order or encouraging or instructing or inspecting the men, he spared Bucephalus, who was now past his prime, and used another horse. But when he was moving into action, Bucephalus would be brought up, and mounting him he would straightway begin the attack.

33.   That day he made a long speech to the Thessalians and other Greeks, and they cheered and shouted to him to lead them against the barbarians. So shifting his lance into his left hand, with his right, Callisthenes says, he appealed to the gods, praying them if he were truly a son of Zeus, to defend and give strength to the Greeks. And the soothsayer Aristander,

wearing a white mantle and a golden crown on his head, rode beside him and pointed out an eagle which rose over Alexander's head and then flew straight towards the enemy. Thereat the beholders were filled with high courage and after heartening and spurring on one another the cavalry charged at a gallop against the enemy, while the waves of the phalanx rolled on.

But before the front ranks came to blows, the barbarians gave way and were fiercely pursued, Alexander driving the beaten troops towards the center, where Darius was. For Alexander had seen him from far off, conspicuous through the deep lines of his royal squadron, a tall and handsome man standing in a high chariot, surrounded by a glittering throng of cavalry massed close around his chariot and drawn up to meet their enemies. On seeing the terrible Alexander draw near them, driving the fleeing soldiers upon those who still stood fast, the majority were panic-stricken and scattered. The best and noblest were cut down in front of the king and fell on top of one another, hindering the Macedonian pursuit by winding themselves in their last struggles around riders and horses.

And now the whole frightful disaster was before Darius' eyes, and the forces placed to guard him were pushed back on him, but it was not easy to turn his chariot and drive off, for the wheels were encumbered by the heaps of corpses, and the horses, caught and hidden behind the mountain of dead bodies, were rearing up and terrifying the charioteer. So he abandoned his chariot and his arms, mounted a mare, which, they say, had lately foaled, and fled. Not even then would he probably have escaped if more horsemen had not arrived from Parmenio, calling Alexander back to his aid, since a large body of the enemy was still standing together and would not give way. On the whole, Parmenio is to be blamed for slowness and inefficiency throughout this battle, whether his courage was sapped by old age, or, as Callisthenes says, he was becoming jealous and resentful of Alexander's authority, dignity, and power. At the time Alexander was resentful at being recalled, but he did not give his soldiers the true explanation and gave as his reason for having the retreat sounded that it was dark and he would stop the slaughter. Then riding himself to the point of danger, he heard on the way that the enemy was completely routed and in flight.

34. This being the end of the battle,[66] it was apparent that the Persian empire was now completely overthrown and Alexander was hailed as king of Asia. He offered magnificent sacrifices to the gods and bestowed on his friends riches and houses and high offices. Anxious to gain honor with the Greeks, he wrote them that all tyrannies were abolished and they were to live by their own laws. To the Plataeans in particular he wrote that their city would be rebuilt, because their ancestors gave their territory to be fought over by the Greeks in their struggle for liberty.[67] He also sent a part of the spoils to the citizens of Croton in Italy in honor of the brave and patriotic athlete Phayllus, who during the Persian invasion, when all the other Greeks in Italy deserted the cause of their fellow Greeks, fitted out a ship at his own expense and sailed to Salamis to take his part in the peril. So warmly did Alexander feel towards every man of valor, and such a preserver and guardian he was of gallant deeds.

35. He now marched through Babylonia, which at once submitted to him. There the most astonishing things he found were a chasm [68] out of which fire poured continuously as from a spring, and, not far from the chasm, a stream of naphtha flowing so abundantly as to form a lake. This naphtha in other respects resembles bitumen but is so inflammable that before a flame touches it, from the mere brightness around the flame, it catches fire and often sets fire to the intervening air. To show Alexander its properties and power, the barbarians sprinkled the street leading to his lodging lightly with the stuff. Then standing at the far end of the street they laid their torches to the sprinkled spots, for by this time it was growing dark. The first spots instantly caught fire and in no perceptible interval of time but as quick as thought the fire had reached the other end, and the street was one unbroken blaze.

Among those who used to wait on Alexander when he was bathing and anointing himself, and furnish pleasing entertainment for his thoughts, was one Athenophanes, an Athenian. This man was once in the bath

---

[66] The battle of Arbela, which marked the end of the far-reaching Persian empire, was fought, near Gaugamela in the Tigris plain, in October 331 B.C.

[67] Alexander is referring to the battle of Plataea, in which the Greeks completely defeated the invading Persians in 479 B.C. See above under *Themistocles*, ch. 16, n. 29.

[68] These phenomena were seen not far from ancient Babylon. They denoted, of course, an area rich in oil.

chamber when a boy called Stephanus, who had an absurdly homely face but sang charmingly, was standing near Alexander. And Athenophanus said, "Would you like, O king, to have us try this substance on Stephanus? For if the fire takes hold of him and does not go out, I would say that unquestionably its power is irresistible and terrible." The boy thereupon eagerly offered himself for the trial, but as soon as he touched the stuff and rubbed himself with it, his body broke into a blaze and was so enveloped in flame that Alexander was terrified and had no idea what to do. Had there not happened to be a group of attendants with pails of water in their hands for the bath, help would have been too late. Even then they put the fire out with difficulty, for the boy's body was all aflame, and afterwards he was in a bad state.

Naturally persons who try to reconcile myths with truth, say that naphtha was the drug with which Medea in the tragedies anointed the crown and the robe.[69] For it was not from those objects nor of its own accord that the flame burst out, but fire was set close to them and the attraction and catching hold were so quick that one could not see them. For the rays and currents of fire which come from a distance bring to some bodies only light and heat; but in things which are dry and airy or sufficiently fatty they collect, set up a fierce blaze, and soon transform the substance completely. There is uncertainty as to the origin . . .[70] or whether the combustible liquid flows out of a soil which by nature is oily and inflammable.

For the soil of Babylonia is very fiery so that often barley grains jump out of the ground and whirl away, as if the heat made the earth vibrate. In the hot season the people sleep on leather bags filled with water. Harpalus, who was left in charge of the district, had a taste for beauty and adorned the king's garden and walks with Greek plants, but although he succeeded with everything else, the soil would not bear ivy. It was always killed because it could not endure the temperature, the earth being hot and the plant loving coolness. If, however, I keep these digressions brief, my annoyed readers will probably find less fault with them.

---

69 See Euripides' story of Medea in his tragedy of that name; also see above, n. 32.
70 There is a gap here in the Greek text; "of naphtha" should surely follow the word "origin." There should then come a "whether" clause, giving one explanation, before the "or whether" clause, which gives another.

36. Alexander then took possession of Susa and found in the palace forty thousand talents in coined money and an untold amount of furnishings and treasure as well. There, too, they say, they discovered five thousand talents' weight of purple from Hermione,[71] which had been stored there for a hundred and ninety years, but which still kept its color fresh and bright. The reason for this is said to be that honey was then used in purple dyes, as was olive oil in white dyes. Both these dyes keep their brilliance clear and lustrous to the sight for an equal length of time. Dinon says too that the kings of Persia had water brought from the Nile and the Danube, and stored away with other things in their treasure house, as if to prove the breadth of their empire and their universal lordship.

37. Persis was hard to invade for the ruggedness of the road and because it was defended by the noblest of the Persians, for Darius had fled there. But a guide appeared to take them in by a circuitous path, not too round about. He was a man who spoke two languages, the son of a Lycian father and a Persian mother. They say that while Alexander was yet a child, the Delphic priestess foretold that a wolf [72] would be his guide on his journey against the Persians. Here there took place a great slaughter of prisoners, for Alexander himself writes that he thought it expedient, and so ordered the men put to the sword. They say that he found as much coined money here [73] as at Susa, and so much other furniture and treasure that it took ten thousand pairs of mules and five thousand camels to carry it away.

Seeing there a great statue of Xerxes, which had been roughly overthrown by the mobs pushing into the palace, Alexander stopped and addressed it as though it were alive. "Shall we go on," he said, "and leave you lying there, because you attacked the Greeks,[74] or shall we set you up again because of your magnificence and gallantry in other ways?"

---

[71] This famous purple dye of antiquity was made from shellfish, caught in this instance in the Hermionic Gulf off Argolis in Greece. The best dye of all came from shellfish from the waters of Tyre.

[72] The word Lycian suggests *lycus*, the Greek word for wolf.

[73] "Here" in this sentence evidently means in Persepolis, where Alexander came into far greater booty than at Susa. Besides jewels and furniture, he is known to have taken 125,000 talents (about $155,000,000) in coin and bullion.

[74] On the invasion of Greece by Xerxes in 480 B.C., see above under *Themistocles*, chs. 6–17.

Finally, after musing a long time, he passed on in silence. Wishing to give his soldiers some rest, since it was now winter, he remained in that place for four months. There is a story that when he first took his seat under the golden canopy on the royal throne, Demaratus, the Corinthian, a devoted friend of Alexander as he had been of Philip, burst into tears, as old men do, and exclaimed that the Greeks had missed a great joy who died before seeing Alexander seated on the throne of Darius.

38. Later, as he was preparing to march on against Darius, it happened that he was present at a drinking feast and carousal of his comrades, to which women came to drink during the revelry with their lovers. Of these women the most famous was Thaïs, an Athenian, mistress of Ptolemy, who later became king. She had been flattering Alexander gracefully and amusing him when, in the midst of the drinking, she was moved to make a speech in a strain suited to the character of her country, but bolder than was natural for one of her profession. She declared that for all she had suffered in her wanderings through Asia she was that day fully repaid, luxuriating in the splendid palace of the Persians, but that it would be still more entertaining to frolic all through the house of Xerxes, who had set on fire and burned Athens. She herself would apply the torch under Alexander's eyes, so that men might tell how the women in his train had inflicted a worse punishment on the Persians for the wrongs of Hellas than all the admirals and generals and commanders had ever done.

As soon as she finished, she was riotously applauded and Alexander's companions heatedly urged him on, until he gave way, leapt from his seat and led the procession, with a garland on his head and a torch in his hand. The others followed with cheers and shouting and romped through the palace, while the rest of the Macedonians, hearing what was afoot, came running gleefully with more torches. For they hoped that the burning and destruction of the palace was the act of a man who had his mind set on home, and was not proposing to live among the barbarians. Some historians say that this was how the deed took place, others that it was done deliberately. But it is agreed that he quickly repented of it and gave orders for the fire to be put out.

39. By nature Alexander was extremely generous, and as his wealth increased he gave away still more. His gifts too were bestowed in the gracious spirit with which donors really confer a pleasure. I shall mention a

few instances. Ariston, chief of the Paeonians, killed an enemy and brought his head and showed it to Alexander. "This, O King," he said, "is a gift which in my country is rewarded with a gold goblet." "With an empty one," said Alexander, laughing, "but I will give you one full of pure wine." Another time, an ordinary Macedonian was driving a mule laden with some of the king's gold; the beast grew tired, and the man took the load on his own back and began carrying it. Alexander saw him toiling under the heavy burden, was told what he was doing, and then, as the man was about to lay down his load, said to him, "Do not be beaten but keep on the rest of the way and take it all to your own tent!"

In general he disliked more those who would not accept his gifts than those who asked for them. To Phocion he wrote a letter, saying that he would not in future consider him his friend if he refused all his presents. To Serapion, a youth who played ball with him, he gave nothing because he asked for nothing. So when Serapion was throwing the ball he would toss it to others; and when the king said, "You are not giving it to me," he answered, "You do not ask for it." At which Alexander laughed and gave him many presents. He seemed once to be angry with Proteas, an amusing joker and fellow drinker. The men's friends interceded for him, he himself pled tearfully for pardon, and Alexander said he forgave him. "Well," said Proteas, "give me some proof of it now." And Alexander ordered that he be given five talents.

What haughty airs his friends and bodyguard put on over the wealth he gave them appears in a letter which Olympias wrote him. "Do find," she says, "other ways of rewarding your friends and those you want to honor. At present you are making them all the equals of kings, building up immense support for them and leaving yourself destitute." Olympias often wrote in this style and he kept her letters secret, except once, when Hephaestion, as he was accustomed to do, opened and read a letter to him, and Alexander did not stop him but took the ring from his own finger and pressed the seal on Hephaestion's mouth. To the son of Mazaeus, chief man at Darius' court, who already was satrap of a province, Alexander offered a second and larger one. The young man refused it with the words, "O King, there was once one Darius, but you now have created many Alexanders."

To Parmenio he gave Bagoas' house at Susa, in which, it is said, he found clothing worth a thousand talents. To Antipater he wrote bidding him keep a bodyguard about his person, because there were plots against him. To his mother he sent many presents, but would not allow her to interfere in affairs of state or war. When she scolded, he bore her anger quietly. And once when Antipater wrote him a long letter denouncing her, he remarked after reading it that Antipater did not know that one of a mother's tears blotted out ten thousand letters.

40. Eventually Alexander perceived that his companions had come to live in excessive luxury and vulgar extravagance. Hagnon of Teos, for instance, had silver nails in his boots. Leonnatus had a string of camels bring him powder from Egypt for use in his gymnastic exercises. Philotas had hunting nets a hundred furlongs long. Most of them used myrrh instead of olive oil when they went to their rubbing and bathing, and took masseurs and chamberlains around with them. Alexander reproved them mildly and reasonably, saying that he was surprised that men who had fought through so many great battles did not remember that those who have labored hard sleep more soundly than those for whom they have labored; and did not see, when they compared their own lives with those of the Persians, that luxury is a very slavish thing and toil peculiarly royal. "How too," he asked, "can a man look after his horse, keep his spear and helmet bright, if he is not used to touching his hands to his own body?" "And do you not know," he said, "that our aim in conquering is not to do the same things as the people we have conquered?"

He then exerted himself still more than before on campaigns and hunting expeditions, exhausting himself and endangering his life, so that a Spartan ambassador, who was with him when he killed a huge lion, said, "You fought well, Alexander, with the lion for your kingdom." Craterus had this hunting scene set up at Delphi, with figures in bronze of the lion, the dogs, the king engaged with the lion, and himself coming to the king's aid. Some of the figures were wrought by Lysippus and some by Leochares.

41. Thus Alexander would run risks exercising himself and stirring up others to be valiant. But his friends, with their wealth and their pomp, now wanted to indulge themselves in comfort and felt abused by his long marches and military excursions, and little by little came to the point of criticizing and speaking ill of him. At first, however, he bore this very good-humoredly, saying that it was a king's fate to treat his subjects well

and have fault found with him in return. Indeed, in the smallest things that concerned his close friends he manifested his great affection and esteem for them. I shall give a few examples.

He wrote to Peucestas to reproach him, because after being bitten by a bear, he had let his other friends know of it but had not told him. "But now," he says, "write me how you are, and whether any of your fellow hunters ran off and deserted you, that I may punish them." To Hephaestion and his companions, who were away on business, he wrote that while they were amusing themselves chasing ichneumons, Craterus had fallen on Perdiccas' spear and been wounded in the thigh. When Peucestas was cured of some illness, he wrote to Alexippus, the physician, to thank him. And when Craterus was ill he had a vision in his sleep, after which he himself offered sacrifices for Craterus, and bade him do the same. He wrote also to Pausanias, the physician, who was proposing to dose Craterus with hellebore, partly to express his anxiety and partly to caution him about the use of the drug. Those who first brought him the news of Harpalus' flight and desertion, Ephialtes and Cissus, he put in chains because he thought they were falsely accusing him. When he was sending home his sick and aged soldiers, Eurylochus of Aegae got his name placed on the list of the infirm. It was then discovered that he had nothing wrong with him. But, he confessed, he was in love with Telesippa, who was going back to the coast, and he meant to go along with her. Alexander then inquired who the girl's parents were and, on hearing that she was a free-born courtesan, said, "You will have my help, Eurylochus, in your love affair, and since Telesippa is freeborn, see if we cannot persuade her either by arguments or by gifts to stay here."

42. It is amazing how he found time to write the letters he did for his friends. For instance, he writes one ordering a search to be made for a boy belonging to Seleucus who had run away to Cilicia, and one praising Peucestas for arresting Nicon, Craterus' slave, and one to Megabyzus about a servant who had taken refuge in a temple, telling him, if possible, to inveigle him outside the temple and then seize him, but not to lay hands on him inside the sanctuary. They say too that at first when he was judging cases punishable with death, he would cover one ear with his hand while the accuser was speaking, in order to keep it open and impartial for the defendant. Later on the number of accusations he heard made

him stern, leading him to believe those that were false because of the many that were true. And especially when he himself was misrepresented, he went out of his mind and was hard and relentless, for he valued his reputation more than his life or his kingdom.

And now [75] he set out after Darius, expecting to fight another battle, but on hearing that he had been captured by Bessus, [76] he sent his Thessalians home, after distributing a bounty of two thousand talents among them, over and above their pay. During his long and painful pursuit of Darius—in eleven days he rode thirty-three hundred furlongs—most of his men collapsed, mainly for want of water. Once he met some Macedonians who were carrying water from the river in skins on the backs of mules. When they saw Alexander faint with thirst, for it was then midday, they quickly filled a helmet with water and brought it to him. He asked them for whom they were carrying the water, and they replied, "To our own sons; but if you live, we can beget other sons, even if we lose these." On hearing this, he took the helmet in his hands, and then looking about he saw the horsemen around him all craning forward staring at the water. Thereat he handed it back without drinking but with thanks to the men who offered it. "For," he said, "if I drink alone, these soldiers will lose heart." As they witnessed his self-control and generosity, they shouted to him to lead them on boldly and lashed at their horses, declaring that they did not consider themselves tired or thirsty or mortal at all while they had such a king.

43. Everyone then was full of ardor. But only sixty men, they say, were with Alexander when he burst into the enemy's camp. Here they trampled over heaps of gold and silver, which had been thrown away, and rode by a crowd of carriages filled with women and children, which were scattering this way and that, without drivers. The leaders in flight they pursued, expecting Darius to be with them. At last he was found, lying in a carriage, his body covered with javelin wounds, almost dead. However, he was able to ask for something to drink, and after swallowing some cold water given him by Polystratus, he said, "Sir, it is the worst of all my hard fortune that I receive a kindness and am unable to repay

---

[75] In the spring of 330 B.C.

[76] Bessus was one of Darius' own high officials, satrap of Bactria, who at this juncture turned traitor to his master.

it. But Alexander will reward you for your courtesy and the gods will reward Alexander for his clemency to my mother, wife, and children. And through you I send him my salute." With these words he took Polystratus by the hand and died.

When Alexander came up, he was plainly grieved at the sad sight, and loosening his own cloak he flung it on the body and spread it over it. And when he captured Bessus, he had him torn asunder. Two straight trees were bent over until they met, and a part of his body was tied to each tree. Then each was let go and sprang swiftly up again, taking with it the part fastened to it. But the body of Darius, laid out as became a king, he sent at that time to his mother, and Darius' brother, Exathres, he took into his own company.

44. He now invaded Hyrcania [77] with a picked force of troops. Here he saw an arm of a sea which seemed to be as large as the Euxine, but was sweeter than the other sea. He could get no certain information about it, but guessed that it was most probably a branch of the Maeotic Lake. Yet natural scientists knew the truth, and many years before Alexander's expedition had stated that this was the farthest north of four gulfs stretching inland from the outer ocean, and had called it both the Hyrcanian and the Caspian Sea.

Here some barbarians unexpectedly came on those who were leading Alexander's horse Bucephalus and captured him. Alexander was furious at this and sent a herald threatening to kill them all, with their wives and children, unless they returned him his horse. But when they came bringing the horse and offering to place their cities in his hands, he treated them all with kindness and paid the captors a ransom for the animal.

45. Thence he marched into Parthia, where, during a time of leisure, he first put on barbarian dress, either because he wished to conform to the customs of the country, believing that similarity of race and habit does much to win a people over, or else because he was attempting in this way to introduce the practice of obeisance among the Macedonians and to accept a change in his own way of life. He did not, however, adopt

[77] Hyrcania lay on the southern shore of the Caspian Sea, which Alexander's men called an overflow from Lake Maeotis, the modern Sea of Azov. These two bodies of water, together with the Euxine, or Black Sea, and "the other sea," or Mediterranean, were to Plutarch four great gulfs stretching inland from an unknown "outer ocean."

the Median garb, which was completely barbaric and strange, nor did he wear trousers or a sleeved jacket or a tiara, designing for himself a good costume, midway between the Persian and the Median—simpler than the first and more dignified than the second. At first he wore this dress only when in company with the barbarians or with his intimate friends at home, but afterwards he was frequently seen in it when riding out and transacting public business.

The sight offended the Macedonians, but they so admired him for his valor that they felt they should give in to him on some matters which added to his pleasure or his renown. For in addition to all his other injuries, he had recently been hit by an arrow in the calf of his leg, so that a splinter of the bone protruded; again, he had been struck on the neck by a stone so that his eyesight was clouded and stayed injured for a long time. Yet he did not stop exposing himself incessantly to dangers, but crossed the river Orexartes, which he took to be the Tanais, put the Scythians to flight, and chased them for a hundred furlongs, though suffering meanwhile from dysentery.

46. There, most writers say—among them, Clitarchus, Polyclitus, Onescritus, Antigenes and Istrus—the Amazon queen came to visit him. But Aristobulus, Chares the court-usher, Ptolemy, Anticlides, Philo of Thebes, and Philip of Theangela, as well as Hecataeus of Eretria, Philip of Chalcis, and Douris of Samos, call the story pure fiction. And Alexander seems to be a witness on their side, for writing to Antipater a full and exact account of his campaign, he says that the Scythian king gave him his daughter in marriage, but he has nothing to say of an Amazon. And many years afterwards, Onescritus, we are told, was reading aloud to Lysimachus,[78] who was then king, the fourth book of his history in which he tells the tale of the Amazon, and Lysimachus asked him with a quiet smile, "Where was I at that time?" Whether one believes or disbelieves that tale, one will not admire Alexander the more or the less.

47. He had some fear that his Macedonians might weary of going on with his expedition. So he left the mass of the army where they were, but kept the best of them with him in Hyrcania, twenty thousand infantry

---

[78] This Lysimachus was not Alexander's tutor, mentioned in ch. 5 and elsewhere, but one of his generals who later became king of Thrace.

and three thousand horse. To them he made a speech, saying that at present the barbarians saw them as in a dream, but that if they should merely create disorder in Asia and then start to leave, the people would set on them at once as if they were women. However, he said, he would let all go who wished to leave, only calling them to witness that he was conquering the world for the Macedonians and they were deserting him and their friends who were willing to keep on with his expedition. He wrote this almost word for word in a letter to Antipater, adding that at the end of his speech the men all cried out that he should lead them wherever in the world he wished. And after these men had met the test, it was no longer difficult to induce the body of the army to go on too, and they followed readily.

He now began to bring his own way of life still closer to that of the inhabitants and to introduce Macedonian customs to them, in the belief that through a mixture and community of habits his empire would stand on a foundation of good will rather than of force, when he was far away. Accordingly, he selected thirty thousand boys and gave orders that they should learn the Greek language and the use of Macedonian arms, and appointed a body of instructors for them. His marriage with Roxana [79] was a love match, for he saw her beauty and grace in a dance at a banquet. Yet it seemed too to fit in well with the designs he had in mind. For the barbarians were pleased with the connection the marriage created and captivated by Alexander's extraordinary self-control in such matters and his refusal to touch unlawfully even the one woman who ever bewitched him.

When he saw that among his closest friends Hephaestion approved of his methods and like him was altering his way of living, but that Craterus adhered to his native customs, he used the former in his dealings with the barbarians and the latter in business with the Greeks and Macedonians. On the whole he loved Hephaestion best, but he respected Craterus, for he thought and was ever saying that Hephaestion was Alexander's friend and Craterus the king's. And for this reason the two men nursed a secret

---

[79] The beautiful Roxana was the daughter of Oxyartes, a Bactrian noble. Alexander married her in 327 B.C. partly, at least, as a measure for reconciling the chieftains of his newly-won northeastern domains. Her son, Alexander IV, was born after Alexander's death. See below, ch. 77. Both he and she were murdered by Cassander's order in 311.

jealousy of one another and often came into collision. Once in India they actually drew swords and fought and each man's friends were coming to his assistance, when Alexander rode up and publicly berated Hephaestion, calling him a senseless madman not to realize that if anyone deprived him of Alexander's favor he would be nobody. In private too he sharply reproved Craterus. He then brought them both together and made peace between them, swearing by Ammon and the other gods that he loved them best of all men, but that if he heard of their quarreling again he would kill them both, or at least the one who began the quarrel. Thenceforth, we are told, they neither said nor did anything to disparage one another, not even in sport.

48. Now Philotas,[80] son of Parmenio, was a man of importance among the Macedonians, for he was considered brave and vigorous, and next to Alexander himself he was the most generous and fond of his friends. They say that once when a comrade of his asked him for money and he ordered his steward to give it to him, the steward said he had none. "What do you mean?" demanded Philotas. "Have you not even a goblet or a cloak?" His haughtiness of spirit, mass of wealth, elaborate care of his person, and mode of life were objectionable, even in a private person, and at this time especially his affectations of majesty and pomp were not tactful but clumsy, offensive, and conspicuous. Even Parmenio once said to him, "O son, pray be not so great!" For a very long time complaints of him had been coming to Alexander himself.

Then after the defeat of Darius in Cilicia, when Damascus was being plundered, among the many captives brought into the camp there was found a girl, a native of Pydna, beautiful to look on, called Antigone. Philotas got her, and as a young man has a way of talking big and boastfully like a great warrior to his mistress over his wine, so he would declare that the greatest of the conquests had been the work of himself and his father. And he would call Alexander a boy, who enjoyed the title of sovereign through their labors. Antigone would repeat his words to one of her intimates, and he to someone else, and at length they came around to Craterus. He took the girl and brought her secretly to Alexander, who, on hearing what she had to say, ordered her to go on meeting Philotas as before, and to come and report to him everything he told her.

---

80 On Parmenio and Philotas see above, chs. 3, 10, 31 ff., and 40.

49. Philotas had no idea of the plot thus formed against him and spent much time with Antigone, during which he made many peevish and arrogant remarks and spoke unsuitably of the king. However, Alexander, even in the face of strong testimony against Philotas, remained silent, whether because he felt certain of Parmenio's loyalty, or because he feared the renown and power of the two men. In the meantime, a Macedonian named Limnus, from Chalaestra, got up a plot against Alexander's life and invited Nicomachus, a young man whose lover he was, to join in the enterprise. Nicomachus refused and told his brother, Cebalinus, of the scheme. He went to Philotas, and urged him to bring them both before Alexander, as persons who had information of great and urgent importance for him, but for some reason or other—for what is not clear— Philotas would not take them to Alexander, saying the king was occupied with affairs of more importance. And twice he behaved in this way. They now grew suspicious of Philotas and turned to another man and by him were conducted to Alexander. First they informed him of Limnus' plot, and then spoke with careful hints of Philotas, how he had twice shown no interest in their report.

At this Alexander was intensely indignant, and when he heard that Limnus defended himself from arrest until the man sent to get him killed him, he was still more disturbed, for he felt the clue to the plot had now escaped him. And in his bitterness against Philotas he drew around himself the men who had long hated him and who now said openly that the king believed too easily that Limnus, a poor fellow from Chalaestra, would have ventured on a scheme of such daring by himself, that he was merely a servant or a tool in the hands of a greater authority, and that investigation of the plot should begin with those persons who had most to gain by keeping it hidden. As the king now lent an ear to this talk of suspicions, they soon brought him a thousand charges against Philotas. Thereupon he was arrested, interrogated, and tortured in the presence of the king's companions, while Alexander listened from behind a hanging curtain. And when, they say, Alexander heard Philotas' piteous and abject entreaties and cries to Hephaestion, he exclaimed, "Such a weakling and coward as you, Philotas, how did you try anything so dangerous?"

When Philotas was dead, Alexander sent at once to Media and had Parmenio executed too, though he had done much good service for Philip, and was the only one of Alexander's older councilors, or the prin-pal one, who encouraged him to cross into Asia. Of the three sons Parmenio had, he had already seen two killed earlier on the expedition, and now he perished with the third. These acts made many of Alexander's friends afraid of him, especially Antipater, who sent messengers privately to the Aetolians to conclude an alliance with them. For the Aetolians too stood in fear of Alexander because they had destroyed the town of Oeniadae, and Alexander on hearing of it had said that not the sons of Oeniadae but he himself would punish the Aetolians.

50. Not long after this occurred the affair of Clitus, which, to those who know only the bare facts, seems more cruel than the death of Philotas. However, if we take into our consideration both the cause and the occasion, we find that the king did not then act deliberately, but that through some evil fortune his rage and intoxication gave Clitus' evil genius an opportunity. This is how it happened. Some men came from the seacoast bringing Greek fruit to Alexander. He admired its bloom and beauty, and called Clitus, meaning to show it to him and share it with him. Clitus happened to be offering sacrifice, but he left his sacrifice and came, and three of the sheep on which libations had been poured followed him. On hearing of this, the king consulted his soothsayers, Aristander and Cleomantes the Spartan. They told him that the omen was bad, and he ordered them to offer sacrifice instantly on behalf of Clitus, for he had himself seen a strange vision in his sleep two days before. Clitus had appeared to him, sitting with the sons of Parmenio in black robes, and all were dead. However, Clitus did not finish his sacrifice but came straight to supper with the king, who had been sacrificing to the Dioscuri.

When the drinking had grown boisterous, some verses were sung, composed by a certain Pranichus, or, as some say, Pierion, for the purpose of shaming and deriding the generals who had lately been beaten by the barbarians. The older men were offended by this and denounced both the author and the singer, but Alexander and his friends were amused and bade the singer continue. Clitus, who was now drunk and naturally of a fierce and stubborn temper, protested that it was not right for Macedonians to be insulted before barbarians and enemies, when in spite of their hard luck, they were far better men than those who were laughing at them. Alexander retorted that Clitus was pleading his own cause when he called cowardice hard luck. At this, Clitus sprang to his feet and exclaimed, "My cowardice at least saved your life, son of the gods, when your back was turned to the sword of Spithridates! [81] By the blood of the Macedonians and my wounds you have grown so great that you now disown Philip and have yourself adopted by Ammon!" [82]

51.   Stung to the quick then, Alexander said, "Villain, do you think you can go about happily saying these things of me and stirring up trouble with my Macedonians?" "But we are not happy," answered Clitus, "even now, for these are the rewards we receive for our toils. We think the happy ones are those who are dead, who died before they saw Macedonians beaten with Median rods and begging Persians to get us an audience with our king." As Clitus used this reckless language, Alexander's companions sprang up to silence him with terms of abuse, and the older men tried to quiet the uproar. But Alexander merely turned to Xenodochus of Cardia and Artemius of Colophon and said, "Do not the Greeks, moving about among the Macedonians, look to you like demi-gods among the wild beasts?" Clitus, however, would not hold his peace, and bade Alexander say out before them all what was in his mind, or else not invite to supper men who were free and used to speaking frankly and keep on living with barbarians and slaves, who would do obeisance to his Persian girdle and white tunic.

Thereat Alexander could no longer control his anger, but hurled one of the apples lying on the table at Clitus and struck him and began to feel for his dagger. One of his bodyguards, Aristophanes, had already taken that away, and the rest surrounded him imploring him to have patience. Upon which he leapt up and shouted a summons in Macedonian to his armor-bearers—a sign of great excitement—and commanded the trumpeter to sound an alarm, giving him a blow because he hesitated and showed reluctance. The man afterwards was highly commended on the score that he more than anyone else saved the camp from being thrown into utter confusion. Clitus would not retract what he had said and his friends with difficulty shoved him out of the hall.

He tried then to reenter by another door, and in a sneering and insolent tone began repeating the lines from Euripides' *Andromache*,[83]

"Alas, in Greece what evil custom reigns!"

[81] See above, ch. 16.   [82] See above, chs. 27 ff.
[83] Euripides, *Andromache*, 683.

So then Alexander snatched a spear from one of the armor-bearers, met Clitus with it as he was drawing back the curtain before the door, and ran him through. As Clitus fell with a loud groan, the king's anger instantly left him, and as he came to himself and saw his friends standing there mute, he pulled the spear out of the dead body and started to thrust it into his own neck. This was prevented by his bodyguard, who grasped his hands and took him by force to his chamber.

52. There he spent the night and the next day, mourning bitterly, until he was so exhausted with crying and grief that he lay speechless, only heaving deep sighs. His friends then became frightened at his silence and broke into the room, but he took no notice of what any of them said until Aristander, the soothsayer, reminded him of the vision he had seen of Clitus and of the bad omen, and declared that all this had been long ago ordained. He then appeared to relax, so they brought in the philosopher Callisthenes, a relative of Aristotle, and Anaxarchus of Abdera.[84] Callisthenes tried by mild and soothing means to relieve the king's anguish, approaching the subject gradually and in a roundabout way, so as not to hurt him. But Anaxarchus, who always took his own way in philosophy and had a name for scorning and disparaging his associates, as soon as he came in, shouted, "This is Alexander, to whom the whole world now looks up! He lies here weeping like a slave, in dread of the law and the reproach of men, to whom he himself should be law and standard of justice, since he has won the right to rule and to be their master. He should not be a slave submissive to idle opinion. Do you not know," he went on, "that Law and Justice sit beside the throne of Zeus to make everything which the sovereign does lawful and right?"

By such reasoning Anaxarchus lightened the king's misery, but influenced his character, making it in many ways more arrogant and lawless. He also cleverly adapted himself to the king and spoiled his intercourse with Callisthenes, which had never been familiar because of Callisthenes' austerity. They say that once at supper they were talking of seasons and the climate thereabout, and Callisthenes agreed with those who called it colder and more wintry there than in Greece. When Anaxarchus, bristling, contradicted him, he said, "But surely you must admit that this country is colder than Greece, for there you would go through the winter

84 On Callisthenes, see above, n. 57; on Anaxarchus, n. 23.

PLUTARCH

54

with only one thin cloak and here you are reclining at table with three rugs spread over you!" This reply made Anaxarchus dislike him still more than before.

53. The other sophists and flatterers of Alexander were jealous too of Callisthenes, because he was much sought after by the young men for his eloquence and was equally popular with their elders on account of his orderly, dignified, and independent way of life. It confirmed what he gave as the reason for his absence from Greece, namely, that he had come to Alexander with a hope of getting his countrymen restored to their homes and his native city rebuilt.[85] But he earned envy by his high reputation, and his behavior also was such as to provoke criticism. For he refused most invitations, and when he did mix in company, by his solemnity and silence he seemed to be disapproving and disliking what the others were doing, so that Alexander himself said of him, "I hate a wise man who not even for himself is wise." [86]

On one occasion, they say, a great crowd had been invited to dine with the king, and Callisthenes was asked, when the cup went around, to celebrate the Macedonians. He was so eloquent on the subject that the company rose and applauded him and threw their garlands to him. On this Alexander's comment was that, as Euripides says, when a man has for his speech "a noble theme, it is not hard to speak well." [87] "But now show your power," he said, "by telling us the faults of the Macedonians, so that they may improve themselves on learning their shortcomings." Thereupon Callisthenes spoke on the opposite side, and went on at length and freely, denouncing the Macedonians. The rise of Philip's power he credited to the discord among the Greeks and quoted the line,

"In a time of dissension a bad man rises to honor." [88]

For this speech the Macedonians hated him profoundly and bitterly, and Alexander said that Callisthenes had displayed not his eloquence but his ill-will towards the Macedonians.

---

[85] Callisthenes' native city, Olynthus, had been destroyed by Philip in 347 B.C.
[86] A line from an unknown play by Euripides.
[87] Euripides, *Bacchae,* 260.
[88] The line seems to be a Greek proverb cast in verse form.

54. The above is the story which, Hermippus says, Stroebus, Callisthenes' reader, told to Aristotle. He says too that Callisthenes knew of the king's estrangement from him, and that two or three times, on leaving the king's presence, he said to himself,

"Patroclus, too, is dead, a far better man than you." [89]

As for Aristotle, he seems to have remarked sagely that Callisthenes had great power as a speaker but no sense. Yet by refusing stoutly and like a philosopher to pay obeisance to Alexander, and by explaining in public what all the oldest and best Macedonians were resenting in secret, he relieved the Greeks from what was a great disgrace and Alexander from a greater, for he prevailed on him not to require the obeisance. But he ruined himself, because to Alexander he seemed to be using compulsion rather than persuasion on him.

Chares of Mitylene tells us that once at a banquet Alexander, after drinking, passed the cup to one of his friends, and he on receiving it stood up facing the hearth shrine and first drank, then did obeisance to Alexander, kissed him and took his seat again. So everyone did the same in turn until the cup came to Callisthenes. The king, who was talking with Hephaestion, did not notice him but after drinking, he went directly towards the king to kiss him. And Demetrius, surnamed Phidon, exclaimed, "O King, do not let him kiss you, for he alone has not paid you obeisance." So Alexander evaded the kiss and Callisthenes said in a loud voice, "Then I will leave, the poorer by a kiss."

55. The breach being thus formed, Hephaestion was at once believed when he declared that Callisthenes had promised him to pay obeisance, and then had broken his agreement. Men too like Lysimachus and Hagnon insisted that the sophist was going about full of grand plans, such as for overthrowing tyranny, and that the young men were flocking to him and following him around as if he were the only free man among all the myriads. So when the plot of Hermolaus and his gang against Alexander was discovered, the falsehoods of Callisthenes' accusers sounded like truth. They said that Hermolaus had inquired of Callisthenes how one might become the world's most famous man, and he had answered, "By killing the world's most famous man." He was even said to have encouraged

---

[89] Homer, *Iliad*, XXI, 107. Achilles speaks these words to Hector.

Hermolaus to make the attempt, bidding him have no fear of the golden couch and reminding him that he would be dealing with a man who was ill and wounded. However, not one of Hermolaus' accomplices, even in extreme necessity, made any mention of Callisthenes.

Even Alexander himself, when writing immediately afterwards to Craterus, Attalus, and Alcetas, says that the youths when put to torture, confessed that they had done this thing by themselves and that no one else knew of it. But writing later to Antipater, he includes Callisthenes among the guilty. "The boys," he says, "were stoned by the Macedonians, but I will punish the sophist, as well as those who sent him to me and those who receive into their cities conspirators against me." In these words certainly he reveals some resentment against Aristotle, for Callis-thenes, because of their relationship, was brought up in his house, for he was the son of Hero, Aristotle's niece. As for Callisthenes' death, some say he was hanged by Alexander, others that he was bound in fetters and died then of disease. Chares says that he was kept in chains seven months after his arrest, in order that he might be tried by the council in Aristotle's presence, but that at the time Alexander was wounded in India, he died of excessive corpulence, sick with lice.

56. All this, however, took place later.[90] In the meantime, Demaratus of Corinth, now an old man, by a great effort came to pay Alexander a visit, and when he beheld him, said that the Greeks who died before seeing him seated on the throne of Darius had been deprived of a great joy.[91] However, he did not long enjoy the king's favor but died of weakness. He was given a splendid funeral and the army erected to him a mound of huge circumference, eighty cubits high. His ashes were taken back to the coast in a four-horse chariot, richly decorated.

57. Alexander was now preparing to cross the mountains into India,[92] but he saw that his army was so encumbered with its masses of booty that it had become unwieldy. So after the wagons had been packed, one morning at daybreak he first had his own wagons and those of his companions burned, and then ordered fire set to those of the Macedonians.

---

[90] The events last mentioned took place early in the year 327 B.C.

[91] For this same anecdote, see above, ch. 37.

[92] Alexander began his invasion of India in the late spring of 327 B.C.

The planning of this measure appears to have been more alarming and difficult than the execution of it proved to be. For only a few soldiers were dismayed, and most of them with enthusiastic shouts and battle cries divided their essentials with those who wanted them, and themselves burned and destroyed their superfluities, thus inspiring Alexander with their spirit of ardor and adventure. Yet already men stood in dread of him, and he was relentless in his punishment of offenders. He put to death Menander, one of his comrades, whom he had made captain of a garrison, on the ground that Menander was unwilling to stay at his post, and Orsodates, one of the barbarians who revolted from him, he shot down himself with an arrow.

When a ewe dropped a lamb that had a head something in shape and color like a tiara and testicles on each side of it, Alexander was horrified at the portent, and had himself purified by the Babylonians, whom he habitually took about with him for such purposes. But talking with his friends he said that he was alarmed not on his own account but on theirs, for fear that if he died, Fate would bestow the power next on some weak and ignoble man.

On the appearance, however, of a better omen he threw off his depression. The Macedonian who had been put in charge of the chamberlains, Proxenus by name, while digging a place for the royal tent beside the river Oxus, uncovered a spring of an oily, fatty liquid. When the top was drawn off, there gushed forth at once a pure, transparent oil, which seemed no different from olive oil in either smell or taste, and in luster and sleekness was the very same. This in a country which produces no olive trees! They say too that the water of the Oxus is itself so soft that it makes the skins of those who bathe in it glossy. Alexander's immense gratification at this discovery is made clear in a letter he wrote to Antipater, in which he mentions it as one of the most significant omens vouchsafed him from the god. The soothsayers, however, regarded it as foretelling a glorious expedition but one that would be toilsome and hard, for oil, they said, had been given men as a help in their labors.

58. Alexander indeed met many perils in his battles on this expedition and received heavy wounds, but the worst damage to his army was caused by their want of necessities and by the hardships of the climate. He himself aspired to conquer fortune by boldness, and power by valor, and

thought no fortress impregnable to brave men or safe for cowards. They say that when he was besieging the steep and inaccessible citadel of Sisimithres, his soldiers lost courage. He asked Oxyartes [93] what kind of man Sisimithres was, and Oxyartes said he was the most utter coward. "Then you are telling me," said Alexander, "that we can take his fortress, since its commander is a shaky thing." So by terrifying Sisimithres he took the place.

When attacking another fortress, similarly steep, and urging on the younger Macedonians, he spoke directly to one named Alexander. "It is surely your duty," he said, "to be a brave man because of your name!" And when the youth fell fighting gallantly, Alexander was deeply grieved. Again, when the Macedonians shrank from approaching the fortress called Nysa because a deep river ran in front of it, he stood on the bank and exclaiming, "Why, wretch that I am, did I never learn to swim?" he immediately started across, carrying his shield. And when he stopped fighting and ambassadors came from the cities he had blockaded to ask for terms, they were first of all astonished to see him without an attendant, wearing full armor. When a cushion was brought him, he ordered the oldest ambassador to take it and sit on it. The man's name was Acuphis and he was so impressed by Alexander's magnificent courtesy that he asked him what he wished his countrymen to do in order to make him their friend. "They must make you their ruler." said Alexander, "and send me a hundred of their best men." Acuphis laughed and replied, "But I will rule better, O King, if I send you the worst men instead of the best."

59. One Taxiles,[94] they tell us, owned a district in India as large as Egypt, with fine pasturage, and one of the richest in fruit. He was a sagacious man too, and after saluting Alexander, he said to him, "Why should we have wars and fight one another, Alexander, if you have not come to deprive us of water or necessary food, the only things for which sensible men must really fight? As for other kinds of wealth and property,, so called, if I am better off than you, I am ready to act generously; or,

[93] Oxyartes, father of Roxana, Alexander later appointed his satrap for northern India.
[94] Taxila, called by the Indians Takshasila, had been the capital city of the Persian satrapy of India, as organized by Darius I, towards the end of the sixth century B.C. It lay a little to the east of the Indus, where its ruins are still to be seen.

if I am poorer, I do not object to feeling grateful for generosity received."
Alexander was delighted, and grasping his hand said, "Now do you
imagine that after such words of friendliness our meeting will end without some kind of contest? No, you shall not get the better of me, for I
will struggle against you and fight you with benefactions, so that good
as you are you shall not outdo me." Alexander then accepted many gifts
but gave Taxiles more, presenting him finally with a thousand talents
in coined money. Thereby he thoroughly annoyed his friends, but made
many of the barbarians feel more reconciled to him.

The best fighters among the Indians were mercenary troops, who
moved from city to city, defending them vigorously and inflicting much
damage on Alexander. So he made a truce with them in one city to permit
them to leave it, and then caught them on the road and killed them all.
This act is like a blot on his military record, for in all other instances he
made war lawfully and as became a king. But the Indian philosophers gave
him as much trouble as the mercenaries, because they reproached the
princes who joined him and encouraged the free populations to revolt.
For this reason he had many of them hanged.

60. His campaign against Porus [95] Alexander himself has described in
his letters. He says that the river Hydaspes [96] ran between the two camps,
and that Porus kept his elephants stationed on the farther bank, to guard
the crossing. So Alexander himself every day had a great noise and din
made in his camp, thus accustoming the barbarians not to be frightened
by it. Then, on a stormy and moonless night, he took a division of infantry and the best of his cavalry and went on some distance from the
enemy and there crossed over to a small island. Rain was falling furiously
and thunder and lightning were crashing over the soldiers, but though
he saw some of them scorched and killed by the thunderbolts, he pushed

[95] Porus, the most formidable of the rajahs Alexander met in India, ruled a region in
the north of the modern Punjab. After his defeat by Alexander at the river Hydaspes,
in the spring of 326 B.C., he became his ally, and to him Alexander committed the
rule of eastern Punjab, when he himself was forced to turn back towards home. But
later Porus was apparently suspected of sympathy with his fellow countrymen in revolt
against the remains of Macedonian control in North India and was assassinated by one
of Alexander's generals.
[96] The Hydaspes is known now as the river Jhelum, a tributary of the Indus in
western Punjab.

on from the island and aimed at the opposite bank. But the Hydaspes, made deep and tempestuous by the storm, was beating against the bank and broke through it, and a great branch of the current began flowing that way. Nor did the bottom between give the men safe footing, for it was slippery and crumbling. And here Alexander is said to have exclaimed, "O Athenians, would you believe what dangers I run to win your praise!"

But that is what Onescritus tells us. Alexander himself says that they let go their rafts, and waded through the breach in the bank with their arms, up to their breasts in water. And after crossing, he says, he led his cavalry twenty furlongs ahead of the infantry, thinking that if the enemy attacked with cavalry he would easily defeat them, and if they were bringing up their men-at-arms, his infantry would reach him first. And one of his plans worked out. For first he routed a thousand horse and sixty chariots which set on him, and then captured all the chariots and killed four hundred riders.

Porus now was informed that Alexander himself had crossed the river, and he advanced with his whole army, except for what he left behind to keep the Macedonians from crossing there. Alarmed though he was at the elephants and at the numbers of the enemy, Alexander himself charged them on their left wing and ordered Coenus to attack on their right. Both wings were beaten, and the defeated men retreated steadily back towards the elephants in the center and crowded in with them. From then on the battle was fought all hand to hand, and it was the eighth hour before the enemy surrendered. This is what the winner of the battle tells of it himself in his letters.

Most historians agree that Porus stood four cubits and a span high,[97] and that because of his bodily size and dignity he looked as well proportioned to his elephant as a horseman to his horse. His elephant was very large, and it displayed exceptional intelligence and concern for the king, defending him and driving back his attackers as long as he was sound and vigorous, but when it saw that the king was exhausted by the onslaught of weapons and his wounds, it was afraid he would fall to the ground, and with its trunk softly took hold of each spear and drew it out of his body. When Porus was captured, Alexander asked him how he should treat him. "Like a king," he answered. Alexander then in-

---

[97] That is, about six feet, three inches.

quired if he had nothing else to say. "Everything," he said, "is in the words, 'like a king.'" So Alexander not only allowed him to rule over his former kingdom, calling him a satrap, but added to it the land of the autonomous peoples whom he had conquered. It was said to contain fifteen nations, five thousand notable cities, and innumerable villages. Over another district, three times as large as that one, he appointed one of his companions, Philip, as satrap.[98]

61. After the battle with Porus, Bucephalus died, not immediately but later. Most writers say he died of wounds for which he was being treated, but according to Onescritus, it was from long service and old age, for he was thirty years old when he died. Alexander was deeply grieved, feeling that he had lost no less than a close comrade and friend. In memory of him he built a city on the Hydaspes and called it Bucephalia.[99] They say too that when he lost a dog named Peritas, which he had reared and of which he was very fond, he founded a city and called it by its name. Sotion says he heard this from Potamon of Lesbos.

62. However, the struggle with Porus had dulled the spirit of the Macedonians, and it put an end to their farther advance into India. For they had had great difficulty repelling him, with his array of twenty thousand infantry and two thousand cavalry, and they vigorously opposed Alexander when he tried to compel them to cross the river Ganges, the width of which, they heard, was thirty-two furlongs, and depth a hundred fathoms. The opposite shore too was covered with hordes of armed men, horses, and elephants. The kings of the Gandarites and the Praesii, they were told, were waiting there for them with eighty thousand horsemen, two hundred thousand infantry, eight thousand chariots, and six thousand war elephants. And this was no exaggeration, for soon thereafter Androcottus, who was king there a little later, presented Seleucus with five hundred elephants, and invaded and subjugated all India with an army of six hundred thousand men.

At first Alexander shut himself up in his tent in disappointment and anger, and lay there feeling no gratitude for what had been accomplished,

---

98 This Philip was a Macedonian and the district he was given to rule was the modern Afghanistan.
99 The city on the site of Alexander's Bucephalia is now known as Jalalpur.

so long as he could not cross the Ganges, regarding a retreat as an admission of defeat. His friends reasoned with him and consoled him, and
his soldiers stood around his door and pled with him in doleful cries.
So in time he responded and prepared to withdraw, meanwhile devising
many deceptive and ingenious tricks to preserve his fame. He had armor,
for instance, and horse mangers made of extra size, and bridles heavier
than ordinary, and left them scattered about behind. He set up altars to
the gods, at which even to this day the kings of the Praesii worship whenever they cross the river, and offer sacrifices in the Greek fashion. Androcottus as a lad saw Alexander, and afterwards, we are told, often said that
he came within an inch of conquering the country, since the Indian king
was hated and despised for his mean disposition and ignoble birth.

63.   Thereafter Alexander grew eager to see the outer ocean,[100] had
many passenger boats with oars and many rafts built, and with them
proceeded in a leisurely manner down the rivers. But his voyage was not
an idle one nor free of fighting, for he would disembark and attack cities
and help himself to everything as he went along. In a fight with the so-
called Malli, who are said to be the most warlike tribe of India, he came
very near being killed. He had driven the men from their city walls by
volleys of missiles, and was the first to set a ladder to the wall and climb
up it. But then the ladder broke and he was struck at from below by
the barbarians who were ranged along the wall beneath him. So, as he
was, he turned and flung himself down into the midst of the enemy,
alone, and by good luck landed upright. And as he stood brandishing
his arms, the barbarians thought an apparition of flashing light passed
before his body, so they at once scattered and fled. But when they saw
only two armor bearers following him, they rushed at him and some
tried to wound him at close quarters, thrusting their swords and spears
through his armor as he defended himself, and one, standing a little
farther away, shot an arrow at him with such strength and force that it
pierced his breastplate and stuck in the bones of his chest. And as he
gave way and shrank before the blow, the man who had hit him ran
at him, drawing a barbarian scimitar, but Peucestas and Limnaeus pro-

---

[100] The "outer ocean," distinguished thus from the Mediterranean, was in this case,
of course, what we now call the Arabian Sea. The rivers down which Alexander sailed
to reach it were the Hydaspes, the Acesines, or modern Chenab, and the Indus.

tected him. Both were wounded and Limnaeus killed, but Peucestas held on and Alexander himself cut down the barbarian.

However, he had been wounded in many places, and finally he was struck on the neck with a club and fell back against the wall, still facing the enemy. But at that moment his Macedonians came swarming around him, seized him, unconscious by now of what was happening about him, and carried him to his tent. Instantly a rumor ran through the camp that he was dead. But with great difficulty and pain they sawed through the wooden shaft of the arrow and managed to take off his breastplate. They then came to cutting out the barbed arrow head, which was sunk in one of his bones. It was four fingers long, they say, and three wide, so when it was being removed, he swooned and came near to dying; but yet he recovered. When he was out of danger, though still weak, having kept himself for a long time under regulation and treatment, he learned from a commotion outside that his Macedonians were longing to see him, and took his cloak and went out to them. And then, after sacrificing to the gods, he boarded ship again and went on down the river, subduing much territory and many cities by the way.

64. He captured ten of the Gymnosophists [101] who had done much to persuade Sabbas to revolt, and made a great deal of trouble for the Macedonians. These men are noted for their terse and pithy answers to questions, and Alexander put insoluble questions to them, saying that he would kill the man who first gave him a wrong answer, and the others the same way, in order. The oldest he ordered to act as judge. He then asked the first which he thought were more numerous, the living or the dead. "The living," he said, "for the dead no longer are." The second was asked which bred the larger animals, the land or the sea; and he said, "The land, for the sea is only a part of it." The third was asked which was the cleverest animal, and he replied, "The one which man has not yet discovered." The fourth was asked the reason why he led Sabbas to revolt, and he said, "Because I wished him either to live nobly or to die nobly."

The fifth was asked which he thought came first, the day or the night, and he answered, "The day, by one day." And he added, as the king

---

[101] Gymnosophist was a name the Greeks gave to the ascetic Indian sages whom they saw wearing little or no clothing. It is composed of two Greek words, *gymnos*, naked, and *sophos*, wise.

showed surprise, that impossible questions required impossible answers. Going on then to the sixth, Alexander asked how a man could best make himself loved. "By being the strongest," he said, "and yet not an object of fear." Of the remaining three he asked one how a man might become a god. "By doing something," he said, "that is beyond a man's power to do." The next he asked which was the stronger, life or death, and he replied that life was, because it endured so much misfortune. And the last he asked how long it was good for a man to live, "As long," he said, "as he does not think death better than life." Thereat Alexander turned to the judge and asked him to pronounce a verdict, but he said that each had answered worse than the other. "Then," said Alexander, "you shall die first for giving such a verdict." "Not so, O King," said the judge, "unless you spoke falsely when you said you would kill first the man who made the worst answer."

65. These men then Alexander dismissed with presents, but to their most famous philosophers, who lived in seclusion, he sent Onesicritus to ask them to come to him. Onesicritus was a philosopher who had belonged to the school of Diogenes the Cynic. Calanus ordered him, very haughtily and rudely, to take off his tunic and listen to him naked; otherwise he would not talk to him, not even if he came from Zeus. Dandamis, he says, was a milder man, and after listening to an account of Socrates and Pythagoras and Diogenes, he said that they seemed to him to have been men naturally good, but to have lived in too great dread of the laws. Others, however, state that Dandamis said only, "Why did Alexander take all this long journey hither?"

But Taxiles did persuade Calanus to visit Alexander. His name was actually Sphines, but because he greeted everyone he met with the Indian word *"Cale,"* instead of with "Hail," the Greeks called him Calanus.[102] It was Calanus, they say, who gave Alexander the illustration of his empire. He laid on the ground a dry, shrunken hide, and then trod on the edge of it. The hide was pressed down in one spot but it rose up in others. He walked around the hide, pressing on it, and showed that the same thing happened every time until he stepped in the middle and held it down there, and then it all lay flat. The figure was meant to show Alex-

---

[102] In Hindu literature his name appears as Kalyana.

ander that he ought to press hardest on the middle of his empire, and not wander a long way off from it.

66. His voyage down the rivers to the sea took seven months.[103] On entering the ocean with his ships, he sailed out to an island which he himself called Scillustis, but others knew as Psiltucis. Here he landed and offered sacrifice to the gods, and examined the nature of the sea and of the seacoast as far as he could reach it. Then, after praying the gods that no man after him might go beyond the bounds of his expedition, he turned homeward. He appointed Nearchus admiral of the fleet and Onescritus chief pilot, and ordered them to sail along, keeping India on the right. He himself marched with his land army through the country of the Oreites and there was reduced to desperate straits, losing such an immense number of men that he brought back not even a fourth of his host from India. Originally it had numbered a hundred and twenty thousand foot and fifteen thousand horse, but they perished from cruel diseases, poisonous food, scorching heat, and most of all from starvation, for they were marching through a wild region with wretched inhabitants, who possessed only a few poor cattle used to eating sea fish, which made their flesh disgustingly rank. Alexander was barely able to get through this region in sixty days. When once he arrived at Gedrosia he was surrounded immediately by an abundance of everything, which the nearby satraps and princes provided for them.

67. After refreshing his troops there, Alexander led them in a joyous revel for seven days through Carmania.[104] He himself was drawn slowly along by eight horses, while he feasted continually night and day with his companions, on a stage erected on a lofty and conspicuous platform. A countless number of wagons followed, some shaded from the sun by purple canopies, others by tree branches, which were kept fresh and green. These carried Alexander's other friends and officers, bedecked

---

[103] Alexander sailed out into the ocean in the midsummer of 325 B.C., having spent nineteen months in India. The island he visited may possibly have been the one now called Cutch.

[104] This revelry may have been an imitation of the riotous return of the god Dionysus from his legendary journey to India. But Arrian, the sober historian, says that the tales of this Bacchanalian procession through Carmania are unsupported by any reliable authority.

with garlands and drinking their wine. Not a shield or a helmet or a pike was to be seen, but along the whole way the soldiers, with their bowls and flasks and horns were dipping out wine from huge jars and mixing basins and drinking each other's health, some as they kept on marching, others lying down meanwhile. The music of pipes and flutes and stringed instruments and the Bacchic hymns of women filled every place. Following this disorderly and straggling march there came the sports of a Bacchic orgy, as if Dionysus himself were there and leading the revel. On reaching the royal palace of Gedrosia, Alexander again halted his army, and held a festival. Once, they say, after drinking, he was watching a contest between choruses when his beloved Bagoas did the best in the singing and dancing. Then in his festal dress Bagoas came through the theater and seated himself beside Alexander. Seeing this, the Macedonians applauded and shouted that Alexander should kiss the boy, until at length he threw his arms around him and kissed him heartily.

68. Here Nearchus and his company came up to join him, and he was keenly interested to hear of their voyage. He had a desire to sail down the Euphrates himself with a great fleet, and then around Arabia and Libya, and so enter the Mediterranean through the Pillars of Heracles.[105] He began building ships of every kind at Thapsacus [106] and collecting sailors and pilots from all directions. But the hardships of his journey back, his wound from the Malli, and the losses in his army, which were said to be tremendous, together with the doubts as to his safe return, had raised a spirit of rebellion in his subjects and had encouraged his generals and satraps to commit many an act of injustice, greed, and insolence. All in all, a restlessness and a longing for change were spreading everywhere. Even against Antipater Olympias and Cleopatra had formed a party and had divided his domain between them, Olympias taking Epirus and Cleopatra Macedonia. When Alexander heard of this, he said that his mother had had the better idea, for the Macedonians would not endure to be ruled by a woman.

For these reasons then he sent Nearchus back to sea [107] and resolved to make war himself all along the coast. He came down from the interior

---

[105] Pillars of Heracles was the ancient name for the Straits of Gibraltar.

[106] Thapsacus, a city on the Euphrates river, lies where it begins to be navigable.

[107] It was now early in 324 B.C.

and punished those of his commanders who had behaved badly. Oxyartes, one of the sons of Abuletes, he killed with his own hand, running him through with a pike. And when Abuletes failed to supply him with any of the necessary provisions, but brought him three thousand talents in coin, Alexander ordered the money thrown down for the horses. When they would not taste it, he said, "So what good is your provision to us?" and sent Abuletes to prison.

69. In Persia, he first renewed the old custom of the kings that whenever they appeared there they would give every woman a gold piece. On that account, we hear, some kings came seldom to Persia, and Ochus [108] not even once, exiling himself out of stinginess from his native land. Next, Alexander discovered that someone had broken into the tomb of Cyrus,[109] and he had the guilty man put to death, though he was a Macedonian of some consequence from Pella, named Polymachus. On reading the inscription on the tomb he ordered it cut in Greek letters as well. It ran as follows: "O man, whoever thou art and from wherever thou comest —for I know that thou wilt come—I am Cyrus, who won the empire for the Persians. Do not then grudge me this little earth which covers my body." These words made a deep impression on Alexander, reminding him of the uncertainty and changefulness of human affairs.

And while they were there, Calanus, who had been suffering for a while from a digestive disorder, asked to have a funeral pile erected for him. He then rode up to it on horseback, offered prayers, poured a libation for himself and threw some locks of his hair on the pyre. Then he climbed to the top and saluted the Macedonians who stood watching, bidding them be of good cheer that day and drink deep at the king's table, adding that he himself would shortly see the king at Babylon. With these words, he sat down and covered his face and did not move as the fire drew near him, but kept the same posture to the end. Thus he sacrificed himself with dignity, in the ancient way of the Indian sages. Many years later, another Indian, in Caesar's retinue,[110] did the same thing at Athens, where to this day they show you what they call "the Indian's tomb."

---

108 Ochus was a name of Darius II, king of Persia from 424 to 404 B.C.
109 The tomb of Cyrus the Great was at Pasargadae, in Persia.
110 That is, Augustus Caesar.

70. But Alexander on leaving the funeral pyre collected many of his friends and officers for supper and proposed a contest in drinking clear wine, with a crown as a prize. The one who drank most, Promachus, drained as many as four pitchers.[111] He won the prize, a crown worth a talent, but he lived only three days afterwards. And Chares tells us that forty-one of the others died of the drinking, for heavy chills attacked them after their orgy.

At Susa Alexander celebrated the marriages of many of his companions, and himself took to wife Statira, Darius' daughter. The noblest of the Persian ladies he assigned to his noblest men, and gave a general banquet too for the Macedonians already married. At this feast, they say, nine thousand guests lay on couches for supper, and to each was presented a golden cup for the libations. All the other appointments were amazingly gorgeous. Alexander even paid the debts of all his guests who owed money to usurers, the whole expense coming to just under nine thousand, eight hundred and seventy talents. But Antigenes, the one-eyed, got his name fraudulently on the roll as a debtor, producing a man who declared he had lent him a sum at the money changer's. The money was paid him, but the deception was soon discovered and the king in anger banished Antigenes from the court and took away his command. However, he was a very fine soldier. When Philip was besieging Perinthus, Antigenes, then a young man, was struck in the eye by a dart from a catapult, but would not allow it to be pulled out or leave the front of the fight until the enemy had been repulsed and shut up inside their walls. So now he was overwhelmed by his disgrace, and was apparently about to destroy himself in his misery and gloom. In fear that this might happen, the king forgot his wrath and told him to keep the money.

71. The thirty thousand boys whom Alexander had left to be trained and taught [112] now looked so manly and were so handsome in appearance and showed such remarkable skill and agility in their exercises that Alexander was delighted with them. But the Macedonians grew disgruntled and fearful that the king would now be less interested in them. So when he sent the sick and disabled among them down to the coast, they said it was an insult and a foul abuse, after using men up in every kind

---

111 This pitcher, or liquid measure, held about three quarts.
112 See above, ch. 47.

of toil, to cast them off now in disgrace and throw them back on their home towns and their parents, no longer what they were when he took them. They therefore told him to send them away and think all Macedonians worthless, now that he had these young dancers with whom to go on and conquer the world. At this Alexander was much irritated and scolded them angrily and at length. He then dismissed them and made guards of Persians, appointing armor bearers and attendants from among them.

When the Macedonians saw him escorted by these men and found themselves shut out from his presence and scornfully treated, they were humbled, and on considering their situation, realized that they had been nearly mad with rage and jealousy. Then, at last, they came to their senses and went to his tent unarmed, clad only in their tunics, and there with wailing and lamentation submitted themselves to him, bidding him deal with them as wicked and ungrateful men. Although he was now softening, Alexander refused to receive them, but they would not go away and for two days and nights persisted in standing thus in front of his tent, mourning and calling on their sovereign. On the third day he came out and seeing them so pitiable and humiliated he wept for a long while. Then after reproving them gently and speaking kindly to them, he sent the useless men home with handsome gifts. He also wrote Antipater that at every public contest and in the theaters those men should sit in the front seats, crowned with garlands. And he had the orphans of those who had fallen put on the pay roll.

72. When Alexander came to Ecbatana in Media, he accomplished his pressing business there, and then was absorbed again with theaters and festivities, for three thousand artists had joined him from Greece. But about that time it happened that Hephaestion fell ill of a fever, and being a young man and a soldier, he would not stand a strict regimen. When once Glaucus, his physician, left him to go to the theater, he went to breakfast, ate a boiled fowl, drank off a big cooler of wine, was taken worse, and soon died.

Alexander went out of his mind with grief. He at once ordered the manes of all the horses and mules to be shorn in sign of mourning, and had the battlements of all the neighboring cities torn down, crucified the poor doctor, and for a long while forbade the playing of flutes and every other kind of music in the camp, until an oracle came from Ammon commanding him to honor Hephaestion and sacrifice to him as to a hero. He then tried to assuage his grief by war and went out on what seemed a hunt and chase after men. He crushed the tribe of the Cossaei, and slew them all, from the youth up. This he called an offering to Hephaestion.

On a tomb and funeral for Hephaestion and their beautification, Alexander was determined to spend ten thousand talents and to have the artistry and originality of the monument exceed the cost. Of all the artists he most wanted Stasicrates, because his designs always had an air of grandeur and boldness and magnificence. Once before this, when talking with Alexander, Stasicrates had told him that of all mountains Athos in Thrace could most easily be worked into the figure and shape of a man; and that if Alexander would give him the order, he would make Athos into a uniquely permanent and striking monument to him, holding in its left hand a city of ten thousand people, while with its right it poured out a copious river flowing to the sea. This suggestion Alexander had refused to consider, but now he began discussing and devising with his artists plans far more strange and costly than that.

73. He was proceeding on to Babylon,[113] when Nearchus, who had joined him again, after sailing through the great sea and up the Euphrates, told him that some Chaldeans had met him with a warning that Alexander should stay away from Babylon. He paid no attention, but went on. On arriving at the walls he saw a flock of crows flying about and pecking at one another. Some of them fell dead beside him. Later he learned that Apollodorus, the commander at Babylon, had been sacrificing, to learn what Alexander's future would be. He then sent for Pythagoras the soothsayer, who admitted that the sacrifice had taken place. Alexander asked how it had turned out, and Pythagoras told him that the victim's liver was without a lobe. "Oh," exclaimed Alexander, "a dread omen!" He did not hurt Pythagoras, but he regretted not obeying Nearchus, and spent most of his time outside Babylon, either in his tent or sailing on the Euphrates.

He was depressed by many omens. A tame ass attacked and kicked to death the largest and finest of the lions he kept. And one day he had taken off his clothes for a rubbing down and was playing at ball when

---

[113] It was now the spring of 323 B.C.

the time came to dress again, and the young men with whom he was playing saw a man sitting silently on the king's throne, wearing his diadem and royal robe. When asked who he was, for a long time the man would not speak, but at length he came to himself and said his name was Dionysius and he was a native of Messene, who had been brought there from the coast on some charge or accusation and for a long time had been kept in chains. But just now the god Serapis had appeared to him, loosed his chains and led him thither, and bidden him put on the king's diadem and robe, take his seat on the throne, and say nothing.

74. When Alexander heard this, he disposed of the man as the soothsayers advised, but he himself grew downhearted, and was less confident now of divine aid, and suspicious of his friends. He became especially afraid of Antipater and his sons, one of whom, Iolaus, was Alexander's head cupbearer. Another, Cassander,[114] had but lately come to Alexander, and on seeing some barbarians paying obeisance to him, he had burst into a loud laugh, for he had been brought up like a Greek and had never seen anything like that before. Thereat Alexander was furious and seizing him by the hair knocked his head violently against the wall.

Another time, when Cassander was about to say something in answer to men who were accusing Antipater of misconduct, Alexander stopped him. "What do you mean?" he said. "Would men come so long a way if they had not been injured and were only false tale-bearers?" When Cassander answered that it looked like false tale-bearing, when they came so far away from the proofs, Alexander laughed and said, "These are the well-known sophisms of Aristotle's pupils, to use for either side of an argument. But if we find that you have wronged these men ever so little, you shall rue it." Altogether, they say, Cassander's spirit was so intimidated by his terrible dread of Alexander that many years later, when he was king of Macedonia and lord of Greece and was walking about in Delphi looking at the statues, on catching sight of one of Alexander he was instantly seized with a shuddering and a trembling, his head swam and with difficulty he regained his composure.

75. When once Alexander had let himself become worried about the gods and fearful in his mind, nothing unusual or strange ever happened,

---

114 On Cassander see above, under *Demosthenes*, ch. 13.

no matter how trifling, that he did not make an omen and portent out
of it. The palace was full of men sacrificing, performing lustrations, and
prophesying. For while it is terrible to have no faith in divine things and
to be contemptuous of them, superstition is also terrible. Like water it
ever seeks the lowest levels, and now it imbued with folly an Alexander
grown timorous.

However, on receipt of the oracle from the god about Hephaestion, he
put by his grief and again took part in sacrifices and drinking feasts. He
gave a brilliant entertainment to Nearchus and his friends, and then
took a bath, as he was accustomed to do on going to bed. Instead, at
Medius' invitation, he went to some revels at his house, and there, after
drinking all the next day, he began to be feverish. He did not drain the
flagon of Heracles, nor was he taken suddenly with a pain in his back,
as if stabbed by a lance, though some writers have thought they must
tell such a story, so as to fashion a tragic and pathetic end to a great drama.
But Aristobulus says he became frantic with fever and drank wine to
quench his parching thirst and then grew delirious and died, on the
thirtieth day of the month Daesius.[115]

76. In the journals the following facts are recorded as to his illness. On
the eighteenth day of the month Daesius he slept in his bath-chamber,
because he was feverish. The next day after bathing he moved to his bed-
room and passed that day playing at dice with Medius. Then in the evening he bathed again, performed the sacred rites, and ate something;
all that night he had a fever. On the twentieth day, after his bath, he
offered his usual sacrifice, and then lay on his couch in the bath-chamber
and devoted his time to Nearchus and his company, listening to accounts
of their voyage and of the great sea. The twenty-first day he spent in the
same way, but his fever increased and he suffered much during the night.
On the following day, though his fever was very high, he had himself
lifted and laid beside the great swimming pool and there he conversed
with his generals about the vacant posts of the command, and how to
find well-tested men to fill them.

On the twenty-fourth his fever was violent and he was carried out to sacrifice. He ordered his chief generals to remain in the palace court, and the

---

[115] June 13, 323 B.C.

commanders of brigades and companies to stay all night outside. On the twenty-fifth day he was carried to the palace beyond the river and there slept a little, but his fever grew no better. When his generals came to his room, he was speechless, as he was also on the twenty-sixth day. So the Macedonians thought he was dead and came clamoring to the palace doors, threatening the attendants until they forced their way in. When the doors were opened to them, one by one they all filed in past his bed, dressed only in their tunics. That day too Python and Seleucus were sent to the temple of Serapis to ask if they should carry Alexander there, but the god answered that they should leave him where he was. And on the twenty-eighth day, towards evening, he died.

77. Most of the above is found thus, word for word, recorded in the journals. No one at the time had any suspicion of poisoning, but five years later, Olympias, acting, it is said, on some information, put a number of men to death and had the ashes of Iolas, who had died, cast to the winds, on the ground that he had poured out the poison. And some say that Aristotle advised Antipater to have the deed done, and that it was entirely through him that the poison was procured. They declare that one Hagnothemis told the story as something he had heard from King Antigonus; and that the poison was water cold as ice from a certain rock in Nonacris, which they gathered like a light dew and kept stored in an ass's hoof, for no other vessel could hold it without splitting because of its coldness and sharpness. Most writers, however, think that the story of the poisoning is completely fictitious, and their view is strongly supported by the fact that though the generals fought one another then for many days, and Alexander's body lay uncared for in warm and stifling rooms, it showed no sign of any such deadly dose but remained pure and fresh.

Roxana was with child and for that reason was treated with reverence by the Macedonians. But she was bitterly jealous of Statira and enticed her by a forged letter into coming to her. And when she had brought her there, she killed both her and her sister, threw their bodies into a well, and filled it up with earth. Perdiccas knew of the crime and was her accomplice in it. He was the one whose power was greatest at first, and he dragged Arrhidaeus around with him, as though he were guarding his royalty. Arrhidaeus was Philip's son by an obscure and common woman called Philinna, and was defective in intelligence because of a bodily disease. This had not, however, attacked him naturally or of its own accord. In fact, they say that as a boy he showed an attractive and noble disposition, but that he was fed drugs by Olympias which damaged him and destroyed his mind.

Caesar

I 0 2 – 4 4 B . C .

1. CAESAR'S [1] wife was Cornelia, daughter of Cinna, who had once been sole ruler of Rome.[2] When Sulla took over control, he could not either by promises or by threats make him put her away, and so he confiscated her dowry. The cause of the enmity between Caesar and Sulla was Caesar's relationship to Marius, for the elder Marius had married Julia, the sister of Caesar's father, and she was the mother of the younger Marius, Caesar's cousin. And even at the first, while Sulla was occupied with his numerous proscriptions, Caesar was not content to be left in the

[1] The abruptness of this beginning and omission of any account of Caesar's birth and upbringing have led many commentators to believe that the opening paragraphs of this life have been lost. Gaius Julius Caesar was of patrician lineage on both sides, though his uncle, the general Gaius Marius, had risen to power as head of the popular party in Rome. See above, *Cicero,* ch. 3. His father died when Caesar was only sixteen and his mother, a woman of exceptional intelligence, had charge of his later training. At seventeen he married as his second wife Cornelia, daughter of Lucius Cinna, the second leader of the popular party. While Sulla, the leader of the aristocrats, was in the East, Marius and his friends made themselves temporarily masters of the city and Caesar was marked for high office. But on Marius' death in 86 B.C. and Sulla's triumphant return to Rome, everything changed, and by 82 Sulla had suppressed all opposition. He recognized the twenty-year-old Caesar as a potentially dangerous rival and without the intercession of his aristocratic relatives and of the College of Vestals might well have included him in the lists of the fatally proscribed. But as it was, Caesar was left to go his own way, preserving a non-committal attitude to both parties, and merely setting out on the usual military and political career of any young Roman aspiring to make something of himself.

[2] Lucius Cornelius Cinna, Caesar's father-in-law, was consul in 86 B.C. In that same year both Marius and Cinna's colleague as consul died, leaving Cinna for the rest of his term sole possessor of official authority.

background but came before the people as a candidate for a priesthood,[3] though he was yet hardly more than a boy. By secret opposition, Sulla made him fail of election and even considered having him put to death. Some said it was not reasonable to kill such a boy as he was, but Sulla told them they were dull if they did not see many a Marius in that boy.

When this remark was reported to Caesar, he went for a while into hiding, wandering about the Sabine country. But then, as he was moving by night to another dwelling place because of an illness, he fell in with some soldiers of Sulla, who were searching the region and arresting the hideaways there. He bribed their commander, Cornelius, with two talents to let him go, and at once made for the coast. Thence he took ship for Bithynia,[4] to join King Nicomedes. He did not remain long with him and on his voyage back was captured off the island of Pharmacusa [5] by pirates, who at that time were masters of the sea, with their great fleets and numberless small boats.

2. At the outset the pirates demanded of Caesar twenty talents for his ransom, but Caesar laughed at them for not knowing who their prisoner was, and voluntarily offered to pay them fifty. Then, after he had dispatched his different companions to various cities to raise the money, he was left with only one friend and two attendants among bloodthirsty Cilicians. Yet he was so contemptuous of them that whenever he had a mind to sleep he would send and order them to be quiet. He spent thirty-eight days with them, taking part in their sports and their exercises as if they were not his jailers but his bodyguard. He wrote poems, too, and speeches which he read to them, and those who did not admire them he would call straight out ignorant barbarians, and would often threaten laughingly to hang them all. The pirates enjoyed it and ascribed his bold talk to simplicity and boyish playfulness.

---

[3] The office of priest in the temple of Jupiter had as much political as religious importance.

[4] A great part of the years 81 to 78 B.C. Caesar spent in Asia Minor serving in campaigns to extend and enforce Roman rule. Nicomedes, king of Bithynia in northern Asia Minor, a faithful ally of Rome, is said to have been much taken by the youthful soldier.

[5] Pharmacusa was a tiny island in the narrow strait between Salamis and the Attic mainland, an excellent lurking-place from which to strike at ships putting in or out of the Piraeus harbor of Athens.

As soon as the ransom came from Miletus and Caesar had paid it and was set at liberty, he manned some vessels in the port of Miletus and went after the pirates. He found them still lying off the island, and captured most of them. Their money he took as booty and the men he deposited in the prison at Pergamum. He then went himself to Junius, governor of Asia, on the ground that he, as praetor, was the proper person to punish them. But Junius, with his eye on the booty, which was considerable, promised only that he would look into the case of the prisoners at his leisure. So Caesar bade him farewell, went back to Pergamum, took out the pirates and crucified them all, as he had often on the island threatened to do, when they thought he was joking.

3. Later, when Sulla's reign was over,[6] Caesar's friends in Rome urged him to return. Instead, he went down to Rhodes, to study in the school of Apollonius, son of Molon, a famous rhetorician, who had Cicero too as a pupil.[7] Caesar had, they say, a remarkable natural gift for political oratory, and worked at it ambitiously, so that unquestionably he made second rank. The first rank he did not try to reach, for he preferred to put his main energies into becoming first a military power. So he did not attain that skill as a speaker for which his natural talents fitted him, since his military campaigns and political activities, which won his supremacy for him, prevented it. And so, at a later time, in his answer to Cicero's *Cato*,[8] he deprecates comparison between the speech of a soldier and the eloquence of an orator who is both naturally talented and spends much time on the subject.

4. On his return to Rome he accused Dolabella [9] of maladministration of his province, and many of the Greek cities furnished evidence to support him. Dolabella was acquitted, but as a return to the Greeks for their zeal in his behalf, Caesar assisted them in their prosecution of Publius Antonius for graft before Marcus Lucullus, the praetor of Mace-

[6] Sulla died suddenly in 78 B.C., while Caesar was still in Asia Minor.

[7] See above, *Cicero,* ch. 4.

[8] See above, *Cicero,* ch. 39.

[9] Gnaeus Cornelius Dolabella, not to be confused with Cicero's profligate son-in-law, had been governor of Macedonia between 80 and 78 B.C. Caesar accused him in 77 of flagrant misconduct in office.

donia.[10] And he made so great an impression that Antonius appealed to the tribunes at Rome, protesting that he could not get justice in Greece against Greeks.

In Rome Caesar gained brilliant renown by his pleadings as advocate, and a wide popularity with the plain people by his friendly way of mixing with them, for he was sociable beyond his years. And by his dinners and entertainments and the general magnificence of his way of living he was gradually increasing his political influence. At first his enemies supposed it would last only until he stopped spending money, and so they disregarded its growth among the people. But eventually his power grew to be great and hard to oppose and it was plain that he was aiming at a total revolution in the state. Then they realized that no beginning of trouble should be thought so small that a continuance of it may not soon make it great, and that from being despised it may become irresistible. The man who apparently was the first to look beneath the surface and fear Caesar's policy, as one fears the smiling aspect of the sea, and to perceive the formidable character concealed under his affable and cheery bearing, was Cicero. He used to say that in all Caesar's plans and political measures he saw a design of tyranny. "And yet," he said, "when I look at his hair, arranged so perfectly, and see him scratching his head with one finger, I cannot believe that this fellow would ever dream of so appalling a crime as the destruction of the Roman state." This anecdote, however, should come later.

5. The first evidence of his popularity with the people Caesar received when he ran against Gaius Popilius for the post of legionary tribune and was elected. A second and more marked evidence he received at the time of the death of his aunt, Julia, Marius' wife, when he delivered an eloquent eulogy of her in the forum, and ventured to display images of Marius in the funeral procession. It was the first time they had been seen since the rule of Sulla, when Marius and his supporters had been pronounced public enemies. Some voices cried out now against Caesar for his act, but the people retorted with wild shouts and hailed him with

---

10 Marcus Lucullus, brother of the more famous Lucius Lucullus (See above under *Cicero,* ch. 29, n. 43.), was an efficient governor of Macedonia as praetor in the year 72. Caesar lost both these cases, but through them he convinced the public of his own hatred of the prevalent corruption of senatorial government in the provinces.

applause, admiring him for bringing back after so long a time, as it were from Hades, the glories of Marius to the city. It was an ancient Roman custom to deliver funeral orations over elderly women,[11] but it was not the rule to do so over young women. Caesar, however, delivered one when his own wife died [12] and this brought him even more popularity and played on the sympathies of the people so that they felt warmly towards him as a man of tender and generous disposition.

After his wife's funeral he went out to Spain as quaestor for the praetor Vetus, for whom he always felt great respect, and whose son he made his quaestor when he, in turn, became praetor. After finishing his quaestorship, he married his third wife, Pompeia. By Cornelia he had had a daughter, who later was married to Pompey the Great. He was so lavish in his expenditure of money that it looked as if he were buying a passing and short-lived fame at a big price, though in truth he was purchasing things of greatest value for very little. They say that before he got any public office he was in debt for thirteen hundred talents. And when he was appointed curator of the Appian Way,[13] he laid out large sums of his own money on it. Again, while he was aedile,[14] he provided three hundred and twenty pairs of gladiators for the shows, and by extravagant outlays on plays and processions and banquets effaced all memory of his predecessors' ambitious exertions. In this way he put the people in such a mood that everyone was looking for new offices and new honors with which to reward him.

6. There were then two parties in the city, that of Sulla, which was still extremely powerful, and that of Marius, which was cowed and scattered and in a forlorn position. This party Caesar aimed to revive and attach to himself, and accordingly, when his magnificent efforts as aedile were at their height, he had images of Marius and trophy-bearing Victories secretly made, and had them set up by night on the Capitol. At dawn the

---

[11] The custom of allowing funeral orations for women was introduced after the capture of the city by the Gauls, as a reward to them for contributing to the ransom demanded by the enemy.

[12] Caesar's second wife, Cornelia, died in 68 B.C.

[13] The Appian Way was the great paved highway which led southeast from Rome through Capua to Brundisium. The duties of curator corresponded roughly to those of a modern road commissioner.

[14] Caesar was aedile for the year 65 B.C.

people saw them there, all gleaming with gold and made with rare
artistry, bearing inscriptions recounting Marius' victories over the Cimbrians. They were astonished at the audacity of the man who had placed
them there, for it was plain who had done it, and the report circulated
rapidly, bringing everyone to see the sight. Some called out that Caesar
was planning to set up a tyranny, restoring honors which had been buried
by laws and decrees, and that this was his test of the people whom he
had been beguiling, to see if they were now so tamed by his ambitious
feats that they would allow him to play with revolution in this style. But
the followers of Marius appeared suddenly in surprising numbers, cheering one another and filling the Capitol with their applause. Many too
shed tears of joy at seeing again the likeness of Marius, and exultingly
praised Caesar as the man who above all was worthy to be his kinsman.

When the senate met to consider the situation, Catulus Lutatius,[15]
who had at that time the greatest name of any man in Rome, rose and
attacked Caesar, using the memorable words, "No longer, Caesar, by
underground approaches but by battering rams you are storming the
republic!" However, Caesar defended himself against his accusations and
won over the senate, at which his admirers were even more elated and
urged him not to relinquish any of his plans. With the people's support,
they said, he would overcome all his enemies and become the chief man
in the state.

7.   About this time Metellus, the Pontifex Maximus, died,[16] and Isauricus
and Catulus were candidates for the office, which was an object of keen
rivalry. They were very distinguished men with great influence in the
senate. However, Caesar would not give it up to them but went before
the people as an opposing candidate. The people's choice seemed to be
equally divided, so Catulus, who was the more likely of the other two
candidates and more worried by the uncertainty, sent to Caesar and tried
to persuade him to resign his ambition, offering him a great deal of money.
Caesar replied that he would go through with the contest even if he had

---

[15] Lutatius Catulus was a respected conservative who had acted as judge at the trial
of the notorious Verres in 70 B.C., when Cicero was prosecuting attorney, and had
opposed Caesar when he argued for a commutation of the death sentence for the followers of Catiline. See above, *Cicero*, chs. 7, 21.
[16] Metellus died in 63 B.C.

to borrow more. On the day of the election, when his mother in tears went with him to the door, he kissed her and said, "Mother, today you will see your son either Pontifex Maximus or an exile." It was a close contest, but when the votes were cast, Caesar was the winner.

At this the senate and the nobility were frightened that he would lead the people on to every form of insubordination. So Piso and Catulus began blaming Cicero for sparing Caesar, when during the trouble over Catiline Caesar had given him a hold on him.[17] For Catiline had planned not only to make changes in the constitution, but to upset the whole government and throw everything into chaos. He himself was banished from the city on being convicted on some minor charges, before the whole extent of his plot had been discovered.[18] But he left Lentulus and Cethegus behind him in the city to carry on the conspiracy. Whether or not they received some secret encouragement and aid from Caesar is unknown. But after they had been forcibly convicted in the senate, and Cicero, as consul, was asking each senator for his judgment on the character of their punishment, all down to Caesar declared for the death penalty. But Caesar rose and delivered a considered speech to the effect that he did not think it lawful or in accord with tradition to put men of high rank and distinguished family to death without trial, except under most urgent necessity. If they were fettered, he said, and kept in prison in whatever cities of Italy Cicero might choose, until the war with Catiline was finished, the senate might then in peace and at leisure decide the case of each one.

8. This proposal seemed so humane, and Caesar's speech for it was so powerful, that not only those who spoke after him took sides with him but many who had already spoken reversed their opinions and went over to him, until the turn came of Cato and Catulus. They vigorously opposed Caesar, and Cato by his speech even aroused some strong suspicion against Caesar himself.[19] So the conspirators were handed over to be executed. And as Caesar was leaving the senate, a number of the young men who were acting at that time as a bodyguard to Cicero crowded together around him, brandishing their naked swords. But Curio, they

---

[17] See above, *Cicero,* ch. 20.

[18] For fuller details of the Catilinian conspiracy see above, *Cicero,* chs. 10 ff.

[19] See below, *Cato the Younger,* chs. 22, 23.

say, threw his toga over Caesar and carried him off. And Cicero himself, when the young men looked towards him, shook his head, either for fear of the people or because he thought Caesar's murder would be utterly wrong and unlawful. But if this story is true, I do not know why Cicero said nothing about it in his book on his consulship.[20] He was blamed afterwards too for not having taken advantage of his excellent opportunity for getting rid of Caesar. But he was intimidated by the people, who were extraordinarily devoted to Caesar.

A few days later Caesar came to the senate and started to defend himself against the charges on which he was suspected, and was answered by a violent uproar. As the senate sat on for a longer time than usual, the people came flocking and shouting and surrounded the senate house calling for Caesar and commanding the senate to let him go. This terrified Cato, who was in dread of a rising of the poorer citizens, who were like firebrands to the entire populace and were pinning their hopes on Caesar. He therefore prevailed on the senate to vote them a monthly ration of corn,[21] a measure which added seven million, five hundred thousand drachmas yearly to the expenses of the state, but which noticeably quieted the widespread fears of the time and broke and dissipated much of Caesar's power at a critical moment, for he was then praetor-elect [22] and more formidable because of his position.

9. No tumults occurred while Caesar was praetor, but a disagreeable event took place in his own family. Publius Clodius [23] was a patrician by birth and conspicuous for his wealth and his eloquence, but in arrogance and recklessness second to none of the notorious villains of the day. This man was in love with Caesar's wife, Pompeia, and she was not averse to him. The guards of the women's apartment were strict, and Caesar's mother Aurelia, a prudent woman, kept the girl always under her eye and made a meeting with Clodius both difficult and hazardous.

Now the Romans have a goddess they call Bona, similar to the Greek Women's Goddess. The Phrygians claim her and say she was the mother of King Midas, the Romans that she is a Dryad nymph, wedded to Faunus, and the Greeks that she is the unnameable one of the mothers

---

[20] Cicero's book on his consulship has not been preserved.

[21] See below, *Cato the Younger,* ch. 26.

[22] Caesar was elected praetor for the year 62 B.C.

[23] On Clodius and the whole of the following episode, see above, *Cicero,* chs. 28, 29,

of Dionysus. This is why the women cover their tents with vine branches while they celebrate her festival, and why a sacred snake is placed beside the goddess in accordance with the myth. It is unlawful for any man to attend her holy rites, or even to be in the house where they are being celebrated. Alone, by themselves, the women perform, they say, many ceremonies connected with those of the Orphics. Therefore, when the time of the festival draws near, the consul or praetor at whose house the celebration takes place and all other males depart, and his wife takes over the place and sets it in proper order. The most important ceremonies are performed at night, and the women are merry at their vigils and have a great deal of music.[24]

10. That year Pompeia was holding the festival, and Clodius, who as yet was beardless and so thought he would not be recognized, put on the dress and ornaments of a girl lute-player and went to the house, to all appearance a young woman. He found the door open and was brought in safely by a maidservant, who knew what was going on. But she ran ahead to inform Pompeia and there was some delay, and Clodius was too impatient to remain where she had left him. He was wandering around the big house, trying to avoid the lights, when a waiting-woman of Aurelia ran into him and challenged him to play, as one woman would with another, and when he refused, she pulled him forward and asked who he was and where he came from. Clodius replied that he was waiting for Pompeia's Abra, that being the maid's name, but his voice betrayed him and the woman instantly sprang back with a scream for the lights and the rest of the company, crying out that she had discovered a man. The women were terrified and Aurelia stopped the rites of the goddess and covered up the sacred objects. She then ordered the doors to be shut, and went through the house with torches, hunting for Clodius.

He was found where he had fled for refuge, in the room of the maid who had let him in, and when the women recognized him they drove him out of doors. They then went straight that very night to their husbands and told them what had happened, and by daybreak the story was running all through the city, how Clodius had attempted something un-

[24] No one knows today precisely what these secret women's ceremonies consisted of, but they seem to have been a development from more ancient fertility rites. See above, *Cicero*, ch. 19. An interesting imaginative description of them, as well as of leading personalities of Caesar's day, may be found in Thornton Wilder's *The Ides of March*.

lawful and had committed an offense not only against the women he had insulted, but against the city and the gods. Accordingly, one of the tribunes began an action against him for sacrilege and the most powerful senators combined against him, testifying that along with his other horrible profligacy, he had committed adultery with his own sister, the wife of Lucullus. In spite of their efforts, the people aligned themselves with Clodius, and were of great service to him with the jurors, who were in panic fear of the masses.

Caesar promptly divorced Pompeia, but when summoned to Clodius' trial as a witness, said he knew nothing about the matters contained in the accusation against him. The answer sounded strange and the prosecutor asked him, "Why, then, have you divorced your wife?" "Because," said Caesar, "my wife should be above suspicion." Some say that Caesar was stating what was actually true; others say that he was acting to please the people, who were bent on saving Clodius. However this may have been, Clodius was acquitted, and the majority of the jurors handed in their verdicts in confused writing, so that they might run no risk from the people by convicting him nor yet spoil their reputations with the nobility by letting him off.

11. As soon as his praetorship expired, Caesar received Spain for his province, but he had difficulties settling with his creditors, who hindered his leaving and were clamorous for money. So he applied to Crassus,[25] then the richest man in Rome, who needed the vigor and warmth of Caesar for his campaign against Pompey. Crassus undertook to pay the most insistent and ruthless of Caesar's creditors, and gave security for eight hundred and thirty talents, whereupon Caesar went off to his province.

There is a story that while crossing the Alps, he was passing a wretched barbarian village with very few inhabitants, and his companions, laughing and joking, asked, "Do you suppose that here too there are men ambitious for offices and struggling to be first, strong men jealous of each other?" To which Caesar replied earnestly, "I would rather be first with these men than second with the Romans." Likewise we hear that in Spain, in a period of leisure, he was reading one of the histories of Alexander, when he sat for a long time in deep thought and then broke into tears

25 On Crassus see above, *Cicero*, n. 18.

When his friends in surprise asked him the reason, he said, "Do you not think it a cause for grief that Alexander at my age was already king of so many nations, and I as yet have accomplished nothing remarkable?" [26]

12. However, as soon as he reached Spain, he started work and in a few days had assembled ten cohorts in addition to the twenty which were already there. He then set out on a campaign against the Calaici and the Lusitani,[27] defeated them and pushed on to the shore of the Outer Sea,[28] subduing tribes which had never before been subject to Rome. After this military success, he did equally well in organizing for peace, establishing harmony between the cities, and, in particular, adjusting differences between debtors and creditors. He arranged that the creditor every year should receive two thirds of his debtor's income, and the debtor the rest of what was his, until in this way his debt was paid. By these measures Caesar gained an excellent name for himself and by the time he left the province he was rich himself, had enriched his soldiers from his conquests, and been hailed by them as Imperator.[29]

13. Now it was the rule at Rome that men who were suing for permission to hold a triumph should stay outside the city, and that those who were standing for election as consul should do so in the city. Hence Caesar was in a quandary. For he arrived just at the time of the consular elections. He sent to the senate a request for permission to stand for the consulship through his friends, in his own absence. But to begin with, Cato insisted on the law and opposed Caesar's request, and then, when he saw that many senators had yielded to Caesar's cajoling, he postponed the decision by using up the whole day in speaking. Thereupon Caesar determined to give up the triumph and make sure of the consulship.

On his entry into the city, he adopted a policy which deceived every-

---

26 Other historians, such as Suetonius, give this incident as occurring seven years earlier, during Caesar's service as quaestor in Spain. He would then have been thirty-four years old, a year older than Alexander was when he died.

27 The Calaici lived in what is now northwestern Spain, and the Lusitani in modern Portugal.

28 The Outer Sea would be, of course, the Atlantic Ocean.

29 *Imperator* under the Roman republic meant simply commander-in-chief. As the republic was transformed into an empire, it came to mean emperor.

one except Cato and which was to bring about a reconciliation between Pompey and Crassus,[30] the two most powerful men at Rome. They had been quarreling, but Caesar now brought them together as friends, centering in himself the combined strength of them both. Thus by an act which was called kind, he altered, unobserved, the form of government. For it was not, as most people supposed, the enmity between Caesar and Pompey which was to cause the civil wars, but rather their friendship, since first they combined to pull down the aristocracy and only then, when that was done, quarreled again with each other. Cato, who often predicted what would happen, got the name at the time of being a sour, meddlesome fellow, but later of being a wise though unsuccessful counselor.

14. Surrounded thus and protected by the friendship of Crassus and Pompey, Caesar entered the contest for the consulship and was overwhelmingly elected, with Calpurnius Bibulus as his colleague.[31] Immediately on his entrance into office he proposed laws which were not what one would expect from a consul so much as from an utterly reckless tribune, out to please the populace by allotments and distribution of land. And when, in the senate, he met with the opposition of the most reputable members, he had the excuse he had long wanted. Loudly calling on everyone to witness that it was against his will that he was driven to the people, but that the senate's rude and insulting conduct forced him to beg the assembly's favor, he rushed out to it, and with Crassus standing on one side of him and Pompey on the other, asked if it would approve his laws. And when the people expressed their approval, he called on them for aid against those who were threatening to oppose him with swords. They promised their help, and Pompey added that he would meet swords with his sword and shield in hand. At this mad and braggart speech, unworthy of the respect in which Pompey was held and unsuited to the reverence due the senate, the aristocrats were distressed, but the people were gratified.

Caesar was bent on making still greater use of Pompey's power. He

---

[30] The understanding which Caesar helped to bring about between Pompey and Crassus was the beginning of the so-called First Triumvirate, the division of supreme power in the state between the three men.

[31] Caesar's first consulship was for the year 59 B.C.

had a daughter Julia,[32] betrothed to Servilius Caepio. He now betrothed her to Pompey and said he would give Pompey's daughter to Servilius, although she too was not free but had been promised to Faustus, Sulla's son. Soon afterwards Caesar himself married Calpurnia, a daughter of Piso, and got Piso elected consul for the next year. At this point again Cato violently protested and exclaimed that it was unendurable to see the chief power of the state prostituted by marriage bargaining and men using women to help one another to provinces and armies and power.

Caesar's colleague, Bibulus, found it useless trying to obstruct Caesar's laws, and he, with Cato, was often in danger of being killed in the forum, so he shut himself up at home for the rest of his term as consul.[33] As for Pompey, soon after his marriage he filled the forum with armed men as an inducement to the people to ratify the law which granted Caesar as his province for five years all Gaul, both on this side and beyond the Alps, along with Illyricum [34] and four legions. When Cato attempted to speak against these provisions, Caesar ordered him taken to prison, thinking he would appeal to the tribunes. When, however, Cato walked off without a word, Caesar saw that not only the nobles were indignant but that the people, who revered Cato for his virtue, were following him in silence with downcast eyes. He therefore asked one of the tribunes secretly to order Cato's release.

Of the other senators very few joined Caesar in the senate; the rest in their resentment kept out of his way. Considius, one of the oldest senators, told Caesar that they did not come because they were afraid of his armed soldiers. "Why, then," said Caesar, "are you not staying at home for the same reason?" "Because," said Considius, "my age makes me fearless, for the little life that is left me is not worth much anxiety." But the most shocking political event of the time seems to have been the election dur-

---

[32] Pompey married Caesar's daughter by Cornelia. The man she was to have married, Servilius Caepio, was uncle of the Marcus Brutus who was later one of Caesar's assassins.

[33] Roman humorists of the time called this the consulship of Gaius Caesar and Julius Caesar, gibing at the complete inactivity of Bibulus.

[34] The province known as Cisalpine Gaul took in most of northern Italy surrounded by the Alps. Transalpine Gaul, the scene of Caesar's spectacular conquests, consisted of more than the territory of modern France, for it reached from the Pyrenees to the Rhine and was bounded on the east by the Alps and the Jura Mountains. Illyricum was the province down the eastern side of the Adriatic.

ing Caesar's consulship of the notorious Clodius as tribune, the man who had outraged the laws of marriage and of the secret rites. But he was elected to bring about Cicero's fall, and Caesar did not set out on his campaign until with the aid of Clodius he had organized a party against Cicero and got him banished from Italy.[35]

15. Such then is the story of Caesar before his Gallic campaigns. But during the wars which he fought thenceforward and the campaigns in which he conquered Gaul,[36] he seems to have made a new beginning and started on a different course of life and fresh accomplishment. As a soldier and a general he showed himself inferior to not one of those who have won most admiration for their leadership and greatness as men. Whether one compare him with the Fabii, the Scipios, and the Metelli, or with men of his own time or a little earlier, such as Sulla, Marius, the Luculli, or even with Pompey himself, whose fame at this time for every kind of excellence in war was springing up and soaring to the skies, Caesar's achievements surpass all theirs. One he outdid in the difficulty of the country where he fought; another in the size of the territory he won; another in the number and strength of the enemies he defeated; another in the strange and treacherous character of the tribes he made friends with; another in the fairness and leniency he showed towards his prisoners; another in the gifts and care he gave to the soldiers who served with him; and all of them in the number of battles fought and of enemies slain. For it was less than ten years that he carried on the war in Gaul, but in them he took by storm over eight hundred cities, subdued three hundred tribes, and at one time or another met in battle three million men, of whom he killed a million in close fighting and took the same number prisoners.

16. His soldiers were so loyal and devoted to him that those who under other generals, on other campaigns, had never distinguished themselves became invincible and irresistible, regardless of any danger to win Caesar glory. One man of that kind was Acilius, who in the naval battle of Marseilles boarded an enemy ship and had his right hand cut off by a sword; with his other kept hold of his shield, striking with it at the

---

[35] See above, *Cicero*, chs. 30, 31.
[36] Caesar's campaigns in Gaul lasted from 58 to 49 B.C.

faces of the enemy, and so drove them all off and took possession of the vessel. Another was Cassius Scaeva, who in the battle of Dyrrachium had an eye put out by an arrow, a shoulder pierced by one javelin and a thigh by another, and on his shield received the blows of a hundred and thirty missiles. He then called to the enemy as if he meant to surrender, but when two of them came near him, he chopped one man's shoulder with his sword, wounded the other in the face and sent him flying, and then, with the aid of his comrades, escaped himself. And once in Britain, when the enemy in front were attacking the centurions, who had stumbled into a swamp full of water, a soldier, as Caesar was watching the struggle, dashed into the midst of it, and after many striking acts of bravery rescued the centurions and put the barbarians to flight. He then threw himself into the muddy stream behind the rest, made his way with difficulty across the swamp, lost his shield, and only by one moment swimming and another wading, got safely over. Amazed at him, Caesar and his companions met him with joyful shouts, but he, utterly downcast and tearful, fell at Caesar's feet, begging his forgiveness for having lost his shield. And again, in Libya, when Scipio [37] had captured one of Caesar's ships in which Granius Petro, a newly appointed quaestor, was sailing, and was treating all the others as his booty but told the quaestor he gave him his life, Granius replied that it was the custom with Caesar's soldiers to give, not to accept safety, and stabbed himself with his sword and died.

17. This spirit and ambition Caesar himself created and fostered in his army, first, by showing through his lavish gifts of rewards and honors that he was not using his wars to collect wealth for his private enjoyment and a life of pleasure, but was holding his plunder as a common prize for valor, and was taking for himself a share no greater than what he gave the soldiers who deserved it. Secondly he never shrank himself from confronting any danger or enduring any toil. The men were not much surprised at his taste for danger, knowing his ambition, but were amazed at his endurance of labor beyond what seemed his body's power to bear, for he was constitutionally thin, had a white, soft skin, suffered from

---

[37] The Scipio mentioned here and again below was Publius Metellus Scipio, a degenerate descendant of a great family, Pompey's colleague as consul in 52 B.C. and an inveterate enemy of Caesar. After Pompey's death he was with Cato in Africa.

headache and was subject to epileptic fits, a disease which, they say, attacked him first in Cordoba.

Yet he did not make his poor health an excuse for self-indulgence, but
used his soldier's life as a means of improving his health. By wearisome
journeyings, frugal diet, constant living in the open air and endurance of
fatigues, he fought with his maladies and hardened his body against
attacks. Most of his sleep he actually took in carriages or litters, turning
even his rest into a progress towards action. By day he would be driving
about to garrisons and cities and camps, one slave, who was used to writing at dictation while traveling, sitting beside him, and one soldier with
a sword, standing behind him. He drove so fast that on his first journey
up from Rome he arrived at the Rhone in seven days. From his boyhood
the handling of horses came easily to him and he used to hold his hands
behind his back, clasp them there and then put his horse to full speed.
On his Gallic campaign he practiced dictating letters on horseback to two
scribes at once, and Oppius says to more. They say too that he was the
first to contrive a way of communicating with his friends by letter, since
he could not wait for face-to-face meetings on pressing problems, because
of the number of his enterprises and the breadth of the city.

Of his indifference to food they give this illustration. The host who
was entertaining him at Milan, Valerius Leo, once set before him asparagus
with a dressing of myrrh instead of olive oil. Caesar ate it without fussing
and scolded his friends for complaining about it. "It should be enough
for you," he said, "simply not to eat what you do not like. A man who
objects to these country manners has country manners himself." Once too
on the road he was driven by a storm into a poor man's hut which had
only a single room, and that barely large enough for one person. He said
to his friends that honors must be granted to the bravest but necessities
to the feeblest, and bade Oppius lie down inside, while he and the rest
slept in the porch at the door.

18.   Now the first of his Gallic wars [38] was against the Helvetii and
Tigurini, who had burned their twelve cities and four hundred villages,
and were moving forward through that part of Gaul which was under

---

[38] Plutarch's prime source for Caesar's campaigns in Gaul was, as ours is today,
Caesar's own account of them in his famous *Commentaries on the Gallic War*.

the Romans, as the Cimbri and Teutones had done long before.[39] They seemed as courageous as their predecessors had been and their equal in numbers, three hundred thousand in all, of whom a hundred and ninety thousand were warriors. The Tigurini were smashed at the river Saône, though not by Caesar in person but by Labienus, whom he sent against them. The Helvetii, however, attacked Caesar unexpectedly on the road as he was leading his army to a friendly city, but he succeeded in escaping to a strong position, where he mustered his troops and lined them up for battle. When a horse was brought to him, he said, "I shall want this after my victory for the pursuit. But now, let us move against our enemy!" With that he led the charge on foot. After a long and stubborn contest, he drove back the enemy's fighting force, but had the hardest struggle around their rampart of wagons, for not only did the men make a stand there and keep on fighting, but their wives and children defended themselves to the death until they too were cut to pieces. The battle lasted almost to midnight. This splendid victory Caesar crowned with another still more splendid, resettling the surviving barbarians who had escaped from the battle, over a hundred thousand of them, and compelling them to re-occupy the land they had deserted and the cities they had destroyed. He did this because he was afraid that if the land were left empty the Germans would cross the Rhine and take it.

19. His second war was directly against the Germans to protect the Gauls, though earlier, in Rome, he had recognized the German king Ariovistus as an ally. The Germans were too disagreeable as neighbors to his subjects, and it looked as if, given an opportunity, they would not remain contented with what they had, but would spread over into Gaul and seize possession of it. Caesar saw that his own officers seemed to dread them, especially those young men of rank who had come out with him, expecting to make their campaign under him a chance for gay living and getting rich. So he called them to a meeting and advised them, since they were so unmanly and soft, to leave him and not run into danger against their will. As for himself, he said, he would take only the tenth legion and set out against the barbarians. He would be fighting an enemy

---

39 Marius' greatest exploit had been his defeat, in 102 and 101 B.C. of the formidable Cimbri and Teutones, who had crossed the Alps and invaded northern Italy and seemed for a time to threaten Rome.

no braver than the Cimbri, and he himself was no worse a general than
Marius. Thereupon, the tenth legion sent deputies to express their gratitude, and the other legions abused their officers. The whole army, now
eager and full of spirit, followed Caesar on a march of many days until
finally they encamped within two hundred furlongs of their enemy.

Ariovistus' resolution was somewhat shaken by the mere approach of
Caesar, for he had not expected the Romans to attack the Germans, whose
advance he did not think they could resist, and he was astonished at
Caesar's daring. He saw too that his army was disturbed. And still more
depressing to German spirit were the predictions of their holy women, who
foretold the future by watching eddies in rivers and read omens in the
whirling and splashing of the currents. They declared that the Germans
must not fight before the new moon shone. When Caesar heard of this
and saw that the Germans were doing nothing, he thought it a good idea
to have the battle while they were not in the mood to fight, instead of
sitting and waiting for their right time to come. Accordingly, he began
to attack their fortifications and the hills on which they were encamped,
thereby exasperating them and provoking them to come down in their
wrath and fight it out. The Germans were completely routed and Caesar
pursued them for four hundred furlongs back to the Rhine, and covered
the whole plain with their corpses and spoils. Ariovistus with a few of
his men escaped across the river. The number of his dead, they say, was
eighty thousand.

20. After finishing with this business, Caesar left his forces among the
Sequani for the winter,[40] since he himself was anxious to put his mind
on what was going on at Rome. He then came down into Gaul along the
Po, which was a part of the province granted him, for the river Rubicon
is the line which divides Italy from Cisalpine Gaul. Establishing his
quarters by the Po, he resumed his activities as a popular politician. Many
persons came to visit him, and he granted each what he asked. Each,
when dismissed, had received something from him and was expectant of
more. Throughout the whole time of his campaigning in Gaul, he went
on in this way unobserved by Pompey, at one moment conquering the
enemy with the arms the citizens gave him, at another captivating and
subduing the citizens with the money he took from the enemy.

40 The winter of 58–57 B.C.

However, when he heard that the Belgae, the most powerful of the Gallic peoples, who occupied a third of all Gaul, had revolted and had collected some myriads of armed men, he immediately turned around and marched back with great speed.[41] He fell on the enemy as they were ravaging the country of those Gauls who were allies of the Romans, and, after a very poor resistance, so routed and destroyed the largest and most concentrated bodies of them that the Romans crossed lakes and deep rivers over the piles of dead bodies. All the rebels who lived by the ocean surrendered without a battle, but with the fiercest and most warlike tribe of that region, the Nervii, Caesar had a struggle. The Nervii lived in thick forests and had hidden their families and property in the depths of the woods, as far as possible from their enemy. Then, suddenly, while Caesar was fortifying his camp and not expecting a battle, they attacked him with a host of sixty thousand men. The Roman cavalry they put to flight and surrounded the twelfth and the seventh legions, killing all the centurions. If Caesar had not seized a shield, pushed through the fighters in front of him and thrown himself on the barbarians, and if the tenth legion, at sight of his danger, had not rushed down from high ground and broken up the enemy's ranks, not a Roman, it seems, would have escaped. But with Caesar's example of daring, they fought, as the saying is, beyond their strength. Even so, they were unable to put the Nervii to flight, but cut them down as they stood defending themselves. Out of sixty thousand only five hundred are said to have survived, and only three of their senators out of four hundred.

21. On receiving news of these victories, the Roman senate voted fifteen days of sacrifices to the gods, a rest from business, and festivity for more days than had ever been voted before. For the danger had seemed very great, with so many tribes revolting at once. And as Caesar was the victor, the people's liking for him made the occasion all the more splendid. Caesar himself, having settled the situation in Gaul, again spent his winter in the country by the Po, carrying on his schemes at Rome. Not only did candidates for office obtain his patronage and get themselves elected by bribing the people with money from him, and then do everything likely to increase his power, but most Romans of high rank and wide

---

[41] The campaign against the Belgae and the Nervii was in the summer of 57 B.C.

influence visited him at Lucca,[42] Pompey, Crassus, Appius, governor of
Sardinia, and Nepos, proconsul of Spain. A hundred and twenty lictors
were there and over two hundred senators.

Their consultations ended in the following agreement. Pompey and
Crassus should be elected the next consuls, and Caesar should have money
and an extension of five more years in his command. To intelligent people it all seemed a very strange affair. For the very men who were getting
so much money from Caesar were now urging the senate to give him
more, as if he were penniless. Or rather, they were compelling the senate
to give it, in spite of its groans over what it was voting. Cato was not
present, for he had been purposely sent away on a mission to Cyprus.[43]
Favonius, a zealous follower of Cato, found he accomplished nothing
by arguing against those measures. So he left the senate abruptly and
called on the people. Nobody would listen to him, for some of them
stood in awe of Pompey and Crassus, while the majority were set to please
Caesar and living in hope of something from him, and therefore would
not stir.

22.   On his return to his troops in Gaul, Caesar found a big war going
on in the country.[44] Two large German tribes had recently crossed the
Rhine to get land. One was called the Usipes, the other the Tenteritae.
In describing the battle he fought with these barbarians, Caesar writes
in his *Commentaries* that while their envoys were treating with him
under a truce, they attacked, with eight hundred men, his five thousand
cavalrymen on the road, and routed them because they were not expecting
anything. They then, he says, sent other envoys to him to try to deceive
him again. But he held these men, and then led his army to attack the
barbarians, convinced that to trust such faithless violators of truces was
folly. Tanusius says that when the senate was voting festivities and sacrifices for his victory, Cato said that he thought they should give Caesar
up to the barbarians and so purify the city from the guilt of his breach
of truce and turn the curse on the man who was to blame.

---

[42] This was in the spring of 56 B.C.

[43] See below, *Cato the Younger*, ch. 34.

[44] Plutarch omits here any mention of Caesar's campaigning in the summer of 56 or
his activity in the following winter. What he now describes is the fighting in the
summer of 55 B.C.

Of the Germans who had crossed the river into Gaul four hundred thousand were slaughtered. The few who recrossed were taken in by the Sugambri, another German tribe, and Caesar seized on this action as a ground for hostilities against the Sugambri. Furthermore, he was eager for the glory of being the first man to cross the Rhine with an army. So he began to build a bridge over the river, wide as it was, and at this spot in its course particularly deep, rough, and turbulent, sweeping along trunks and boughs of trees to break down and tear away the supports for the bridge.[45] Caesar had a rampart of heavy timbers planted across the bed of the river to catch these logs, and thus bridled and yoked the onrushing current. And within ten days he had his bridge finished, a sight past all belief.

23. When now he took his troops across the river, no one dared to oppose him, and even the Suevi, the leading tribe of the Germans, retired with their possessions into deep, wooded valleys. Accordingly, after ravaging and burning their country and putting heart into the faithful friends of the Romans, Caesar withdrew back into Gaul, having spent eighteen days inside Germany.

His expedition against Britain too was famed for its audacity, for he was the first to embark with a fleet on the western ocean and to sail through the Atlantic Sea with an army for war. The island too is larger than commonly believed and has been a subject of much dispute among countless historians as to whether or not its name and story were fabrications of something that never existed. In his effort to take it, Caesar extended the supremacy of Rome beyond the borders of the known world. He crossed twice over to the island [46] from the opposite coast of Gaul, and worsted the enemy in many battles but won little reward for his men, for there was nothing worth taking from a people so miserably poor. He then brought the war to an end, though not as he would have

---

[45] The point where Caesar crossed the Rhine is presumed to be near the modern Coblenz, not many miles from where the American army crossed the river in World War II.

[46] On Caesar's first expedition to Britain, in the autumn of 55 B.C., he did little more than land on the coast of Kent. On his second trip, in 54, he took with him five legions and two thousand horse and penetrated apparently beyond the Thames, but retreated before a determined British resistance in a country of trackless swamps and forests. The king here mentioned was known to the Romans as Cassivelaunus.

wished; he took hostages from the king, imposed tributes, and then sailed off. Back in Gaul he found letters from his friends in Rome, about to be carried over to him, informing him of the death of his daughter. She died in child-birth, in Pompey's house. Pompey's grief was great, and so was Caesar's. Their friends too were much distressed, perceiving that the connection which alone preserved the ailing state in peace and harmony had now been broken. For the child also died, outliving its mother by only a few days. In spite of the tribunes' opposition the people carried Julia to the Campus Martius, and there her obsequies were held and there she lies.

24.   Caesar's army was now so large that he was obliged to disperse it through many different winter quarters, while he himself, as he habitually did, departed for Italy. But then all Gaul broke out again in rebellion, and powerful armies scoured the country attacking Roman fortifications and destroying their winter camps. The largest and strongest band of rebels, under Abriorix, wiped out Cotta and Titurius with their army, and the legion under Cicero [47] was surrounded and besieged by sixty thousand men and came near being captured by storm, since the Romans were all wounded and exhausted by their gallant defense.

When the news was reported to Caesar, he was a long way off, but he promptly turned back and collecting seven thousand men in all, hastened to release Cicero from his state of siege. The besiegers learned of his approach and went to meet him, expecting to crush him entirely and scornful of the smallness of his force; but Caesar deceived them by constantly evading them until he found a place advantageous for one who was fighting a host with a handful. There he fortified a camp, but still kept his men from fighting and had them build the ramparts higher and strengthen the gates as if they were terror-struck. These tactics served to make the enemy scornful of him, and they rashly attacked him in scattered groups; then he sallied out, put them to flight, and killed many of them.

25.   By this victory he put a stop to the many uprisings of the Gauls in those parts, as also by his traveling about everywhere during that winter

---

[47] The Cicero here mentioned was Quintus Cicero, brother of Marcus Tullius Cicero, the orator.

and keeping a sharp watch on everyone who acted as if restless. There came from Italy three legions to take the place of the men he had lost. Pompey lent him two of those under his command, and one was raised freshly in Gaul along the Po. But farther away the seeds of the greatest and most perilous of all the wars ever waged in Gaul were sprouting.[48] They had long been sown and cultivated secretly by the most powerful men in the most warlike tribes. Now the movement gathered strength from the crowds of young men who came in from every direction with their arms, from the great wealth that they had collected, from the strength of the cities and from the difficulties the country presented to invaders. It being the season of winter, too, the rivers were frozen, the forests covered with snow, the plains turned into lakes by winter streams which were swerving out of their courses. All these things made it seem quite impossible for Caesar to interfere with the insurgents' plans. Many were the tribes in revolt, but at the front were the Arvenni and the Carnuntini. They had chosen Vercingetorix to have full command of the war, whose father the Gauls had put to death because they thought he was playing the tyrant.

26. Vercingetorix now divided his force into many parts, appointing officers for them, and began taking over the whole country around as far as the valley of the Saône. It was his plan, now while there were men in Rome combining against Caesar, to stir up all Gaul to fight. If he had done this a little later, when Caesar was engaged in the civil war, Italy would have been as seriously alarmed as she was by the Cimbri. But now Caesar, the man with a natural talent for making the best use of every weapon in war, especially of an opportunity, on hearing of the revolt, immediately started out over the same roads by which he had come, and by the speed of his march through the bitter winter weather showed the barbarians that an undefeated and invincible army was on its way against them. For in regions which it was incredible that one of his couriers or letter carriers could have reached for a long while, he would appear with all his army, spoiling the country, wrecking their strongholds, subduing their cities, and receiving into his protection those who came over to him.

But this situation lasted only until the tribe of the Aedui joined the war against him. They had hitherto called themselves brothers of the Romans,

[48] Plutarch leaves out here the events of the year 53 B.C., and goes on to 52.

and had been signally honored by them, and now their defection to the rebels caused great depression among Caesar's troops. Accordingly he moved from there and was crossing the territory of the Lingones, intending to join the Sequani, who were friends and formed a bulwark between Italy and the rest of Gaul. But there the enemy fell upon him and hemmed him in with their many myriads. He was resolved to fight the battle through, and on the whole won the day, defeating the barbarians after a long time of heavy slaughter. At first, however, he appears to have found the going hard, and the Arverni show a short sword hanging in a temple, which they say was taken from Caesar. He himself saw it later and smiled, and when his friends urged him to have it taken down, he refused, for he regarded it as sacred.

27. Most of the barbarians who escaped that day fled with their king to the city of Alesia.[49] Caesar laid siege to it, though it was thought to be impregnable because of the height of its walls and the number of its defenders. And then from outside there descended on him a danger too great to describe. The best warriors from all the tribes of Gaul gathered and came to relieve Alesia, three hundred thousand of them. And inside the city there were not less than a hundred and seventy thousand. Thus Caesar was caught and shut in between two huge armies, and forced to build two walls to protect himself, one towards the city and the other facing those who had come to its aid, since, if these two armies were to unite, his cause would be totally lost.

For many reasons naturally the peril that confronted Caesar before Alesia spread his fame abroad, for it gave rise to deeds of daring and skill such as no other of his struggles produced. Especially one should admire the way in which he fought and disposed of so many tens of thousands outside the city without those inside becoming aware of it, and, more, without even the Romans who were guarding the wall facing the city learning of it. For they knew nothing of his victory until they heard the mourning of the men in Alesia and the wailing of the women who had seen on the farther side Romans carrying into their camp masses of

---

[49] The Gallic hill-town of Alesia is represented now by the small village of Alise-Ste Reine, not far from the headwaters of the Seine. Some excavation has been done on the site and the ruins of Caesar's siege walls have been discovered.

shields decorated with silver and gold, and breastplates stained with blood, as well as goblets and tents of Gallic make. As quickly as a phantom of a dream, that mighty force dissolved and disappeared, the greater part of it slain in battle. The troops in Alesia, too, after making considerable trouble for themselves and for Caesar, at length surrendered. And the leader of the whole war, Vercingetorix, put on his handsomest armor, trimmed up his horse, rode out through the gate, and circled around Caesar where he sat. Then springing down from his horse, he threw off his suit of armor, and sat down at Caesar's feet, remaining there quietly until he was turned over to be kept guarded for Caesar's triumph.[50]

28. Long before this Caesar had resolved to make an end of Pompey, just as Pompey of course had resolved to do with him. For now that Crassus, who had been watching them both, had been killed by the Parthians,[51] it remained for the one who aspired to be greatest to overthrow the one who already was, or for the one who was now the greatest to save himself from downfall by getting rid in time of the one he feared. This fear had but recently occurred to Pompey, for until then he had looked down on Caesar, thinking he would find no difficulty in disposing of a man whom he himself had raised up. But Caesar from the beginning had made his plan and, like an athlete, having first retired a long distance off and there got practice in the Gallic wars, had trained his troops and built up his own reputation, and so lifted himself by his exploits to a point where he could match the successes of Pompey.

He made use of devices offered him, some by Pompey himself and some by the times and by the bad state of government at Rome. Under it candidates for office set up tables in public places, where they bribed the populace shamelessly, who, thus hired, went down to the forum and fought for their paymaster, not with votes but with bows and arrows, slings, and swords. Often they polluted the rostrum with blood and corpses before they departed, leaving their city to anarchy, like a ship

---

[50] Vercingetorix was kept in chains until, six years later, he was brought out to grace Caesar's great triumph, after which he was put to death.

[51] Crassus was invading Mesopotamia with his army in 53 B.C., when he was cut off in the desert by Parthian bowmen and killed.

tossing on the sea without a pilot. All who had any wisdom would have been thankful to have nothing worse descend on them than a monarchy as a result of such terrible folly and so wild a storm. There were many who actually ventured to say publicly that the state could be cured only by a monarchy, and that they ought to accept that remedy, when it was offered them by the mildest of physicians—a hint at Pompey.

And Pompey, though putting on a show in words of declining the crown, by his behavior did more than anyone to get himself appointed dictator. So Cato, perceiving his intention, persuaded the senate to name him sole consul, to placate him with a more lawful kind of monarchy that he might not resort to violence to get a dictatorship. They also voted him more time as governor of his provinces. He had two, Spain and the whole of Libya, which he administered through legates, keeping armies there too. For their maintenance he received a thousand talents from the public treasury every year.

29.   So Caesar began sending to Rome and canvassing for a consulship and likewise for a continuance of his government of his provinces. At first Pompey kept silent but Marcellus and Lentulus [52] set up an opposition. They hated Caesar for many reasons and now did everything, fitting and unfitting, to embarrass and shame him. They took away Roman citizenship from the people of New Como,[53] a colony newly planted by Caesar in Gaul. And Marcellus, when he was consul, had beaten with rods a senator from there who had come to Rome, telling him that he was putting these stripes on him as a sign that he was not a Roman, and ordering him to go back and show them to Caesar.

Since Marcellus' consulship, Caesar had been sending down funds from Gaul in a stream for everyone in public life to draw upon, and had freed the tribune Curio from numerous debts and had presented the consul Paulus with fifteen hundred talents, out of which Paulus had beautified the forum by building his basilica, a famous monument which filled the

---

[52] Gaius Claudius Marcellus, a warm friend of Cicero and Pompey and opponent of Caesar, was consul for 50 B.C. See above, *Cicero,* ch. 44. Lucius Cornelius Lentulus, a more hotheaded friend of Pompey, was consul in 49 and did a good deal to precipitate the civil war which then broke out. See below, chs. 30 and 31.

[53] There was an old Celtic settlement at Como, on the lake of that name. In 59 B.C. Caesar had planted a colony from Rome near by, which he called New Como.

place of the Fulvia.[54] Pompey now took alarm at this combination and both he and his friends worked openly to have a successor appointed to Caesar in his command. He sent too and demanded from Caesar the soldiers he had lent him for his wars in Gaul. Caesar sent them back, after first giving each man a present of two hundred and fifty drachmas.

But the officers who brought them back to Pompey spread tales among people about Caesar which were neither fair nor honest, and they misled Pompey himself with ill-founded hopes. For they told him that Caesar's army was longing for him and that, though Pompey's position at Rome was precarious because of the lurking jealousy there against him, the troops in Gaul were ready to join him and once they crossed into Italy would promptly declare for him, so weary were they of Caesar's endless campaigns, and so suspicious and fearful that he was aiming at a monarchy. Pompey was fooled by these stories and therefore neglected to organize an army, as if he had nothing to fear. By speeches and resolutions he seemed indeed to be getting the better of Caesar, having measures voted against him, for which Caesar cared not a whit. They say, in fact, that one of Caesar's captains sent by him to Rome, as he stood before the senate house and heard that the senate would not prolong Caesar's term of office, clapped his hand on the hilt of his sword and said, "But this will!"

30. Certainly the demands Caesar made had a striking appearance of fairness. For he proposed that he should lay down his arms and that Pompey should do the same, both thus becoming private citizens, and that then they should see what honor their fellow citizens would give them. But if, he said, they took from him his authority while they confirmed Pompey in his, they would be branding one as a tyrant and making a tyrant out of the other. When Curio in Caesar's name laid these proposals before the people, he was tremendously applauded, and some even showered wreaths of flowers on him as though he were a victorious athlete. Antony, who was then a tribune,[55] produced in the people's pres-

---

54 The basilicas of Roman cities were stately halls, with high central roofs and lower side aisles, built usually near a forum and used as headquarters for business and social intercourse of all kinds. They were later taken as models for early Christian churches. The remains of the basilica of Paulus Aemilius, called the Basilica Aemilia, may still be seen to one side of the Roman forum. It replaced a basilica built in 179 B.C.

55 For Mark Antony and his part in the following narrative, see below, *Antony*, ch. 5.

ence a letter from Caesar on the subject and read it aloud, in spite of the consuls.

But in the senate, Scipio, Pompey's father-in-law,[56] moved that if Caesar did not lay down his arms by a set day, he should be declared a public enemy. And when the consuls put the question, whether they would order Pompey to dismiss his troops, and again, whether they would order Caesar to do the same, very few voted for the first measure, and all but a few for the second. But when Antony again proposed that both should resign their commands, all were unanimously in favor of it. Scipio, however, was violently opposed, and the consul Lentulus shouted that what they needed against a robber was arms not votes. At this the senate broke up and its members put on clothes of mourning for their disagreement.

31. But then letters came from Caesar which seemed still more moderate in tone, for this time he offered to give up everything else, asking only that Cisalpine Gaul and Illyricum, with two legions, should be granted him to hold until he became candidate for a second consulship. Cicero, the orator, who had just returned from Cilicia and was laboring for a reconciliation, tried to induce Pompey to relent. But Pompey, though yielding on every other point, was determined to deprive Caesar of his soldiers. Cicero then urged the friends of Caesar to give in and agree to a settlement on terms of the said provinces and only six thousand soldiers.[57] Pompey was inclined to soften and allow him that many, but the consul Lentulus would not allow it. He insulted Antony and Curio and drove them with abuse out of the senate, thus providing Caesar with the most plausible of all the pretexts by which he inflamed the passions of his troops. He pointed to the men of high standing and office who had fled from Rome in hired wagons, dressed as slaves. For in their terror they had been putting on slaves' clothes and stealing out of Rome.

32. Now there were with Caesar not more than three hundred horse and five thousand foot, for the rest of his army he had left beyond the Alps, to be brought on by men he sent for that purpose. But he saw that

---

[56] After the death of Julia, Caesar's daughter, Pompey had married Cornelia, daughter of his friend Publius Scipio.

[57] The Roman legion at this time consisted of six thousand men. Cicero's compromise proposal, therefore, meant allowing Caesar one legion instead of two.

the start and first step of the enterprise before him did not at the moment require a great army, but rather astounding daring and quickness in seizing the opportunity, and that it would be easier to stun his enemies by an unexpected movement than to defeat them by an attack in full force. Accordingly he ordered his chief officers and centurions to take their swords, but no other weapons, and occupy Ariminum, a large Gallic city,[58] avoiding bloodshed and disturbance as far as possible. He put Hortensius in command of the force.

He himself spent that day in public, visiting and watching some gladiators who were exercising. A little before evening he made his toilet, went to the dining hall, and talked briefly with those whom he had invited to dinner. As it grew dark, he rose and courteously bade his guests wait for him, for he would be back. Previously, however, he had told a few of his friends to follow him, not all by the same route, but one by one road, another by another. He himself got into one of the hired wagons, and first drove down another road and then turned off toward Ariminum. But when he came to the river called the Rubicon, which divides Cisalpine Gaul from the rest of Italy, and drew nearer to the fateful act, he grew reflective and was shaken by the magnitude of what he was daring. He stopped the wagon and halted while for a long time he debated with himself in silence, his mind swaying this way and that and his resolution taking many forms. For some time too he shared his uncertainties with his friends who were with him—among them Pollio Asinius—calculating the great evils which his crossing of the river would bring on mankind and how great would be the fame of it transmitted to posterity.

At last, in a sort of passion, as if casting aside calculation and throwing himself on the future, he uttered the words with which men commonly announce a plunge into dark and reckless fortunes, "Let the die be cast!" [59] and dashed across. Going on then with a rush the rest of the

58 Ariminum, now called Rimini, a Gallic town and important harbor on the Adriatic coast, lay within the area of Italy proper and outside the province of Cisalpine Gaul, therefore outside Caesar's lawful territory for any display of arms. Its inhabitants had obtained Roman citizenship about 89 B.C.

59 The Rubicon marked the exact frontier between Italy and Cisalpine Gaul. A law forbade any general on a return from his province to cross the frontier into Italy without first laying down his arms. The date of Caesar's crossing of the Rubicon was January 10, 49 B.C.

way, before dawn he entered and took Ariminum. There is a story that the night before he crossed the Rubicon he had an impious dream. He thought he was having unspeakable relations with his own mother.

33. On his seizure of Ariminum it was as if war had been let loose through wide-open gates over all the earth and sea together, and the laws of the state were annihilated along with the boundaries of the provinces. One would have thought that not merely men and women were streaming in panic through Italy, as at other times, but that the very cities themselves had risen and fled from their sites and were passing through one another. Rome was swamped by the flood of people fleeing from the neighboring towns. Unwilling to obey an official or to heed words of reason, she herself came near being wrecked by her disunity in the surging of that great tempest. For conflicting emotions and violent passions were seething everywhere. Those who were pleased would not keep silent, and at many spots in Rome collided with those who were terrified and dismayed, and, being sanguine themselves as to the future, were quick to pick a quarrel.

Pompey himself was thunderstruck and beset by people from every side. Some took him to task for having strengthened Caesar against both himself and the supremacy of the state. Others blamed him for allowing Lentulus to insult Caesar, when he was giving way and proposing fair terms of agreement. Favonius bade him stamp with his foot on the ground, because once in an arrogant speech in the senate he had told them not to trouble or be concerned about preparations for war. When it came he would stamp on the earth with his foot and Italy would be filled with armies. Yet even now Pompey had the advantage over Caesar in the size of his forces, but nobody would let the man use his own judgment. At length, overwhelmed by the many false and alarming reports that the war was already closing in on him and carrying all before it, he succumbed and was swept away by the general current. He proclaimed a state of anarchy and left the city, with orders for the senate to follow and for no one to stay behind who preferred his country and his liberty to tyranny.

34. The consuls now fled, without making even the usual sacrifices before going. So did most of the senators, taking whatever of their own goods they could get hold of, almost like robbers, as though the stuff

were the property of someone else. Even some, who had previously been all for Caesar, now lost their bearings for fright and were carried away, though not needing to be, on the stream of the huge tide. Saddest of all was the spectacle of the city as the great storm grew nearer, left adrift like a ship deserted by her pilots, to crash against whatever she met. But though their departure was so calamitous a thing, these people still believed that for Pompey's sake exile was their duty to their country, and quit Rome as though it were Caesar's camp. Even Labienus, one of Caesar's closest friends, who had been his legate and had fought with him most valiantly all through his Gallic wars, now deserted him and went to Pompey. However, Caesar sent all Labienus' money and baggage after him.

He then marched on Domitius,[60] who commanded thirty cohorts and was holding Corfinium, and pitched his camp near the city. Domitius, in despair over his position, asked his physician, who was a slave, for poison, and took the dose given him and drank it, to kill himself. But soon afterward he heard that Caesar was treating his prisoners with extraordinary clemency and then he mourned for himself and regretted his hasty decision. His physician, however, consoled him by telling him that what he had drunk was a sleeping potion, not a poison. So, much rejoiced, he rose from his bed, went to Caesar and clasped his hand, though he soon left him for Pompey. The news of these events brought to Rome made men more hopeful and some of those who had fled now returned.

35. Caesar took Domitius' troops into his service, as well as all the others that were being raised for Pompey in the cities which he captured by surprise. Then, since he had now a large and formidable army, he marched against Pompey himself. However, Pompey did not await his attack but fled to Brundisium, sending the consuls on ahead of him with a force to Dyrrachium. A little later, as Caesar approached, he put to sea himself, as I will describe in detail in my life of him. Caesar would have pursued him immediately but lacked ships, so he turned back to Rome. In sixty days he had made himself master of all Italy without bloodshed.

---

60 This was Lucius Domitius Ahenobarbus, Cato's son-in-law, an aristocrat, who until now had opposed both Pompey and Caesar. He was later killed fighting for Pompey at Pharsalus. See above, *Cicero,* ch. 38. Corfinium, since destroyed, was a city of central Italy, hardly more than seventy-five miles east of Rome.

He found the city calmer than he had expected, and many senators
there. To them he talked in a reasonable and courteous way, proposing
even that they send someone to Pompey with fair terms for a peace.[61]
But no one listened to him, whether it was that they were afraid of
Pompey, whom they had deserted, or that they did not think Caesar
meant what he said and was only putting up a pretense of honeyed words.
But when the tribune Metellus tried to prevent him from taking money
out of the public reserve funds,[62] and quoted several laws forbidding it,
Caesar replied that arms and laws had each their own time. "And if
what I do displeases you, get out of my way for the present. War does
not want free speech. When we have reached some agreement and I have
laid down my arms, then you shall come forward and stand for the people. And in saying this," he went on, "I am waiving my own just rights;
for you are in my hands, you and all of the party against me, who are my
prisoners."

With these words to Metellus, he walked to the door of the store room,
and when the keys could not be found, sent for smiths and ordered them
to break down the door. Metellus again opposed him and some encouraged
him to do so, but Caesar, drawing himself up, threatened to kill him if he
did not stop his annoying interference. "And this, you know, young man,"
he added, "I find more distasteful to say than to do." At that remark
Metellus was frightened and left, and thereafter Caesar was readily and
promptly supplied with everything he needed for the war.

36. He first led an expedition into Spain, having decided to drive out
Afranius and Varro,[63] Pompey's legates there, and after making himself
master of their forces and of the provinces, then to march against Pompey,
leaving no enemy in his rear. He was often personally in danger from
ambuscades, and his army seriously so from hunger, but he never gave
up pursuing, challenging, and encircling the enemy, until by sheer

---

[61] Caesar himself gives a summary of his speech to the senate in his *Civil War*, I, 32.

[62] This public reserve fund, kept in the temple of Saturn, was never to be touched
except in a dire emergency. The senate had supplied Pompey with money for his wars
out of the ordinary treasury.

[63] This was Marcus Terentius Varro, a man of encyclopedic learning, and a highly
esteemed writer on many subjects. After Pharsalus Caesar forgave him for his loyalty
to Pompey and employed him in collecting a great public library.

strength he had taken over their camps and their armies. The leaders escaped to Pompey.

37. On Caesar's return to Rome, Piso, his father-in-law, advised him to send envoys to Pompey to discuss terms for an agreement, but Isauricus, to gratify Caesar, opposed the idea. He was next chosen dictator by the senate, whereat he called home the exiles, restored to full rights the children of those who had been penalized in Sulla's time, relieved the debtors by a method of lowering interest, and undertook a few other public measures of the same sort. Then in eleven days he resigned his dictatorship, had himself and Servilius Isauricus proclaimed consuls, and set out on his campaign.

He marched so fast that he left the bulk of his army behind him, and with only six hundred picked horsemen and five legions, put to sea in early January, the month which to Athenians would be Poseideon. Crossing the Ionian Gulf he took Oricum and Apollonia, and sent his ships back to Brundisium for the soldiers left behind. These men, on the road, had been complaining of Caesar, for they were now past their bodily prime and wearied by his endless wars. "Where now, and to what end," they said, "will this man take us, rushing us about and treating us as though we were tireless, inhuman things? Even a sword wears out at last, and shield and breastplate are given some rest when they have been used so long. Do not our wounds, at least, make Caesar realize that he is commanding mortal men, and that as mortals born we suffer and feel pain? Not even a god can control the winter season and the time of storms at sea. But this man runs risks not like one chasing his enemies but like one flying from them." Grumbling like this they proceeded slowly on to Brundisium, but on their arrival, when they found that Caesar had crossed the sea, their feelings abruptly changed, and they reproached themselves as traitors to their emperor and reproached their commanders too for not hastening their steps. Sitting on the cliffs they looked out towards the sea and Epirus for the ships that would transport them over to Caesar.

38. Meanwhile, at Apollonia, Caesar had not a force with him equal to fighting the enemy, and the troops from Brundisium were long in arriving. He was therefore in considerable perplexity and embarrassment, and without telling anyone, he conceived a wild plan to go back to Brun-

disium in a twelve-oared boat, even though the sea was swarming with the great fleets of the enemy. So one night, disguising himself in a slave's dress, he went aboard, flung himself down as a person of no importance, and lay quiet. But as the river Aous was carrying the boat down to the sea, the morning breeze, which generally made the water smooth at the river's mouth by driving back the sea waves, was stilled by a strong wind which blew in that night from the sea. So the river, resisting the influx from the sea and the clash of waves, was very rough, beating about in a roar with powerful eddies, and the pilot could make no headway. Accordingly, he ordered his sailors to turn about and go back. But on seeing this, Caesar made himself known and took the hand of the terrified pilot, saying, "Come, my good man, have courage and fear nothing. You are carrying Caesar and Caesar's fortunes in your boat." At this the sailors forgot the storm, and laying to with their oars, did their best to drive on down the river. At the river's mouth they shipped floods of water and were in grave danger, and since it was impossible to go on, Caesar very unwillingly permitted the pilot to turn back. On his reappearance his soldiers met him in crowds, full of chiding, and indignant because he did not believe that with them alone he could win his victory, but was worried and risking his life to bring over those who were absent, as though he distrusted the men who were with him.

39.   Soon afterward Antony sailed in from Brundisium with his troops, and Caesar, now confident, challenged Pompey to battle. He, however, was in a favorable situation and had plentiful supplies coming to him by sea and by land, whereas Caesar, from the first, was poorly off and later was extremely hard pressed for lack of provisions. But his soldiers chopped up a kind of root, mixed it with milk and ate it, and once even made bread of it, and dashing over to the enemy's outposts, threw some loaves inside and tossed some back and forth, declaring that as long as the earth produced such roots, they would keep on besieging Pompey. Pompey would not let either the loaves or those words be reported to his army, for the bulk of his soldiers were dispirited and dreaded the fierce temper and endurance of their enemies as though they were wild beasts.

There were continual skirmishes around Pompey's fortifications and in all Caesar had the advantage, except in one, when his soldiers were badly routed and he was in danger of losing his camp. For that time, as Pompey attacked, no one stood firm; the trenches were filled with dead, and more were falling around their own ramparts and bulwarks, to which they had been driven back in a disorderly flight. Caesar met the fugitives and tried to turn them around, but he had no success, and when he started to seize the standards, their bearers threw them down, so that the enemy took thirty-two of them. Caesar himself barely escaped being killed. A tall, powerful soldier dashed past him in flight and he put his hand on him, ordering him to stop and face the enemy; but the man, driven frantic by the danger, raised his sword to strike. However, Caesar's shield-bearer struck him first and cut off his arm at the shoulder. So surely did Caesar feel he was failing that when Pompey, whether through over-caution or by some accident, did not follow up his great victory, but retired after shutting the fugitives in behind their ramparts, he said to his friends on leaving them, "Today victory would have gone to the enemy, if they had had a victor leading them."

Going by himself then to his tent, he lay down and spent that most unhappy of all nights in bitter reflection, sure that his generalship had been bad. For while a rich country lay before him and all the wealthy cities of Macedonia and Thessaly, he had failed to carry the war there and had stationed himself here by the sea, which his enemies commanded with their ships, so that for lack of necessities he was held fast, besieged instead of using his army to be the besieger. So he tossed about, miserable over the uncertainty and difficulty of his situation, and the next day broke camp, determined to lead his troops up into Macedonia against Scipio. He would then either lure Pompey into following him to a region where he would fight without getting supplies, as he did now from the sea, or else he would overpower Scipio if he were left alone to defend himself.

40. This move encouraged Pompey's army and the officers who were with him to stick close to Caesar, whom they took to be beaten and retreating. Pompey himself was cautious about risking a battle for so vast a stake, and since he was well furnished with everything for the time being, he decided to wear down and weaken the strength of his enemy, which could not last long. For though the best men in Caesar's army had experience and a boldness in battle that was irresistible, with all their long marches and pitching camps and siege fights and night watches, they were

wearing out with age, growing too heavy in body for labor, and out of infirmity losing their alacrity. At that time, too, a kind of plague, they say, spread through Caesar's army, brought on by the strangeness of the food. And, most serious of all, Caesar was so short of money and provisions that everyone thought his army would soon be breaking up of its own accord.

41.   For these reasons Pompey preferred not to fight and Cato praised him, for he was anxious to spare his fellow citizens. When he saw the heaps of the enemy who had fallen in battle, to the number of a thousand men, he covered his face and went away in tears. But he was the only one. The rest all abused Pompey for postponing the battle and tried to spur him on by calling him "Agamemnon" and "King of Kings," as if they knew he did not want to divest himself of the sole command and enjoyed having so many officers under him flocking to his tent. Favonius, assuming Cato's freedom of speech, grumbled like a fool because that year too they would not get a taste of the figs of Tusculum on account of Pompey's love of authority. And Afranius, who had lately arrived from Spain, where he had done so poorly as a general, on being accused of betraying his army for a bribe, asked why they were not fighting the merchant who had bought Pompey's provinces from him. Driven on by all these sneers, against his will Pompey set out in pursuit of Caesar to bring on a fight.

Caesar meanwhile was encountering difficulties on most of his march, for no one would let him have provisions, and he was universally despised because of his recent mishap. However, after he took Gomphi, a Thessalian city, he not only had food for his army, but cured his men unexpectedly of their sickness. For they found there plenty of wine and drank freely of it, and then, reveling and rioting along the way, they dispelled and got rid of their ailments by their drinking, for they changed the condition of their bodies.

42.   When, however, the two armies entered the plain of Pharsalus and set up camp there, Pompey's thoughts returned to their earlier course. He had unlucky visions and a dream in his sleep. He thought he saw himself in his theater, applauded by the Romans. . . .[64] But his companions were

---

[64] There is a gap here in the Greek text where we should have the substance of Pompey's dream. It may be found, however, in Plutarch's *Life of Pompey,* ch. 68.

so bold, and looked forward so hopefully to victory that Domitius, Spinther, and Scipio were squabbling furiously as to which should have Caesar's post of Pontifex Maximus, and many were sending to Rome to rent or preempt houses suitable for consuls and praetors, expecting to hold such offices immediately after the war. The cavalry were most on fire for the battle, being sumptuously equipped with splendid armor, well-fed horses, and handsome looks. They were proud too of their numbers, for they were seven thousand as against Caesar's thousand. In numbers the infantry also were unevenly divided, Pompey's forty-five thousand being arrayed against Caesar's twenty-two thousand.

43. Caesar now called his soldiers together and told them that Cornificius was close by with two legions and that fifteen cohorts more under Calenus were camped at Megara and Athens, and asked if they wished to wait for them or to risk a battle by themselves. The soldiers shouted that they did not wish him to wait, but to manage his strategy so as to bring them to grips with the enemy as soon as possible. When he was conducting the purification of his army and had sacrificed the first victim, the augur said to him that within three days he would fight a critical battle with his enemy. But when Caesar asked him if he saw any favorable sign in the victims as to the outcome, he replied, "You can answer that question better for yourself. The gods point to a great change and overturn of the present state of things. So if you think you are prospering in your present situation, look for a turn of fortune to the worse; but if you are badly off, expect something better." The night before the battle, as Caesar was going the round of the sentries about midnight, there was seen in the heavens a fiery torch which seemed to pass, brilliantly flaming, over Caesar's camp and then fall down on Pompey's. And in the morning watch they perceived a panic-like confusion in the enemy's camp. However, Caesar was not planning to fight that day, but was starting to break camp in order to go on towards Scotussa.[65]

44. His tents were already taken down when his scouts rode up with the news that the enemy was descending the hills for a battle.[66] But at

[65] Scotussa was a small town lying to the northeast of Pharsalus, on Caesar's road up to Macedonia.

[66] The battle of Pharsalus was fought on August 9, 48 B.C.

this he was delighted, offered his vows to the gods, and set his legions in line, arranging them in three divisions. Domitius Calvinus he put in charge of the center, Antony took the left wing, while he himself commanded the right, where he expected to fight with his tenth legion. But on seeing that the enemy's cavalry were moving up opposite that point and fearing their numbers and dazzling appearance, he gave orders that six cohorts of his own horse should come quietly around to him from the rear, and stationed them back of the right wing with instructions as to what they should do when the enemy cavalry attacked. Pompey himself commanded his right wing, Domitius the left, and Scipio, Pompey's father-in-law, the center. All Pompey's cavalry were massed at his left wing with the idea of surrounding Caesar's right and scattering completely the troops protecting the general, for they were sure that no infantry formation, however deep, could withstand them, but that at the onset of such a body of horse they would be utterly shattered and broken.

As both sides were preparing to sound the attack, Pompey sent orders to his legionaries to stand with arms ready and wait in close ranks to meet the enemy's charge until the men were within a javelin's throw. Caesar says [67] that here too Pompey made a mistake, not realizing that the first impetuous crash at a run adds power to a soldier's blows and fires and fans his courage to full heat. As Caesar was moving his legion into action and going forward to the front, he noticed one of his centurions, a man loyal to him and experienced in war, encouraging his men and challenging them to a contest in valor. Caesar called him by name and said, "What hope have we, Gaius Crassinius, and how high is our courage?" And Crassinius, waving his right hand, shouted back loudly, "We shall win a famous victory, Caesar, and you shall praise me this day, whether I live or die." So saying, he dashed ahead on a run against the enemy, carrying with him the hundred and twenty soldiers under him. He cut through the first rank and was pushing on, laying many low, when he was stopped by a thrust of a sword through his mouth, the point coming out at the nape of his neck.

45. As the infantry then clashed together and fighting began in the center, Pompey's cavalry rode proudly out from their left wing, spreading their squadrons apart to enclose Caesar's right. Before they charged,

---

[67] See Caesar, *Civil War*, III, 92.

Caesar's cohorts galloped out from their post, not hurling their javelins, as they were used to doing, nor striking at their enemies' thighs and legs, but aiming at their eyes and mauling their faces. This Caesar had instructed them to do, for he anticipated that men who were unfamiliar with wars and wounds, and were young and vain of their youth and beauty, would be especially wary of such an onslaught and fail to stand up under it, out of dread both of their immediate danger and of some future humiliation. And so it turned out. They could not bear the thrust of the javelins up into their faces and did not dare look the blades in the eye, but veered off and covered their heads to protect their features. And at length, after thus throwing themselves into disorder, they turned and disgracefully fled, and so ruined their whole cause. For the cohorts who had defeated them straightway surrounded Pompey's infantry, fell on them in the rear, and began cutting them to pieces.

When Pompey on the other wing saw his cavalry scattered in flight, he was no longer himself and quite forgot that he was Pompey the Great. Much like a man whose wits have been darkened by God, he went silently back to his tent and sat down there, waiting for what would happen, until his army was beaten and the enemy appeared on the ramparts and were struggling with their defenders. Then, as if coming to his senses, he uttered, they say, only these words, "What! Even to my camping ground!", pulled off his general's garb, and putting on garments suited to a fugitive, slipped away. What happened to him afterwards, and how he surrendered to the Egyptians and was killed, I shall tell in my *Life of Pompey*.[68]

46. When Caesar arrived at Pompey's entrenchments and saw the bodies of the enemy already lying dead and the slaughter still going on, he said with a groan, "This is what they wanted! They reduced me to this necessity. For I, Gaius Caesar, conqueror in great wars, would have been condemned in their courts if I had once disbanded my troops." Asinius Pollio says that Caesar spoke these words at the time in Latin, but wrote them down later in Greek. He also says that the majority of the dead were slaves, killed at the taking of the camp, and that not more than six thousand soldiers fell. Most of the prisoners captured alive Caesar drafted

---

[68] Plutarch, *Life of Pompey*, 77–80.

into his legions, and many men of distinction he pardoned, among them
Brutus, who afterwards killed him. It is said that Caesar was much troubled when after the battle Brutus did not appear, and when he was
brought before him safe and well, Caesar was immensely relieved.

47. There were many omens that foreshadowed this victory, the most
remarkable of which was recorded at Tralles.[69] In the temple of Victory
there, there stood a statue of Caesar, and the ground about it naturally
was solid, the surface paved with hard stone. But out of it, they say, a
palm tree sprang up beside the base of the statue. In Padua, one Gaius
Cornelius, who had a high reputation as a seer, a fellow citizen and acquaintance of the historian Livy, happened that day to be sitting among
his birds of augury. First, Livy says,[70] he saw it was the hour of the
battle, and said to the people there that even then the event was taking
place and the men were meeting in action. Then taking another look and
observing the signs, he sprang up joyously and cried, "You are conquering, Caesar!" The bystanders were astonished, but he took the garland
from his head and said with an oath that he would not put it on again
until the facts had testified to his art. At least Livy positively states that
the story is true.

48. Caesar gave the Thessalian people their liberty in honor of his victory, and then went on in pursuit of Pompey. On reaching Asia [71] he
freed the Cnidians as a compliment to Theopompus, the collector of fables,[72] and exempted all the inhabitants of Asia from a third of their
taxes. He reached Alexandria just after the murder of Pompey and turned
away horrified from Theodotus, who brought him Pompey's head. But
he accepted Pompey's seal ring and wept over it. All Pompey's companions and associates who were roaming around the country and being

---

[69] Tralles was a town in Lydia, Asia Minor.

[70] Livy's account of this incident was contained probably in Book III of his *History*,
which has since been lost.

[71] Caesar crossed the Hellespont into Asia Minor and there met Gaius Cassius, one of
his future murderers who had been working against him, but who now surrendered
and was pardoned.

[72] Theopompus of Chios (fourth century B.C.) was the author of two long and diffuse
histories.

taken prisoner by the king,[73] he treated well and won over to his side. To his friends in Rome he wrote that the greatest and sweetest joy he had in his victory was this—saving the lives of citizens who had always fought against him.

As to the war in Egypt,[74] some say that it was unnecessary, except as a result of his infatuation for Cleopatra, and both discreditable and dangerous. Others blame the king's party, and principally the eunuch Pothinus, the most powerful man in the country, who had lately murdered Pompey and banished Cleopatra. He was now plotting secretly against Caesar, and for that reason, they say, Caesar began thenceforward to spend his nights at drinking parties to protect himself. In his public behavior Pothinus was unendurable too, many times affronting and insulting Caesar by both word and act. He had the poorest and oldest grain measured out for Caesar's soldiers, and then told them they must take it and be satisfied, for they were eating what belonged to other men. At banquets he set the table with wooden and earthen dishes, explaining that Caesar had taken all the gold and silver ones as payment of a debt. For the father of the present king had been in debt to Caesar for seventeen million, five hundred thousand drachmas. Much of this sum Caesar had previously forgiven the king's children, but he now claimed ten million with which to feed his army. Pothinus told him to go off now and look after his important affairs and he would later be paid his money with thanks. Caesar answered that he had not the slightest need of Egyptian counselors, and secretly he sent for Cleopatra to return from the country.

---

[73] The king of Egypt at this time was the fifteen-year-old Ptolemy XIII (63–47 B.C.), who three years before had succeeded his father Ptolemy XII Auletes, and shortly afterwards had married his sister, the ambitious, nineteen-year-old Cleopatra. Before Caesar's arrival, however, under the influence of the eunuch Pothinus, he had banished her from his court.

[74] The so-called Alexandrian War, described below, was a confused conflict in which financial, political, and personal interests all were involved. Caesar needed money and may have expected to get in Egypt a part of what Ptolemy XII had promised him, when in 59 B.C., during Caesar's consulship, he was recognized as friend and ally of Rome, and, a few years later, was helped by Rome to regain his throne, from which he had been driven by his rebellious subjects. The Egyptians, probably with reason, suspected Caesar meanwhile of political designs on their country. And after his meeting with Cleopatra another of his aims seems to have been to restore her to her position as queen and co-ruler with her brother.

49. Accordingly, Cleopatra, bringing the Sicilian Apollodorus alone of all her friends with her, came down in a small boat and landed at the palace at dusk. As it was impossible for her to enter unseen in any other way, she got into a bedding sack and stretched out at full length, and Apollodorus fastened the sack up with a strap and carried it through the door to Caesar. He was, they say, captivated at first by this scheme of Cleopatra's, which showed her to be an audacious wanton, and then further enslaved by the charm of her society. Eventually he reconciled her and her brother, so that she was to share the royal power with him.

While everyone was feasting in honor of the reconciliation, a slave of Caesar, his barber, a fellow whose exceptional cowardice made him let nothing go unexamined, and who kept his ears open and was into everything, discovered that Achillas, the general, and Pothinus, the eunuch, were framing a plot against Caesar. On learning this, Caesar placed a guard around the banquet hall, and had Pothinus put to death. Achillas, however, fled to his camp and began a war against Caesar which was troublesome and difficult, since with so small a force Caesar had to defend himself against so large a city and army. In this struggle he was threatened first with being cut off from the water, for the canals were closed by the enemy. Next, an attempt was made to seize his fleet, and he was compelled to fight this danger by fire, which spread from the dockyards and destroyed the Great Library.[75] Thirdly, in a battle fought around the Pharos,[76] he jumped from the causeway into a small boat and was going to the help of his soldiers, but the Egyptians came sailing up on him from every direction and he threw himself into the sea and barely escaped by swimming. On this occasion, it is said, he had a number of papers in his hand which he would not let go, pelted though he was by missiles and deep in the water. He held the papers above the surface with one hand and swam with the other. His little boat had been sunk at once.

[75] The library of Alexandria, founded by the first two Ptolemies, at the opening of the third century B.C., was the most famous library of antiquity. At this time it was only damaged. Not until the fire of 651 A.D. was it completely destroyed.

[76] On the Pharos and the causeway that connected it with the city of Alexandria, see above, *Alexander,* ch. 26.

Finally, after the king had left him and joined his enemies, he attacked and defeated them in a battle in which many fell and the king himself disappeared.[77] Then leaving Cleopatra queen of Egypt, he started for Syria. She soon afterwards gave birth to a son by him, whom the Alexandrians called Caesarion.

50. From Syria Caesar went on into Asia, where he heard that Domitius had been defeated by Pharnaces, son of Mithridates,[78] and had fled from Pontus with a few men; and that Pharnaces, taking full advantage of his victory, was already in possession of Bithynia and Cappadocia, had his eye on so-called Lesser Armenia, and was stirring up the kings and tetrarchs in those parts. So immediately Caesar marched against him with three legions, fought a great battle with him near the city of Zela, sent him flying out of Pontus, and left nothing of his army. In describing to Amantius, one of his friends at Rome, the zest and speed of that battle, Caesar used just three words, "[I] Came, saw, conquered." [79] In Latin these words, each with the same ending, have a terseness which is extraordinary.

51. From there, crossing to Italy, he went up to Rome at the end of the year for which he had been appointed Dictator a second time. That office had never before been held for an entire year.[80] He was then elected consul for the following year. He was, however, much criticized because when his soldiers revolted and killed two men of praetorian rank, Cosconius and Galba, he penalized them only so far as to address them as "citizens" instead of as "soldiers." He then gave them each a thousand drachmas, and allotted them a wide expanse of land in Italy. He was

---

[77] The unhappy boy, Ptolemy XIII, was drowned in the Nile.

[78] Pharnaces II was the son of Mithridates the Great (c.132–63 B.C.), king of Pontus, who at the height of his power had ruled over most of Asia Minor, the Aegean Islands, and Greece but had been conquered and his kingdom shattered by Pompey. His son was trying to make use of the time afforded by the war between Caesar and Pompey to build up again something like his father's dominion.

[79] The Latin words are *"Veni, vidi, vici."* Neither the Greek words into which Plutarch translated them nor the English have that conciseness and repetition of sound which make the Latin so striking and memorable.

[80] Soon after the battle of Pharsalus, in 48 B.C., the senate had appointed Caesar for the second time dictator for a year.

blamed also for the misbehavior of Dolabella,[81] the avarice of Amantius, the drunkenness of Antony, as well as for Cornificius' rebuilding of Pompey's house and refurnishing it, as if it were not good enough for him. The Romans were irritated by all these things. But though Caesar was not ignorant of what went on and disliked it, in the existing state of politics he was obliged to use that kind of men as his assistants.

52.   Cato [82] and Scipio, after the battle of Pharsalus, fled to Libya and there with the help of King Juba, got together a considerable force. Caesar now decided to start a campaign against them, and so at the winter solstice crossed over to Sicily. Anxious to crush at once all hope in his officers' minds of dallying and wasting time there, he planted his own tent on the shore, and as soon as the wind was right went on board and set sail with three thousand infantry and a few horsemen. He landed them without being discovered and then put back again, in fear for the greater part of his force; but he met them already on the sea and conducted them all to camp.

He then heard that his enemies were being heartened by an ancient oracle to the effect that it was the destiny of the family of the Scipios always to be victors in Libya. Consequently he began both making disparaging jests about the Scipio who commanded the enemy and seriously claiming the forecast for himself. It is hard to say which method he used more. He had with him, for instance, a man, otherwise contemptible and insignificant, who was of the house of the Africani, Scipio Sallutio by name. This man he would post in the forefront of his army in battle, as if he were a general, and require him to attack the enemy often and act eager to fight.

But there was neither food enough for his men nor forage for his beasts of burden. They were even forced to feed the animals seaweed, after washing out the salt and mixing it with a little grass for sweetening. The Numidians too were constantly appearing in swarms on fast

---

[81] Publius Cornelius Dolabella, Cicero's son-in-law, was one of the ruined spendthrifts who thought to retrieve their fortunes by joining Caesar's party in the civil war. However, on Caesar's murder he was one of those who at first supported the conspirators, though Antony soon bought him off by allowing him to assume the office of consul for the rest of the year 44 B.C. See above, *Cicero*, ch. 43.

[82] On Cato's efforts to muster resistance to Caesar in the province of Libya, see below, *Cato the Younger*, chs. 56, 57.

horses, thus keeping a hold on the country. Once Caesar's cavalrymen happened to be amusing themselves with a Libyan, who was showing them how he danced and played the flute at the same time amazingly well, and the men were sitting enjoying themselves on the ground, having turned their horses over to their attendants, when the enemy suddenly surrounded and fell upon them, killed some and drove the rest headlong back to their camp. Had not Caesar himself with Asinius Pollio come from the entrenchments to their aid and stopped their flight, the war would have been over. And once in another battle, when the enemy was winning the struggle, Caesar is said to have seized the fleeing standard bearer by the neck, turned him around, and said, "There is the enemy!"

53. Encouraged by his advantages, Scipio decided to risk a decision by battle. So leaving Afranius encamped in one place and Juba in another, a little way apart, he himself began building fortifications for a camp above a lake near the city of Thapsus, as a starting point for all his forces to go out to fight, and also as a shelter. While Scipio was at work on that scheme, Caesar was making his way with incredible speed through wooded country which contained approaches no one knew about, and thus he got around some of the enemy and attacked the rest in front. Having put them to flight, he seized on the favorable moment and the tide of good fortune and went on to capture the camp of Afranius, meeting no resistance, and then, still unresisted, sacked the Numidian camp from which Juba had fled. So in a brief portion of a single day he took three camps and slaughtered fifty thousand of the enemy, with a loss of less than fifty of his own men.[83]

This is the account which some give of that battle. Others say that Caesar himself was not in the fight, but that just as he was ordering and lining up his army, he was taken with his chronic distemper,[84] and feeling at once that a seizure was coming on, before his mind, already shaken, was utterly confused and obsessed by the disease, he had himself carried to a nearby tower, where he stayed quietly through the battle. As for the men of consular rank who escaped from the field, some killed themselves when they were taken, and others Caesar had put to death.

[83] The battle of Thapsus, which marked the end of resistance to Caesar in the south, took place in April, 46 B.C.

[84] Caesar is said to have been subject to epileptic attacks.

54.   He was now ambitious to take Cato alive and so hurried on to Utica, for Cato was defending that city and had had no hand in the battle. On hearing that Cato had killed himself,[85] he was plainly disappointed, though for what reason is not clear. He certainly said, "Cato, I grudge you your death as you grudged me the chance to save your life." Yet the speech he wrote afterwards against the dead Cato contains no indication of clemency or of willingness to forgive. And why would he have spared the living Cato when he poured out on him dead such a torrent of wrath? Yet there are those who infer from his leniency to Cicero and Brutus, and to thousands of others who fought against him, that his speech was composed not out of animosity to Cato but to promote his own political ambitions.

The reason they give is the following. Cicero had written an eulogy of Cato and given the name of *Cato* to it,[86] and many were excitedly reading it, as was natural in the case of a work by the most skillful of orators on the noblest of subjects. But it annoyed Caesar, who considered Cicero's praise of a man whose death he had caused to be an accusation of himself. Accordingly, he composed an answer in which he put together a mass of charges against Cato, and called his book *Anti-Cato*. And both these compositions had eager readers on Caesar's account as well as on Cato's.

55.   On his return to Rome from Libya, Caesar immediately made a vainglorious speech to the people about his victory, declaring that he had conquered a country vast enough to provide yearly for the public stores two hundred thousand Attic bushels of grain and three million pounds of olive oil. He then celebrated three triumphs, one for Egypt, one for Pontus, and one for Libya, the last not for his victory over Scipio but, professedly, for his conquest of King Juba. On that occasion, a child Juba, son of the king, was carried in the triumphal procession. He was the most fortunate captive taken, for though born a Numidian barbarian, he was to be numbered among the most learned historians of Greece.[87]

---

[85] See below, *Cato the Younger,* ch. 65. Scipio attempted to escape to Spain, but when in danger of falling into Caesar's hands, he also stabbed himself.

[86] See above, *Cicero,* ch. 39.

[87] This child grew up in Italy to become Juba II (c.50 B.C.–c.22 A.D.). At the age of about twenty, he was granted his father's kingdom of Numidia and later that of Mauretania. He was also a traveled man of letters, who endeavored to introduce Greek and Roman culture into Africa, and the author of histories of Rome, Libya, Arabia, and Assyria, none of which has survived.

After his triumphs, Caesar gave generous largess to his soldiers, and entertained the people with banquets and shows, feasting the whole population together on twenty-two thousand dining couches.[88] He held gladiatorial contests too and naval combats in memory of his daughter Julia, long ago dead. After the shows he had a census taken, but instead of the previous three hundred and twenty thousand they counted only one hundred and fifty thousand. So great was the loss caused by the civil war and so large a portion of the Roman people had it consumed, to say nothing of the disasters to other parts of Italy and to the provinces.

56.   When all this was over and Caesar had been declared consul for the fourth time, he led an expedition to Spain against Pompey's sons. Although they were still young, they had assembled a surprisingly large army, and had exhibited a courage worthy of commanders, so that Caesar found himself in extreme danger. The great battle was fought near the city of Munda [89] and Caesar saw his men hard pushed there and putting up a poor defense. Dashing with a shout through the ranks of his soldiers, he asked whether they were not ashamed to take and deliver him into the hands of boys. At length with a mighty effort he drove off the enemy, killing more than thirty thousand of them, and losing a thousand of his own best soldiers. As he left after the battle he said to his friends that he had often fought for victory, but that this was the first time he had fought for his life. He won that victory on the day of the feast of Bacchus,[90] the day on which they say the great Pompey, four years before, set out for the war. As for Pompey's sons, the younger escaped, but within a few days the head of the elder was brought by Didius to Caesar.

This was the last war Caesar fought, and the triumph he celebrated for it displeased the Romans more than anything else he had done. For this was no victory over foreign generals or barbarian kings, but the total destruction of the sons and family of the bravest of the Romans, who had met with calamity. It was unseemly too to hold a triumph over the woes of one's own country and to exult at deeds for which the sole excuse before gods and men was that they were done under necessity. Before this time Caesar had never even sent a messenger or dispatches to an-

---

[88] A dining couch would usually accommodate three persons.
[89] The city of Munda was in southeastern Spain, near present-day Malaga.
[90] March 17, 45 B.C.

nounce to the public a victory in the civil wars and out of delicacy had refused to receive any honor for them.

57. Nevertheless, his countrymen submitted to the man's good fortune and accepted the bridle, and, regarding monarchy as a relief from the miseries of civil war, made him dictator for life. It was admittedly a tyranny, for the monarchy in addition to being absolute now became permanent. This first honor Cicero proposed for him in the senate, and it was perhaps not too great for the man, but others kept adding extravagant honors and vying with each other in suggesting them. Thereby they made Caesar detested and odious, even to the most moderate sort of men, because of the absurd lengths to which they went in voting honors for him. Some think that his enemies worked with his flatterers to put the votes through, in order to have as many grounds as possible for an attack on him and the most serious reasons, apparently, for attempting to kill him.

For, in every other respect, after the close of the civil war, Caesar's behavior was irreproachable, and with good reason, seemingly, they voted to build a temple to Clemency as a thank offering for his mildness. He pardoned many of those who had fought against him, and to some he actually gave offices and honors besides, as he did to Brutus and Cassius, both of whom became praetors. Nor would he permit the statues of Pompey to lie thrown down from their pedestals, but set them up again, at which Cicero said that by restoring Pompey's statues Caesar had firmly planted his own.[91] His friends thought he should have a bodyguard and many of them offered their services, but he would not hear of it, saying it was better to die once than to live always expecting death. He thought his noblest and surest protection would be the good will of the people and tried to surround himself with that and to win them back to him with feasts and distributions of grain. To appease his soldiers, he organized new colonies, the most famous of which were at Corinth and Carthage. In the past, these two cities, as it happened, had been captured at the same time, and now they were simultaneously rebuilt.[92]

---

[91] See above, *Cicero*, ch. 40.

[92] Both cities had been taken by Romans a century before, in 146 B.C., and both were restored in 44.

58. To some of the nobility he promised future consulships and praetorships, while others he pacified with a variety of honors and positions of influence. To all he gave hope, for his ardent wish was to rule over willing subjects. So when the consul Maximus died, he appointed Caninius Revilius consul for the one day still left of his term of office. But when the crowds were going, as usual, to welcome the new consul and escort him about, Cicero said, "Let us hurry, or the man will be out of office!"

But Caesar's many achievements did not beguile his naturally great energy and ambition into merely enjoying what he had already won, but served rather as incentives and stimuli to go on, fostering in him ideas of still grander accomplishments and a passion for new glory, as if he had exhausted what he already had. He felt, indeed, something like a jealousy of himself, as of another man, a sense of rivalry between his past exploits and what he was yet to do. For he was planning and preparing to take an expedition against the Parthians, and after conquering them to march through Hyrcania, and by way of the Caspian Sea, the Caucasus, and the coast of the Black Sea, to attack Scythia. He would then subdue the countries bordering on Germany and Germany itself, and return to Italy through Gaul.[93] Thus he would join in one this circle of his empire, bounded on all sides by the ocean.

While this expedition was going on he meant to have the Corinthian Isthmus dug through and had already appointed Anienus to superintend the work. He had also a plan to turn the Tiber, just beyond the city, into a deep channel, bending it towards Circaeum to make it enter the sea at Tarracina, and thus furnish a safe and easy entrance for merchants coming to Rome for trade.[94] Furthermore, he would drain the marshes around Pomentium and Setia, and make a solid plain which would give means of support to many thousands. He would also build dikes to hold back

---

[93] By enclosing this great circle of countries in one empire Caesar would have outdone Alexander, uniting most of Europe and the North African coast with something like half of Alexander's conquests in Asia.

[94] The bringing of the Tiber down southward through this low, swampy country to a mouth at Tarracina would have provided not only a better harbor and entrance to the river way to Rome but would have facilitated the draining of what has since been known as the Pontine Marshes, a project which the twentieth century has finally seen carried out.

the sea where it came nearest to Rome, clear the coast at Ostia [95] of hidden reefs, and construct ports and roadsteads adequate for every kind of shipping. All these things he had in preparation.

59. The reformation of the calendar [96] and rectification of the error in the reckoning of time were objects of congenial and scientific study by him, and when carried through were of the most gratifying utility. For in very ancient times not only were the cycles of the lunar and the solar years confused at Rome, so that sacrifices and festivals, moving slowly, at last fell in opposite seasons of the year, but in that period too people had no way of computing the years correctly. Only the priests knew the actual time, and they would all of a sudden, without warning anyone, slip in an intercalary month called Mercedonius.[97] King Numa is said to have been the first to insert this month, thus inventing a poor and temporary expedient to cure the errors that arose in the returning cycles, as I have explained in his *Life*.[98]

Caesar laid the problem before the ablest philosophers and mathematicians, and out of the systems they proposed he put together one of his own, a more exact method of correction than any other. The Romans use it down to the present time, and apparently are more successful than other nations in avoiding the errors caused by the inequality of the cycles. However, even this achievement gave offense to people who envied him and resented his power. Cicero, the orator, they say, when someone observed that Lyra [99] would be rising the next morning, answered, "Yes,

---

[95] Ostia was the old port of Rome, on the south bank of the Tiber, near its mouth.

[96] By his authority as Pontifex Maximus Caesar instituted what was to be known to succeeding centuries as the Julian Calendar. The old Republican Calendar had made the year ten days too short, so that by Caesar's time it was almost three months ahead of the true solar year. He, first, had inserted in the year 46 B.C. days enough to bring it to a total of 445 days. Thereafter the year was set at 365 days, with an extra day in February every four years. This gave a year only eleven minutes and twelve seconds too long, an error which was finally rectified by Pope Gregory XIII, in 1582.

[97] The simplest way to set right a calendar made up of years which had been reckoned too short had been to insert every now and then in the middle of a year an extra or so-called intercalary month, consisting of the number of days needed to make the calendar fit again with the courses of the sun.

[98] See above, *Numa*, ch. 18.

[99] Lyra was the classical name for a small, triangular constellation of stars in the northern sky, thought to suggest the lyre of Orpheus or of Hermes.

because that is the order,"—as if men were under compulsion to accept even that event.

60. But the most open and venomous indignation against him was caused by his desire to be king. It was the first offense he gave to the common people and a plausible excuse for men who had long been secretly cherishing a hatred of him. Persons who wanted to procure him that honor spread in public a story that the Sibylline Books [100] predicted that Parthia would be conquered when the Romans invaded it under a king, but not till then. And once, when Caesar was on his way down from Alba to the city, they ventured to greet him as king; but the people showed their displeasure, and Caesar, annoyed, said his name was not king but Caesar. As everyone then kept silent, he passed on looking not very pleasant or happy. Another time, the senate had been voting him some extraordinary honors, and he happened to be sitting above the rostrum when the consuls and praetors came toward him with all the senate following them. He did not rise from his seat but, as if he were receiving private individuals, merely told them that his honors needed diminishing more than increasing. His manner irritated not only the senate but the people as well, for they thought that the city had been insulted in the person of the senate, and all who were not obliged to stay went gloomily home.

Caesar himself, perceiving his mistake, at once turned to go, and throwing his cloak off from his neck called out to his friends that he was ready to offer himself to anyone who would like to stab him. Later on he excused himself on the ground of his malady, saying that sufferers from it were apt to be shaky in their senses if they stood while talking to a crowd, and soon began trembling and growing dizzy, and so to fainting and unconsciousness. This was not the true explanation, however. Instead, he had fully intended to rise as the senate approached, but one of his friends, or rather, they say, one of his flatterers, Cornelius Balbus,[101] checked him with the words, "Remember that you are Caesar, and expect to be treated with respect as their superior."

[100] On the Sibylline Books see above, *Numa,* ch. 22, n. 43.
[101] Balbus was a native of Spain who had won Roman citizenship by his military prowess. At first an adherent of Pompey, he gradually shifted to Caesar and after Pharsalus became one of his chief advisers.

61. Added to this offensive behavior was his defiance of the tribunes. The festival of the Lupercalia [102] was being celebrated, a festival which many writers say was in old times a shepherd rite and had some relation also to the Arcadian Lycaea. Bands of young noblemen and magistrates then run naked through the city, joking and laughing, and striking everyone they meet with shaggy strips of hide. Many women, even of high rank, deliberately go to meet them and hold out their hands to the lash, as boys do in school, convinced that those who are pregnant will thus be aided to an easy birth, and the childless to pregnancy. Caesar was looking on at this performance, seated on the rostrum on a golden throne and decked out in a robe of triumph. Antony was one of those who ran in the sacred race, for he was a consul, and when he came charging into the forum the crowd parted before him. He was carrying a diadem, wound around with a wreath of laurel, which he held out to Caesar. There was a little clapping of hands, but not loud, and all arranged beforehand. But when Caesar pushed the diadem away, the whole multitude broke into applause. Again Antony offered it and a few clapped, and again on Caesar's refusal of it everyone applauded. The experiment having thus failed, Caesar rose and ordered the wreath taken up to the Capitol.

Next Caesar's statues were seen crowned with royal diadems and two of the tribunes, Flavius and Marullus, went up to them and pulled them off. Then on learning who first had saluted Caesar as king, they committed them to prison. And the people followed, cheering and calling the tribunes Brutuses, because it was Brutus who ended the line of kings and transferred the power from a monarch to the senate and the people.[103] But at this Caesar was angry and removed Flavius and Marullus from office. In his accusation of them he berated the people sharply and repeatedly called the tribunes "brutes" and "Cymaeans." [104]

---

[102] The Lupercalia was a fertility festival, held on February 15, whose origins went back to prehistoric times. The name suggests a connection with a wolf god, something to be feared and propitiated by a small, pastoral community. For a further description of the rites see below, *Antony,* ch. 12.

[103] Lucius Junius Brutus in Roman tradition was the patriot who led the popular uprising which drove out King Tarquin after the outrage his son had inflicted on the matron Lucretia, and thus put an end to monarchy at Rome.

[104] The Latin word *brutus* means stupid; the natives of Cyme, a town on the coast of Asia Minor, had a reputation for being dull-witted.

62. Such incidents turned the people's thoughts to Marcus Brutus,[105] who on his father's side was said to be descended from the first Brutus, and on his mother's side from the Servilii, another distinguished house. He was also a son-in-law and nephew of Cato. But the honors and favors he had received from Caesar had dulled now any desire he might have had to attempt the overthrow of the new monarchy. Not only had he been pardoned at Pharsalus after Pompey's flight, along with many of his friends at his beseeching, but Caesar had shown great confidence in him. He held at this time the most prominent of the praetorships and was slated for the consulship three years later, being preferred to his rival Cassius.[106] For Caesar, they say, had declared that Cassius had put in the fairer claim to the position, but that he could not pass over Brutus. And once when some men were warning him against Brutus, and the conspiracy was already under way, he would not listen, but laying his hand on his body, said to the tale-bearers, "Brutus will wait for this skin of mine," meaning that Brutus deserved his office because of his honesty, and that to get office he would not become an ungrateful scoundrel.

However, the men who were set on change looked to Brutus as the only or at least the best person to bring it about, though they did not venture to speak to him directly. At night they strewed papers over his praetor's platform and the chair where he sat to judge, most of them containing words like, "You are asleep, Brutus," or "You are no Brutus." And Cassius saw that Brutus' ambition was being somewhat stirred thereby and he began to urge him more than he had done before, and to incite him on, for he had himself some private grudges against Caesar, on grounds I have mentioned in my *Life of Brutus*.[107] Caesar did suspect Cassius and said once to his friends, "What do you think Cassius wants?

[105] Marcus Junius Brutus (c.85–42 B.C.), son of an earlier tribune Brutus, had won a name at this time for high, moral integrity and impressiveness as a speaker. In his younger days, he had been associated with the republican Cato, and during the civil war had fought for Pompey, but after Pharsalus had been pardoned by Caesar, as noted above. He had married as his second wife Cato's daughter Porcia.

[106] Gaius Cassius Longinus, a hard-headed, rather cynical man, had earned some military reputation by his defense of Syria against the Parthians after the collapse of Crassus and his army. In the civil war he had commanded Pompey's fleet but, like Brutus, he had been pardoned after Pharsalus. In 44 B.C., he was praetor in charge of the court for foreigners at Rome.

[107] Plutarch's *Life of Brutus*, chs. 8, 9.

I like him none too well; he is too pale." Again, they say, when a false
story reached him that Antony and Dolabella were planning a revolution,
his remark was, "I am not much afraid of these fat, long-haired fellows,
but more of those pale, lean ones," meaning Cassius and Brutus.

63. Fate, however, it seems, is less something unforeseeable than something unescapable, for marvelous portents and apparitions are said to
have appeared. Flashes in the sky, widespread noises by night, and wild
birds swooping down into the forum are perhaps not worth mentioning
in connection with so grave an event. But Strabo, the philosopher, tells
of many men all afire who were seen moving in, and of a soldier's slave
who threw a mass of flame off his hand and seemed to onlookers to be
burning himself. Yet when the flame went out, there was nothing wrong
with the man. He says too that when Caesar was offering a sacrifice, the
heart of the victim could not be found, and that this was a dire omen,
since no animal in nature can exist without a heart.

There are many who tell this story. A soothsayer warned Caesar to be
on guard against a great danger on the day in the month of March which
Romans call the Ides. When the day came, and Caesar was setting out
for the senate, he met the soothsayer and greeted him with amusement,
saying, "The Ides of March are here." To this the soothsayer replied
softly, "Yes, they are here, but they have not yet gone." The day before,
Caesar was at dinner with Marcus Lepidus and happened to be signing
letters, as he used to do while reclining at table. The conversation turned
on the question of what kind of death was best, and before anyone else
could speak he called out, "One which is unexpected." That night, as he
was sleeping as usual beside his wife, all the doors and windows of the
room flew open together. Startled by the noise and by the radiance of
the moon shining down on him, he looked at Calpurnia and saw she
was fast asleep but muttering indistinct words and inarticulate groans in
her dream. For she dreamt that she held Caesar murdered in her arms
and was weeping over him.

Others, however, say that this was not the vision the woman had. There
had, by vote of the senate, been placed a pediment on Caesar's house as
an ornament and mark of distinction, as Livy says. This in her dream
Calpurnia saw torn down, and accordingly, she thought, she grieved and
wept. And so when day came, she entreated Caesar, if possible, not to

go out, but to put off the senate meeting. And if he cared nothing for her dreams, he should inquire by some other method of divining and sacrificing what the future was bringing him. Caesar himself, too, it seems, felt some suspicion and dread, for never before had he detected in Calpurnia any womanish superstition, and now he saw that she was deeply distressed. And when the soothsayers, too, after sacrificing many victims, told him that the omens were unfavorable, he determined to send Antony to dismiss the senate.

64.   But at this point stepped in Decimus Brutus, surnamed Albinus,[108] who was so trusted by Caesar that in his will he had made him his second heir. He was taking part in the conspiracy of the other Brutus and Cassius, and was afraid that if Caesar escaped that day their plot might become known. So he made fun of the soothsayers and reproved Caesar for giving the senate cause for spiteful criticisms of him, for they would think he was playing with them. They had, Brutus said, convened at his bidding and were all eager to vote to proclaim him king of the provinces outside Italy, with the right to wear a diadem whenever he went anywhere but in Italy, on sea or on land. But if someone should tell them now, as they were taking their seats, to go home and come back again when Calpurnia happened to have better dreams, what would his enemies say? And who would listen to his friends when they tried to explain that this was not slavery and tyranny? If Caesar was thoroughly convinced that the day was inauspicious, it would be better for him to go himself and speak to the senate, and then postpone the meeting. And as he said this, he took Caesar by the hand and began leading him on. He had gone only a little way from his door when a slave belonging to someone else, anxious to get to Caesar but prevented by the pressure of the crowd around him, forced a path into the house and put himself in Calpurnia's hands, telling her to keep him until Caesar's return, for he had important things to say to him.

---

108 Decimus Brutus Albinus had a record of service under Caesar in his Gallic wars and of command of Caesar's fleet during the civil war. In 46 B.C. Caesar had made him governor of Cisalpine Gaul and promised him the consulship for 42. Caesar's first heir was his youthful great-nephew, Octavian, spoken of below as the "young Caesar." See above, *Cicero,* ch. 44.

65.   Then Artemidorus, a Cnidian by birth, a teacher of Greek philosophy
and for that reason an intimate friend of some of Brutus' followers, so
that he knew most of what was afoot, came bringing in a small roll the
information he intended to give Caesar. And when he saw that Caesar
handed each roll as he received it to the attendants about him, he came
up very close and said, "Read this, Caesar, by yourself and quickly, for
it is about serious matters which concern you." Caesar then took the roll,
and was about to read it, but was prevented by the throng of people who
came up to him, though he started to do it several times. So holding and
keeping only that roll, he walked on into the senate. Some, however, say
it was another man who gave him the roll, and that Artemidorus did not
come near reaching him, but was shoved back all along the road.

66.   Now it may be that these things happened independently. But the
hall which saw that struggle and that murder, and where the senate met
that day, contained a statue of Pompey and had been built by Pompey
as an ornamental addition to his theater. That certainly proved that some
divinity was at work summoning and guiding the deed to take place
there. They say, too, that just before the attack Cassius was gazing at
Pompey's statue and silently invoking his aid, even though he was himself a devotee of the doctrines of Epicurus.[109] But at this critical moment,
apparently, when the terrible event was actually at hand, religious emotion
took the place of his earlier cold reasoning.

Brutus Albinus now got hold of Antony, who was loyal to Caesar and
a man of vigor, and purposely detained him outside in a long conversation. Caesar, however, went in and the senate rose to do him honor. Some
of Brutus' party then took their stand behind his chair, while others
advanced towards him, as if to join Tillius Cimber in a petition on behalf
of his exiled brother. They all began imploring Caesar together and following him to his chair. But on taking his seat he rejected their petition,
and as they pressed more strenuously on him, he grew angry with one
and another. Thereat Tillius took hold of his toga with both hands and
pulled it down from his throat. That was the signal for the attack.

First, Casca struck him on the neck with his sword, a blow neither
fatal nor deep, for naturally he was nervous at the start of so terrific a

---

[109] As an Epicurean Cassius would not believe in the survival of Pompey's spirit after
death or in any divine aid.

deed of daring. At this Caesar turned around and clutched and held the knife, and both cried out almost in unison, the injured man in Latin, "You damned Casca, what are you doing?" and his assailant in Greek to his brother, "Brother, help!" Thus the struggle began, and those who were not in the plot were so shocked and horrified at what was taking place that they dared not fly or go to Caesar's aid or even make a sound. Those who were prepared for the murder bared their swords, so that Caesar was surrounded on all sides, and whichever way he turned to look he met stabs from blades aimed at his face and eyes. So driven back and forth like a wild beast, he was caught by everyone's hands, for everyone had to join in the sacrifice and take part in his death. For that reason Brutus too gave him one blow in the groin.

Some say that Caesar was defending himself against the rest, shouting and dodging this way and that, but on seeing that Brutus had drawn his sword, he pulled his toga over his head and sank, whether by chance or because his murderers pushed him there, against the pedestal on which Pompey's statue stood. It was bathed in his blood, so that it looked as if Pompey himself were presiding over this revenge on his enemy, who now lay at his feet panting under the rain of wounds. For they say he received twenty-three. And many of his assassins were wounded by one another as they persisted in stabbing at that one body so many times.

67. When Caesar was completely disposed of, Brutus came forward as if to say something about what they had done, but the senators, without waiting to listen, rushed through the doors and fled, thereby spreading excitement and bewildered terror among the people. Some shut up their houses, and others left their counters and shops and ran to the spot to see what had happened and then, having seen, ran away. Antony and Lepidus, the chief friends of Caesar, stole off and took refuge in other men's houses. But Brutus and his followers, as they were, still hot from the slaughter, marched in a body from the senate house to the Capitol, brandishing bare swords, not like fugitives but radiant and confident, calling the people to liberty and inviting the noblest of those they met to join them. And some did go up to the Capitol with them and mixed with them as if they had had a hand in the deed and were claiming credit for it. Among these men were Gaius Octavius and Lentulus Spinther. Later they paid a penalty for their pretensions, for they were put to death by

Antony and the young Caesar. They did not even enjoy the glory which they died to win, for no one ever believed them. Even those who punished them did so not for what they did, but for what they wished they had done.

The next day Brutus came down and addressed the people, who listened to his words without expressing either approval or indignation at what had been done, but indicating by their hushed silence that they both pitied Caesar and respected Brutus. The senate attempted a general amnesty and reconciliation of parties. They voted that Caesar should be honored as a god and that not the smallest measure he had taken while in power should be altered; to Brutus and his companions they awarded provinces and appropriate honors. So everyone supposed that the situation was stabilized and settled in the best way.[110]

68. When Caesar's will was opened and it was discovered that he had given every Roman a handsome present,[111] and when the people beheld his body, as it was carried through the forum, lacerated by wounds, they kept no longer within the bounds of orderliness but piled up around the body benches, railings, and tables from the forum, set fire to them and burned it there. Then catching up the flaming brands, they ran to the houses of the murderers to set them on fire, while others rushed up and down the city looking for the men to seize and tear them to pieces. But they found none of them, for they were all well protected.

One Cinna,[112] a friend of Caesar's, happened, they say, to have had a strange dream the night before. He thought that he was invited by Caesar to dine with him, and that he excused himself, but that Caesar pulled him along by the hand against his will and in spite of his resistance. When he heard that Caesar's body was being burned in the forum, he got up and went there to pay his respects, although he was somewhat alarmed by his dream and was also ill of a fever. And one of the crowd who saw him told his name to another who asked him, and he repeated it to another.

---

[110] See below, *Antony*, chs. 14–16.

[111] To every citizen Caesar left three hundred sesterces and to the public at large his gardens on the Tiber.

[112] This was Gaius Helvius Cinna, one of the tribunes for the year 44 B.C. and a staunch friend of Caesar. The mob mistook him for Lucius Cornelius Cinna, the brother of Caesar's first wife, a praetor that year, who had expressed approbation of Caesar's assassination.

And at once the rumor spread through the mob that he was one of Caesar's murderers. In fact, there was among the conspirators a man of the same name of Cinna. So believing that this man was he, they suddenly sprang at him and tore him to pieces between them. At this, Brutus and Cassius were thoroughly frightened and within a few days left the city. What they did and what they endured before they died is told in the *Life of Brutus*.

69. When Caesar died he was full fifty-six years old; he had outlived Pompey, though by not much more than four years. As for the position and power he had sought all his life through such heavy perils, he had barely attained them and had as yet reaped no fruit of them save the empty name and the glory which had aroused the jealousy of his fellow citizens. Yet his guiding genius which attended him through life followed him even after he was dead, as an avenger of his murder, driving on and tracking down his assassins on every land and sea until not one was left, and even those who in any way whatever were involved in the deed or shared in the planning had met their punishment. The most remarkable of humanly inflicted penalties was that which befell Cassius. After his defeat at Philippi [113] he killed himself with the same dagger he had used against Caesar. Among signs from heaven there was the great comet which shone brilliantly for seven nights after Caesar's murder and then vanished. There was also the dimming of the sun's light. For all through that year its orb rose pale and without radiance, and the heat from it was feeble and ineffective, so that the moving air was murky and heavy because of the weakness of the warmth that passed through it. And the fruit, half-ripe and green, withered and dried up because of the chill in the atmosphere.

In particular, the specter which appeared to Brutus showed that Caesar's murder was displeasing to the gods. This is the story. When Brutus was preparing to take his army across from Abydus [114] to the other continent, he was lying one night as usual in his tent, not asleep but pondering over the future. For Brutus, they say, was the poorest sleeper of all the generals and by nature the most wakeful. He thought he heard a noise by the

---

113 On the plain outside the city of Philippi in Thrace, in the year 42 B.C., the armies of Octavian and Antony finally defeated the forces of Brutus and Cassius.

114 Abydus was a town on the Asiatic side of the Hellespont.

door and looking towards the light of his lamp, which was now going out, he beheld a terrifying sight, a man of phenomenal size and cruel countenance. He was struck dumb at first, but on seeing that the figure neither moved nor spoke, but stood silently by his bed, he asked who he was. The specter answered, "Your evil genius, Brutus. You will see me at Philippi." To which Brutus replied bravely, "I will see you," and the spirit immediately disappeared.

When the time arrived, and he ranged his forces against Antony and Caesar at Philippi, he was victorious in the first battle, dispersed the enemy in front of him, and pillaged Caesar's camp. Before the second battle, the same specter visited him again at night, though not to say anything to him. However, Brutus knew what fate had decided and threw himself headlong into the melée. Yet he did not fall fighting. After his army was in flight, he got away up a steep pitch of ground and there stabbed himself in the breast with his naked sword, assisted, so they say, by a friend to drive it in, and thus he met his death.

Demetrius

3 3 6 - 2 8 3 B . C .

1. THOSE who first observed a relationship between our arts and
our bodily senses were correct, I think, in remarking on the power of dis-
crimination they both have. Through that power, equally in each case, we
are by nature able to recognize opposites, for the power is common to
them both. But they differ in the end for which they use the distinctions
they draw. Our senses are as ready to perceive black as white, bitter as
sweet, or soft and yielding things as hard and rough ones, for their function is to receive impressions from everything with which they come in
contact and convey each impression as they feel it to the mind. But the
arts exist to select by reason and accept just what is congenial to them,
and to avoid and reject what is alien. The first class of objects they study
carefully for their own sake, the second incidentally, so as to guard against
them. Thus the art of healing incidentally studies the character of disease
and the art of music discord, in order to produce their opposites. And the
highest arts of all—self-control, justice, and wisdom, which decide not
only what is honorable, righteous, and useful, but also what is hurtful,
shameful, and wrong—do not recommend an innocence which prides itself on inexperience of evil, but think it folly to be ignorant of what it
much behooves all men who would live rightly to know. So the ancient
Spartans at their feasts used to compel their helots to drink heavily of
unmixed wine, and then would bring them into the dining halls to show
their young men what drunkenness was like.

I do not think that the demoralization of some men for the instruction
of others is either humane or politically expedient, yet, since there are men
who have led ruthless lives and through sheer power and mighty deeds

have become famous in wickedness, I may perhaps without harm include
a pair or two of them in my biographies—not, by Zeus, to amuse and
entertain my readers by putting variety into my narrative, but to be like
Ismenias the Theban, who would present to his pupils both good and bad
flute players and say, "You must play like this," and again, "You must
not play like this." Antigenidas too thought that the young would more
enjoy listening to good flute players if they first had experience of listening
to bad. So I believe we shall be more interested to watch and imitate the
better lives if we are not without some record of ignoble and inglorious
ones. This book, then, will contain the life of Demetrius, the city-besieger,
and of Antony, the high commander, men who bear signal witness to the
truth of Plato's words [1] that great natures produce great vices as well as
great virtues. Both alike were passionate lovers, hard drinkers, able soldiers, free-handed, extravagant, and haughty. Their fortunes were likewise similar. Not only throughout their lives did they win great successes
and meet great failures, achieve many conquests, and lose as much again,
fall crashing unexpectedly, and unexpectedly rise once more, but in death
they were alike—one a captive in the hands of his enemies, the other on
the edge of the same disaster.

2.   Antigonus [2] had two sons by Stratonice, daughter of Corrhagus, one
of whom he named Demetrius, after his brother, and the other Philip,
after his father. This is what most historians say, though some assert that
Demetrius was not the son but the nephew of Antigonus. His own father
died, they declare, when Demetrius was very young, whereupon his
mother at once married Antigonus, and he was commonly regarded as
Antigonus' son. Philip was a few years younger than he, but he died.

   Demetrius grew up to be a tall man, though not so tall as his father.

---

[1] It is impossible to say what passage Plutarch refers to here.

[2] Antigonus (c.382–301 B.C.), son of Philip, a Macedonian noble, was one of Alexander's strong generals, whom he made satrap of Phrygia and who helped hold all
Asia Minor for Alexander until the latter's death. His friend Antipater, who then represented Alexander's empire in Greece and Macedonia, put Antigonus at the head of the
army for Asia, where he showed his abilities by setting up a strong government and
defeating rebels and upstarts. For eighteen years he ruled a considerable part of Alexander's Eastern empire, assuming the title of king in 306. But at length Ptolemy in
Egypt, Cassander, Antipater's son, in Macedonia, and Seleucus in Babylonia united to
crush him, and at the battle of Ipsus in Phrygia he was defeated and killed. See below,
ch. 29.

His face was of such amazing and extraordinary beauty that no sculptor or painter ever did it justice. There was grace in it and power and majesty and charm, and blended with the fire of youth a certain heroic look and royal dignity, hard to portray. So too his nature and disposition were such as to make men both dread and love him. For he was the most engaging of companions and most fastidious of princes during the times he spent drinking and living luxuriously; on the other hand, when it came to action, he was most wholehearted and energetic in his persistence and vigor. Above all other gods he strove to imitate Dionysus, since he was both terrible in war and, when war was over, delightfully ready to turn peace into joy and happiness.

3. Demetrius was exceptionally devoted to his father, and by his care for his mother showed that the honor he paid Antigonus came from true affection, not from a wish to cater to his father's power. Once when Antigonus was occupied with an embassy, Demetrius came in from hunting. He went up to his father, kissed him, and then, just as he was, still carrying his spears, sat down beside him. And when the ambassadors had received their answers and were about to depart, Antigonus said in a loud voice, "And, gentlemen, take this report home about us, that this is the way we live with one another," as if he thought his harmony with his son and trust in him were a strong proof of the strength of his monarchy. So completely isolating a thing is kingship and so beset by distrust and malice that this oldest and greatest of Alexander's successors exulted in the fact that he was not afraid of his son, but let him come near him with a spear in his hand. But his house was, so to speak, the only one that for generations went unpolluted by crimes of that kind; or rather, Philip [3] was the only one of Antigonus' descendants to kill his son: almost all the other dynasties record numerous murders of sons and mothers and wives. As for the murder of brothers, like the axioms of geometricians, that came to be accepted as a common rule for kings to protect their own safety.

4. The following instance may be cited to show that in the beginning Demetrius was by nature humane and good to his friends. Mithridates,

---

[3] The reference is to Philip V, king of Macedonia 221–179 B.C., who had his son put to death on a charge of treasonable relations with the Romans, with whom he was struggling during the greater part of his reign.

son of Ariobarzanes, was a companion of his, a comrade of the same age. He was also one of Antigonus' attendants, and neither was nor was supposed to be disloyal. But in consequence of a dream, Antigonus became suspicious of him. For Antigonus dreamed that he was walking through a fine large field, sowing it with gold dust. At first a golden crop sprang up, but soon afterwards he returned that way again and saw nothing but stubble. In his annoyance and disappointment, he heard some men saying that Mithridates had reaped the golden harvest and had then departed for the Black Sea. Antigonus was upset by his dream and having sworn his son to secrecy, told him of it, adding that he had made up his mind to put the fellow out of the way for good and all. At hearing this Demetrius was deeply grieved, but when Mithridates came as usual to spend a while with him, he dared not, because of his oath, breathe a word to him or warn him by voice of his danger. However, little by little, he drew him away from his friends and when they were alone together, before Mithridates' eyes he traced on the ground with the spike on the end of his spear, "Fly, Mithridates!" Mithridates understood, and escaped that very night to Cappadocia. And fate soon fulfilled for Antigonus the vision he had had, for Mithridates gained possession of a wide and handsome territory and founded the line of kings of Pontus, which, in its eighth generation was overthrown by the Romans.[4] This story illustrates Demetrius' natural disposition towards generosity and justice.

5. But even as the elements in nature, according to Empedocles,[5] are driven by love and strife to clash and fight with one another, especially those elements which touch or are close together, so all the successors of Alexander were continually at war, and those who were near neighbors in activity and location were the more open and heated enemies. And thus it was then between Antigonus and Ptolemy.[6]

---

4 A Roman army under Pompey, in 63 B.C., overthrew Mithridates VI and broke up his kingdom, which at that time took in far more than Pontus. See above, *Caesar,* n. 78.
5 Empedocles (c.493–c.433 B.C.), the famous Sicilian philosopher and poet, was the first Greek to propose a pluralistic theory of reality. According to him, the universe consisted of eternal material elements forever being driven together and forced apart by the two forces of Love and Strife. His theories led the way to the atomic system of Democritus and Epicurus.
6 Alexander's general Ptolemy, who obtained Egypt as his province at Alexander's death, founded the Ptolemaic dynasty there.

Antigonus himself was busy in Phrygia, but hearing that Ptolemy had crossed by way of Cyprus and was plundering Syria and luring and compelling the cities to join him, he sent his son Demetrius to oppose him. Demetrius, who was but twenty-two years old, had never before had complete charge of a campaign where great forces were involved. Being young and untried and pitted against a warrior trained in the school of Alexander, who had waged many hard wars alone, he was beaten and defeated near the city of Gaza, with a loss of five thousand killed and eight thousand taken prisoners.[7] He lost even his tent and his funds and in general all his personal equipment. These articles, together with his friends, were sent back to him by Ptolemy, with a kind and courteous message to the effect that they need not fight for everything at once but simply for glory and empire.

On receiving such consideration, Demetrius prayed the gods that he might not be long in Ptolemy's debt for it, but might soon repay him in like coin. And he took his defeat not like a boy, foiled at the outset of his enterprise, but like a sober general, experienced in the changes of fortune. He set to work collecting more soldiers and getting ready more arms, keeping meanwhile a firm hold over the cities and exercising his new troops.

6. When Antigonus heard of the battle he remarked that Ptolemy had beaten beardless boys but was now to fight with men. However, in order not to humiliate or crush his son's spirit, he acceded to his request to be allowed to fight again by himself, and let him do it. And not long afterward Cilles, a general of Ptolemy, appeared with a huge force for the purpose of chasing Demetrius quite out of Syria, contemptuous of him for his earlier defeat. But Demetrius fell on him suddenly, threw his army into a panic, captured his camp with the general in it, took seven thousand soldiers prisoner, and seized a vast quantity of loot. He was delighted at his victory, not for the wealth he would keep but for what he would give back, and rejoiced not so much over the riches and glory his success had brought him as over his repayment of Ptolemy's benevolence and the favor he had done him.

He did not, however, do this on his own responsibility, but wrote first to his father. Since he gave him permission and told him to dispose of

---

7 The battle of Gaza took place in the spring of 312 B.C.

everything as he chose, he gave lavish presents also to Cilles and his friends and sent them back to Ptolemy. By this defeat Ptolemy was forced out of Syria, and Antigonus was brought down from Celaenae, delighted at the victory and eager to see his son.

7. Thereafter Demetrius was sent to subdue the so-called Nabataean Arabs,[8] and ran into dangerous regions with no water. By his coolness and courage he amazed the barbarians, took a mass of booty from them as well as seven hundred camels, and then returned.

Then Seleucus,[9] who had earlier been driven out of Babylonia by Antigonus and had later retaken the kingdom by his own strength and was still in possession of it, set off in force to reduce the tribes bordering on India and the provinces around Mount Caucasus. Thereat Demetrius, hoping to find Mesopotamia undefended, suddenly crossed the Euphrates, took Babylonia by surprise, drove Seleucus' garrison out of one of its two fortresses and after subduing it thoroughly planted seven thousand of his own troops there. He told his men to appropriate for their use or to carry off everything in the country they could take or drive away, and then returned to the coast. Actually he left the authority of Seleucus more firmly established there than before, for by plundering the country he seemed to be admitting that it belonged no longer to him or to his father. As Ptolemy, however, was now besieging Halicarnassus,[10] he went promptly to that city's aid and saved it.

8. He won great glory by this gallant action and he with his father next conceived the grand idea of liberating the whole of Greece, which had been enslaved by Cassander [11] and Ptolemy. None of the kings ever waged

---

[8] The Nabataean Arabs inhabited the northwest corner of the Arabian peninsula, running back from the Red Sea.

[9] Seleucus I (c.358–280 B.C.) one of Alexander's officers and companions, on Alexander's death obtained the satrapy of Babylonia. After having lost his province to Antigonus and then regained it, he conquered Media and built up a territory of his own, which he expanded toward the west after the death of Antigonus. He built the city of Antioch and founded the dynasty of enlightened Seleucid Hellenistic kings who ruled a great part of Alexander's Asiatic empire until the warlike Parthians took over the lands east of the Euphrates and the Romans under Pompey annexed Syria.

[10] Halicarnassus, on the southwestern coast of Asia Minor, was a long march from Babylonia.

[11] On Cassander, son of Antipater, see above, *Demosthenes,* n. 22.

a more just or honorable war than this, in which Antigonus and his son spent on the Greeks, for their renown and honor, the wealth they had collected while subjugating barbarians. They decided to go first with their fleet to Athens. One of Antigonus' friends said to him that if they took that city, they must keep hold of it themselves, because it was the gangway into Greece. Antigonus rejected this suggestion, saying that the sound and unshakable gangway into a country was the good will of its people; and that Athens, as the watch-tower of the world, would blaze out the glory of their deeds to all mankind.

Demetrius then set sail for Athens with five thousand talents of silver and a fleet of two hundred and fifty vessels. Demetrius of Phalerum was then in charge of the city for Cassander, and a garrison had been placed in Munychia.[12] By good luck and good management Demetrius appeared off the Piraeus on the twenty-sixth day of Thargelion,[13] without anyone being aware of his approach. And when his ships were sighted near by, everyone thought they were Ptolemy's and prepared to welcome them. But at length the officers in command realized their mistake and began taking measures of protection and all was in confusion, as is natural when men are compelled to defend themselves against enemies unexpectedly descending on them. For Demetrius had found the entrances to the harbors open and sailed straight in and now could be seen by all signaling from his ship a request for quiet and silence. When this had been brought about, he bade a herald beside him proclaim that his father had sent him thither in an auspicious hour to set the Athenians free, drive out the Macedonian garrison, and restore to them their laws and the government of their fathers.

9.   On hearing this the majority of the people instantly threw down their shields and with shouts and applause called on Demetrius to come ashore, hailing him as savior and benefactor. The Phalerian's party too thought they must accept this new potentate, even though he might have no intention of fulfilling his promises. They therefore sent deputies to entreat for them. Demetrius met them pleasantly and sent back with them

12 Munychia was the name of a steep hill to the east of the Athenian harbor of Piraeus, on which a citadel had been built. After Alexander's death the Macedonian rulers of Greece had kept a garrison there.

13 The month of Thargelion ran from about May 15 to June 15. The year was 307 B.C.

one of his father's friends, Aristodemus of Miletus. Then after the change of government, the Phalerian Demetrius was more afraid of the Athenian citizens than of the enemy, and Demetrius was considerate of him and out of respect for his courage and good reputation had him conveyed, as he wished, in safety to Thebes. For himself, Demetrius declared that, eager as he was to view the city, he would not do so until he had liberated it entirely by expelling the Macedonian garrison. Meanwhile he surrounded Munychia with a trench and a rampart, and then sailed to attack Megara, which had also been garrisoned by Cassander.

But on hearing that Cratesipolis, who had been a wife of Alexander, son of Polyperchon, and was a celebrated beauty, was staying at Patrae,[14] and would not be displeased to see him, he left his army at Megara and went off with a few light-armed followers. On arrival he left their company and pitched his tent some distance away, so that the lady might not be seen when she came to visit him. But some of the enemy discovered it and swooped suddenly down on him, and he in terror snatched up a little cloak and took to his heels and escaped, barely missing ignominious capture as a result of his reckless behavior.

However, Megara was taken, and the soldiers were starting to sack the city, when the Athenians vigorously interceded for it and saved it. Demetrius expelled the garrison and freed the town. While doing this he remembered the philosopher Stilpo,[15] who was famed as one man who had chosen the life of tranquillity. So he sent for him and asked him if anyone had stolen anything from him. "No one has," replied Stilpo; "I saw no one taking away knowledge." However, almost all the slaves were stolen, so when Demetrius finally, on his departure, tried once more to establish friendly terms with the philosopher and said, "I am leaving your city free, Stilpo," "Quite true," he answered, "for you have left us not a single slave."

10. Demetrius now returned to Munychia, encamped before it, annihilated the garrison, and demolished the fort. And then, at the welcoming summons of the Athenians, he took the road into the upper city and as-

---

14 Patrae, the modern Patras, lay across the Peloponnesus from Megara, near the mouth of the Corinthian gulf.

15 Stilpo (c.380–c.300 B.C.) was head of a popular school of philosophy at Megara, where much was made of the teachings of Diogenes the Cynic, especially of his doctrine of detachment from earthly things.

sembling the people there, restored to them the government of their fathers. He promised too that his father would send them a hundred and fifty thousand bushels of grain and a supply of ship timber, enough for a hundred triremes. It was fourteen years since the Athenians had lost their democratic constitution.[16] In the interval since the Lamian war and the battle of Crannon the government had been called an oligarchy, but prac tically it was a monarchy under the domination of the Phalerian.

But after Demetrius had shown himself so splendidly generous in his benefactions, the Athenians made him unpopular and obnoxious by voting him the most extravagant honors. They were the first to address Antigonus and Demetrius as kings, a title which they had always scrupled to use and which was by that time the one distinctive mark of royalty still left to the descendants of Philip and Alexander. Other men, it seemed, should not touch or share it. The Athenians too were the only people to call Antigonus and Demetrius Savior Gods. They even put an end to their own ancient method of naming each year after an archon, and instead elected annually a priest of the Savior Gods and set his name at the head of decrees and contracts. They also voted to have images of Antigonus and Demetrius woven into the sacred robe, along with the images of other gods.[17] They consecrated the spot where Demetrius first stepped down from his chariot and built an altar on it which they called the altar of Demetrius the Descender. They also added two to the number of their tribes, naming them Demetrias and Antigonis, and raised the number of the senators from five to six hundred, because each tribe had fifty senators.

11. But the most fantastic idea of Stratocles [18]—for it was he who in· vented these ingenious and excessive forms of flattery—was his motion that all delegations sent by decree at public expense to Antigonus or De metrius should be called not ambassadors but sacred envoys, like the men

16 The end of Athenian democracy was reckoned as coincident with the escape of Antipater from the town of Lamia, where the Greek rebels had been besieging him, and his defeat of their forces at the battle of Crannon, 323–322 B.C. See above, *Demosthenes,* n. 47.

17 A sacred robe was carried in solemn procession at the Panathenaic festival every fifth year, and offered to the goddess Athene on the Acropolis. In it were woven scenes from the stories of her mighty deeds.

18 Stratocles had been one of Demosthenes' opponents at the trial of Harpalus. See *Demosthenes,* ch. 25. He now became an obsequious devotee of Demetrius.

who in the name of the cities take the ancient sacrifices to Delphi and to
Olympia during the great Hellenic festivals. In his other behavior too
Stratocles acted with brazen effrontery. He lived an unscrupulous life and
seemed to be copying the vulgar ribaldry of old Cleon [19] in bandying words
with the people. He had taken and kept a mistress named Phylacion, and
one day, when she had bought in the market some brains and necks for
dinner, he said, "Why, you have bought us just such things as we politicians play ball with!"

At the time of the Athenian defeat in the sea-fight off Amorgus,[20] before the reporters of the news reached the city, he set a garland on his head
and drove through the Ceramicus [21] announcing that Athens had been
victorious. He then moved a sacrifice for good tidings, and had a public
distribution of meat among the tribes. Shortly after, when the men arrived
bringing back their scattered ships from the battle and the people angrily
turned on him, he faced their clamor coolly. "Well," he said, "how has it
hurt you, if for two days you have been happy?" Such was the imperti-
nence of Stratocles.

12.   But there were other things, "hotter even than fire," as Aristophanes
says.[22] Another man went beyond Stratocles in servility by moving that
whenever Demetrius visited Athens, they should receive him with the
same rites of welcome they would pay to Demeter or Dionysus, and should
give to the citizen who outdid the rest in the beauty and costliness of his
reception money from the public treasury for an offering. And, finally,
they gave the name Demetrion to the month Munychion, and the name
Demetrias to the last day of a month, "the old and the new," and changed
the name of the festival of the Dionysia to Demetria.

At most of these changes there were signs of the gods' displeasure. The

---

[19] Cleon, a fifth century Athenian politician, succeeded Pericles as leader of the people's
party. See above, *Pericles,* n. 67.

[20] In 322 B.C., the year after Alexander's death, when the Athenians were hoping to
throw off the Macedonian yoke, their fleet was defeated by the fleet of Antipater off
Amorgus, an island in the south Aegean Sea.

[21] The Ceramicus, or potters' quarter, was an area on the northwest of Athens which
included land both within and without the city walls, where in early times the potters
had settled, attracted by its excellent clay soil and water supply. The agora, or market
place, lay within the Ceramicus.

[22] *Knights,* 382.

sacred robe, in which the Athenians had voted to have the figures of Demetrius and Antigonus woven beside those of Zeus and Athene, was torn by a violent gust of wind as it was being borne in procession through the Ceramicus; and all around the altars to them the ground sprouted masses of hemlock,[23] although in much of the country it will not grow at all. On the day of the festival of the Dionysia the procession had to be given up on account of the unseasonably icy weather. A severe frost blasted with cold not only every vine and fig tree but even most of the young grain in the blade. Hence Philippides, an enemy of Stratocles, put these lines on him into a comedy:

> "On his account the frost did blast our vines,
> For his irreverence the robe was rent,
> Because he gave gods' honors unto men.
> 'Tis this destroys a people, not a comedy."

Philippides was a friend of King Lysimachus,[24] who for his sake conferred many benefits on the Athenians. Lysimachus thought it a happy omen to meet or catch a glimpse of Philippides before undertaking anything or starting on a campaign. In general too, Philippides was popular because of his character, for he was no meddler and affected none of a courtier's officious ways. Once Lysimachus, meaning to show his friendship, said to him, "Philippides, what of my possessions may I share with you?" "Anything, O King," replied Philippides, "except your secrets." This man I deliberately contrast with Stratocles, the man of the stage with the man of the rostrum.

13. But the most extraordinary and preposterous honor suggested for Demetrius was proposed by Dromoclides of Sphettus, when the dedication of some shields at Delphi was being discussed. He moved that they should procure an oracle from Demetrius! I will set down the very words of the decree, which ran as follows: "May fortune be kind.[25] It is decreed by the people that a man be elected by the people from the Athenians to go

---

[23] To a Greek the hemlock meant a poisonous plant, from the juice of which was made a lethal drink administered to criminals under sentence of death.

[24] Lysimachus, another of Alexander's companions in Asia, succeeded to a province made up of Thrace and northwest Asia Minor. Later he combined with Seleucus to defeat Antigonus, and eventually took Macedonia and Thessaly away from Demetrius.

[25] These first words were a formula, usually placed at the head of state documents.

to the Savior, and after sacrificing and obtaining good omens ask the Savior how the people may most reverently and honorably and speedily bring about the restoration of their offerings to their places. And whatever response he gives, the people will do as he directs." With this travesty of adoration they eventually wrecked Demetrius' reason, which was at no time over strong.

14. While he was still living on at Athens he married Eurydice, a widow and a descendant of old Miltiades.[26] She had been the wife of Ophelas, the ruler of Cyrene, and after his death had returned to Athens. The Athenians took this marriage as a mark of favor and honor to their city. Demetrius, however, was rather free with his marriages and had many wives at once. His greatest respect and honor he gave to Phila, because she was both the daughter of Antipater and had been the wife of Craterus,[27] the one of all the successors of Alexander who had left the most good will behind him among the Macedonians. While still very young, it seems, Demetrius had been persuaded by his father to marry this woman, though she was not his age, but older. And when he expressed some unwillingness, his father, they say, whispered in his ear Euripides' line,

"Where profit lies, there one should wed, be it natural or not,"

substituting cleverly "one should wed" for the original form "one should serve." [28] So superficial, however, was any respect which Demetrius paid to Phila or to his other wives that he felt no restraint about keeping great numbers of courtesans and as many free women. As regards addiction to this sort of pleasure, he had the worst reputation of any king of his time.

15. His father now summoned him to fight Ptolemy and take Cyprus.[29] He had to obey, but was reluctant to drop the war for the liberty of Greece, which was a nobler and more illustrious struggle. So first he sent to

---

[26] Miltiades (c.550–489 B.C.) was the famous hero general who won the battle of Marathon.

[27] Craterus, the most capable, probably, of all Alexander's generals, had been appointed by him in 324 B.C. to conduct home the Macedonian veterans and to take Antipater's place as regent of Macedonia and Greece. He was killed three years later in one of the first battles over the division of Alexander's empire.

[28] The line referred to is from some lost play by Euripides.

[29] Demetrius' defeat of Ptolemy of Egypt and conquest of the important island of Cyprus took place in 306 B.C.

Cleonides, Ptolemy's general, who commanded garrisons at Sicyon and Corinth, offering him money to let those cities go free. But Cleonides refused and Demetrius then hurriedly set sail, and picking up more forces proceeded to Cyprus. There he fought a battle with Menelaus, Ptolemy's brother, and quickly defeated him. Then Ptolemy himself arrived with a great land army and fleet and there followed an exchange of threats and braggadocio, Ptolemy ordering Demetrius to sail off before his host assembled and overwhelmed him, Demetrius declaring he would let Ptolemy go, provided he agreed to withdraw his garrison from Sicyon and Corinth. And not only the combatants themselves but other magnates waited in great expectancy for the uncertain outcome of the impending conflict, feeling that not only Cyprus and Syria but world mastery would pass at once to the victor.

16. Ptolemy now advanced with a hundred and fifty ships, sending word to Menelaus to put out from Salamis with sixty ships and when the battle was hottest, attack the fleet of Demetrius from behind, so cutting them off and throwing them into disorder. Demetrius sent only ten ships to oppose these sixty, for the mouth of their harbor was so narrow that a small number could close it. He himself got his land force into line, spreading it out along the promontories which jutted into the sea, and then put out with a hundred and eighty ships. He attacked with great energy and violence, and completely routed Ptolemy. When all was lost Ptolemy fled in haste with only eight ships, for that few were all that were left of his whole fleet. Of the rest some were wrecked in the sea battle, and seventy were captured with their crews. As for the crowds of servants, friends, and women, which were in transports near by, and the arms, money, and military engines which had belonged to Ptolemy, absolutely not one escaped Demetrius. He took everything and had them conveyed to his camp.

Among the prisoners was the celebrated Lamia, once much sought after as an artist, for she was considered an admirable flute player, and later a brilliant courtesan. By now her beauty was fading and Demetrius was much younger than she, yet she so captivated and enthralled him by her charm that while other women yearned for love of him, he was her lover only. After this sea battle, Menelaus held out no longer but surrendered Salamis to Demetrius, with his ships and his land army of twelve hundred cavalry and twelve thousand heavy infantry.

17. This noble victory Demetrius made still nobler by his generosity and humanity. He gave the enemy's dead a handsome burial and let all his prisoners go free. He sent a present to the Athenians of twelve hundred suits of armor from the spoils. To his father, as a messenger to announce his victory, he sent Aristodemus of Miletus. Of all his courtiers this man was the boldest flatterer, and on this occasion, it appears, he planned to perpetrate a piece of flattery greater than any he had achieved before. After the voyage from Cyprus, he did not allow his ship to touch land, but gave orders to the men to cast anchor and all stay quietly on board, while he himself got into a small boat, rowed ashore alone, and walked up to Antigonus' palace. Antigonus was in suspense, waiting to hear of the battle, and feeling as men naturally feel in a struggle for such important stakes. And now when he heard that Aristodemus had come, he was more nervous than ever and had difficulty keeping himself in his palace. He sent servants and friends one after another to find out from Aristodemus what had happened. But Aristodemus answered not a word to any of them, and walked on with a grave face, in total silence. Utterly terrified and unable to bear it any longer, Antigonus met Aristodemus at the door. The latter by now was surrounded by a great crowd of people rushing to the palace. And as he came up to it, he stretched out his hand and called in a loud voice, "Hail, King Antigonus! We have defeated Ptolemy in a sea battle and are masters of Cyprus, and have taken sixteen thousand, eight hundred soldiers as prisoners!" To which Antigonus answered, "Hail to you also, by Zeus! But for thus torturing us you shall be punished, and wait long before getting your reward for the good news."

18. Thereafter, for the first time, the people addressed Antigonus and Demetrius as kings. The friends of Antigonus crowned him at once, and he sent a diadem to his son with a letter in which he addressed him as king. The Egyptians on hearing of it, proclaimed Ptolemy king too, that they might not seem to be dispirited by their defeat. And so out of rivalry the practice spread to the other successors of Alexander. For Lysimachus then began wearing a diadem, and Seleucus as well, in the presence of Greeks. For among the barbarians Seleucus had already borne himself as a king. Cassander, however, although the others wrote to him and spoke of him as king, went on writing his letters simply in his own name, as he used to doing.

The assumption of this title resulted in more than merely an additional name or change of style. It stirred up thoughts in its wearers, gave them exalted ideas, and made them haughty and pompous in their ways of living and intercourse with other people, even as tragic actors suit their gait, voice, attitude at table, and manner of speech to the costume they are wearing. The kings became more severe too in their administration of justice, discarding the efforts to conceal their power which had previously made them more lenient and easygoing with their subjects. So great was the influence of a flatterer's single word, and so great the change it brought throughout the world!

19. Elated by the success of Demetrius at Cyprus, Antigonus undertook immediately a further campaign against Ptolemy. He himself led the army on land, while Demetrius, with a large fleet, accompanied him on the sea. But how this expedition was to turn out Medius, a friend of Antigonus, saw in a dream. He thought that Antigonus with all his army was running a race down a track and back again. At first he ran stoutly and fast, but then, little by little, his strength gave out, and at last, after rounding the turn, he grew so weak and out of breath that he found it hard to finish. And indeed Antigonus on land met with many difficulties, and Demetrius was imperiled by a terrible storm at sea and then cast ashore in a rocky region without harbors. Thus he lost many ships and Antigonus returned without achieving anything.

He was now close to eighty years of age, and his size and weight of body, even more than his age, made him unfit for further campaigning. He accordingly made a habit of relying on his son, who by dint of his good fortune and experience was now managing successfully the most important affairs, and whose luxuries and extravagances and orgies did not worry him. For though in peace time Demetrius lived riotously, spending his time on pleasures without restraint or measure, when war came, he was as sober as a man more naturally cautious.

They say that once, during the time that he was notoriously under Lamia's influence, on his coming home from a journey and kissing his father, Antigonus said laughing, "I think, my son, you are kissing Lamia." Another time, when Demetrius had spent several days in a debauch, he gave as excuse that he had been disabled by a flux. "So I heard," said Antigonus. "But was it Thasian or Chian wine that flowed?" Again, being told that his son was ill, Antigonus went to see him and met a certain beauty at the door. But he went in, sat down by his son's bed, and took his hand. "The fever," said Demetrius, "has just left me." "Of course, my boy," said Antigonus. "I met it just now going out the door." Thus gently did he bear with Demetrius' faults because of his accomplishments in many fields.

The Scythians have a custom of twanging their bowstrings while they are drinking and carousing, as though calling to their valor even while it is relaxed in pleasure. But Demetrius would give himself up whole heartedly at one time to pleasure and at another to seriousness, keeping the one quite distinct from the other. He was none the less an expert in preparations for war.

20.   Men considered him, in fact, as a general even more gifted in equipping an army than in handling one. He wanted always an abundance of everything, in case of need, and he had never too much of constructing great ships and siege engines, or of gazing delightedly at them. He was naturally talented and fond of planning, and did not waste his ability on useless toys or pastimes, like other kings who play on the flute or paint or work in metal. Aeropus, the Macedonian, for example, whenever he had leisure, would spend it making small tables and stands for lamps. And Attalus Philometor cultivated poisonous herbs, not only henbane and hellebore, but also hemlock and aconite and dorycnium. He would sow and plant them himself in the royal gardens, and make a business of knowing their juices and fruits and of gathering them in their season. The kings of Parthia prided themselves on whetting and sharpening the points of their javelins with their own hands.

When Demetrius turned craftsman, it was as a king should, on a magnificent scale. His creations combined loftiness of conception and design with excellent ingenuity, so that they looked worthy not only of being invented and financed by a king but of being his handiwork. They astonished even his friends by their size, and fascinated even his enemies by their beauty. And this is more truth than imagination. His enemies stood along the shore marveling at his fifteen and sixteen-banked galleys as they sailed by, and his "city-takers" were a spectacle to the very men he was besieging, as their conduct made evident. Lysimachus, who was Demetrius' bitterest enemy among the kings and had taken sides with the Cilicians when he was besieging Soli, sent and asked him to show him his engines of war and his ships out at sea. When Demetrius had shown them to him, he went away full of admiration. The Rhodians too, after standing a long siege by him, when finally they came to terms, asked for some of his siege engines that they might keep them as a memento of his power and of their own courage.

21. Demetrius went to war with the Rhodians [30] because they were allies of Ptolemy, and brought up against their walls his largest city-taker. It had a square base, each side measuring forty-eight cubits at the bottom. It was sixty cubits in height, with its upper sides contracting and narrower than the base. Inside it was walled off into many storeys and chambers, with windows opening out of each storey on the side towards the enemy, through which were hurled missiles of all kinds, for it was manned by soldiers used to every species of fighting. It neither shook nor tipped when it was moved but upright on its base rolled steadily onward, with a great rumbling and momentum that filled the minds of watchers with both terror and pleasure. For Demetrius' own use in this war two iron coats of mail were brought from Cyprus which weighed only forty pounds each. Their maker Zoilus, in order to show their strength and power of resistance, ordered a dart from a catapult shot at one of them from a distance of only twenty paces. Where it struck, the iron remained unbroken, showing only a slight scratch, such as might be made by an engraver. This coat Demetrius himself wore. The other was worn by Alcimus of Epirus, the stoutest and best fighter of the men with him. He had been the only one with armor that weighed a hundred pounds. The others had armor weighing but fifty pounds. He fell fighting near the theater at Rhodes.

22. The Rhodians, however, defended themselves with great spirit, and Demetrius was accomplishing nothing worth mention. Yet he went on with the war in wrath because they had seized a boat bringing him letters, bedding, and garments from his wife Phila, and, just as it was, had sent it to Ptolemy. Therein they did not follow the courteous example of the Athenians, who, when Philip was at war with them, captured some of his letter carriers and read all their letters but the one from his wife Olym-

---

[30] Demetrius' famous siege of Rhodes lasted for nearly a year, 305–304 B.C.

pias. This they did not open but sent on to him with the seal unbroken.

However, indignant as he was at their conduct, Demetrius would not stoop to retaliate, although shortly afterwards the Rhodians gave him an opportunity to do so. For it happened that Protogenes of Caunus [31] was painting a picture of Ialysus for them, and Demetrius captured the painting, almost finished, in one of the city's suburbs. The Rhodians sent a herald to beg him to spare the picture and not destroy it, to which he answered that he would burn his father's portrait before he would so splendid a work of art. It took seven years, they say, for Protogenes to finish it. Apelles tells us that when he first saw it he was so struck with wonder that his voice failed him, but at length he exclaimed, "Great was the labor and wondrous is the masterpiece!" Yet it had not, he thought, the charm through which his own paintings touched heaven. This picture, after being taken to Rome and deposited in the same place as the others, was destroyed by fire.[32]

The Rhodians continued to hold their own in war, and at length Demetrius, who wanted an excuse for putting an end to it, was induced by a delegation of Athenians to make peace on condition that the Rhodians became allies of Antigonus and Demetrius, except when they fought against Ptolemy.

23. The Athenians next called on Demetrius, for Cassander was besieging their city. So he came sailing up with three hundred and thirty ships and a large infantry force and not only drove Cassander out of Attica but pursued him in flight as far as Thermopylae and defeated him there. He then occupied Heraclea, which joined him of its own free will, and took over six thousand Macedonians, who changed to his side. On his way back he freed the Greeks south of Thermopylae, made an alliance with the Boeotians, and captured Cenchreae. He then stormed Phyle and Panactum, fortresses of Attica, which had been garrisoned by Cassander, and restored them to the Athenians.

And they, although they had already poured out and exhausted on him

---

[31] Protogenes was a well-known painter of the late fourth century. He is known to have painted portraits of Aristotle's mother and of Antigonus, among others.

[32] Cicero saw and admired the painting at Rhodes, but when Pliny the Elder wrote, in the century after Christ, it had been brought to Rome and placed in the temple of Peace. Pliny, *Natural History*, XXXV, 10, 36.

every form of adulation, once more contrived fresh, new ways to flatter him. They assigned him the rear chamber of the Parthenon for his lodging, and there he stayed and Athene was said to be receiving him as her guest, though he was a very disorderly guest and did not comport himself as behooved one in the house of a virgin. Once when his father Antigonus heard that his son Philip was stationed in a house where there were three young women, he said nothing to Philip himself but sent for his quartermaster and in Philip's presence said to him, "Listen! Please move my son out of his narrow quarters!"

24. Demetrius, who owed Athene reverence, if for no other reason, at least as his elder sister—for so he liked to have her called— [33] so polluted the Acropolis with his wanton behavior with freeborn boys and women of the city that the place seemed quite pure when he had as companions in dissipation only the well-known courtesans, Chrysis, Lamia, Demo, and Anticyra. For the city's sake it is unfair to go closely into details, but the courage and modesty that were shown by Democles should not pass unrecorded. He was still a young boy, but Demetrius had noticed his title which betokened good looks, for he was called Democles the Beautiful. He was caught by none of the many advances, gifts, and threats Demetrius made to him, and finally stayed away from the training grounds and the gymnasium, and went to a private bath house to bathe. And there Demetrius, who had been watching his chance, surprised him alone. The boy, seeing no one near and the plight he was in, pulled off the lid of the copper cauldron and sprang into the boiling water, killing himself. He suffered what he did not deserve, but he showed a spirit worthy of his country and of his own beauty.

Not so Cleaenetus, son of Cleomedon, who managed to have his father let off from a fine of fifty talents by producing before the people a letter from Demetrius, thereby disgracing himself and creating disturbance in the city. The people released Cleomedon from his fine but passed a decree that no citizen should bring a letter from Demetrius before them. But when Demetrius heard of this he resented it strongly, and the people were frightened again and not only revoked their decree, but put to death some of those who had proposed and advocated it, and banished others.

[33] As a Savior God, Demetrius could regard himself as a younger brother of the goddess Athene.

In addition, they voted that the people of Athens had resolved that whatever was the command of King Demetrius would be both righteous towards the gods and just towards men. And when one of the nobler citizens remarked that Stratocles was mad to make such a motion, Demochares of Leuconoe said, "He would certainly be mad, if he were not mad," for Stratocles made a great fortune out of his flatteries. Demochares was accused in court for his remark and sent into exile. So it went with the Athenians who had thought that after they were rid of the Macedonian garrison they would have their freedom.

25. Demetrius next went down to the Peloponnesus [34] where he met with no resistance, for his enemies deserted their cities and fled before him. He made allies of so-called Acte and of Arcadia, all but Mantinea, and he liberated Argos, Sicyon, and Corinth by giving their Macedonian garrisons a hundred talents to leave. At Argos, where the festival of Hera was going on, he acted as president of the games and attended the public assemblies of all the Greeks. He married there too Deidamia, daughter of Aeacides, king of the Molossians, and sister of Pyrrhus.[35] He told the people of Sicyon that they had their city in a wrong place for a city, and persuaded them to move to where they now live. And with the site he changed the name of the city, which he called Demetrias instead of Sicyon. At a general congress held on the Corinthian Isthmus, where crowds of men came together, he was proclaimed chief commander of Greece, as Philip and Alexander had been before him.

However, he considered himself much superior to either of them, elated as he was by his constant good fortune and control over events. Admittedly Alexander never denied any other king's right to the royal title, nor did he proclaim himself king of kings, even while he was bestowing on many a man the name and state of king. But Demetrius would jeer and laugh at those who called anyone king save himself and his father, and at banquets he enjoyed hearing toasts drunk to Demetrius, the King, Seleucus, the Master of the Elephants, Ptolemy the Admiral, Lysimachus the Treasurer, and Agathocles of Sicily, Lord of the Isles. The other kings all laughed at the reports of his doings, except Lysimachus, who was angry

---

[34] This was in the spring of 303 B.C.

[35] Pyrrhus (319–272 B.C.), king of Epirus, was trying to Hellenize his country, and also expand its boundaries. Later he was to come into conflict with Demetrius.

that Demetrius thought him a eunuch—for it was apparently the custom to have eunuchs as treasurers. Indeed Lysimachus hated him more bitterly than anyone else did. Sneering at his passion for Lamia, he used to say that now for the first time he had seen a whore playing a part on a tragic stage.[36] But Demetrius declared that his whore was more chaste than Lysimachus' Penelope.

26. Later, as Demetrius was preparing to return to Athens, he sent on word that he wished to be initiated immediately into the mysteries, and to go through every grade from the lowest to the highest without delay. Such haste was not lawful and had never been practiced before, for the lesser mysteries were celebrated in the month of Anthesterion,[37] the great in Boedromion, and the greatest at least a year after the great. Yet when Demetrius' letter was read, only Pythodorus, the torchbearer in the mysteries, dared to oppose his wish, and he got nowhere. On Stratocles' motion the people voted to call the current month, which was Munychion, Anthesterion, and consider it such. Demetrius was then admitted to the lesser rites at Agra, after which Munychion was converted from being Anthesterion to Boedromion and Demetrius received the next grade of initiation; and then the highest grade as well. For this reason Philippides, in his scathing lines on Stratocles, wrote,

> "Who crowded a year into a single month";

and, in allusion to the lodging of Demetrius in the Parthenon,

> "Who treats the Acropolis like a wayside inn
> And brings his harlots to the Virgin's home."

27. But of all the outrageous and lawless performances of Demetrius at this time in the city, not one, they say, offended the Athenians so much as his ordering them to raise in haste two hundred and fifty talents for him, and then, when by harsh and stringent exactions they had collected the money and he saw it all together, his commanding them to give it to

---

[36] Disreputable or vulgar persons never figured in Greek tragedy. They were material kept strictly for the comic stage.

[37] Anthesterion was the Attic eighth month, approximately February 15 to March 15, Boedromion the third month, from mid-September to mid-October, Munychion the tenth, from mid-April to mid-May.

Lamia and the courtesans with her to buy soap. The shame was more galling to the people than the cost and his words than what he did. Some, however, say that it was the Thessalians, not the Athenians, whom he treated in this way.

Besides all this, Lamia herself once on her own account wrung money from many citizens, when she was preparing a dinner for the king. The dinner was so famous for its costliness that Lynceus of Samos wrote a description of it. So too a comic poet cleverly called Lamia a real "city-taker." [38] And Demochares of Soli called Demetrius "the Myth" because he had a Lamia.[39] Not only Demetrius' wives but his friends as well were made jealous and resentful of Lamia by the wealth and devotion he showered on her. Some of them once went on an embassy from him to Lysimachus, and he in a moment of leisure showed them some deep scars on his thighs and shoulders made by a lion's claws, and told them about his fight with the beast when King Alexander put him in the same cage. And they laughed and said that their king too bore on his neck the marks of a terrible beast, a Lamia.

The surprising thing was that Demetrius, who in the beginning had objected to Phila because of her age, kept on so long being captivated by Lamia and in love with her, though she was now well past her prime. Once when she was playing the flute at dinner, Demetrius asked Demo, whom they called Mania, "What do you think of her?" "An old woman, my king," she replied. Another time, when sweets were placed on the table, Demetrius said to her, "Do you see how many things Lamia sends me?" "My mother," retorted Demo, "will send you more, if you will sleep with her too." A saying of Lamia's has been recorded about the well-known judgment of Bocchoris. A certain Egyptian was enamored of the courtesan Thonis and offered her a huge sum for her favors. Then in his sleep he thought he had them and his passion cooled, whereupon Thonis sued him in court for the promised price. On hearing the case, Bocchoris ordered the man to bring into court the exact sum he had offered, in a box, and to wave it back and forth in his hand. The courtesan would have its shadow, for the appearance is a shadow of the reality. Lamia did not

---

[38] The allusion is of course to Demetrius' great machine, as described in ch. 20.
[39] The Lamia of Greek myth was a monster who fed on human flesh.

think this judgment fair, because the courtesan's desire for money was not satisfied by its shadow, as the young man's passion was by his dream.

28. But the fortunes and deeds of the man whose story we are telling carry us back as it were from the comic to the tragic stage. For all the other kings now combined against Antigonus and united their forces to attack him. At this Demetrius took leave of Greece and joined his father,[40] whom he found beyond his years on fire for the war, and was thereby much heartened. It actually seems that if Antigonus had only made some small concessions and put some check on his excessive love of power, he might have kept his supremacy as long as he lived and left it to his son. But he was harsh and disdainful by nature, and in his speech no less truculent than in his acts. Thereby he antagonized and stirred up against himself many young and powerful men. He said that he would scatter their confederacy, like a flock of crows, with a stone and a shout.

He had under him more than seventy thousand foot, ten thousand cavalry, and seventy-five elephants, while his enemy's army numbered sixty-four thousand foot, five hundred more cavalry than he had, four hundred elephants, and a hundred and twenty chariots. As they approached each other, the character of Antigonus' expectations, though not of his resolve, seemed to alter. As a rule he was proud and exultant in time of conflict, making pompous speeches in a loud voice, and often, when the enemy was close at hand, by a jest or bit of humor showing his own confidence and his scorn of them. This time, however, he was seen to be very thoughtful and silent; he merely exhibited his son to the people and named him his successor. But what most surprised everyone was his conferring with Demetrius alone in his tent, for it was not his habit to hold secret consultations even with his son. Instead, he kept his own counsel and made his plans by himself and then gave out his orders publicly. They say that once when Demetrius was a boy, he asked his father when they would be moving, and he answered, annoyed, "Are you afraid that you will be the only one not to hear the trumpet?"

29. On this occasion the spirits of both were depressed too by sinister omens. Demetrius dreamed that Alexander appeared before him in shining armor, and asked what would be their watchword for the battle. When

---

[40] It was late in the year 302 B.C.

Demetrius replied, "Zeus and Victory," Alexander said, "Then I shall leave you and go to your foes. They will welcome me." [41] Then Antigonus, stepping out of his tent as his phalanx was forming in line, tripped and fell flat on his face and hurt himself badly. However, he rose and lifting his hands to heaven, prayed the gods to grant him either victory or else a painless death before his defeat.

When the battle began,[42] Demetrius with the largest and best squadrons of horse charged Antiochus, the son of Seleucus, and fought brilliantly until he had routed the enemy, but then pursued them with such mistaken violence and eagerness that he threw away his victory. For he was unable to turn back and rejoin his infantry because the enemy's elephants had been moved up between him and them. Seleucus saw that Demetrius' phalanx was left without cavalry to protect it and though not actually attacking it, he kept the men fearful of an assault. And then riding around them, he offered them a chance to change sides. That, in fact, is what they did. A considerable section of Antigonus' army broke away and voluntarily went over to Seleucus, while the rest fled. A crowd of his enemies now made for Antigonus and one of his attendants said to him, "My king, they are headed for you!" "Who else but me," he replied, "is their target? But Demetrius will come to my rescue." He hoped to the end for his son's appearance and kept looking about for him. Finally a shower of darts was hurled at him and he fell. The rest of his friends and followers now deserted him, and only one, Thorax of Larissa, stayed by his corpse.

30. Thus the battle was decided and the victorious kings carved up the whole realm of Antigonus and Demetrius like a vast carcass, and each took his portion, annexing it to the provinces he already had. Demetrius, with five thousand infantry and four thousand cavalry, fled, and drove straight for Ephesus. Everyone there thought that in his need for money he would not spare the temple,[43] and he himself was afraid that his soldiers might start plundering. So he went on through as quickly as possible and sailed over to Greece, setting his chief hopes now on Athens. For he had left ships there, and funds, and his wife Deidamia, and he supposed

---

[41] That is, they should have been using Alexander's old battle cry, "Alexander and Victory!"

[42] This was the battle of Ipsus in Phrygia, 301 B.C.

[43] The magnificent temple of Artemis, the patron goddess of Ephesus.

he could find no surer refuge from adversity than in the loyalty of Athens.

But as he was passing the Cyclades an embassy of Athenians met him and asked him to stay away from the city, for the people had voted to admit none of the kings, and they had sent off Deidamia with honor and a suitable escort. At this, Demetrius, who had borne his other calamities with serenity and through all the collapse of his fortunes had never been cowardly or ignoble, burst into a passion of wrath. That the Athenians should unexpectedly turn false and their seeming friendship prove in action hollow and unreal was a bitter disappointment to him. But an extravagant outlay of honors is, it seems, a very poor sign of a people's good will towards its king or ruler, for the beauty of such honors lies in the motive of those who confer them. And fear makes them untrustworthy, for the same honors may be voted by a people in fear and a people in affection. Hence wise men look not at the statues, paintings, and deifications which their people offer them but at their own deeds and achievements, and then either trust the honors as genuine or distrust them as fruits of compulsion. For many times, in the very midst of conferring honors, a people hates the greedy and arrogant receiver who takes them from unwilling givers.

31. However, Demetrius considered that he was being abominably treated. But since he could make no reprisal, he sent a mild reply to the Athenians, chiding them gently and asking to have his ships sent back to him, one of which was the vessel with thirteen banks of oars. On obtaining them, he coasted on down to the Isthmus, where he found his affairs in a bad way. For everywhere his garrisons were being driven out, and in general the country was going over to his enemies. So he left Pyrrhus in charge of Greece, and himself weighed anchor and sailed up to the Chersonese.[44] There by ravaging Lysimachus' territory he both supplied and held together his troops, who were beginning to recover their spirits and again prove themselves far from despicable. The other kings sent no help to Lysimachus, thinking him as obnoxious as Demetrius, and more to be feared because he was more powerful.

Not long afterward, Seleucus sent a request for the hand of Stratonice, the daughter of Demetrius and Phila. He already had a son, Antiochus, by Apama, the Persian, but he thought his empire would require more than one heir and he wanted the alliance with Demetrius, because he saw

---

[44] This was the Thracian Chersonese, beside the Hellespont, the site of modern Gallipoli.

that Lysimachus was taking one of Ptolemy's daughters for himself and the other for his son Agathocles. To Demetrius a marriage alliance with Seleucus was an unexpected piece of good luck and he took the girl and sailed with his entire fleet to Syria. On the way he was obliged to touch at several places and he stopped awhile in Cilicia. Pleistarchus was holding that country, which had been assigned to him by the kings after their battle with Antigonus. Now Pleistarchus was Cassander's brother and he regarded these descents of Demetrius upon his coasts as trespass on his domain and was anxious to remonstrate with Seleucus for making peace with the common enemy without the other kings. So he went up to see him.

32. But on hearing of Pleistarchus' movements, Demetrius left the coast for Quinda, where he found twelve hundred talents of its stores still remaining. He took them into his possession, got them aboard ship without interference and hurriedly put back to sea. His wife Phila now joined him, and at Rhossus [45] he met Seleucus and the two were soon holding meetings in royal style, without trickery or suspicion. First Seleucus feasted Demetrius in his tent in his camp, and in return Demetrius received Seleucus on board his thirteen-banked galley. There were entertainments and conferences and days spent together without bodyguards or arms, until finally Seleucus took Stratonice and went off in grandeur to Antioch. Demetrius then made himself master of Cilicia and sent his wife Phila to her brother Cassander, to answer any accusations made by Pleistarchus. Meanwhile Deidamia came from Greece to Demetrius, but soon after her arrival she sickened and died. Through the mediation of Seleucus, however, friendship was proclaimed between Demetrius and Ptolemy, and a marriage was arranged between Demetrius and Ptolemais, Ptolemy's daughter.

Thus far, Seleucus had behaved very handsomely. But then he asked Demetrius to give up Cilicia for a sum of money, and when he refused, angrily demanded the surrender of Tyre and Sidon. His conduct now seemed ruthless and unscrupulous, as though he, who had already acquired control of the whole vast stretch from India to the Syrian Sea, was so poor and beggarly still as to have to harry a man who was his father-in-law, and had suffered such a downfall of fortune, over two cities! He was a

---

[45] Rhossus lay probably on the northwest coast of Syria, below Antioch.

shining instance of the person warned by Plato [46] not to make his possessions more but his desires less, if he wished to be truly rich; since he who sets no bounds to his covetousness is never secure from penury and want.

33. Demetrius, however, was not daunted, but said that not even if he lost ten thousand more battles at Ipsus would he want Seleucus as a son-in-law for pay. He strengthened his cities with garrisons, and hearing that Lachares [47] had taken advantage of the internal divisions at Athens to make himself tyrant there, he thought that if he appeared before the city, he might now take it easily. He crossed the sea in safety with a large fleet, but off the coast of Attica ran into a heavy storm in which he lost most of his ships and many men with them. He himself escaped and began a war of sorts on the Athenians. But making no headway there, he sent men to collect another fleet for him, and meanwhile proceeded himself to the Peloponnesus and laid siege to Messene.

But there, during an assault on the walls, he was in peril of death, for he was struck in the face by a dart from a catapult which pierced through his jaw into his mouth. He recovered, however, and after forcing the submission of several insurgent cities, he again invaded Attica, took possession of Eleusis and Rhamnus, and laid waste the country. He captured a ship too, bound for Athens with a cargo of wheat, and hanged the merchant owner and the pilot. Thereat all other ships turned back in fright, and famine was severe in the city, which was starved for other things as well as food. A bushel of salt sold for forty drachmas, and a peck of wheat for three hundred. A short breathing space was given the Athenians by the appearance near Aegina of a hundred and fifty ships sent by Ptolemy to aid them. Then swarms of ships arrived for Demetrius from the Peloponnesus and from Cyprus, so that in all he had three hundred assembled, and Ptolemy's ships fled. At this, the tyrant Lachares abandoned the city and departed.

---

[46] The passage in Plato which Plutarch here has in mind is not known.

[47] Lachares was an Athenian general who after Demetrius' defeat at Ipsus made friends with Cassander. Seizing the opportunity offered by the disorders at Athens, he made himself tyrant, with the support of mercenary troops who had been bought with gold stripped from Athene's statue. But he was not able to hold out against the siege of the city by Demetrius and his other enemies, and in 294 B.C. fled to Boeotia.

34. Thereupon the Athenians, although they had voted death to anyone who even spoke of peace and coming to terms with Demetrius,
hastily opened their nearest gates and sent ambassadors to him, expecting
no mercy from him but driven by their destitution. Among many other
painful incidents, they say, the following had occurred. A father and
son in a state of despair were sitting in a room, when a dead mouse
fell from the ceiling and at sight of it both started up and fought with
each other for it. This was also the time, they tell us, when the philosopher Epicurus [48] kept his disciples alive on beans, which he counted out
and divided among them.

Such then was the condition of the city when Demetrius entered it
and ordered everyone to assemble in the theater. He placed a ring of
armed men around the stage structure, and surrounded the stage itself
with his bodyguards; then he himself stepped out, like the tragic actors,
through a side entrance at the rear. The Athenians were more terrified
than ever, but his first words put an end to their fears. For he refrained
from any harshness of voice or sternness of speech and merely reproached
them mildly in a friendly way and said he forgave them. He then presented them with a hundred thousand bushels of grain and appointed
to office men popular with the people. So Dromoclides, the orator, seeing
that the people in their glee were making all kinds of propositions and
were keen to do more than simply praise Demetrius through their mouth-
pieces on the rostrum, moved that the harbors of Piraeus and Munychia
be turned over to him as king. The vote was passed, and Demetrius on
his own account placed a garrison on the Museum [49] too, to keep the
people from throwing off the rein again and giving him more trouble
with his enterprises.

35. Now that he had Athens, Demetrius at once made plans to attack
Sparta. He met the King of Sparta, Archidamus, near Mantinea, defeated
and routed him in battle, and then invaded Laconia. He fought a second
engagement near Sparta itself, in which he captured five hundred men
and killed two hundred. It looked then as if he as good as had the city

---

[48] In 306 B.C. the famous philosopher Epicurus (341–270 B.C.) had moved to Athens
and set up with his friends a school of the simple life, in a garden which he bought for
the purpose.
[49] The Museum was a small hill southwest of the Acropolis, dedicated to the Muses.

in his hands, a city which up to that time had never been taken. But to no king did fortune seem to bring such great and rapid changes, and in no other man's career did she so often toss him from littleness up to greatness, from splendor down to abjectness, and from insignificance back up to the heights of power. So, they say, in his times of adversity he would quote the line of Aeschylus,[50]

"Thou kindlest me to flame; thou dost, it seems, extinguish me."

Thus now, when all seemed so auspicious for the expansion of his rule and power, Demetrius received news, first, that Lysimachus had seized all his cities in Asia, then, that Ptolemy had taken Cyprus, except for the one city of Salamis, and, further, that in his siege of Salamis he had caught Demetrius' mother and children. Yet like the woman in Archilochus,[51] Fortune,

"The crafty, in one hand bore water and in the other, fire,"

and while with these disastrous and fearful tidings she drew him off from the Spartans, a moment later she bestowed on him fresh hopes for new and wonderful achievements, as follows.

36. Cassander had died, and the eldest of his sons, Philip, after reigning a short time over the Macedonians had also died, and the surviving sons were fighting for the succession. One of them, Antipater, murdered his mother, Thessalonice, and the other, Alexander, called in Pyrrhus of Epirus and Demetrius from the Peloponnesus to help him. Pyrrhus was the first to arrive, but he cut off a large slice of Macedonia as the price of his assistance, making himself at once a formidable neighbor to Alexander. And the young man was still more afraid of Demetrius because of his reputation and renown, and as Demetrius on receipt of his letter set out with his army to come to him, he met him at Dium, greeted him cordially, but explained that the situation no longer required his presence. As a result they both grew suspicious of each other. As Demetrius was on his way to a dinner to which the young man had invited him, some one warned him of a plot brewing to assassinate him while they were drinking. Demetrius showed no concern, but delayed going for a little while

---

[50] The line is in one of the fragments of a lost play by Aeschylus.

[51] Archilochus was a seventh-century Aegean poet.

and ordered his commanders to keep their men under arms, and all his retinue of attendants and slaves, who far outnumbered Alexander's, to go with him to the hall and remain there until he rose from the table. Alarmed by these precautions, Alexander and his company did not dare to try anything, and Demetrius excused himself on the ground that his health did not permit him to drink, and left early.

The next day he prepared to start, telling Alexander that fresh troubles called him away and asking him to pardon his sudden departure, promising that he would make him a longer visit some other time. Alexander was much relieved, for he thought Demetrius was leaving the country of his own free will and not as an enemy, but he escorted him as far as Thessaly. On reaching Larissa, each again invited the other to a banquet, both plotting murder, and thus Alexander was delivered into Demetrius' hands. For he was loath to be on his guard openly, lest he should warn Demetrius to be on guard against him, so he met first the fate he was devising for another man, while he was still planning to do something to prevent the other man's escape. Since Demetrius invited him to dinner he went, but when Demetrius in the middle of dinner rose to his feet, Alexander in alarm started up also and followed on Demetrius' heels to the door. As Demetrius reached the door with his own bodyguard beside it, he said simply, "Cut down whoever follows me," and walked quietly out. And Alexander was cut down by the guard, as were those of his friends who ran to his aid. One of them, the story is, said as he lay dying that Demetrius had gotten ahead of them by one day.

37. That night was naturally one of uproar and confusion, and at daybreak the Macedonians were still in a tumult and afraid of the army of Demetrius. But when no one alarming attacked them and Demetrius sent them a message that he would like to meet them and explain what had happened, they plucked up courage and prepared to receive him in a friendly way. When he appeared, he did not need to make long speches, for the Macedonians hated Antipater, the murderer of his mother, and knew not where else to look for a better ruler. So they now proclaimed Demetrius king of the Macedonians and with him returned at once to Macedonia.[52] The Macedonians at home were not displeased by the change, for they always remembered with loathing the crimes Cassander

52 These events took place in 294 B.C.

committed after the great Alexander's death. And wherever some memory of the elder Antipater's justice still lingered, Demetrius reaped the fruit of it, for his wife Phila was Antipater's daughter, and he had a son by her, an heir to his dominion, who was already a grown lad, accompanying his father on his campaign.

38. And now that Demetrius had met with so brilliant a piece of good fortune, he had news that his mother and children had been set at liberty and that Ptolemy had given them presents and shown them honor. He heard also that his daughter who had been married to Seleucus was now the wife of Seleucus' son Antiochus,[53] with the title of Queen of the Barbarians of Upper Asia. It seems that Antiochus fell violently in love with Stratonice, who was still a girl, though she had already had a child by Seleucus. He was miserable and tried in many ways to curb his passion, until at last, blaming himself for his wicked desires, incurable sickness and folly, he resolved to find some means of putting an end to his life. Pretending an illness, he thought he would kill himself quietly, going without help and abstaining from food.

Erasistratus, his physician, had no difficulty in seeing that he was in love, though whom he loved it was harder to guess. So, wishing to find out, he spent his days continually in Antiochus' apartment, and when any of the young men or women came in, he watched his countenance closely and observed the parts and movements of the body which naturally express most sympathy with the yearnings of the spirit. When any other visitor appeared Antiochus was unmoved, but when Stratonice came to see him, as she frequently did, either by herself or with Seleucus, then all those symptoms mentioned by Sappho [54] were visible in him, a stammering voice, fiery blushes, failure of vision, sudden sharp sweats, irregular thumping of the heart, and finally, as his soul was overwhelmed beyond resistance, bewilderment, stupefaction, and pallor. Reasoning further,

---

53 Antiochus I (324–261 B.C.), the son of Seleucus I and his Bactrian wife, Apama, was put by his father in charge of his eastern territories, and after his father's death succeeded to the whole of his dominions. He pursued a policy of conciliation with Macedonia and let much of Asia Minor and Syria slip from his hold, while he devoted himself to founding cities and establishing colonies of Greek soldiers in Persia, Media, Bactria, and other lands beyond the Euphrates.

54 Fragment 2.

Erasistratus thought that the king's son, if he were in love with any other woman, probably would not persist in silence about it until he died.

It seemed to him hard to explain this state of things to Seleucus, but trusting to his affection for his son, he risked it one day and told him that love was the young man's ailment, a helpless and incurable love. Seleucus in astonishment asked why it was incurable. "Because, by Zeus," said Erasistratus, "he is in love with my wife." "Well, then Erasistratus," said Seleucus, "will you not give her up to my son since you are my friend, seeing too that he is our only reliance in these storms of trouble?" "But you, who are his father," said Erasistratus, "would not do it, if Antiochus had set his heart on Stratonice." "My friend," replied Seleucus, "would that some god or man could suddenly turn and direct his passion towards her! As for me, I would rejoice to let my kingdom go, if I could thereby keep Antiochus."

As Seleucus, with deep feeling and many tears, said this, the physician took him by the hand and told him he did not need Erasistratus, for as father and husband as well as king he was the best physician for his house. Thereupon Seleucus summoned an assembly of all his people and announced his will and purpose to appoint Antiochus king of all Upper Asia and Stratonice queen, they both to be joined in marriage. He added that he thought his son, who was accustomed to obeying and submitting to him in everything, would not oppose him in this marriage, and if his wife hesitated to agree to it as unlawful, he appealed to his friends to teach her and persuade her to believe that what seemed right and expedient to the king was honorable and lawful. With this justification then, they say, the marriage of Antiochus and Stratonice took place.

39. After thus winning Macedonia, Demetrius took over Thessaly as well. And since he had most of the Peloponnesus, and Megara and Athens on the other side of the Isthmus, he marched next against the Boeotians. At first they accepted a fair agreement for friendship with him, but then Cleonymus of Sparta made his entry into Thebes [55] with an army, and the Boeotians took heart, and Pisis of Thespiae, who was their leader at the time in renown and influence, also encouraged them. Accordingly, they revolted. But when Demetrius brought up his war engines against

---

[55] Thebes was the principal city of Boeotia. Cassander had partially rebuilt it after its total destruction by Alexander. See above, *Alexander*, ch. 11.

Thebes and began a siege of the city, Cleonymus was frightened and slipped out, and the Boeotians in a panic surrendered. Demetrius stationed garrisons in their cities, levied a considerable tribute, and left Hieronymus the historian [56] as their supervisor and governor. He got thereby a name for mildness, in particular by his treatment of Pisis. For on capturing him, he did him no injury but spoke to him amiably and appointed him polemarch of Thespiae.

Not long afterward, Lysimachus was taken prisoner by Dromichaetes, whereat Demetrius started off in haste for Thrace, hoping he might find it undefended. But the Boeotians then revolted again, and news came at the same time that Lysimachus had been released. Demetrius therefore promptly turned back, enraged, and found that the Boeotians had been beaten in a battle by his son Antigonus. So again he laid siege to Thebes.

40.   However, Pyrrhus was now overrunning Thessaly, and appearing as far south as Thermopylae. So Demetrius left Antigonus to go on with the siege, and himself set out against Pyrrhus. Thereupon Pyrrhus beat a hasty retreat, and Demetrius, leaving ten thousand infantry and a thousand cavalry in Thessaly, went back to the siege of Thebes. He brought up against it his famous city-taker, but because of its weight and size, it could be moved only laboriously, and a little at a time, so that in two months it came on barely two furlongs. The Boeotians too made a vigorous defense, while Demetrius frequently compelled his soldiers to fight and risk their lives out of obstinacy more than from necessity. Antigonus saw many of them fall and said in distress, "Why, father, do we allow these men to be sacrificed, when there is no need of it?" But Demetrius answered him sharply, "Why do you worry about it? Do you have to find rations for the dead?" Yet not wishing to be thought wasteful of other men's lives and not of his own, Demetrius was quick to share their dangers in battle, and he was pierced through the throat by a javelin.

Yet, though suffering much, he did not let go, but eventually took Thebes for the second time.[57] On his reentry into the city, the citizens were desperate with terror, for they were sure he would punish them

---

[56] Hieronymus of Cardia wrote an important history of the successors of Alexander, which has not survived He entered the service of Antigonus and was with him in the fatal battle of Ipsus in 301 B.C.

[57] This siege had lasted almost a year. The city was taken in 290 B.C.

severely. But he put to death only thirteen, banished a few, and pardoned all the rest. Thus it happened that Thebes, which had not yet been ten years rebuilt, was twice captured during that time.

Then as the time for the Pythian games arrived, Demetrius took a most unprecedented step. Since the passes around Delphi were manned by Aetolians, he held the games and festival at Athens, insisting that it was right that Athenians should pay special honor to Apollo, who was a patron of their city and the reputed founder of their race.

41. From Athens Demetrius went back to Macedonia. But he was not born for a life of quiet, and he saw too that his men were more attached to him when away on campaigns, and more troublesome and restive at home. So he started a war on the Aetolians. He devastated their country, then left Pantauchus there with a large part of his army, and marched to attack Pyrrhus. But Pyrrhus was on his way to attack him, and they missed each other. Demetrius went on to plunder Epirus, and Pyrrhus fell on Pantauchus, and in a battle in which the two commanders met and exchanged blow for blow, defeated him, captured five thousand prisoners and killed many of the rest.

This defeat did great damage to Demetrius, for Pyrrhus was not so much hated for the suffering he had inflicted as admired for accomplishing so much by his own strength, and from that victory he acquired a great and glittering name in Macedonia. Many Macedonians began to say that in Pyrrhus alone of all the kings did they see any likeness to the great Alexander in daring, whereas the others, in particular Demetrius, merely mimicked his state and pomp, like actors on a stage. There was, in fact, much of the tragic theater about Demetrius, who wore not only wonderful cloaks and diadems, broad hats with double crowns, and purple robes woven with gold, but on his feet shoes of purple felt embroidered in gold. A cloak was being woven for him which took a long time, a gorgeous piece of work on which were depicted the earth and the heavenly bodies. It was left behind unfinished when Demetrius' fortunes fell, and no one ever ventured to wear it, although not a few of the later kings of Macedonia were fond of ostentation.

42. Not only did this outward show of his irritate the Macedonians, who were not accustomed to it, but his luxurious way of life was offensive to them, and most of all his unapproachability and the difficulty of speak-

ing to him. For he either granted no interviews, or else was severe and harsh with the persons he saw. He kept an embassy of Athenians, whom he cared more about pleasing than any other Greeks, waiting for two years. When a single ambassador arrived from Sparta, he took it as a sign of disrespect and was indignant. But when he said to the man, "What do you mean? Did the Spartans send but one ambassador?", he made him a smart and laconic reply, "Yes, O King, to one king."

One day Demetrius was riding out, seemingly in a more affable humor than usual, and less averse to listening to his subjects. A number of people ran forward to hand him written petitions. He accepted them all and folded them together in his cloak, whereat the people were pleased and followed along after him. But when he came to the bridge over the Axius, he opened out his cloak and tossed all the petitions into the river. This act was bitterly resented by the Macedonians, who felt they were being insulted instead of governed. They recalled, or listened to those who recalled, how reasonable Philip had been in such matters, and how approachable. One day an old woman waylaid Demetrius as he was passing and begged him repeatedly for a hearing. And on his saying he had no time, she shrieked, "Then do not be a king!" Stung sharply by her words, after thinking them over, he returned to his palace, and postponing everything else for many days spent all his time on those who wanted audience with him, beginning with the old woman.

Indeed nothing is so much a king's duty as the work of doing justice. For "Ares is a tyrant," as Timotheus says,[58] but "Law is king of all," according to Pindar. And Homer says that kings receive from Zeus not city-takers or bronze-beaked ships for their defense and guard, but ordinances of justice, and he calls not the most warlike or most unjust or most bloodthirsty king the friend and disciple of Zeus but the most just. Demetrius, on the other hand, reveled in a title totally unlike those given to the king of the gods. For Zeus is called City Guardian and City Preserver, but Demetrius City Besieger. Thus when evil, swayed by blind power, invaded the territory of what had once been good, it blackened his fame with injustice.

---

[58] The quotations from Timotheus and Pindar are among the fragments of Greek lyric poetry we still possess. The first allusion to Homer is based on *Iliad*, I, 238, 239; the second on *Odyssey*, XIX, 179, a description of Minos of Crete, who for his justice as king in this world was made judge of souls in the underworld after death.

43. Then Demetrius fell dangerously ill at Pella,[59] and came near to losing Macedonia, for Pyrrhus rapidly overran it and got as far as Edessa. However, as soon as Demetrius was stronger, he easily drove Pyrrhus out and made terms of a sort with him, for he did not wish to be hindered by constant collisions and local fights with his troublesome neighbor from carrying out what he had most in mind. And this was nothing less than the recovery of the whole realm that had been his father's. His preparations were equal to the greatness of his design and his undertaking, for he had already collected an army of ninety-eight thousand foot, as well as close to twelve thousand horse. At the same time he was laying the keels for a fleet of five hundred ships, some at the Piraeus, some at Corinth, some at Chalcis, and some at Pella. He visited every place himself, directing what had to be done and taking part in the planning.

Everyone was amazed not only at the number but at the size of his vessels. Ptolemy Philopator later built one of forty banks, which measured two hundred and eighty cubits in length and forty-eight cubits to the top of the stern, in height. That ship had a crew of four hundred sailors besides the oarsmen, and four thousand oarsmen, and in addition could take on her gangways and decks almost three thousand soldiers. But she was for show only and differed little from a fixed structure on land, meant for exhibition, not for use, and was moved at great risk and labor. The beauty of Demetrius' ships did not spoil them for fighting, nor did their elaborate equipment interfere with their usefulness; indeed their speed and power were more spectacular than their size.

44. However, while this great armament, such as no man had possessed since Alexander, was being got ready to attack Asia, the three kings, Ptolemy, Seleucus, and Lysimachus, leagued together against Demetrius. They sent a joint message to Pyrrhus, urging him to attack Macedonia and disregard the truce by which, they said, Demetrius had not guaranteed him against war but had secured for himself the right to go to war with whomever he chose. Pyrrhus agreed to their proposal, and Demetrius, while still in the midst of preparations, found himself encircled by a huge war. For at the same time Ptolemy sailed to Greece with a big fleet and

---

[59] Pella, at this time the capital city of Macedonia, lay on a lake from which a navigable stream ran to the sea, fifteen miles away.

tried to start a revolt, and Lysimachus from Thrace and Pyrrhus from nearby Epirus invaded Macedonia and pillaged the country. Leaving his son to command in Greece, Demetrius himself went to the help of Macedonia, and made first for Lysimachus. But then he had word that Pyrrhus had taken the city of Beroea.[60] The news spread quickly to the Macedonians and there was an end of Demetrius' good order. The camp was full of tears and wailing and anger and curses against him. The men would not stay together and were set on leaving, professedly to go home, but in reality to join Lysimachus.

Demetrius accordingly decided to get as far away as possible from Lysimachus, and to turn his attention to Pyrrhus, for Lysimachus, he thought, was a fellow countryman, and popular with many Macedonians because of his service to Alexander, whereas Pyrrhus was a stranger and a foreigner and they would not respect him more than they did himself. However, in these calculations he was much deceived. He moved down near Pyrrhus and encamped beside him. But his soldiers had always admired Pyrrhus' brilliance in war, and for a long time had been accustomed to regarding the strongest in battle as the most fit to be king. They now learned that Pyrrhus was lenient with his prisoners, and as they were searching eagerly for a way to shake off Demetrius and join Pyrrhus or someone else, they kept deserting. At first they went secretly, a few at a time, but soon the whole camp was openly in commotion and disorder. At last some of the men ventured to approach Demetrius and advise him to leave and save himself, for the Macedonians, they said, were tired of fighting to maintain him in luxury.

Compared with the harshness of the rest, Demetrius thought these men spoke very fairly. So he went to his tent, and not like a king but an actor exchanged his theatrical robes of state for a dark cloak and slipped away unobserved. Immediately the mass of his soldiers started to loot, pulling down his tent and quarreling with each other over it, but then Pyrrhus appeared, took over control without a struggle, and occupied the camp. He and Lysimachus divided the whole kingdom of Macedonia between them, after Demetrius had ruled it firmly for seven years.[61]

---

60 Beroea was on the way up to Pella, not more than twenty-five miles distant.
61 Demetrius' reign over Macedonia lasted from 294 to 287 B.C.

45. Thus Demetrius fell from power and took refuge in Cassandrea.[62] His wife Phila was sunk in grief and could not bear to see him, the most wretched of kings, again a plain man and a fugitive. She gave up all hope, hating his fortune, which was more persistent in bad times than in good, and so drank poison and died. But Demetrius was resolved to hold on still to what was left of the wreckage, and he went on to Greece and began collecting his generals and friends there.

The Menelaus of Sophocles [63] applies the following image to his own fortunes:

> "But my fate on the massive wheel of God
> Is ever whirling, ever shifting form,
> E'en as the moon's face on two balmy nights
> Can never be or look to be the same.
> For out of darkness first she comes forth young,
> Her face the fairer as it opens full,
> But when she seems most queenly to our sight,
> She shrinks again and vanishes away."

The same simile might be used even better for the fortunes of Demetrius, their waxings and wanings, their enlargings and shrivelings, for even now when his light seemed to fail completely and be quite extinguished, it shone out again and gathering strength little by little, fulfilled all his hopes. At first he went around visiting the cities like a private citizen, with none of the insignia of royalty. And one who saw him in that garb at Thebes, quoted appropriately the lines of Euripides: [64]

> "The god's form he has changed for that of man,
> And comes to Dirce's well, Ismenus' stream."

46. But now he began to hope for a way back to a kingdom and gathered around him again a body and form of royalty and restored to the Thebans their constitution. The Athenians, however, had revolted from him and deprived Diphilus, who had been named priest of the Savior Gods, of the

---

[62] Cassandrea was a new city, founded by Cassander on an arm of the peninsula of Chalcidice stretching into the Aegean.

[63] *Menelaus* is one of the plays of Sophocles, of which only fragments have survived.

[64] Euripides, *Bacchae,* 4, 5. The well of the nymph Dirce was on Mount Cithaeron in southern Boeotia, and the little river Ismenus flowed near by. These words are spoken in the first person by the god Dionysus, who has come in human guise to visit the Thebans.

right to give his name to the year, and had voted to elect archons again as in the days of their fathers. And on seeing that Demetrius was becoming stronger than they had anticipated, they had sent for Pyrrhus from Macedonia. So Demetrius turned on Athens furiously, and began a vigorous siege of the city. But the people sent him the philosopher Crates,[65] a man of high reputation and influence, who partly by his appeals for Athens and partly by pointing out to Demetrius what his best course was, persuaded him to raise the siege. Collecting then all the ships he had and taking eleven thousand infantry and his cavalry on board, he sailed for Asia, to wrench Lydia and Caria away from Lysimachus.

At Miletus he was met by Eurydice, a sister of Phila, who brought with her one of her daughters by Ptolemy, Ptolemais, who had earlier been promised to him through the mediation of Seleucus. Demetrius married her, Eurydice giving her to him. Immediately after the marriage he set himself to getting hold of the cities of Ionia, many of which joined him of their own accord, while many others he compelled to submit. He captured Sardis, and some of Lysimachus' generals deserted to him, bringing troops and money.

But when Agathocles, Lysimachus' son, came to meet him with a large force, he withdrew into Phrygia with the idea, if he could reach Armenia, of then stirring up Media to revolt and occupying the interior provinces, where a fugitive commander could find numerous places of refuge and retirement. But Agathocles followed him, and Demetrius, though victorious in their skirmishes, was cut off from food and forage and reduced to great straits. His soldiers too began to suspect that he was making for Armenia and Media. At the same time famine was wearing on them, and through a mistake that occurred at the crossing of the river Lycus, a large body of men were swept away by the current and lost. Yet the men did not quite stop joking, and one of them posted on the front of Demetrius' tent the first lines of the *Oedipus,* slightly altered: [66]

> "O child of blind and old Antigonus,
> To what place have we come?"

[65] Crates (c.365–285 B.C.) was a Cynic philosopher who lived a life of voluntary poverty and won the popular love by going about as a consoler in trouble and a peacemaker between enemies.

[66] Sophocles, *Oedipus Colonus,* 1, 2. The name Antigonus has been substituted for the Oedipus of the original.

47. Finally pestilence attacked them on top of the famine, as usually happens when men must eat whatever they find; and after losing at least eight thousand men in all, Demetrius gave up his project and led the remainder back. He went down then to Tarsus, and would like to have spared that country, which was at the time under Seleucus, and so have avoided giving him offense. But that was impossible, for his soldiers were in desperate need and Agathocles had blocked the passes of the Taurus against him. He therefore wrote a long letter to Seleucus, lamenting first his own sad fortunes, and then entreating and beseeching him to take pity on a man of his own family, who had suffered enough to make even his enemies feel compassion for him.

Seleucus was somewhat moved by this letter and wrote to his generals in that district to supply Demetrius himself with royal abundance and his troops with provisions in plenty. But now Patrocles, a man counted sagacious and a trusted friend of Seleucus, came to him and said that the expense of supporting Demetrius' troops was negligible, but that it was not wise to allow Demetrius himself to stay on in the country, since he had always been the most strenuous of kings and addicted to tremendous enterprises, and he was now in circumstances that would drive even naturally moderate persons to rashness and violence. Impressed by this reasoning, Seleucus started for Cilicia at the head of a large army. Surprised and frightened by this rapid change in him, Demetrius retreated to the strongest footholds in the Taurus Mountains, and sent messengers to Seleucus earnestly requesting to be allowed to acquire a small kingdom among the independent barbarians, where he might live out his life at rest from wandering and flight. But if not that, he asked him to provide his army in Cilicia with food for the winter, and not to drive himself out empty-handed and completely destitute, and throw him to his enemies.

48. But Seleucus was suspicious of everything, and sent Demetrius word that he might, if he liked, winter for two months in Cataonia,[67] but he demanded his chief friends as hostages. At the same time he blocked the passes leading into Syria. Thus Demetrius, surrounded now and attacked from every quarter like a wild beast, was compelled by necessity to fight. He overran the country, and when Seleucus attacked him, he met him

[67] Cataonia, a district in Cappadocia, was in wilder country than Cilicia and farther back from the sea.

and always came out ahead. When the scythed chariots were sweeping down on him, he stood his ground, and he drove off the detachments that were blocking the passes into Syria and got control of those. Once more he was all elated in spirit, and seeing that his soldiers had recovered their confidence, he prepared to fight the battle out with Seleucus for the supreme prize. Seleucus himself was now in difficulties. For he had rejected Lysimachus' offer of assistance, since he distrusted and feared him, and he dreaded a struggle with Demetrius alone, by himself. He was afraid of his desperation and the incessant alternations of his fortune, which carried him from the lowest ebb of poverty to the highest summit of success.

But at this crisis, Demetrius fell gravely ill and was thereby terribly weakened in body and utterly ruined in his prospects. Some of his soldiers deserted to the enemy and some strayed off. After forty days he had barely recovered enough to take his remaining troops and start—as far as the enemy could see or guess—for Cilicia. Then, in the night, without sound of trumpet, he began marching in the other direction, crossed the Amanus Mountains, and began plundering the country below as far as Cyrrhestica.[68]

49.   Soon afterward Seleucus appeared and pitched his camp close by, but Demetrius got his men up at night and moved to surprise him. Seleucus and his army were asleep, unaware of his coming. But some deserters arrived and warned him of his danger, and leaping up in terror he ordered the trumpet sounded, meanwhile pulling on his boots and shouting to his companions that a savage wild beast was attacking them. Demetrius, however, perceived from the noise his enemies made that they had been warned, and quickly marched his men back again. At daybreak Seleucus pressed forward against him, but he sent one of his officers to his other wing, where he routed the enemy in part. At this point, however, Seleucus himself dismounted, took off his helmet, and with only a light shield in his hand went up and confronted Demetrius' mercenary troops, showing himself to them and calling on them to join him. They surely knew, he said, that he had for a long time been sparing them, not

---

[68] That is, instead of moving northwest into Cappadocia, where Seleucus wanted him to be, Demetrius marched southeast into Cyrrhestica, a district of northern Syria, from which Seleucus was determined to exclude him.

for Demetrius' sake but for their own. Thereupon they all greeted him, hailed him as king, and flocked over into his army.

Demetrius now realized that the last of his many vicissitudes of fortune had come upon him, and abandoning the fight he fled towards the passes of Amanus. With a few friends and followers he plunged into a thick wood and waited for the night, hoping to be able to take the road to Caunus [69] and so push through to the sea, where he expected to find his fleet at anchor. But when he discovered that between them they had not funds enough even for the next day, he tried to make other plans.

Then Sosigenes, a friend, arrived with four hundred gold pieces in his girdle. With this help they hoped they could get through to the sea, and as it grew dark, they set out for the passes. But the enemy were burning fires along the passes, so that they despaired of escaping by that road and went back again to the same place in the wood—not all of them, for some had slipped away and those who were left were not so ardent as before. One of them now dared to speak out and say that Demetrius ought to give himself up to Seleucus. Demetrius drew his sword and started to kill himself, but his friends surrounded him and bade him take heart, and prevailed on him to do as the man advised. So he sent Seleucus a message putting himself in his hands.

50. On receipt of it, Seleucus said that Demetrius was saved not by his own good fortune but by that of Seleucus, which, besides her other gifts, was granting him a chance to display humanity and kindness. Summoning his stewards, he bade them erect a royal tent and do everything else to prepare for a magnificent welcome and entertainment. With Seleucus there was a certain Apollonides who had been a close friend of Demetrius, and Seleucus sent him off at once to cheer and encourage Demetrius, since the man he was to confront was his kinsman and son-in-law. As it became known that this was Seleucus' attitude, first a few of his friends and then most of them rushed off to Demetrius, vying with one another as to who should get there ahead, for they expected that he would instantly become the greatest man at court.

But this zeal on the part of his friends converted the compassion of Seleucus into jealousy, and enabled the ill-natured and malicious to pervert and defeat the king's generous intentions. They frightened him into be-

---

[69] Caunus, a small city on the coast of southwest Asia Minor, was a long march away.

lieving that, with no delay, as soon as Demetrius was seen in his camp, there would be a great rising of troops for him. So just as Apollonides, full of joy, had reached Demetrius and others were arriving with wonderful stories about the magnanimity of Seleucus, and Demetrius himself after all his dire misfortunes and failures, even though he had looked on his surrender as an act of shame, was changing his mind and plucking up courage and confident hope, Pausanias appeared with a thousand soldiers, horse and foot together. With them he abruptly surrounded Demetrius, and then, sending the rest away, took him, not into the presence of Seleucus but off to the Syrian Chersonese. There for the rest of his life he was kept under a strong guard. An adequate staff of attendants came to him from Seleucus and a liberal provision of money for his support was made for him daily. Royal walks and paths and parks, with wild beasts, were arranged for him. Any friend who was a fellow exile was permitted to visit him whenever he wished, and men came to him from Seleucus bringing pleasant messages and telling him to keep up heart, for as soon as Antiochus and Stratonice arrived he would be released.

51. In this helpless situation Demetrius now sent word to his son and to his friends and commanders at Athens and Corinth, warning them to put no faith in any dispatches from him or in his seal, but to regard him as dead and to hold his cities and the rest of his possessions for his son Antigonus. But Antigonus, grieved to hear of his father's captivity, put on mourning and wrote to the other kings, and to Seleucus himself, pleading and offering to give up whatever was left of their possessions, and above all proposing himself as a hostage in his father's place. Many cities and magnates joined in the petition, but not Lysimachus, who promised to pay Seleucus a large sum of money if he would kill Demetrius. But Seleucus, who had always been on his guard against Lysimachus, at this suggestion thought him still more disgusting and barbarous. However, he let the time go by with Demetrius still captive, keeping him for his son Antiochus and Stratonice, that the gift of liberty might come from them.

52. In the beginning Demetrius bore up manfully against his adversities, and soon grew used to enduring captivity, taking exercise of one kind or another, hunting as much as he could, and riding. Then, gradually, he found these occupations boring and distasteful and took to drinking and

dice, and spent most of his time at them. Either he was trying to escape from thoughts on his present situation, which haunted him when sober, and to deaden his mind with wine, or else he felt that this was the life he had long been wanting and seeking, but which he had missed through his folly and vain desire for glory, bringing thus much trouble on himself and others. In arms and fleets and camps he had looked for the best in life, which now, unexpectedly, he discovered lay in ease and rest and repose. For what other ends indeed do wretched kings go through their wars and dangers? But they are both wrong and foolish, for not only are they aiming for luxury and pleasure, instead of for virtue and nobility, but they do not even know how to feel true pleasure or enjoy real luxury.

Demetrius was confined for three years [70] in the Chersonese, and then fell ill from inertia and surfeit of food and wine, and died at the age of fifty-four. Seleucus was greatly blamed for his death, and he deeply regretted the suspicions he had entertained about Demetrius, and his failure to imitate Dromichaetes, a Thracian barbarian, who had treated Lysimachus, when he captured him, so generously and so royally.

53.   Even the funeral of Demetrius had something of the tragic theater about it. His son Antigonus, on learning that his father's ashes were being sent to him, put out with all his ships and met them at the islands. He received them in a golden urn and placed them on board the largest of his flagships. At every port they touched, the citizens either laid garlands on the urn, or sent men in mourning dress to take part in the escort back to Greece and in the burial rites. When the fleet arrived at Corinth, the urn was conspicuous to see on the ship's poop, decked out with a king's purple robe and a diadem, and surrounded by young men in arms as a bodyguard. The most famous flute-player of that time, Xenophantus, was sitting close to it playing a solemn melody, to which the rowers kept time in rhythm. The beat of their oars, like funeral mourning, answered the strains of the flute. But to the crowds who gathered at the shore the most pitiful and woeful sight was that of Antigonus himself, bowed down with tears and grief. Honors and garlands were heaped on the ashes at Corinth, after which Antigonus took them for burial to Demetrias, the city to which Demetrius had given his name, when he built it up from the villages around Iolcus.

---

[70] From 286 to 283 B.C.

The children whom Demetrius left were Antigonus and Stratonice by Phila, two sons called Demetrius, one surnamed the Thin, by an Illyrian woman, and one who became ruler of Cyrene, by Ptolemais. By Deidamia, he had Alexander, who lived all his life in Egypt. It is said too that he had a son Corrhagus by Eurydice. His line came down in succession reigning over Macedonia until it ended with Perseus,[71] under whom the Romans conquered the country. And now that the Macedonian play is finished, it is time to bring on the Roman.

[71] Perseus (c.213–165 B.C.), the last of the independent kings of Macedon, made a vain attempt to revive the imperialist policy of his forefathers in Greece, Thessaly, ar Thrace, and was finally defeated by the Romans at Pydna in 168 B.C.

Antony

c. 82-30 B.C.

1. ANTONY'S grandfather was the orator Antonius, who was put to death by Marius for having joined Sulla's party. His father was Antonius, called the Cretan, a man not very famous or distinguished as a public figure, but benevolent and good, and remarkably liberal in his giving, as one may tell from a single instance. He was not rich and for that reason was often checked by his wife in his acts of generosity. So one day when a close friend came to him asking for money and he had no money, he ordered a young slave to pour water into a silver bowl and bring it to him, and when it was brought, he wet his chin as if he were going to shave. He then on some excuse sent the boy away and presented the bowl to his friend, telling him to make use of it. Later when a strict search was being made for it among the slaves, and Antonius saw that his wife was angry and about to have them put to the torture, one by one, he admitted what he had done, and by his pleading soon won her forgiveness.

His wife was Julia, of the house of the Caesars, a woman who could compare with the noblest and most prudent of her day. She brought up her son Antony after his father's death. She then married Cornelius Lentulus, who was put to death by Cicero for having been a member of Catiline's conspiracy,[1] an act which seems to have been the cause and starting point of Antony's bitter hatred of Cicero. For Antony says that he would not even give up the corpse of Lentulus until his mother begged it of Cicero's wife. Yet this statement is obviously false, for not one of those whom Cicero punished at that time was denied burial.

---

[1] See above, *Cicero*, ch. 22.

2. Antony, they say, was a brilliant youth, but his intimacy with Curio [2] affected him like a disease. For Curio knew no restraint in his own pleasures, and to make Antony easier to handle he plunged him into a life of drinking and dissipation with women and extravagant, unbridled expenditures. As a result Antony fell heavily into debt, too far for his years, since he owed two hundred and fifty talents. Curio went surety for the whole amount, but when his father heard of it, he drove Antony from his house. For a short time Antony was mixed up in the activities of Clodius,[3] the most impudent and rascally demagogue then agitating the state; but soon growing weary of his folly and alarmed at the size of the group that was combining against him, he left Italy for Greece and spent some time there, training his body in military exercises and studying oratory. He adopted what was called the Asiatic style of oratory, which was popular at that period, and which had a striking similarity to his own mode of life, being boastful, ostentatious, full of empty flourishes and erratic aims.

3. When Gabinius,[4] a proconsul, was sailing for Syria, he tried to persuade Antony to accompany him on the expedition. He refused to go as a private but on being appointed commander of cavalry, he went along. He was sent first to capture Aristobulus,[5] who was stirring the Jews to revolt. Antony was the first man to mount Aristobulus' high fortifications, and he drove him from all of them. He then met him in battle and with

---

[2] Gaius Scribonius Curio was one of the able but dissipated and reckless young aristocrats of the time, who later sold his allegiance to Julius Caesar. At the outbreak of the civil war he was appointed by Caesar praetor for Sicily and held that island for him, but later he crossed over to Africa to attack Pompey's forces there and was defeated by King Juba of Numidia, and killed.

[3] On Clodius see above, *Cicero*, chs. 28-35 and *Caesar*, ch. 10.

[4] Aulus Gabinius was a man of the popular party who had filled many offices. He had been consul in 58 B.C., when Cicero was exiled, and through Clodius' influence had now been awarded the province of Syria. In 55, he restored Ptolemy XII of Egypt to his throne, in return for a large bribe, but was soon afterwards summoned to Rome to be prosecuted for corruption, and banished. On Caesar's accession to power he recalled Gabinius and made him one of his lieutenants. See below, ch. 7.

[5] Aristobulus, a prince of the Maccabaean line in Judaea, had been captured and carried to Rome by Pompey in 63 B.C. Six years later he escaped and made his way back to Judaea, and was stirring up hostilities against Roman rule when he was again captured and sent back to Rome by Gabinius. Caesar released him in 49 and sent him home once more, but on the way he was poisoned by agents of Pompey.

the small force he had with him put to flight a much more numerous enemy, killing all but a few. Aristobulus himself he captured with his son.

After this, Ptolemy tried to prevail on Gabinius with a bribe of ten thousand talents to join him in an invasion of Egypt and recover his kingdom for him. Most of his officers opposed the idea, and Gabinius himself was somewhat afraid of that war, though utterly fascinated by the ten thousand talents. Antony, however, was eager for grand exploits and anxious to stand well with Ptolemy, so he helped to persuade Gabinius and get him started on the campaign. But more than the actual war they dreaded the road to Pelusium,[6] which lay through deep and waterless sand, along the Ecregma and the Serbonian marshes. The Egyptians call these the blasts of Typhon,[7] but apparently it is swampland left behind by the Red Sea as well as water that has filtered through where the isthmus dividing that sea from the Inner Sea is the narrowest. Antony was sent on with the cavalry and he not only occupied the straits, but took Pelusium, which is a large city, with its garrison. Thus he both made the road safe for the main army and gave its general a confident hope of victory. His enemies too received some benefit from Antony's love of glory, for when Ptolemy entered Pelusium and in his rage and resentment was starting a massacre of the Egyptians, Antony objected and stopped him.

Thereafter, in their many hard battles and skirmishes he performed numerous deeds of daring and shrewd generalship, the most outstanding of which was his surrounding and encircling the enemy from the rear, thereby giving the victory to the soldiers in front, for which he received fitting honors and marks of distinction. Nor did his humanity towards the dead Archelaus [8] go unnoticed. In his lifetime Archelaus had been a close comrade of Antony, who had later been obliged to fight against him, but when he fell and Antony found his body, he gave it a handsome and royal

---

[6] Pelusium, a frontier town on the eastern branch of the Nile delta, would be the first place of importance they would reach as they emerged from the desert road down from Syria.

[7] Typhon, the malicious brother of the gods Isis and Osiris, was the Egyptians' evil deity. His name was therefore given to the wasteland between the Red Sea and the Mediterranean. See below, *Isis and Osiris,* ch. 49.

[8] Archelaus, a so-called son of Mithridates, king of Pontus, had married Berenice, the older daughter of Ptolemy XII and the sister of Cleopatra, who had been acting queen of Egypt during her father's banishment. Archelaus was killed defending Egypt against Antony.

burial. So he left behind him a great reputation among the people of Alexandria, and the Romans on the expedition regarded him as their shining light.

4. He had a figure of noble dignity, and with his well-shaped beard, broad forehead, and beaked nose men said he had the powerful look of Heracles in his portraits and statues. There was an old story that the Antonii were Heracleidae and descended from Anton, Hercules' son, a story which in Antony's opinion was confirmed by his physical appearance, as I have said, and by his dress. For always, whenever he expected to be seen by a large number of people, he wore a tunic girded up to his thigh, a large sword hanging at his side, and a thick cloak around his shoulders. And even the traits that to some people seemed obnoxious, his bragging and joking and prominent wine goblet, his sitting down beside a man as he ate, or standing to eat at a soldiers' table, all created an amazing liking and affection for him among his soldiers. Even his love affairs had something engaging about them, and through them too he won popular favor, for he helped other men in their affairs and bore good humoredly their jests about his own.

His liberality and his way of doing favors for his soldiers and friends with no mean or stingy hand gave him an excellent start towards power, and when he had become great, raised his power still higher, though it was always being shaken by his too numerous faults. I will give you one instance of his freehandedness. He ordered two hundred and fifty thousand drachmas, a sum the Romans call a *decies,* paid to one of his friends. His steward, astonished at the amount, laid out the coin in plain sight to show him the size of the gift. Antony, going by, asked what that was and when the steward replied that it was the gift he had ordered, Antony saw through his unwillingness and said, "I thought a decies was more. This is too little, so add to it as much again!"

5. These stories, however, belong to a later time. When the Roman state finally broke apart and the aristocratic party declared for Pompey, who was then in the city, and the people's party summoned Caesar, who was with his army in Gaul, Curio, Antony's friend, who had changed sides and was now supporting Caesar, brought Antony over to him too. And Curio used the great influence he had with the populace, through his eloquence and through the bountiful funds supplied by Caesar, to get

Antony made tribune of the people [9] and later one of the priests who divine the future by birds and whom the Romans call augur.

As soon as he took office, Antony was of great help to the men in the government who were working for Caesar. First, when Marcellus the consul was for handing over to Pompey the troops already assembled and empowering him to raise more, Antony opposed him and proposed instead a decree that the forces assembled should go by ship to Syria to assist Bibulus, who was fighting the Parthians, and that the troops which Pompey was raising should not belong to him. Secondly, when the senate would not receive Caesar's letters nor permit them to be read, Antony, by the authority of his office, read them aloud himself, and so changed the minds of many who heard him and were convinced by what Caesar wrote that he was asking only what was just and reasonable.

Finally, however, when two questions were put to the senate, one, whether they wished Pompey to disband his troops, the other, whether Caesar should do the same, only a few favored having Pompey lay down his arms, and all but a few favored having Caesar do so. But Antony rose and asked whether the senate would require both Pompey and Caesar to lay down their arms and disband their forces. This proposal they accepted enthusiastically, and with loud praises for Antony, they demanded the taking of the vote. But the consuls withheld their consent; so the friends of Caesar made still other proposals, which sounded reasonable. These Cato opposed, and Lentulus, as consul, expelled Antony from the senate. He went out, cursing them all fluently; then dressing himself as a slave, he hired a carriage with Quintus Cassius, and started off to find Caesar. When they reached his presence they cried out that affairs at Rome were now in utter disorder, since even tribunes had no liberty of speech, and everyone who spoke a word on the side of justice was driven out at the risk of his life.[10]

6.   Thereupon, Caesar took his army and invaded Italy. Consequently Cicero in his *Philippics* wrote that as Helen was the cause of the Trojan War, so was Antony of the civil war,[11] but on that point he was manifestly deceived. For Gaius Caesar was not so susceptible a man or so easily

---

[9] Antony was tribune in 50 B.C.

[10] On these events, see above, *Caesar,* chs. 30 ff.

[11] See *Philippics,* II, 22, 55.

influenced by anger as to lose all his power of reason. If he had not long before resolved to take this step, the mere sight of Antony in a menial's dress and Cassius seeking refuge with him, in a hired carriage, would not have made him seize that moment to make war on his country. It merely furnished a pretext and a plausible reason for war to one who had long wanted an excuse for it. What led Caesar to war against all mankind was what led Alexander before him and Cyrus in old times, an insatiable love of authority and a feverish desire to be first and greatest, and this he could not be if Pompey were not overthrown.

So he came and took possession of Rome, and drove Pompey out of Italy. He then decided to turn against Pompey's forces in Spain, and later, when he had a fleet ready, to cross to Greece and attack Pompey himself. Accordingly, he entrusted Rome to Lepidus,[12] who was praetor, and the army and Italy to Antony, who was tribune. With the soldiers Antony was soon popular, for he exercised with them, in many ways lived with them, and made them presents as far as his means then allowed; but to everyone else he was hateful. He was too indolent to pay attention to persons with injuries, he was surly listening to those who came to him, and he had the name of seducing other men's wives. In general, Caesar's power, which seemed anything but a tyranny when he exercised it, was made odious by his friends. And of these friends, Antony, who had the highest position, committed apparently the gravest faults, and so received the most blame.

7.   On Caesar's return from Spain, however, he overlooked the charges against Antony, and since he found him energetic, brave, and a good commander, he was right to do so. Caesar himself then crossed the Ionian Sea from Brundisium with a few troops,[13] and sent the boats back, with orders to Gabinius and Antony to get their men on board and make for Macedonia at full speed. But Gabinius was afraid of the voyage, which was hazardous in the winter season, and started leading his army a long way around, by land. Antony, however, was alarmed for Caesar, surrounded

---

12 Marcus Aemilius Lepidus, a member of Caesar's party, was chosen by him as his colleague in the consulship for the year 46 B.C. After the murder of Caesar, he attached himself to Antony and became one of the Second Triumvirate which divided the world between himself, Antony, and Octavian.

13 See above, *Caesar*, ch. 37. It was now the year 48 B.C.

by a host of enemies. So he drove off Libo, who was blockading the mouth
of the harbor of Brundisium, encircling his triremes with swarms of light
boats, took eight hundred horse and twenty thousand infantry on board,
and put out to sea.

When the enemy caught sight of him, they started in pursuit, but he
escaped that danger for a blustering south wind raised high waves and
swept their triremes into the trough of the sea. He was driven with his
ships towards a steep and rocky coast and had not a hope, when all at
once there blew from the bay a hard southwest breeze and the waves began
running from the land out to sea, and Antony steered away from the shore
and sailed proudly on, seeing the coast covered with wreckage. For the
wind cast up there the triremes which were pursuing him, and many
were broken to pieces. He collected many prisoners and much booty,
captured Lissus,[14] and gave Caesar great encouragement by arriving at
that critical time with so fine a force.

8.   In all the following struggles, which were many and incessant, Antony distinguished himself. Twice when Caesar's soldiers were flying
head over heel, he met and turned them around, compelled them to stand
and fight their pursuers again, and so won the day. After Caesar, he was
the most talked of man in camp. And Caesar showed his opinion of him,
for when he was preparing for the final decisive struggle at Pharsalus and
had taken the right wing for himself, he put Antony, as the best warrior
he had, in command of the left. After the victory, when he had been
proclaimed dictator, he set out himself in pursuit of Pompey, but appointed Antony master of the horse and dispatched him to Rome. This
post is second when the dictator is present, but in his absence it is first
and well nigh the only one. For once a dictator is chosen, only the tribune's
office continues; all other offices cease to exist.

9.   Dolabella [15] was tribune at that time, a young man longing for change.
He proposed a measure for annulling debts, and set out to persuade Antony, who was a friend of his and who always liked standing well with
the crowd, to join with him and support it. But Asinius and Trebellius [16]
advised Antony against it, and a terrible suspicion then happened to grip

---

[14] Lissus was a town on the coast of southern Illyria.
[15] This was Publius Dolabella, Cicero's notorious son-in-law. See above, *Cicero*, n. 74.
[16] These were friends of Antony, about whom not much else seems to be known.

him, that he was being wronged by Dolabella in his wife. He took the idea hard, and drove his wife from his house, though she was his cousin, the daughter of Gaius Antonius who was consul with Cicero. He then took Asinius' side and attacked Dolabella, who had men occupying the forum in order to push through his law by force. So the senate had voted that Dolabella must be resisted by arms, and Antony attacked him, and in the fray killed some of Dolabella's men and lost some of his own.

But this act brought down on Antony the popular resentment, while well-behaved and discreet citizens disliked his way of living altogether, as Cicero says.[17] In fact, they detested him, hating his drinking at all hours, his wild extravagance, his orgies with women, his spending the day in sleeping, or in wandering about muddled and nauseated, and the night at revels and shows, or at the nuptials of buffoons and jesters. The story is told that once after he had feasted and drunk all night at the marriage of Hippias the buffoon, the people called for him in the forum early the next morning, and he came still gorged with food and vomited into his toga, which a friend held up for him. The buffoon Sergius was one of those who had most influence over him, as had Cytheris too, from the same training school, a popular little woman whom he carried around with him in a litter when he visited the cities. As many attendants accompanied her litter as escorted that of his mother. People were irritated too by the sight of the golden goblets he took with him on his travels as though on a religious procession, his setting up of tents on the way, his holding of costly banquets by groves and rivers, his chariots drawn by lions, and his quartering of prostitutes and lute-players in the houses of sober men and women. They thought it outrageous that while Caesar, away from Italy, had but the sky for a roof, and with vast toil and danger was clearing up the remains of the war, these other men, because of his labors, were living in a luxury that was an insult to their fellow citizens.

10. Antony's conduct appears to have aggravated also the party quarrels at Rome and to have encouraged the soldiers in acts of shocking violence and greed. On that account, when Caesar came home he pardoned Dolabella, and when elected consul for the third time, he chose not Antony but Lepidus for his colleague. When Pompey's house was offered for sale, Antony bought it, but when he was asked to pay for it, he was offended.

---

17 Cicero describes Antony's debaucheries with much virulence in *Philippics*, II.

He says himself that the reason he did not join Caesar on his Libyan expedition was that he was getting no reward for his earlier achievements. However, it looked as if Caesar had cured him of much of his folly and dissipation by not letting his sins go unnoticed. For he now gave up his scandalous way of life, turned his mind to marriage and took to wife Fulvia, widow of Clodius, of the popular party. She was a woman not interested in spinning or housewifery, nor was she content with managing one ordinary husband. Her ambition was to rule a ruler and command a commander. Cleopatra was indebted to Fulvia's teachings for Antony's submissiveness to a woman's control, for she received him all tamed from the first and trained to obey a mistress.

He used to try playfully with boyish tricks to make Fulvia merrier. Once, for example, when he had gone out with a great crowd to meet Caesar after his victory in Spain, a report suddenly reached Italy that Caesar was dead and that his enemies were approaching. Antony returned to Rome, put on a slave's dress and went to his house at night, saying he had brought a letter from Antony to Fulvia. Still all wrapped up, he was brought to her, and she, in a state of great anxiety, before taking the letter, asked him if Antony was still alive. In silence he held out the letter, but as she was beginning to open and read it, he threw his arms around her and kissed her. This little anecdote, out of many, I cite as an illustration.

11.   When Caesar came back from Spain,[18] all the leading men went many days' journey to meet him, but it was now Antony whom he markedly honored. On his way through Italy, he had Antony in his chariot with him, and behind them came Brutus Albinus [19] and Octavian, his niece's son, who was later called Caesar and ruled over the Romans for a very long time. Then when Caesar was named consul for the fifth time, he at once selected Antony as his colleague. For himself he preferred to resign the office and give his place to Dolabella, and he proposed it to the senate. But as Antony was violently set against the idea, and said much that was bad of Dolabella and had as much said of him, Caesar, embarrassed by their unruly behavior, dropped the matter for the time being. Later when he came before the assembly to proclaim Dolabella consul, Antony called out that the omens were unfavorable. Caesar then yielded

---

[18] Caesar's final return from Spain, after his victory over Pompey's sons, was in 45 B.C.
[19] On Decimus Brutus, see above, *Caesar,* ch. 64.

and gave up Dolabella, to the latter's indignation. But apparently Caesar was as disgusted with Dolabella as he was with Antony. For they say that when someone was denouncing both of them to him, he remarked that he was not afraid of those fat, long-haired fellows, but of the pale, lean ones, meaning Brutus and Cassius, who were to conspire against him and kill him.[20]

12. Without meaning it, Antony gave Caesar's enemies their most plausible argument against him. The Romans were celebrating the feast of the Lycaea, which they call the Lupercalia, and Caesar, decked out in triumphal robes, was sitting on the rostrum, watching the runners. These runners are youths of noble birth and a few of the magistrates, who have all been anointed with oil and carry strips of leather with which they strike in fun whomever they meet.[21] Antony was among those running, but ignoring the ancient rules, he wound a garland of laurel around a diadem and ran with it up to the rostrum. There he was lifted up by his fellow runners and placed it on Caesar's head, implying thus that he should be king.

When Caesar, pretending modesty, refused to accept it, the people were pleased and clapped their hands. Antony again held out the diadem, and Caesar again pushed it away. The struggle went on for some time, with only a few of Antony's friends applauding his attempts to force the diadem on Caesar, and all the people shouting and applauding when Caesar rejected it. This was surprising too, since in actual fact they were submitting to kingly rule, yet the name of king they abhorred, as though it meant the destruction of their liberty. At length, Caesar, disappointed, got up from the rostrum, and pulling his cloak away from his neck, called out that he offered his throat to anyone who cared to strike a blow. The garland, which now was laid on one of his statues, was torn off by some tribunes, and the people hailed them with applause; but Caesar deposed them from office.

13. These incidents all gave strength to the party of Brutus and Cassius, and when they were counting up the friends they could trust for their undertaking, they inquired about Antony. The others were for adding

---

[20] See above, *Caesar,* ch. 62.
[21] On the Lupercalia, see above, *Caesar,* ch. 61.

him to their number, but Trebonius [22] opposed it. For, he said, when they went to meet Caesar on his way back from Spain, Antony shared his, Trebonius', tent and traveled with him, and he tried him out coolly and cautiously. Antony, he said, understood him, but made no response to his overtures. However, he did not report their talk to Caesar, but faithfully said nothing about it. Thereupon the conspirators made a plan to kill Antony after they had made away with Caesar; Brutus stopped that, pleading that the act they were daring in defense of law and justice should be kept pure and clear of injustice. But since they feared Antony's strength and the influence of his office, they delegated some of the conspirators to detain him and, when Caesar went into the senate house and the deed was about to take place, to start an earnest conversation with him outside, and so hold him there.

14. All this was accomplished as planned and Caesar fell in the senate house. Antony immediately put on slave's dress and went into hiding. When he learned that the murderers were attacking no one else but were collecting on the Capitol, he prevailed on them to come down and receive his son as a hostage. He himself entertained Cassius at supper, while Lepidus took Brutus. He also convened the senate and spoke of an amnesty and of a distribution of provinces among Brutus, Cassius, and their accomplices. The senate confirmed his proposals, voting also not to alter anything that Caesar had done. So Antony left the senate with his prestige high, for it seemed as if he had prevented a civil war and had managed a situation of much difficulty and extraordinary complexity with great sagacity and statesmanship.

But from sober counsels of this sort he was soon swept away on the current of popular fame, and began to think that if Brutus were disposed of, he himself would certainly be the first man in Rome. Now it happened that when Caesar's body was being carried out for burial, Antony delivered the customary eulogy over it in the forum. He saw that the people were deeply stirred and fascinated by his words, and proceeded to mingle with his praises of Caesar compassion and horror at the woeful deed. As he ended his speech, he waved above them the clothing of the dead man,

---

[22] Gaius Trebonius had worked for the First Triumvirate and later been made by Caesar his legate in Gaul. But though he was always treated generously by Caesar, he became one of the conspirators who murdered him.

blood-stained and torn by the swords, and called the perpetrators of the deed villains and assassins.[23] He got the people in such a state of frenzy that they piled up benches and tables and burned Caesar's body in the forum, and then snatching up flaming faggots from the pyre, ran to the houses of the murderers to attack them.

15. Thereat Brutus and his company left the city, and the friends of Caesar joined to support Antony. Caesar's wife Calpurnia trusted him and had most of the money in her house transferred to Antony's, to the amount of four thousand talents. He took over also Caesar's papers, containing notes of his decisions and opinions, and he inserted entries in them, thus naming many officials and many senators of his own choice. He ordered some men back too from exile and released some from prison, as though Caesar had commanded it all. So the Romans, in sarcasm, called all those men Charonites,[24] since, when challenged to prove their rights, they referred to a dead man's notes. Everything else Antony managed in autocratic style, being consul himself and having his brothers too in office, Gaius as praetor and Lucius as tribune.

16. While things were in this state, young Caesar, son of the dead Caesar's niece and designated heir of his estate, as we have said, arrived in Rome from Apollonia, where he was staying at the time of his uncle's death. He at once paid his respects to Antony as his uncle's friend, and then reminded him of the money deposited with him. For according to the instructions in Caesar's will he was obliged to give every Roman seventy-five drachmas.[25] At first, Antony was scornful of him as a mere boy, and told him he was out of his mind and that without good judgment and good friends the succession to Caesar was a burden too heavy for him to bear. And as the youth would not yield and kept demanding the money, Antony went on freely insulting him in word and in act.

When he stood for election as tribune, Antony opposed him, and when he tried to dedicate his uncle's golden chair, as the senate had ordered,

---

23 Several ancient writers have described the speech which Antony made on this occasion. The speech which Shakespeare puts into his mouth in *Julius Caesar,* Act III, Scene 2, is probably based on this passage in Plutarch, which Shakespeare knew in North's translation.

24 In Greek mythology Charon is, of course, a god of the lower world, who ferries souls across to Hades. The parallel Roman god was Orcus.

25 On Caesar's will, see above, *Caesar,* ch. 68.

Antony threatened to send him to prison if he did not stop playing up to the people. But when the young man turned to Cicero and the others who hated Antony and through them secured the good will of the senate, while he himself was winning the people and bringing in soldiers from the colonies, Antony was alarmed and held a conference with him on the Capitol, and they made peace. As Antony was asleep that night, he dreamed a strange dream. He thought his right hand was struck by a thunderbolt. And a few days later a report reached him that young Caesar was plotting against him. Caesar tried to clear himself, but he did not convince Antony, and the breach between them widened again. Both now went rushing around Italy, endeavoring by offers of large pay to bring out the soldiers who were now settled in the colonies, and to outdo the other in attracting troops who were still under arms.

17. Of the men in Rome Cicero was then the most influential, and he was stirring up everybody against Antony. He finally persuaded the senate to vote him a public enemy, to send young Caesar the *fasces* and other insignia of a praetor, and to order Pansa and Hirtius, who were consuls that year, to drive Antony out of Italy. In a battle with Antony near the city of Mutina,[26] they had Caesar with them and he fought for them. They defeated Antony, but were both killed themselves.

Antony was now a fugitive and beset by many difficulties, the worst being famine. But by nature he was at his best in adversity, and in time of trouble came nearest to being a good man. It is common enough for people balked by misfortune to see what the good way is, but not all in calamity have strength enough to imitate what they admire and to refrain from what they disapprove, and some out of weakness give way even more then to their old habits, and are too feeble to use any judgment. Antony, however, at this time, set a wonderful example to his soldiers. After such a life of extravagant luxury as he had led, he drank dirty water cheerfully and lived on wild fruits and roots. It is said that they ate bark too, and while crossing the Alps devoured animals never before tasted.

18. Their design was to meet the troops which Lepidus commanded in those regions, for he was supposed to be Antony's friend and through

---

[26] Mutina, the modern Modena, was a city on the great highway through Cisalpine Gaul. The battle was fought in 43 B.C.

Antony's help he had profited a good deal from Caesar's friendship. But when Antony came and camped near him, he met with no kindliness. He decided then on a bold step. His hair had been left unkempt and his beard allowed to grow long ever since his defeat. Now throwing on a dark cloak he went up to Lepidus' rampart and began to speak. Many of the soldiers were touched by his appearance and moved by his words, and Lepidus in alarm ordered the trumpets to sound all together to keep him from being heard.

The soldiers now pitied him all the more, and set up communication with him secretly, sending Laelius and Clodius to him in the dress of women camp followers. They urged Antony to attack their fortifications boldly, for there were many, they said, who would welcome him and would even kill Lepidus, if he wished it. Antony would not consent to their touching Lepidus, but the next morning he started to cross the river with his army. He was himself the first man to wade in, and as he pushed over to the other side, he saw that already numbers of Lepidus' soldiers were holding out their hands to him and breaking down their ramparts. On entering the camp he took possession of everything, but behaved with great courtesy towards Lepidus, embracing him and calling him father. And though in fact he was complete master of the field, he went on giving Lepidus the name and honor of a general. His conduct brought Munatius Plancus also over to him—for he was in the neighborhood with a considerable force. Being thus raised anew to a position of power, Antony crossed the Alps back into Italy, bringing with him seventeen legions of infantry and ten thousand horse. Besides these he left to guard Gaul six legions under Varius, one of his friends and boon companions, known as Cotylon.

19. Meanwhile Caesar was no longer interested in Cicero, who, he saw, was intent on saving liberty, and through his friends he proposed to Antony that they come to terms. So the three men met on a small island in the middle of a river and conferred together for three days. About everything else they soon agreed and divided the whole empire among themselves as if it were their paternal estate, but a dispute as to which men they would have killed caused them a great deal of trouble. Each one wanted to get rid of his enemies and preserve his relatives. At length their vindictiveness against those they hated made them forget honor to kins

folk and loyalty to friends. Caesar gave up Cicero to Antony and Antony
let him have Lucius Caesar, who was his uncle on his mother's side.
Lepidus was allowed to put his brother Paulus to death, though some say
that Lepidus handed his brother over to Caesar and Antony, who were
insisting on his death. Nothing, I think, was ever more brutal or savage
than this exchange. For by trading murder for murder they did to death
both those whom they surrendered and those whom they took into their
own charge, but their wrong to their friends was worse, for they destroyed
them without hating them.

20.   On top of this agreement, the soldiers around them there demanded
that Caesar should strengthen this friendship by marriage and take to wife
Clodia, a daughter of Fulvia, Antony's wife. This also being agreed to,
three hundred men were proscribed and executed by them.[27] When Cicero
was murdered, Antony ordered his head cut off and the right hand with
which he had written his speeches against him,[28] and on their being
brought to him, he looked at them with delight and laughed gleefully
again and again. Then when satiated with the sight, he ordered them
fastened above the rostrum in the forum, as if he were insulting a dead
body and not displaying his own arrogance in good fortune and making a
disgrace of power. His uncle, Lucius Caesar, when he was being hunted,
fled to his sister for refuge, and when the executioners were at her door
and about to force their way into her room, she stood in the doorway
spreading out her arms and crying over and over, "You shall not kill
Lucius Caesar unless you first kill me, the mother of the dictator!" By
this means she got her brother away and saved his life.

21.   The rule of the triumvirate was in most respects detested by the
Romans. Antony bore most of the blame, because he was older than Caesar
and more powerful than Lepidus. As soon as he had thrown off his troubles, he flung himself into his old pleasure-loving, dissolute way of life. In
addition to his general bad reputation, he made himself much hated on
account of the house he lived in. It had belonged to Pompey the Great,
a man who was admired as much for his seriousness and his orderly and

---

[27] According to the historians Appian and Dion Cassius, the number of proscribed
persons was much larger.
[28] See above, *Cicero*, ch. 48.

democratic way of life as for his three triumphs. So it displeased the citizens to see that house closed much of the time to commanders, officers, and ambassadors, who were rudely driven from its doors, but crowded with actors, jugglers, and drunken panderers, on whom was spent most of the money acquired by violence and cruelty. For the triumvirs not only sold the estates of those whom they murdered, bringing false accusations against their wives and children, and piling on them every sort of tax, but hearing that there had been money deposited with the Vestal Virgins by both foreigners and citizens, they went and took it away. Antony could never get enough, and so Caesar at last called for a division of funds. They divided the army too between them, and both took their troops to Macedonia against Brutus and Cassius, leaving the charge of the city to Lepidus.

22.   Crossing the sea they started military operations and encamped near the enemy, Antony opposite Cassius and Caesar opposite Brutus. Caesar, however, did nothing of importance and it was Antony who gained all the victories and successes. In the first battle [29] Caesar was completely defeated by Brutus, lost his camp, and only by flight escaped his assailants, though he writes himself in his *Memoirs* that he retired before the battle on account of a dream which one of his friends had. But Antony vanquished Cassius, although some authors say that Antony was not in the battle, but only came up afterwards when his men were already hot after the enemy. At his own entreaty and command Cassius was killed by Pindarus, one of his faithful freedmen, without knowing that Brutus had been victorious. A few days later they fought a second battle in which Brutus was defeated and then killed himself. And Antony carried off most of the credit for that victory, especially since Caesar was ill at that time.

Standing over the corpse of Brutus, Antony upbraided him mildly for the death of his brother Gaius, whom Brutus had put to death in Macedonia to avenge Cicero; but he blamed, he said, Hortensius [30] more than he did Brutus, and ordered him slain at his brother's tomb. Over the body of Brutus he threw his own purple cloak, worth a great deal of money, and ordered one of his freedmen to see to its burial. He afterwards found

[29] This was the first battle of Philippi, fought in 42 B.C. The second, in which Brutus was defeated, followed almost at once.
[30] Quintus Hortensius, son of the famous orator and rival of Cicero, had served under Caesar in important posts, but after his murder had sided with Brutus.

out that the man had not burned the cloak with the body and had appropriated much of the sum meant for the burial, whereat he put him to
death.

23.   Thereupon Caesar went back to Rome, no one thinking he would
live long on account of his illness. Antony went on into Greece with a large
army, intending to levy tribute on all the eastern provinces, for the triumvirs had promised every soldier five thousand drachmas and so had
to take more strenuous measures to raise money and collect contributions.
With the Greeks he behaved at first politely and courteously. His jovial
spirits indeed made him enjoy listening to learned conversations and
looking on at games and religious ceremonies. In his court decisions he
was fair, and he enjoyed being called a Graecophile, and still more an
Athenophile, and made many gifts to the city. When the people of Megara
wanted to compete with Athens in showing him something handsome
and asked him to come and see their senate house, he went and looked
at it, but when they asked him what he thought of it, said, "Small, and
out of repair." He had the temple of Pythian Apollo measured, as though
intending to finish it; in fact, he promised the senate that he would.

24.   But then he left Lucius Censorinus in charge of Greece and crossed
to Asia,[31] and helped himself to the wealth he found there. Kings thronged
to his door, and wives of kings, rivaling one another in their gifts and
their beauty, offered themselves to his seductions. And while Caesar at
Rome was being worn out with party strife and war, Antony himself
was basking in great peace and leisure, being carried by his passions back
to his familiar ways of life. Lute players such as Anaxenor, flute players
such as Xuthus, Metrodorus, a dancer, and a swarm of similar Asiatic
entertainers, far outdoing in their gluttony and ribaldry the harpies from
Italy, poured in and took up quarters in his court. It was unendurable
how everything was wasted on those orgies. All Asia, like the city of
Sophocles,[32] was filled "both with the burning of incense, and

> With paeans too and the sound of heavy groaning."

So on Antony's entry into Ephesus, women clad like Bacchae, and men
and boys like Satyrs and Pans led the way. And the city was filled with

[31] Antony moved over to Asia Minor in 41 B.C.
[32] The city was Thebes. Sophocles, *Oedipus Rex*, 4.

ivy and thyrsus wands,[33] harps, flutes, and psalteries, while the people hailed Antony as Dionysus, Joy Giver and Gracious One. He was that, it is true, to some, but to more he was Devourer and Savage One.[34] For he robbed well-born men of their possessions and squandered them on knaves and flatterers. Some of them would ask him for the property of men still living, on the pretense that they were dead. A house belonging to a citizen of Magnesia Antony presented to a cook who had pleased him, they say, by a single successful supper. But at last, as he started to impose a second levy on the cities, Hybreas ventured to speak on behalf of Asia, using words which were plain, and yet did not displease Antony's hot temper. "If," he said, "you collect taxes twice in one year, you can create for us also two summers and two harvests." In bold and matter-of-fact language he went on to say that Asia had paid him already two hundred thousand talents. "If you have not received them, demand them of those who took them; but if you did receive them and now have them not, we are ruined." His words had a strong influence on Antony, for he was ignorant of much of what was happening, not so much because of his indolence but because in his simplicity he trusted those about him.

For there was simplicity in his character and slowness of perception, though when he did realize his errors, he was deeply penitent and ready to ask pardon of those he had wronged. He was free-handed both in the restitutions he made and in the punishments he inflicted, but he went to more extremes in his conferment of favors than in his infliction of punishments. His rude manners in sport and joking carried their own remedy with them, for a man might return his jokes and his rudeness, and he enjoyed being laughed at as much as laughing at others. This disposition was the cause of many of his disasters, for he never imagined that those who used such free language in jesting with him would flatter him in serious talk, and so he was easily taken in by their adulation, not knowing that some persons mix bold speech, like a tangy sauce, with their flattery, to take away its nauseating quality. They chatter impertinently at table to make it seem that, when they are obsequious in important matters, it is not because as courtiers their aim is to gratify their superior but because they are overwhelmed by his wisdom.

---

[33] The thyrsus was a slender wand wreathed with ivy and grape leaves, and with a pine cone at the top, carried usually by worshipers of Bacchus.
[34] Dionysus, or Bacchus, had these and various other names.

25. Such then was Antony's disposition. The final catastrophe was the awakening of his love for Cleopatra, which aroused and maddened to frenzy many passions that had hitherto been concealed and lying dormant in him, and vanquished and destroyed whatever of goodness and sane judgment still tried to resist them. This was the way she captured him. As he was preparing for the Parthian war he sent her orders to meet him in Cilicia to answer the charges made against her of collecting and supplying Cassius with large sums for his war. Dellius, whom Antony sent, when he saw her face and observed her cleverness and craftiness in conversation, knew at once that Antony would never dream of doing anything to such a woman, and that she would be all powerful with him. He turned therefore to paying court to the Egyptian, and to persuading her, in the words of Homer,[35] to go to Cilicia "bedecked in her fine array," and fear nothing from Antony, who was the gentlest and kindest of generals.

She was persuaded by Dellius, and judging by the effects her beauty had had earlier on Gaius Caesar and on Gnaeus, Pompey's son, she was sanguine that she would easily win over Antony. For the other men had known her when she was still a girl and inexperienced in affairs, but she would go to Antony at an age when women are at the height of their most brilliant beauty and keenest too in their understanding.[36] Accordingly, she got ready a quantity of presents and money and ornaments, such as might be expected from one of her lofty station and flourishing kingdom; but she based her hopes, as she went, principally on herself and the witcheries and charms of her own person.

26. She received many letters from Antony and his friends summoning her to appear, and she was both scornful and amused at the man. She sailed up the river Cydnus [37] in a barge with a gilded stern, purple sails spread, and rowers plying silver oars to the sound of a flute in tune with pipes and lyres. She herself lay under a gold-spangled canopy, adorned as Aphrodite in her pictures, while boys, looking like painted Cupids, stood on either side to fan her. The most beautiful of her handmaids, arrayed like Nereids and Graces, were stationed some at the tillers, others at the

---

[35] *Iliad*, XIV, 152. The words are used of Hera, adorning herself for a meeting with Zeus.   [36] Cleopatra was twenty-eight at this time and Antony about forty-two.
[37] The river Cydnus, later called Tersus, flows down from the mountains of Cilicia past the city of Tarsus, where Antony awaited Cleopatra, to the sea.

ropes. Wonderful perfumes from many incense fires spread to the river banks. One crowd of people followed her, on both sides of the river, up from its mouth, and another crowd came down from the city to see the spectacle. The mob in the market place at Tarsus too streamed away, until finally Antony was left alone seated on his tribunal. And the tale spread everywhere that Aphrodite was coming to make merry with Bacchus for the good of Asia. Antony now sent and invited Cleopatra to dinner, but she requested him to come instead to her. So, wishing to show his good nature and friendliness, he promptly obeyed and went. He found the preparations too splendid to be described, and was especially astonished by the number of the lights. Such myriads of them, they say, were hanging and sparkling on every side, in such curves and relations to one another to form squares and circles, that the sight was rare and lovely to see.

27. The next day, Antony feasted her in turn, and aspired to surpass her in splendor and refinement, but in both respects he was outclassed and vanquished. He himself was the first to jeer at the scantiness and clumsiness of his entertainment. Cleopatra saw in Antony's gibing much of the vulgar soldier, and adopted the same free and saucy manner towards him. Now her beauty, they say, in itself was not so far beyond compare or so striking as to astound those who saw her, but her conversation had an irresistible charm, and the combination of her appearance with her persuasive way of talking and with the character that somehow pervaded all her intercourse with people had something fascinating about it. There was sweetness too in the sound of her voice, and her tongue, like an instrument with many strings, she could turn fluently to whatever language she chose. With few barbarians did she ever converse through an interpreter, and to most of them she made her replies without help, as, for instance, to Troglodytes, Hebrews, Arabs, Syrians, Medes, and Parthians. She is said to have known the speech of many other peoples besides, though the kings, her predecessors, had not troubled to learn even the Egyptian tongue, while some of them had given up the Macedonian.[38]

28. She made now such a conquest of Antony that, while his wife Fulvia in Rome was struggling with Caesar to protect his interests, and a Par-

---

[38] The Ptolemaic dynasty of Egypt, it will be remembered, was Macedonian in origin.

thian army was hovering around Mesopotamia, and the Parthian king's generals had made Labienus [39] commander-in-chief and were about to invade Syria—he let himself be carried off by her to Alexandria. And there, amusing and diverting himself like a young man of leisure, he consumed and wasted on pleasure what Antiphon called the most precious treasure of all, which is Time. They formed a kind of club called the Inimitable Livers, and every day they feasted one another, squandering incredible sums. Philotas, the physician at Amphissa, used to tell my grandfather Lamprias that he was then a young man in Alexandria learning his profession, and that he became well acquainted with one of the royal cooks and was invited by him to take a look at their lavish preparations for dinner. He was conducted accordingly into the kitchen, where on seeing the enormous profusion of everything, with eight wild boars roasting, he wondered at the number of the guests. The cook laughed and said that the dinner party was not large, only about twelve, but that every dish set before them must be at the very pitch of perfection, which is over in a moment of time. It might be that Antony would call for dinner at once, and then after a few moments, if it so happened, he might postpone it and ask for a glass of wine or fall into conversation with someone. "Consequently," he said, "not one but many dinners are prepared, for the exact time of serving is hard to guess." This was Philotas' story.

He said too that in course of time he became one of the attendants on Antony's eldest son, whom he had by Fulvia, and used to dine with him and his other companions, when the boy did not dine with his father. On one occasion a physician present was boring the company at dinner by his bragging, and Philotas shut him up with this sophism: "To a man a little feverish one should give cold water, but every man who has a fever is feverish; hence to every man who has a fever one should give cold water." The man was bewildered and said no more, and Antony's son, much pleased, laughed and said, "Philotas, I make you a present of all the things here," and he pointed to a table covered with a number of large tankards. Philotas accepted his good will but was far from imagining

---

39 This Quintus Labienus was the son of the Labienus who served under Julius Caesar in Gaul. After Caesar's death the son was sent East by Brutus to get help against young Caesar, and Antony. He invaded Syria at the head of a Parthian army, defeated Antony's representative there and advanced into Asia Minor, where in 39 B.C. he was overcome and killed.

that a boy of that age had the power to give away things of such value. A little later, however, one of the slaves brought the tankards to him, packed in a container, and told him to seal it. And when he held back and was afraid to take it, "What are you afraid of, fellow?" said the slave. "Do you not know that the giver is Antony's son and that he can make presents of that many things, even if they are solid gold. But if you take my advice, you will sell them all back to us for money. For it might be his father would miss some of the pieces, which are old and valued for their workmanship." Stories like these, my grandfather used to say, Philotas would relate on every occasion.

29. But Cleopatra, by distributing her flattery not, as Plato says,[40] in four ways, but in many, and by constantly introducing some fresh pleasure and charm into Antony's occupations, whether serious or mirthful, got him completely under her sway, never leaving him day or night. She played at dice with him, drank with him, hunted with him, watched him as he took his exercise in arms. And at night, when he would go and stand at the doors and windows of common people and make fun of those inside, she would go with him on these escapades, dressed as a serving girl. Antony too would try to pose as a slave. So invariably he would get back some jeers and often blows before he went home, though most people guessed who he was. All in all, the Alexandrians were amused by his foolery and joined in his games in a light and refined way, for they liked him and said that he wore his tragic mask with the Romans but his comic mask with them.

To describe his frolics at length would be a great waste of time. Once he was fishing and had bad luck and was annoyed because Cleopatra was there. So he ordered the fishermen to dive down and fasten secretly to his hook some fish which had already been caught. Two or three times he drew these up, but the Egyptian lady was not deceived. Pretending to be full of admiration, she told her friends about it and invited them to come the next day and see. A crowd went out on the fishing boats, and when Antony lowered his line, she ordered one of her slaves to get ahead of him, swim to his hook and stick on it a smoked fish from Pontus. Antony, sure he had something, then drew up his line and naturally there was great laughter. But Cleopatra said, "Turn over your fishing rod to the

40 Plato, *Gorgias,* 464.

fishermen of Pharos and Canopus, general! The things you are after are cities, kingdoms, and continents."

30. While Antony was thus diverting himself with trifles and boyish pranks, two messages arrived: one from Rome, that Lucius his brother and Fulvia his wife, having first quarreled with one another and then gone to war with Caesar, had lost the struggle and were in flight from Italy; the other, no pleasanter, that Labienus in command of the Parthians was conquering Asia from the Euphrates and Syria as far as Lydia and Ionia. With difficulty, then, like a man aroused from sleep after a heavy debauch, Antony set out to meet the Parthians and got as far as Phoenicia. Then Fulvia sent him a letter full of lamentation, and he turned his course towards Italy, taking with him two hundred ships. On the voyage, however, he picked up some friends who had fled from Italy, and heard from them that Fulvia had been the cause of the war. For she was naturally an interfering and high-handed woman, and she had hoped that if any commotion arose in Italy, it would drag Antony away from Cleopatra. And then it happened that Fulvia, who was sailing to meet him, fell ill and died at Sicyon.

The time was therefore opportune for a reconciliation with Caesar. And when Antony arrived in Italy, Caesar evinced no intention of bringing any charges against him, and Antony laid on Fulvia the blame for whatever might have been charged against him. Their friends would not allow any scrutiny of this excuse, but brought the two together. And so they now divided up the empire, making a boundary out of the Ionian Sea and assigning what was east of it to Antony and what was west to Caesar. They allowed Lepidus to have Libya, and for the consulship it was settled that friends of each should hold the office in turn, when they did not want it for themselves.[41]

31. This agreement was considered fair, but it needed some stronger security, which fortune now provided. Octavia was a sister of Caesar, older than he and by another mother, for she was Ancharia's daughter, and he, born later, was Atia's son. Caesar was extremely fond of his sister, and she was, as they say, a wonder of a woman. Her husband, Gaius Mar-

---

[41] This agreement, renewing the Second Triumvirate, was reached at Brundisium in the winter of 40–39 B.C.

cellus, had died a short time before this, and she was a widow. And Antony, now that Fulvia was dead, was considered a widower, even though
he did not disavow his connection with Cleopatra. He did not, however,
profess to be married to her and his reason was still struggling at this
point with his love for the Egyptian. Everyone was trying to promote his
marriage with Octavia, in the hope that she, with her great beauty, dignity and intelligence, when wedded to Antony and loved by him, as such
a woman naturally would be, could preserve harmony and be their salvation in everything. When then both men were satisfied they went up to
Rome and celebrated Octavia's nuptials. The law did not allow a widow to
remarry until her husband had been dead ten months, but the senate by a
decree removed the time barrier for them.

32. Sextus Pompey [42] was then holding Sicily and raiding Italy, and with
his fleets of pirate ships, led by the brigands Menas and Menecrates, had
been making the sea unsafe for other vessels. But he seemed to have a
friendly feeling for Antony, for he had received Sextus' mother when she
fled from Rome with Fulvia, and so, Antony thought, they might come
to terms with him. They all met at the promontory and pier of Misenum,[43]
near which Pompey had his fleet anchored, while the troops of Antony
and Caesar were drawn up along the shore. There it was agreed that
Pompey should have Sardinia and Sicily, keep the sea clean of pirates
and send up to Rome a fixed quantity of grain; and then they invited
one another to dinner. Lots were cast and it fell to Pompey to feast them
first. When Antony asked him where they would dine, "There," said
Pompey, pointing to the admiral's ship with its six banks of oars, "for
that is the only ancestral home which is left to Pompey." This he said as a
reproach to Antony, who then owned the house which had belonged to
his father Pompey.

But he brought his ship in to anchor, put up a kind of bridge as a passageway over from the promontory, and received the other two on board
with a hearty welcome. When the gaiety was at its height and jests about

[42] This was the younger son of Pompey the Great, who with his brother had fought
Julius Caesar in Munda, Spain. He had escaped from the battle to continue from
Sicily the struggle against Caesar's heir.
[43] Misenum was a headland and a port on the western coast of Italy, north of Naples.
It was, however, merely a seaside resort until under Augustus it was made the chief
naval station of Rome.

Cleopatra and Antony were passing freely, Menas the brigand came up
to Pompey and said, so that the others did not hear, "Do you want me to
cut the ship's anchor ropes and make you lord not of Sicily and Sardinia,
but of the Roman state?" On hearing this Pompey reflected for a short
time and then said, "You should have done it, Menas, without speaking
to me beforehand. But now let us be content with what we have. Oath-
breaking is not for me." So after being feasted in his turn by the other
two, Pompey sailed back to Sicily.

33. This peacemaking over, Antony sent Ventidius [44] on into Asia, to
check the farther advance of the Parthians, while he, to please Caesar,
was being made priest in place of the elder Caesar.[45] And so with everything else of importance in the political field, they acted together in an
atmosphere of friendliness. But in any playful contests, Antony was continually beaten, to his great annoyance. He had with him an Egyptian
diviner, one of those who cast nativities, and he, whether to please Cleopatra or in good faith, spoke freely to Antony, saying that his fortune,
though brilliant and splendid, was being obscured by that of Caesar. He
therefore advised Antony to get as far away as possible from that young
man. "For your genius," he said, "is afraid of his, and though proud and
lofty whenever it is by itself, when his is near, it is humiliated and abject."
And little incidents that happened seemed to confirm the Egyptian's
words. For they say that whenever in play they cast lots or threw dice
for something that had come up, Antony was the loser. Frequently they
matched cocks and fighting quails, and Caesar's were always victorious.

These trifles irritated Antony, though he did not show it, and made
him pay more heed to the Egyptian. At length, committing affairs at
home to Caesar, he left Italy and took Octavia, who had meanwhile borne
him a daughter, to Greece. While wintering in Athens, he had news of
the first successes of Ventidius, how he had defeated the Parthians in
battle and killed both Labienus and Pharnapates, the ablest of King

---

44 Publius Ventidius, a native of western Italy, came first to Rome as a prisoner of war.
When released, like many other impoverished Italians, he joined Julius Caesar's party
and fought in the civil war. After Caesar's death he raised three legions to fight under
Antony. His commission from Antony to drive the Parthians out of Asia Minor gave
him a chance for real military achievement, and after his victories he was given a
Parthian triumph at Rome.
45 That is, he was created Pontifex Maximus, as Julius Caesar had been.

Hyrodes' generals. To celebrate this victory Antony gave a feast to the Greeks and acted as games-master for the Athenians. Leaving at home his insignia as general, he appeared with the wands of a games-master, in a plain gown and white shoes, and, when necessary, he took young wrestlers by the neck and separated them.

34. Then as he was preparing to set out for the war, he took a garland from the sacred olive tree [46] and in obedience to an oracle, filled a vessel with water from the Clepsydra,[47] and carried it with him. In the meantime, Pacorus, the Parthian king's son, with a large army had again marched against Syria, but Ventidius met and routed him in Cyrrhestica [48] and slaughtered a huge number of his men. Pacorus himself fell among the first. This victory, which became highly celebrated, gave the Romans full satisfaction for their downfall under Crassus, and once more confined the Parthians within Media and Mesopotamia, for they had been thoroughly defeated in three successive battles.

Ventidius gave up, however, all idea of pursuing the Parthians farther, for he was afraid of Antony's jealousy, but he attacked and subjugated the people who had rebelled against Rome, and laid siege to Antiochus of Commagene [49] in the city of Samosata. Antiochus now offered to pay a thousand talents and submit to Antony's dictates, but Ventidius told him to send his proposal to Antony, who by then was drawing near. But he would not allow Ventidius to make peace with Antiochus, because he wished that this one achievement at least should bear his own name, and that not every success should be Ventidius' work. The siege, however, took a long time, for the inhabitants despaired of making peace and turned to fighting with all their might. Antony got nowhere with it, and at last, ashamed and remorseful, was thankful to make peace with Antiochus for three hundred talents. Then, after settling some small affairs in Syria, he went back to Athens, conferred suitable honors on Ventidius and sent him home for his triumph.

Ventidius is the only man up to our day who ever celebrated a triumph

---

[46] An olive tree sacred to Athene stood on the Acropolis by the Erechtheum.

[47] A sacred spring, below the ancient gateway to the Acropolis.

[48] Cyrrhestica was a district in northern Syria.

[49] Antiochus, king of Commagene, the northernmost district of Syria, had had his rule confirmed by Pompey in 64 B.C. He had supported Pompey in his war with Julius Caesar, and was now against the triumvirs, the heirs to Caesar's power.

over the Parthians. He was a man of obscure birth, but through his friendship with Antony he enjoyed opportunities to do great deeds. Of these opportunities he made excellent use and thus substantiated the general report of Antony and Octavius Caesar—that they accomplished more with armies commanded by others than by themselves. For Sossius, Antony's general in Syria, had great success, and Canidius, whom Antony left in Armenia, subdued the Armenians, and also the kings of the Iberians and the Albanians, and penetrated to the Caucasus. Whereupon the name and renown of Antony's power spread far among the barbarians.

35.   But Antony was once more irritated against Caesar by some false stories, and with three hundred ships he sailed back to Italy. As the people of Brundisium would not admit his fleet, he went on to anchorage at Tarentum. From there, at her request, he sent Octavia, who had come with him from Greece, to see her brother. She was with child, having already borne Antony two daughters. On her way she met Caesar, and after first winning over his friends Agrippa and Maecenas,[50] she implored him with many pleadings and entreaties not to let her become an utterly miserable woman after being the most happy. For now, she said, all men looked up to her as the wife and sister of the two great commanders. "But if," she said, "the worst prevails and war comes, one of you—I know not which—is fated to win, and one to lose. In either case my lot will be wretched."

Moved by her words, Caesar came on in peaceful fashion to Tarentum, and the population there saw a beautiful sight—a great army lying tranquil on land, a swarm of ships riding quietly off shore, and the commanders and their friends meeting one another like comrades. Antony gave a banquet first, and Caesar agreed to it for his sister's sake. It was then decided that Caesar should give Antony two legions for the Parthian war, and that Antony should give Caesar a hundred bronze-beaked galleys. Apart from these negotiations, Octavia asked her husband for twenty light boats for her brother, and her brother for a thousand soldiers for her husband. So they parted, and Caesar busied himself at once with his war

---

[50] Marcus Agrippa had been a fellow student with the young Caesar at Apollonia and remained his close friend through life. Gaius Maecenas, an Etruscan, the famous patron of men of letters, became Caesar's counselor in affairs of state.

against Sextus Pompey to conquer Sicily, while Antony entrusted Octavia and his children by Fulvia to Caesar's care and crossed back to Asia.

36. But the dread poison that had long lain dormant in him—his passion for Cleopatra—which seemed to have been put to sleep and exorcised away by wiser reflection, flared up again and gathered strength as he approached Syria. And finally, like the stubborn and ungovernable beast in the soul, of which Plato speaks,[51] he spurned all good and wholesome considerations and sent Fonteius Capito to bring Cleopatra to Syria. On her arrival he bestowed on her no mere trifle to add to her domain, but Phoenicia, Coele Syria, Cyprus, much of Cilicia, and, furthermore, the part of Judaea which grows balsam, and all of Arabia Nabataea which slopes towards the Outer Sea. These gifts deeply displeased the Romans. He had conferred tetrarchies and kingdoms of great nations on many private persons, and had taken kingdoms away from many monarchs, as for instance from Antigonus the Jew, whom he had tried and beheaded, the first king to be punished in that way; but nothing stung the Romans as did the shame of these honors paid to Cleopatra.

He increased the scandal by acknowledging his two children by Cleopatra, one of whom he named Alexander and the other Cleopatra, giving one the surname of Sun and the other of Moon. He was good at glossing over disgrace, and he said that the greatness of the Romans' power was shown not by what they took from people but by what they gave, and that by their successive begettings of many kings they were broadening the scope of noble families. In this fashion his own ancestor had been begotten by Hercules, who did not limit his progeny to a single womb. Nor was he afraid of laws like Solon's or of rules for procreation, but he gave free rein to nature and left behind him many beginnings and foundations of families.

37. Then Phraates killed his father Hyrodes [52] and seized the kingdom, and many other Parthians fled. Among them was Monaeses, a man of

---

[51] See Plato, *Phaedrus*, 254.

[52] Phraates IV of Parthia, a cruel and treacherous man, killed his father Hyrodes in 36 B.C. Hyrodes was the king who had inflicted the crushing defeat on Crassus (see above, *Caesar*, ch. 28). The war with the Parthians, which Antony left unfinished, was not actually concluded until 20 B.C., when Augustus himself journeyed to Asia Minor, made peace, and established a Roman protectorate over the country.

power and high standing, who came as a fugitive to Antony. Antony saw in Monaeses' fate a resemblance to that of Themistocles,[53] and comparing his own opulence and magnanimity with that of the Persian kings, he presented him with three cities, Larissa, Arethusa, and Hierapolis, which formerly was called Bambyce. But Phraates sent Monaeses an offer of amnesty and Antony was glad to have him go home, for he had resolved to deceive Phraates with pretenses of peace. He asked, however, for the return of the standards captured from Crassus, as well as of his men who still survived.

He then sent Cleopatra back to Egypt and went on through Armenia and Arabia to where his forces were assembled with those of the allied kings. Of them there were many, the greatest of all being Artavasdes, king of Armenia, who brought six thousand cavalry and seven thousand foot. Here Antony reviewed his army. Of the Romans proper there were sixty thousand foot, besides the cavalry counted as Roman, and ten thousand Spaniards and Celts. Of other nations there were thirty thousand, including cavalry and light-armed troops.

Yet all this preparedness and power, which alarmed even the Indians beyond Bactria and shook the whole of Asia, were wasted on Antony, they say, because of Cleopatra. For in his eagerness to spend the winter with her, he started the war prematurely, and conducted it in a confused way. He was not in control of his own reasoning powers but, as though bewitched by drugs or magic, was forever looking longingly towards her, more intent on a speedy return to her than on defeating the enemy.

38.   In the first place, then, he should have wintered in Armenia and rested his army there, worn out as it was by a journey of eight thousand furlongs, and then at the beginning of spring, before the Parthians had stirred out of winter quarters, have occupied Media. But he could not wait and immediately led his army along, keeping Armenia on the left and skirting Atropatene,[54] laying waste the whole countryside. Secondly, the engines he needed for sieges were conveyed in three hundred wagons, among them a battering ram eighty feet long. Not one of them, if lost, could be replaced in time to use, since this inland country produced no wood of proper length or hardness. Yet in his haste he left them all be-

---

[53] See above, Themistocles, ch. 29.

[54] This was a province of Media bordering on the Caspian Sea.

hind as impediments to speed, though he set a guard under Statianus over the wagons. He himself now laid siege to Phraata, a large city, where the king of Media's wives and children were. The demands of that siege proved at once what an error he had committed in leaving his engines behind, so, as he moved up closer, with great labor and loss of time he began to erect a mound against the wall. Meanwhile Phraates came down with a large army, and on hearing that the wagons which carried the machines had been left behind, sent a large detachment of cavalry to seize them. They surrounded and killed Statianus and ten thousand of his men. The engines they captured and destroyed. They took many prisoners too, among whom was King Polemon.[55]

39. This unexpected blow at the outset of the campaign naturally upset Antony's followers. The Armenian king Artavasdes, despairing of Roman success, took his troops and departed, though he had been the main cause of the war. The Parthians now flaunted themselves before the besiegers in gaudy array, threatening and insulting them.[56] So Antony, anxious that his soldiers should not remain despondent in inactivity or grow even more cast down, took ten legions and three cohorts of heavyarmed men and all his cavalry and led them off to forage, with the idea that thus he would certainly lure out the enemy into a regular battle. And at the end of one day's march, he saw that the Parthians were circling around him and aiming to attack him on the road. Thereat he posted inside the camp the signal for battle, but had the tents pulled down as if he were planning not to fight but to retire. Then he led his troops past the barbarians' line, which was shaped like a crescent, first giving orders that his cavalry should charge as soon as they thought the foremost Parthians were within reach of their own heavy infantry.

To the Parthians, as they stood in formation, the orderliness of the Romans seemed beyond telling, and they watched them marching past, spaced equally apart, without confusion or sound of voice, waving their javelins. But when the standard was raised and the cavalry facing about

---

[55] Polemon I had recently been made king of Pontus by Antony. He ransomed himself from the Parthians and remained loyal to Antony until after the battle of Actium, when he made terms with Octavian.

[56] The Parthians at this time were a semi-nomadic people, expert horsemen, whose fighting tactics seem to have been similar to those of the North American Indians of the western plains.

with a shout hurled themselves on the enemy, they received the attack and repelled it, even though the Romans were at once too close to allow the use of arrows. When, however, the heavy infantry joined in the melée with shouting and clashing of arms, the Parthians' horses were frightened and fell back and the Parthians fled before coming to close quarters. Antony pressed hard in pursuit, with high hopes that by that battle he had finished the whole or most of the war. His infantry kept up the chase for fifty furlongs, and the cavalry for three times that distance. But on summing up the number they had slain and captured they found they had but thirty prisoners and eighty corpses, and were all baffled and dismayed. For they considered it terrible that in their victory they had killed so few and in their defeat around the wagons they had lost so many.

The next day they got ready and took the road back towards Phraata and their camp. But on their way they met the enemy again, at first a few, then more, and finally all of them, and they, as though fresh and unvanquished, yelled at them and fell on them from every quarter, so that it was with difficulty and great exertion that they got safely to their camp. Then the Medes made a raid on their rampart and stampeded its defenders, and Antony in a rage treated the cowards to what is called decimation. He divided them all into tens and put to death the one in each ten who was chosen by lot. For the rest he ordered rations of barley instead of wheat.

40. The war was now a burden to both sides, and a continuation of it looked even more arduous. Antony expected a famine, for it was no longer possible to go foraging without having many men wounded or killed. As for Phraates, he knew that his Parthians could stand anything but hardships and exposure in winter air, and had fears that if the Romans stayed stubbornly on, his troops would desert him. Already the air was growing chilly after the summer equinox. Accordingly, he planned the following stratagem. The Parthians of greatest experience were to grow less ferocious in their attacks on the Romans during their foraging expeditions and in other encounters, allow them to take some things, and call out praises of their valor as brave fighting men, who were rightly admired by their own king. Later, riding up closer and quietly putting their horses beside the Romans', they were to revile Antony because, when Phraates was anxious to make peace and spare the lives of so many good men, An-

tony was not giving him an opening, but was sitting there, waiting for those cruel and mighty enemies, Hunger and Winter, from which it would be a task to escape, even with a convoy of Parthians.

Their words were reported by many to Antony, and his mind was relieved by hope. Yet he sent no herald to the Parthian until he had inquired of these so friendly barbarians whether they were truly expressing the thought of their king. They declared that they were, and urged him to feel no fear or distrust. Thereupon he sent some of his companions to repeat his demand for the return of the Roman standards and captives, so that he might not be supposed to be completely satisfied with merely a safe escape. But the Parthian king told him to let that subject drop, meanwhile promising him peace and safety as soon as he started to withdraw. And within a few days, Antony had his baggage brought together and was breaking camp. But though he had great powers of persuasion when addressing the people, and was more skillful at leading an army by eloquence than any man of the time, his power to encourage his soldiers now deserted him for shame and despondency, and he bade Domitius Ahenobarbus speak to them for him. Some of the men took this amiss, thinking it a sign of his contempt for them; but most of them were deeply moved and understood the reason. Therefore they thought they should be even more respectful and obedient to their general than before.

41.   Antony was intending to lead his troops back by the route over which they had come, through a flat, treeless country. But a Mardian native, a man well acquainted with the habits of the Parthians, who had earlier proved himself loyal to the Romans in the battle over the war engines, now came to Antony and advised him on his retreat to keep close to the mountains on his right, and not to expose an army of heavy-laden infantry to so large a body of mounted bowmen in the bare, wide stretches. This was the very thing, he said, which Phraates had in mind when by his friendly conversations he had induced Antony to lift the siege. He himself, he said, would guide them by a shorter road, where there was an abundance of provisions. On hearing this, Antony deliberated what to do. He did not wish to appear to mistrust the Parthians after making a truce with them, yet he approved of the shorter road and the prospect of marching past inhabited villages. He therefore asked the Mardian for a pledge of good faith, and the man offered to let himself be bound in chains until

he led the army safely into Armenia. And in chains he was their guide for two days peacefully.

On the third day, when Antony had stopped thinking of the Parthians and was advancing carelessly and confidently, the Mardian observed that an embankment along the river had been recently broken through, and that a great stream of water was pouring out towards the road over which they must march. He realized that it was the work of the Parthians, turning the river their way to hinder and delay their march, and he warned Antony to look out and be alert, for the enemy was not far off. And just as Antony was marshaling his infantry and arranging that his spearmen and slingers should charge out through them against an enemy, the Parthians appeared and began riding around them with the aim of encircling the army and throwing it into disorder on every side. Whenever the Roman light-armed troops charged out against them, the Parthians wounded numbers of them with their arrows. However, the Parthians were wounded as severely by the lead bullets and javelins of the Romans and so they would retire. Then they would attack again, until finally the Celts combined their horses into one battalion and scattered them, and there was no further sign of them that day.

42. Having learned from this encounter what he must do, Antony covered not only his rear but both flanks as well with a force of javelin men and slingers, and thus led his army in the form of a square. The cavalry had orders to repel the enemy's attacks but after driving them off not to pursue them far. In consequence the Parthians during the next four days suffered as much damage as they inflicted, grew less venturesome, and were making the winter an excuse for plans to go home. However, on the fifth day, Flavius Gallus, a good and energetic soldier who held a high command, came to Antony and asked him for more light-armed troops from the rear and some cavalry from the van, with which to win a big victory. Antony gave him what he asked and then, when the enemy attacked, he repulsed them but did not draw back, as on former occasions, and lead them towards the heavy infantry, but stood his ground and engaged with them in a more dangerous way. The commanders at the rear saw that he was being cut off from them and sent to call him back, but he paid no heed. They say that Titius the quaestor seized hold of the standards and started to turn them around, berating

Gallus for wasting the lives of so many brave men, but as Gallus berated him in turn and called on those around him to stand fast, Titius went back.

As Gallus was pushing forward against the enemy at his front, he was surrounded all unaware by a swarm from the rear. Attacked now by missiles from every direction, he sent for help. The infantry commanders, of whom Canidius was one, a man of great influence over Antony, appear to have made a serious error. They should have turned their whole phalanx against the enemy, but they sent only a few at a time to Gallus' aid, and only as those were defeated sent others, and so before they realized it, they came near to losing the whole army by defeat and flight. Antony himself, however, quickly appeared from the front with his men-at-arms and stopped the fugitives, and the third legion forced its way through them against the enemy and kept them from pursuing farther.

43. At least three thousand were killed and five thousand wounded were carried to the tents. Among them was Gallus, shot through the body with four arrows, and he did not recover. Antony went about visiting the men and encouraging them, with sympathetic tears in his eyes. They cheerfully grasped his hand and begged him to go and look after himself and not worry about them. They called him commander-in-chief and said that as long as he was well they were safe. All in all, it seems that no general in those days ever collected an army more distinguished for brave deeds, endurance, and vigor. And as for the respect Antony's troops felt for him as their leader, and their willing obedience, and the way in which all alike, good soldiers and bad, officers and privates, valued honor and favor from him more than life and safety—even the ancient Romans had nothing to surpass it. For this there were many reasons, as I have said before: his noble birth, powerful eloquence, simplicity, love and lavishness of giving, and geniality on occasions of pleasure or when mingling with his men. At this time too, by his sympathy with the weariness and pain of the sufferers and his furnishing them with whatever they needed, he made the sick and wounded even more eager to serve him than those who were whole and well.

44. But the Parthians, who previously had been feeling exhausted and inclined to give up, were now so elated by their victory and so contemptuous of the Romans that they camped for the night close to the Roman army, in expectation of soon plundering their empty tents and their

baggage, while the Romans took to their heels. At dawn they gathered for the assault, in far greater numbers than ever before. There are said to have been as many as forty thousand horsemen, for their king had sent even those who customarily guarded his person, believing that success was now certain and sure. The king himself was never present at a battle. Antony wished now to address his soldiers and asked for a dark cloak that he might look more pathetic to them. But his friends were against that idea and he came forward in a general's purple cloak and made his harangue, praising those who had fought victoriously, and upbraiding those who had fled. The former urged him to keep up his courage, and the latter in apology offered themselves for decimation, if he chose, or any other kind of punishment. Only they besought him not to trouble or grieve over them. At this Antony lifted up his hands and prayed the gods that if any retribution were due for his earlier successes, it might fall on him alone, and that to the rest of his army might be granted safety and victory.

45. The next day they went on under stronger defenses, and when the Parthians made their attack, they were greatly surprised. For they thought they were riding up to plunder and pillage, not to fight, and when they met a shower of missiles and saw the Romans sturdy and refreshed and full of ardor, their energy flagged again. However, when the Romans were coming down some steep hills, they set on them, shooting at them as they slowly proceeded. Then the shield-bearers faced about, enclosing the light-armed troops within their ranks, dropped on one knee and held their shields out in front of them. The rank behind held their shields out over the first, and the next rank did the like for them. This formation very much resembles a roof and makes a striking appearance and is the best coverage against arrows, which glance off it. But the Parthians thought that the Romans' dropping on their knees was a sign of fatigue and collapse; so throwing away their bows, they gripped their spears and rode in to close quarters. But then, shouting their battle cry, the Romans sprang instantly to their feet and with their javelin thrusts killed the Parthians in the lead and put all the rest to flight. The same thing happened too on other days, as little by little the Romans moved along their way.

Famine, however, afflicted the army, for it obtained little grain by fighting and was not supplied with implements for grinding. Most of what they had had they had left behind, since some of their pack animals were dead and others were carrying the wounded and sick. An Attic quart of wheat, they say, sold for fifty drachmas, and barley loaves for their weight in silver. The soldiers resorted to greens and roots, but found few with which they were familiar and were forced to try things they had never tasted before. So they chanced on an herb which caused madness followed by death. A man who ate it lost all his memory and understanding. One task only obsessed him, to move and turn over every stone as if he were accomplishing something of great importance. The plain was covered with men stooping down to the ground, grubbing around stones and moving them about. At length they vomited bile and died, for wine, the one antidote, was lacking. When many were dying like this, in the midst of the Parthians' persistent attacks, Antony, we hear, would often cry out, "O, the Ten Thousand!" in heartfelt admiration of Xenophon's army, which had even a longer journey to make from Babylon to the sea, and fought with enemies many times more numerous, and nevertheless got home safe.[57]

46. But now the Parthians, being unable to throw the Roman army into disorder or to break its ranks, and being by this time often defeated and put to flight, again began mixing peaceably with the detachments who went out after fodder or grain. They would point to the loosened strings of their bows and say that they were going back home and that this was the end of their fight to defend themselves. A few Medes, they said, would still follow the Romans for a day or two, not annoying them at all, but simply protecting the more distant villages. With these words they coupled signs of greeting and friendliness, so that once more the Romans grew cheerful and confident, and Antony, hearing of it, was on the verge of deciding on the route across the plains, since the road through the mountains was said to be waterless. But as he was about to take that course, there came to the camp a man named Mithridates, a cousin of the Monaeses who had been with Antony and had received three cities from him as a gift.[58] He asked for someone who could speak the Parthian or

[57] Xenophon's story of the march of ten thousand Spartan soldiers through hostile Persian country from Babylon to the sea is told in his *Anabasis*.

[58] See above, ch. 37. Nothing is known of this Mithridates or of his cousin Monaeses except what Plutarch tells in these chapters and below in ch. 48.

the Syrian language. Alexander of Antioch, a comrade of Antony, went to him and the man told him who he was and mentioned Monaeses as the person responsible for his coming. He then asked Alexander if he saw in the distance a range of lofty hills. When Alexander said he saw them, Mithridates went on, "Under those hills the Parthians in full force are waiting in ambush for you. For the great plains border on those hills, and they expect you to be allured by them and to turn towards them, leaving the road through the mountains. That road undoubtedly means thirst and fatigue, to which you are now accustomed. But if Antony takes the way of the plains, he may be sure that the fate of Crassus is waiting for him there."

47. With these words he departed, and Antony, hearing of it, was disturbed and called his friends together, with the Mardian who was their guide and who was himself of that same opinion. For he knew that even without an enemy, they would wander painfully and blindly over the trackless plains, and he explained that the rough path through the mountains presented no hardships except lack of water for one day. So Antony changed his plan and took his army along the mountain road by night, after ordering every man to carry water with him. Most of them had no pails and therefore filled their helmets with water and carried it that way, while others had it in skins.

Hardly had they started than the news was brought to the Parthians, and contrary to their custom they set out that night to pursue them. As the sun was rising, they overtook the Roman rear, which—what with sleeplessness and fatigue—was in a bad way, for they had marched that night two hundred and forty furlongs, and they had not expected the enemy to overtake them so quickly and hence were disheartened. The fighting too increased their thirst, for they had to keep defending themselves while they trudged on. The marchers in the van came to a river whose waters were cold and clear, but salty and poisonous. When drunk they immediately produced pains and cramps in the bowels and a burning thirst. The Mardian had warned them against this too, but none the less the soldiers shoved away those who tried to prevent them, and drank. Antony went around imploring the men to hold out a little longer, telling them that there was another river not far off which was drinkable, that the rest of the way beyond it was too rough for horses, so that the enemy would certainly turn back there. At the same time, he called in the men who were out fighting, and gave the signal for setting up tents, so that the troops might have some respite in the shade.

48. However, as they were putting up the tents, and the Parthians as usual were beginning to withdraw, Mithridates suddenly appeared again and told Alexander, who came to meet him, that he advised letting the army rest a short time, then getting it on its feet and hurrying to the second river. For the Parthians, he said, would not cross that river and would pursue them only that far. Alexander took the message to Antony, and brought back from him a quantity of gold goblets and bowls, of which Mithridates took as many as he could hide in his clothing and rode away. Then, as it was still daylight, they broke camp and set off again. The enemy did not annoy them, but that night, by their own doing, was the most wretched and appalling of any they passed through. For the men began killing and robbing whoever had any silver or gold, and seizing the property that was being carried by the pack animals. Eventually they fell on Antony's baggage carriers and cut up the tankards and costly tables and divided them among them.

The whole army now fell into a great uproar and began drifting this way and that, for they thought then that the enemy had attacked them and that they were being beaten and scattered. Antony called for one of his freedmen, Rhamnus by name, who was in his bodyguard, and made him swear that whenever he should give him the order, he would run him through with his sword and cut off his head, so that he would neither be captured alive by the enemy nor be recognized after he was dead. His friends broke into tears, but the Mardian tried to encourage him by telling him that they were close to the river, for a moist breeze was blowing from that direction, and a cool air on their faces made breathing pleasanter. He said too that the time they had been on the march confirmed his reckoning, for there was not much left of the night. Meanwhile other messengers reported that the turmoil was due to the greed and misbehavior of their own troops. So to bring the mob back into ranks after its disorder and demoralization, Antony had the signal given for setting up camp.

49. Day was now breaking, and the army was beginning to recover some order and calm, when the Parthians' arrows began falling on the

rear guard and the light-armed troops were given the signal for battle. But the Roman heavy infantry again covered the men with their shields as before, and so stood off the assault of the Parthian archers, who did not dare to come up near. And in this fashion the front ranks advanced little by little and the river came into view. On reaching it Antony drew up his cavalry to hold off the enemy and sent his sick and wounded across first. And shortly, even those who were fighting had an opportunity to drink without fear. For when the Parthians saw the river, they unstrung their bows and bade the Romans pass over boldly and complimented them much on their valor. So they crossed in comfort and rested for a time, and then took the road again, still not trusting the Parthians in the least. On the sixth day after their final battle they arrived at the river Araxes, which is the boundary between Media and Armenia. Its depth and turbulence made it look dangerous, and a rumor went around that the enemy were lying in ambush there and would fall on them while they were crossing; but they reached the other side in safety and found themselves in Armenia, and like men at sea on seeing land again, they fell on their knees and wept and embraced one another for joy. As they went on, however, through a fertile land and after their long privations had everything in abundance, they fell ill with dropsies and dysenteries.

50.   While there, Antony held a review of his forces and found that he had lost twenty thousand foot and four thousand horse, not all killed by the enemy but more than half by disease. They had indeed marched all the way from Phraata in twenty-seven days and had defeated the Parthians in eighteen battles, but their victories had not been effective or lasting, because their pursuits had been brief and incomplete. So, obviously, Artavasdes the Armenian kept Antony from putting an end to that war.[59] For if the sixteen thousand horsemen whom he took out of Media, armed in the same style as the Parthians and accustomed to fighting them, had stayed with Antony to cut down the fugitives after the Romans had beaten them in battle, they could not have rallied after their defeats and plucked up boldness again so repeatedly. For that reason, the whole army in anger tried to induce Antony to punish the Armenian.

On prudent reflection Antony did not reproach him for his treachery or withdraw the friendliness and honor he was used to paying him, not

---

[59] After the battle of Actium, Cleopatra had Artavasdes beheaded.

then, while his own army was weakened and destitute of supplies. But later he again invaded Armenia [60] and by a profusion of promises and invitations persuaded Artavasdes to come to a meeting, and then he seized him and carried him in chains down to Alexandria, and celebrated his triumph. This was one of his acts which most offended the Romans, his entertaining the Egyptians, for Cleopatra's sake, with the stately and solemn ceremonials which belonged to his own country. It, however, took place later.

51. Pressing on now through heavy winter weather and endless snow storms, Antony lost eight thousand men more by the way before he reached the seacoast with a few survivors. There in a little place called White Village, lying between Sidon and Berytus, he awaited the arrival of Cleopatra. As she was slow in coming, he grew distracted with anxiety and soon gave himself up to heavy drinking. Yet he could not endure sitting long at table, but between drinks would jump up often to see if she were in sight. At last she sailed into harbor, bringing a quantity of clothing and money for the soldiers. Some say, however, that Antony got the clothing from her but that he took the money from his own personal funds and distributed it in her name.

52. A quarrel now broke out between the Median king and Phraortes,[61] the Parthian, originating, they say, in a dispute over the Roman booty and creating in the Mede a fearful suspicion that he might be about to lose his dominions. Accordingly he sent and invited Antony to come up, telling him he would join him with his own troops in a war against Phraortes. Antony's hopes were thereby raised high. For the one thing he seemed to have lacked to defeat the Parthians, namely a plentiful supply of horsemen and archers, he saw now provided for him, and himself in the position of granting, not of asking a favor. So he began preparations to march up again through Armenia, and after joining forces with the Mede near the river Araxes, then to resume the war.

53. At Rome Octavia was growing anxious to go to Antony and Caesar had given his consent, not, most writers say, with the idea of pleasing his

---

[60] This later invasion of Armenia was in 34 B.C. in connection with Antony's trip to Parthia before his final return to Alexandria.

[61] Phraortes is evidently a misspelling for Phraates.

sister, but so that if she were insulted or neglected he might have a proper reason for starting a war. On her arrival at Athens [62] she received a letter from Antony telling her to stay there and informing her of his proposed expedition to Media. She saw through his excuse and was pained by it, but still wrote him inquiring where she should send the things she was bringing him—a large supply of clothing for his soldiers, herds of pack animals, money, and presents for the officers and friends with him, and in addition two thousand picked soldiers, fitted out as praetorian cohorts with excellent armor. One Niger, a friend of Antony, was sent by her to tell him these things and he added the praises of her which she so richly deserved.

But Cleopatra saw that Octavia was now on her way to come face to face with her, and feared that if to her nobility of character and Caesar's influence she added the pleasure of her company and services to Antony, she would be invincible and regain complete mastery over her husband. Accordingly Cleopatra pretended to be madly in love with Antony, made herself thin by meager diet, looked rapturous when he entered the room, and woebegone and languishing when he left. She arranged that he should see her in tears, which she would wipe away and try to hide, as if she did not wish him to notice them. She behaved in this way as he was planning his expedition up from Syria to join the Mede. Obsequious servants, too, were busy in her behalf, upbraiding Antony as a hard, unfeeling man, who was killing a mistress devoted to him alone. Octavia, they said, who had married him for reasons of state at her brother's command, was enjoying the title of wife. But Cleopatra, though queen of so many nations, was called simply Antony's love, and did not reject or disdain that name so long as she could see him and live with him. If she were forced away from him, she would not survive.

At length they had him so softened and weakened that he was terrified that she might kill herself, and returned to Alexandria, putting the Mede off until summer, though Parthia was said to be in a state of great unrest. However, he did go up then and came to friendly terms again with the king, betrothed one of the king's daughters, still a child, to one of his sons by Cleopatra, and returned to Alexandria, his mind now occupied with the civil war.

[62] Octavia came to Athens in 35 B.C.

54. In Caesar's opinion Octavia had been insulted, and when she came back to Rome from Athens, he ordered her to live in her own house. But she refused to leave her husband's house, and implored her brother, if he had not on some other score resolved on a war with Antony, to overlook his behavior to her, for it was an indecent thing to have said that the two greatest Roman commanders had plunged their country into civil war, one out of passion for a woman, the other out of jealousy for a woman. Those were her words and she enforced them by her behavior. For she lived in her husband's house as if he were there with her, and cared for the children, both her own and those Fulvia had borne him, in a generous and honorable fashion. She received also the friends of Antony whom he sent to Rome on business or to try for office, and helped them to get from Caesar what they wanted.

But unintentionally she was damaging Antony by her conduct, for he was hated for mistreating such a woman. He was hated too for his distribution of honors among his children at Alexandria, which seemed a theatrical and gaudy show and a sign of his hostility to the Romans. In the crowded gymnasium at Alexandria he had set up two gold thrones on a silver platform, one for himself and one for Cleopatra, with other thrones lower down for his sons. He first proclaimed Cleopatra queen of Egypt, Cyprus, Libya, and Coele Syria, with Caesarion as fellow king. He was supposed to be the son of Julius Caesar, who had left Cleopatra with child. He next proclaimed his sons by Cleopatra kings of kings. To Alexander he assigned Armenia, Media, and Parthia, when he conquered it; to Ptolemy, Phoenicia, Syria, and Cilicia. At the same time he introduced his sons, Alexander dressed in Median costume, with a tiara and high cap, Ptolemy in boots, short mantle, and broad-brimmed hat topped by a diadem. The latter was the dress of the Macedonian kings who succeeded Alexander the Great, and the former that of the Medes and Armenians. And after the boys had embraced their parents, one was given a bodyguard of Armenians, and the other of Macedonians. Both on that and on other occasions when she appeared before the people, Cleopatra wore a robe sacred to Isis, and assumed the name of the New Isis.

55. All these doings Caesar reported to the senate and denounced them frequently in the assembly, trying to excite the people against Antony. But Antony too sent counter charges against Caesar. The most serious of

them were, first, that after taking Sicily from Sextus Pompey, Caesar had not given a share of the island to Antony; second, that after borrowing ships from him for the war, Caesar had not returned them; third, that after deposing his colleague Lepidus from office and degrading him, Caesar was keeping hold of Lepidus' army and territory and the revenues which had been assigned to him; and, finally, that Caesar had divided nearly all Italy up in allotments for his own soldiers, and had left nothing for Antony's men. These charges Caesar answered by saying that he had removed Lepidus from his office for misbehavior. As for what he had acquired by war, he would share it with Antony, whenever Antony shared Armenia with him. Further, Antony's soldiers had no claim to Italy, for they had Media and Parthia, which they had added to the Roman possessions by their brave fighting under their commander.

56. Antony heard of all this while he was still in Armenia, and immediately he ordered Canidius to take sixteen legions and proceed down to the sea. He himself took Cleopatra with him and went to Ephesus, where his navy was assembling from every direction, eight hundred battle ships with their cargo boats. Cleopatra furnished two hundred of them, as well as twenty thousand talents and supplies for all the army for the war. Then, persuaded by Domitius [63] and some others, he commanded Cleopatra to sail back to Egypt and there await the outcome of the war. But she was afraid that under Octavia's influence he would again make peace with Caesar, and so by lavish bribes she prevailed on Canidius to speak to Antony about her and tell him that it was not fair to drive away from the war a woman whose contributions to it were so great, nor was it to his advantage to dampen the ardor of the Egyptians, who made up a large part of his naval force. Also, that he could not see that Cleopatra was inferior in intelligence to any of the kings who were joining Antony's army. She had ruled her great kingdom for a long time by herself, and through her close association with him had learned how to handle affairs of large importance.

These arguments succeeded, since it was fated that everything should pass to Caesar, and with their combined fleets, they set sail for Samos and there took their ease. For while all the kings, potentates, and tetrarchs, nations, and cities between Syria, Maeotis, Armenia, and Illyria had re-

---

[65] This was the Domitius Ahenobarbus who spoke to Antony's army for him in ch. 40.

ceived orders to send or bring supplies for the war, all Dionysiac artists [64] were being summoned to meet at Samos. And while well nigh the whole world around was resounding with lamentation and groans, one island for many days was tuneful with flutes and stringed instruments. Theaters were filled and choruses were competing for prizes. Every city sent an ox as a contribution to the sacrifices, and kings rivaled one another in giving presents and entertainments. And people began to ask themselves, "What will the conquerors be like after their victories, if they celebrate their preparations for war so extravagantly?"

57. At the end of these diversions, Antony gave Priene to the Dionysiac artists for a dwelling place, and himself took ship for Athens where he again was absorbed in sports and shows. And Cleopatra, jealous of the honors bestowed on Octavia by the city, for Octavia was much beloved by the Athenians, attempted to win over the people by her profuse generosity. So they voted her honors and sent a deputation to her house to bring her the vote. Antony, as an Athenian citizen, was one of them, and standing before her he made the speech in the name of the city. He then sent men to Rome to evict Octavia from his house. She left it, they say, taking all Antony's children with her, except his eldest son by Fulvia, who was with his father, and sorrowfully mourning that she would be considered one of the causes of the war. But the Romans were pitying Antony, not her, especially those who had seen Cleopatra and knew that she was neither more beautiful nor more youthful than Octavia.

58. On hearing of the speed and extent of Antony's preparations, Caesar became alarmed that he might have to fight the decisive battle that summer.[65] For he was deficient in many things, and the people were resenting his levies of taxes. In general, the citizens were being forced to pay a fourth of their income, and the freedmen an eighth of their property. They were all crying out against Caesar and disturbances for that reason were breaking out all over Italy. It is therefore regarded as one of Antony's gravest mistakes, that he put off the war for that season. He thus gave Caesar time to finish his preparations and the people's excitement a

---

[64] The great festival of Dionysus at Athens was the origin of Greek drama; these artists would be actors.

[65] That is, the summer of 32 B.C.

chance to quiet down; for while the taxes were being collected they were irritated, but once they had paid they stopped agitating.

Titius and Plancus, friends of Antony and men of consular rank, who had been insulted by Cleopatra, because they had strongly opposed her accompanying the expedition, now deserted to Caesar, and told him about Antony's will, the provisions of which they knew. The will was in the keeping of the Vestal Virgins, and when Caesar asked for it, they would not give it to him, but if he were determined to take it, they bade him come and do so. So he went and took it, and first read it through by himself, marking some culpable passages. Then he convened the senate and read it to them, to the displeasure of most of them, for they thought it strange and shocking to call a living man to account for things he wished done after his death. However, Caesar dwelt heavily on the provisions for Antony's burial, since they specified that his body, even if he died in Rome, after being carried in state through the forum, should then be sent to Cleopatra at Alexandria.

Calvisius, a comrade of Caesar, brought forward the following charges also against Antony with regard to Cleopatra: he had given her the libraries from Pergamum,[66] containing two hundred thousand volumes; at a banquet, before many guests, he had risen and rubbed her feet, to carry out some pledge or wager he had made; he had allowed the Ephesians in his presence to hail Cleopatra as sovereign; and frequently while sitting on his tribunal, judging cases of tetrarchs and kings, he had received tablets of love from her, set in onyx or crystal, and had read them. And once when Furnius, a man of eminence and the ablest speaker in Rome, was arguing, and Cleopatra was carried in a litter through the forum, at sight of her Antony sprang up, left the court, and hanging on to her litter, escorted her home.

59. However, most of Calvisius' tales were thought to be inventions, and Antony's friends went around Rome pleading with the people for him. And they sent one of their number, Geminius, to beg Antony not to

---

[66] Pergamum, the capital city of a Hellenistic kingdom of the same name in western Asia Minor, had become in the third and second centuries before Christ one of the most beautiful cities of the Greek world, famous for its art and its culture, and for the magnificent library collected by its kings, second only to the library at Alexandria. Attalus III, king from 138 to 133 B.C., had left the kingdom by will to Rome.

allow himself to be voted out of his office and denounced as an enemy of Rome. But when Geminius arrived in Greece, he was suspected by Cleopatra of being an agent of Octavia. He was continually ridiculed at table and insulted by being seated in the lowest places. Yet he bore it and waited for a chance to talk with Antony. But once at supper he was ordered to say why he had come, and he answered that the rest of his message he would keep for a sober hour, but that, drunk or sober, one thing he knew, which was that all would be well if only Cleopatra were sent back to Egypt. At this Antony was furious, but Cleopatra said, "You have done well, Geminius, to admit the truth without being tortured." And a few days later Geminius fled and went back to Rome.

Cleopatra's flatterers drove away many of Antony's other friends, who could not abide the drunken gambols and heavy ribaldry. Among these friends were Marcus Silanus and Dellius the historian. Dellius says that he was afraid too of a plot by Cleopatra against him, of which Glaucus the physician told him. For he had annoyed Cleopatra at supper by saying that while their cups were being filled with sour wine, Sarmentus at Rome was drinking Falernian. Sarmentus was one of Caesar's young favorites, whom the Romans call "delicacies."

60. But when Caesar had made preparation enough, a vote was passed for a war against Cleopatra; also, to deprive Antony of the authority he had abandoned to a woman. Caesar added that Antony had been poisoned and was no longer his own master, and that the enemy they would be fighting would be Mardion the eunuch, Pothinus, and Iras, Cleopatra's hairdresser, and Charmion, who among them managed the principal business of the government.

The following omens are said to have appeared before the war. Pisaurum, a city situated near the Adriatic, where a colony had been established by Antony, was swallowed up by chasms which opened in the earth. From one of the stone statues of Antony at Alba sweat dripped for many days, and did not stop when it was wiped off. In Patrae, while Antony was there, the Heracleum was burned by lightning. And at Athens, the Dionysus in the Battle of the Giants [67] was blown down by winds and fell into the theater. Now, Antony claimed to be descended from Hercules

---

[67] The Battle of the Giants was one of the figure groups which decorated the south wall of the Acropolis.

and to resemble Dionysus in his way of life, as I have said. He was addressed as the New Dionysus. The same storm at Athens brought down also, from among many statues which were not disturbed, the colossal figures of Eumenes and Attalus,[68] which were inscribed with Antony's name. Cleopatra's flagship was called Antonias, and a bad sign was seen there. Some swallows had made a nest under the poop and other swallows attacked them and drove them out and killed the fledgelings.

61. But now the antagonists were coming together for the conflict. Antony had no less than five hundred ships of war, among which were many vessels of eight and ten banks of oars, gorgeously fitted out as for a festival. He had an army of one hundred thousand infantry and twelve thousand horse. The subject kings who fought with him were Bocchus, king of the Libyans, Tarcondemus, king of Upper Cilicia, Archelaus of Cappadocia, Philadelphus of Paphlagonia, Mithridates of Commagene, and Sadalas of Thrace. These were with him in person, while from Pontus Polemon sent an army, and Malchus one from Arabia, and Herod the Jew one, as did also Amyntas, king of Lycaonia and Galatia. Assistance came likewise from the king of the Medes. Caesar had two hundred and fifty ships of war, eighty thousand infantry, and about the same number of horsemen as his enemy. Antony's domain extended from the Euphrates River and Armenia to the Ionian Sea and Illyria, Caesar's from Illyria to the Western Ocean, and from the ocean back to the Tyrrhenian and Sicilian seas. Caesar had the part of Libya lying opposite to Italy, Gaul and Spain, as far as the Pillars of Hercules, Antony the part from Cyrene down to Ethiopia.

62. But Antony was by now so completely the mere adjunct to a woman that although on land he was much superior to his enemy, yet to please Cleopatra, he wished the victory to be won at sea; and this in spite of the fact that he saw that his captains, for want of crews, were scraping together out of long-suffering Greece vagabonds, mule-drivers, harvest-hands, and boys, and that even so their ships were not adequately manned, but most were deficient in something, and were also hard to manage at sea. Caesar's ships, on the contrary, had not been built to show off their

---

68 These may have been statues of the father and son, Attalus I and Eumenes II, kings of Pergamum, who were both renowned as patrons of Greek civilization and art.

height and bulk, but were easy to steer and swift and perfectly manned. He kept his fleet together in Tarentum and Brundisium, and now sent to Antony to ask him to waste no more time but to come on with his forces, and he would give them unobstructed ports and roadsteads and would himself retire with his coastal army a day's journey by horse inland from the sea, until Antony had landed in safety and set up camp. In a boastful reply Antony challenged Caesar to single combat, though he himself was the older man. If he refused that, Antony proposed fighting their battle out at Pharsalus,[69] as Caesar and Pompey had done earlier. But while Antony was lying at anchor near Actium, where Nicopolis now stands, Caesar took the initiative by crossing the Ionian Sea and seizing a place in Epirus called Torune (Ladle). Antony's friends were uneasy at this because their land forces would be late in arriving, but Cleopatra, mocking, said, "What is so terrible in Caesar's sitting on a ladle?"

63. At daybreak the enemy's fleet advanced and Antony was alarmed for fear they might capture his ships while still empty of fighting men. He accordingly armed the rowers and stationed them on the decks to make a show. He then assembled his ships at the mouth of the gulf of Actium,[70] their oars on either side lifted and ready for a stroke, their prows facing the enemy, as if they were well manned and prepared to fight. Deceived by this stratagem, Caesar withdrew. And Antony seemed again to show cleverness in enclosing their water supply within defenses and thus cutting the enemy off from it, since other places in the neighborhood had little water and that not good. He was magnanimous too in his treatment of Domitius, contrary to Cleopatra's judgment. For when Domitius, all in a fever, got into a small boat and made off to Caesar, Antony, though taking his desertion hard, sent all his baggage and his friends and slaves after him. Soon after the discovery of his faithlessness and treachery, Domitius died of remorse.

There were desertions too among the kings, and Amyntas and Deiotarus went over to Caesar. And since Antony's navy was poor in every respect and too far from ready to be serviceable, he was compelled to put his mind

---

[69] A battle at Pharsalus would have been a land battle. By bringing his fleet over from Italy and seizing a port on the coast of Epirus, a little way above Actium, where Antony's ships were lying, Caesar made sure that the battle would be fought at sea.
[70] That is, the Ambracian Gulf, on the southern border of Epirus.

on his land forces. Canidius, the commander of the army, had a change of opinion in the face of danger, and now advised Antony to send Cleopatra away and retreat to Thrace or Macedonia and there settle the issue in a land battle. Dicomes, king of the Getae, was promising to come to their aid with a large army, and it would be no disgrace to yield the sea up to Caesar, who had had much practice on it in the Sicilian war. It would, however, be a preposterous thing for Antony, who had had the widest experience in land warfare, to make no more use of his strong and well-equipped host of infantry than to parcel them out among his ships and so fritter away their power. In spite of all these considerations, however, Cleopatra won her contention that the war should be decided by the ships, though already she was contemplating flight and placing her own forces, not where they would be useful as a help to victory, but where they could most easily escape in case of defeat.

There were two long walls extending down from the camp to the navy quarters, between which Antony was used to going back and forth quite unsuspectingly. A slave told Caesar that it would be possible to seize Antony as he was walking down between the walls, whereupon he sent men to lie in ambush for him. They almost succeeded but sprang out too soon and caught only the man who was walking ahead of Antony. He himself had a narrow escape by running.

64. Now that it had been resolved to fight on sea, Antony burned all but sixty of the Egyptian ships. He then manned the best and largest of those, which had from three to ten banks of oars, and put on board twenty thousand heavy-armed soldiers and two thousand bowmen. They say that an infantry centurion there, a man who had fought many battles for Antony and was worn and exhausted in body, as Antony went by him, broke into a wail and said, "Commander, why do you think poorly of these wounds and this sword and put your hopes in trashy planks of wood? Let Egyptians and Phoenicians fight on sea, but give us land, on which we are accustomed to stand and die or else to vanquish our enemies!" To this Antony made no answer, but by a look and a gesture merely bade the man be of good courage, and passed on. He had not much hope himself, for when the masters of his ships proposed leaving their sails behind, he ordered them put on board and taken with them, with the remark that they must not let a single enemy fugitive escape.

65.   On that day and the three following days the waves were high under a strong wind and the sea too rough for fighting. But on the fifth day,[71] the weather was calm and the sea tranquil, and the struggle began. Antony and Poplicola took the right wing of his fleet, Coelius the left, and in the center were Marcus Octavius and Marcus Insteius. Caesar put Agrippa on his left wing and kept the right for himself. Canidius was in command of Antony's land army, and Taurus of Caesar's. They both drew up their troops by the sea and stood quiet. As for the principals themselves, Antony went all around his ships in a rowboat, instructing the soldiers, because of the weight of their ships, to fight holding their positions as if they were on land. The captains he ordered to stand the shock of the enemy's attack as if they were lying still at anchor, and to maintain their guard of the narrow and crooked mouth of the gulf. Caesar, they say, left his tent while it was still dark, and was on his way to visit his ships when he met a man driving an ass. He asked the fellow his name, and he, recognizing Caesar, replied, "My name is Good Luck and my ass's name is Victor." So when later Caesar decorated the spot with the beaks of ships, he set up bronze statues of an ass and a man.

After inspecting the rest of his line of ships, he was rowed in a boat to his right wing and from there was surprised to see the enemy lying motionless in the narrow channel, for they looked like ships moored at anchor. For a long while he actually believed that to be the case and kept his own ships about eight furlongs away from their foes. At the sixth hour a sea breeze sprang up, and Antony's men grew impatient at the delay, and trusting to the height and size of their vessels to make them irresistible, they set their left wing in motion. Caesar was delighted at the sight, and directed his right wing to row backward, with the aim of drawing the enemy's ships still farther out from the gulf and its narrow entrance, and then sailing around them with his own light boats and getting in close to them, because their ponderous size and the smallness of their crews made them ineffective and slow.

66.   Though the struggle was now commencing to be a hand-to-hand contest, there was no ramming or smashing of ships, for Antony's had no impetus because of their weight, which is what chiefly makes the blows of the beaks effective, and Caesar's not only avoided charging

---
[71]The day was September 2, 31 B.C.

prow against prow on the solid masses of rough bronze, but did not even dare to ram Antony's galleys on the sides. For their own beaks would easily have been broken off by striking against vessels built of great square timbers, fastened together with iron. Thus the engagement resembled a land battle, or, to speak more exactly, a siege fight. For three or four of Caesar's ships would be closing in at the same time around one of Antony's, and the men were all fighting with wicker shields and spears and poles and flaming missiles, and Antony's soldiers were shooting catapults too from wooden towers.

Agrippa now began extending his left wing in an encircling movement and Poplicola was compelled to advance to resist him, and so became separated from his center; this was in some confusion and closely beset by Arruntius' [72] ships. But the sea fight was still undecided and the prospect looked the same for both sides, when all at once Cleopatra's sixty ships were seen hoisting their sails to leave, and slipping through the middle of the combatants. They had been stationed behind Antony's great ships and created a commotion as they made their way through. The enemy beheld them with astonishment sailing away with a fair wind, headed for the Peloponnesus. And at this crisis Antony made it plain that he was no longer governed by the principles of a commander or of a true man, or even by his own, but that, as someone once said in jest, the soul of the lover lives in another person's body. He was dragged away by the woman as if he had grown to be a part of her and moved along with her. He at once spied her ship sailing off, and forgetting everything else, he betrayed and forsook those who were fighting and dying for him, boarded a five-banked galley, with only Alexas the Syrian and Scellius accompanying him, and hastened to follow her who had already ruined him and would now add to his ruin.

67. Cleopatra recognized him and raised a signal on her ship, and so when he came up, he was taken on board. But he did not see her nor was he seen by her. He went forward alone to the prow and sat by himself in silence, holding his head in both hands. Meanwhile Liburnian ships from Caesar's fleet were observed pursuing them, but Antony ordered the vessel turned to face them, prow on, and thus held them off, all but the ship of Eurycles, the Laconian. He pressed on defiantly, brandishing a spear on

---

72 Arruntius was in command of Caesar's center.

his deck, as if to hurl it at Antony. Standing at his prow, Antony asked, "Who is this who pursues Antony?" "I," he replied, "am Eurycles, son of Lachares, who by the help of Caesar's good fortune am avenging my father's death." Lachares had been beheaded by Antony for being involved in a case of robbery. However, Eurycles did not ram Antony's ship, but struck the other admiral's ship—for there were two—with his bronze beak and made it spin around. And as it swung over sideways, he captured it and one of the others, which carried valuable furniture for household use. When Eurycles was gone, Antony once more flung himself down in the same position and sat motionless. For three days he stayed by himself in the prow, whether angry with Cleopatra or ashamed to go to her, and then turned in at Taenarum.[73] There the women who attended on Cleopatra first brought them to speak with one another, and then prevailed on them to dine and sleep together.

Already a number of their cargo boats and some of their friends were gathering around them after their defeat, bringing news that the fleet was lost, but that they thought the land army still kept together. Thereupon Antony sent messengers to Canidius with orders to withdraw as fast as possible with the army through Macedonia into Asia. For himself, he was planning to cross from Tenaerum to Libya, but first he selected one of the cargo ships which was carrying a great sum of money and precious royal utensils of gold and silver, and gave it to his friends in common, telling them to divide up its contents and see to their own safety. They were tearfully for refusing the gift, but he consoled and besought them with much kindliness and affection, and induced them to depart. He wrote too to Theophilus, his steward in Corinth, to keep the men safe and hide them until they could make their peace with Caesar. This Theophilus was the father of Hipparchus, who had immense influence on Antony and who was the first of all his freedmen to go over to Caesar; he later settled in Corinth.

68. This now was Antony's situation. At Actium the fleet had held out for a long time against Caesar and only after suffering heavy damage from a high head sea had reluctantly, at the tenth hour, given up the fight. Not more than five thousand men were dead, but three hundred ships

---

[73] Taenarum was a port at the tip of the central promontory which runs south from the Peloponnesus.

had been taken, as Caesar himself has recorded. Not many persons knew of Antony's flight, and those who heard the story could not at first believe that he had gone and left nineteen legions of undefeated infantry and twelve thousand horse, as if he had not again and again met both kinds of fortune and were not inured to vicissitudes in a thousand battles and wars. His soldiers longed for him and expected him to appear shortly from somewhere; and such was their loyalty and courage that even when the report of his flight was confirmed, they kept together for seven days and paid no attention to the messages Caesar sent them. But at last, after their general Canidius had stolen away by night and abandoned the camp, since they were without supplies and had been betrayed by their commanders, they joined the conqueror.

Caesar next sailed to Athens, and after reaching an agreement with the Greeks, distributed the grain which was left after the war among the cities, which were in a miserable state, stripped of money, slaves, and beasts of burden. My great-grandfather, Nicarchus, used to tell us how all the citizens [74] had been forced to carry on their shoulders a fixed measure of wheat down to the sea near Anticyra, speeded along by whips. They had carried down one load in that manner, the second had already been measured out and they were about to start off again, when the news came that Antony was beaten. This was the saving of the city, for at once Antony's stewards and soldiers fled and the people divided the grain among themselves.

69. On his arrival in Libya, Antony sent Cleopatra on to Egypt from Paraetonium, and himself was free to enjoy solitude in plenty, roving and wandering around with two friends, a Greek rhetorician called Aristocrates, and a Roman, Lucilius, of whom I have written elsewhere. [75] At Philippi, in order to let Brutus escape, he had pretended to be Brutus and so surrendered to the pursuers. For this brave act Antony had spared his life, and he remained faithful and devoted to Antony up to the last.

When the man to whom he had entrusted his troops in Libya took them over to Caesar, Antony started to kill himself, but was stopped by his friends and then brought to Alexandria. There he found Cleopatra

---

[74] Presumably this was the city of Chaeronea. Like the other Greek cities it was being drained of food, money, and slaves, to supply Antony's army.
[75] Life of Brutus. ch. 50.

venturing on a large and hazardous enterprise. The isthmus which sep-
arates the Red Sea from the sea at Egypt is considered the boundary
between Asia and Libya. In the narrowest part, where it is most com-
pressed by the two seas it is three hundred furlongs wide. Here Cleopatra
was attempting to have her fleet lifted out of the water and dragged across.
Then, after letting her ships down into the Arabian Gulf,[76] with much
money and a large force she proposed to find a place to settle outside
Egypt and thus escape from slavery and war. But the Arabs from around
Petra set fire to the first ships as they were being dragged up on land, and
Antony still believed that his army at Actium was holding on. So she gave
up the attempt and merely set guards to defend the approaches to Egypt.
But Antony left the city and the companionship of his friends and built
for himself a house in the sea, at Pharos, on a pier which he extended out
into the water. There he lived, a fugitive from men, declaring that he preferred and was imitating the life of Timon,[77] since he had suffered like
Timon. He too had been wronged by his friends and had met with ingratitude, and so had come to hate and distrust all men.

70. Now Timon was an Athenian who lived about the time of the
Peloponnesian War, as one may learn from the plays of Aristophanes and
Plato. In them he is depicted as crabbed and misanthropic and as avoiding and resisting all association with men. Yet he was fond of Alcibiades,
who was then a bold young fellow, and would embrace him warmly.
Apemantus wondered at this and asked the reason, and Timon said that
he loved the lad because he knew he would be a source of great harm to
the Athenians. This Apemantus was the only one whom he would sometimes permit to approach him, because he was like him and an imitator
of his way of life.

Once, during the festival of the Libations,[78] when the two were feasting by themselves, Apemantus said, "How pleasant, Timon, is our sym-

---

[76] Arabian Gulf was another name for the Red Sea.

[77] The misanthropic Timon of Athens seems to have lived in the time of Pericles but
nothing definite is known of him beyond the jests ascribed to him by Aristophanes
and Plato, the comic poet, and later by Plutarch and Lucian. Shakespeare drew his
material for *Timon of Athens* from the passage here and from Lucian's dialogue,
Timon or the Misanthrope.

[78] The second day of the festival of Dionysus was called Libation Day, for on it
libations were poured to the dead.

posium!" "It would be," answered Timon, "if you were not here." They say too that once at an Athenian assembly, Timon ascended the rostrum, and the strangeness of his appearance created a dead hush and great expectancy. Thereupon he said, "Men of Athens, I have a small plot of ground and a fig tree growing in it, on which many of our fellow citizens have already hanged themselves. I am now proposing to build a house on that ground and wish to give public notice of my intention, so that if any of you choose, you may hang yourselves before the fig tree is cut down." At his death he was buried at Halae, by the sea. The shore in front of his tomb slid away and the sea came in around it and made it inaccessible to man. On it was the inscription:

"Here do I lie who have now broken off a life doomed to ill.
   Ask not my name, but as evil you are, may your death be evil."

This inscription, they say, he composed during his lifetime; but the one more commonly known is the work of Callimachus:

"Timon, a hater of men, here I dwell; but pass on;
   Fling many a curse at me, only pass on."

71. So much for Timon—a little of the much that might be said. To Antony now Canidius came bringing the news of the loss of his forces at Actium. He heard too that Herod the Jew, with some legions and cohorts, had gone over to Caesar, that the rest of the princes were likewise forsaking him, and that nothing was left of what had been his outside Egypt. However, none of those things distressed him but as if he gladly put off hope so that he might also put off care, he quit his abode in the sea, which he called his Timoneum, and was taken by Cleopatra into her palace. There he led the city back to feasting and drinking and dispensing of gifts. The son of Cleopatra and Caesar he registered among the young men,[78] and on Antyllus, his son by Fulvia, he conferred an adult's toga, without a purple border, and these were occasions for banquets and revels and festivals all over Alexandria.

---

[79] That is, among the *ephebi,* or young Greeks of age for preliminary training in military service. The purple bordered toga was worn by Roman boys until they reached manhood. The adult citizen's toga was all white, unless as a curule magistrate he obtained the right to a purple border again. Caesarion, it may be seen, was being brought up as a Greek, Antyllus as a Roman.

With Cleopatra he now broke up the club of the Inimitable Livers and formed another, no way inferior to it in refinement and luxury and extravagance, which they called the club of the Comrades in Death. They and their friends now enrolled themselves as intending to die together, and meanwhile spent their days gaily in a succession of dinner parties. Cleopatra was collecting all kinds of deadly poisons, and trying out the painlessness of each by giving them to prisoners condemned to death. Finding that the quick poisons made death harder by the pain they caused and that the gentler poisons were slow to act, she next tried venomous animals, watching them herself as they were matched one against another. She kept at this every day and saw almost every kind, and found that the bite of the asp brought on a drowsy numbness and languor, with no spasms or groaning, but a light perspiration on the face and an easy dulling and relaxing of the senses, which resisted all efforts to arouse and revive the victim, who seemed like one in deep slumber.

72. At the same time, they both sent ambassadors to Caesar in Asia, Cleopatra asking for the kingdom of Egypt for her children, and Antony requesting to be allowed to live as a private person in Athens, if forbidden to stay in Egypt. Since their friends were now few and they themselves distrustful, owing to all the desertions, they sent Euphronius, the children's teacher, on the embassy. For Alexas of Laodicea, who had been introduced to Antony at Rome through Timagenes and had more influence on him than any other Greek, and who also had been one of Cleopatra's strongest instruments in thwarting Antony and overcoming the arguments that rose in his mind for a return to Octavia, had been sent to King Herod to keep him from changing sides. And he had stayed there and betrayed Antony, and then had had the effrontery to come before Caesar, relying on Herod's protection. However, Herod was no help to him, and he was immediately imprisoned and then taken in bonds to his own country, where by Caesar's orders he was put to death. Such was the penalty Alexas paid to Antony for his treason, while Antony was still living.

73. Caesar, however, would not listen to the pleas on Antony's behalf, but to Cleopatra he sent an answer to the effect that she would receive fair treatment provided she would either have Antony killed or else turn him out. He sent back too with the ambassadors one of his freedmen,

Thyrsus, a quick-witted fellow, and one who would persuasively transmit messages from a youthful general to a haughty woman, exceedingly proud of her beauty. This man's interviews with Cleopatra were longer than those of the rest and she paid him marked honors, so that Antony grew suspicious and seized him and had him whipped. He then sent him back to Caesar, to whom he wrote that Thyrsus had annoyed him by his impertinent and saucy manners, at a time when misfortune had made him quick to be annoyed. "But if you object at all to what I did," he wrote, "you have my freedman, Hipparchus. Hang him up and flog him, and so we shall be even." But thereafter Cleopatra set about allaying his grievances and suspicions and paid excessive attention to him. She kept her own birthday simply and in a manner suitable to her condition, but Antony's birthday she celebrated with immense splendor and prodigality, so that many of the guests who came to the supper poor men went home rich. Meanwhile, Caesar was called back to Rome by Agrippa, who wrote him often that affairs there were in great need of his presence.

74. For a time, therefore, war was delayed. But when the winter had passed, Caesar advanced on Egypt again through Syria and his generals through Libya. Pelusium was taken and there was a rumor that Seleucus had surrendered it with Cleopatra's consent, but she let Antony put Seleucus' wife and children to death. For herself she had a tomb and monument built of extraordinary beauty and height, near the temple of Isis, and there she now collected the most precious of the royal hoards, gold, silver, emeralds, pearls, ebony, ivory, and cinnamon, and on top of all this a mass of kindling and tow. Caesar was alarmed for the treasure, afraid that in a desperate fit the woman would destroy it all by fire; so, as he moved on with his army towards Alexandria, he kept constantly sending ahead to her messages of friendliness and hope. But on his taking up a position near the hippodrome, Antony came out to meet him and in a brilliant fight routed Caesar's cavalry and chased them back to their camp. Elated by this victory, he appeared at the palace still in his armor and embraced Cleopatra, and presented to her the one of his soldiers who had fought most ardently. And she, as a reward, gave the man a gold breastplate and helmet. He took them—and by night deserted to Caesar.

75. Once more then Antony sent Caesar a challenge to single combat. But Caesar's sole reply was that there were many ways for Antony to die.

Aware that there was no death more honorable for him than one in battle, Antony now determined to launch an attack by land and sea together. And at dinner, they say, he bade the slaves pour out the wine and feast him more cheerily than usual, for no one could tell whether they would be doing the same thing tomorrow, or would be serving other masters, while he himself was lying dead and turned to nothing. But seeing his friends in tears at his words, he said that he would not lead them out to a battle in which he would be looking for a glorious death instead of for their safety and victory. That very night, they say, when it was about half gone, and the city was lying quiet and gloomy with dread of what was to come, suddenly sounds of music from every kind of instrument were heard, and the shouting of a multitude with Bacchic cries and satyrs leaping, as if some company of revelers were leaving the city with a huge din. They took their way through the middle of the city to the outer gate which opened towards the enemy, where the tumult grew loudest, and then they rushed out. Those who pondered over the sign thought it meant that the god whom Antony believed he most resembled and to whom he was closest was now abandoning him.

76. At daybreak [80] Antony posted his infantry on the hills before the city, and then watched his ships, which were putting out and advancing against those of the enemy, and while waiting to see them do something important, remained still. But the crews on his ships, as soon as they drew near, saluted Caesar's crews with their oars, and when they returned the salute, changed sides, and all the ships together as one fleet sailed up towards the city, prow after prow. Hardly had Antony beheld this than his cavalry deserted him and joined the enemy, his infantry was defeated, and he retreated into the city, crying out that he had been betrayed by Cleopatra to those with whom he was fighting for her sake. She, in fear of his anger and despair, took refuge in her tomb and let down the hanging doors, which were reinforced with bars and bolts. She then sent messengers to tell Antony that she was dead. He believed the message and saying to himself, "Why still keep on delaying, Antony? Fate has taken your only remaining excuse for loving life," retired into his chamber. As he unloosed his breastplate and took it off, he said, "O Cleopatra, I do not grieve to lose you, for I shall soon arrive where you are. But I grieve

[80] The day was August 1, 30 B.C.

that so great a general as I was has been discovered to have less fortitude than a woman."

Antony had a faithful slave named Eros, to whom he had long before given orders to kill him, if there should be need of it; and he now demanded the execution of this promise. Eros drew his sword and raised it as if he would strike his master, then turned his face away and killed himself. As he fell at his feet, Antony exclaimed, "Well done, Eros! Though you could not do it yourself, you teach me what I must do," and stabbing himself through the belly, he fell on his couch. The wound was not at once fatal, and so, as the flow of blood stopped when he lay down, he came to himself and begged those about him to give him the final stroke. But they fled from the chamber and left him calling and writhing, until the scribe Diomedes came from Cleopatra with instructions to bring him to her in her tomb.

77. On learning then that she was alive, Antony commanded his attendants to lift him up, and he was carried in their arms to the door of the tomb. Cleopatra, however, did not open the doors but appeared at a window, from which she let down ropes and cords. These they tied around Antony, and she and two women drew him up. They were the only persons she had taken with her into the tomb. Those who were there say that no sight was ever more pitiful than that, as, stained with blood and fighting with death, Antony was drawn up, stretching out his hands to her, even as he swung in the air. For the women the task was not easy, and hardly could Cleopatra with clinging hands and straining face pull up the ropes, while the watchers below called directions to her and shared her suffering.

When in this way she had got him up and laid him down, she tore her robes over him, and with her hands beat and lacerated her breasts, wiping some of his blood off on her face, and calling him master, husband, and chief commander. She was near to forgetting her own troubles in compassion for his, but Antony stopped her wails and asked for a drink of wine, whether because he was thirsty or because he hoped thereby to be more quickly released. While drinking it, he advised her to take steps for her own safety, if that were possible without disgrace, and among all Caesar's companions to trust Proculeius most. She should mourn his own latest misfortunes, but count him happy for the good things fortune had granted him. He had been of all men most illustrious, had wielded the greatest power, and though now he had been overcome it was not ignobly, a Roman by a Roman.

78.   Barely was he dead when Proculeius came from Caesar. For after Antony had stabbed himself and while he was being conveyed to Cleopatra, Derketaeus, one of his bodyguard, snatched up his sword and hid it and slipped away with it. Then running to Caesar, he was the first to tell him of Antony's death, and he showed him the blood-stained sword. On hearing the news, Caesar withdrew into his tent and shed tears for a man who had been his kinsman by marriage, his colleague in office, and his companion in many struggles and enterprises. Then he took their correspondence and called for his friends, and read the letters aloud to show how sensibly and fairly he had written, and how rude and insolent had always been Antony's replies.

He then sent Proculeius with orders especially to get hold, if possible, of Cleopatra alive. For he was alarmed about her treasures, and he also thought it would much enhance the glory of his triumph to lead her in it. But Cleopatra refused to put herself into the hands of Proculeius. However, they talked together after he had come close to the front of the tomb and was standing outside by a door which opened on the ground. It was strongly barred, but provided a passageway for a voice. They had a talk, and she asked that her children be given her kingdom, and Proculeius bade her keep up heart and trust Caesar in everything.

79.   Proculeius then inspected the place and reported to Caesar, and Gallus was sent to have another interview with her. He too came to the door and deliberately held her there in conversation for a long time. Meanwhile, Proculeius set up a ladder and stepped in through the window through which the women had drawn up Antony and he ran quickly down to the door where Cleopatra stood listening to Gallus, taking two attendants with him. One of the women shut in with Cleopatra cried out, "Poor Cleopatra, you are caught alive!" At this Cleopatra turned around, and seeing Proculeius, started to stab herself, for she chanced to be wearing at her girdle a dagger such as brigands wear. Instantly Proculeius sprang down to her, grasped her in both arms, and said, "You are wronging yourself, Cleopatra, and Caesar too by trying to rob him of a great chance to show his goodness, and giving him, the most lenient of com-

manders, the name of a faithless and implacable foe." So saying, he took the dagger from her hand and shook her dress to see if she were hiding any poison. Caesar sent also one of his freedmen, Epaphroditus, with orders to keep her alive under the closest surveillance, but in other respects to allow her whatever would give her comfort and pleasure.

80. Caesar himself now rode into the city conversing on the way with Areius the philosopher,[81] to whom he had already given his right hand that he might be conspicuous at once among the Alexandrians and be admired for the special honor Caesar was showing him. He then entered the gymnasium and ascended a tribunal which had been erected for him. The people were terrorstruck and threw themselves on their faces before him, but he ordered them to rise and said he acquitted them of all guilt, first for the sake of their founder, Alexander the Great; second, because he so marveled at the beauty and greatness of their city; and third, to please his comrade Areius. That was an honor Caesar paid Areius, and he obtained Caesar's pardon too for many other men. Among them was Philostratus, a man cleverer at ex tempore speaking than all the sophists who ever lived, but who claimed without warrant to belong to the Academy. Caesar despised his character, and would not listen to his pleas. But Philostratus, who had a long white beard, put on a dark cloak and walked behind Areius, declaiming the line,

"Wise men will save wise men, if wise they be." [82]

When Caesar heard of this performance he pardoned Philostratus, but more for the purpose of saving Areius from jealousy than Philostratus from fear.

81. As for Antony's children, Antyllus, his son by Fulvia, was betrayed by his tutor Theodorus and killed. After the soldiers had beheaded him, the tutor took off the priceless stone he wore about his neck and sewed it into his own belt. He later denied having done this, but was convicted of it and crucified. Cleopatra's children were kept with their caretakers under guard, and received liberal treatment. But Caesarion, who was said

---

[81] Areius, of the Stoic school of Alexandria, is said to have been one of the younger Caesar's earlier teachers.

[82] A line from some poet now unknown.

to be Caesar's son, was given large funds and sent by his mother to India, by way of Ethiopia. But another tutor like Theodorus, named Rhodion, persuaded him to go back to Egypt, telling him that Caesar would invite him to assume a kingdom. While Caesar was considering the question, they say, Areius remarked, "Too many Caesars are not a good thing." [83]

82. So, later, after Cleopatra's death, Caesarion was executed. Many persons, both kings and generals, asked for Antony's body to give it burial, but Caesar did not take it away from Cleopatra. It was interred by her own hands, richly and royally, and she was given everything she wished to use. But as a result of so much grief and pain together—for her breasts were injured and inflamed by the blows she had given them— she was attacked by a fever and welcomed the excuse it furnished her for going without food, and so escaping from life with no interference. She had with her too a physician, a good friend of hers, called Olympus, to whom she told the truth, and whose advice and assistance she relied on for quietly putting an end to herself, as Olympus himself says in a history of those events which he published. But Caesar grew suspicious and began assailing her with threats and fears for her children, to which she succumbed as to an engine of war, and yielded her body to be tended and fed as they desired.

83. A few days later Caesar himself came to see and cheer her. As it happened, she was lying on a shabby mattress bed, and at his entrance she sprang up, clad only in a tunic, and fell at his feet. Her hair and face were in wild disorder, her voice shook and her eyes were sunken in her head. The marks of blows showed plainly on her breast, and altogether her body seemed in no better condition than her spirit. Yet her charm and confidence in her beauty were not entirely extinguished, and even in that state shone out from within her and revealed themselves in the mobility of her features. When Caesar had bidden her lie down and had taken a seat near her, she began a kind of justification of her acts, attributing them to necessity and fear of Antony. But as Caesar answered and confuted her at every point, she swiftly changed her tune and tried to stir his pity by entreaty, like one clinging desperately to life.

Finally she gave him a list she had of the mass of her treasures, and when Seleucus, one of her stewards, charged her with concealing and

[83] A play on a line from the *Iliad*, "Too many rulers are not a good thing."

keeping back some of them, she sprang up, seized him by his hair and rained blows on his face. And when Caesar smilingly stopped her, she said, "But is it not terrible, Caesar, now that you have deigned to come to me and speak with me in my wretched condition, that my slaves should denounce me for putting by some women's ornaments—not, I assure you, for my unhappy self, but so that I may give a few trifles to Octavia and your Livia, and through them make you gracious and more lenient to me?" This speech pleased Caesar, for he thought it showed decisively that she wished to live. Accordingly, after saying that he left those matters to her, and that in all other respects he would be more generous to her than she had ever expected, he departed, imagining he had deceived her; whereas he was deceived instead.

84.   There was a young man of note among Caesar's companions, one Cornelius Dolabella, who had a tender feeling for Cleopatra. He now in compliance with a request from her, sent her word secretly that Caesar was preparing to move with his land forces back through Syria, and had decided to send her and her children away in three days. On hearing this, she first requested Caesar to allow her to pour libations on Antony's tomb and when he gave permission, she had herself borne to the tomb accompanied by her women. There she embraced the urn and cried, "Dear Antony, I buried you a little while ago with hands still free; I now pour out libations for you as a captive, and so guarded that I cannot with blows or tears disfigure this slave's body of mine, which is being preserved for the triumph over you. Expect no more honors or libations, for these are the last which Cleopatra brings you. Nothing parted us from one another while we lived, but in death we are threatened with exchange of habitation. You, the Roman, will lie here, and I, forlorn creature, in Italy, winning just that much of your country as my portion. But if the gods of your country have any might or power—for the gods of this country have betrayed us—forsake not your own wife while she lives, and let no triumph be held over you through me, but hide me and bury me here with you! For of all my myriad afflictions none has been so grievous and terrible as this short time I have lived without you!"

85.   Amid such lamentations, she garlanded and kissed the urn. She then ordered a bath to be made ready for her and after bathing lay down and ate an excellent lunch. A man from the country came bringing a basket,

and when the guards asked what was in it, he opened it and taking off the leaves showed them a dish full of figs. The guards admired their beauty and size, and the man, smiling, told them to take some, so they trusted him and let him go in. After eating, Cleopatra took a tablet which she had already inscribed and sealed and sent it to Caesar. She then dismissed all her attendants except her two favorite women and shut the doors.

But when Caesar opened the tablet and read her plaintive prayers and entreaties that he would bury her with Antony, he instantly guessed what had happened. At first he was for going himself to her rescue but then he sent others to hasten with all speed and make inquiries. But the harm had been quickly done. Although they went on a run and found the guards still aware of nothing, when they opened the doors, they found Cleopatra lying dead on a golden couch, attired like a queen. And as for her two women, the one called Iras was dying at her feet, and Charmion, already staggering and scarcely able to hold up her head, was trying to arrange the diadem on Cleopatra's head. One of the men exclaimed angrily, "A grand deed this, Charmion!" "Most grand, indeed," she answered, "and fitting for the descendant of so many kings." She said no more but fell there beside the couch.

86. They say that the asp was brought with the figs and leaves and lay hidden under them. Those had been Cleopatra's orders, so that the snake might fasten on her before she knew it. But as she lifted up some of the figs, she saw it and said, "So here it is," and baring her arm offered it to be bitten. Others say that the asp was kept shut up in a water pitcher, and that Cleopatra stirred it up with a golden distaff and irritated it until it sprang up and clung to her arm. But the real truth no one knows. For it was also said that she carried poison around in a hollow comb, which she concealed in her hair. However, no spot or other mark of poison broke out on her body, nor was the snake seen inside the palace, though some said they had noticed tracks of it near the sea, where the windows of Cleopatra's chamber overlooked the water. Some say further that on Cleopatra's arm were seen two light and faint punctures, and that apparently is what Caesar believed. For in his triumph a figure of Cleopatra was carried, with the asp clinging to her. Such are the accounts given of the event.

Caesar was disappointed at the woman's death, but he admired her greatness of spirit and ordered her body buried with Antony's in royal magnificence. Her women also were given honorable burial by his command. At her death Cleopatra was thirty-nine years of age, had reigned as queen for twenty-two years, and had shared her rule with Antony for more than fourteen.[84] Antony, by some counts, was fifty-six, by others, fifty-three. The statues of Antony were now torn down but those of Cleopatra remained in place, because Archibius, one of her friends, paid Caesar two thousand talents that they might not suffer the same fate as Antony's.

87. By his three wives Antony left seven children. Antyllus, the eldest, was the only one put to death by Caesar. The rest Octavia took and brought up with her own. Cleopatra, Cleopatra's daughter, she married to Juba,[85] the most polished king of the day, and Antony, Fulvia's son, she made so great a man that after Agrippa, who stood first in Caesar's esteem, and Livia's sons, who stood second, young Antony was considered to stand third and actually did. Octavia had by Marcellus two daughters and one son, Marcellus, whom Caesar made both his son and his son-in-law. One of the daughters he gave to Agrippa. But Marcellus died soon after his marriage, and it was hard for Caesar to choose from his other friends a son-in-law whom he could trust. So then Octavia proposed that Agrippa should marry Caesar's daughter and put away her own. First, she persuaded Caesar and then Agrippa, after which she took her own daughter back and married her to young Antony, and Agrippa married Caesar's daughter.

Antony left two daughters by Octavia, one of whom became the wife of Domitius Ahenobarbus, and the other, Antonia, famed for her beauty and intelligence, married Drusus, son of Livia and Caesar's step-son. From their marriage came Germanicus and Claudius, and Claudius was afterward emperor. Of the children of Germanicus, Gaius made an excellent emperor for a short time, but then was killed with his wife and child. Agrippina [86] had a son, Lucius Domitius, by Ahenobarbus, and later

---

[84] Plutarch's chronology is in error here. Their period together was eleven years.

[85] On Juba II, king of Numidia and Mauretania, who was taken as a child captive to Rome and educated there, and who later worked to spread Roman culture in North Africa, see above, *Caesar,* ch. 55.

[86] This was Agrippina, called the Younger, daughter of Germanicus. She was married first to the son of Domitius Ahenobarbus, just mentioned, by whom she had a son who became the emperor Nero. After her husband's death, she was married to her uncle, the emperor Claudius.

married Claudius Caesar. Claudius adopted her son and called him Nero Germanicus. This Nero was emperor in my time. He slew his mother and by his insane folly came near to wrecking the Roman empire. He was fifth in order of succession from Antony.

Comparison of Demetrius and Antony

1. TO BOTH these men came great changes of fortune, but let us first consider the origins of their power and renown. In Demetrius' case they were won by his father and inherited from him, for Antigonus was the strongest of Alexander's successors and before Demetrius came of age he had invaded and conquered the greater part of Asia. But Antony's father, though a popular man, was no soldier, and left him no great heritage of fame. Yet Antony had the daring to reach out for the empire of Julius Caesar, to which by birth he had no right, and made himself heir to what Caesar had built up with such toil before him. Starting from only his own resources, he grew so strong that he could divide the world into two parts, choose one and pick the grander of the two. Even without his presence, through his assistants and deputy generals he defeated the Parthians many times, and drove the barbarous tribes in the Caucasus region as far as the Caspian Sea.

Even the things for which he was blamed were proofs of his greatness. Demetrius' father was much pleased to have his son marry Phila, Antipater's daughter, in spite of her age, because he regarded her as his son's superior, whereas Antony's marriage to Cleopatra was a reproach to him, though she was a woman who outshone all the princes of her time, except Arsaces,[1] in power and magnificence. But Antony had made himself so great that he seemed worthy of greater things even than he himself desired.

---

[1] Arsaces is probably another name for Phraates IV, king of Parthia, Antony's enemy.

2. As for their determination to acquire empire, Demetrius is not to blame for attempting to conquer and rule over peoples used to submission to kings. But it was cruel and tyrannical of Antony to enslave the Roman people, who had just escaped from the absolutism of Caesar. The greatest and most brilliant of his exploits, his war against Brutus and Cassius, was fought to deprive his country and his fellow citizens of their liberty. But Demetrius, even before he was compelled by fortune, made a practice of liberating Greeks and expelling the garrisons from their cities, not like Antony, who was proud of having slain in Macedonia the men who had set Rome free. As for one of the qualities for which Antony is especially praised, his love of lavish giving, Demetrius far surpassed him in that and made more gifts to his enemies than Antony made even to his friends. Antony, indeed, received much credit for ordering Brutus' body to be suitably attired and buried, but Demetrius held funerals for all of his enemy's dead, and sent his captives back to Ptolemy with money and presents.

3. Both were arrogant in prosperous times and abandoned themselves to luxury and pleasure. Yet no one can say that Demetrius was ever so immersed in gaiety and lovemaking as to lose a chance for action. It was when he had plenty of leisure that he brought in his enjoyments; he diverted himself with his Lamia, like the mythical creature, only when he was very jovial and drowsy. But when he was preparing for war, no ivy wreathed his spear, no myrrh scented his helmet, nor did he go forth to his battles from a woman's chamber, sleek and blooming. He put a quietus on revels and a stop to Bacchic orgies and became, as Euripides says,[2] "a follower of unhallowed Ares." He never tripped once through his own negligence or love of pleasure.

Antony, on the other hand, like Heracles in the paintings where we see Omphale stealing his club and pulling off his lion's skin, was many a time disarmed and bewitched by Cleopatra, and persuaded to let mighty enterprises and necessary campaigns drop from his hands, to wander about and play with her on the seashore by Canopus and the tomb of Osiris. And at the last, like Paris, he ran away from battle to sink upon her breast, though Paris fled to Helen's chamber only after he had been de-

---

2 The phrase is from some lost play of Euripides.

feated, whereas Antony, by turning tail to pursue Cleopatra, thereby threw away the victory.

4. Also, in marrying several wives, Demetrius did nothing forbidden, but only what had become usual for the kings of Macedonia since the days of Philip and Alexander, and what Lysimachus and Ptolemy did. And all the women he married he treated with honor. But Antony, first of all, had two wives at once, a thing which no Roman had ever dared to do; and then he ejected his Roman and lawfully wedded wife to please the foreigner who was living with him contrary to the laws. So marriage did no harm to Demetrius but the gravest harm to Antony.

Yet with all his licentiousness Antony never added sacrilege to his misdemeanors as Demetrius did. Historians say that dogs are debarred from the whole Acropolis because they copulate most openly of all animals. But Demetrius consorted with prostitutes inside the Parthenon itself and debauched many Athenian women there. And the vice which one would think belonged least with such sensuous indulgence, the vice of cruelty, was mingled with Demetrius' love of pleasure, for he permitted or rather compelled the most beautiful and modest of the Athenians to die a pathetic death in order to escape his violence. In brief, Antony wronged himself by his wanton behavior, but Demetrius wronged others.

5. In his conduct towards his parents Demetrius was irreproachable, whereas Antony gave up his mother's brother so that he might kill Cicero, an act so vile and brutal that he would scarcely be pardoned for it even if Cicero's death had been the price of his uncle's life. Both men perjured themselves and broke treaties, Antony when he seized Artabazus, and Demetrius when he murdered Alexander. But for Antony there is the excuse, acknowledged to be valid, that Artabazus had deserted and betrayed him in Media; while Demetrius, many say, fabricated false charges on which to act and denounced a man whom he had wronged. He was not protecting himself against one who had wronged him. Again, the successes of Demetrius were all won by himself in person. On the other hand, Antony's finest and greatest victories he won through his generals, in his own absence.

6. They both brought about their own ruin, though in different ways. Demetrius was left forsaken, because his Macedonians deserted him, but

Antony was the deserter, flying from men who were risking their lives for him. So Demetrius is to be criticized for making his soldiers so hostile to him, and Antony for betraying so much evident love and devotion. As for their deaths, neither was admirable, but Demetrius' death was the more discreditable. For he allowed himself to be taken prisoner, and was content to gain three years of life in confinement, being tamed, like a wild beast, by wine and gluttony. Whereas Antony took his own way out—a cowardly, pitiful, and ignoble way to be sure, but at any rate before his enemy could make his body captive.

Cato the Younger

95-46 B.C.

1. THE family of Cato won its first fame and renown through his great grandfather Cato, who by his virtue gained great reputation and influence among the Romans, as I have related in his life.[1] The death of his parents left this later Cato an orphan, along with a brother, Caepio, and a sister, Porcia.[2] He had also a half-sister, Servilia, born of the same mother. They all were brought up in the house of their uncle on their mother's side, Livius Drusus,[3] who was then a political leader. He was a most able speaker and in general a man of great wisdom and as lofty a spirit as any Roman of the day.

They say of Cato that even from his childhood, in voice and looks and in his childish amusements, he gave indication of a determined and inflexible nature, completely steadfast. He would set about accomplishing his aims with an energy beyond his years. To persons who tried to flatter him he was rude and refractory and still more obstinate with those who would frighten him. It was hard to make him laugh, though his face

---

[1] Marcus Porcius Cato, the subject of this biography, known also as Cato Uticensis, from the city where he died, was the great grandson of Cato, surnamed the Censor (234–139 B.C.), a famous Roman statesman and general of the period of the Second and Third Carthaginian Wars. The family was plebeian. Plutarch has also a life of the elder Cato.

[2] Cato's father died first, leaving two children, Cato and Porcia. His mother then married Quintus Servilius Caepio and had two more children, Caepio and Servilia, before she also died.

[3] Through most of his life Marcus Livius Drusus had been a supporter of the aristocratic party, but by the time the children came to his house he had become an agitator, like the Gracchi, for social reform.

occasionally broke into a smile, nor was he quickly made angry, though once angered he was difficult to pacify.

So when he came to learn, he was stubborn and slow of understanding, but what he understood he held tenaciously in his memory. This is generally the case in nature. Those who have good natural capacity recollect things more readily, whereas those who learn with toil and effort remember them longest, for each thing they learn is, as it were, branded on their minds. It seems as if Cato's dislike of being persuaded made his learning even more laborious, for to learn is to accept something, and to be quickly persuaded is characteristic of persons who can put up little resistance. For this reason young men are more easily persuaded than old men, and sick persons than those who are well. In short, where there is least ability to doubt, acceptance comes easiest. However, they say that Cato was obedient to his tutor and would do whatever he was ordered to do, but that he would inquire the reason for everything and be ever asking why. But his tutor was a pleasant man, more inclined to explain than to use the rod. His name was Sarpedon.

2. While Cato was still a child, the allies [4] of Rome were exerting themselves to get Roman citizenship and a certain Pompaedius Silo, a man of high standing, who had fought in the war and was a friend of Drusus, spent some days with him. During that time he made friends with the children and one day he said to them, "Come, beg your uncle to help us in our struggle for citizenship!" Caepio smiled and promised, but Cato made no answer and looked fixedly and grimly at the strangers. Pompaedius then said, "But you, young man, what do you say to us? Can't you, like your brother, speak to your uncle for the strangers?" As Cato still did not speak, but by his silence and his expression showed that he refused Pompaedius' request, Pompaedius lifted him up and held him through a window as if he would let him drop, and commanded him to promise or he would throw him down, at the same time making his voice rough and shaking the boy's body again and again as he held him through

---

[4] These were the *socii* or Italian allies of Rome who had accepted Roman leadership and furnished troops for Roman wars, in return for which they were now claiming the rights of citizenship and equality in the Roman state. Their struggle culminated in the so-called Social War, at the end of which full citizenship was granted them by the laws of 90 and 89 B.C.

the window. When for a long time Cato had stood this test, uncowed
and fearless, Pompaedius set him down and said softly to his friends,
"What luck it is for Italy that he is a child; if he were a man, I think
we should not get a single vote from the assembly." [5]

Another time, a kinsman of his on his birthday invited Cato and other
boys to supper and to pass the time they were all playing games in one
part of the house, young and old mixed together. The game was make-
believe accusations and trials and leading off convicted ones to prison.
One of the convicted boys, a handsome child, was taken by an older boy
and shut up in a room, and from there called out to Cato for help. Cato
perceiving quickly what was happening went to the door, shoved aside
those who stood in front of it and tried to stop him, and took the child
out. He then went indignantly home, followed by some of the other boys.

3. He became very well known. When Sulla was assembling and training the highborn lads for presenting the sacred game of boys on horseback, which they call the Troja,[6] he selected two as leaders. The boys
accepted one of them on his mother's account, for she was Metella, Sulla's
wife, but the other, a nephew of Pompey named Sextus, they refused to
take, and would not practice under him or follow him. Sulla then asked
whom they wanted, and they all shouted, "Cato," and Sextus himself gave
way and surrendered the honor to him, as deserving it better.

As it happened, Sulla was an old friend of Cato's father, and he sometimes had him and Caepio brought to him and talked with them, a friendliness he showed to very few because of the weight and dignity of his
power and authority. Sarpedon felt that these meetings much enhanced
both the prestige and the safety of the boy and he was constantly bringing Cato to pay his respects to Sulla at his house, which at that time
looked precisely like an inferno, owing to the throngs of people being
brought there to be tortured.[7] Cato was in his fourteenth year, when,
seeing the heads of men reputedly distinguished which were being carried

---

[5] This incident must have occurred, if at all, before Drusus' death in 91 B.C. Cato then
could not have been more than four years old, too young to understand political questions but old enough to resent and hold out against a stranger's bullying.

[6] The Troja was a mock battle of Roman boys, either on foot or on horseback, the
origin of which as a religious ceremonial went back, according to legend, to Aeneas.
There is a description of it in Vergil's *Aeneid*, V, 553 ff.

[7] On Sulla and his proscriptions, see above, *Cicero*, n. 8.

out, and hearing the stifled moans of others present, he asked his tutor, "Why does nobody kill this man?" "Because, my boy," said Sarpedon, "they fear him more than they hate him." "Why, then," said Cato, "did you not give me a sword that I might kill him and free my country from slavery?" On hearing his speech, and seeing also the look full of anger and determination on Cato's face, Sarpedon was so alarmed that he watched him thenceforward carefully and was on guard to keep him from any rash attempt.

When he was still a little boy and people asked him whom he loved best, he would reply, "My brother." When they asked him whom second best, he would say again, "My brother," and so for third best, until after many more such answers, the questioners left off asking. And as he grew to manhood, this fondness for his brother was intensified. When he was twenty years old, he would not dine, or leave town, or step out into the forum without Caepio. But his brother used perfumery and Cato refused it, and was strict and austere in his whole way of living. So when Caepio was complimented for being sober and moderate, he would admit that he might be so, provided he was measured against other men. "But when," he would say, "I compare my life with Cato's, I look to myself no better than Sippius," naming a man notorious for his luxury and effeminacy.

4. After Cato was made priest of Apollo, he changed his home, took his portion of the paternal inheritance, which amounted to a hundred and twenty talents, and began living still more frugally. He had Antipater of Tyre, a Stoic philosopher, as his intimate companion and concentrated especially on the study of ethics and politics. He was possessed, as it were, by an enthusiasm for every virtue, but devoted above all to the goodness of inflexible justice, which is not to be swayed towards leniency or favoritism. He practiced also the kind of speaking which is effective in public, thinking that in political philosophy, as in a great city, there would be call for some kinds of contentiousness. Yet he did not practice his exercises in company with other young men, nor did anyone ever hear him declaiming. And to one of his friends who said, "Men are finding fault with you, Cato, for your silence," he replied, "I only hope they do not find fault with my life. I shall begin to speak when I am sure not to say what is better unsaid."

5. The so-called Porcian Basilica had been built and dedicated by the elder Cato, when he was censor.[8] The tribunes were accustomed to do their business there, and as they thought one of the pillars was in the way of their seats, they decided to take it down or else move it to another spot. Their decision brought Cato for the first time, reluctantly, into the forum. For he opposed the tribunes and won admiration by the proof he gave of eloquence and high spirit. His speech had nothing juvenile or affected about it, but was straightforward, soundly reasoned, and blunt, and still it had a grace, charming to hear, which masked the sternness of his sentiments. And his character, appearing through it all, made his austerity seem somehow attractive and smiling and not repulsive to people. His voice was loud and resounding enough to be heard by the great assemblage, with a strength of tone which did not break or wear down, for he frequently spoke all day long without tiring.

On this occasion, however, after winning his case, he went back once more to silence and training. He hardened his body by energetic exercises, teaching himself to bear both heat and snow with uncovered head, and to walk the roads in all seasons with no carriage. His friends who went on trips with him would go with horses, and many a time he would join each of them in turn and chat with them, he on foot and they riding. In times of illness he showed remarkable endurance as well as self-control. If he were feverish, he would spend the day alone by himself, allowing no one to come near him until he felt a definite relief and knew the disease was leaving him.

6. At dinners he used to throw dice for his portion, and if he lost, and his friends still urged him to choose first, he would say it was not right to do so against the will of Venus.[9] In the beginning, after drinking once, he would rise from the table, but as time passed he let himself drink a good deal, and often sat over the wine until daybreak. His friends gave as the reason for this change the political and public labors with which he filled his days and which kept him from literary pursuits. So at night over wine he would converse with the philosophers. Hence, when one Memmius said in company that Cato spent all his nights drinking, Cicero added, "You failed to say that he spends all his days throwing dice!"

---

[8] In the year 182 B.C. Porcius was the family name of the Catos.
[9] The highest throw of dice was known as the Venus throw.

In general Cato believed that the course he took should run quite contrary to the customs and ways of living of the time, which he regarded as corrupt and needing a thorough reformation. When he saw that a garish red and vivid purple was the fashion, he would wear a dark shade. And often after breakfast he would go out into the public street without shoes or tunic. Nor was he working to get a reputation by so strange a habit, but accustoming himself to be ashamed only of what was shameful, and to despise all other sorts of disgrace. When a legacy worth a hundred talents came to him from a cousin Cato, he converted it into money and offered the use of it without interest to any friend who needed it. Some of them were pledging lands and slaves to the public treasury, and he supplied them with what they wanted and made good their pledge.

7. When he thought he had reached the age for marriage, having as yet never known any woman, he betrothed himself to Lepida. She had earlier been promised to Metellus Scipio,[10] but since Scipio had refused to take her and the engagement was broken, she was now free. But before the marriage Scipio changed his mind again, did everything to regain the girl, and finally succeeded. Cato was furious at this, and in his anger tried to take his case to court. When his friends stopped him, still full of youthful indignation, he took to writing iambic verses, in which he hurled many an insult against Scipio in the bitter style of Archilochus,[11] though without his license and scurrility. He then married Atilia, daughter of Serranus. She was the first but not the only woman he ever knew, for he was less fortunate than Laelius, the friend of Scipio Africanus, who during his long life knew but one woman, the wife he married in his youth.

8. When the Servile War broke out, which they called the war of Spartacus,[12] and Gellius was in command, Cato joined the service as volunteer

10 Metellus Scipio, a rapacious and dissolute young man, fought under Pompey at Pharsalus, and fled from there to Africa, where eventually he found himself an ally of Cato. See below, chs. 47, 56 ff.

11 Archilochus, a seventh-century Greek poet, was famous for his creation of new styles in meter and subject matter.

12 Spartacus, a gladiator from Thrace, led a revolt of Thracian, Celtic, and German gladiators, slaves, and fugitives, which broke out first in Capua in 73 B.C. and defeated in turn seven Roman armies sent to suppress it. He was at last caught and killed by Crassus in southern Italy, in 71 B.C., and the surviving rebels were crucified or otherwise exterminated by Crassus and by Pompey, on his way back from Spain.

for his brother's sake, since his brother Caepio was a tribune. He had not, however, the chance to exhibit as much as he wished his zeal and disciplined courage, because the war was badly misdirected. But in the midst of the conspicuous effeminacy and self-indulgence of those who went on that campaign he showed such good discipline, self-control, courage, and intelligence in every situation that he seemed in all respects the equal of the elder Cato. Gellius listed him for prizes and conspicuous honors, but Cato would not receive or consent to them, insisting that he had done nothing to deserve them. Consequently he was thought very eccentric. When the law was passed that candidates for office should not be accompanied by prompters,[13] he was standing for the tribuneship, and was the only candidate to obey the law. He made a business of greeting and addressing the people he met without anyone's prompting. Yet those who praised him resented him, for the more they saw the rightness of what he was doing, the more they disliked the difficulty of imitating it.

9. On being chosen tribune [14] he was sent to Macedonia to join the praetor Rubius. His wife, it is said, was weeping for grief, and one of Cato's friends, Munatius, said to her, "Atilia, cheer up! I will take care of him for you." "Surely he will," said Cato, and when they had gone a day's journey, immediately after supper he said to Munatius, "Come, Munatius, and keep your promise to Atilia. Do not leave me day or night!" Thereupon, he gave orders that two beds be placed in the same room, and thus Munatius always slept guarded—as a joke—by Cato. Attending him were fifteen slaves, two freedmen, and four friends. They rode on horseback and Cato always went on foot, but he would fall in with each in turn and talk to him.

When he arrived at the camp, where there were several legions, the general appointed him to the command of one of them. Thereat, thinking it a petty and useless thing to display his own valor, which was that of one man only, he became above all ambitious to make the men under him like himself, not by divesting his authority of everything terrifying about it but by bringing reason to support it. So with the help of reason he

---

[13] These "prompters" were men who went about the streets with candidates to tell them the names of the persons they were meeting, so that they might appear to know them.

[14] About 67 B.C.

persuaded and instructed his men at every turn and followed their conduct with honors and punishments. It was really difficult to say whether
he made his soldiers more peaceable or more warlike, more ardent or
more just; they showed themselves so formidable to their enemies and so
courteous to their allies, bold but not to do wrong and eager to earn praise.
And what Cato cared least about, fame and favor and deep respect and
affection from his soldiers, came to him in abundance. For he was ready
to take his share of the toil he required of them, and in his dress and way
of life and method of travel he made himself more like them than like
the other officers, whereas in character and high purpose and eloquence he
was superior to all the titled commanders and generals. Hence without
knowing it he created among his men this high regard for himself. A true
desire to be valiant grows only out of a strong affection and esteem for
one who shows himself valiant. Those who praise brave men without
loving them may respect their fame but do not really admire their bravery
or imitate it.

10. Cato now heard that Athenodorus,[15] surnamed Cordylion, who had
a wide knowledge of Stoic philosophy, was living in Pergamum. He was
an old man and had been obstinately repulsing all the friendly advances
of magnates and kings. So Cato thought he would accomplish nothing by
sending or writing to him. But as he had a two-months' furlough granted
him by law, he sailed over to Asia to see him, trusting to his good qualifi-
cations to save him from failure to reach his goal. He met Athenodorus,
argued successfully with him, induced him to change his resolution and
brought him back to camp with him, overjoyed, and pluming himself on
taking a most noble captive, more distinguished than the nations and
kingdoms which Pompey and Lucullus were then conquering with their
armies.

11. While Cato was still serving in this campaign, his brother, who was
on his way to Asia, fell sick at Aenus, in Thrace. A letter came promptly
to Cato, and though a heavy gale was blowing at sea, and there was no
ship of proper size at hand, he put out with only two friends and three
slaves in a small cargo boat, from Thessalonica. He barely escaped drown-

---

15 Athenodorus, called Cordylion, a Stoic philosopher, had been head of the great library
at Pergamum. He later moved to Rome and died in Cato's home.

ing and by some marvelous luck reached land in safety, but Caepio had just died. He seemed to bear this loss with more grief than philosophy, not only giving way to laments and depths of sorrow as he embraced his brother's body, but spending great sums on his burial and providing incense and rich garments to be burned with the corpse. He had a monument too of polished Thasian stone, which cost eight talents, set up in the market place of Aenus.

There were people who criticized these things, as not consistent with Cato's usual controlled behavior, not realizing how much tenderness and devotion were mixed with the man's inflexibility and stern resistance to pleasures, fears, and begging petitions. Cities and princes sent him many gifts for the funeral in honor of the dead. From none of them, however, would he accept money, but he did take incense and adornments, paying the price of them to those who sent them. When the inheritance came to him and to Caepio's little daughter and was being divided, he did not ask back anything of what he had spent on the funeral. Although that was his behavior then and always, there was a man who wrote that he had his brother's ashes strained through a sieve, to find any gold that had been melted down.[16] So sure was this writer that not only his sword but also his pen were never to be called to account or punished for what he said!

12. When Cato's service in the army was over, he was sent on his way not with merely the usual good wishes or praises, but with tears and insatiable embraces. The soldiers threw their cloaks down under his feet for him to walk on, and kissed his hands, things which Romans of that time did for only a few of their chief commanders. But before taking up political life he wished to travel and make a study of Asia, and see for himself the customs and ways of living and strength of each province. At the same time, he thought, he would satisfy Deiotarus of Galatia,[17] a guest friend of his father, who was begging him to make him a visit.

For his travels Cato made the following arrangements. In the morning he would send his cook and bread-maker ahead to the place where he intended to lodge that night. They would enter the city quietly, in an orderly way, and if there were no family friend or acquaintance of Cato

---

16 This mysterious writer was Julius Caesar, in his *Anti-Cato*. See above, *Caesar,* ch. 54.
17 Deiotarus, tetrarch of Galatia in Asia Minor, was a loyal ally of the Romans all through their wars in that region, and in 63 B.C. the senate gave him the title of King.

there, they would prepare for his reception at an inn, without disturbing anyone. If there were no inn, they would then apply to the magistrates for hospitality and accept gratefully whatever they offered. But often they were received with distrust and disrespect because they made no commotion and used no threats in their applications. Then Cato would find them with their work undone, and he would look more insignificant than they did, as he sat silently on his baggage, giving the impression of a poor bashful fellow. However, he would then summon the magistrates and say, "You wretches, stop being so inhospitable! Not all your visitors will be Catos! Try to conciliate by some friendliness the power of those who want only an excuse to take by force what you do not give them willingly."

13. In Syria, they say, he had an amusing experience. As he was entering Antioch, he saw near the gates outside the city a throng of people lined up on either side of the road. Among them, in one group, were standing young men in military cloaks, and in another, boys in gay array. Some, who were priests of the gods or magistrates, were wearing white robes and crowns. Cato could only think that the city was staging this honorable reception for him, and was annoyed with the servants he had sent on ahead for not having prevented it. But he told his friends to dismount and went forward with them on foot. Then, as they approached, the one who was arranging all this pomp and placing the crowd in order, an elderly man, came forward to meet Cato, holding a wand and a crown in his hands. And without a word of greeting he asked him where they had left Demetrius and when he would be there. Now Demetrius had been one of Pompey's slaves who, at that moment, when the eyes of all men, so to speak, were fastened on Pompey, was being courted far above his merits because of his considerable influence over his former master. Cato's friends fell into such a fit of laughter that they could not control themselves, even while they were walking through the throng. But Cato at the time was much upset and exclaimed, "O unhappy city!" and nothing more. Later, however, he, too, would laugh at the incident when he recalled it and told the story.

14. But Pompey himself corrected the men who out of ignorance were so disdainful of Cato. For when on reaching Ephesus he went to pay his respects to Pompey as his elder and much his superior in fame and in command of larger forces, Pompey at sight of him did not wait or allow

him to come forward, while he himself remained seated, but sprang up
as though in deference to a superior, and gave him his hand. And then
and there, in the midst of his warm greeting to Cato and still more after
Cato had left, he sang the praises of his goodness and valor. Thenceforth
everyone knew better and paid attention to Cato, admiring the qualities
in him which previously they had scorned, noting his gentleness and his
breadth of mind.

Yet it was plain that Pompey's enthusiasm for him was more a matter
of expediency than of affection. All knew that he admired him when
present, but was relieved when he departed. For the other young men
who came to him he was eager to keep by him and wanted their companionship, but he did not ask Cato to stay. Instead, as if he were somehow accountable to him while he was there, he was glad to have him go.
And still Cato was almost the only one of those who were leaving for
Rome to whom he commended his wife and children. They, however,
were related by blood to Cato. Thereafter the cities vied strenuously with
one another in offering him honors and dinners and invitations, so that
he bade his friends keep watch on him, lest unwittingly he might make
good the prophecy of Curio. This Curio, who was a friend and comrade
of Cato, disliked his austerity. He asked him once whether after serving
his time in the army, he would enjoy seeing Asia. And when Cato said
he certainly would, Curio replied, "You are right; for you will be more
agreeable when you come back, and more tame." Something like that
was what he said.

15. Deiotarus, the Galatian, now an old man, had sent for Cato, wishing to put his children and his household under his protection. On his
arrival, however, he offered him all kinds of presents, persistently beseeching and imploring him to accept them. He so irritated Cato that
though he had reached there in the evening, he stayed only a night, and
went off about the third hour of the next day.[18] After a day's journey,
he found at Pessinus more gifts waiting for him there, and a letter from
the Galatian begging him, if he would not accept them himself, at any
rate to allow his friends to take them. For, he wrote, they quite deserved
some good treatment from him if Cato's own means did not go so far.

---

[18] That is, about nine in the morning; the Greeks counted the hours beginning with
sunrise, while the Roman hour count began at midnight.

But Cato would not give in even to these pleadings, though he saw that some of his friends were weakening and grumbling at him. He declared that there would always be a good excuse for bribe-taking, and that his friends would share in whatever he got honorably and justly. And so he sent the gifts back to Deiotarus.

When he was on the verge of sailing for Brundisium, his friends thought he should have Caepio's ashes put in another boat, but he said he would part with his life sooner than with those ashes, and set out. And actually, they say, it turned out that he had a very perilous crossing, though the others got over fairly comfortably.

16. On his return to Rome he spent his time either at home in the company of Athenodorus, or in the forum helping his friends. The office of quaestor was open to him, but he would not stand for it until he had read the laws governing the quaestorship, and learned all the details of the office from persons who had held it, and formed some conception of its powers. Then as soon as he was installed in the position, he made great changes in the assistants and clerks in the treasury. They were men long familiar with the public accounts and the laws relating to them, and when they received as superiors youths so utterly ignorant and inexperienced that they needed teachers and tutors themselves, they did not give up their power to them, but were themselves the superiors. Cato, however, set energetically about his task, and since he had not merely the name and title of quaestor but the mind and reasonable judgment of one, he thought it his duty to treat the clerks as the assistants which they really were. In some cases he convicted them of wrong practices and in others he corrected mistakes due to ignorance. They were stubborn men who tried to wheedle and ingratiate themselves with the other quaestors while they fought with Cato. But the leader of them he found guilty of a breach of faith in a case involving an inheritance and had him expelled from the treasury. A second he had tried for fraud.

Yet Lutatius Catulus,[19] the censor, undertook to defend him. He was a man of great influence from his office and much greater from his goodness, for he was esteemed above all other Romans for his justice and wisdom. He was an admirer too of Cato and a companion in his way of living.

---

[19] Lutatius Catulus, a respected aristocrat, was censor in 65 B.C. For other mention of him, see above, *Caesar*, ch. 6.

But when the case was going against him in court, he begged openly to have the clerk let off from punishment. Cato tried to stop him from doing this, and when he persisted, Cato said, "It would be a scandal, Catulus, if you, who are the censor and must pass judgment on our lives, were turned out of court by our officers." At these words from Cato, Catulus looked at him as if he were going to retort but said nothing, and whether in anger or in shame went off in silence, there being nothing else for him to do. However, the clerk was not convicted, for the votes for condemning him were but one more than the votes for acquittal, and Marcus Lollius, a colleague of Cato, who had been prevented by illness from attending the trial, was sent for by Catulus to come and give the man his support. So, though the trial was over, Lollius was carried there in a litter and cast the vote which acquitted. But Cato would not employ the clerk or pay him his wages, or take any count whatever of Lollius' vote.

17. After thus humbling the clerks and reducing them to obedience, he managed his department as he wished, and in a short time made the treasury more respected than the senate, so that everyone thought and said that Cato had brought to it the dignity of the consulship. In the first place, he found that many persons owed old debts to the state, and that the state was in debt to many others, and he put an end at the same time to the wrongs the state was suffering from and the wrongs it was committing. From its debtors he vigorously and inexorably insisted on payment, and to its creditors he promptly and cheerfully made payment, and the people were impressed when they saw those who were expecting to rob the state paying their debts in full, and the others getting back money they never expected to see. Many too had been filing documents without going through the proper forms, and previous quaestors were used to accepting false decrees which favored some petitioner. But nothing of that kind could happen without Cato's discovering it. In fact, in the case of one decree, when he was doubtful whether it had been passed, even though many testified that it had, he would not trust them or register it until the consuls came and swore that it was valid.

There were many agents too whom Sulla had paid for killing men on his list of proscribed, at the rate of twelve thousand drachmas apiece. Everyone detested them as accursed and blood-polluted, but no one dared to punish them. Cato, however, called each one to account, as having public money unlawfully in his possession, and made him return it, at the same time reproaching him severely for his wicked and unlawful deed. That accomplished, the same men were immediately accused of murder and brought before the judges, already prejudged in a way, and punished. Thereat the whole people rejoiced, feeling that with them the tyranny of that time had been blotted out and Sulla himself visibly punished.

18. The people were won too by Cato's assiduity and untiring diligence, for none of his colleagues came earlier to the treasury than he or left it later. He never omitted attending any meeting of the people or of the senate, for he feared and was on guard against men who were ready to do others a favor by voting for cancellations of debts and taxes or for indiscriminate grants. By displaying a treasury honest and inaccessible to intriguers, and likewise full of money, he taught men that the state could be rich without wronging anyone. At first some of his colleagues disliked him and thought him too harsh, but later they grew fond of him, since he took on himself in place of them all the odium incurred by refusals to give out public money or make dishonest decisions. He provided them with a defense against those who would force their demands on them. "It is impossible," they could say, "for Cato is against it."

On the last day of his office he was accompanied back to his house by almost all the citizens. Then, however, he heard that a group of powerful men who were intimates of Marcellus [20] had fallen on him at the treasury and were surrounding him and compelling him to record a release from some debts that were due. Now Marcellus had been a close friend of Cato from boyhood and with him had been an excellent quaestor, but by himself he was easily led, out of modesty, to be too kind to petitioners and too prone to grant every favor. So Cato at once went back to the treasury and found that Marcellus had been coerced into recording the release. Thereupon he asked for the tablets and erased what Marcellus had written, while Marcellus stood by in silence. This done, Cato led him away from the treasury and took him home. Neither then nor later did Marcellus utter a word of complaint, but he remained a close friend of Cato all through. And not even after he had finished his term as quaestor did Cato leave the treasury unguarded, but slaves of his were there daily, making

---

[20] This may have been Gaius Claudius Marcellus, who, like Cato, was a friend of Cicero and Pompey, and dreaded Caesar.

copies of transactions. For himself he bought for five talents books which contained records of public business from Sulla's time down to his own quaestorship, and he constantly had them in his hands.

19.   He used to be the first to arrive at the senate, and the last to depart. Often while the others were taking their time to assemble he would be sitting quietly reading, holding his toga in front of his book. He never left the city when the senate was in session. Later, when Pompey and his partisans saw that he could never be persuaded or compelled to take a hand in the unjust measures on which they were bent, they would contrive to draw him away to act as an advocate or arbitrator or business advisor for a friend. But Cato soon recognized their schemes, refused all their suggestions, and made it a rule to do nothing else while the senate was meeting. It was not to gain reputation or wealth, nor was it accidentally or by chance, as it was with some others, that Cato plunged into a politi-cal career. He chose politics as the proper occupation of a good citizen, and believed it was his duty to put his mind on the common interest more than a bee does on its honey. He took pains therefore to have events which took place in the provinces, and decrees and trials and important meas-ures reported to him by his friends and connections everywhere.

He once took up cudgels against Clodius [21] the demagogue, who was creating disturbances and excitements as a prelude to serious uprisings, and was spreading slander about the priests and priestesses, among them Fabia,[22] sister of Cicero's wife Terentia, who was in actual danger. But he covered Clodius so thoroughly with shame as to compel him to slink out of the city. When Cicero thanked him, Cato said he should keep his gratitude for the city, since it was for its sake that he had done what he had for the public. In this way he gained a great name, such that a speaker at a trial where but one witness was being produced said to the judges that it was not right to rely on a single witness, not even a Cato. And many people, when referring to weird and incredible things, would say, as if it were a kind of by-word, that the story was not to be believed, even though Cato told it. Again, when a dissipated spendthrift was delivering

---

[21] On Publius Clodius Pulcher and his unscrupulous career, see above, *Cicero,* chs. 28, 29, and *Caesar,* chs. 9, 10.
[22] Fabia was a Vestal Virgin. The charge that she had been guilty of unchastity was not proved.

a speech in the senate on frugality and temperance, Annaeus rose and said, "Who can stand you, friend, dining like Lucullus, building like Crassus, and haranguing like Cato?" Other worthless and dissolute men too, who yet were dignified and severe in their speech, were called Catos in derision.

20. Many people urged him to stand for election as tribune, but he thought it not right to squander the power of a great and mighty office, any more than that of a strong medicine, on matters which were not essential. He was free at that time from public business and so, taking books and philosophers with him, he started for Lucania, where he owned lands and a pleasant place of residence. But on the road he met a long line of beasts of burden and luggage and attendants and heard that Metellus Nepos [23] was on his way up to Rome, prepared to stand for the tribuneship. At this he halted without speaking, and after hesitating a short while ordered his people to turn back. When his friends showed some surprise, he said, "Do you not know that even by himself Metellus is dangerous because of his violence? And now that he comes at Pompey's direction, he will fall on the state like a thunderbolt and upset everything. So it is no time for a vacation or absence from home. We must get the better of this man or die honorably struggling for our liberty." However, his friends persuaded him to go on first to his country place, but he stayed only a short time and then returned to the city. He arrived in the evening and as soon as it was dawn went down into the forum to stand as a candidate for a tribuneship as a would-be opponent of Metellus. For the power that office gives is more preventative than constructive. If all the tribunes but one should vote for a measure, the decisive power is his who refuses to consent.

21. At first there were few of Cato's friends about him, but when his intention was made public all the men of character and standing came quickly hurrying, and cheered and encouraged him. He would be receiving no favor, they said, but conferring a great one on his country and on all really respectable citizens, for he had many times refused the office, when it would have been his with no trouble, and now he was standing

---

[23] Quintus Metellus Nepos came to Rome as Pompey's agent in 63 B.C.

for it at a risk to himself, to fight for freedom and the state. So many, they say, crowded up around him in their enthusiasm and affection that he was in danger and could scarcely get through the crowd into the forum. He was then elected tribune with Metellus and others.[24]

But on noting that the elections for consuls were being accompanied by bribery, he reproved the people, and at the close of his speech swore that he would prosecute the briber, whoever he was, excepting only Silanus,[25] because of their relationship. For Silanus was the husband of Cato's sister Servilia. Accordingly, he passed over Silanus, but prosecuted Lucius Murena on the charge of having obtained his election as consul along with Silanus by bribery. There was a law by which the accused always could hire a man to keep watch on his accuser, in order to find out what materials he was getting together and preparing for the prosecution. So one was hired by Murena to follow Cato around and keep watch on him. But when he saw that Cato was doing nothing crafty or unlawful, but was proceeding honorably and considerately, in a fair and honest way, with the prosecution, he felt such respect for his noble spirit and character that he would come up to him in the forum or go to his door and ask him whether he planned to do any business that day with the prosecution; and if Cato said no, the man would trust him and go away.

In the course of the trial, Cicero, who was then consul and an advocate for Murena, brought out Cato's devotion to the Stoics, and had much to say in ridicule and jest of those philosophers and their so-called paradoxes, which made the judges laugh. Whereat Cato, they say, smilingly remarked to those near him, "Friends, what a humorous consul we have!" [26] Murena was acquitted, but he did not feel the resentment towards Cato which a bad or a foolish man would have done. During his consulship he would go to Cato for advice on the most important questions, and in other ways he showed his respect and confidence in him. The reason for this was Cato himself, for though on the tribunal and in the senate he was severe and formidable in his insistence on justice, away from there, he was benevolent and friendly in his manner to everyone.

---

[24] The number of tribunes at this time was ten.
[25] Silanus and Murena were consuls in 62 B.C. At his trial Murena was defended by Hortensius and Cicero. Cicero's speech for Murena has survived.
[26] For the same anecdote, see *Comparison of Demosthenes and Cicero,* ch. 1.

22. Before he took office as a tribune and while Cicero was consul, he upheld his authority in many struggles, and by his action with regard to Catiline, the most important and noble of his career, he put an end to that crisis.[27] Catiline was the man who attempted to overthrow and completely revolutionize the Roman state, and stirred up both insurrections and wars. He was convicted by Cicero and fled the city. But Lentulus and Cethegus and many others of their party took up the conspiracy and, accusing Catiline of cowardice and want of spirit, began plotting themselves to burn down the city and wreck the empire and were instigating tribal revolts and wars with other nations.

Their scheme, however, was discovered, and Cicero laid the situation before the senate. Silanus, who spoke first, declared that in his opinion the men ought to suffer the extreme penalty, and those who spoke after him in turn agreed with him, until it came to Caesar. But when Caesar rose, being a skillful speaker and wishing to promote change and agitation in the state, as material for his own designs, rather than let them be suppressed, he spoke at length persuasively and in a tone of humanity. He would not have the men put to death without a trial, but was for confining them under guard; and he so worked on the sentiment of the senate, which was afraid of the people, that even Silanus retracted what he had said and declared that he had not recommended death but only imprisonment, since that to a Roman was the extreme penalty.

23. But after this transformation had taken place and all the senators were making haste to approve the milder and more merciful procedure, Cato rose to state his opinion and plunged at once into a wrathful and passionate speech. He denounced Silanus for changing his mind, and attacked Caesar, whom he charged with aiming to overthrow the state under a popular pretense of humanity. He was trying, he said, to frighten the senate in a situation where he himself was the one to be afraid and be thankful, if he got off unpunished and escaped suspicion. For he was openly and blatantly trying to rescue the common enemies of them all, and admitting that he felt no compassion for his country, so noble and so great, which had come so near to destruction. He was weeping and lamenting for men who should never have been born or grown up,

---

[27] For further details, see above, *Cicero*, chs. 10–22, and *Caesar*, ch. 7.

and whose death would deliver the city from much bloodshed and peril.

This is the only speech of Cato, they say, which has been preserved, and it was due to the consul, Cicero, that it was saved. He had previously taught those secretaries who were especially rapid writers to use symbols which served to compress the sense, and then had these men dispersed here and there through the senate house. Up to that time the Romans had not trained or even possessed what we call shorthand writers, but that day, they say, the first move towards employing some such method was made.[28] At any rate Cato won his case and changed the senate's verdict again, so that they condemned the men to death.

24. And since we must not omit even small indications of character, when attempting to draw, as it were, a portrait of a soul, there is a story that while Caesar that day was in the thick of a hot argument with Cato and the senate was absorbed in watching the two men, a small tablet was brought in to Caesar from the outside. Cato tried to make that incident seem suspicious, and insinuated that some conspirators were behind it, and called on Caesar to read his letter aloud. At this Caesar handed the tablet to Cato, who was standing near him. But it was an amorous note to Caesar from Cato's sister Servilia, who was in love with him and had been seduced by him. When Cato read it, he threw it back to Caesar, saying, "Keep it, sot!" and returned to his original argument.

As regards the women of his family Cato appears to have been thoroughly unfortunate. For this sister had a bad name for her relations with Caesar, and the other Servilia, also a sister of Cato,[29] was even worse behaved. She had been married to Lucullus,[30] a man of the highest standing in Rome, and had borne him a child, and then was sent out of his house for licentiousness. And—the greatest shame of all—not even Cato's wife Atilia was clear of the same stain. Although he had two children by her, he was obliged to divorce her for improper conduct.

---

[28] There are grounds for thinking that the Romans had used shorthand before this time.

[29] Cato had two half-sisters named Servilia.

[30] For Lucullus, see above, *Caesar,* ch. 10. He had married Cato's half-sister after his divorce from the notorious Clodia.

25. He then married Marcia, a daughter of Philippus, a woman apparently decorous, but about whom there was a great deal of talk. This part of Cato's life, like a play, has been much discussed and is hard to understand. However, what happened was the following, according to Thrasea,[31] who relies on Munatius, Cato's friend and constant companion. In the throng of devotees and admirers of Cato were some more distinguished and eminent than others. One of these was Quintus Hortensius, a man of fine reputation and upright character, who wanted not merely to be a close friend and comrade of Cato but to unite his whole household and family somehow with Cato's in a tie of relationship. To this end he tried to persuade Cato, whose daughter Porcia was the wife of Bibulus and had borne him two sons, to give her next to him, as excellent soil in which to beget children. "To the popular way of thinking," he said, "such a thing may seem strange, but by nature it is not good nor is it advantageous to the state that a woman at the height of her youth and beauty should suppress her powers of fruitfulness and lie idle, or else bring her husband too many children and so weigh down and beggar him. For worthy men to have offspring in common would make virtue more plentiful and widespread in their families. The state itself too would be knit close together by their alliances." If Bibulus was deeply attached to his wife, he, Hortensius, would return her as soon as she had borne him a child, and he would thus be more nearly connected both with Bibulus and with Cato in a community of children.

Cato answered that he loved Hortensius and would value a common bond of relationship with him but that he thought it strange to speak of marrying his daughter, who had been given to another. At this Hortensius altered his proposal, uncovered his whole design, and had the daring to ask for Cato's own wife, who was still young enough to have children, while Cato had heirs enough.[32] And it cannot be said that he did this because he believed that Cato neglected her, for they say that Marcia was with child at the time. However, seeing Hortensius' ardor and eagerness, Cato did not refuse, but said that Philippus, Marcia's father, must also give his consent. So there was a meeting with Philippus and he agreed but would take no part in the ceremony, unless Cato himself were present

31 Publius Thrasea Paetus, a student of Stoic philosophy, wrote a life of Cato. He was executed in 66 A.D. by Nero.
32 See above, *Numa, Comparison,* ch. 3, for an account of a similar arrangement.

and joined in giving her away.[33] This event took place later, but since I was discussing the women of Cato's family, I thought best to tell of it here.

26.   Lentulus and his associates had now been executed, and Caesar, because of the rumors and the accusations brought against him before the senate, had taken refuge with the people and was stirring up and winning to himself the numerous diseased and corrupt elements in the state. Cato then, in alarm, prevailed on the senate to try winning back the poor and landless mob by giving them a share in the distribution of grain, the cost of which came yearly to twelve hundred and fifty talents. By this liberality and bounty the menace of Caesar was undoubtedly dispelled.

But then Metellus, who had entered promptly on his office of tribune, began holding turbulent meetings of the people, and he proposed an edict summoning Pompey the Great to hasten back to Italy [34] with his forces, to take over the protection of the city, which, he said, was in danger from Catiline. It was a plausible proposal, but the real object and aim of the edict was to put everything in Pompey's hands and surrender the supreme power to him.

When the senate met, however, Cato did not in his usual way launch a violent attack on Metellus, but offered him much sensible and appropriate advice, turning finally to pleading with him, and praising his family for having always been on the aristocratic side. Metellus was thereby much emboldened, and despising Cato as a terrified weakling, he broke out in fantastic threats and reckless speeches, expecting to put his whole plan through by force in spite of the senate. Then Cato changed his manner and voice and language and ended by declaring to everyone that as long as he lived Pompey should not enter the city with an army. As a result of this scene the senate concluded that neither speaker was in a sound state of mind or reasoning soberly, but that Metellus' policy was a madness which by its extreme wickedness would lead straight to chaos and destruction of everything, whereas Cato's was a passionate virtue, fighting for honor and justice.

---

[33] It seems that Cato himself must have first divorced Marcia. Otherwise her father could hardly have married her to another man. Divorce in Rome at this time required no formalities, merely a declaration by one party or both, oral or in writing, that the marriage was at an end.

[34] The year was 62 B.C. Pompey had just completed his conquest of the kingdom of Mithridates in Asia Minor, and was on his way home.

27. But when the people went to vote on the edict, there were armed strangers and gladiators and slaves drawn up in the forum to support Metellus. A considerable section of the people too wanted Pompey back in hope of a change, and Caesar, who was then praetor, showed great strength. As for the leading citizens, though they joined Cato in his indignation at all this wrongdoing they did not in his efforts to resist. So a deep depression and alarm took possession of his household. Some of his friends sat up without food all night in baffled talk with one another about him, while his wife and sisters wailed and wept. Cato himself, however, spoke to them all fearlessly and cheerfully and tried to console them. He had dinner as usual, and after the night was over was wakened from a deep sleep by Minucius Thermus, one of his colleagues.

They then went down with a few companions into the forum, where many met them and warned them to be on their guard. Pausing then, Cato saw the temple of Castor and Pollux [35] surrounded by armed men, its steps guarded by gladiators, and Metellus himself sitting at the top with Caesar. Thereat, he turned to his friends and exclaimed, "O what a bold and a cowardly fellow, to muster such an army against one unarmed, empty-handed man!" At the same time he walked straight ahead with Thermus. The men standing on the steps made way for them, but let no one else pass, except that Cato with some difficulty grasped Munatius' hand and brought him along. Then walking directly up the steps, he sat himself down as he was between Metellus and Caesar, thus cutting off their further exchange of talk. This move disconcerted Caesar and Metellus, but the better citizens saw and admired Cato's look and high spirit and courage, and drew nearer, calling out to him to keep up heart, and to each other to stand together and not betray their liberty or the man who was struggling to defend it.

28. The attendant now produced the edict, but Cato would not let him read it, and when Metellus took it and began to read, Cato snatched the paper from him. Metellus, who knew the law by heart, then began to repeat it, but Thermus shut his mouth with his hand and stopped his voice.

[35] The temple of the Dioscuri, the twin hero gods, stood on the south side of the forum, where three of its columns still stand. In front of it was a platform from which addresses were often made to the people.

At length Metellus saw that a fight was being put up which was too much
for him and that the people were impressed and turning towards their
rightful leaders, so he sent orders to his men-at-arms, who were some
distance off, to come on at a run with frightening yells. This they did and
everybody scattered but Cato, who stood there alone, pelted though he
was with stones and sticks from above, until Murena, whom he had
before denounced and prosecuted, came to his aid and held his toga in
front of him and called out to those who were pelting him to stop. Finally
he persuaded Cato to leave, and putting his arm about him led him into
the temple of Castor and Pollux.

But when Metellus saw the area around the rostrum deserted and his
opponents fleeing through the forum, he was sure he had won the day,
and commanded his men-at-arms to withdraw. He then came forward
in the proper way and attempted to get the edict passed. But the opposition recovered quickly from their flight and came on again, shouting
loudly and boldly. Metellus and his partisans now were alarmed, thinking
that their enemies had obtained arms from somewhere with which to
attack them. So not one stood his ground, but they all fled from the rostrum. When they were thus dispersed, Cato came forward and praised
and encouraged the people, and the majority were ready to put down
Metellus by whatever means. The senate too met and proclaimed anew
that it would support Cato and fight against the edict, which it said would
bring discord and civil war into Rome.

29. Metellus himself was still unshaken and audacious, but he saw that
his followers were desperately afraid of Cato and thought him quite invincible. So he sprang abruptly down into the forum and calling the
people together delivered a long and bitter invective against Cato, crying
out that he would now flee from his tyranny and from the conspiracy
against Pompey, and that the city would soon repent of dishonoring so
great a man. And soon afterwards, he started off for Asia to lay all this
report before Pompey. Now Cato's reputation stood high for having relieved the tribunes of a great anxiety, and in a measure broken the power
of Pompey in the person of Metellus. He was still more respected when he
would not let the senate degrade and depose Metellus, as it was about to
do, but spoke against such a step and won them over. For the common
people thought it not humane or fair to trample on and insult an enemy

who was already thoroughly defeated, and wise men considered it right and prudent not to enrage Pompey.

Meanwhile, Lucullus returned from his campaign—the conclusion and glory of which Pompey seems to have snatched from him—and was dangerously close to not having a triumph,[36] for Gaius Memmius had formed a party hostile to him among the people and brought charges against him, though more to please Pompey than out of any enmity on his own part to Lucullus. Cato, however, was related to Lucullus, who had married his sister Servilia; and he thought too that he was being shockingly treated. So he took a stand against Memmius, thus exposing himself to a host of slanders and misrepresentations. At last an attempt was made to turn him out of his office, on the ground that he was acting as a tyrant, but he was so far victorious that he forced Memmius to drop his charges and give up the struggle. So Lucullus had his triumph, and thereafter held on still more tightly to Cato's friendship, regarding it as his great bulwark and protection against Pompey's power.

30. And then Pompey came back in might from his campaign [37] and the magnificence and enthusiasm of his reception convinced him that he would get everything he asked from his fellow citizens. He therefore sent ahead to the senate a demand to postpone the elections for consul so that he might be there and assist Piso [38] in his candidacy. Most of the senators were ready to consent, but Cato, who did not consider the postponement a very important matter but who was anxious to cut short Pompey's maneuverings and hopes, opposed the proposition and so changed the senators' attitude that they voted it down. At this Pompey became seriously uneasy, for he realized that he would find Cato very obstructive if he were unable to make him his friend. He therefore sent for Cato's comrade, Munatius, and asked through him for the older of Cato's two marriageable nieces as a wife for himself and the younger for his son.

---

36 Lucullus returned in 66 B.C., but had to wait three years for his triumph. Gaius Memmius was a tribune in 66, and in that capacity opposed Lucullus' claim. But Memmius was later involved in some electioneering scandals for which he was banished in 53. To him Lucretius dedicated his great work, *On the Nature of Things.*

37 Pompey came back in 62 B.C.

38 Lucius Calpurnius Piso was the father of Caesar's wife Calpurnia. Piso was in the main loyal to Caesar, but his record as governor of Macedonia was so shameless that he was excoriated by Cicero in several orations, and was recalled.

Some, however, say that the proposal was not for Cato's nieces but for his daughters.

When Munatius brought the message to Cato and his wife and sisters, the women were delighted at the prospect of an alliance with so great and distinguished a person. But Cato, without hesitation or reflection, said in a sudden passion of heat, "Go, Munatius, go, and tell Pompey that Cato is not to be caught by an approach through the women's apartments, but that he values highly Pompey's good will, and if he does right, Cato will give him a friendship more to be trusted than any marriage connection. But he will not give hostages for Pompey's glory, which may be his country's hurt."

The women were disappointed by this reply, and Cato's friends criticized it as both rude and arrogant. The next thing, however, was that Pompey in an effort to obtain the consulship for one of his friends,[39] sent out money to the tribes; and the bribery was barefaced, for the money was counted out in his gardens. Cato then remarked to the women that anyone connected with Pompey by marriage would inevitably have shared in the obloquy of such doings, and they confessed that he had done wisely to reject Pompey's advances. Yet if one is to judge by the result, it appears that he made a fatal mistake in not accepting that marriage alliance and allowing Pompey to turn to Caesar and contract a marriage which combined the power of himself and Caesar, and came near to wrecking the Roman state, and did overthrow the constitution. None of these things, it may be, would have happened, if Cato had not been so alarmed by Pompey's small offense as to permit him to commit the enormous one of uniting his power with that of another man.

31.   These events, however, were still to come. Previously, Lucullus got into a quarrel with Pompey over the arrangements that had been made in Pontus, for each of them wanted his own acts ratified. Cato defended Lucullus, who was clearly being wronged, and Pompey lost his case in the senate. He then set out to make himself popular with the people, and for the army proposed a division of land. But at this point, too, Cato opposed him and prevented the passing of the measure, whereat Pompey took up Clodius, the most brazen demagogue of the time, and won over

39 The friend was Lucius Afranius, who was elected consul in 61 B.C. to serve in the year 60.

Caesar. And in a way Cato himself brought this last about. For Caesar, on his return from his praetorship in Spain,[40] was anxious to stand for the consulship and at the same time was asking for a triumph. But by a law candidates for office must be there in the city, while men expecting to hold a triumph must remain outside the walls. Caesar therefore requested the senate's permission to canvass for the office through agents. Many senators were willing to let him do it, but Cato spoke against it. and when he saw that they were for pleasing Caesar, he used up the whole day in talking, and so thwarted the senate's wishes. Caesar then gave up hope of celebrating his triumph, moved into the city, and at once attached himself to Pompey and stood for the consulship. On his election as consul, he gave his daughter Julia as wife to Pompey, and the two now combined against the state, the one introducing laws providing for distribution of land allotments to the poor, and the other on hand with support for the measures. But the followers of Lucullus and Cicero joined with Bibulus, the other consul, to oppose them. Among them Cato was foremost, for he already suspected that the loving partnership of Caesar and Pompey boded nothing good. He was not, he said, afraid of the distribution of land, but of the price that would be demanded for it by those who through it were courting the people's favor.

32. By his speeches Cato brought the senate to unanimous agreement; and many an outside citizen stood with him, irritated by Caesar's strange behavior. For political tricks which only the most impudent and unscrupulous tribunes had used to win popularity, Caesar, with the aid of his authority as consul, was now employing to ingratiate himself with the people. And when Caesar's party became alarmed, they resorted to violence. First a basket of dung was flung over Bibulus as he was going down to the forum; then a mob attacked his lictors and smashed their fasces. Finally weapons were thrown and many persons were wounded. Then everybody fled running from the forum, except Cato, who last of all walked slowly away, turning back to protest to his fellow citizens.

After this demonstration Caesar's partisans not only got the law passed for the distribution of land, but also a vote that the entire senate should solemnly swear to maintain the law and help enforce it, if anyone dis-

---

[40] Caesar returned from Spain in 60 B.C., and was elected consul for the following year. On these events, see also, *Caesar*, ch. 13.

obeyed it. They also imposed heavy penalties on senators who refused to swear. So they all perforce took the oath, having in mind what happened to Metellus [41] in the old days, when the people allowed him to be exiled from Italy because he would not swear to uphold a similar law. For the same reason the women of Cato's household wept and urgently implored him to yield and take the oath, as did also his friends and intimates. But the person who did most to persuade and influence him to take the oath was the orator Cicero, who pointed out that for him to think that he alone could refuse to obey the general decision and try to ignore what had been done and could not be altered was senseless and mad. For him now too to desert the city for which he was doing everything, and surrender her to her foes, as if he were glad to be through with struggling to protect her, would be the worst of misfortunes. For even if Cato did not need Rome, Rome needed Cato, and so did all his friends. Among them, Cicero said, he himself was foremost, for it was he against whom Clodius was plotting, attacking him directly through his authority as tribune. By these and similar arguments and entreaties, they say, both at home and in the forum, Cato was softened and compelled reluctantly to relent. But he was last of all to come forward to take the oath, except for Favonius, one of his close friends.

33. Thus encouraged, Caesar introduced another law for the division of nearly all Campania [42] among the poor and destitute. No one spoke against it except Cato, and Caesar had him taken from the rostrum to prison. However, he paused not at all in his bold speech, but as he walked along kept on talking about the law and advising the people to stop that kind of legislating. The senate followed with eyes downcast, together with the best of the people, who were displeased and troubled, though they said nothing; and Caesar did not fail to see their disapproval. However, he was stubborn, expecting Cato to appeal and beseech him, and so had him still led on. But when it was plain that Cato had no intention of doing any such thing, Caesar was overcome by the shame and dishonor of his position, and himself stealthily got one of the tribunes to rescue Cato.

---

[41] Quintus Metellus, known as Numidicus for his triumph in 108 B.C. over Jugurtha, king of Numidia, went into exile rather than swear to enforce a law of which he disapproved.

[42] Campania was a rich and fertile district to the south of Rome; it included the region around the Bay of Naples.

Yet by these laws and their other favors the people were beguiled, and they voted Caesar the government of Illyria and all Gaul, with an army of four legions, for five years, though Cato warned them that by their votes they themselves were planting a tyrant in their citadel. Against the law, too, they moved Publius Clodius from the patrician to the plebeian class and then made him a tribune. In order to purchase the banishment of Cicero, Clodius' policy was to do anything to placate them. And they elected as consuls [43] Calpurnius Piso, the father of Caesar's wife, and Aulus Gabinius, a man "out of Pompey's lap," as those said who knew his habits and manner of life.

34. But though Caesar and his party had thus got control of things, and had made one half of the citizens submissive by favors and the other half by terror, they still dreaded Cato. For even on the occasions when they got their way against him, it was with difficulty and hard work and some shame and disgrace that they forced their proposals through, and this was unpleasant and vexatious. And Clodius had no hope of getting rid of Cicero so long as Cato was in Rome, and that, above all things, he was aiming to do.

Accordingly, as soon as he was in office he sent for Cato and made him a proposition. He said that he considered him the cleanest handed of any Roman, and was ready to give proof of his belief by deed. A crowd of men were asking for the appointment to Cyprus and the court of Ptolemy,[44] and begging to be sent out. But he thought Cato the only one worthy of it, and was glad to offer him the favor. But Cato cried out that the thing was a snare and an insult and not a favor, to which Clodius scornfully and arrogantly replied, "Well, if you will not accept it as a favor, you shall go as a punishment." He then went straight to the people and had an edict passed to send out Cato. But when Cato was leaving Rome, Clodius gave him neither ship, nor soldier, nor assistant, except for two clerks, one of whom was a thief and a scoundrel and the other a client of Clodius. And as if he had given him too small a task in the mission to Cyprus and Ptolemy, he instructed him also to get the exiles from Byzan-

---

[43] For the year 58 B.C.

[44] This was a younger brother of Ptolemy Auletes, king of Egypt and father of Cleopatra. Ptolemy of Cyprus was deprived of his kingdom in this year by a decree of the Roman assembly put through by Clodius. By the end of the year the island had become a Roman province.

tium restored, his idea being to keep Cato out of the way for the longest
possible time while he was tribune.

35.   Under this compulsion to leave, Cato advised Cicero, who was being
threatened with banishment, not to be the cause of any quarreling, nor to
plunge the city into fighting and bloodshed, but to yield to the emergency
and become again the savior of his country. He also sent Canidius, one
of his friends, on ahead to Cyprus and tried to persuade Ptolemy to surrender the island without a struggle, assuring him that he would not
have to live without money or honor, for the Roman people would bestow on him the priesthood of the goddess at Paphos.[45] Cato himself
meanwhile stayed in Rhodes making his preparations and waiting for
an answer.

At this same time Ptolemy, king of Egypt, who had quarreled with
his citizens and left Alexandria in anger, was on a voyage to Rome, expecting that Pompey and Caesar with an armed force would restore him
to his throne. He wished, however, to have a talk with Cato, and therefore
sent him a message, supposing that Cato would come to him. But Cato
happened then to be taking a treatment of purging, and sent word back
that Ptolemy must come to him if he wished to see him. When the king
arrived, Cato did not go to meet him or even rise from his seat, but greeted
him as if he were any casual visitor, and bade him be seated. Ptolemy
was at first put out by this behavior and astonished at the haughtiness
and stateliness of Cato's manner in view of the plainness and common-
ness of his equipment. But when he began to discuss his affairs with him,
he heard words that were extremely sagacious as well as bold.

For Cato blamed him for his situation, and pointed out how much
happiness he had left behind, and to how much humiliation and hardship
he was exposing himself among the corrupt and greedy magnates of Rome,
who would hardly be satisfied if all Egypt were turned to silver. He advised Ptolemy to sail home and make peace with his subjects, and said he
was ready to sail back with him and help him to make the peace. The king
came to his senses, as though from a fit of insanity or delirium, and realizing the honesty and wisdom of Cato's advice, resolved to follow it. But

---

[45] Paphos was a city near the west coast of Cyprus which contained a famous shrine
to the goddess Aphrodite, who was supposed to have risen from the sea not far away.
The priesthood carried with it lands, slaves, wealth, and great dignity.

then his friends persuaded him to revert to his original plan. As soon, however, as he arrived in Rome and began walking up to the door of an official, he groaned over his own folly, believing that he had rejected not a good man's advice but the prophetic warning of a god.

36. Meanwhile Ptolemy of Cyprus, luckily for Cato, killed himself by taking poison. He was said to have left a large amount of treasure, so Cato decided that while he went himself to Byzantium, he would send his nephew Brutus to Cyprus, because he did not altogether trust Canidius. Then, after settling the trouble between the exiles and the people of Byzantium, he left that city at peace and sailed for Cyprus. There he found a great mass of royal paraphernalia, goblets, tables, precious stones, and purple robes, which had to be sold and converted into money. Cato was anxious to manage everything with precision, raise the price of every article to the highest point, see to it all himself, and keep the most careful accounts. He did not trust the men who were familiar with the market, but suspected everyone alike, assistants, criers, purchasers, and friends. Finally by talking himself in private to the purchasers and leading each one on to bid, he got most of the saleable stuff sold. But by his methods he offended all his friends, who felt he distrusted them, and angered Munatius, the most intimate of them all, nearly beyond healing. When Caesar wrote his invective against Cato, he was most scathing in this part of his denunciation.

37. Munatius, however, writes that his anger against Cato was caused not by Cato's distrust of him but by his lack of consideration for him, and by his own jealousy of Canidius. Munatius himself brought out a life of Cato, which Thrasea followed closely. In that he says that he reached Cyprus later than the rest and found no accommodation prepared for him, and on presenting himself at Cato's door he was turned away because Cato was discussing something in the house with Canidius. And his mild complaint to Cato met with no mild reply, for Cato told him that too much love, as Theophrastus said, often results in hatred. "And now you too," went on Cato, "with all your great devotion to me, are annoyed because you think I pay you less respect than I should. But I do employ Canidius more than others because I have now had experience of him and trust him. He came here at the beginning and is showing himself honest."

Cato said this to him, Munatius writes, when they were alone together, but Cato later repeated it to Canidius. On hearing that he had done this, Munatius no longer went to dine with Cato when he was invited, or to consult with him. And when Cato threatened to require surety of him, as Romans used to do in the case of persons disobedient to orders, Munatius, regardless of his threat, took ship and departed and remained angry for a long time.

Later yet, Marcia, who was still Cato's wife, spoke to him on the subject. And it happened that both Cato and Munatius had been invited to supper by Barca. Cato came in late, after the others were seated, and asked where he should sit. Barca told him to sit where he liked and Cato, after looking around the room, said he would sit by Munatius. He then went and sat down by him, but showed him no other mark of friendliness during the supper. But Marcia, Munatius says, appealed to Cato again, and he wrote Munatius that he wished to see him about something. So Munatius went early in the morning to Cato's house and was kept by Marcia until all the others had left. And then Cato came in and throwing both arms around him embraced him like an affectionate friend. Such episodes I think are no less revealing for the perception and understanding of a man's character than his great deeds done in public. So I have related this at considerable length.

38. Cato collected in Cyprus almost seven thousand talents of silver, and dreading the long voyage ahead had a number of chests prepared, each of which held two talents and five hundred drachmas. To each chest he had fastened a long rope, at the end of which was tied an immense piece of cork, so that if the ship were wrecked, the corks, with their ropes attaching them to the chests below, would show where they lay. The money, except for a little, was conveyed safely, but the two books in which he had the accounts of his whole administration carefully written down were both lost. A freedman of his, Philargyros by name, took one of them, and sailed from Cenchreae,[46] but his boat capsized and he lost both the books and his cargo. The other Cato himself carried as far as Corcyra, where he set up his tent in the market place. But it was cold and the sailors for that reason lit many fires during the night, and the tents caught fire and the book disappeared. The royal stewards who were with Cato would have stopped the mouths of enemies and traducers, but

---

[46] Cenchreae was the name of one of the harbors of Corinth.

still the loss stung him. For he was ambitious to produce his accounts, not as a proof of his trustworthiness but as an example to others of exactitude; accordingly he felt mortified.

39. The Romans got wind of his arrival with the ships and all the officials and priests, the entire senate, and a great crowd of people went to meet him at the river, so that both banks of the Tiber were covered and his voyage up to the city was like a triumph in pomp and splendor. Yet to some it seemed rude and ungenerous that, though the consuls and the praetors were there in the crowd, he neither came ashore to greet them nor halted in his course, but through a roar of applause swept past the bank where they stood in a royal galley of six decks, and never stopped until he had brought his fleet to anchor in the dockyard. But when the money was carried through the forum, the people were astonished at the amount of it, and the senate met and voted that along with suitable commendations a special praetorship [47] be conferred on Cato, and that when attending public spectacles he might wear a purple-bordered robe. Cato, however, declined these distinctions, but after testifying before the senate to the diligence and fidelity of Nicias, the steward of the royal possessions, he persuaded it to give him his freedom. Philippus, Marcia's father, was then consul, and in a way the dignity and power of his office took in Cato, too, while Philippus' colleague honored Cato as much for his high character as Philippus did for his relationship to himself.

40. Meanwhile Cicero had returned from the exile into which he had been driven by Clodius, and was exerting much influence. In Clodius' absence he forcibly took down and destroyed the tablets recording Clodius' term as tribune, which Clodius had inscribed and placed on the Capitol.[48] When the senate assembled to discuss his action, Clodius spoke in accusation. Cicero replied that inasmuch as Clodius had become tribune illegally, all that had been done and recorded during his term must be null and void. But while Cicero was still speaking, Cato objected, and finally rose and said that although he was sure that there was nothing wholesome or good in Clodius' administration, still if one annulled everything that Clodius did as tribune, then all his own work in Cyprus would be annulled

---

[47] Cato was only thirty-eight at this time, too young under ordinary circumstances for the responsible office of praetor.

[48] See on all this, above, *Cicero*, chs. 30-34.

and his commission there would be illegal, since an illegal magistrate had got it assigned to him. It was not illegal for Clodius to be chosen tribune, after his transfer, permissible by law, from a patrician to a plebeian family. If Clodius, like others, had been a bad tribune, they should call him to account for his misbehavior, but not blot out the office which had suffered from his wrongdoing. This speech made Cicero angry with Cato and for a long time he stopped treating him as a friend. Later, however, they were reconciled.

41. Then Pompey and Crassus had a meeting with Caesar,[49] who crossed the Alps, and they made a plan that the two should stand together for a second consulship. When they were settled in office, they would have the people vote Caesar another period of command as long as his first, and themselves the largest provinces, with money and troops. It was a conspiracy for the division of sovereign power and the overthrow of the constitution. Many honest men at that time were preparing to be candidates for the consulship, but on seeing Pompey and Crassus canvassing, they gave up the idea, all but Lucius Domitius, the husband of Cato's sister Porcia. Cato persuaded him not to draw back and retire, since the struggle was not for office but for the liberty of Rome. And in fact the word went around among the still sober-minded party in the city that the consular office must not be permitted to become too domineering and oppressive through a union of the power of Pompey and Crassus, but that one of them must be kept out of it. Accordingly, they rallied to Domitius, urging and encouraging him to maintain his opposition and assuring him that many who were then silent through fear, would support him with their votes.

Pompey's partisans were afraid of just that and laid an ambuscade for Domitius as he was going down to the Campus Martius by torchlight early one morning. First, the torchbearer, who stood close to Domitius, was struck, and fell and died, and after him quickly all the rest were wounded and fled, but Cato and Domitius. For Cato kept hold of Domitius, though he himself had been wounded in the arm, and called on him to stay and, as long as there was breath in him, not desert the struggle for freedom against the tyrants, who were showing how they would use their authority by their approach to it through such dastardly crimes.

---

[49] Their meeting was at Luca, in 56 B.C. See above, *Caesar,* ch. 21.

42. Domitius, however, would not face the danger and fled to his house for refuge, and Pompey and Crassus were elected consuls.[50] Yet Cato did not give up the struggle but came forward himself as candidate for a praetorship, because he wished to have a foothold for wrestling with them and not as a private citizen to oppose magistrates. But Pompey and Crassus dreaded this move too, for they thought that the praetorship in Cato's hands would become a match for the consulship. So first they suddenly convened the senate without the people knowing anything of it, and got a vote passed that the men elected as praetors should take office at once, without waiting for the lawful time to pass within which those who had been bribing the people were liable to trial. Then when through this vote they had made bribery free from accountability, they produced helpers and friends of their own as candidates for the praetorship. In person they passed out money, and in person they were on hand when the votes were cast.

But the virtue and good name of Cato promised to triumph even over all these stratagems, for the people's reverence for him made them think it terrible to sell him by their votes, when the right thing for the city would be to buy him for its praetor. So the first tribe called upon voted for him, whereupon Pompey abruptly announced a lie, namely, that he had heard thunder, and by that mean trick dissolved the assembly. For they used to regard such signs as inauspicious and would conclude no business after a signal like that from the gods. But again Pompey and his party lavished money on bribes, and drove the best men away from the Campus Martius, and thus by sheer violence brought about the election of Vatinius as praetor instead of Cato. At this, they say, the men who had been selling their votes so wickedly and illegally skulked away in haste, but the others collected and were voicing their indignation when one of the tribunes on the spot turned the meeting into an assembly and Cato appeared before them. As if inspired by the gods, he predicted everything that would happen to the city, and tried to arouse the citizens against Pompey and Crassus, who, he said, were conniving at such crimes and devising such a policy as made them afraid of Cato, lest as praetor he put a curb on them. And then at the end he was escorted home by a crowd greater than that which accompanied all the elected praetors together.

---

50 They were elected for the year 55 B.C.

43. Gaius Trebonius [51] next proposed a law for the division of the provinces between the consuls, to the effect that one should have the government of Spain and Libya and the other of Syria and Egypt, and that both might make war on whomever they chose and attack and conquer them with forces on sea and land. Other men had now given up as hopeless all opposition and efforts to stop the course of events and would not even speak against the measure, but Cato mounted the rostrum before the vote was taken, and at his request was reluctantly granted leave to speak, and spoke for two hours. After he had spent that much time on lengthy arguments, explanations and predictions, they would not let him speak longer, though he was still for keeping on, and an attendant went up to him and pulled him down. But from where he stood on the ground, he kept on shouting, and had people listening and sympathizing with his indignation. So the attendant again took hold of him, led him off and put him outside the forum. But the moment he was let go, he turned back and struggled to get to the rostrum, crying out to the people to stand by him. The same thing took place several times, and at last Trebonius, exasperated, gave orders to take him to prison. But a crowd followed him, listening to his words as he walked along, so that Trebonius in a fright let him go.

In this way Cato used up that day. But during the following days Pompey's agents intimidated some of the citizens, bought up others by favors and bribes, with armed men prevented one of the tribunes, Aquilius, from leaving the senate house, threw Cato himself out of the forum when he shouted that it thundered, and after wounding a good many persons and even killing some, forcibly carried through the law. As a result, a mob gathered and was furiously stoning Pompey's statues, but Cato came up and stopped them. But when next a law was proposed giving Caesar his provinces and armies, Cato no longer appealed to the people, but to Pompey himself, formally assuring and warning him that he was now, without realizing it, taking Caesar on his shoulders and that when he began to feel the weight of the burden and find it too heavy for him he would neither be able to get rid of it nor go on bearing it, but would collapse with it on the state. Then he would recall Cato's advice and see

---

[51] Gaius Trebonius was a tribune in 55 B.C. and a useful tool of the triumvirs, Pompey and Crassus. Later he served as legate for Caesar in Gaul, but he was one of the conspirators who planned his murder.

that it had been as much in Pompey's interest as it was honorable and right. Pompey heard these warnings often but paid no attention and put them out of his mind. He did not believe there would be a change in Caesar, for he had faith in his own power and good fortune.

44. For the following year [52] Cato was chosen praetor. It looked, however, as if he were not so much adding to the dignity and importance of the office by his good conduct of it as he was detracting from it by shaming it. For he frequently went out to his tribunal wearing neither shoes nor tunic, and in that shape presided at capital trials involving eminent men. Some say too that after lunch, when he had drunk wine, he would go on with business; but that certainly is not true. But the people were being corrupted by bribes from men who were seeking office, and who went about the buying of the masses as though it were a regular trade, and Cato was bent on eradicating the disease completely from the state. He therefore persuaded the senate to pass a decree that all magistrates elected, even if no one accused them of misdoing, must themselves come forward before a sworn court and present an account of their election.

At this the candidates for offices were indignant, and still more indignant were the masses who took the bribes. So, in the early morning when Cato went out to his tribunal, a throng fell on him, shouting, cursing, and pelting him with stones, so that everybody fled from the tribunal and he himself was shoved away from it and was pushed around by the mob, and with difficulty got his hands on the rostrum. But then he rose to his feet and by the firmness and courage of his appearance at once gained control of the riot and stopped the yelling. He said what was appropriate, the people listened quietly, and the disturbance was entirely over. But when the senate was praising him, he said, "I cannot praise you for leaving a praetor in danger alone, and doing nothing to help him."

But every candidate for office was in a dilemma, for they were afraid to use bribery themselves but afraid too of being defeated if their rivals used it. Accordingly, they agreed to meet in one spot, and each put down one hundred and twenty-five thousand drachmas in money, all then to stand for office honestly and lawfully. Whoever broke his word and used bribes should forfeit his money. Having reached this agreement, they chose Cato to hold the money and act as umpire and witness, and bringing

---

[52] Cato was praetor in 54 B.C.

their money they were for depositing it with him. They wrote out their agreement too in his presence. However, though he accepted sureties for the money, he would not receive it.

When election day came, Cato took his place beside the presiding tribune and watched the vote. One of the pledgers he found cheating, and ordered him to turn over his money to the rest. But they, after expressing their admiration of Cato's integrity, remitted the penalty, feeling that they had satisfaction enough from the offender. This action of Cato created much ill feeling and resentment in the rest of the citizens, for it looked as if he were assuming the power of the senate, the courts, and the magistrates.

For no virtue by the fame and the trust which it brings with it arouses more envy than justice, because both power and trust follow it, especially among the masses. The people do not merely honor just men, as they do the brave, or respect them, as they do the wise, but love them, and put confidence in them and trust them. They are afraid of brave men and distrust wise men. They think, moreover, that such men owe their superiority to nature rather than to their own will, bravery being a certain impetuosity, and wisdom a strength of soul, whereas it is possible for anyone who chooses to be just. So they abhor injustice particularly as a wickedness without excuse.

45. Hence all the big men were against Cato, feeling that he had put them to shame. Pompey saw Cato's reputation threatening an end to his own power, and was continually setting men on to slander him. Among these was Clodius, the demagogue, who had again drifted over to Pompey, and was crying out against Cato for having stolen quantities of treasure in Cyprus, and for being an enemy of Pompey because Pompey had refused to marry Cato's daughter. But Cato replied that with neither a horse nor a soldier he had collected from Cyprus more wealth for Rome than Pompey had brought back from his many wars and triumphs after ransacking the whole world; and that he had never desired a marriage connection with Pompey, not because he considered Pompey unworthy, but because he recognized the difference between their political aims.

"For my part," Cato went on, "I declined a province offered me after my praetorship, but Pompey took several, some of which he still keeps and some he bestows on others. He has now lent Caesar a force of six thousand infantry to use in Gaul. Caesar did not ask them of you citizens, nor did Pompey lend them with your consent, but forces like this, and arms and horses are now exchanged as gifts between men in private station. And though he has the titles of general and commander in chief, he has put others in charge of his armies and provinces, while he himself settles down close to the city, directing parties at the elections and fomenting disturbances, from all of which it is clear that by means of anarchy he is intriguing for a kingdom for himself."

46. Thus Cato defended himself against Pompey. Marcus Favonius [53] was a comrade and devoted friend of his, as Apollodorus of Phalerum is said to have been of Socrates in the old days. He was an excitable man, quickly stirred by argument, which affected him not gradually or mildly but, like unmixed wine, maddened him. He was being defeated as a candidate for the aedileship, when Cato, who was at the election, observed that the writing on the voting tablets was all in one hand. He exposed the cheat, and by appealing to the tribunes stopped the election. Later, when Favonius had been chosen aedile, Cato both superintended the shows in the theater and looked after the other business of the office. To the actors he presented crowns, not of gold but of wild olive, as is the fashion in Olympia, and instead of costly presents, he gave the Greeks beets, lettuce, radishes, and pears, and the Romans, jars of wine, pork, figs, melons, and bundles of wood. Some laughed at these thrifty gifts, but others were respectful, watching Cato's austere and sober manner change to a pleasant humor.

Favonius himself finally joined the crowd and sitting among the spectators applauded Cato and shouted to him to give the prizes and the honors to the best performers, and urged the spectators to shout the same, as though he were turning all his authority over to him. Meanwhile, in the other theater, Curio, Favonius' colleague, was giving an expensive entertainment, but the people left him to go over to where Cato was, and joined heartily in the game Favonius was playing as a private citizen, while Cato acted as master of sports. Cato's aim was to disparage the habit of costliness, and to show that in play one should be playful, making it an occasion

---

[53] Marcus Favonius, called "Cato's ape," was aedile in 52 B.C. When it came to the choice between Caesar and Pompey, he followed Pompey and fled with him after the battle of Pharsalus.

of simple mirth rather than of elaborate and lavish preparations and expenditure of vast thought and energy on things of no value.

47. Then Scipio, Hypsaeus, and Milo [54] stood as candidates for the consulship. They employed not only those unlawful methods which were
now familiar in the political arena, that is, the use of gifts and bribes, but
with insane recklessness were pressing on, by dint of armed force and
murder, towards a civil war. Some people therefore were demanding that
Pompey take charge of the elections. Cato at first opposed the demand,
saying that the laws ought not to base their security on Pompey, but
Pompey on the laws. However, when there had been no government for
a long time, and three armies were surrounding the forum daily, and
the anarchy was almost past stopping, he decided that the situation should
be put in the hands of Pompey by the willing consent of the senate before
extreme necessity compelled them. In this way, by choosing the most moderate of illegal measures as a cure for the chaos in the highest quarters,
he would be bringing in the monarchy himself instead of letting civil
strife run on until it ended in monarchy. So Bibulus, a kinsman of Cato,
said in the senate that in his opinion they should elect Pompey sole consul,
for then under his dispensation either matters would be set right, or else
the state would submit to the strongest man in it. And Cato rose and
quite unexpectedly spoke in favor of the proposal, advising any government as better than no government, and adding that he believed that
Pompey would deal excellently with the existing situation and protect
the state entrusted to his charge.

48. Thus Pompey was appointed consul and he at once asked Cato to
come to him in the suburbs. On his coming Pompey received him like a
friend, embracing him, clasping his hand and expressing his gratitude.
He then invited him to become his adviser and coadjutor in office. But
Cato answered that he had not at the outset spoken out of hatred for
Pompey, nor now out of partiality for him, but always for the good of the
state. In private now, he said, he would give Pompey his advice when
invited to do so; but in public, even uninvited, he would certainly con-

---

[54] For Metellus Scipio, see above, ch. 1 and n. 10. Annius Milo was the notorious ruffian who quarreled with Clodius, and after five years of riotous warfare murdered him,
in January, 52 b.c., while the disorders described here were preventing the regular
consular elections. Scipio and Plantius Hypsaeus were Pompey's candidates.

tinue to say what he thought right. And this he did, as he said he would. In the first place, when Pompey was proposing to issue laws prescribing new penalties and severe punishments for the men who in the past had bribed the people, Cato bade him disregard the past, and put his mind on the future. For, he said, it would not be easy to determine the point at which the inquiry into past offenses should stop, and if penalties were prescribed after the crimes, it would be a shocking way to treat men, to punish them by a law which they were not breaking when they committed their crimes. Then when many prominent men were on trial, some of them friends and relatives of Pompey, Cato noticed that he was relenting in many instances, and reproached him seriously and tried to rouse him to his duty.

And after Pompey had forbidden by law the usual delivery of panegyrics on men on trial, he himself wrote a panegyric on Munatius Plancus [55] and presented it at his trial. But Cato, who happened to be one of the jurors, closed his ears with his hands and stopped the reading of the testimonial. After the speeches had been made Plancus got Cato taken off the jury, but he was convicted nevertheless. In general Cato was a puzzling proposition for the defendants in lawsuits, and hard to handle. They neither wished to permit him to be one of their jurors nor did they dare to challenge him. For a good many men were condemned because their objections to Cato made it seem that they had no confidence in the justice of their own cases. Some of them had friends scolding them hotly, as if it were a great disgrace to refuse to accept Cato as a juror when he was named.

49. Meanwhile Caesar, though taken up with his legions in Gaul and busy with his wars, was employing gifts and money and friends to advance his power at Rome. And now the warnings of Cato began stirring Pompey out of the deep incredulity he had maintained until then, and he had visions of peril. But he was still hesitant and weakly procrastinating when it came to attacking and checking a menacing danger, so Cato resolved to stand as candidate for the consulship, that he might either

---

[55] Munatius Plancus (not to be confused with the Munatius in chs. 9, 30, 36) was tribune in the year 52 B.C., and had much to do with stirring up lawlessness in the city. Under Pompey he was tried and condemned, but under Caesar his civil rights were restored.

strip Caesar of his armies or convict him of conspiring against the state. The rival candidates, however, were both popular men, and Sulpicius[56] had benefited a great deal from Cato's reputation and influence in the city. So he seemed then to be behaving unfairly as well as ungratefully, but Cato did not blame him. "What wonder is it," he said, "if a man will not give up to another what he considers the greatest of all good things?"

But Cato had persuaded the senate to vote that the candidates for the office should themselves interview the people in person, and not solicit or communicate with them through agents going about to represent them. By this he had irritated the populace still more, for he not only kept them from getting money for their votes but also from doing favors, and so made them both poor and unrespected. In addition, Cato was not persuasive when speaking for himself, for he preferred to maintain in his deportment the dignity of his own character rather than affect the manner of a consul, greeting everyone and clasping their hands. Nor would he let his friends do the things by which the mob is humored and captivated. He therefore failed to get the office.

50. The event brought disappointment and regret tinged with shame not only to the defeated candidates but to their friends and relatives for many days afterwards. But Cato bore his defeat so casually that after anointing himself he first played a game of ball in the Campus Martius, and then after luncheon, went down to the forum, as was his custom, without either shoes or tunic, and walked about with his friends. Cicero, however, criticized him for not making more effort, when the situation called for a consul like him, and not trying to win the people by friendly mingling with them; also for taking no interest in the future and abandoning the struggle, although he had been a candidate twice for the praetorship. Cato, however, said that he had lost the praetorship not because the majority decided against him, but because they were coerced or corrupted, whereas in this consular election there had been no cheating, and he knew that he had displeased the people by his manners. But those no sensible man would change, merely to make himself attractive, nor, while he kept them as they were, would he subject himself to another such ordeal.

---

[56] Servius Sulpicius Rufus had been a fellow student of Cato, and his friend; now he was Caesar's candidate.

51. As for Caesar, he was fighting warrior nations and winning strenuous victories. It was even reported that he had attacked Germans during a truce, and had killed three hundred thousand.[57] Most persons then thought that the people should offer sacrifices of rejoicing, but Cato was urgent that they give Caesar up to the tribe against whom he had committed that crime, and not take his guilt on themselves or have it fall on the city. "However," he went on, "let us sacrifice too to the gods, for they are not turning their vengeance on the soldiers for the general's folly and madness, and they are sparing the city."

Thereupon Caesar wrote a letter and sent it to the senate, where it was read aloud, full of vicious tirades against Cato. But Cato rose and calmly, with no outburst of anger or vindictiveness, but as if he had reasoned it all over beforehand, argued that the charges against him were abusive and scurrilous and showed a kind of childishness and vulgarity in Caesar. He proceeded to analyze Caesar's policies from the beginning, revealing his whole design, as if he were not his enemy but his fellow conspirator and accomplice. He told them that it was not the sons of Germans or Celts that they had to fear but Caesar himself, if they were wise. He stirred and aroused the senate so that Caesar's friends regretted that they had had his letter read there, thus furnishing Cato an opportunity for his just reply and truthful accusations. Nothing, however, was done; it was simply said that it would be well to give Caesar a successor.[58] But when Caesar's friends demanded that Pompey too should likewise lay down his arms and give up his provinces, or else Caesar would not, Cato cried out that now had come to pass what he had foretold. The man was now openly using the power he had got, by deceiving and tricking the state, to coerce them. But outside the senate house, Cato could do nothing, for the people all along had wanted Caesar to be at the head of things, and while the senate was convinced by Cato, it was afraid of the people.

52. But when Caesar seized Ariminum,[59] and news came that he was marching with an army on Rome, then everyone looked to Cato, the common people and even Pompey too, for Cato alone from the beginning

---

[57] See above, *Caesar,* ch. 22.

[58] See above, *Caesar,* ch. 30.

[59] Caesar's crossing of the Rubicon and capture of Ariminum took place in 49 B.C. See above, *Caesar,* ch. 32.

had seen Caesar's plans and had been first to announce them publicly. And Cato said, "If any of you men had taken to heart what I was always predicting and advising, you would not now be terrified of one man or resting your hopes on one man." And Pompey said that Cato had spoken like a prophet, whereas he himself had acted like a friend. Cato then advised the senate to place everything in Pompey's hands, for the men who had done the great harm should be the ones to stop it.

But Pompey had no army in readiness, and he saw that the troops he was then levying were not eager to fight; so he left Rome. Cato had decided to follow him into exile, and therefore sent his younger son to Munatius in Bruttium to be out of danger, but the elder he kept with him. And as his household and daughters required someone to take care of them, he took Marcia, who was now a widow and very wealthy, again as his wife. Hortensius at his death had made her his heir. Over this arrangement Caesar berated Cato unsparingly, accusing him of avaricious bargaining in the marriage.[60] "Why," said Caesar, "did he have to give up his wife, if he wanted her, or why should he take her back, if he did not want her? Unless he first offered the woman to Hortensius as a bait when she was young, just to take her back when she was rich." To these insinuations Euripides' lines well apply: [61]

> "First, then, what can't be said; among such things
> I place calling you coward, Hercules."

For to accuse Cato of sordid greed is like imputing cowardice to Heracles. But whether in other respects the marriage was right is open to question. However, as soon as he had married Marcia, he turned over his house and daughters to her, and himself hastened after Pompey.

53. From that day forward, they say, Cato never cut his hair or his beard or wore a garland, but kept until his death the one attitude of grief, dejection, and mourning for the calamities of his country, whichever party won or lost. At the time, however, he had Sicily allotted him as his province, and crossed over to Syracuse. There he learned that Asinius Pollio [62]

---

60 The reference here is to some passages in Caesar's *Anti-Cato*. See above, ch. 25.
61 Euripides, *Heracles*, 173, 174.
62 Gaius Asinius Pollio, historian and poet, was a close friend of Julius Caesar and fought under him in Africa and Spain. After Caesar's death, he took the side of his heir, Octavian.

had arrived at Messana with troops from the enemy, and sent to ask the reason for his coming. But Pollio in turn asked Cato the reason for the transformations in the state. Cato then heard that Pompey had abandoned Italy entirely and was camping at Dyrrachium, whereupon he said that the ways of the gods were devious and obscure. For as long as Pompey was acting selfishly and dishonestly, he was invincible; but now, when he was anxious to save his country and fight for its liberty, his luck had deserted him. Pollio, Cato said, he could drive out of Sicily, but another and larger army would be coming on after him and he did not wish to ruin the island by involving it in war. So, after advising the Syracusans to save themselves by joining the winning side, he sailed away.

After his arrival at Pompey's camp, he clung always to one idea, to put off the war, because he hoped for a settlement and did not want the state to be defeated in the struggle and suffer the worst of fates, that is, have its future determined by the sword. To that end he persuaded Pompey and his council to take various decisions, such as not to sack any city subject to Rome, and not to kill any Roman save in the line of battle. These resolutions brought honor to Pompey's side, and led many to join it, attracted by his fairness and humanity.

54. Next, Cato was sent to Asia to assist those who were collecting boats and an army there, and he took with him his sister Servilia and her child by Lucullus. For Servilia, now that she was a widow, followed Cato about, and effaced much of the scandal created by her wanton life by accepting his guardianship of her own accord and adapting herself to his wandering existence. But Caesar said vile things of Cato even in his relation to her. In most ways, apparently, Pompey's generals did not want Cato's assistance, so after securing the allegiance of Rhodes, he left Servilia and her child there and returned to Pompey, who by now had gathered around him a splendid infantry and naval force. On that occasion, especially, Pompey seems to have demonstrated his opinion of Cato. For he considered giving him the command of the fleet, which numbered as many as five hundred ships of war, besides great quantities of Liburnian galleys, scouting ships, and open boats. However, he soon realized or was reminded by his friends that Cato's one chief aim in his whole political career was to set his country free, and that if he were made head of so great a force, the day he defeated Caesar he would begin demanding that

Pompey too lay down his arms and obey the laws. So Pompey changed his mind, although he had already talked with Cato on the subject and had appointed Bibulus admiral.

Yet he never saw Cato's ardor dampened by this treatment. There is a story that when Pompey was trying to stir up his troops to a battle before Dyrrachium, he ordered all the commanders to say something to hearten the men, and the soldiers listened listlessly and in silence. But when Cato's turn came, last of all, he spoke to them feelingly, on lines drawn from philosophy, of liberty, valor, death, and glory, and at the end turned his speech into an invocation to the gods, as there present and watching over their struggle on behalf of their country. And there was such acclamation and such a thrill through the excited army that all the officers were full of hope as they set out to face the battle. And they defeated Caesar's men and put them to flight, though the genius of Caesar robbed them of complete victory, for he took advantage of Pompey's caution and distrust of success. All this, however, I have told in the *Life of Pompey*.[63] But while everyone else was jubilant and magnifying the victory, Cato was weeping for his country and mourning for that disastrous and fatal love of power, seeing how many brave citizens had already fallen by one another's swords.

55.   Pompey then broke up camp to pursue Caesar into Thessaly, leaving behind at Dyrrachium a mass of arms and supplies, along with many kinsmen and friends. Over everything there he appointed Cato commander and guardian with fifteen cohorts of soldiery, for he both trusted and feared him. In case he were defeated, he believed that Cato would be his firmest reliance, but in case of victory, he was sure that Cato would not, if he were with him, let him run things as he chose. He made many other prominent men, too, stay behind at Dyrrachium with Cato.

After the defeat at Pharsalus, Cato made up his mind that if Pompey were dead he would take over to Italy the people he had with him but would thenceforth himself live in exile, as far as possible from Caesar's tyranny. But if Pompey were alive, he would use every means to keep the army together for him. Accordingly, he crossed to Corcyra, where the fleet lay. There he would have given up the command to Cicero, who was of consular rank, while he had been only a praetor. But Cicero refused to accept it and set off for Italy. Cato saw then that Pompey's son, in his

---

[63] *Life of Pompey*, ch. 65. See also above, *Caesar*, ch. 39.

stubbornness and ill-timed pride, was bent on punishing everyone who left him and would lay hands on Cicero first of all. So he reasoned with him in private and thereby undoubtedly saved Cicero from death and made the others secure.

56. He judged now that Pompey the Great would escape to Egypt or Libya, and being in haste to join him, he put to sea with all his company, first giving permission to all who were not keen to join his expedition to depart or stay behind. But on reaching Libya, as he was sailing along the coast, he met Sextus, Pompey's younger son, who told him of his father's death in Egypt. All were grieved, but no one, now that Pompey was dead, would even hear of any other commander while they had Cato. So pitying these brave men, who had given proof of their loyalty, and ashamed to leave them destitute and helpless in a strange land, Cato undertook the command and led them along to Cyrene. There the people took them in, though a few days before they had shut their gates against Labienus.[64]

And there he heard that Scipio, Pompey's father-in-law, had been welcomed by King Juba, and that Attius Varus, who had been appointed governor of Libya by Pompey, was with them with his army. He thereupon set out to reach them by land, in the winter season, after collecting a host of asses to carry water, and a great many cattle. He took chariots with him too, and also the people called Psylli,[65] who cure the bites of snakes by sucking out the poison and charm and stupefy the snakes themselves by their incantations. The march took seven days without a break; Cato himself walked at the head of his men, riding neither horse nor pack animal. And he continued to sit at table as he had done since the day he heard of Pharsalus, a sign of sorrow which he added to the rest. He never lay down except to sleep. He spent the winter there in Libya and then led out his army, which by then numbered almost ten thousand.

57. But things were not going well between Scipio and Varus, and as a result of their disputes and quarreling they were both trying to ingratiate themselves with Juba, whose pompousness and arrogance over his wealth

---

64 Labienus had been one of Caesar's trusted officers in Gaul, but after the outbreak of the civil war he had joined Pompey. From Pharsalus he fled to Africa, and after the defeat at Thapsus, he escaped to Spain and was killed fighting there.
65 The people called Psylli are mentioned by Herodotus, who says, however, that in his day they had all been lost in the desert sands. *Histories*, IV, 173.

and power were making him unbearable. Before he had his first interview
with Cato, Juba had his own seat placed between Scipio's and Cato's.
When, however, Cato noticed this, he lifted his own seat and moved it to
the other side, thus putting Scipio in the middle, though Scipio was his
enemy and had published an abusive book about him. Yet people give
Cato no credit for his action at this time, though they criticize him because when in Sicily he was walking with Philostratus,[66] he put him in
the middle, to do honor to philosophy. But now he put a rein on Juba,
who had all but made Scipio and Varus his satraps, and brought them
both to terms. Everyone wanted Cato to take the command, Scipio and
Varus above all, for they were resigning and offering to surrender their
authority to him. But he said he would not break the laws to uphold
which they were fighting a transgressor of them, nor would he set himself,
a propraetor, above a present proconsul. For Scipio had been appointed
proconsul and the troops were encouraged by his name, for they thought
that with a Scipio leading them in Libya they would be sure of success.

58. On assuming command, however, Scipio was at once ready to please
Juba by a massacre of all the people of Utica,[67] from the young men up,
and the destruction of their city for having favored the cause of Caesar.
But Cato would not permit that, and with loud and solemn protests in
the council and appeals to the gods he, though with difficulty, delivered
the people from this savagery. Then partly at the citizens' request and
partly at the demand of Scipio, Cato agreed to keep watch over the city,
so that neither voluntarily nor involuntarily should it fall into Caesar's
hands. For the place was in every way valuable to those who held it, as
well as self-sufficient, and now it was still more strengthened by Cato. He
brought in grain in huge quantities and fortified the walls by erecting
towers and building deep ditches and stout palisades in front of the city.
The young men of Utica he kept stationed at the palisades, having first
taken their arms from them. The rest of the inhabitants he held inside
the city, taking great care, however, that they should not be wronged or
ill-treated by the Romans. He also sent out a large supply of arms, pro-

---

[66] Philostratus, an Egyptian, was an unworthy but ostentatious member of the Platonic
school of philosophy. For his later association with Antony and Cleopatra, see above,
Antony, ch. 80.
[67] Utica, an ancient Phoenician colony, was strategically situated on the north coast
of Africa, twenty-seven miles northwest of Carthage.

visions, and grain to the Romans in camp, and altogether made the city a storehouse for the war.

The advice he had earlier given Pompey and now gave Scipio—not to try battle with a man experienced and terrible in war, but instead to rely on time, which wears away all the vigor wherein the strength of a tyranny lies—Scipio obstinately scorned. He wrote once to Cato, upbraiding him for cowardice, because not only was he satisfied to be himself inside city walls, but he was not even letting others use their minds boldly to meet the emergency. To this Cato replied that he was ready to take the infantry and horse he had brought to Libya, and cross with them over to Italy, thus compelling Caesar to change his tactics and drawing him away from Scipio and Varus to attack him. When Scipio scoffed at this idea too, Cato obviously regretted his refusal of the command, for he saw that Scipio would neither handle the war well, nor, if he should, surprisingly, win it, would he be moderate in his victory towards his fellow citizens. He came consequently to the opinion and said to his close friends that there were no good hopes for that war, because of the inexperience and rashness of the commanders; and that even if by some stroke of good luck, they should crush Caesar, he, Cato, would not live in Rome but would flee from Scipio's ruthlessness and cruelty, for already he was muttering fierce and tremendous threats against many persons.

It all turned out even worse than he had foreseen. Late in the evening a messenger who had been three days on the road, came from the camp to report that a great battle had been fought at Thapsus,[68] their cause was completely lost, Caesar was in possession of their camp, Scipio and Juba had escaped with a few men, and the rest of their army was destroyed.

59. This report falling suddenly on the city, the inhabitants, as was natural at night and in wartime, were almost frantic and could scarcely keep themselves within the walls. But Cato came forward and throughout that night, as he met people rushing about and crying, he took hold of them and with calming words soothed their distracted fears and panic, telling them that things were perhaps not so bad and the report had been exaggerated. So he quieted the tumult, and at daybreak he proclaimed a meeting in the temple of Jupiter of the three hundred men who formed

---

[68] The battle of Thapsus, on the North African coast, which ended any hope of resistance to Caesar, was fought in 46 B.C.

his senate, Romans who were in business in Libya as merchants and money-lenders, and all the Roman senators who were there, with their sons. While they were still assembling, Cato appeared, unexcited and tranquil, as if nothing extraordinary had happened, holding a book in his hand from which he was reading. It was a register of his war engines, arms, grain, bows, and heavy infantry.

When they were all assembled, he began by praising at length the zeal and fidelity of the three hundred, which they had shown by helpful aid with money, labor, and advice. He then exhorted them not to spoil their prospects by trying to save themselves, every one separately, by flight or escape. If they kept together, he said, Caesar would be less contemptuous of them as enemies, and more ready to pardon them, if they submitted. He urged them to talk over their situation together, assuring them that he would not blame them whatever they decided. If they turned and chose the lucky side, he would ascribe their changing to necessity; but if they stood firm in the face of terrors, and accepted danger in the fight for liberty, he would not only praise them but be proud of their courage, and himself become their leader and fellow-fighter, until they had tried what was to be the final fate of their country—their country, which was not Utica or Adrumetum [69] but Rome, which had many a time by her might raised herself out of more cruel disasters.

Many circumstances, he said, favored their deliverance and safety, chief among them the fact that they were fighting a man who was pulled in many opposite directions by the demands of his situation. For Spain had gone over to the younger Pompey, and Rome herself had not yet fully accepted the strange bridle, but was restive under it, and ready to rise up solidly at any turn of affairs. Nor was danger a thing to fly from. Their enemy could teach them that, for he was unsparing of his life in committing the most horrible crimes, not like them for whom success would mean the end of war's uncertainties in a peaceful life, and failure the end in a glorious death. However, he said, they must talk it over by themselves, and he joined them in praying that in view of their earlier valor and zeal their decision might be for the best.

60. With this speech by Cato, some were merely steadied, but the majority, realizing his fearlessness and nobility and generosity, came near

---

[69] Adrumetum was another Phoenician port on the coast, a few miles south of Carthage.

forgetting the peril they were in, and looked to him as the one invincible leader, superior to every fortune. They entreated him to make what use of their persons, possessions, and arms he thought fit, because it was better to die while obeying him than to save themselves by betraying such virtue. Someone then suggested that they vote to give freedom to the slaves, and most were for assenting. Cato said he would not do that, because it was not lawful or fair, but if the owners of their own accord let them go, all of military age would be accepted. Many owners promised to do that, and he had the names of all who volunteered written down. He then withdrew. Shortly afterward letters came to him from Juba and Scipio. Juba was in hiding on a mountain with a few men, and he asked Cato what he had decided to do, for if he were abandoning Utica, he, Juba, would wait for him, and if he were standing a siege there, he would come to his aid with an army. Scipio was lying in a ship by a headland not far from Utica, waiting anxiously in the same way.

61. It seemed wise to Cato to detain the letter carriers until he was sure of the action of the three hundred. For whereas the men from the Roman senate were eager to help, and immediately set about freeing and arming their slaves, the three hundred who were merchants and money-lenders and had most of their property in slaves, did not long feel the effect of Cato's speech, which soon passed off. As porous bodies readily take in heat and give it out again and grow cool as soon as the fire is removed, so these men at sight of Cato warmed up and broke into flame. But when they reasoned about it by themselves, their dread of Caesar overcame their respect for Cato and honor. "Who are we," they said, "and who is the man whose orders we are refusing to obey? Is he not Caesar, on whose shoulders has fallen the whole might of Rome? Not one of us is a Scipio, a Pompey, or a Cato. At this critical time, when all men in their fear are thinking more timidly than brave men should, at this time shall we fight to defend the Romans' liberty, and make war in Utica against one from whom Cato and the great Pompey fled, forsaking Italy. Shall we free our slaves to oppose Caesar, we who ourselves will have only so much freedom as he may choose to allow us? No, poor wretches, let us see ourselves as we are, implore the conqueror's pardon and send delegates to plead with him." This was the course recommended by the most moderate of the three hundred. The majority were plotting against the senators, with

the idea that if they seized them, Caesar's anger against themselves would be appeased.

62. Cato suspected the change in them but did not accuse them of it. However, he wrote to Scipio and to Juba to stay away from Utica, because he distrusted the three hundred, and he sent the letter carriers away. And then the horsemen who had escaped from the battle, quite a number of them, came riding to Utica, and sent three of their men to Cato, though not with the same message from them all. One group of them was set on going to Juba, another on joining Cato, but still others were afraid to come into Utica. On hearing all this, Cato ordered Marcus Rubrius to see to the three hundred and quietly take the lists of those who were freeing their slaves, without forcing anyone. He himself, with the Roman senators, went outside the city and met the cavalry commanders and begged them not to desert all those senators, nor to select Juba for their leader in place of Cato. They might save themselves along with saving others if they came into a city which was impregnable and contained grain and other provisions enough for many years. The senators joined in this petition with tears. Thereupon the commanders conferred with their men and Cato with the senators sat down on a mound and waited for their answer.

63. At this point Rubrius arrived, angrily charging the three hundred with fomenting disorder and tumult by their rebellious behavior and throwing the whole city into confusion. At his news the other Romans were in utter despair and fell to weeping and wailing. Cato tried to cheer them, and sent orders to the three hundred to wait for his return. Then the cavalry leaders came back with an unreasonable demand. They did not, they said, want Juba for a paymaster, nor were they afraid of Caesar, if they had Cato to lead them, but to be shut in with the people of Utica, fickle Phoenicians, was terrifying. Even if they were quiet now, as soon as Caesar appeared, they would turn traitors and lend him a hand in his attack. So if anyone wanted the horsemen to stay and help in the war, he must first expel or kill all the Uticans, and then summon them to a city clear of both enemies and barbarians. This proposition Cato thought horribly savage and barbarous, but he answered mildly that he would consult with the three hundred.

But on his return to the city he found the men there no longer inventing pretexts or excuses out of respect for him, but undisguisedly angry that anyone should be trying to compel them to fight Caesar, when they were neither able nor willing to do so. Some were even muttering about the Roman senators, that since Caesar was approaching they should be kept inside the city. Cato ignored this talk, as though he did not hear it, and indeed he was a little deaf. But when someone came and reported to him that the horsemen were leaving, he was afraid that the three hundred might go entirely wild over the senators, and so rose up with his friends and started to walk out to the men. And finding that they had already gone away, he took a horse and rode after them. They were glad to see him come riding up and welcomed him and urged him to save himself with them. But then, they say, Cato broke into tears, and with hands outstretched pled with them for the senators, even trying to turn back some men's horses and taking hold of their arms, until he had prevailed on them to stay there that day at least, to ensure a safe escape for the senators.

64. When he came back bringing the horsemen with him, and had some posted at the gates and others appointed to guard the citadel, the three hundred were afraid that they might be punished for their disloyalty. They sent to Cato and prayed him earnestly to come to them. The senators, however, crowded around him and would not let him go. They would not, they said, give up their preserver and savior to faithless traitors. For by that time evidently everyone in Utica alike had recognized clearly the goodness of Cato, and loved and admired him, knowing that there was no admixture of falsehood or deceit in anything he did. But long before the man had resolved to kill himself, and now he was laboring desperately and spending his thought and pains on others, in order that he might get them all established safely before he set himself free from living. In fact, his intention to die was no secret, although he did not speak of it.

He now encouraged the senators, and then obeyed the call of the three hundred. He went alone to them, and they expressed their gratitude and begged him to use them in every way, and to trust them. If they were not Catos and had not the lofty mind of Cato, he should pity their weakness. They had now decided to send to Caesar and entreat his pardon, but it was for Cato first and foremost that they would make their plea.

If they could not persuade him to grant that, they would not accept any mercy he might offer them, but as long as they had breath they would go on fighting for Cato.

In reply, Cato praised their good will, but said that for their own safety's sake they must send quickly, and must not ask anything for him. Vanquished men must entreat and wrongdoers beg pardon. But for himself he had not only gone unvanquished all his life, but even now was victorious as far as he wished to be, surpassing Caesar in the field of honor and justice. Caesar was the man who was captive and vanquished; for his crimes against his country, which he had long denied, had now been revealed and proven.

65. With these words to the three hundred he left them, and then heard that Caesar with all his army was already on the way. "Ah," he said, "he expects to find us men!" Turning to the senators he urged them not to hesitate but to make their escape while the horsemen were still waiting there. He then closed all the city gates but the one leading down to the sea, and on the shore front he divided the boats among the men under his command and tried to maintain order, putting a stop to misconduct, suppressing riots, and giving out supplies to those who had none. Marcus Octavius [70] with two legions was encamped nearby, and he sent a message to Cato, asking him to define for him the boundaries of his command. Cato sent him no answer, and said to his friends, "Well, can we wonder that our cause is lost, when we see the love of power persisting in us, even as we near the verge of destruction?"

At that point he heard that the horsemen were leaving the city, and were seizing and driving off the property of the people of Utica, as if it were war booty. So he hurried hot foot out to them, snatching the plunder from the first he met. The rest all made haste to throw away or put down what they had taken, and they rode off in silence with shamed and downcast looks. Cato next assembled the Uticans in the city and asked them not to provoke Caesar against the three hundred, but to act together to procure safety for each other. From there he went back to the shore, supervising the embarkation there, and embracing and escorting on board all of his friends and acquaintances whom he could persuade to leave. But his son

---

70 Marcus Octavius was another of Pompey's officers who fled to Africa after Pharsalus. He fought later, at Actium, in 31 B.C., under Antony against Caesar's successor.

he did not urge to go aboard, nor did he think he ought to dissuade him from standing by his father.

There was one Statyllius, a man young in years but ambitious to be strong in character and to imitate Cato's coolness. Cato thought he should go, for he was well known as a hater of Caesar. When he refused, Cato looked at Apollonides the Stoic and Demetrius the Peripatetic and said, "It is your duty to soften this obstinate fellow, and make him do what is best for him." He himself was busy that night and the greater part of the following day helping others to get away and finding supplies for those who needed them.

66. Lucius Caesar, a relative of Julius Caesar, was planning to go as an ambassador to him to intercede for the three hundred, and he asked Cato to help him frame a persuasive speech to use on their behalf. "When I plead for you," he said, "it will be right for me to fall at Caesar's knees and grasp his hands." But Cato would not permit him to do that. "For," he said, "if I wished to be saved by Caesar's grace, I ought to go myself, alone. But I do not wish to be beholden to the tyrant for one of his unlawful acts; and it is unlawful for him to spare, as though he were their master, the lives of men over whom he has no right to rule. However, let us consider, if you like, how you may get your pardon for the three hundred."

After conferring with Lucius on this subject, he presented his son and his friends and talked with them on many topics. He told the lad never to take part in politics, since circumstances no longer allowed him to do so as befitted a Cato, and to do so in any other way would be disgraceful. And towards evening he went off to the bath. While bathing, he remembered Statyllius, and called out loudly, "Apollonides, did you bring Statyllius down from his high horse and send him off? And has the fellow sailed without ever bidding me farewell?" "Not at all," said Apollonides, "though we talked to him for a long while. But he is lofty and not to be budged, and says he will stay and do whatever you do." At this, they say, Cato smiled and remarked, "Well, that will be seen before long."

67. After his bath he dined with a large company, sitting as he had made it his habit to do after Pharsalus; for he never reclined after that except to sleep. All his friends were at dinner with him and the magistrates of Utica. After dinner the drinking went on with much literary and agreeable conversation, one philosophic proposition after another going the

rounds, until the discussion reached the so-called "paradoxes" of the Stoics, to wit, that the good man alone is free and the bad are all slaves. To these the Peripatetic naturally raised objections, whereat Cato fell on him with great vehemence, and in a loud harsh voice insisted on his own argument to the bitter end, showing extraordinary depth of feeling, so that everyone realized that he had decided to end his life and release himself from his troubles. After his speech they all were silent and depressed, and Cato tried to revive their spirits and quiet their suspicions by again asking questions. He expressed his concern too over what was then happening, saying that he was afraid for those who were on the sea, and afraid too for those who were making their way through a waterless and barbarous desert.

68. Thus the dinner ended, and Cato then took his customary after-dinner walk with his friends and gave the officers of the guard the necessary orders. Then he retired to his room, first embracing his son and each of his friends with more than his usual affection, thus arousing again their suspicions of what was to come. On entering his chamber he lay down and took in his hands Plato's dialogue *On the Soul*.[71] He read through the greater part of it and then looked up over his head, and not seeing his sword hanging there, for his son had removed it while he was still at dinner, he called a slave and asked who had taken his sword. The slave did not reply, and Cato went back to his book. But a little later, as if he were not in haste or impatient but was merely inquiring about the sword, he bade the slave bring it.

There was some delay and no one brought it, and having read the book through, he again called his slaves, one by one, and raising his voice demanded the sword. One of the slaves he struck on the mouth and bloodied his own hand. By now he was angry, and shouted loudly that he was being betrayed unarmed to the enemy by his son and his slaves, until his son, weeping, hurried in with his friends and embraced him with lamentation and beseeching. But Cato stood up and looked sternly around and said, "When and where, without my knowing it, have I been proved so insane that no one tries to instruct or enlighten me on subjects on which I seem to have reached a wrong conclusion, but I am prevented

---

[71] That is, Plato's *Phaedo*, which records Socrates' last conversation in prison with his friends, and his death.

from using my own judgment and deprived of my arms? Why, noble son, do you not also bind your father's hands behind his back, until Caesar comes and finds him unable to defend himself? I do not need a sword to kill myself, when I can do it by holding my breath a little while or by striking my head once against the wall."

69. As Cato said this, the youth went out sobbing, and all the rest too, except Demetrius and Apollonides, who stayed behind. To them he began to speak in milder tones. "So you too think it right," he said, "to keep a man of my age alive by sheer force, and to sit here in silence as guards over him? Or have you stayed to argue that it is not a shocking or a shameful thing for Cato, when he has no other way of safety, to wait for what his enemy may grant him? Then why do you not speak and convince me of it and teach me a new doctrine, that we may discard our old opinions and principles with which we have lived thus far, and be made wiser through Caesar and so more grateful to him? For myself indeed I have come to no decision, but when I have decided, I must have the power to do what I have made up my mind to do. I shall make my decision with your help, in a way, for I shall decide with the help of the doctrines which you too as philosophers accept. Leave me then and be of good heart, and tell my son not to try coercing his father when he cannot persuade him."

70. To this Demetrius and Apollonides made no answer, but withdrew weeping. The sword was then sent in by a small child, and Cato took it and drew it out and looked at it. Seeing that the point was sharp and the edge still keen, he said, "Now I am my own master," and laid it down. He began reading his book again, and is said to have read it all through twice. He then fell into a heavy sleep so that persons outside his chamber heard him. About midnight he called his freedmen, Cleanthes, the physician, and Butas, who was his chief assistant in public business. He sent Butas down to the harbor to inquire if everyone had got off well and then to report to him. He gave his hand to the physician to bandage, for it was inflamed from the blow he had given the slave. This made them all happier, for it looked as if he were now thinking of living. In a short time Butas returned with the news that all had got away except Crassus, who was detained on some business, and that he too was about to go aboard. However, a violent storm and strong wind were making the sea

very high. Hearing this Cato groaned in pity for those out at sea and sent Butas down again to the shore, to learn if anyone had been driven back and stood in need of necessities, and to bring him word. But by now the birds were beginning to sing, and he dropped off again to sleep for a little.

When Butas returned and reported that all was quiet at the harbor, he told him to close the door and threw himself down on his bed as if he were going to sleep for the rest of the night. But when Butas had gone, Cato drew out his sword and stabbed himself below the chest. His hand, however, was not as strong as usual, owing to the inflammation, and his sufferings were not over at once. In his death struggle he fell off the bed and made a noise by knocking down a geometer's abacus which stood beside it. His servants heard him and called out, and his son and friends instantly hurried in. They saw him stained with blood and the greater part of his bowels protruding, but still alive with his eyes open. They were all appalled, but the physician went up to him and tried to replace the bowels, which were still whole, and sew up the wound. But when Cato came to himself and realized what the physician was doing, he pushed him away, tore at his bowels with his hands and so broke his wound open, and died.

71. Sooner than one would suppose that the people in the house could have heard of the tragedy, the three hundred were at the door, and shortly after the citizens of Utica had collected. With one voice they called Cato their benefactor and savior, the only free man, the only unconquerable one. And they went on doing this, even when the news came that Caesar was approaching. Neither fear of the victor nor wish to propitiate him nor their own mutual differences and quarrels put a stop to their desire to do Cato honor. They dressed his body sumptuously, had a fine procession, and buried him near the sea, where now a statue of him stands with sword in hand. Then they turned to thinking how to save themselves and their city.

72. Caesar had heard from men who came to him that Cato was staying on in Utica and not trying to escape, though he was sending the others away, and that he was going about fearlessly himself, with his son and his companions. He found it hard to understand what the man had in mind, but he had the highest opinion of him and made haste to get on

with his army. When he heard of Cato's death, he made, they say, just this one comment, "O Cato, I grudge you your death, for you have grudged me the saving of your life." In fact, if Cato could have borne to have his life saved by Caesar, men would not have thought he had sullied his own fame so much as enhanced Caesar's. What would have happened, however, we cannot tell, though it seems likely that Caesar would have been considerate.

73. Cato died at the age of forty-eight. His son was never injured by Caesar, but he is said to have been easy-going and not above reproach in his behavior with women. He was a guest, in Cappadocia, of Marphadates, one of the royal family, who had an attractive wife; and he spent more time with them than it was correct to do. So writers made fun of him in lines like these,

> "Tomorrow Cato goes away, after staying thirty days,"

and,

> "Porcius and Marphadates, two friends, one soul."

For the wife of Marphadates was named Psyche,[72] and again,

> "Nobly born and famed is Cato, and he has a royal soul."

But all such ill report he blotted out and erased by the bravery of his death. For he fought at Philippi in defense of liberty against Caesar and Antony, and when the battle line was giving way, he thought it unworthy to flee or try to hide. Instead, he shouted a challenge to the enemy, showing himself in front of them and spurring on those who were standing with him. Thus he fell after astounding his antagonists by his valor. Cato's daughter was still more distinguished for intelligence and courage. She was the wife of the Brutus who killed Caesar and she took part in the conspiracy and died in a manner worthy of her noble birth and high spirit, as I have described in the *Life of Brutus*.[73] Statyllius, too, who said that he would imitate Cato, was prevented at the time by the philosophers from taking his life, as he wished to do, but later he proved most faithful and helpful to Brutus, and died at Philippi.

---

[72] The Greek word, *psyche,* corresponds to our English, soul.

[73] In chs. 13 and 53 of this life, Plutarch tells how Porcia stabbed herself in the thigh, thus proving to her husband that she deserved to be taken into the secrets of the conspiracy against Caesar, and how, after Brutus' death, she killed herself by holding a hot charcoal in her mouth until it suffocated her.

ESSAYS

Rules for Husband and Wife

1. $\mathbf{P}$LUTARCH to Pollianus and Eurydice, health and happiness:
  Now that the ancient ceremonies are over, in which the priestess of Demeter joined you together and shut you into your chamber, I think a discourse on a subject which touches both of you and is in tune with your nuptial song may be of some use to you and chime in too with convention.

2. In music they used to call one of the themes for flutes the Mating Horse, for the tune seemed to excite desire in horses and stimulate them when they were mating. In the domain of philosophy, though there is many a noble subject for discussion, none is more worth serious consideration than marriage, for it can spread a charm over those who are entering on a life in common and make them gentle and amenable to one another. So I have drawn up a summary reminder of what you, who were brought up in philosophy, have often heard, arranging it in the form of brief comparisons that it may be the better remembered, and I send it as a gift to you both together.
  And I pray the Muses to attend you and assist Aphrodite, for it is no more their duty to provide you with harmonious lyres and lutes than to see that your house is in tune through reason, concord, and philosophy. The ancients set a figure of Hermes beside Aphrodite, to signify that pleasure in marriage depended much upon reason. They gave a place too to Persuasion and the Graces, to show that married people were to get what they wanted from one another by persuasion, not by wrangling and bickering. . . .

3. Married people, especially at the outset, should beware of disagreements and collisions, observing that household implements made in sections are at first easily wrenched apart by any chance blow, but in course

of time, when their joints have become compacted, they can hardly be loosened even by fire and steel.

4. As fire kindles easily in chaff or on a wick or in rabbit's fur, but goes out quickly if it finds no other material which can hold and feed it, so the ardent love of newly married people, which blazes up so fiercely out of their youth and beauty, must not be thought of as durable and lasting, unless it has food in character, and taking hold of the rational mind, arrives at a state that will last.

5. By fishing with poisoned bait you may catch a fish quickly and get hold of it easily, but it makes the fish uneatable and bad. So women who lay artful traps for their husbands with potions and charms, and win mastery over them by pleasure, have stupid and spoiled fools to live with. The men bewitched by Circe did her no good, nor could she make any use of them after they were turned into swine and asses, whereas she fell passionately in love with the prudent Odysseus, who was wise with her.

6. Women who would rather lord it over fools than listen to sensible men are like those who would rather lead blind men on a road than follow persons with eyesight and knowledge. . . .

11. As when two voices sing in unison the tune is carried by the bass, so in a well-managed household, though everything is done by mutual consent, the husband's leadership is apparent, and his wishes consulted. . . .

12. The Sun triumphed over the North Wind.[1] For when it blew a terrible blast, and tried to force the man to remove his cloak, he only wrapped it more tightly around him. But when the hot Sun came out after the wind, the man grew warm, then scorching hot, and then stripped off his tunic as well as his cloak. Most women behave in the same way. If their husbands try to curtail by force their luxury and extravagance, they resent it and fight stubbornly against it, but if they are convinced by reasoning, they quietly drop their expensive ways and keep within moderation. . . .

---

[1] Plutarch repeats here one of the well-known fables of Aesop, who was a slave, born on the island of Samos in the sixth century B.C. As early as the fifth century the great mass of Greek popular fables was attributed to him.

14. A mirror decorated with gold and precious stones is of no use unless it reflects a true likeness. So there is no advantage in having a rich wife unless she adapts her life to her husband's and her disposition is harmonious with his. If when a man is joyful, the mirror gives back an image of gloom, and when he is depressed and sad, it shows him looking merry and grinning like a dog, it is quite perverse and worthless. So is the wife worthless and tactless who frowns when her husband is in the vein for mirth and jollity, and jokes and laughs when he is serious. In one case she is being disagreeable, in the other callous. Just as geometricians say of lines and surfaces that they do not move by themselves but only in connection with the bodies of which they are a part, so the wife ought to have no feeling of her own, but share in her husband's gravity or playfulness, anxiety or laughter.

15. Men who do not like to see their wives eating in their company are teaching them to gorge themselves when alone. So too those who are never gay with their wives and never joke and laugh with them are teaching them to seek their pleasures away from them.

16. The kings of Persia have their lawful wives sitting beside them at dinner and eating with them, but when they have a mind for sport and drinking, they send them away and call their singing girls and concubines. They are right in so doing, for thus they do not mix their wives up with licentiousness and drunkenness. Similarly, if a private citizen is loose and wanton in his amusements and misbehaves himself with a prostitute or a maid servant, his wife should not be too vexed or angry, but reason that it is respect for her that makes him vent on another all his lustful depravity.

17. Kings who are fond of the arts make many persons artists, those fond of learning make many scholars, and those fond of athletics make many athletes. So a man fond of physical beauty makes a wife who spends her whole time beautifying herself, a man of pleasure makes her a dissolute harlot, and one who loves goodness and honor makes her intelligent and decorous. . . .

19. The wife ought not to make friends of her own but in common with her husband enjoy his friends. Now the gods are our first and greatest friends. Accordingly the wife ought to worship only the gods her husband

recognizes, and shut the door tight on all weird rites and strange superstitions, for no god is pleased with stealthy and secret worship from a wife.

20.   Plato says [2] that the state where the words "mine" and "not mine"
are seldom heard is happy and fortunate, because the citizens there treat
everything of importance as common property. Far more essential is it
that in marriage these words should have no place. For, as doctors say
that blows on the left shoulder are felt also on the right, so is it good
when the wife sympathizes with her husband's interests and the husband with his wife's. Like ropes, which by being intertwined get strength
from one another, the marriage tie is reinforced by an exchange of mutual
good will. Nature unites us through our bodies, taking a portion from
each of us and blending them together to produce an offspring common
to both, so that neither can discriminate or tell his own part in it from
the other's. And the best way for married persons is to have the same
partnership in property and throw all their possessions into one common
stock, combining them so that here too neither one will think of one part
as his own and another as the other's, but each will consider the whole as
his own and nothing as the other's. But as we call the mixture of water
and wine wine, even when the greater part is water, so we should say that
the house and property belong to the husband, even when the wife con-
tributes most of it.

21.   Helen was fond of wealth, Paris of pleasure, whereas Odysseus was
prudent and Penelope wise. So the marriage of the last two was happy
and enviable, while that of the first two brought an Iliad of woe on Greeks
and barbarians.

22.   The Roman [3] who was taken to task by his friends for sending away
a chaste, rich, and blooming wife, held out his shoe and said, "Now this
is new and fine to look at, but nobody knows where it pinches me!" A
wife ought not to trust to her dowry or her family or her beauty, but to
things which touch her husband more vitally, namely, her congenial disposition and companionability, her capacity for making everyday life
neither tiresome nor harassing, but harmonious, cheerful, and agreeable.
For as doctors are more afraid of fevers that spring from obscure sources

---

[2] *Republic*, V, 462.
[3] The following anecdote is told by Plutarch again in his *Life of Aemilius Paulus*.

and grow worse gradually than of those that come from obvious and sudden causes, so the petty and constant daily squabbles of husband and wife, which the world knows nothing about, are what set them widest apart and spoil their life together. . . .

25.   Socrates used to advise the homely young men who looked at themselves in the mirror to make up for their defects by their virtue, and the handsome young men not to disgrace their beauty by bad behavior. So too it is good for the mistress of the house, when she has her mirror in her hands, if she is plain, to say to herself, "What would I be, if I were not virtuous?" and if she is fair, to say, "What would I not be, if I were virtuous too?" For a plain woman to be loved for her character is a greater thing than to be loved for one's beauty. . . .

28.   Plato advised Xenocrates,[4] who had rather a harsh disposition but in other respects was a good and honorable man, to sacrifice to the Graces. I think that a virtuous wife especially needs graces in her relations with her husband so that, as Metrodorus said, "she may live pleasantly with him, and not be cross because she is virtuous." A frugal wife should not neglect neatness, nor a loving wife cheerfulness, for peevishness makes a good wife wearing, and untidiness disgusts one with parsimonious living.

29.   The wife who is afraid to laugh and make a joke with her husband lest he think her bold and wanton is no different from one who will not put oil on her head lest he think she uses perfumes, and will not wash her face lest he think she paints. But we see all the poets and orators, even those who abhor a vulgar, crude, or affected style of speech, still endeavoring artfully to move and sway their audiences by the tales they tell, their handling of them, and the characters they describe. And so the mistress of the house, while she shuns and repudiates everything extravagant, false, and showy, as she should do, must all the more use art with her husband in the graces of her disposition and everyday life, and accustom him to what is honorable but is also pleasant. If, however, the wife is by nature austere, uncompromising, and grim, the husband should make the best of it, and say as Phocion [5] did, when Antipater ordered him to

---

[4] We do not know from which work of Plato Plutarch took this story.

[5] Phocion was an Athenian general who, after Alexander's death, stood for a policy of peace with Antipater and Macedon. See above, *Demosthenes,* ch. 27.

do something dishonorable and improper. Phocion said, "You cannot have me as a friend and a flatterer both." So the husband must reason about his virtuous and austere wife, "I cannot have the same woman both as wife and as mistress."

30. It was an old custom among Egyptian women not to wear shoes,[6] so that they would have to stay at home all day. And most women, if you strip them of their golden shoes, bracelets, anklets, purple robes, and pearls, will stay indoors.

33. Rich men and kings who honor philosophers add grandeur both to the philosophers and to themselves. But philosophers who pay court to the rich do not exalt the rich any higher and they lower themselves. The same happens with women. If they submit to their husbands they are praised, but if they try to rule over them they make a worse mistake than the husbands do who let themselves be ruled. However, the husband should rule his wife, not as a master does his chattel, but as the soul governs the body, by feeling with her and being linked to her by affection. He can care for his body without being a slave to its pleasures and desires, and so he can rule his wife and cheer and satisfy her.

34. The philosophers tell us that some bodies are composed of separate parts, as a fleet is, or an army; others of connected parts, as a house is, or a ship; others grow knit together, as every living creature is. In much the same way the marriage of lovers is a growing together, that of persons who marry for a dowry or for children is one of connected parts, and that of persons who merely sleep together is one of separate parts, which may be said to live in the same house but not to live together. The scientists say that when liquids are mixed, the mixing extends to every particle in them. Thus with married people there should be a complete union of bodies, wealth, friends, and relatives. Hence the Roman lawyer forbade husbands and wives to exchange presents with one another, not that they should not share anything with each other, but that they should think of all their possessions as belonging to them both. . . .

35. At Leptis, a city in Libya, it is an old custom for the bride the day after her marriage to send to the bridegroom's mother's house and ask for a bowl. His mother does not lend her one, and says she has not got

---
[6] It is doubtful that this was a widespread custom.

one, so that from the start the bride knows that her mother-in-law nas a stepmotherly mind. Then if later she should be harsher still, the bride would not be indignant or take it ill. Any wife ought to understand this feeling and try to cure the cause of it. It is the mother's jealousy of her son's wife because of his affection for her. The one cure for this situation is for her, while she builds up in her husband a close affection for her, not to divert or weaken his love for his mother.

36. Mothers seem to love their sons best as able to be of help to them, and fathers their daughters as needing their help. Perhaps too it is in com-pliment to one another that each wishes to show that he admires and loves most the characteristics of the other sex. This, however, is probably a debatable point. But it is courteous of the wife to show greater deference to her husband's parents than to her own, and if anything distressing happens to tell them of it rather than her own people. For trust, it seems, begets trust, and love, love.

37. The generals of the Greeks in Cyrus' army ordered their men to receive the enemy in silence if they came up shouting, but if they came up silently, to rush out against them with a shout. Sensible wives, when their husbands are storming with rage, keep still, but when they are silent, talk to them consolingly and appease them. . . .

40. Hermione speaks the truth, I think, when she says:

"The visits of bad women ruined me." [7]

Such a catastrophe, however, does not come about simply but only after a dispute with her husband and jealousy have opened not only a wife's doors but her ears to such women. But that is the very time when a woman of sense will close her ears most carefully, and be on her guard against whisperers, so that fire may not be added to fire. She should have ready in mind the words of Philip, who, when his friends were trying to stir him up against the Greeks, on the ground that he was treating them well and yet they were maligning him, answered, "What would they do then, if I treated them badly?" Whenever the shrews start saying to a woman, "How badly your husband treats you, his loving and virtuous wife!" let

---

[7] Euripides, *Andromache,* 930.

her answer, "How would he act then, if I began to hate him and played him false!"

41. A man once caught sight of his runaway slave, some time after he had escaped, and chased him, but the slave got away and took refuge in a treadmill.[8] "Where else," the man said, "would I have preferred to find you?" So let a wife who out of jealousy is furiously entering a plea for divorce say to herself, "Where else would my rival be more pleased to see me and what would she rather have me doing than nursing my bitterness, breaking with my husband, and abandoning my home and my chamber?" . . .

44. They say the cat is driven frantic by the smell of perfumes. If it so happened that women were similarly driven wild and beside themselves by perfumes, it would be cruel for their husbands not to abstain from using them, but for a brief pleasure to themselves make their wives suffer in that way. And now since they suffer quite as much, not when their husbands use perfumes but when they go with other women, it is unfair to grieve and upset them so seriously for the sake of a trivial pleasure, and not to treat them as well as beekeepers treat their bees, because bees are supposed to be irritated and quick to sting men who have been with women. Husbands, that is, should be pure and clean from association with other women when they come to their wives.

45. Those who are going near elephants do not wear bright-hued clothes, nor do those who are handling bulls wear red, for those colors make the brutes very savage. Tigers, they say, go quite mad at the beating of drums and tear themselves to pieces. Similarly, some men cannot bear the sight of scarlet and purple gowns, and others are exasperated by cymbals and drums. Then what dreadful harm would it do their wives to abstain from those things, and not vex or provoke their husbands but live with them comfortably and pleasantly? . . .

47. Plato [9] used to advise old men particularly to be modest before young men, so that they might respect them; for when the old are immodest, they inspire no respect or deference in the young. The husband should remember this and be as respectful to his wife as to anyone, knowing that

---

[8] Sending slaves to toil in a treadmill was a common punishment.
[9] *Laws.* 729.

their chamber will be for her a school either of good behavior or of license. And he who indulges in the pleasures from which he debars his wife is the same as one who orders her to fight to the death against enemies to whom he has himself surrendered.

48. As for love of ornament, do you, Eurydice, read and try to remember what Timoxena [10] wrote to Aristylla. But you, Pollianus, need not imagine that your wife will abstain from fine clothes and extravagance if she sees that you do not despise those vanities in others, but enjoy gold cups, frescoed houses, handsome trappings for your mules, and collars for your horses. You cannot banish extravagances from the women's side of the house when it is flaunted everywhere in the men's apartments.

Moreover, Pollianus, you are now old enough for the study of philosophy. So you should now perfect your character by training it in logical argument and solid reasoning, and associate and converse with persons who can help you. And for your wife, gather from every quarter whatever is excellent, as the bees do, and bring it and share it with her, and discuss it with her, making the best doctrines dear and familiar to her. For to her

> "Father thou art, and mother dear,
> And brother too besides." [11]

It is splendid to hear a wife say, "Husband, you are to me guide, philosopher, and teacher in things most beautiful and divine."

Such studies in the first place draw women away from follies, for a woman who is learning geometry will be ashamed to appear as a dancer, nor will she have faith in charms and spells as long as she is being charmed by the words of Plato and Xenophon. And if someone professes to be able to bring the moon down from the sky, she will laugh at the ignorance and stupidity of women who believe such nonsense. For she knows something of astronomy and has heard the story of Aglaonice, the daughter of the Thessalian Hegetor, who was well informed on the subject of total eclipses of the moon, and knew beforehand the time when the moon was due to be overtaken by the shadow of the earth. So she

---

[10] Timoxena was the name of Plutarch's wife. We know nothing of Aristylla.

[11] The lines are adapted from the *Iliad*, VI, 429–30. The words there are spoken by Andromache to Hector.

tricked other women and persuaded them that she herself was pulling it down from the sky.

No woman, they say, has ever had a child without intercourse with a man, but they do have shapeless, fleshy growths in the womb, which come of themselves from an infection, and are called "moles." We must guard against something similar happening in women's minds. For if they do not receive the seeds of good learning, and do not share in their husband's education, they conceive by themselves many weird and distorted ideas and feelings.

As for you, Eurydice, try your best to become acquainted with the sayings of the wise and the good, and have ever on your tongue those words which you learned as a girl with us, so that you may make your husband's heart glad, and win other women's admiration for being in yourself so wonderfully and nobly adorned. You cannot take and put on without paying a large sum this rich woman's pearls or that foreign woman's rich gowns, but the ornaments of Theano,[12] Cleobuline, and Gorgo, wife of Leonidas, Timoclea, sister of Theagenes, Claudia of ancient time, Cornelia, daughter of Scipio, and of all other women who have been revered and famous, in these you may array yourself without money and without price, and thus made beautiful lead a distinguished and a happy life. For if Sappho plumed herself so much on the charm of her verses as to write to a rich woman,

> "Dead thou shalt lie in thy tomb
> Nor shall any remember thee there,
> For no share hast thou had in the roses
> That grow in Pierian fields," [13]

—why will you not have a better right to think highly and proudly of yourself for having shared not only in the roses but in the fruits which the Muses bring and freely bestow on all who admire learning and philosophy?

[12] Theano was the wife of the philosopher Pythagoras. Cleobuline, the daughter of the sage, Cleobulus, was famous for her learning and courage. Gorgo, the daughter of a Spartan king, was wife of Leonidas, who held Thermopylae against the Persians. For Timoclea see above, under *Alexander,* ch. 12. Claudia was the first Roman woman to volunteer to tow a ship carrying the image of the goddess Cybele up the Tiber to Rome. Only a perfectly chaste woman could move the ship. For the story, see Livy, *Histories,* XXIX, 14. Cornelia, the mother of the Gracchi, the young would-be reformers of Rome, said of her sons, "These are my jewels."

[13] Pieria, a region in northern Thessaly, was known as the birthplace of Orpheus and the Muses.

Letter of Consolation to His Wife

1. PLUTARCH to his wife, greeting:

The messenger you sent me to tell me of the death of our little girl seems to have missed his way on the road to Athens, but I heard the news from our granddaughter when I reached Tanagra. I suppose the funeral has already taken place, and I hope everything was done in a way to give you the least pain both now and in time to come. And if you left undone anything you wished to do, and are waiting to hear my opinion and think your grief will be lighter when it is done, do that too without elaborateness or superstition, both of which things would be quite unlike you.

2. Only, dear wife, take thought for both me and yourself in your sorrow at what has happened. I know and appreciate how severe is our loss, but if I find you overwhelmed with misery, it will distress me even more than the blow itself. Yet I am not made of oak or of stone, as you know, who have shared with me in the rearing of our many children, all brought up at home by ourselves. But this one I know was especially dear to you —the daughter you were longing for after four sons—as indeed she was to me, and so I gave her your name.[1] But the bereavement falls peculiarly hard on you who have a tenderness for children like her, with their pure and simple gaiety and no touch of passion or fretfulness. She had by nature a wonderfully happy disposition and a sweet temper, and her generous and winning ways both charmed us and gave us a sense of her real kindness of heart. For she used to tell her nurse to give her breast not only to other babies but to her favorite toys and playthings, out of her lovingness inviting them as it were to her own table, sharing her good things with them, dividing her greatest treasures with those who were pleasant to her.

---

1 Timoxena, as we see later on.

3. But I see no reason, dear wife, why these and like traits in her character which delighted us in her lifetime, should now, when we recall them
to memory, grieve and harrow us. I cannot fear that if we cease to grieve
we may also cease to remember, and be like Clymene,[2] when she says,

> "I hate a curving bow of cornel wood,
> And would banish athletics forever,"

because she shunned and dreaded whatever reminded her of her son,
since it brought heartache with it, and we naturally avoid anything that
gives us pain. But since it was our greatest joy to embrace and watch
and listen to her, so her memory, still living and dwelling with us, should
give us more—many times more—gladness than sorrow. And some of
the arguments we have so often used to comfort others will probably help
to keep us in our time of need from sitting down and wailing and drowning the memory of those happy days in vast floods of grief.

4. Those who were at the funeral tell me admiringly that you put on no
mourning, and imposed on neither yourself nor the maids any gloomy
marks of woe, and that there was no ostentatious expenditure of money
at the burial, but that everything was done in good order and silently in
the company of our relatives. But I was not surprised to hear that you,
who were never one for display at a theater or in a procession and thought
extravagance for pleasure was wrong, were still simple and frugal in a
time of sadness.

For a wise woman ought not only "in Bacchic revels"[3] to keep her
sanity, but control her surges of sorrow and upswellings of grief, and
fight, though not, as most people think, against a natural love, but against
an ungoverned soul. We sympathize with love in the regret and honor
and remembrance it pays the dead; but an unappeasable passion of mourning, which vents itself in loud shrieks and laments, is as unseemly as a
loss of control in pleasure, and claims our forgiveness only because of
the bitter pain, in place of joy, which causes the unseemliness. For how
unreasonable it is to suppress loud outbursts of laughter and mirth, and

---

[2] Clymene was the mother of Phaethon, who attempted to drive the chariot of his
father, the Sun, and was killed, in order to save the world from disaster, by a thunderbolt from Zeus. The lines quoted here are from a lost play of Euripides, *Phaethon,*
fragment 785.
[3] Euripides, *Bacchae,* 317.

then let loose with no restraint the tides of lamentation and tears which rise from the same source! Or for men to quarrel with their wives over their perfumes and purple gowns, and yet allow them to go about in mourning, wearing garments dyed black, sitting about huddled and shapeless, and lying down in wretchedness! Or, worst of all, for husbands to interfere and stop their wives if they punish the servants and maids severely or unfairly, and yet permit them to punish themselves ruthlessly and cruelly in times of suffering and calamity, when what they need is gentleness and affection.

5.   But between us, dear wife, there never was need for contention, nor do I think there ever will be. Every philosopher with whom we are well acquainted has been amazed at your economy in dress and thrifty way of living, and every citizen has observed how simply you appear at ceremonials and sacrifices and theaters. Already under similar affliction you have shown your steadfastness, when you lost the eldest of our children, and again when our handsome Chaeron left us. I remember that some guests were with me on my way up from the sea when I learned of the boy's death, and they then came on, with some others. On seeing the absolute quiet and tranquillity of the household, they thought, as they afterwards told some other people, that no disaster had happened, and that the report was certainly untrue. So carefully had you ordered everything in the house, at a time when there would have been plenty of excuse for disorder! Yet you had nursed that son at your own breast and had borne the lancing of the nipple for a bruise it received. That was noble and truly loving conduct!

6.   Most mothers we see take their children in their arms as playthings only after they have been washed and dressed up by others. If they die, they burst out in loud and showy grief, not because they loved them so much—for love is reasonable and beautiful—but because their intense desire for vainglory, mixed with a little natural affection, makes them keenly disappointed and unreasonable and hard to console. Aesop seems to have known of these things, for he says that when Zeus was dividing honors among the gods, Grief appeared and demanded his. Zeus granted it, but added that it would come only from those who chose and were willing to pay it. At the start this is what happens. Everyone of his own accord takes Grief into his house. When, however, in course of time, it has settled there and become a familiar inmate of the house, it is not to be

dislodged, however much people may wish to be rid of it. So we must fight it off at our door, and not weaken our defenses by putting on mourning, or cutting our hair, or making similar signs of sorrow.

For the repetition every day of these insistent reminders of loss contracts and narrows the mind and makes us unsocial and bitter and apprehensive, so that, beleaguered and haunted by grief, we no longer laugh, or endure the light, or the tables of our friends. Following on this sad state of things comes neglect of our bodies and dislike of ointments and bathing and other comforts of life, whereas a soul in distress ought to have the very opposite treatment and get help from a well-fortified body. For sorrow is softened considerably and soothed, like sea in calm weather, when pervaded by a sense of bodily ease. But if the body becomes parched and aching with hardships, and sends up nothing soothing or healthful to the soul but only pains and suffering, like sharp and nauseous exhalations, the soul cannot easily recover itself however we may wish it would. So deep becomes the misery in a soul that is so ill-treated.

7. Nor would I hesitate to say that the most formidable part of it all is "the visits of unscrupulous women," [4] their chatter and chorus of lamentation, by which they encourage and fan the fires of sorrow, and keep them from being stifled by others or by oneself. I know what a struggle you had lately when you went to assist Theon's sister, and fought with the visitors who came in from outside with their cries and their wailings, in their folly adding fuel as it were to her flames of grief. When people see their friends' houses ablaze they put them out as quickly and as energetically as they can, but when their friends' souls are burning, they only bring more kindling. When a man has something wrong with his eyes, they do not let him put his hands to them, even if he wishes to, nor do they themselves touch the inflamed part. But when a person in trouble sits and gives himself up to every chance comer, like a stream to be stirred up and riled, his suffering grows from a slight pricking and discomfort to be a dire and woeful calamity. I know, however, that you will be on your guard against these things.

8. Try, by carrying yourself back in memory, to return often to the time before this child was born, when we had no complaint against Fortune, and compare our situation now with what it was then, as though

---

[4] Euripides, *Andromache*, 930. On this subject, see *Rules for Husband and Wife,* ch. 40.

it had merely become again the same as it was. For, dear wife, we shall seem to be regretting the birth of our little daughter if we think of our situation before her birth as happier than it is now. Not that we should wipe from our memories the two years between, when she was alive, but consider them as a gift of grace and special joy. We must not call a blessing a great affliction because it was short, nor be unthankful for what was given us because Fortune did not grant us all we hoped for. If we always speak well of Deity, and are cheerful and content with Fortune, we shall have a fair and pleasant reward. For one who in a position like ours mostly tries to remember his blessings, and turns and diverts his mind from the dark and distressing things in life to what is bright and splendid, will either cure his grief altogether or else make it seem insignificant and pale in comparison with his comforts. As perfume is pleasant to the nose and a remedy for disagreeable smells, so the thought of past happiness in present trouble is a valuable support to those who would neither shut out of their memory the good things that are past, nor always and everywhere be complaining of Fortune. Certainly it does not behoove us to go disparaging our own past life because, like a book, it has one blot in it, while all the other pages are bright and clean.

9. You have often heard that happiness is a result of right thinking that produces a steadfast state of mind which the vicissitudes of Fortune cannot seriously disturb. Nor can they bring confusion and uncertainty into our lives. But if, like most people, we too must be swayed by external events, count up just what we have had from Fortune, and make our various acquaintances judges of our felicity, I ask you to disregard the tears and laments of the women now with you, which by a poor custom they shower on everybody. Consider rather how envious they all are of you still, for your children, your house, your way of life. It would be strange if when others would gladly choose your lot, even taking into account our present sorrow, you should be bemoaning and resenting it, and because of this sad loss refuse to see how much comfort there is in what is still left to us. Like those who quote the imperfect and faulty verses of Homer and overlook the many great passages in his poems, you would be counting up and making much of the trials of life, while paying no attention to the mass of your blessings. It would be like stingy misers, who heap up riches and have little use for them while they have them, but wail and mourn when they are lost.

If your heart aches for our child, dying unmarried and childless, you may consider yourself better off than others in that you have missed neither of those experiences. And they are not such great joys to those who are deprived of them, nor such trifles to you who have had them. She has gone to a place where there is no sorrowing, and she wants not our sorrow. Indeed what grievance have we on her account, if no sorrow now can touch her? The loss even of important things has no power to grieve us when we have arrived at the point where we do not need them. Timoxena has lost only little things, for she knew only little things and found amusement in little things. The things she had no knowledge of and which had not entered her mind, how can we say she has lost them?

10. You are hearing from some people, who persuade many to believe them, that the dead have no feeling or consciousness at all. But I know you are kept from believing that by your father's teaching and by the mysteries of Dionysus, into which we have both been initiated. Remember that the soul, which is immortal, is in the condition after death of a bird that has been caught. If it has lived many years in its body, and during this life has been tamed by its many activities and long continued habits, it drops down again and a second time enters a body, and does not free itself from entanglement in the changes and chances which come with birth. Do not imagine that old age is despised and derided only for its wrinkles and its white hair and physical weakness. The worse feature of it is that it dulls the soul's memories of the other world, and makes it content with things here, and cramps and presses down on it, compelling it to keep the form which it has got from the body in previous experiences.

But the soul, . . .[5] captivated and possessed by better things, soars up as it were from a soft and easy starting point on towards its destined goal. As when someone puts out a fire, and lights it again at once. It is soon rekindled, and blazes up once more quickly, . . .[6]

"How to pass swiftly through the gates of Hades," [7]

---

[5] There is a gap here in the Greek text. The sense of the omitted words was probably "which has been but a short time in the body and is still," etc.

[6] Another gap in the Greek text. The sense must have been roughly, "so a soul which has lingered but a few years in the darkness of this life is soon back in the brightness of the other life. It has discovered," etc.

[7] Theognis, 427. Theognis, a Greek poet of the sixth century B.C. left a collection of lines of verse which were often quoted by other writers.

before a great love for this world grew up in it, and it became fond of the body, and enfeebled as though by a poison.

11.   The truth of this belief is borne out by our inherited and time-honored customs and laws. When our little children die no libations are poured out or other rites performed for them, such as are usually performed for their elders who die. For they have no share in the earth or in things of the earth. We do not linger over their tombs and monuments and the laying out of their bodies, nor do we sit long beside them. Our laws do not allow it for little children, holding it impious to mourn so deeply for those who have departed to a better and diviner life and country. . . .[8] And since it is harder to disbelieve them than to believe, let us outwardly keep the commandments of the laws and inwardly be even more stainless and pure and wise.

---

[8] A third gap in the Greek, with no indication of what is missing.

Topics for Banquets (Symposiacs)

BOOK I

QUESTION I: *Should We Talk Philosophy at a Banquet?*
SPEAKERS: Aristo, Plutarch, Sossius Senecio, Crato.

1.   THE first question of all is whether we should talk philosophy at a dinner party. I remember that at Athens once, after dinner, the question was raised whether it was right over the wine to start a philosophical discussion, and what limit to set to it. Aristo was there and exclaimed, "In heaven's name, are there any who would not give philosophy a place at our wine?" And I replied, "Indeed there are, my friend, and some who in solemn banter tell us that philosophy, like the lady of the house, should make not a sound at wine-time, and that the Persians were right in not letting their wives, but only their mistresses, drink and dance with them. They think we should imitate them and bring musicians and players to our feasts, but ban philosophy, as too stiff to be merry with us, while we are in no mood to be serious with her. Isocrates,[1] the Sophist, when they begged him to say something at a banquet, answered simply, 'Now is not the time for what I can do well, and the things it is time for I cannot do well.'"

2.   Then Crato called out: "By Dionysus, he was right in refusing to speak, if what he would have spouted were pompous periods sure to ruin a feast of the Graces! But I do not think there is the same reason to forbid philosophy as there is to allow no rhetoric at a feast. For philosophy is a different thing; it is an art of living, and hence should not be banished from any scene of amusement or pleasure which we enjoy, but be there at them all, to keep us moderate and aware of what is fitting, un-

---

[1] Isocrates (436–338 B.C.) was a highly-respected teacher of rhetoric at Athens.

328

less we think we ought not to admit wisdom or justice to our table but sneer at their solemn faces. Of course, if, like the men who received Orestes,[2] we had to eat and drink in silence in a judgment-hall, that might be a lucky cloak for our ignorance. But Dionysus is a loosener and releaser from every restraint, and especially removes bridles from the tongue, and gives the voice complete freedom. So I think it stupid and absurd to deprive our most talkative time of our best conversation, to discuss in schools behavior at banquets and what makes a good table companion and how one should take wine, and then deny philosophy a place at our table, as if she were unable to confirm in action what she teaches in words."

3.   You then said that we ought not to argue against Crato on this point but inquire instead what kind and quantity of philosophical talk should be allowed at a feast, so as to anticipate that humorous jibe at lovers of wrangling and sophistry,

"Come now to dinner, that we may fight it out."

Since you were urging the rest of us to speak, I said, first, that I thought we should have to consider the company present. "For if the greater part of the guests are learned men, as they were at Agathon's party,[3] men like Socrates, Phaedrus, Pausanias, and Eryximachus, and again at Callias' feast, Charmides, Antisthenes, Hermogenes, and others like them, we will permit them to reason and philosophize as freely as we let Dionysus frolic with the Muses and the Nymphs, since the latter make wine wholesome and pleasant to the body, and the former cheering and delightful to the spirit. And if there should be a few uneducated persons present, surrounded by a crowd of scholars, like consonants by vowels, they will take part with voice and understanding not altogether helpless.

"If, however, the majority is made up of men who like the sound of any bird, any fiddlestring, any stick of wood better than the voice of a philos-

---

[2] According to Aeschylus' version of the Orestes story, he was cleared of blood guilt for the slaying of his mother Clytemnestra by the Athenian court of the Aeropagus, constituted for that purpose by Athene. During the sitting of the court silence was commanded in the judgment hall by the goddess herself. See Aeschylus, *Eumenides,* 569 ff.

[3] The reference is to the brilliant gathering described by Plato in the *Symposium.* Callias' feast is the setting for Xenophon's *Symposium.*

opher, Pisistratus [4] found a good way. He had a dispute once with his sons, but when he heard that his enemies were crowing over it, he convened an assembly and announced that he had tried to persuade his sons to take his point of view, but since they were obstinate, he would yield and take theirs. So a philosopher among dinner companions who have no ears for his discoursing changes his tune and follows them, enjoying their amusements so long as they do not go beyond propriety, knowing very well that while men have to practice rhetoric by speaking, they may philosophize in silence or while they are amusing themselves, or, by Zeus, while they are being laughed at or laughing. For not only is it, as Plato says, [5] 'the worst form of injustice to put on an appearance of being just when you are not,' but the height of wisdom to philosophize without appearing to do so, and while playing to be doing what serious men do. Like the Bacchae, in Euripides, [6] who without swords or armor lacerated their assailants with their wands, so the true philosophers, even in the midst of joking and laughter, in some way or other stir and arouse their companions who are not entirely insensitive."

4. There are topics of conversation at dinner, I think—some of which history gives us and others one can find in what is going on at the moment—which furnish many illustrations for philosophy and many for religion, and stimulate to courageous and high-minded action or to kind and bountiful deeds. A man who talks of such things with no apparent design may teach the drinkers something and rid the entertainment of some of its worst features. Those who mix eloquence with the wine and sprinkle with ideas the dry floors of the dovecotes for the purpose of instilling good will and friendliness into the feasters, are imitating Homer's Helen, [7] who put a drug into her pure wine. (They are not aware that that tale came a long way around from Egypt to find its consummation in fittingly beautiful words.) Helen then tells the men, as they drink, about Odysseus, "what that mighty man did and dared, when he inflicted on himself degrading stripes." Hers was undoubtedly a drug that ban-

---

[4] Pisistratus was the tyrant who in spite of determined opposition ruled Athens, with some intermissions, from 560–527 B.C.

[5] *Republic,* II, 361.   [6] Euripides, *Bacchae,* 736.

[7] *Odyssey,* IV, 219–264. The men for whom Helen drugged the wine were her husband Menelaus and their guest, young Telemachus, who had come to ask for information about his father, Odysseus.

ished sorrow and pain, and a word spoken at the right time to ease their griefs and enhance the exploits of which they were speaking.

The men who give pleasure talk philosophy with reverence, but carry on their discussion in an attractive way instead of by dint of hard demonstrations. You see how Plato, in the *Symposium,* does not insist on proof or stir up the dust, or take a tight and inescapable grip on his opponent, as he usually does, but with easier steps, through examples and legendary tales, he leads his friends to believe him.

5. The discussion must be of the simpler sort, the problems intelligible, and the questions asked courteous, and not too intricate, so as not to embarrass or antagonize the less educated. It is customary for feasters to limber up their bodies with a dance and a chorus, but if we try to compel them to get up and either fight a battle or pitch quoits, our symposium will not only be tiresome, but may do harm. Light discussion stimulates our minds agreeably and profitably, but what Democritus called "contentious" and "whip-waving arguments," [8] which involve the participants in elaborate and obscure problems, and are of no interest to onlookers, should be barred. Our talk should be like wine, something shared by all, of which everyone partakes.

Those who propose difficult questions seem no better fitted for society than Aesop's fox and crane.[9] The fox poured his rich soup out over a flat stone, and laughed at the crane, for with her long narrow bill she could not get a taste of the running broth. But the crane, in her turn, played a joke on the fox by serving him a supper in a flagon with a long narrow neck, into which she could easily thrust her bill, while the fox got none of her fragrant meal. Just so, when philosophers at a banquet plunge into subtle problems of logic they are a trial to the crowd who cannot follow them. And when the crowd, in its turn, becomes absorbed in frivolous songs, silly gossip, coarse and ribald stories, the whole aim of a banquet together is spoiled, and Dionysus dishonored.

When Phrynichus [10] and Aeschylus brought tragedy to discourse of

---

[8] Democritus, Fragment 150.

[9] On Aesop and his fables, see above, *Rules for Husband and Wife,* ch. 12, and n. 1.

[10] Phrynichus and Aeschylus were the two poets who at the beginning of the fifth century B.C. created the tragic drama of Athens as a feature of the quadrennial festival of Dionysus. Their subjects were drawn from both history and mythology. None of Phrynichus' plays has come down to us.

myths and sufferings, men asked, "What has this to do with Dionysus?"
For to sing, probably the so-called drinking songs, while the great bowl
stands in the midst and the garlands are being distributed with which
the god crowns us to set us free, is neither beautiful nor fitting for his
feast. . . .[11]

---

[11] The rest of this passage is obscure. Probably some words or clauses have been lost.

The Eating of Meat[1]

PART I

1. YOU ask me why Pythagoras[2] abstained from eating meat. For my part I wonder what was the disposition, idea, or motive of the first man who put to his mouth a thing slaughtered and touched with his lips the flesh of a dead animal. How he could set out tables of stale corpses and then give the name of food and victuals to things which but a little before were lowing and bleating and moving and seeing; how his sight could endure the spectable of butchering, skinning, and mangling them, how his nose could bear the scent; and why his mouth did not sicken at the filthiness of chewing other creatures' sores and swallowing the saps and juices of their fatal wounds.

> "The raw hides crawled, the flesh upon the spits,
> Roasted as well as raw, bellowed like cattle lowing."[3]

These lines are but fiction and myth, but a meal is really horrible when the eater was hungry for animals still mooing, and directed which birds still alive and chirping he must have to gorge on, and ordered the seasonings and ways of cooking and serving them up at table. We ought to be inquiring who first started this custom, not who in late times gave it up.

2. Actually, the reason why those primitive people first started the eating of flesh was probably their utter poverty. It was not that their life was one of lawless appetites or that they had grown arrogant over their

---

[1] This essay, divided into two parts, may have been notes for two lectures delivered by Plutarch at Rome. See Part II, 1.

[2] Pythagoras, the Greek philosopher and mathematician, taught an austere and semi-monastic way of life.

[3] Homer, *Odyssey*. XII, 395–6.

superfluity of necessities, and thence had arrived at this unnatural and inhuman kind of enjoyment. Could they at this moment recover consciousness and voice, they would say:

"How happy are you now living and beloved of the Gods! How wonderful is the age of the world on which you have fallen, who gather and share among you an endless portion of all the good things which spring up for your use! How abundant is the fruit of your vines! How much wealth comes from your fields! How much sweetness you may pluck from your trees! You may live sumptuously without polluting yourselves. Whereas our lot fell in the most dismal and terrifying age of time, and because we were first to be born we were plunged into a state of deep and helpless wretchedness.

"As yet a mist covered the heavens and the stars were blurred by dense and inseparable clouds of moisture and fire and stormy winds. As yet the sun was not settled in an unwavering and steady

> 'course which marked out
> Morning and evening, nor did he bring back in order
> The seasons in garlands of fruit-bearing buds.
> The land too was ravaged' [4]

by wild inundations of rivers; and much was formless with swamps and lay utterly waste in deep mud, barren thickets, and forests. Hunger allowed us no time, for seed-time did not then exist nor harvest at the yearly seasons. What wonder if we resorted to animal flesh, contrary to Nature, when our food was mud and gnawing the bark, and when it was great luck to find a sprouting grass or the root of a reed? The day we tasted and ate an acorn, we danced for joy about an oak, calling it 'life-giver,' 'mother,' and 'nourisher.' Our life knew that festival, but all other days were full of pain and gloom.

"But what folly and madness drives you who are living now to defile yourselves with blood, when you have an abundance of everything you need? Why falsely pretend that the earth is unable to maintain you? Why dishonor Demeter, the lawgiver, and treat with disdain the mild and gentle Bacchus, as though what you receive from them were not sufficient? Are you not afraid to mix your cultivated crops with blood and butcher's work? You call snakes, leopards, and lions savage but your-

---

4 The lines may be a quotation from Empedocles.

selves are smeared with gore, and fully as cruel as they. For to them killing means necessary food, whereas to you it means luxury."

3. As a matter of fact, we do not eat the lions and wolves against which we have to defend ourselves. We let them alone, but catch and kill the harmless and gentle creatures which have neither stings nor fangs to bite with, and which, by Zeus, Nature seems to have created for their beauty and their grace. . . .

4. But nothing abashes us, neither the beauty of a color, nor the charm of a musical voice, nor the alertness of disposition, nor the cleanliness of habit, nor the extreme intelligence of the poor beasts. For the sake of a titbit of meat, we rob a soul of sun, light, and the length of life for which it was born and for which Nature reared it. And then we fancy that its cries and shrieks are merely inarticulate sounds, and not prayers, entreaties, and reasonable pleas, as it says, "I appeal not against your necessity, but your callousness. Kill what you need for food, but do not kill for more delicate food!" O the cruelty of it! It is terrible to see the tables set of rich people who keep butchers and cooks of dead meat, but more terrible to see them cleared away, for what is left over is more than what is eaten. These animals then died uselessly. Other people dislike dead bodies and object to them when they are set before them, and will not have them carved and cut up, but made no objection when they were still alive.

5. I call it absurd for these men to say that Nature started the habit. It is not natural for man to eat meat. This is shown first of all by the shape of our bodies. The human body has no resemblance to that of a carnivorous creature. It has no hooked beak or sharp talons or pointed teeth, no stout stomach or hot breath able to convert and dispose of such heavy and fleshy fare. . . .

And if you insist it is your nature to eat such food, do you yourself then kill first what you want to eat. Do it yourself without the help of a chopping-knife, club, or axe, but as wolves, bears, and lions do, who kill for themselves all they devour. Bite an ox to pieces with your teeth, or a pig with your jaws, tear a lamb or a hare to shreds and eat it quickly, still alive, as they do. If you wait until the dying animal is quite dead and are ashamed to enjoy the flesh while the spirit is still in it, why against Nature see food at all in a living thing? Actually, no one wants to eat even a dead and lifeless thing as it is, but they boil it and roast it and transform it with heat and sauces, changing and altering and smothering the taste of gore with thousands of sweet spices, so that the palate, being thus deceived, may accept this uncongenial fare. An amusing story is that of the Spartan who bought a little fish at an inn and gave it to the innkeeper to prepare. But when he asked for cheese and vinegar and olive oil, the Spartan said, "But if I had those things I should not have bought a fish." We are become so gross with this unholy blood-shedding that we call flesh a delicacy, and then must add more delicacies to it, mixing oil, wine, honey, pickles, and vinegar with Syrian and Arabian spices, as though, now that it is really dead, we would embalm it. Yet when the tissues are thus dissolved and made soft and in a way corrupted, it is a task for us to absorb them, and when absorbed they cause us severe discomfort and sickening indigestion.

6. . . . Not only is this meat-eating unnatural for our bodies, but by clogging and cloying them, it does our spirits harm. For though wine and servings of meat may make a body strong and sturdy, they disable the mind. Not to offend the athletes, I will cite examples only from my own country. The people of Attica call us Boeotians dense and dull-witted and stupid, chiefly because of our gluttony. . . . An eye swimming in too much moisture is blinded for its proper work. When we gaze at the sun through a fog or a mass of swirling vapors, we see it not clear and bright, but far off and dim, with failing beams. So in a muddy and glutted body, weighted down with heavy and alien nourishment, a brilliant and splendid mind must be dulled and confused and go wandering after trivial and insignificant objects, since it has not the sight and vigor for important things. . . .

PART II

1. My reason now calls on me to return with fresh ideas and energy to my yesterday's discussion of meat-eating. It is hard (as Cato said) to talk to stomachs which have no ears, and after they have already drunk the draught of custom, which, like that of Circe, is

> "A drink of pangs and griefs and sorcery and anguish."

And it is no easy task to pull the hook of meat-eating out of men caught and impaled on luxury. We should be fortunate if, like the Egyptians who ripped the bowels out of their corpses and cut them in bits before the sun and then cast them away as the cause of all the sins the man had committed, we could cut out our gluttony and blood guiltiness and keep the rest of our lives pure. For the stomach itself is not guilty of bloodshed, but is made guilty by our greed. If a sinless life is impossible, with custom so strong, we can, by Zeus, at least feel shame enough to lead our sinful lives by this rule. We will eat meat, but only to feed our hunger, not for self-indulgence. We will kill an animal, but only in sorrow and pity, not abusing and tormenting it, as is often done in these days by men who in the slaughter of boars thrust red-hot irons into them, so that the blood as it flows out and tries to cool the heat of the iron plunged into it may make the flesh tender and delicious. Others jump on and kick the dugs of farrowing sows, so as to mingle in the birth pains the blood and milk and gore of the little pigs, all, O expiating Zeus, being murdered together that we may eat the creature when most inflamed. And others sew up the eyes of cranes and swans, then shut them up and fatten them in darkness, so making their flesh rich with various mixed and savory foods.

2.   From all of which it is quite clear that it is not for needed nourishment or necessity but out of sheer gluttony, vanity, and wastefulness that men have made a diversion of brutality. Just as love, in women who cannot be satisfied with pleasure, tries everything and wanders around debauched, until at last it falls into unspeakable lusts; so, intemperance in food, when it passes beyond nature and necessity, looks for variety to tempt its appetite in cruelty and viciousness. For our senses, when once they fail to keep within their natural limits, become all of them sick and perverted and out of control. Thus a diseased ear makes nothing of music, but exhausted and unstrung, it yearns for what is low, bungling, or effeminate amusement. Such ears have taught our eyes not to enjoy Pyrrhic dances [5] and pantomimes and stately choric marches and statuary and paintings but to prefer a more costly spectacle of human death and slaughter and wounds and battles. And so our wicked feasts are followed by licentious living.

3.   What kind of meal is not too costly? That for which no living thing is put to death? Do we reckon a soul a small expense? I am not speaking

---

[5] The Pyrrhic dance was a bold and dashing war dance. The other things listed were all objects of beauty which a wholesome eye would delight in.

of a mother's or a father's or a friend's or a child's soul, as Empedocles was,[6] but of one that still shares in feeling, seeing, hearing, imagination, and intelligence, which it has received from Nature in order to obtain what belongs to it, and avoid what does not. And ask yourself which philosophers do more to civilize us, those who tell us to eat children, friends, fathers, and wives, because they are dead, or Pythagoras and Empedocles, who teach us to be just even towards the other members of creation. . . .

4. Who in later times decided that we owed no justice to dumb animals?

> "Who first forged by the road a brutal knife
> And first with it shed blood of plowing oxen."

It all began in the same way that tyrants began to slaughter men. At Athens the first man they put to death was the worst of their informers, who everyone said deserved it. The second was the same sort of man, and so was the third. But after that, the Athenians were accustomed to bloodshed and looked on passively when Niceratus, son of Nicias, and the general Theramenes, and Polemarchus the philosopher were executed. In the same way the first animal killed and eaten was a wild and mischievous beast, and then a bird or a fish was caught. And murder, being thus tried and practiced on creatures like these, arrived at the laboring ox, and the sheep that clothes us, and the cock that guards our house. And little by little, our desires hardening, we proceeded to the slaughter of men, and wars and massacres.

One may not prove that souls in their rebirths inhabit different bodies in turn and that what is now rational becomes at another time irrational, and what is now wild becomes tame, and that Nature changes and gives to everything a new abode.

> "In a strange coat of flesh she clothes them all." [7]

Yet we should be persuaded to abandon this wicked habit by the fact that it brings sickness and heaviness upon the body, and eventually destroys the soul by making it less averse to lawlessness and war. For custom now makes it impossible for us to entertain a guest or celebrate a wedding or spend time with our friends without shedding blood and killing something.

---

[6] Empedocles, Fragment 442. [7] Ibid., Fragment 414.

5. And if the proof of what men say about the transmigration of souls into bodies does not compel our belief, still the bare possibility of it should make us very cautious and fearful. Suppose that in night fighting between armies a soldier threatens with his sword a man who has fallen and whose body is concealed by his armor, and then hears someone say that he does not know surely but thinks it likely that the man lying there is the soldier's son or brother or father or tent-mate. Which would be better? To admit his suspicion might be wrong and treat an enemy as a friend, or to despise the warning as uncertain and not worth believing, and kill his comrade as an enemy? . . .

Peace of Mind

1. **P**LUTARCH to Paccius,[1] greeting:

It was late when I received your letter, asking me to write you something on peace of mind, and on the passages in the *Timaeus* which require fuller explanation. And about that very time our friend Erotas felt he must take ship quickly for Rome. He had had a letter from the powerful Fundanus, urging haste, as is his wont. So I had not the time I would have wished to do what you wanted, and yet could not bear to have you see a man just come from us with wholly empty hands. Accordingly I gathered up from my notes some I had happened to make for myself on peace of mind, for I thought you did not want this to be merely an essay to be listened to as an exhibit of fine writing, but as something helpful for use. . . .

2. The man who said that anyone who expected to get peace of mind must have little to do either in public or in private life, first of all makes that peace a costly article, if we must buy it at the price of doing nothing. It sounds like advice to sick people,

"Lie still, poor wretch, in your bed," [2]

though really the stupor induced by idleness is a bad remedy for the body. And it is a poor physician for the soul who would free it of trouble and anxiety by prescribing a soft and lazy life, leaving our friends and relatives and country in the lurch. Besides, it is not true that persons with

---

[1] This essay, in the form of a letter addressed to Paccius, one of Plutarch's noble friends at Rome, suggests that Plutarch had read earlier Epicurean and Stoic treatments of the same subject. His essay, however, appealed to Christians of that time and later, as the others did not. It was used and quoted by church leaders, such as St. Basil and St. Chrysostom.

[2] Euripides, *Orestes,* 258.

little to do are peaceful in their minds. If it were, women would be serener than men, since they mostly lead lives of inactivity, and nowadays, as Hesiod [3] says, the north wind

> "Comes not near a soft-skinned maiden";

yet griefs and troubles and petty spites, more than one could describe, springing from jealousy or superstition or ambition or empty vanity, inundate the women's part of the house. And Laertes, who had lived for twenty years alone in the country,

> "With but an old woman to serve as his handmaid,
> To set on his board his meat and his drink," [4]

and who was in exile from his country, his house, and his kingdom, had sorrow and despondency as companions in his leisure. . . . So even Epicurus [5] thinks that men who love honor and glory should not idle their lives away, but use their natural talents in politics and public service, since they are likely to be more fretted and harmed by inaction than by not getting everything they work for. . . .

3. There are people quite certain that there is a kind of life which is carefree. Some of them think the farmer's is, others the bachelor's, others the king's. Menander [6] reminds us of them, when he says,

> "Phania, I thought they were rich
> Who never were forced to borrow,
> Nor groan at night, nor toss up and down,
> Sighing 'Alas,' but sweetly and gently
> Slept the night through."

But he then goes on to say that he sees the rich suffering the same as the poor.

> "Trouble and life, he says, are akin.
> In luxurious lives or in lives of great honor
> Trouble is there, and in lives that are poor
> Stays with them to the end."

---

[3] *Works and Days,* 519.

[4] *Odyssey,* I, 191–2.

[5] Fragment 555.

[6] Fragment 28.

But we are like people at sea, timid and seasick, who think they will find it easier if they change from a sailboat to a galley, and then if they change again to a trireme, but gain nothing thereby, for they take their fears and their qualms with them. So changes in manner of life do not cure the sorrows and disturbances of the soul, which come from lack of experience and reflection or from inability or ignorance of how rightly to enjoy the present. These are afflictions of both rich and poor; they trouble both the married and the unmarried. They make some men shun the forum, but find retirement unbearable; they make others work for introductions at court, and on their arrival straightway find they care nothing for it.

"The sick are peevish in their helplessness," [7]

for the wife bothers them, and they blame the doctor, and they find the bed uncomfortable, and, as Ion [8] says,

"The friend who visits them is tiring,
And yet they do not like his going."

However, when the illness is over, and the man in better shape, sweet health returns and makes all things pleasant and acceptable. He that yesterday loathed eggs and fine meal loaves and sesame cakes will today eat eagerly and with appetite coarse bread with olives and cress.

4. But reason, if inbred in us, creates contentment and a readiness to accept vicissitudes in every kind of life. . . . It was a burden to Agamemnon to be king over so many subjects,

"Here you see Atreus' son, Agamemnon, on whom forever
Zeus has sent cares without end." [9]

On the other hand, Diogenes, when he was being sold, sat down and kept jeering at the auctioneer, and would not stand up when bidden, but said jokingly with a laugh, "Suppose it were a fish you were selling—?" And Socrates in prison talked philosophy with his friends. But Phaethon,[10] after ascending to heaven, wept because nobody gave him his

---

[7] Euripides, *Orestes,* 232.
[8] Fragment 56.
[9] *Iliad,* X, 88–9.
[10] For the story of Phaethon, see above, *Letter of Consolation,* ch. 3, n. 2.

father's horses and chariot. As, then, the foot shapes the shoe, and not the shoe the foot, so does the disposition make the life similar to itself. . . .

5. Plato [11] compared life to a game of dice; we ought to throw in whatever way promises gain, but, having thrown, make the best of whatever turns up. It is not in our power to decide what the throw will be, and it is our duty, if we are wise, to take in a right spirit what fortune sends, and adjust the situation to everyone participating, so that what was lucky may do them the most good, and what was not may do them the least harm. . . .

6. So we ought first to cultivate and practice a habit of adapting ourselves to circumstances, like the man who threw a stone at his dog, and missed it but hit his stepmother and cried out, "Not so bad!" In that way we may put a different face on fortune when things turn out wrong. Diogenes was sentenced to banishment. "Not so bad," for it was after his banishment that he began to be a philosopher. . . . What keeps us from imitating men like them? Have you failed to win an office? You can live in the country and manage your own affairs. Did you court the friendship of a great man and meet with rebuff? You can live now free from risks and exertions. Or have you been involved in business that kept you busy and anxious? "Even warm water will not make the limbs so soft," according to Pindar,[12] as glory and honor, with some power, make "labor sweet, and toil no toil." [13] Or have you met with bad luck or opprobrium because of some other man's slander and envy? The breeze is favorable to waft you to the Muses and the Academy, as it did Plato when he was suffering from the break in his friendship with Dionysius.[14]

It does indeed help one in keeping a quiet mind to observe how famous men have borne unflinchingly the same troubles that you have. Is your childlessness a grief to you? Look at the kings of the Romans, not one of whom left a son to inherit his kingdom. Do you find your poverty pain-

---

[11] *Republic*, X, 604.

[12] *Nemean Ode*, 4, 4.

[13] Euripides, *Bacchae*, 66.

[14] In the course of his travels after the death of Socrates, Plato visited Sicily and became adviser to Dionysius I, tyrant of Syracuse. His ideas, however, did not please Dionysius, who sent him away in disgrace. Twice, later in his life, Plato revisited Sicily, and attempted to influence for good the son and successor of Dionysius I, Dionysius II, but both times he failed, and even had difficulty in getting back to Athens in safety.

ful? But what Boeotian would you rather be than Epaminondas? [15] What
Roman than Fabricius? "But my wife has been seduced!" Have you never
read that inscription at Delphi,

> "Agis, king of land and sea, erected me";

and have you not heard that his wife Timaea was seduced by Alcibiades,[16]
and in whispers to her handmaidens called the child she bore Alcibiades?
But this ill fortune did not prevent Agis from being the most renowned
and greatest Greek of his time. Nor did the licentiousness of his daughter
prevent Stilpo [17] from leading the merriest life of all contemporary
philosophers. . . .

7.   Many people are irritated and exasperated both by what is wrong in
their friends and intimates, and by the misdeeds of their enemies. Back-
biting and anger and envy and malice and jealousy and ill-will are characteristics of persons destined to some disaster, and foolish men are
troubled and worried by them. Take, for instance, the quarrels of neighbors, the peevishness of friends, and the wickedness of those in charge of
the state. You seem to me considerably upset by them, like the doctors
in Sophocles,[18] who

> "With bitter physic would purge the bitter bile."

So indignant and bitter are you at people's weaknesses and infirmities,
which is not reasonable of you. . . .
    But if you accept things as they are, and, as the surgeon does with his
forceps and bandages, as far as possible show yourself cheerful and calm,
your happiness in your own state of mind will be greater than your distress at the other people's disagreeable shortcomings, for you will think
of them simply as barking dogs, doing what is natural for them to do. . . .
Look, is it not unreasonable to allow ourselves to be so annoyed and vexed
because everyone who has dealings with us and comes near us is not good
and charming? Let us see to it, dear Paccius, that we are not, unawares,

---

15 The Theban hero Epaminondas in 371 B.C. broke the military power of Sparta;
Fabricius, between 282 and 278 B.C., led the Roman armies in the defeat of the invader Pyrrhus. Both men were celebrated for their austerity and integrity.
16 For this story of Alcibiades, see above, *Alcibiades,* ch. 23.
17 Stilpo (c. 380–300 B.C.) was head of a philosophical school at Megara.
18 Fragment 770.

really criticizing and fearing, instead of the general faultiness of the people we meet, just that in them which touches ourselves, our motive then being selfishness, not a hatred of evil. . . .

8. Let us resume our argument. When we are in a fever everything tastes sour and unpleasant, but when we see others eating and enjoying the same things, we no longer blame our food and drink but our disease. And so we shall stop blaming and worrying over the state of the country, if we see others cheerfully and gaily putting up with it.

It is good too for our peace of mind, in the midst of disturbing events, not to overlook all our advantages and comforts, and to lessen our troubles by mixing them with our blessings. When our eyes now are dazzled by things too bright, we turn them away and ease them by looking at fresh green grass, but our minds we keep strained over painful things, and compel them to brood on unhappy ideas, wrenching them by force away from what is pleasanter. Yet we might aptly apply here what was said to the meddlesome man,

> "Malign intruder, why so keen to spy
> A neighbor's fault, while seeing not your own?"

. . . Folly it is too to go on grieving over things we have lost, without rejoicing over what we have left. But like small children, who, if one of their many playthings is taken away by anyone, cry and scream and throw the rest away too, so we, when fortune robs us of a treasure, wail and mourn and treat everything else as worthless to us.

9. "Well, what blessings have we?" someone may say. Well, what have we not? One has a reputation, another a house, another a wife, another a good friend. When Antipater of Tarsus before his death was reckoning up his pieces of good fortune, he did not omit even the delightful voyage he had had from Cilicia to Athens. So we too should not overlook common pleasures but take account even of them, be glad that we live and are well and see the sun, that there is no war going on or civil strife, that the earth is open to the farmer's tilling and that whoever wills may fearlessly sail the sea, that we are free to speak and act or to be silent and idle. We shall get still more contentment from the possession of these blessings, if we imagine ourselves without them and remind ourselves often how people who are ill long for health, and people at war for peace, and an

unknown stranger in a great city for name and friends, and how miserable it is to be deprived of what we have once had. Then all these good things will not seem great and precious to us only when they are gone, and nothing while we have them. For absence of a thing does not actually add anything to its value.

Nor should we go about acquiring things we regard as valuable, and always be trembling for fear of losing them because they are valuable, and yet, while we have them, neglect and think little of them. We should use them constantly for our pleasure and enjoy them, so that we may bear their loss, if that happens, with more equanimity. Most people, however, as Arcesilaus said, think they must be looking closely and in every detail at other people's poems and paintings and statues, studying them with the eyes of the body and the mind, but never glance at their own lives, which contain much to give them joy. They are forever gazing abroad and admiring other people's reputations and fortunes, as adulterers admire other men's wives and despise their own.

10.   But it is a great help towards peace of mind to look for the most part at home and at things around us, or if not, to turn our thoughts to people worse off than ourselves and not, as many do, compare ourselves only with those who are better off. As, for example, men in chains think their fellows are happy who are released, and released prisoners think freemen are, and freemen citizens, and citizens the rich, and the rich satraps, and satraps kings, and kings the gods, for by then they want to hurl thunderbolts and flash lightning. So always yearning for something above them, men are never thankful for what they have. . . . But one whose mind thinks wholesome thoughts does not sit down despondent and miserable if he is less renowned or less rich than some of the myriads of mankind the sun looks down upon, "who feed on the fruits of the whole world," [19] but goes on his way singing praises of his divinity and his life, because it is in so many ways fairer than that of countless thousands. . . .

Whenever, then, you are brimful of admiration for someone carried by in his litter, who seems a greater man than yourself, lower your eyes and look at his bearers. And when you think, as the man from Hellespont did,[20] that Xerxes was a marvel for crossing the straits on his bridge of

[19] Simonides, Fragment 5, 17.
[20] Herodotus, *Histories,* VII, 56.

boats, look at the men who dug through Mount Athos under the lash, and at those whose ears and noses were cut off because the bridge was broken by the waves. Consider their state of mind too, how they think your life and your position marvelous. When Socrates heard one of his friends saying how expensive Athens was, how "Chian wine costs a mina, a purple robe three minas, a half pint of honey five drachmas," he took him to the bread shops. "Half a peck of barley meal for an obol? Athens is cheap!" Then to the vest maker. "A sleeveless vest for only ten drachmas? Athens is cheap!" So when we hear anyone saying of us that we live in a small way and are terribly unfortunate because we are not consuls or governors, we may answer, "We live in a grand way and our lot is enviable. We do not beg, we bear no heavy burdens, we toady to no one."

11.   But since in our folly we are used to living more with an eye to other people than to ourselves, and human nature is so jealous and covetous that it rejoices less in its own blessings than it is pained by those of others, do not only look at the much-vaunted splendor of the men you envy and admire, but open and draw, as it were, the gaudy curtain of their pomp and show, and step inside. You will see that they have much to vex and distress them. The well-known Pittacus,[21] renowned for his fortitude, wisdom and justice, was once entertaining some guests, when his wife came in in a rage and upset the table. The guests were in consternation, but he said, "Every one of you has some trouble, and he who has only mine is very well off." . . . There are many such cases, unknown to the public, among the rich and the famous and even among kings, for pride throws a veil over them.

"O happy son of Atreus, child of fate, blest is thy lot." [22]

Congratulations like this come from outside, through a halo of arms and horses and war, but the inward voice of suffering testifies against such vainglory:

"A heavy doom is laid on me by Zeus, the son of Cronos." [23] . . .

---

21 One of the so-called Seven Wise Men of Greece.

22 *Iliad*, III, 182. The line is addressed to Agamemnon.

23 *Iliad*, IX, 18. This is Agamemnon speaking of himself.

By reflections like these one may wean oneself from the discontent with one's own lot and the belittlement and disparagement of one's own possessions which come from too much admiring one's neighbor.

12.   Another thing which is a serious hindrance to our peace of mind is failure to proportion our desires to our means, and spread of too much sail, as it were, in hopes of great things. Then, when unsuccessful, we blame Heaven and fortune and not our own folly. For a man is not unfortunate who tries to shoot an arrow with a plow, or to hunt a hare with an ox, nor has he an evil spirit opposing him if he fails to catch deer with fishing nets and seines, but in his silly stupidity he has attempted the impossible. Self-love is mainly to blame, making people desire to be first, ambitious in all they do, and insatiably eager to snatch hold of everything. They want not only to be rich and learned and strong and convivial and attractive, and friends of kings and governors of cities, all at the same time, but they are dissatisfied if their dogs and horses and quails and cocks are not the finest and the best. Dionysius the Elder was not content with being the most powerful tyrant of his time, but because he could not sing better than Philoxenus the poet, or beat Plato in dialectics, he was so angry and exasperated that he sent the one to labor in his stone quarries, and the other as a slave to Aegina. . . . Yet even among the gods one has one function and another another. One is called the god of war, another the god of prophecy, another the god of wealth, and Aphrodite, since she takes no part in feats of war, is despatched by Zeus to marriages and bridals.

13.   There are some pursuits which cannot be carried on together, but are by their very nature exclusive of one another. For instance, training in oratory and the study of mathematics require time and leisure, whereas political influence and the friendship of kings are not won without activity in public affairs and constant work. Wine and much eating of meat make the body strong and vigorous, but blunt the intellect. Continuous attention to the making and saving of money increases one's wealth, but disdain and scorn of riches are a great help to philosophy. All things, therefore, are not in everyone's power, and we should heed the maxim inscribed in Apollo's temple, "Know thyself," and act so as to carry out our natural bent, and not let ambition drag us and force our nature into some other kind of life. . . .

He who chafes and frets because he is not at the same time a lion "reared on the mountains, exulting in his strength," [24] and a little Maltese dog cherished in the lap of a rich widow, is out of his senses. Not a bit wiser is the man who would like to be an Empedocles, or a Plato, or a Democritus, writing about the universe and the true nature of things, and at the same time to be married like Euphorion to a rich old woman, and to revel and drink like Medius with Alexander, and who is sore and hurt if he is not also admired for his wealth, like Ismenias, and for his valor, like Epaminondas. Yet runners in a race are not upset because they do not carry off the wrestlers' crowns, but are delighted with their own. . . .

Men who have such respect for their own walk in life will not be envious of their neighbors'. We do not nowadays expect a vine to bear figs nor an olive grapes, yet if we have not at one and the same time the distinction of being both rich and learned, both generals and philosophers, both flatterers and outspoken, both thrifty and extravagant, we blame and scold and despise ourselves for living a maimed and imperfect life. We see, however, that nature teaches us the same lesson. She has provided that different animals eat different kinds of food, and has not made all carnivorous or seed-gatherers or root-diggers. So too she has given to mankind various means of getting a livelihood, "one by keeping sheep, another by plowing, another by fowling, while another is fed from the sea." [25] We ought therefore to select the calling appropriate for ourselves and work hard at it, and leave other people to theirs, . . .

14. Every man has in himself stores of content or discontent, and the jars containing blessings and evils do not stand on the threshold of Zeus,[26] but are here in our own minds, as may be seen from the differences in our attitudes. For foolish men overlook and disregard their present blessings, because their thoughts are always intent on the future, but the wise keep the past clearly in mind through memory. To foolish people the present, which allows us but the briefest instant to touch it and then slips from our grasp, does not seem to be ours or to belong to us at all. Like the rope-maker depicted in Hades who permits an ass to eat up his rope

---

[24] *Odyssey*, VI, 130.
[25] Pindar, *Isthmian Odes*, 1, 48.
[26] An allusion to *Iliad*, XXIV, 527–533. See below, *Exile*, ch. 4.

as fast as he plaits it, so with most people, a stupid and ungrateful forget-fulness has possession of them, and wipes from their minds every past accomplishment, success, pleasant holiday, piece of good luck or happi-ness, breaking the unity of life, which comes from weaving of the past into the present. For by separating yesterday from today, as if it were something different, and tomorrow, likewise, as if it were not the same as today, it soon makes what is now happening into what has never taken place, by not recalling it. Those in the schools who deny the growth of bodies on grounds of the continual flux of substance, make each of us in theory different from himself, and, therefore, a different man.[27] So those who do not keep or store in memory things that are past, but let them float away, actually leave themselves vacant and empty daily, while they cling to tomorrow, as if what happened last year or day before yesterday or even yesterday mattered nothing to them, or had not happened to them at all.

15. This habit, then, is one interference with peace of mind, and another still worse is the way in which, like flies that slide down the smooth sur-face in mirrors, and stick fast in rough spots and cracks, men glide over the cheerful and agreeable things in their lives, and snarl themselves up in memories of unpleasant things. . . . As Euripides [28] says,

> "There may no separate good and ill be here,
> But only mixture of the two, and rightly."

And we ought not to be disheartened or despondent at what is wrong, but, like musicians who always blur over their worse playing with their better and drown what is poor in what is excellent, we should make our checkered life into something harmonious and congenial to us. . . .

16. At our birth we received the mingled seeds of every experience and for that reason lead lives that are very uneven. The sensible man prays for good things, but expects the contrary, and makes the most of either, avoiding too much of anything. . . . For we may not only admire but imitate the attitude of Anaxagoras, which made him exclaim at the death of his son, "I knew I had begotten a mortal." We may apply it too to every

---

[27] Perhaps a reference to the Epicureans, who taught that the atoms of which all bodies are composed are continually in motion, forever building up and breaking down.
[28] Fragment 21.

contingency. "I know that my wealth is ephemeral and insecure." "I know that those who gave me my office can take it away." "I know that my wife is good but still a woman, and that my friend is only a man." "An animal is by its nature changeable," as Plato [29] said. For such a prepared frame of mind, if anything undesirable happens, it is not unexpected. It does not meet trouble with "I would not have thought it!" or "I was looking for something different!" or "This I was not expecting!" It stops the throbbings and palpitations of the heart, and puts a prompt quietus on anything frantic or hysterical.

Carneades [30] suggests that in a time of great calamities the thing that produces shock and despair is wholly and entirely the unexpected. . . . The poet [31] has shown us graphically how powerful may be something unexpected. For Odysseus broke into tears when his old dog wagged his tail, but was nothing like so moved when he sat by his weeping wife, for to her he had come with his emotions under control of his reason and fully prepared, whereas he had not expected the dog and came on him suddenly, without looking for him.

17. . . . As for the things which seem to pain us by their very nature, such as sickness, anxieties, and the deaths of friends and children, there is that line of Euripides,[32]

"Alas—yet why alas? We but suffer what comes to mortals."

And no reasoning is of such help, when sorrow suddenly descends on us, as that which reminds us of the common and natural necessity to which man through his body is exposed. But that is the only handle he gives to fate, since in the chief and most important things he stands secure. . . . For fortune can afflict us with disease, take away our money, calumniate us to the people or the tyrant, but it cannot make a good and brave and high-souled man bad and cowardly and ignoble and malicious, nor deprive him of the disposition which, as long as he keeps it, is of more value to him in the conduct of his life than is a pilot to a ship at sea. For a pilot cannot calm the wild wind and wave, nor can he in his need find a harbor wherever he wants it, nor can he await events

---

[29] *Letters,* XIII, 360.
[30] Carneades was founder of the New Academy at Athens.
[31] *Odyssey,* XVII, 300; XIX, 209.
[32] *Bellerophon,* Fragment 300.

boldly, without trembling, though as long as he has not despaired, he uses his skill,

> "Scudding on with his great sail lowered to the shorter mast,
>   Above a sea dark as Erebus,"

and while it still rises above the billows, he sits there shivering and quaking. But a wise man's mind keeps him calm, for the most part, even in the face of bodily ailments, for he cuts out the causes of disease by his temperance and sober living and labor in moderation, and if some trouble starts to appear from outside, he sails around it as though it were a rock. "Prompt to act he passes by it with nimble helm," as Asclepiades puts it. And if some unexpected and tremendous gale sweeps down on him and proves too much for him, the harbor is near, and he can swim away from his body, as from a leaky boat.

18.   For it is fear of death, and not desire of life, that makes the foolish man hang on to his body, clinging to it, as Odysseus did to the fig-tree [33] in terror of Charybdis that lay below.

> "Where the wind neither let him stay nor sail on,"

and he was indignant at one, and afraid of the other. But a man who has some understanding of the nature of the soul, and who reflects that the change it undergoes at death is either to something better or at least to nothing worse, has in his fearlessness of death a great help to peace of mind in life. . . .

He who said, "I have anticipated you, O fortune, and shut off every way by which you can creep in on me," was not trusting to bolts or keys or walls, but to convictions and reasons which are within grasp of all who want them. Nor should we despair or disbelieve those who tell us these things, but admire and emulate them and be inspired by them, and observe and test ourselves in trivial matters with a view to those that are serious. We should not avoid or refuse that self-examination, or try to evade it by saying, "Nothing probably can be more difficult." An unexercised inertia and softness are the results of that spirit of self-indulgence which occupies itself always with the easiest task, and sheers away from the disagreeable to what is pleasant. But the soul that is compelled by reason to train itself to face steadily sickness and grief and exile will find in

---

[33] *Odyssey*, XII, 432.

what appears hard and dreadful much that is deceitful and empty and hollow, as reason will show in each case.

19. Yet many shudder at that line of Menander,[34]

"No man can say, 'I shall not suffer that.' "

They do not know how great a help it is to serenity of mind to practice and become able to look at fortune with open eyes, and not build up in themselves fine and pretty fancies, like a person reared in the shade on a multitude of hopes which are always giving way and never hold out against anything. We can answer Menander's line,

"No man can say, 'I shall not suffer that,' "

for anyone can say, "I will not *do* that. I will not lie. I will not be a sluggard. I will not cheat. I will not be a schemer." And that which is in our power is not a small but a great aid to peace of mind. So, on the contrary,

"The consciousness that I have done terrible deeds," [35]

like a sore in the flesh, leaves in the mind a regret which is forever wounding and piercing it. . . . Neither a costly house, nor a heap of gold, nor pride of race, nor high office, nor charm nor eloquence of speech, make life so peaceful and serene as a soul pure of evil acts and desires, having as its spring of life a nature steadfast and undefiled. From it flow noble deeds, bringing with them an inspired and joyful energy, together with loftiness of thought and a memory sweeter and more lasting than the hope which Pindar [36] says is the support of old age. . . .

20. I am much taken with Diogenes' remark to the stranger whom he saw at Sparta dressing himself ostentatiously for a feast, "Does not a good man think of every day as a feast?" And a very splendid feast, if we see it rightly. For the world is a most holy and divinely beautiful temple, into which man is introduced at his birth, not to behold motionless images made by hands, but things which the mind of God has prepared as visible copies of things of the mind, as Plato says, and which have innate in them the principle of life and motion—sun, moon, and stars, and riv-

---

34 Fragment 355, 4.
35 Euripides, *Orestes, 396.*
36 Fragment 214.

ers gushing fresh waters, and the earth the sustainer of plants and animals. Life is an initiation into all these things, and as the most revealing of initiations it should be full of peacefulness and delight. . . .

But men shame the festivals which God provides for us and the mysteries to which he leads us and pass their time chiefly in lamentation and heaviness of heart and carking cares. . . . They will not listen when other men call on them with reasoning that would enable them to endure the present without repining, remember the past with gratitude, and go forward to the future fearlessly and without suspicion, in glad and radiant hope.

Exile[1]

1.   THEY say that the best and surest words are those which come to men's aid in adversity, as their best friends do, and are useful. For many of the people who visit and talk with unfortunates do them more harm than good. They are like persons unable to swim but trying to rescue the drowning, who get entangled with them and sink with them to the bottom. The words of friends and persons who want to be helpful should be heartening, and not mere condolences for the sufferer's trouble. In times of calamity we do not need people to weep and wail with us like choruses in a tragedy, but people to speak plainly to us and show us that grief and discouragement over anything is wrong and useless and foolish, and that our whole situation, when examined and laid bare by the light of reason, warrants our saying to ourselves, "You have suffered nothing so terrible if you do not pretend you have." [2] It is silly not to ask our body how far actually it is hurt, and our mind if it is any the worse for what has happened, but to allow outside sympathizers and fellow mourners to make us miserable.

2.   So, alone by ourselves, let us test the weight of our misfortunes, as if they were loads for us to carry. Our body may be weighed down by a burden of some kind wearing on it, but our soul many times adds to that burden a heaviness of its own. A stone is by nature hard and ice by nature cold, and they do not receive their solidity or their coldness, probably, from outside. But when it is a matter of exiles and disgraces and loss of honors, or of their opposites, crowns and offices and front seats at the

---

1 Banishment for a longer or shorter period was a common form of punishment imposed on persons who had incurred the displeasure of the governing powers in Greece or Rome. An essay on exile would therefore find plenty of readers.

2 Menander, *The Arbitration,* Fragment 179.

theater, it is not their intrinsic nature but our opinion of them that is the gauge of our joy or sorrow over them, and each man makes them for himself light or heavy, easy or hard to bear. We may listen to Polynices' answer to the question,

> " 'What is't to lose one's country? Is it catastrophe?'
> 'Utter catastrophe, and worse in fact than in word.' " [3]

But compare him with Alcman,[4] as the poet has described himself in the epigram.

"Sardis, my father's ancient home, had I grown to manhood in thee,
I should have worn gold as a priest of Cybele,
And beaten beautiful drums. But now the name they call me is Alcman,
And my country is Sparta, the land of the tripod.
And there I have learned how to sing to the Muses of Greece who have
    made me greater
Than were ever the tyrants Dasycles or Gyges."

Thus the very same thing is in one man's estimation good, and an excellent institution, and in another's bad and pernicious.

3.   But grant that exile is, as many people say and sing, a great hardship. Many foods are bitter, or sharp and biting to the taste, but by mixing with them something sweet and agreeable we take away their unpleasantness. There are colors too, trying to the eyes, which confuse and dazzle us by their harshness and glare. If we can remedy that by a mixture of shadow, or by turning our eyes to something green and soothing, we can do the same with misfortunes, mixing with them the goodly and pleasant things we still enjoy, such as wealth, friends, leisure, and an abundance of the necessaries of life. . . .

4.   The man in the comedy who is exhorting an unfortunate friend to take courage and bear up against fortune, when asked how this is to be done, replies, "As a philosopher." So let us too brace ourselves manfully, like philosophers, against fate. But

"How against Zeus when he raineth? How against fierce Boreas?"

---

[3] Euripides, *Phoenician Women,* 388-9. In the play, Jocasta is asking her long vanished son, Polynices, what it is like to live in exile.

[4] Alcman, a poet of the seventh century B.C., according to this fragment was banished from Sardis and found a home in Sparta.

Why, we make for a bath, a coat, or a house; we do not sit down in the
rain and cry. So you, more than most, can revive and warm yourself in
the chill of adversity, needing no other aid, but recalling sagely your
present blessings. . . . As for those two jars, which Homer [5] says are
stored in heaven, one full of good fortunes and one of bad, it is not Zeus
who presides over the dispensing of them, allotting to some men a mixture
of pleasant things and to others streams of unmitigated evil, but ourselves.
For wise men make life happier and more endurable by lightening their
troubles with remembrance of their blessings, whereas most people, like
sieves, let the worst things remain and stick to them while the best slip
through.

5.   Hence, even should we fall into any real trouble or disaster, we should
find cheer and courage in the good things that still are left to us, allaying
outward calamity by inward strength. And as for things which are not
by their nature evil but are made painful wholly and entirely by sheer
imagination, we should treat them as we do masks that frighten children
—bring them near, put them in the children's hands, and turn them over
until we accustom them not to mind them. So by bringing our trouble
close to us and using our reason we may discover how ephemeral and
flimsy and exaggerated it is.

Such is now your present banishment from what you call your fatherland. For in nature there is no fatherland or private house or field or
forge or surgery, as Ariston [6] said, but all such things invariably origi-
nate in or take their names from a person who inhabits or makes use of
them. And man, as Plato [7] says, is "not an earthy or a motionless but a
heavenly plant," the body holding the head as erect as if it rested on a
root and was turned up to heaven. So Heracles said and said well,

"Argive or Theban am I, but I vaunt not either one,
For wherever a Greek tower stands there to me is my country." [8]

But better still, Socrates said that he was not an Athenian or a Greek but
a citizen of the world, as a man might say he was a Rhodian or a Corin-

---

5 *Iliad*, XXIV, 527-33.

6 Ariston, a Stoic philosopher of the third century B.C. taught that the end of human
life was complete indifference to worldly things.

7 *Timaeus*, 90.

8 Stobaeus, *Anthology*, III, 735.

thian, because he did not shut himself up inside Sunium and Taenarum and the Ceraunian mountains.

> "See you this boundless reach of sky above,
>   And how it holds the earth in its soft arms?" [9]

These are the boundaries of our country, and within them no one is either an exile or a stranger or an alien, for there are the same fire, water, and air, the same rulers, controllers, and governors, the sun, the moon, and the morning star, the same laws for all under one appointment and one ordinance, the summer and winter solstices, the equinoxes, the Pleiades and Arcturus, the seasons of sowing and of planting. And there is one supreme king, God, "who holds in his hand the beginning and middle and end of all that is, and moves about accomplishing everything in due order in accordance with his nature; and Justice follows him to punish transgressors of the divine law." [10] All men by nature obey her when they deal with all other men as fellow citizens.

6.   As for your not living in Sardis, that is nothing. Neither do all the Athenians live at Collytus, nor all the Corinthians at Cranium, nor all the Spartans at Pitane. Are all the Athenians strangers and exiles who moved from Melita to Diomis, where, they say, the month and the festival of Metageitnion [11] are named after their migration, and who serenely and cheerily accept and are content with their new neighbors? You would not say so. What part of the inhabited earth or of the whole world is really far distant from another part, when the mathematicians declare that it is all a mere point compared to the heavens? Yet, we, like ants or bees driven out of their one ant-hill or hive, are in agony and feel utterly lost, not knowing or having learned how to make and look on all things as our own, as in truth they are. But we laugh at the stupidity of one who says that the moon at Athens shines brighter than the moon at Corinth, though in a way we feel the same ourselves, and, in a strange land, we wonder whether the earth, the sea, the air, the sky, are not different from those we are familiar with. Nature leaves us free and unrestricted, but we

---

[9] Euripides, Fragment 941.
[10] Plato, *Laws,* IV, 716.
[11] Metageitnion, the Greek month which included the latter half of August and the first half of September, meant literally "change neighbors."

bind and cramp, immure and force ourselves into small and scanty spaces. . . .

7. . . . It is surely more proper and more pious to say that whoever has the good fortune to be moderately well provided with the necessaries of life is nowhere a stranger, nowhere without city and hearth, if only he has, besides these essentials, reason and sense as anchors to steady him, so that he can moor himself in any harbor. For a man who hast lost his wealth it is not easy to accumulate more quickly, but every city soon becomes his own country when he has learned how to treat it as such, and has roots capable of living and finding nourishment and growing everywhere, as Themistocles [12] and Demetrius of Phalerum had. The latter after his banishment became the favorite friend of Ptolemy of Alexandria, and not only lived a life of plenty, but sent gifts to the Athenians. And when Themistocles was being entertained at the king's expense, he is said to have remarked to his wife and children, "We should have been ruined, if we had not been ruined." . . .

8. However, if you look at the facts apart from pure fancy, a man who belongs to one city is in his own eyes a stranger and an alien to all others. For it does not seem to him honorable or right to desert his city and live in another. "Sparta was your lot; make her beautiful," [13]—even though she is inglorious or weak or torn by internal factions or far from prospering in her policies. But when fortune deprives a man of his own city, she gives him the right to choose any one he likes. The Pythagoreans have an excellent maxim, "Choose the best life, and habit will make it pleasant." So in such a case it is wise and right to say, "Choose the best and pleasantest city; time will make it your country"; and a country that will not keep distracting you and bothering you and giving you orders: "Pay taxes. Go on an embassy to Rome. Entertain the prefect. Take your turn at public service." Any sensible person, not quite a fool, who remembered these things, would prefer to be an exile and live on an island, even Gyarus or Cinarus,

"Rugged and barren and hard to plant with trees." . . .

---

[12] See above, *Themistocles,* ch. 29, and *Demetrius,* ch. 52.
[13] Euripides, Fragment 723.

9.　I think you have seen Naxos;[14] if not, then Hyria, which lies nearby.
The former was the home of Ephialtes and Otus,[15] and the latter of Orion.
. . . Tiberius Caesar [16] spent the seven years before his death on Capri,
and the sacred governing power of the world, enclosed in his breast, during all that time never changed its abode. However, the cares of empire
pouring in on him from all sides, kept his island repose from being tranquil and calm. But one who can land on a small island and be rid of big
troubles is a wretch if he does not often say or sing to himself those lines
of Pindar,[17]

"Yearn not, heart, for the slender cypress or for the fields of Crete, near Ida.
　Small is the plot of earth given me, but here I am strong, free from
　　sorrow and strife,"

and from ordinances of governors, and service in political emergencies,
and state functions, hard to avoid.

10.　For if the saying of Callimachus seems good, "Do not count wisdom
by a Persian measuring-line," much less should we count happiness by
measuring-lines and parasangs. Even though we live on an island only
two hundred furlongs long, and not, like Sicily, four days' sail around,
ought we to wail and lament as if fate were being cruel to us? For how
does abundance of room ensure one a carefree life? Do you not hear
Tantalus saying in the tragedy,

　　　　　"I sow a field that takes twelve days to cross,
　　　　　　The Berecyntian land?" [18]

And shortly after he says,

　　　　　"My fortunes, which were once as high as heaven,
　　　　　　Now to the ground are fallen and say to me,
　　　　　　'Learn not to make too much of earthly things,' " [19]

---

[14] Naxos was one of the most rich and fertile of the Aegean islands; Hyria was a
beautiful section of Boeotia.
[15] Ephialtes and Otus were sons of the sea-god Poseidon; Orion was a mighty hunter,
early identified with a special constellation of stars.
[16] Tiberius had a morbid fear of assassination and left Rome to spend the last years of
his life on the island of Capri.
[17] Fragment 154.
[18] Aeschylus, Fragment 158.
[19] Aeschylus, Fragment 159.

The Academy was a little place bought for only three thousand drachmas, but it was the habitation of Plato and Xenocrates and Polemon, who taught and lived there the whole time, except for one day a year, when Xenocrates went into the city to celebrate, it was said, the new tragedies at the festival of Dionysus. Theocritus of Chios twitted Aristotle with liking to live at the courts of Philip and Alexander, and choosing instead of the Academy a home at the mouth of the Borborus. There is a river near Pella which the Macedonians call Borborus. . . . Among his illustrious men Homer mentions four who dwelt on islands, Aeolus, beloved of the gods, the most wise Odysseus, the brave hero Ajax, and Alcinous, kindest to strangers.

11. When Zeno heard that the only ship he had left had been lost at sea with all its freight, he said, "Fortune, you are doing me a kindness, limiting me to a threadbare cloak and the life of a philosopher." And a man not an utter fool or mad about crowds would, I think, not blame Fortune much for confining him on an island. He might even praise her for relieving him from great troubles and anxieties, wanderings in foreign countries, perils by sea, and uproars in the forum, and for giving him a secure, quiet, undistracted, private life, including within a narrow circle everything he needs. For what island has not a house, a place to walk, a bath, and fish and hares for those who want hunting and sport?

The greatest of blessings, peace, which other men frequently thirst for, is yours to keep. They, when they try to play at checkers and enjoy the privacy of their homes, are tracked down by informers and busybodies, who chase them out of their suburban houses and gardens and drag them forcibly to the forum or the court. Whereas on an island no man comes to bother or to dun you or to borrow money or to beg you to go surety for him or to canvass for him. Only the best of your friends and relatives out of good will and affection sail over to see you. The rest of your life is free, inviolate, and sacred, if you wish or have learned how to live in leisure. But a man who thinks people are happy who are always racing around the country, and spending most of their lives in inns and ferry boats, is like one who thinks the planets are happier than the fixed stars. Yet every planet keeps to its post, revolving through one sphere, as on an island. "For," as Heraclitus [20] says, "the sun will never transgress its bounds; and if it does, the Furies, the ministers of Justice, will find it out."

[20] Fragment 94.

12.   . . . But just as Archilochus [21] overlooked the fruitful fields and
vineyards of Thasos, and abused the island as rocky and uneven, saying,

"Like an ass's backbone she stands, crowned with wild forest,"

so we, fixing our eyes on but one aspect of exile, the ignominy of it, overlook its freedom from cares, its leisure, its liberty. Yet people thought the
kings of Persia were happy, passing the winter in Babylon, the summer
in Media, and the sweet season of spring at Susa. An exile may attend the
mysteries at Eleusis, the high festival of Dionysus at Athens, go on to the
Pythian games at Delphi, and the Isthmian games at Corinth, provided
he is fond of sightseeing. If not, he has leisure, can take walks, read, sleep
undisturbed, and say like Diogenes, "Aristotle dines when Philip chooses,
Diogenes when Diogenes chooses," for no business, no ruler, no prefect
interferes with his habitual way of life.

13   For this reason you will find few of the wisest and most intelligent
men buried in their own countries. Most of them without anyone's compulsion weighed anchor, shifted their course and removed, one to Athens,
one away from it. Who ever has spoken so glowingly of his country as
Euripides [22] did?

"First we are not a people assembled from elsewhere,
     But we are indigenous, while others from other cities
     Like chessmen find themselves moved from place to place,
     And as strangers are transported hither from foreign climes." . . .

"And also, my lady, to boast a little besides,
     We have o'er our earth a sky well-tempered for man,
     So that we suffer not overmuch from hot or cold weather,
     And all the most beautiful things in Greece or in Asia
     We procure them and have them to attract all other men here."

Yet the author of these lines went off to Macedonia and lived all the latter
part of his life at the court of Archelaus. . . . As for the sacred and divine
breath of the Muses, "the singer of Phrygian battles," Homer, did not

---

21 Archilochus was a seventh-century B.C. Greek poet; only a few eloquent fragments
of his work have survived.
22 Fragment 981.

many cities dispute for him because he was not a eulogist of one city? And many and great are the honors paid to hospitable Zeus.

14. If anyone says that these men went off hunting for fame and honors, go to the philosophers and their schools and studies at Athens. Count over the men at the Lyceum, the Academy, the Porch, the Palladium, the Odeum. If you prefer and admire above all the Peripatetic school, Aristotle came from Stagira, Theophrastus from Eresus, Strata from Lampascus, . . . If you like the Stoics better, Zeno was from Citium, Cleanthes from Assus, Chrysippus from Soli, . . . while the Athenian Archedemus moved to Parthia, and left a successor to the Stoic school at Babylon. Who banished these men? No one; it was their own pursuit of peace and quiet, which no one at all well known or powerful can get at home. . . .

In my opinion too the Muses aided our old writers to complete their finest and most distinguished works by making banishment helpful to them. Thucydides, an Athenian, wrote his history of the war between the Peloponnesians and the Athenians in Thrace, near the forest of Scapte, Xenophon wrote at Scillus in Elis, . . . and Bacchylides the poet in Peloponnesus. All these and many more, though banished from their own countries, did not despair or abandon themselves to grief, but cheerfully took their exile as an opportunity given them by fortune. For this, even now that they are dead, they are everywhere remembered, whereas not a word survives of anyone of those who were their rivals and brought about their banishment.

15. So the man is ridiculous who thinks that any ignominy attaches to exile. What say you? . . . Themistocles did not lose in exile the glory he had won among the Greeks, but added to it among the barbarians. And there is no one so lacking in spirit and so ignoble as to wish he had been Leobates the prosecutor instead of Themistocles the exile, or Clodius, who got Cicero banished, instead of the banished Cicero, or Aristophon the accuser instead of Timotheus, who had to leave his country. . . .

17. But is not exile a matter of reproach? It may be among fools, who jeer also at the beggar, the bald man, the dwarf, and even, by Zeus, at the foreigner and resident alien. But those who are not swayed by appearances admire good men, even if they are poor or strangers or exiles. Do we not see how everyone reveres the Parthenon and the Eleusinian temple

and the Theseum? Yet Theseus [23] was an exile from Athens, though it is owing to him that men now live in Athens, and he was banished from a city which he had himself built and dwelt in. . . . If you then are taunted with being an exile, answer, "The father of the glorious victor Heracles was an exile. And Cadmus,[24] the grandfather of Dionysus, was sent from home to find Europa and never came back. 'A Phoenician born, he changed his race and went to Thebes, and from him came the Bacchic Dionysus, the exciter of women, who delights in their frenzied worship!' " As for what Aeschylus [25] hints at darkly in the line,

"Apollo the pure god, exile from heaven,"

let me keep a religious silence, as Herodotus [26] says.

Empedocles [27] begins the exposition of his philosophy with

"An ordinance there is of necessity, a decree of the gods long ago.
Whenever a man in his sin stains his hands with the blood of another,
The demons, ancient of days, lay hold of his life, and three times
A thousand years he must wander, far off from the gods who are blessed.
E'en such an exile am I from the gods, and a wanderer."

And in these words he is speaking not only of himself, but passing by himself he is telling us that we too are strangers and exiles in this world. "It was not," he is saying, "the mixture, O men, of blood and of breath that made the beginning and substance of your souls, though your earth-born and mortal body is framed of those things. But your soul has come hither from another place," and he speaks tenderly, in the gentlest of words, of its birth in a strange country.

In truth the soul is an exile and a wanderer, driven from home by divine edicts and decrees, and then, as if in a sea-girt island, joined to a body, like an oyster to its shell, as Plato [28] says. Hence it does not recall or remember the great honor and bliss from which it came. It exchanged,

---

[23] Theseus was the legendary founder of the Attic state and slayer of the Minotaur. At the end of his reign he was forced to flee, and died in exile.
[24] In Greek legend Cadmus was the son of Agenor, king of Tyre. He was the founder of the city of Thebes, and his daughter Semele became the mother of the god Dionysus.
[25] Aeschylus, *Suppliants,* 214.
[26] Herodotus, *Histories,* II, 171.
[27] Fragment 115.
[28] *Phaedrus,* 250.

not Sardis for Athens, nor Corinth for Lemnos, but heaven and the moon for earth and the life on earth. Here, however, if it shifts but a little way from spot to spot, it finds it hard and feels it strange and withers like a miserable plant. To a plant one soil is more favorable than another, and it grows and buds better in it. But no place can take away a man's happiness, nor his virtue nor his power of thought. It was in prison that Anaxagoras wrote his book on squaring the circle, and that Socrates, while he drank the hemlock, discoursed of philosophy and urged his friends to be philosophers; and they thought him happy. Whereas Phaethon and Tantalus, who rose to heaven, fell on terrible misfortunes, the poets tell us, through their folly.

Superstition

THE flood of ignorance and misunderstanding of the gods has divided from the very beginning into two separate streams. One, flowing as it were over stony ground, has in hard dispositions produced atheism; the other, as if over moist soil, has in tender minds produced superstition. Now all false opinion, especially on matters of this kind, is harmful; but when accompanied by emotion, it is still more harmful. For such emotion is, it seems, an inflammation of the error, and just as dislocations of the joints, when there is laceration, are harder to handle, so derangements of the soul, when there is emotion, are more difficult to cure.

One man thinks that atoms and void are the original elements of the universe.[1] His theory is false but it produces no wound, no quickened heartbeat, no painful agitation. Another man thinks that to be rich is the greatest good. This fallacy has poison in it, eats into his soul, excites him, allows him no sleep. It fills him with tormenting desires, pushes him down precipices, chokes him, takes away his power to speak his mind. Again, some persons believe that virtue and vice are corporeal,[2] a gross piece of ignorance, presumably, yet not worth tears and lamentations. But when we hear judgments and declarations like this,

> "O poor virtue! So thou wert but a name,
> And I pursued thee as reality," [3]

and gave up the wrongdoing which was making me rich, and dissipation, which is the parent of all pleasure,—such sentiments we ought both

---

[1] An allusion to the atomic theory of Epicurus.

[2] The reference is to the Stoics, who called the universe all material, though matter to them was very different from the Epicurean atoms.

[3] These lines seem to be spoken by Heracles in some unknown play.

to pity and to hate. For their presence in the soul breeds many diseases and emotions like worms and vermin.

2. And so with the subjects of our discourse. Atheism, which is a faulty idea that nothing exists blessed and incorruptible, leads one around apparently through disbelief in divinity to a state of indifference. Its object in not believing in gods is not to be afraid of them. Superstition, on the other hand, as its very name [4] indicates, is an emotional state or conception which produces a fear that humiliates and crushes a man. He believes that there *are* gods, but that they are spiteful and malevolent gods. The atheist is seemingly unmoved in the presence of Deity; the superstitious man is moved but in a wrong and perverted way. In one man ignorance has produced a denial of the power which succors him; in the other it has created a notion that the same power does him harm. Hence atheism is reason deluded, superstition an emotion growing out of deluded reasoning.

3. Debasing indeed are all emotional maladies of the soul, though in some there is pride, loftiness, and exultation, rising out of their fantastic quality, and none of them but contains, so to speak, some impulse to action. It is, in fact, the general fault of emotions that with their compulsion to be doing something they push hard on and strain the reasoning power. But only fear, which is as deficient in courage as in ability to reason, is both irrational and impotent, baffled and hopeless. Its faculty of fettering the soul at the same time that it keeps it agitated we call terror and dread.

Now of all kinds of fear the most paralyzing and the most helpless is superstitious fear. He who takes no voyages has no fear of the sea, and he who will not go soldiering has none of war. He who stays at home is not afraid of brigands, he who is penniless of a blackmailer, he who holds no office of envy. A man who lives in Gaul has no dread of earthquakes, or a dweller in Ethiopia of lightning. But one who fears the gods fears everything, earth, sea, air, sky, darkness, light, sound, silence, and dreams. Slaves in slumber forget their masters; sleep lightens the weight of the prisoners' chains. In sleep men feel no more the inflamed flesh of their wounds, the sharp gnawing of ulcers in their bodies, and all their other torturing pains.

---

[4] The Greek word for superstition means by derivation "fear of divinity."

   "Dear balm of sleep, true medicine for disease,
   How sweet thy coming, at my time of need." [5]

But superstition does not permit one to speak so, for it alone makes no
truce with sleep. It grants the soul no chance to breathe and take courage
by relieving it of its cruel and harrowing notions of God. In the sleep of
the superstitious as in the realms of the damned, hair-raising visions and
terrific phantoms loom up, and scenes of punishment, which keep the
wretched soul on the rack, scaring sleep away from it by dreams. Thus
it lives scourged and tormented by itself as though by some executioner,
compelled to obey strange and dreadful commands.

 And when the dreamers wake, they do not make light of or laugh at
their visions or realize that none of what horrified them was true. Instead, they strive to escape from the shadowy illusion, which was not
really anything harmful, and go on deluding and exhausting and exciting
themselves, running to sorcerers and cheats, who say to them,

   "If a specter in sleep brought terror to you,
   And you met with the train of Hecate from Hades,"

call for the old witch who breaks spells, or dip yourself in the sea, or
spend a day squatting on earth." "O Greeks, who learn barbarians' evil
ways," [6] with your superstitious mud-smearings, wallowings in the mire,
washings, fallings on your faces, shameful sittings about, extraordinary
prostrations! "Sing with your mouths right" was the direction once
given to harpists by men who tried to observe the established rules of
music. We, on our part, ask men to pray to the gods with mouths truthful and right, but not to examine the tongue which is laid on the sacrificial
entrails to see whether it is clean and straight, while twisting and defiling
their own tongues with strange names and barbaric phrases, shaming
and violating the ancient divine dignity of our religion.

 The comic poet, speaking to persons who overlay their bedsteads with
gold and silver, has said somewhere, amusingly,

    "The one free gift the gods have given us
    Is sleep; why make it cost so much to you?"

---

[5] Euripides, *Orestes*, 211-2.
[6] Ibid., *Trojan Women*, 764.

And to the superstitious man one may say, "The gods have bestowed on us sleep as a time of rest and forgetfulness of troubles. Why then make it a perpetual torture chamber for yourself, from which your poor soul can never escape to some other sleep?" Heraclitus says that men inhabit one world common to them all, but when they sleep each wanders away into a world of his own. But the superstitious man inhabits no world in common with other men, for when awake he is not using his intelligence, and when asleep he is never free from his distresses. His reason is always dreaming, his fear is always awake; escape and change are both impossible.

4. Polycrates [7] was a frightful tyrant at Samos, and Periander another at Corinth; yet no man was afraid of them once he had moved away to a free city, ruled by a democracy. But when one fears the government of the gods as a gloomy and implacable tyranny, where shall he go, where can he flee, what land or what sea can he find where the gods are not? Into what corner of the universe, poor wretch, can you creep and hide yourself, and be sure you have escaped from God? Even slaves who despair of freedom are allowed by the law to demand to be sold, and thereby to change their present master for one who may be milder. But superstition permits one no change of gods, nor can a man find a god whom he will not fear when he is terrified of the gods of his fathers and his family, shudders at his own saviours, and trembles with dread at the gracious beings from whom we ask wealth, prosperity, peace, concord, and success in whatever we do and say that is good. The same people consider slavery a calamity, and say,

> "For man and woman 'tis a dreadful fate
> To be enslaved and have a cruel master."

But how much more appalling do you think is the suffering of those who can never escape, never slip away, never rebel? For a slave there is an altar of refuge, and even for brigands many shrines offer a sanctuary. Fugitives from their enemies take courage if only they can lay hands on a statue or a temple of a god. But these are the very things the superstitious man most shivers at, dreads, and fears, the things in which others who anticipate dangers put their trust! You cannot drag the superstitious

---

[7] Polycrates was a powerful ruler of the island of Samos in the late sixth century B.C., Periander a ruthless tyrant of Corinth about sixty years earlier.

man from the shrines, but it is there that he is punished and suffers for his fears!

Why go on at length? "The end of life for all mankind is death"; [8] but for superstition not even death is the end. It reaches beyond the boundaries of life into the other side, making terror last longer than life, and adding to death the spectacle of eternal woes, telling men that when their earthly troubles cease, they are entering on others that will never cease. Far down below are opened the gates of Hades; rivers of fire and streams from the Styx flow side by side; the darkness is full of ghosts of many a fantastic shape, with hideous looks and piteous voices. There are judges and executioners, yawning gulfs and chasms, crammed with countless horrors. So unhappy superstition, through an excessive anxiety to avoid everything that appears terrifying, unwittingly makes itself a victim of every sort of misery.

5. Atheism is tormented by none of these evils. Its ignorance is deplorable, and to see wrongly or to be quite blind to things of the greatest moment is a disaster to the soul. It is as though it had put out the brightest and most important of its many eyes, its concept of God. But superstition, as I have already said, is accompanied from the first by strong emotion, pain and agitation and abject enslavement. Music, says Plato,[9] the creator of harmony and order, was given by the gods to man not in order to amuse him and tickle his ears but to disentangle gently, bring around, and restore to its proper place again whatever in his body was maladjusted and disturbing to the courses and harmonies of his soul, and which often for lack of art and grace became unruly and mischievously lawless. Yet

"Whatsoe'er Zeus loveth not,"

says Pindar,[10]

"Flees in panic when it hears
The Muses call."

Actually it is exasperated and irritated by it. Tigers, they say, if drums are beaten around them, go wild and mad and finally tear themselves

8 The quotation is from Demosthenes' *Oration XVIII, On the Crown*, 97.

9 The following is a free adaptation from Plato's *Timaeus*, 47.

10 *Pythian Odes*, I, 13.

to pieces.[11] But persons who because of deafness or injury to their ears are merely indifferent and insensible to music, are less unfortunate.

It was a calamity for Tiresias [12] that he could not see his children or his friends, but it was worse for Athamas and Agave to see them in the shape of lions or deer. And for Heracles in his madness certainly it would have been better not to see his sons or to know they were there than to destroy his best beloved like enemies.

6. Well, does it not seem to you that the state of atheists, compared to that of superstitious people, shows the same sort of difference? The former do not see any gods at all, the latter believe that they exist but are evil; the former ignore them, the latter conceive as fearful what is really benign, tyrannical what is fatherly care, hurtful what is loving concern, and savage and brutal what is wrath long delayed. They have faith in metal workers, sculptors, and wax modelers, who make images of the gods in human form. They have such images made and adorn and worship them, and despise the philosophers and statesmen who would explain to them that to the majesty of God belong goodness, magnanimity, kindness, and a protective care for man.

The atheists then are utterly blind, with no faith in those who could help them, whereas the superstitious are timid and frightened of their helpers. In general, atheism is absence of feeling for the divine and utter ignorance of the good, superstition is a multitude of feelings and a suspicion that the good is bad. The superstitious are afraid of the gods and yet fly to the gods for refuge; they flatter them, and revile them; they pray to them, and blame them for their troubles. It is the common lot of men not to be happy always and in every thing.

> "Ever are they young and free from ill,
> Unacquainted they with toil and care,
> Dreading not the roaring flood of Acheron,"

---

[11] See above, *Rules for Husband and Wife,* ch. 45.

[12] In Greek mythology Tiresias was the blind prophet of Thebes; Athamas, a king who in a fit of madness killed his own son, taking him for a wild stag. Agave, daughter of Cadmus, in a Bacchanalian frenzy, killed her son, the king of Thebes, believing him to be a lion. The hero Heracles slew his own wife and children, not knowing what he did. In each of these three cases the madness was sent by an offended god.

says Pindar,[13] of the gods. But human experiences and actions are mixed with chance and accident, which flow now in one direction and now in another.

7. Then let us contemplate, first, the atheist in misfortune and observe how he behaves. If, as usual, he is a self-controlled man, notice how he takes his calamity quietly, and sets about obtaining for himself assistance and consolation. And if he is an impatient and excitable person, listen how he lays all the blame on fortune and chance, and exclaims that nothing is ruled by justice and providence, but that all human life sweeps along in bewildering confusion and disorder.

This is not the way of the superstitious man. If the most trifling mishap befalls him, he sits down and builds up on the basis of his trouble a series of great and cruel and inevitable disasters yet to come, and takes on a heavy burden of fears, apprehensions, suspicions, and agitations, bemoaning himself with every sort of wail and lamentation. It is not man, nor fate, nor occasion, nor himself that he blames, but God, to whom he attributes everything. From God, he says, a heaven-sent stream of catastrophe has come pouring down upon him. He is, he thinks, not merely unlucky but hateful to the gods, and therefore is being chastised and punished. Everything he suffers he deserves because of his sin.

Then the atheist, when he is sick, counts up and calls to mind his times of over-eating and over-drinking, irregularities in his way of living, too heavy exertions, or unaccustomed changes of climate and place. When he gets into political trouble and falls out of favor with the populace, or into bad odor with the governor, he looks for the reason in himself and his surroundings.

> "Where did I err? What did I do?
> What duty did I leave undone?" [14]

But to the superstitious man every infirmity of body, loss of money, death of children, misfortune or failure in public office, are "blows from God," or "assaults of an evil spirit." Consequently, he does not dare help himself or try to find compensation or remedy for what has happened, or stand up against it, lest he should seem to fight against God and resist

---

[13] Fragment 143.
[14] *Golden Verses,* ascribed to Pythagoras, 42.

his chastisement. If he is sick, the physician is shoved out of his house; if in sorrow, the philosopher who comes to advise and comfort him has the door shut on him. "Let me alone, good fellow," says he, "to suffer my punishment, impious and accursed as I am, and hateful to all the gods and divinities!"

When a man who does not believe that gods exist is in grief or great suffering of some other kind, it is possible to wipe away his tears, trim his hair, and remove his cloak; but what words can you use to a superstitious man, or in what way can you help him? He sits outside his house, dressed in sackcloth and girdled with filthy rags. Many a time he rolls naked in the mire, confessing aloud his sins and transgressions. He ate this or drank that, or walked on a road forbidden by the spirit. If he is more fortunate and has but a mild form of superstition, he sits in his house, being fumigated and purified, while the old women, as Bion says, "bring whatever they happen to have and tie and hang it on him, as if he were a peg."

8.   Tiribazus,[15] they tell us, when the Persians were trying to arrest him, being a very strong man, drew his sword and fought desperately. But when they protested and called to him that they were acting by the king's orders, he immediately threw down his sword and gave them his hands to be bound. Is not this like the thing that happens with these men? Other men fight hard against calamities and push their way through troubles, devising for themselves ways of escape and means of averting whatever they dread. But the superstitious man listens to nobody, and says to himself, "This thing you are suffering, poor wretch, comes from Providence and the will of God." So he casts away all hope and submits, and shuns or repulses whoever tries to aid him.

Superstition turns many an ordinary evil into something fatal. Midas of old became dispirited and depressed, apparently by dreams, and grew so despondent that he killed himself by drinking bull's blood. Aristodemus,[16] king of the Messenians in the war against the Spartans, when his dogs began howling like wolves, and wild grass grew up around his paternal hearth, and the diviners showed alarm at the omens, lost all

---

15 Tiribazus was one of the great officers of King Artaxerxes II, who in his old age was convicted of treachery and put to death.

16 Aristodemus led the Messenians in their first war of resistance against the rising power of Sparta.

courage and hope and slew himself with his own hand. It had been better, perhaps, for Nicias,[17] general of the Athenians, to have got rid of his superstition in the way that Midas and Aristodemus did than to be so terrified by the shadow on the moon in an eclipse that he sat still while the enemy was building a wall around him, and finally fell into their hands along with forty thousand men, slaughtered or captured alive, and perished ingloriously. The cutting off of light caused by the earth's passing between the sun and the moon is nothing frightful, nor is the creeping of a shadow over the moon at the proper time in its rotations. What was frightful was the darkness of superstition that fell on the man, confusing and blinding his judgment under circumstances which desperately required clear thinking.

> "Glaucus, see, e'en now deep ocean is with billows tossed and torn,
> and around the Gyrian peaks a dark cloud rises to the sky,
> Signal of storm . . . ;[18]

The pilot, seeing the oncoming tempest, prays, it is true, for deliverance and calls on the Saviour Gods,[19] but while he prays he hauls to his rudder, lowers the yard and furls the big mainsail and so makes his escape from the darkening sea. Hesiod [20] bids the husbandman, before plowing and sowing, "to pray to Zeus of the underworld and to holy Demeter," but with his hand on the plow handle. Homer says [21] that Ajax, when about to fight in single combat with Hector, bade the Greeks pray to the gods for him, and then, while they were praying, put on his armor. Agamemnon, too, after he had commanded his fighters

> "Each one to sharpen well his spear, and brace his shield," [22]

then asked of Zeus

> "Grant me to raze to the ground the palace of Priam," [23]

---

[17] Nicias led the disastrous Athenian expedition to Sicily, towards the end of the Peloponnesian War.

[18] A fragment from the poet Archilochus. See above, *Exile*, n. 23.

[19] The Saviour Gods for seamen were the deified brothers, Castor and Pollux.

[20] *Works and Days*, 465-8.

[21] *Iliad*, VII, 193–5.

[22] Ibid., II, 382.

[23] A loose rendering of *Iliad*, II, 413–5.

for God is the hope of courage, not an excuse for cowardice. Yet the Jews,[24] since it was their Sabbath, sat still in their places while the enemy was setting up ladders and seizing the walls, and did not stir but remained there, held together by their superstition, as though in one wide net.

9. Such then is the way of superstition under circumstances and on occasions called unfavorable and critical, but even under pleasanter conditions it is no better than atheism. The pleasantest times of all to people are the festivals and banquets at the temples, the initiations and Bacchic rites, and prayers and adoration of the gods. Watch the atheist on such occasions, laughing his senseless and sardonic laughter at what is going on, and remarking, perhaps, in an undertone to his friends that men are crazy fools to think that by doing such things they are honoring gods. His scorn, however, gives him no pain.

The superstitious man, on the contrary, yearns to be happy and enjoy himself but cannot.

> "With smoking incense is the city filled;
> With hymns and cries of woe together mingled!" [25]

And so is the soul of the superstitious man. He turns pale under his crown of flowers, is terrified while he sacrifices, prays with a faltering voice, scatters incense with trembling hands, and all in all proves how mistaken was the saying of Pythagoras that we are at our best when approaching the gods. For that is the time when the superstitious are most miserable and most woebegone, approaching, as they do, the halls and shrines of the gods as though they were dens of bears, or holes of serpents, or lurking places of monsters of the deep.

10. I am therefore surprised when people say that atheism is impiety and do not say that superstition is. Anaxagoras [26] was tried for impiety because he said the sun was a stone, though no one called the Cimmerians [27] impious because they were sure there was no sun at all. What do you say?

---

[24] The reference seems to be to the taking of Jerusalem either by Pompey in 63 B.C., or by Antony in 38 B.C.

[25] Sophocles, *Oedipus Rex*, 4.

[26] Anaxagoras, philosopher and astronomer, was banished from Athens on a charge of impiety. See above, *Pericles*, ch. 4.

[27] For Homer's account of the Cimmerians, see *Odyssey*, XI, 13-19.

Is a man wicked who thinks there are no gods? Then are not the notions of one who thinks they are what the superstitious say they are far more wicked? For my part I should much rather have men say of me that I was never born at all and that there was no Plutarch than say "Plutarch is an inconstant, fickle man, easily made angry, vindictive over accidents, fretted by trivialities. If you invite others to dinner and omit him, or if you are busy and do not call at his door, or fail to speak to him when you meet him, he will clutch you around the body and bite you through, or he will seize your small child and beat it to death, or he will turn the animal he owns into your crops, and spoil your harvest."

When Timotheus at Athens was singing a hymn to Artemis and calling her

> "Ecstatic, prophetic, frantic, demented,"

Cinesias the song-writer stood up from among the audience and cried, "May you have a daughter like that!" But in fact superstitious people do imagine things like that and worse about Artemis.

> "Whether hastening from a strangled corpse,[28]
> Or from watching a woman in childbed pain,
> Whether come from wherever a dead man lies,
> Defiled thou hast entered this shrine,
> Or whether from where the three roads meet
> Thou are drawn hither for cleansing rites,
> Since thou wast near to the murderer." [29]

No more suitable than these are the ideas they have about Apollo, about Hera, about Aphrodite. They tremble with horror at all of them.

What did Niobe say about Leto [30] so blasphemous as that which superstition makes silly folk believe about her, namely that because Niobe exulted over her, she had the wretched woman's

> "Six daughters and six sons in blooming youth,"

[28] These lines, in an old Doric dialect, have come down in various forms. They are perhaps taken from some ritual chant used in the worship of Artemis.

[29] Cruelties like these were actually attributed to divinities in some tales of Greek mythology.

[30] Niobe, mother of twelve, boasted that she was at least the equal of Leto, who had borne but two children, the gods Apollo and Artemis. Thereupon every one of her children was shot dead by the arrows of Leto's son and daughter.

shot dead? So greedy was she to make others suffer, and so unforgiving! If the goddess was really angry and hated effrontery, resented being maligned, and did not smile at human ignorance and blindness but detested it, she should have shot those who falsely ascribed to her such cruelty and spite, and repeated and recorded such stories.

We condemn the rage of Hecuba as something barbarous and savage when she says,

> "I would I might eat his liver,
> Grinding it with my teeth." [31]

But the superstitious think that if anyone eats sprats or anchovies, the Syrian goddess [32] gnaws at his shinbones, inflames his body with sores, and withers up his liver.

11. Is it then wicked for a man to tell evil things of the gods, but not wicked to believe them? Or is it the belief that makes the words of the slanderer offensive? We consider slander a sign of hostility, and those who speak ill of us we regard as our enemies, because we think they believe ill of us. And you see what kind of beliefs the superstitious have about the gods—that they are hasty, faithless, fickle, revengeful, cruel, and quick to take offense—whence it must follow that a superstitious man both hates and fears them. How can he help it, when he thinks that the worst of his troubles have come to him through them, and will come through them again? Hating and fearing the gods, he is then their enemy. But even though he fears them, he worships them, offers sacrifices to them, and spends time in their temples. Yet this is not so strange, for people pay homage to tyrants, curry favor with them, and erect gold statues to them, while silently hating them and "shaking their heads." [33] Hermolaus [34] was an attendant on Alexander, Pausanias one of Philip's bodyguard, and Chaereas one of Caligula's, yet each of them undoubtedly said, as he followed his lord's train,

> "Vengeance I surely would take, if I had the power."

---

[31] Homer, *Iliad,* XXIV, 212.

[32] This is the Lydian goddess Cybele, who was known in Greece as early as the fifth century B.C. and later had her worshipers in Rome.

[33] A phrase from Sophocles, *Antigone,* 291.

[34] Hermolaus, Pausanias, and Chaereas were all guilty of taking part in conspiracies to kill their sovereigns.

The atheist thinks there are no gods, the superstitious man wishes there were none, but believes in them unwillingly because he is afraid not to believe. And as Tantalus [35] would be glad to get out from under the rock suspended over him, so would the superstitious man rejoice to be rid of the fear by which he feels as oppressed as Tantalus by his rock. He would call the state of the atheist happy, because it is a state of liberty. So as things are, the atheist will have nothing to do with superstition, but the superstitious man by choice would be an atheist. Yet he is too weak-minded to believe about the gods what he would like to believe.

12. Again, atheism was in no way responsible for superstition, whereas superstition supplied the seed from which atheism sprang, and when it appeared, furnished it with an excuse, not, indeed, a true or a sound one, but one not devoid of plausibility. For it was not because the atheists had discovered anything faulty in the heavens, or inharmonious or disorderly in the stars, or in the seasons, or in the revolutions of the moon, or in the movements of the sun about the earth, the "makers of day and night," or in the growth of living things, or of crops, that they decided against the existence of gods in the universe. But it was the ridiculous acts and emotions of superstition, its phrases and gesticulations, magic spells and incantations, runnings hither and yon, drum-beatings, impure purifications, and obscene consecrations, its barbaric and uncouth penances and self-abasements at shrines—it was these things that gave some men an excuse to say it was better there should be no gods at all than gods who took pleasure in receiving such worship, gods so arrogant, so petty, and so quickly offended.

13. Would it not have been better for the Gauls and the Scythians to have had no idea or image or record of gods at all, than to believe there were gods who delighted in the blood of human slaughter, and regarded it as the most perfect sacrifice and holiest rite? And, again, would it not have profited the Carthaginians to have taken Critias or Diagoras [36] for their lawgiver at the beginning, and believed in no god or divinity, rather than sacrifice such victims as they used to offer to Cronos?

---

[35] For revealing secrets entrusted to him by Zeus, Tantalus was punished in the lower world in various ways. Among other torments he had a huge rock suspended over his head, forever threatening to crush him.

[36] Critias and Diagoras were famous fifth-century atheists. Human sacrifices were offered by the Carthaginians to their gods as late as the time of Christ.

It was not, as Empedocles described it in his attack on men who sacrificed living beings,

> "Changed in form is the son beloved, whom the father,
> Praying, lifts up and stabs. Poor fool!"

But with their eyes open, and knowingly they offered their own children, and childless persons would buy babies from the poor and slaughter them like so many lambs or young birds. The mother stood by, without a tear or a moan, for if she uttered one moan or shed one tear, she had to forfeit the price they gave her and the child would be sacrificed all the same. The whole place in front of the god's statue was filled with the din of flutes and drums, so that the sound of wailing should not be audible.

Suppose the Typhons [37] or the giants had driven out the gods and were now reigning over us. What sacrifices other than these would they wish, or what other rites would they demand? Amnestris, wife of Xerxes,[38] had twelve men buried alive as offerings on her behalf to Hades, the god who Plato says is humane and wise and rich, controlling the souls of the dead by persuasion and reason, whence he has the name of Hades.[39] Xenophanes, the philosopher, on seeing the Egyptians beating their breasts and mourning at their festivals, gave them sensible advice. "If these beings are gods," he said, "do not mourn for them; if men, do not sacrifice to them."

14. But no malady is so variable, so charged with emotion, so compounded of ideas opposed to and conflicting with one another, as superstition. We should try, therefore, to avoid it and choose a way that is safe and wholesome, not like men who run headlong, wildly back and forth to escape an attack of highwaymen or of wild beasts or a fire, and stumble into pathless wildernesses full of pitfalls and precipices. For in that way some who try to get clear of superstition fall into a hard and stubborn atheism, and pass by the true religion which lies between.

---

37 On Typhon, see *Isis and Osiris*, chs. 49 ff. The Giants in Greek mythology represented the brutish and irrational powers in nature, which were overcome and expelled from Olympus by the gods of intelligence and world order, led by Zeus.

38 This story is told by Herodotus, *Histories*, XII, 114.

39 An attempt to derive the name of Hades from an old Greek verb, *hadein*, to please.

The Tardiness of God's Punishments [1]

2. PATROCLEAS said: "The delays of God and his slowness in punishing the wicked seem to me very extraordinary. For a long time I have disliked hearing those words of Euripides, [2]

'He lingers; such is the nature of the gods above.'

For indeed it is not right for God to be sluggish in his dealings with the wicked, who are themselves neither sluggish nor dilatory in doing mischief, but are impelled to commit crime by swift and passionate impulses. Certainly, as Thucydides [3] says, 'it is the vengeance which follows close on iniquity which puts a prompt stop to the career of men who are making great profits out of successful villainy.' There is no obligation like that to do justice. When postponed it weakens all the hopes of the person wronged and leaves him wretched, and heightens the boldness and recklessness of the wrongdoer; whereas punishments that confront immediately all acts of lawlessness are checks also on future crime and may bring great encouragement to the victims. . . .

"What good was the punishment of Aristocrates to the Messenians who were killed before it happened? . . . This, I think, and nothing else is what wicked men tell themselves when encouraging themselves to commit crimes, namely, that the fruit of their knavery is ripe that moment and foreseeable, and the punishment will come late, long after they have had their enjoyment."

3. As Patrocleas finished speaking, Olympichus plunged into the argument. "How strange, Patrocleas," he said, "is the procrastination and

---

1 This dialogue was composed at Delphi, during one of Plutarch's stays there as a priest of Apollo. The persons conversing with him are his brother Timon, and two friends, Patrocleas and Olympichus.
2 *Orestes*, 420.   3 *History of the Peloponnesian War*, III, 38, 1.

tardiness of the gods in these matters, since by their dilatoriness they destroy belief in providence. And the fact that calamity does not fall on the wicked at once after every misdeed, but only long afterward, allows them to class it as a piece of bad luck, call it an accident, not a punishment, and profit not at all by it. They are sore at what happens to them, but they do not repent of what they did. It is as with a horse; the lash and spur that follow immediately on his blunder or disobedience correct and recall him to his duty, but all the whipping and loud shouting which come later seem to him to be for some other reason than to teach him, and hence they pain without educating him. . . . So I cannot see what good there is in these so-called mills of the gods which grind so slow and leave justice obscured, and destroy all fear of evil doing."

4. When he stopped and I was pondering what he had said, Timon spoke up. "Shall I," he asked, "cap their questioning now with a problem of mine, or shall I let you first work on theirs for a while?" "Why," said I, "let in a third wave to drown my reply, if I am not able to drive back the first two, or to find an escape from their accusations?

"But let us begin as if standing on our hearthstone shrines and feeling the ancient reverence for divinity which is felt also by the philosophers in the Academy, and not presume to argue over these things. For it is better for men who know no music to descant on musical subjects and for those who never saw a war to talk of arms than for us, who are but mortal men, to try to penetrate the ways of gods and spirits, like persons with no knowledge of the arts trying to grasp the mind of artists through fanciful guesses as to their probable meaning. It is not for a layman to understand a physician's reason why he did not operate earlier but later, or why he did not cauterize yesterday but did today. Nor is it easy or safe for a mortal to say anything of God save that he knows best the time to cure a man of his evil and administers his punishment as a medicine to each. It is not the same amount for everyone nor is it given at the same time, nor is it the same medicine. . . . What wonder then, when the actions of men are so hard for us to comprehend, that it is not easy for us to say why the gods visit their punishments on sinners sometimes late and sometimes soon.

5. "I say this, however, not as an excuse for running away from argument, but to win your consent that our discussion may keep its eyes fixed on its goal while proceeding bravely to find a reasonable solution to the

difficulty. First of all, consider this, that God, according to Plato, when he set himself in the midst of the world as a pattern of all that is good, implanted human virtue, which in some measure is like himself, in those who were able to follow him. . . . Now there is no greater joy that a man can get from God than by studying and imitating the goodness and beauty in him, to become himself established in virtue. Therefore God inflicts his punishments on the wicked without haste, though in due course of time, not because he is afraid of committing an error or of repenting if he should punish swiftly, but because he would cure us of brutality and cruelty in punishing, and teach us that we should not in anger, at the top of our heat and excitement, when our temper outruns our judgment, fall on persons who have injured us as if we were satisfying our hunger and thirst, but should copy his gentleness and forbearance, resort to justice duly and in order, but grant time to allow for a little repentance.

"It is not, as Socrates said, so bad for a drunkard to tumble into muddy water and drink it as it is for one whose mind is turbid and fouled with anger and rage, before it settles and becomes clear again, to wreak vengeance on the body of a relative and kinsman. . . . The words of men when recalled to our minds, and their acts when reported to us, can temper in us the harshness and violence of our passion. How much more then ought we, as we behold God, with whom there is no fear or remorse for any of his deeds, deferring nevertheless his punishments and biding his time, to be slow ourselves to act in such matters, and view as an aspect of divine virtue the patience and long-suffering of which God gives us an example. By his punishment he reforms a few, but by his tardiness to punish he helps and admonishes many.

6. "In the second place, consider this, that human punishments contemplate only inflicting pain in return for an injury received, and making the offender suffer severely. Beyond that they do not go, which is the reason why they chase after wrongdoers, like barking dogs, and hunt down wrongs as soon as committed. But God, apparently, when he takes a sick soul into his justice, scrutinizes the emotions in it, whether they give evidence of an inclination to repent, and he grants time to those whose wickedness is not unmixed with good or incorrigible. . . . So he does not inflict punishments on all in the same way. The incurable soul he lops off quickly and removes altogether from life, since the continuance of its existence in wickedness is extremely harmful to others and most harmful

of all to itself. But to those whose errors are probably a result of ignorance of the good rather than of choice of the vicious, he grants time to change, though if they remain obdurate, he punishes them too. He has no fear of their escaping him.

"Think how often the character and life of a man change! . . . Suppose someone had killed Miltiades [4] when early in life he was a tyrant in the Chersonese, or had caught and murdered Cimon when he was committing incest with his sister, or had banished Themistocles from Athens when he was carousing and rioting through the agora, as, later, Alcibiades was banished, should we not have lost Marathon, the Eurymedon, and lovely Artemisium?—-

> 'Where the sons of Athens laid
> The famed foundations of their freedom.' [5]

"For great natures produce nothing puny. The vigor in them is too intense to lie still, and they toss about on a surging sea until at length they arrive at a stable and settled character. A person with no experience in agriculture would not choose a piece of ground which he saw all overrun with brush and weeds, infested with wild beasts, and soggy with streams and mire, but to one who has learned how to recognize and judge these things they are proofs of the strength, fertility, and richness of the soil. So great natures may blossom out at first in many strange and odious ways, and we, annoyed by their unpleasantness, think we must check them immediately and make an end of them. But the wiser judge, who discerns the goodness and nobility behind their misbehavior, waits for age, which is the season of reason and virtue, to come to their rescue, when their nature will produce its proper fruit.

7. "This too on the same point. Do you not think that some Greeks have done well to copy the Egyptian law which prescribes that if a woman with child is sentenced to die, she shall be reprieved until the child is born?" "Most certainly," they said. "Then," said I, "though a man cannot bear children, yet if he is able, with time, to bring to light some secret

---

[4] Miltiades was the general under whom the Athenian army defeated the invading host of Persians at Marathon, in 490 B.C. His son, Cimon, completely destroyed the Persian fleet in or about 468 B.C. Themistocles was responsible for the building of the Athenian fleet which defended the approaches to Athens and later won the victory of Salamis. See above, *Themistocles,* chs. 12 ff.

[5] Pindar, Fragment 77.

scheme or conspiracy, or to discover and reveal some hidden peril, or to offer some wholesome advice, or to invent something very important, is it not better that he should be useful and wait a while for his punishment than be summarily executed? It seems so to me," I said. "And to us too," said Patrocleas. "Think carefully," I went on. "If Dionysius [6] at the beginning of his tyranny had suffered according to his deserts, not a Greek would have settled in Sicily, which was being ravaged by Carthaginians. . . .

"God evidently has made use of some wicked men as popular chastisers of other wicked men, and then has destroyed them. I think he does that with most tyrants. For as the gall of a hyena and the spit of a seal and other substances from vile monsters contain something that heals diseases, so God sends to people who need sharp punishment a harsh and implacable tyrant or a stern and oppressive governor, and does not remove the cruel tormentor until he has cured and purified the nation of its sickness. . . . The farmer never cuts out the thorn until it injures the asparagus, and the Libyans never burn the dry stalks until they have collected from them all the laudanum. So why is it strange if God does not pull up the tough and troublesome root of a renowned and royal race before he has reaped from it its proper fruit? For it would have been better for the Phocians to lose ten thousand of Iphitus' horses and oxen, and for still greater sums of gold and silver to vanish at Delphi than that Odysseus [7] and Asclepius should not be born, and all the others who after being wicked rascals became good and great benefactors to men. . . .

9. "I am saying all this," I went on, "as I think rightly, on the hypothesis that there is some delay in the punishment of the wicked. . . . But wickedness creates pain and punishment for itself; not at some later time but in the very moment of its pride it pays the penalty of wrongdoing. . . . It is an accomplished builder of a wretched and shameful life, full of terrors and regrets and bitter suffering and never-ceasing anxieties. Yet there are people like children who on seeing rogues in the theaters in golden

---

[6] Dionysius I of Syracuse (c.430–367 B.C.) was the tyrant who built up the Greek settlements in Sicily and drove back the Carthaginians.

[7] Odysseus stole the horses of Rhesus, king of the Thracians, not of Iphitus, king of the Phocians (*Iliad*, X, 474-81). Phlegyas, grandfather of Asclepius, was said to have once set fire to Apollo's temple at Delphi, and for that and other crimes was put in the depths of Tartarus among the most hardened criminals. *Aeneid*, VI, 618-20

tunics and purple cloaks, dancing with crowns on their heads, admire and look on them often as blissfully happy, until they see them goaded and scourged, with fire rising from their gay and costly garments. Thus many a wicked man, with trappings of great houses and distinguished offices and authority, is being punished without anyone knowing it, until he is found murdered or thrown down a precipice—which indeed one would not call punishment so much as an end and completion of his punishment.

"Herodicus the Selymbrian fell ill of consumption, an incurable disease, but was the first man to combine gymnastics with medicine, Plato [8] says. However, in so doing he only made death last a long while both for himself and for others who were sick in the same way. So wicked men who congratulate themselves on escaping immediate trouble, receive a longer and not a slower punishment, not later but more spun out. It is not after they are old that they are punished but they grow old being punished. When I say 'a long time,' I am speaking in terms of ourselves. For to the gods every period of human life is as nothing; and to say it is 'now, not thirty years ago,' is the same as to say it is 'in the afternoon, not in the morning' that the criminal is to be tortured or hanged. In truth the man is shut up in his life as in a jail that allows no movement or escape, while yet he feasts and is full of business, receives gifts and favors, and plays at games, like the men who play dice or checkers in a prison, while the rope dangles over their heads.

10. "Doubtless men condemned to death do not seem to be punished until the executioner has chopped off their heads, and one who has drunk hemlock but is still walking around and waiting for the heaviness to appear in his legs seems not to be punished until he lies unconscious in the rigidity of death—that is, if we regard the last moment of punishment as the only punishment, and ignore the sufferings in between, the fears, apprehensions, and regrets, with which every wicked man is tormented for his misdeeds. As if we did not call a fish caught that has swallowed a hook until we see him cut up and baked by the cooks! . . . For visions in dreams and apparitions by day, oracles and descents underground,[9] all objects that appear to be sent by God, raise tempests and horrors in the souls of the guilty. They say that Apollodorus in his sleep

---

[8] *Republic*, III, 406.
[9] The priestess at Delphi, to receive the message of the god, went down into a special chamber beneath the temple floor. See below, *The Passing of the Oracles*, n. 17.

once saw himself being flayed by the Scythians and then boiled, and that his heart cried out to him from the kettle and said, 'I am the reason you suffer all this.' Again he saw his daughters running in a circle around him, their bodies on fire and blazing. And Hipparchus, the son of Pisistratus, shortly before his death, saw Aphrodite throwing blood out of a bottle in his face. . . .

11. "Hence if nothing befell the soul after death and that event was the end of both rewards and punishments, one might say that divinity was treating easily and indulgently those malefactors whom he punished promptly by slaying them. . . . For wherever avarice, empty voluptuousness, pure hatred, ill-will and malice dwell together, there, if you look, you will find superstition skulking, and weakness in the face of difficulty, and cowardly terror of death, and sudden collapses of energy, and pride in glory obtained by false pretenses. . . . When a scoundrel does restore something left him in trust, or goes security for an acquaintance, or serves his country honorably and creditably, he is at once regretful and vexed at what he has done, because his mind is forever wavering and shifting. . . . For my part, if it is right for me to express an opinion, I believe that there is no need for either God or man to punish evildoers but that their lives are sufficient, all distraught and ruined as they are by their own villainy.

12. "But see," I said, "has not my talk run on too long?" "Perhaps," said Timon, "in view of what is ahead of us and the length of what there is still to say. For now, like an enemy biding his time, I am raising our last difficulty, since the first have been fairly well disposed of. Euripides is outspoken in his indictment of the gods for laying the sins of the fathers on the children. Think whether we who are silent should not blame them too. For if the guilty have already paid their penalty, there is no need of further punishing the innocent, since it is not fair to punish even an offender twice for the same crimes. And if out of leniency the gods have neglected punishing the guilty but later exact the penalty from persons who are blameless, they are hardly justified in atoning for their tardiness by a subsequent act of injustice. . . .

"Not even the devoted lovers of Alexander, among whom I am one, can justify his laying waste the town of Branchidae [10] and slaughtering

---

[10] This town, also called Didyma, was a few miles from the important city of Miletus in Asia Minor. In his *Alexander,* Plutarch makes no mention of this slaughter.

its inhabitants of every age because their forefathers had once betrayed the temple at Miletus. Agathocles, tyrant of Syracuse, when the Corcyraeans asked why he was plundering their island, laughed mockingly at them and said, 'Because, by Zeus, your forefathers entertained Odysseus.' And when the Ithacans also protested because his soldiers were carrying off their flocks, 'Your king,' he said, 'came to our island and put out the eyes of our shepherd.' [11] . . .

"Now what is reasonable or just in all this? We do not approve of the Thracians who to this day beat their wives to punish them for their treatment of Orpheus,[12] nor of the barbarians along the Po, who wear mourning in grief for Phaethon,[13] they say. That seems to me even more ridiculous since the people who were living at the time took no notice of Phaethon's disaster and now, five or ten generations after it, they have begun changing their clothes and sorrowing for him. However, this is merely folly, nothing terrible nor irremediable. But the wrath of the gods, why should it at first go underground, like some rivers, and then long afterwards break on other men's heads, bringing with it the extreme penalty of death?"

13.   He stopped but I was afraid that he would begin again and produce more and weirder strange stories, so I asked him at once, "Well, do you think that everything you have said is true? . . . Most of your instances sound like myths and fiction. But recall the feast of Theoxenia [14] which we lately celebrated, and the noble portion which was borne away and proclaimed to be the share of the descendants of Pindar. How reverent and charming an act you thought that was!" "Who would not," he said, "have been delighted at that graceful tribute, so ancient, simple, and Greek, unless he had what Pindar [15] himself called, 'a black heart, forged at a cold flame'?"

"Then I shall refrain," I said, "from mentioning the similar procla-

---

11 The reference is to Odysseus' putting out the eye of the Cyclops, Polyphemus. *Odyssey,* IX, 377-90.

12 One of the myths about Orpheus told of his being killed by Thracian women in a religious frenzy.

13 On Phaethon, see above, *Letter of Consolation,* n. 2.

14 The Theoxenia at Delphi was a spring feast at which Apollo himself was supposed to be present. Pindar had been the greatest of Boeotian poets. Hence the honor paid to his descendants.

15 Fragment 123.

mation made in Sparta, to honor 'the descendants of the Lesbian singer,' in memory of old Terpander.[16] For it is the same kind of story. As for you, I know you think yourself above all other Boeotians, because you come of the race of the Opheltiadae; [17] and among the Phocians you are superior because of Daiphantus. . . ." "You have," he said, "reminded us of high distinctions, quite proper for philosophers." "Stop then, sir," said I, "your rancorous accusations of the gods and do not resent the fact that some descendants of wicked and vicious parents are punished, or else stop celebrating and praising the honors paid to nobility of birth. For if we wish to preserve rewards for an ancestry of valor, we cannot, in logic, think that punishment for their wrongdoing should be cut short, but must agree that it should last as long as the reward, and requite them all in turn according to their deserts. So a man who is happy to see the descendants of Cimon honored in Athens, but distressed and indignant at the banishment of the descendants of Lachares [18] and Aristion, is either too soft-hearted and easygoing, or, more probably, too censorious and critical of God. One moment he blames him if the sons of an unjust and bad father seem to be prospering, and again he blames him if the race of the wicked is cut off and disappears from the earth, finding fault with God alike when the children of a good father suffer adversity and when the children of a bad father do. . . .

15. "However, the popular guilt of whole cities is clearly a subject for justice. For a city is one continuous body like an animal. It does not, in its changing ages, cease to be itself or become something different again and again with time, but is always alike in its feelings and peculiar to itself, and always takes blame or praise for everything it does or has done as a community, as long as the community acts and binds itself together in its web as a unit and maintains itself so. . . .

16. "And if a city is one continuing body, so certainly is a race of men, starting from one beginning, and carrying on a power and a community of spirit which grows with it. And what is thus begotten is not like a piece of handicraft, separate from what begot it, for it sprang from it, was

---

[16] Terpander, a poet and musician of the seventh century B.C., came from the island of Lesbos but spent much of his time in Sparta.

[17] The Opheltiadae were the royal family of Nemea, in the northern Peloponnesus.

[18] On Lachares, see below, *Isis and Osiris*, n. 13.

not made by it. Thus it has and contains within itself a part of that from which it came, whether it is deservedly punished or whether it is honored. If it did not seem too frivolous of me, I should say that it was a greater injustice when the Athenians melted down the statue of Cassander,[19] and when the Syracusans cast out the body of Dionysius, than when they penalized their posterity; for the statue had nothing in it of the nature of Cassander, and the soul of Dionysius had abandoned his body. Whereas in Nisaeus, Apollocrates, Antipater, Philip, and others, similarly sons of wicked fathers, there had grown up and still existed the dominating force of their fathers, not dormant or idle, but something by which they lived and grew and ordered their lives and thought. Nor is it surprising or strange if, as the offspring of such parents, they felt as they did. . . ."

17.   While I was still speaking, Olympichus interrupted me. "It looks," he said, "as if in this argument you were assuming a very important hypothesis, that is, the duration of the soul." "And you," I said, "are granting it, or, rather, have granted it. Our discussion from the beginning up to now has proceeded on the assumption that God awards to us what accords with our deserts." "Then," he said, "do you think it follows from the fact that God watches over us and allots to us everything in our lives that therefore our souls last on, either altogether indestructible or at least surviving after death for a time?" "No, my friend," I answered. "But is God so trivial and such a waster of energy that if we had nothing divine in us, nothing in the least resembling his permanence and strength, and were like the leaves which, as Homer [20] says, are all soon withered and gone, he would give such thought to us, like the women who tend and cherish their gardens of Adonis in little pots? Would he plant ephemeral souls in soft flesh, with no firm root in life, to bloom and then, suddenly, to perish on any chance excuse?

"Disregarding, if you please, the other gods, consider just our own god here. Does it seem to you likely that if he knew that the souls of the dead vanished quickly away and breathed out from our bodies like mist or smoke, he would order so much propitiation of what is gone and such great gifts and honors paid to the dead, thereby deluding and cheating

---

[19] On Cassander and the Athenians, see above, *Demosthenes*, n. 22; ch. 31.
[20] *Iliad*, VI, 146-9.

us who trust him? For my part, I would never deny the immortality of the soul until someone like Heracles [21] stole the tripod of the priestess and overthrew and destroyed the oracle. For as long as we have so many wise oracles even in our time, like those, they say, that Corax of Naxos [22] received, it is impious to declare that the soul dies. . . .

18. "One and the same reason," I said, "confirms both the providence of God and the duration of the soul, and it is not possible to admit one if you deny the other. And if the soul lives on after death, it is still more probable that it then receives both punishments and rewards. For throughout this life the soul is contending like an athlete and when the struggle is finished, it obtains whatever it deserves. What punishments and what rewards for things done in this life the soul receives there, alone by itself, are nothing to us who are living. We have no belief in them and they are hidden from us. But the penalties that pass on down through the children and the family and are plainly visible to us here are a restraint and curb on many an evildoer. I have a story which I lately heard which indicates that there is no punishment more humiliating or more painful than the sight of one's offspring suffering for one's sins, and that, if the soul of a godless ruffian looking back to earth were to see, not his statues overturned or his dignities reversed, but his children, friends, and kindred in great trouble on account of him and suffering his punishments, no one again could persuade him to be unscrupulous and wicked and despise the honors of Zeus. But I fear you would think it only a myth. . . .

19. "Bion [23] indeed says that in punishing the children of the wicked God is more absurd than a physician who, when a father or a grandfather fell ill, gave his medicine to his son or grandson. That situation is rather different, though in some respects comparable. For one man by taking treatment cannot cure the disease of another, and one man's sore eyes and fever are not made better by seeing another man plastered with ointment. But the punishments of malefactors are inflicted in public because by

---

[21] See below, *The Passing of the Oracles,* n. 13.

[22] Plutarch goes on to explain that Corax of Naxos was the man who killed the poet Archilochus in battle and was at first ordered into banishment by the Delphic oracle, but later at his entreaty was allowed to go down to Taenarum and sacrifice to Archilochus' spirit.

[23] This Bion was probably the third-century lecturer who preached a cheerful and cynical type of atheism.

seeing justice accomplished in due order other men may learn self-restraint from their sufferings. So Bion was mistaken in finding in his comparison a real resemblance to what we are looking for.

"A man may, however, fall ill with a troublesome but not incurable disease, and then through weakness and lack of self-control fail to support his body in resisting the malady and die. His son does not seem to be sick, but he has a tendency to the same disease. A good physician or relative or trainer or master, learning of it, will restrict him to a plain way of living, forbid rich food, sweetmeats, drinks, and women, give him tonics regularly, make him work hard at exercises, and thus expel and scatter the little seed of serious illness, not permitting it to develop into something big. Do we not ourselves urge all who come of diseased fathers or mothers to watch and look out for themselves, and not be careless but get rid at once of the first sign of trouble coming in from outside, taking it while it is easy to throw off and has not a firm hold on them?" "We certainly do," they said.

". . . Is it then a duty," I asked, "to tend and guard the child of a sickly body, but let one who has an innate bent for evil grow and expand his character in his youth, and wait until he openly displays his feelings, 'and reveals the malignant fruit of his heart,' as Pindar [24] says?

20. ". . . The cubs of bears and the young of wolves and apes at once reveal their inborn characters without disguise or concealment, but the nature of a man when confronted by our customs and beliefs and laws is often to conceal his vices and imitate nobility, so that either he ends by actually wiping away and cleansing himself of the inward stain of his ugly disposition, or else for a long while he goes on secretly practicing his villainy under cover, as it were, and deceiving us who take little notice of all his malevolent pricks and stings. For we believe that men are lawbreakers only when they are breaking the law, bad only when they are acting impudently, and cowards only when they are running away. As if a silly man should suppose that scorpions had stings only when they stung, and vipers venom only when they bit! The evil man is evil not only when he breaks out into crime; he has the wickedness in him from the first and seizing his means and opportunity, the thief proceeds to steal and the tyrant to violate the law.

---

[24] Fragment 211.

"However, God is not ignorant of any man's nature and disposition, for he observes the soul more than he does the body, nor does he always wait to punish until violence has actually been done and blasphemy spoken and lewdness committed. For he is not avenging himself on the wrong-doer for any harm that he himself has suffered, nor is he angry with the brigand for violence done to himself, nor does he hate the adulterer for an insult to himself, but often he punishes the adulterer, the money-grabber, and the wrongdoer to cure them and eradicate the evil in them, as if it were epilepsy, before it takes possession of them.

21. "But a few minutes ago we were incensed because the gods were slow and late in chastising the wicked, and now we are so because they curb and punish the nature and disposition of some sinners before they commit crime. We accuse them, not knowing that many times a villainy planned but as yet secret is worse and more dreadful than one already committed and plain in sight. We cannot comprehend the reasons why it is better to bear with some who have already committed crimes and put a stop to others who are only contemplating them. . . .

"So too the gods do not always visit the sins of the parents on the children,[25] but if a good son comes of a worthless father, as a healthy son may of a father who is diseased, he is exempted from the penalty inflicted on his family, as if lifted by adoption out of that unfortunate state. But when a young man treads in the footsteps of a criminal line, it is surely just that he should succeed to the punishment of its iniquity, as to a debt attached to his inheritance. Antigonus [26] was not punished for the crimes of Demetrius, nor, among ancient heroes, was Phyleus for Augeas, nor Nestor for Neleus, because though their fathers were wicked, they were virtuous themselves. But justice has pursued those who by nature enjoyed and took kindly to their inherited wickedness, vengeance overtaking them at their approach to sin.

"And the warts, moles, and freckles of the fathers, though not visible on their children, may later reappear on the children of their sons and daughters. A Greek woman who bore a black infant, and was tried for adultery, proved that she was the great-granddaughter of an Ethiopian.

---

[25] Euripides, Fragment 580.
[26] This is Antigonus II (c.320–239 B.C.), the son of Demetrius, whose life by Plutarch is given above. A brave and honest man and a philosopher, Antigonus built up the strength of Macedon again after its years of exhausting wars.

One of the children of Pytho the Thisbean, who died recently and was said to be descended from the Sown-men,[27] had the print of a spear on his body. After all this time it reappeared and started up again, as out of the depths of his likeness to his race. So often the first states and reactions of a soul cover up and hide the sources of its being, but later, in other ways, its nature breaks out and shows its propensity to vice or to virtue." . . .

---

[27] "Sown-men," or *Sparti,* was the name given in Greek mythology to the armed soldiers who sprang from the dragon's teeth which the hero Cadmus sowed in the course of his founding of Thebes. They were all said to be marked with a spear print on their bodies.

The Passing of the Oracles[1]

Persons taking part in the dialogue: Lamprias, Cleombrotus, Didymus, Philip, Demetrius, Ammonius, Heracleon.

1.   THERE is a story, dear Terentius Priscus, that some flocks of eagles and swans once flew in from the farthest ends of the earth towards the center and met at Delphi, at the so-called navel-stone.[2] Later, Epimenides of Phaestus [3] tried to test the story by asking the god about it, but he received a vague and indefinite response. Whereupon he said,

> "So there is no navel-stone, center of earth and ocean;
> And if there is, it's known to gods but hidden from mortals."

In all likelihood the god was simply trying to discourage him from tampering with an ancient myth, as though it were a painting which he was trying to test by touching it.

2.   But shortly before the Pythian games which were held under Callistratus, in our own day,[4] it chanced that two venerable men, coming from opposite ends of the world, also met at Delphi. They were Demetrius the grammarian,[5] on his way home from Britain to Tarsus, and Cleom-

---

[1] This essay in the form of a letter from Plutarch's brother Lamprias to his friend Terentius Priscus is interesting because of the prominent part played by oracles in Greek history and because of Plutarch's own position as priest at the great oracle at Delphi.
[2] Navel, or *omphalos*, was the name given in Greek antiquity to a large stone of a rounded conical shape which was looked on as the center of the locality where it was found. The most famous *omphalos* was that which stood in the forecourt of Apollo's temple at Delphi and was regarded as marking the center of the earth.
[3] Epimenides of Phaestus was a Cretan famed as a religious teacher and miracle-worker.
[4] That is, 83–84 A.D.
[5] This Demetrius may have been the traveler who dedicated two stone tablets now in the museum of York, England.

brotus the Spartan, who had traveled a great deal in Egypt and through the land of the cave dwellers and had sailed beyond the Persian Gulf. He was not a merchant but liked seeing things and accumulating knowledge. He had wealth enough and thought it not important to have more than enough; so he spent his time in that sort of occupation and was compiling a history as material for a philosophy, which would have as its aim a theology, as he called it. He had shortly before visited the shrine of Ammon and, on the whole, had evidently not been much struck by things there.[6] . . .

5. When Ammonius stopped speaking, I said, "I wish you would tell us about the oracle of Ammon, Cleombrotus. For in old times the divinity there had a great reputation, but now it seems to be waning."

As Cleombrotus did not answer and had his eyes fixed on the ground, Demetrius said: "There is no need of asking and speculating about the state of things in Egypt when we see the decline of the oracles in this country, or rather, the complete disappearance of all but one or two. We should be looking for the reasons why these here have grown so feeble. Why mention any others, when in Boeotia, which used to be a land of many tongues because of all its oracles, they have now vanished entirely, just as if they were streams of water and a great drought of prophecy had spread over the land. Nowhere now, except at Lebadia, does Boeotia offer anything to those who want to draw from the wells of prophecy. As for the rest, silence has descended on some and total extinction on others.

"Yet at the time of the Persian Wars Boeotia had many oracles, highly renowned, that at Ptoüm [7] as famous as that of Amphiaräus. . . . The oracle at Tegyrae, the place where they tell us Apollo was born, was flourishing too at that time. Two streams flow by it, one of which the inhabitants still call the Palm and the other the Olive. During the Persian Wars, while Echecrates was priest, the god there foretold victory and strength in war for the Greeks. During the Peloponnesian War, after

---

[6] Lamprias now tells of his meeting with Ammonius, Demetrius, and Cleombrotus outside Apollo's shrine.

[7] Ptoüm was a mountain in Boeotia on which stood a shrine to Apollo. Amphiaräus was a son of Apollo who was swallowed up in the earth as a result of a thunderbolt from Zeus. An oracle commemorated the spot. Tegyrae was a town in Boeotia.

the people of Delos had been driven from their island,[8] an oracle, they say, was brought to them from Delphi, commanding them to find the place where Apollo was born and offer certain sacrifices there. They were surprised to hear this and wondered if it were true that the god had not been born on their island but somewhere else. And then the Delphic priestess sent them another oracle to the effect that a crow would tell them the spot.

"So they went on their way and when they reached Chaeronea they heard the woman innkeeper talking about the oracle to some strangers who were going to Tegyrae. And as the strangers were leaving and saying goodbye to the woman, they called her by her name, which was Crow. Thereupon the Delians understood the oracle and offered sacrifices at Tegyrae, and soon afterward were able to return to Delos. There have been manifestations since at those oracles, but now they have ceased. So it is right to inquire here, at Apollo's temple, into the reasons for the change."

6. By that time we had walked some way from the temple and were at the doors of the Cnidian treasury hall.[9] We went inside and saw sitting and waiting for us there the friends to whose houses we were going. Everywhere it was quiet because it was then the hour for a rub-down, or else for watching the athletes. Demetrius smiled and said to them: " 'Shall I tell you a lie, or give you the truth?' [10] You look to me as if you had nothing in particular to talk about. I see you sitting here entirely at your ease, with your faces all relaxed."

"Yes," replied Heracleon of Megara, "for we are not trying to find out which of the two l's in *ballo* [11] it loses in its future tense, nor from what positives 'worse' and 'better' and 'worst' and 'best' are formed. These and the like abstruse problems may make a face tense and set, but there are others we can consider in a philosophical spirit without knitting our

---

[8] Their expulsion took place in 421 B.C. The island of Delos was the traditional birth-place of Apollo and his sister Artemis.

[9] Around the shrine at Delphi stood a number of small buildings put up by various cities, islands, and other communities, for the storage of their archives or other treasures, and for the use of their citizens when visiting the oracle. The foundation stones of the treasury of the city of Cnidos may still be seen.

[10] Demetrius accosts them with a familiar line from the *Odyssey*, IV, 140.

[11] The verb *ballo*, throw, in its future tense is *balo*.

brows, and look into them calmly without frowning fiercely and growing cross with our companions."

"Then take us in," said Demetrius, "and with us the problem which has just now occurred to us. It is connected with this spot, and since it involves the god it is of interest to everyone. But take care not to knit your brows over it!"

7. When then we had joined them and were seated among them, Demetrius announced the problem. At once the Cynic Didymus, called Planetiades, sprang to his feet, pounded the floor two or three times with his staff, and cried, "Ah, this is a difficult question you have brought us and one calling for deep investigation! You are wondering why with so much wickedness spread everywhere, not only Modesty and Just Indignation have, as Hesiod foretold,[12] forsaken the life of humanity but the Providence of the gods has gathered up its oracles from all lands and departed! On the contrary, I propose you inquire why this oracle here has not also fallen silent and Heracles or some other god has not carried off the tripod,[13] harried as it is now with the shocking and blasphemous questions which people put to the god. Some quiz him as if he were a Sophist, others beg him for information about treasure troves or about legacies or about illegal marriages. Therewith they prove that Pythagoras was quite wrong in saying that men are at their best when they draw near the gods, for they bring to the god in all their nakedness the diseases and turmoils of the soul which they would do well to disown and conceal, even before an older man."

He wanted to say more but Heracleon took hold of his shabby coat [14] and I, who was about the most intimate with him of anyone, said, "O dear Planetiades, stop provoking the god. For he is serene and mild,

'And has been judged most gracious to mortal man,'

as Pindar [15] says. And whether he is the sun, or the lord and father of the sun and of things that lie beyond our sight, he is not likely to refuse

---

[12] *Works and Days,* 199.

[13] There was a legend that Heracles in his rude and ignorant youth tried to seize and carry away the tripod on which the Delphian priestess sat when delivering oracles. There is a representation of this attempt on a frieze now in the museum at Delphi.

[14] A shabby coat would be one mark of a professed Cynic.

[15] Fragment 149.

to speak to men even in our day, when he is the cause of our birth and growth and of our being and our power to think. Nor will Providence, who, like a benign and kindly mother, does everything for us and watches over us, become vindictive at this one point, the prophetic oracles, and take away what she gave us in the beginning, as if there were not more wicked men living then than now. For the population was larger, when the oracles were set up in so many spots around the world. Come, sit down again and make a Pythian truce [16] with wickedness, which you are always out to punish by words every day, and search with us for some other reason for the so-called passing of the oracles. But keep the god gracious and do not vex him!" By saying this I accomplished this much, that Planetiades went out through the door without another word.

8.   We were quiet for a little while and then Ammonius turned to me and said: "But watch what we are doing, Lamprias, and see to it that we do not make the god out as having no part in the change. For the man who thinks that the oracles which have ceased to speak have done so for some other reason, and not by the will of God, gives us ground for suspecting that their origin and continuance were not due to the god but came about in some other way. Yet certainly no other greater or higher power exists able to destroy and wipe out a work of God, which is what prophecy is. I did not like what Planetiades said for several reasons; in particular for the inconsistencies he attributes to the god; how at one time he has him abhorring and disowning evil and at another time admitting it to his presence, as if some king or tyrant shut out wicked men at certain doors and at others let them in and did business with them.

"Now measure and suitability and proportion and entire self-sufficiency are characteristics of the works of the gods. Taking this principle to start with, we should next observe that in the general depopulation which ancient conflicts and wars have brought to nearly all the world, Greece has suffered most, and that now the whole country could scarcely raise three thousand men-at-arms, which is what the one city of Megara sent to fight at Plataea. We should then have a definite basis for correct reasoning. For the god's abandonment of many oracles is nothing but his confirmation of the desolation of Greece. Who would use the oracle if there were one at Tegyrae, as formerly there was, or at Ptoüm, where

---

[16] The Pythian truce was the sacred truce observed by every Greek community during the Pythian games, which were held every four years in Apollo's honor at Delphi.

you now may see a fellow pasturing his herds? As for this oracle here, the oldest in time and the most famous by reputation, they tell us that for a long while it was kept deserted and unapproachable by a terrible beast, a serpent. They do not, however, grasp correctly the reason for its lying unused, but have it quite wrong. It was the desolation which attracted the serpent, and not the serpent which caused the desolation.

"When Greece, by the will of God, was mighty in cities, and the land was filled with men, they employed two prophetesses here, whom they sent down in turn,[17] and a third was selected to be held in reserve. Whereas now there is only one prophetess and we do not protest, for she is sufficient for our needs. There is no fault to be found with the god, for the prophesying we have and continue to have is enough for everyone and sends everyone away with his questions answered. Agamemnon [18] had nine heralds and still had difficulty in keeping the assembly in order because of its size, whereas here, in a few days, you will see one voice reaching everyone in the theater. So, at that time, prophecy required more voices to speak to more people; but now, on the contrary, we should be surprised at the god if he permitted his oracular judgments to flow out wasted, like water, or to echo, like rocks in a wilderness, only the voices of shepherds and their flocks."

9. When Ammonius had finished and I still did not reply, Cleombrotus said to me, "You have then already granted his point, that the god both creates and destroys these oracles?" "Not I," I said. "I maintain that no prophetic shrine or oracle is ever closed by action of the god. He creates and furnishes us with many kinds of good things, but to some of them nature brings corruption and decay; or rather, the matter composing them, which is a form of decay, disintegrates often and destroys the thing created by the higher power. In this way, I think, there come to be later the darkenings and endings of prophetic forces, since, though the god bestows many fair gifts on men, he bestows nothing immortal, and as Sophocles [19] says, 'the gifts of the gods die, though the gods never!' But their presence and power, as the wise men are always saying, we must

[17] The most sacred spot in the temple, where the priestess sat over a cleft in the rock, was on a lower level than that of the temple floor. She went down to it by steps in one corner.

[18] *Iliad*, II. 96.

[19] Fragment 311.

look for in nature and matter and ascribe the origin of those things to God, as is right. . . ."

10. "That is true," said Cleombrotus, "but to grasp and define how and to what extent Providence should be regarded as acting is hard. Some make the god out simply as the cause of nothing, and others as the cause of everything together, and they all stray far off the proper balance. Those who say that Plato,[20] by discovering the element underlying all created objects, which they now call 'matter' or 'nature,' freed the philosophers from many grave dilemmas are correct. But in my opinion those who set a race of demigods between gods and men solved more and graver problems, for they discovered something that in its way linked our whole community together. Their doctrine may have come from the magi who follow Zoroaster, or it may be Thracian from the time of Orpheus, or Egyptian or Phrygian, as one might suppose on seeing so many observances connected with death and mourning taken from the rites of both those countries, mingled with the ceremonies we perform at our obsequies here. Among the Greeks, Homer seems to use both names indiscriminately and to speak at times of the gods themselves as demigods. Hesiod was the first to outline clearly and definitely the four races of rational beings: gods, then demigods, then heroes, and finally, men. On that hypothesis, apparently, he worked out his idea of transmigration, the golden race changing one by one into many good demigods and demigods into heroes.

"Others believe in a different kind of transmigration of bodies and spirits alike. As we see water generated from earth, air from water, and fire from air, as the substance of them moves upward, so, we are told, the better souls of men win a transformation into heroes, and from heroes into demigods. And a few of the demigods in the long course of time through virtue become purified and take on complete divinity.[21] But in some cases it turns out that they cannot control themselves but give way to weakness and hence are clothed again in mortal bodies and lead a dim and murky life, like vapor.

---

[20] As, for example, in the *Timaeus,* 48 ff.

[21] Heracles, Minos, Castor, and Pollux are examples in Greek mythology of human beings who rose to the ranks of heroes and demigods and even in some cases to full divinity.

11. "Hesiod also thinks that with the passage of certain cycles of time death comes even to the demigods, and speaking in the person of a Naiad, he suggests what that time may be.

" 'Nine generations long is the life of the cawing crow,
   Nine generations of robust men. And four crows' lives
   Make up the life of a stag; three stags the full age of a raven.
   Nine lives of a raven make up the life of a phoenix; ten lives
   Of a phoenix have we, fairhaired nymphs, the daughters of Zeus, aegis-
      bearer'. . . .[22]

12. "I hear things like these," said Cleombrotus, "on many sides. . . . And whether the time in which the spirit of a demigod or a hero changes its life is longer or shorter, fixed or indeterminate, no less can it be shown on the testimony of ancient wisdom that there exist natures in the borderland, as it were, between gods and men, who have the feelings of mortals and undergo necessary changes, but whom it is right for us, after the custom of our fathers, to regard as demigods, to give them that name and revere them.

13. ". . . . So let us not listen to persons who say there are oracles not divinely inspired, or ceremonies and mystic rites in which the gods are not concerned, but on the other hand, let us not fancy that the god has his dwelling at the oracle and is present and taking part in whatever goes on there. Let us assign such duties, as is right, to the ministers of the gods, who act as their servants and scribes, and think of some demigods as stewards of the sacred deities and organizers of their mysteries, and of others as going about as avengers of haughty and wicked behavior. Others still Hesiod [23] addresses very reverently as

'Givers of wealth, possessing therein a privilege of holy kings,'

as if doing good were kingly. Among demigods as among men there are differences of virtue. In some there lingers only a feeble and hazy remnant of irrational impulse as a faint survival, but others have a great deal of it, hard to suppress. Traces and symbols of all these things are preserved and kept alive in many places, scattered here and there through sacrifices and ceremonies and myths. . . .

---

[22] Hesiod, Fragment 183.
[23] *Works and Days,* 123, 126.

15. "As for the many tales they tell and sing about in legends and in hymns, thefts and wanderings of gods, their hidings and flights and servitudes, these were never things done to gods or happening to them. They belonged to the demigods and are remembered because they showed virtue and might. Aeschylus [24] was not speaking piously when he said,

'Holy Apollo, god exiled from heaven.' . . .

"And now let us venture to say, as many have done before us, that when the demigods appointed to take charge of prophecy and oracles fail to do so, the oracles themselves utterly fail, and when the demigods flee or move elsewhere, the oracles lose all their power. But when after a long time the demigods appear again, the oracles, like musical instruments, sound again, since those who speak through them are there and in charge of them."

16. Cleombrotus having finished his remarks, Heracleon said, "There is no profane or unhallowed person here, or one whose ideas of the gods are incompatible with ours. But let us keep watch on ourselves, Philip, lest without our realizing it we make too great and too unwarrantable assumptions during our argument."

"You are right," said Philip, "but which of Cleombrotus' propositions troubles you most?"

"That it is not the gods," said Heracleon, "who preside at oracles, since, properly, the gods are free from cares of earth, but that it is demigods, ministers of the gods, seems to me a reasonable proposition. But to grab handfuls of sins and crimes and god-impelled wanderings out of lines from Euripides, and load them on these demigods, and on top of that to assume they are mortal and die like men, I consider hasty and unwarranted."

At this Cleombrotus asked Philip who the young man was and from where he came. On learning his name and his city, he said, "We realize, Heracleon, that we have drifted into strange arguments. But it is not possible to reach probable truth on great subjects without making use of great hypotheses. And you yourself without realizing it are retracting something you have already granted. For you admit that demigods exist, but by insisting that they are never wicked and never mortal you make

---

[24] *Suppliants*, 214.

them demigods no longer. For how are they different from gods if in substance they are imperishable and in character they are sinless and serene?"

17. As Heracleon pondered over this question in silence, Philip said, "Not only Empedocles, Heracleon, but Plato and Xenocrates and Chrysippus have told us of wicked demigods. Democritus, too, by praying that he might meet with benign spirits showed that he knew of other stubborn spirits with vicious dispositions and impulses.

"As for death among such beings, I once heard a story from a man who was not a fool or a deceiver. He was Epitherses, the father of the orator Aemilianus, whom some of you have heard, and he was a fellow citizen of mine and a teacher of grammar. He said that once, on a voyage to Italy, he was traveling in a ship that carried merchandise and a large number of passengers. It was evening, when near the Echinades Islands [25] the wind dropped and the ship drifting on drew near to Paxi. Most of the passengers were still awake, and many were still sipping their after-dinner wine. Suddenly from the island of Paxi a voice was heard calling loudly for Thamus, so that they were all surprised. For Thamus was an Egyptian pilot, not known by name to many of those on board. Twice he was called and did not answer, but the third time he replied to the caller, who then raising his voice, said, 'When you are opposite Palodes proclaim that Great Pan [26] is dead!'

"On hearing this, said Epitherses, they were all thunderstruck, and debated among themselves whether it would be better to obey the order or to disregard and ignore it. And Thamus decided that if the wind were blowing, he would sail past and say nothing, but if it were calm and the sea quiet, he would call out what he had heard. As he came opposite Palodes, there was neither wind nor wave; so standing on the stern, facing the land, he shouted what he had heard: 'Great Pan is dead!' Even before he had finished, there rose a great moan of sorrow and astonishment from not one but a multitude of voices. There were many people on board the ship, so that the story spread quickly in Rome and Thamus was sent

---

[25] A cluster of small islands off the west coast of Greece.

[26] The god Pan, half man and half goat, was originally an Arcadian god of herdsmen, but he came to be worshiped in other lands as the god of woods and pastures. The story which Plutarch tells here had wide circulation, and Christians accepted it as a sign of the passing of the pagan divinities at the coming of Christ.

for by Tiberius Caesar. And Tiberius put such faith in his tale that he had an inquiry and search made for information about Pan. The scholars, a crowd of whom were at the court, thought that probably he was the son of Hermes and Penelope." [27] Philip had some witnesses too among the men with us that day who also had heard the man Aemilianus.

18. Demetrius now said that among the islands close to Britain there were a number scattered and barren, some of which were named after demigods and heroes. He himself had sailed on an imperial commission to the nearest of these solitary islands for information and an inspection. It had only a few inhabitants, all holy men, held inviolate by the Britons. Soon after his arrival there was a great storm, with numerous portents. Winds tore over the earth and lightning fell from the sky. When it was quiet, the islanders said that some mighty spirit had passed away. "For," they said, "as a lamp, when it is being lit is not frightening, but when it goes out it seems to startle many people, so with great souls. They kindle at first gently and harmlessly, but their extinction and death, as now, brings winds and tempests and often infects the air with poisonous influences." . . .

19. Cleombrotus then took up the thread of talk and said, "I myself could tell more stories like these, but for our purpose it is enough to state that nothing contradicts them or prevents their being true. In fact, the Stoics,[28] as we know, believe that what we are saying applies not to demigods alone but that only one out of the great throng of gods is eternal and deathless. The rest, they think, were born and will perish. We need not mind the jeers and ridicule of the Epicureans,[29] which they are so bold as to turn on the whole idea of Providence, dubbing it a myth. We say their 'infinity' is a myth, in which among a multitude of worlds there is not one governed by divine reason, but all are produced by chance cohesion of particles. . . ."

---

27 Pan was commonly called the son of Hermes. His mother was sometimes one woman, sometimes another.

28 The Stoic doctrine of one supreme and eternal Reason running through the universe and manifesting itself as Providence came near to a monotheistic conception.

29 According to the Epicureans, this world and countless other worlds are composed of an infinite number of hard, invisible atoms, drifting through infinite space, and by accidental collisions linking together to form objects, souls as well as bodies, everything, indeed, that exists.

20. When he had finished speaking, Ammonius said, ". . . But Cleombrotus ought rightly to go on again with the story he was telling us, about the departure and flight of demigods."

21. Thereat Cleombrotus said: "I shall be surprised if you do not think it much stranger than anything said so far. Yet it seems to square with natural science, and Plato has given us warrant for it, not by any definite statement but as part of a vague idea, which he cautiously suggested in his enigmatic fashion. . . . So I do not hesitate to give you some account of a barbarian whom I found after many wanderings and the payment of large sums for information. He was near the Persian Gulf, where once every year he meets with people. The rest of his time he spends, he says, with roving nymphs and demigods. I had great difficulty in finding him, but then I had a talk with him and he was very friendly. . . .

"His learning and his knowledge of history he keeps with him always, but one day in every year he is inspired to prophesy and goes down to the sea and foretells the future. Potentates and royal scribes come to him there, and afterward depart. His power to prophesy he ascribes to the demigods. He had much to say about Delphi and had heard all the stories they tell here of Dionysus and the sacred rites. They were, he declared, all great tales of demigods, including those told about the Python.[30] His slayer was not afterward banished for nine years nor did he go to Tempe, but on being sentenced he passed to another world. After nine cycles of great years he came back from there purified and truly Phoebus,[31] and took over the oracle which until then had been guarded by Themis.[32] . . . However, the honors men used to pay to the demigods have become meagre and obscure or have been discontinued entirely in cases where they have moved to another world. . . ."

22. Cleombrotus paused and we all thought his story extraordinary. But then Heracleon asked what it had to do with Plato and in what way he had furnished a basis for it, and Cleombrotus replied, "You recall that he decided definitely against an infinity of worlds but that he was not

---

[30] The Python was a terrible serpent or dragon which had possession of Delphi until it was killed by Apollo. To purify himself from the pollution Apollo was said to have been banished to Tempe for eight years.

[31] Phoebus is a Greek adjective meaning radiant. It was a common epithet for Apollo.

[32] Themis, goddess of law and justice, was also on occasion a prophetess.

sure about a limited number. He even admitted the possibility of assuming as many as five worlds, one for each element, although for himself he believed in but one." . . . .

"It looks to me," I said, "as if we had now dropped our discussion of oracles, had finished with it, and were moving on to another topic equally large."

"We have not dropped it," said Demetrius, "but we are not passing over this new question, which also interests us. However, we shall not linger long over it but touch on it just enough to decide what the probabilities are. Then we will revert to our original problem."

24. "First of all then," said I, "the reasons that keep us from having an infinite number of worlds do not prevent us from having more than one. For God and prophecy and Providence can be in more worlds than one and chance may play a very small part in them. The majority of the most important things may still go through their rise and their changes in an orderly manner, which is impossible in an infinity. Besides, it is more reasonable to believe that our world is not the only-begotten and solitary work of God. For he is perfectly good and lacks none of the virtues, least of all justice and kindliness, which are the fairest and do most become the gods. And God by his nature possesses nothing aimless which he does not put to use. Hence there exist other gods and other worlds outside ours, for whom he employs his social virtues. . . .

25. "There is a dread which some people especially feel, and therefore they insist that all matter was exhausted in making one world, for if something were left over outside they think it might shake our world's framework by obstructing or striking it. But they are wrong in being so afraid. For though there are more worlds than one, each has received its own substance and matter in limited measure and bounds, and nothing is left over like a remnant unassigned or unorganized to crash into it from outside. For the Reason that provides for each world and controls the matter distributed to each will not permit anything to stray away and wander off and smash into another world, or anything from another world to smash into it, because nature contains no boundless and infinite quantity or any irrational and disordered motion. When there is an emanation from some worlds to others, it is undoubtedly congenial and pleasant, mingling harmoniously with everything, like the blending rays

of the stars. The worlds themselves rejoice, beholding one another with friendly eyes, and furnish the many good gods in each with places for their genial visiting. . . .

29. "And why be daunted by the ideas of the Stoics, who ask how, if there are many worlds, there can still be but one Destiny and one Providence and not many Zeuses and Zens.[33] If, in the first place, it is absurd to imagine many Zeuses and Zens, the Stoics' ideas are certainly far more absurd, for they set up an infinite number of suns and moons and Apollos and Artemises and Poseidons in their infinite orbits of worlds. Besides, what is the need of many Zeuses, even if there are more worlds than one? Why not have in each world another chief god and ruler of that whole, possessing mind and reason, like him who among us is called Lord and Father of all?

"Or why should not all worlds be subject to the destiny and providence of Zeus, and he oversee and guide them all in turn, providing them all with primal energies and material seeds and rational ends for what they do? Have we not here often a single body made up of separate bodies, such as an assembly, an army, a chorus, each member of which has the power of living, thinking, and learning, as Chrysippus supposes? Then is it impossible that in the whole universe there should be ten worlds, or fifty, or even a hundred, using one reasoning faculty and ordered by one government? . . . .

30. ". . . The Zeus of Homer [34] turned his gaze a little way from Troyland as far as Thrace and the nomad peoples around the Danube. But the true Zeus has a fair and worthy variety of sights in many worlds. His eyes are not fixed on an infinite void outside, nor on himself and nothing else, as some [35] have supposed, but he looks down on countless works of gods and men and the movements and courses of stars in their cycles. For divinity does not dislike changes but takes much pleasure in them, if we are to judge by the concourses and revolutions of the things we see in the sky. . . ."

38. When I had finished, Demetrius said, ". . . 'But we must carry our discussion back,' as Euripides [36] says, to our original topic. And what we

---

[33] Zen was another form of the name Zeus.   [34] *Iliad*, XIII, 3.

[35] This may be a reference to Aristotle's self-centered god. See his *Metaphysics*, XII, 9.

[36] Fragment 970.

said then—that it is when the demigods depart and leave the oracles that
they lie idle and voiceless, like musicians' instruments—brings up another
and greater problem as to the means and power they employ to make the
prophets and prophetesses entranced by their inspirations and receptive
to their visions. We cannot blame the demigods' departure for the silence
of the oracles, unless we are sure of the way by which through their presence and authority they made them active and vocal."

Ammonius then broke in and said, "But do you think that the demigods are anything else but souls on their rounds, 'clad in mist,' as
Hesiod [37] says? . . . It is neither unreasonable nor strange if souls meeting souls should impart to them visions of the future, just as we communicate with one another not altogether by voice but by writing or by
merely a touch or a glance, and so reveal much about the past and predict
the future. Unless, Lamprias, you have another suggestion to make. A
report reached us not long ago that you had had a lengthy conversation on
the subject with some strangers at Lebadia, but the man who told us
remembered none of it accurately."

"No wonder," I said, "for there were many events and much business
going on in the middle of it. Prophesyings and sacrifices were taking
place, which made our talk disconnected and fragmentary."

"But now," said Ammonius, "you have listeners with leisure, eager
to inquire and learn about this and that. Strife and contentiousness are
forbidden and full sympathy and freedom of speech, as you see, are guaranteed for every word you say."

39.   The others too called on me to speak, so after a few minutes of silence
I went on, ". . . If souls who have been separated from the body or have
never had any body whatever are demigods, according to you and the
divine Hesiod,[38]

'Holy dwellers on earth and guardians of men who are mortal,'

why deny to souls still in bodies that power by which demigods are able
to foresee and predict the future? It is not likely that on leaving their
bodies souls acquire powers or faculties which they did not possess before.
They have always possessed them, but as long as they are linked to bodies
these powers are weaker. In some persons they are entirely undiscernible

---

[37] *Works and Days,* 125.
[38] Ibid., 123.

and concealed, in others they are feeble and dim, and as ineffectual and slow as men are when peering through a fog or moving in water. They need a great deal of care, the restoration of all that belongs to them, and removal and cleansing from what has been smothering them.

"The sun does not become radiant when it breaks through clouds but is always radiant, though in a fog it looks to us blurred and dim. So the soul does not acquire the prophetic power after it passes out of the body, as out of a cloud, but has it even now, when it is blinded by being mixed and combined with mortality. We should not be surprised at this or incredulous, for we can see in the soul, if nothing else, at least the power which is the counterpart of prophecy and which we call memory, and we know how much it does to save and preserve things past or rather things that have been. For nothing of all that has happened is or subsists now, but the moment it takes place it is gone—deeds and words and feelings alike. Time, like a flowing stream, bears all away. But this power of the soul, I do not know how, lays hold of things no longer here and bestows on them appearance and being. . . .

40. "Souls have also the prophetic power, innate and faint and scarcely perceptible, but they often feel it blossoming and shining in dreams, and sometimes at death, when the body is purified and attains a state of being right for it. . . . Of itself the body often attains that state. . . . And the earth exudes many streams of power, some hysterical, unwholesome, or deadly, others good, gentle, and beneficent, as proved by the experience of those who encounter them. The prophetic stream or vapor is completely divine and holy, whether it comes to us directly through the air or in running water. When absorbed into the body it forms with the soul a new and peculiar combination of being, the special nature of which it is hard to describe clearly, though a discussion may reveal many analogies. . . .

42. "Nor is it strange if though the earth sends out many streams, only this one kind makes souls ready for inspiration and visions of the future. Legend certainly confirms my argument. For here, they tell us, the power of the place showed itself first when a shepherd happened on it and then uttered words of inspiration. His companions at first scorned them but later, when what he had predicted took place, they were confounded. The most learned men at Delphi preserve the memory of his name,

which they say was Coretas. For myself I strongly believe that the soul forms a close union with the prophetic stream, such as sight has with light, which is similar in properties. Though the eye has the power of seeing, it is useless without light, and the prophetic power of the soul, like an eye, needs something akin to it to kindle it and set it aflame. Men of earlier generations, many of them, thought that Apollo and the sun were one and the same god, but those who understood and appreciated a fair and true analogy thought that as body was to soul, the thing seen to the mind, and light to truth, so was the power of the sun to the nature of Apollo. They declared that the sun was his offspring begotten, forever being born of one who forever is. And the sun kindles and draws out and stimulates the power of sight in our senses, just as Apollo does the prophetic power of the soul.

43. ". . . But in the case of powers that issue from the earth it is likely that there are disappearances in one place and new arrivals in another, here changes in the locality and there changes in the stream, and that such cycles should often revolve in the long course of time. We infer this from what we see going on around us. We have noted in lakes and rivers, and still more in hot springs, how some have disappeared and vanished completely and some have slipped away and gone underground and then come back again, appearing and flowing out in the same places, or near by. We know too how mines have become exhausted in recent times, such as the silver mines in Attica and the copper lode in Euboea, from which they used to forge the cold-tempered blades of swords. . . .

44. "The followers of Aristotle [39] maintain that exhalations are the cause of all such changes in the earth and that natures of that kind must necessarily die down, change place, and break out vigorously again. The same may be taken as true of prophetic vapors, that their power too is not everlasting or ageless but is subject to change. Tempests of rain probably drown them and thunderbolts disperse them. Most of all when the earth quakes deep down and sinks into rubble in its depths, the vapors shift their location or disappear altogether. Here in Delphi, they say, there still remain marks of the great earthquake that once destroyed the

---

[39] The scientific followers of Aristotle might be expected to give a physical explanation for all phenomena. See Aristotle, *Meteorology*, I. 3.

city. And at Orchomenos,[40] they say, during a pestilence, when many people died, the oracle of Tiresias ceased completely and to this day is still unresponsive and dumb. Whether the same fate has befallen the oracles in Cilicia, as we hear it has, you, Demetrius, can tell us better than anyone."

45.   "I do not know the situation there now," Demetrius said, "for, as you know, I have been away a long time. But when I was there, the oracle of Mopsus [41] and that of Amphilochus were both still flourishing. I visited Mopsus' oracle and have a remarkable incident to tell of it. The ruler of Cilicia was once divided in his mind on religious matters. He was weakly sceptical, I think, and on every subject arrogant and flippant. He had about him some Epicureans who reasonably enough had learned from their natural science to be contemptuous, as they themselves admitted, of things like oracles. And he sent a freedman to Mopsus' oracle like a spy into the enemy's country, providing him with a sealed tablet inside which he had written a question. No one else knew what it was.

"The fellow spent the night, as the custom is, in the sacred enclosure and slept, and in the morning reported the following dream. He thought a beautiful man stood beside him and uttered one word, 'Black,' and no more, and at once was gone. It seemed a strange story and left everyone much perplexed, but the ruler on hearing it, was amazed and prostrated himself in worship. Then he opened the tablet and showed the question he had written there: 'Shall I sacrifice to you a white bull or a black?' So the Epicureans were confounded and the ruler himself offered the sacrifice and ever after was reverential to Mopsus."

46.   With this story Demetrius paused, and I, expecting to wind up the discussion, looked back at Philip and Ammonius, who were sitting together. But they seemed to me anxious to say something more, and I hesitated again. Whereupon Ammonius said, "Philip has something yet to say on what we have been talking about, for he thinks, as most people do, that Apollo is not a different god but the same as the sun. But I have an important question to ask on a very important subject. A little while

---

40 Orchomenos was an ancient city of Boeotia. Tiresias, the blind seer of Thebes, had an oracle in the neighborhood.
41 In post-Homeric Greek legend, Amphilochus and Mopsus were wandering diviners and founders of oracular shrines in Asia Minor.

ago, I know not how, we yielded to argument and abruptly transferred the power of prophecy from the gods to the demigods. And now, apparently, we are forcing out the demigods in their turn, driving them too from the oracle and the tripod here, and explaining away the source, or rather the existence and the power of prophecy, by ascribing it to winds and vapors and exhalations. For the minglings and heatings and hardenings we have been talking of take the glory that much more away from the gods and imply some such doctrine as to the cause of everything as Euripides [42] puts into the Cyclops' mouth,

> 'The earth must needs, whether she will or not,
> Bring forth the grass which fattens these my flocks.' . . .

"But when I consider how much help this oracle has been to Greeks during wars and foundations of cities, in seasons of pestilence and failure of crops, I think it terrible to attribute its discovery and origin not to God and Providence but to chance and accident. And I wish," he said, "that Lamprias would speak to us now on this subject. Will you wait?"

"Yes, certainly," said Philip, "and so will we all. For this discussion has stirred every one of us."

47. I turned to him then and said, "Not only am I stirred, Philip, but also filled with confusion, if before so many good men as you are I seem to be pluming myself crudely on the plausibility of my logic and destroying and disturbing some beliefs about the Deity which were framed in truth and sanctity. But I shall defend myself by calling on Plato as my witness and advocate in one. He criticized old Anaxagoras [43] because he was too much obsessed by physical causes and was forever tracing out or searching for the power of necessity expressing itself in the behavior of bodies, and was ignoring the questions of 'why' and 'by whom,' which are the most important in any inquiry as to causes and origins. Plato was the first or most persistent of the philosophers to follow up both lines of investigation, ascribing to God on the one hand the origin of all reasoning activities but not on the other hand robbing matter of its place in the necessary causes of the world as it now exists. He realized that this visible and beautifully ordered universe was not simple and unalloyed, but had its source in matter interwoven with reason.

---

[42] Cyclops, 332-333.
[43] Phaedo, 97.

"Look first at the case of artists, and take as example the famous stand and base of the mixing-bowl here, which Herodotus [44] called the 'bowl-pedestal.' Its material causes were fire and iron and softening by fire and tempering by water, without which there exist no means of producing such a work. But the overruling cause which set all these things in motion and worked through them was art and reason. The maker and creator of the portraits and likenesses here has his name inscribed,

> 'Polygnotus,[45] a Thasian by birth and Aglaophon's son,
> Painted the sack of the citadel of Troy.'

as you may see written here. But without pigments ground together and blended with one another nothing could have produced this magnificent composition. Does a man then who tries to get at its material cause, looking for and showing how the red earth of Sinope behaves and changes when mixed with yellow ochre, or the pale earth of Melos when mixed with lamp-black, deprive the artist of his glory? . . .

48. "In general, every type of creation has, as I say, two causes. The very early theologians and poets chose to center their attention on the greater cause alone, using these words to cover everything that happens,

'Zeus the beginning, Zeus midway, and everything comes from Zeus.' [46]

But as yet they made no approach to the necessary, physical causes. On the other hand, the men who came after them and who are called physicists have turned away from the beautiful and divine cause and seen everything in terms of bodies and the behavior of bodies, their collisions and movements and combinations. Accordingly the reasoning of both eras is deficient in what it should have included. The one ignores or overlooks the 'through whom' and 'by whom,' the other the 'from what' and 'through what.' And he who first comprehended clearly both agencies, and to the rational creator and mover added, as indispensable material, the underlying substance which he acts upon, acquits me of all charge of misrepresentation. For we do not make prophecy godless and irrational

---

[44] *Histories,* I, 25.
[45] Polygnotus was a celebrated Greek painter of the fifth century B.C. He decorated the treasury of Cnidos at Delphi, mentioned earlier.
[46] *Orphic Fragments,* VI, 10.

when we give it the soul of man as material and the inspiring air and exhalation as the instrument or plectrum with which to play upon it. . . .

50. "I think too that the exhalation is not always the same under all conditions but that it has its times of weakening and again of strength. To prove this I have witnesses, many foreigners and all the attendants at the shrine. The chamber where they seat those who are consulting the god is sometimes filled—though not often or at fixed seasons, but occasionally and as it happens—with a fragrant air like a breath of the sweetest and most costly perfumes, as if wafted from a source in the inner sanctuary. This flowering, probably, is caused by the warmth of some other force created there.

"If this does not appear to you credible, you will admit that the priestess herself is affected by emotions and circumstances, differing from time to time, in that part of her soul with which the inspiring vapor comes in contact, and that she does not always maintain one mood, like a harmony, unchanged in every situation. Many annoyances and vexations of which she is aware and more of which she is unaware affect her body, and when obsessed by them it is better for her not to go to present herself to the god, since she is not altogether pure—like an instrument well strung and tuned—but is excitable and unstable. . . .

51. "When the visionary and prophetic power of foretellers of the future is in a state to combine harmoniously with the inspiring vapor, as with a drug, the inspiration must come; but when it is not, the inspiration does not come, or it comes maddening and ravaging and distracting, as we know it did to the priestess who died recently. . . . She went down to the oracle, they say, unwillingly and with no zest for it, and immediately at her first replies it was plain from the harshness of her voice that she was not responding rightly. Like a hard-driven ship she was impelled by a dumb and malignant wind. Finally she became quite hysterical and with an inarticulate and terrifying shriek rushed towards the exit and flung herself down, and the delegates to the shrine fled, along with the prophet Nicander and the holy men who were present. A little later they went in and took her up. She was conscious, but she survived only a few days.

For these reasons they guard the chaste body of the priestess and have her live entirely away from contact or intercourse with strangers, and take the omens before consulting the oracle with the idea that the god sees clearly when she is in a propitious mood and temper for submitting to the inspiration without being hurt. . . . The power is in reality from the gods and demigods, yet it is not unfaltering or deathless or ageless, lasting on so into that unending time when all things between earth and moon grow weary, according to our reckoning. There are men who declare that even things above the moon cannot endure that time, but grow faint in the face of the everlasting and the unending, and pass through incessant changes and rebirths.

52. "Questions like these," I said, "I challenge you and myself to reflect upon often, for there are many contrary opinions and signs pointing in opposite directions, which this occasion does not permit us to follow up. So let us postpone them to another time, as also Philip's query about the sun and Apollo."

Isis and Osiris [1]

45. ... WE shall not ascribe the origins of the universe to inanimate bodies, as Democritus [2] and Epicurus do, nor make one Reason and one Providence, which overrules and contains all things, the creator of universal matter, as the Stoics do; for it is equally impossible for anything bad to exist where God is the cause of all things, and for anything good to exist where he is the cause of nothing. The harmony of the world is, as Heraclitus says, like that of a bow or a harp, alternately tightened and relaxed; and according to Euripides,

> "Nor good nor bad is to be found alone,
> But there is mixture, which is surely well." [3]

This very ancient opinion has been handed down from the theologians and lawgivers to the poets and philosophers. In its origin it goes back to no one author, but the conviction it has produced is strong and indelible, and is everywhere expressed, by barbarians as well as by Greeks. One may hear it not only in common talk and story but also in mysteries and sacrifices.

According to it the world is neither suspended on high without intelligence, reason, or guidance, nor yet is there only one Reason, which directs it on its course with a rudder, as it were, or a strict rein. On the

---

[1] The following selection from Plutarch's essay on Egyptian religious practices and beliefs is an interesting early study in comparative religion and the philosophy of religion.

[2] Democritus and Epicurus were the famous founders of the atomic school of philosophy. See above, *The Passing of the Oracles,* notes 28 and 29.

[3] *Aeolus,* Fragment 21.

416

contrary, it contains many elements, and is compounded of evil as well as of good. Or rather, to put it simply, Nature produces here nothing but what is mixed with something else. Not that there is a single storekeeper who draws and dispenses our human lots in one mixture [4] out of two different casks, but that all comes from two contrary causes and opposing powers, one of which leads us to the right in a straight line, and the other turns us contrarywise, backward.

For human life is a mixture, and so is the universe. If it is not all so, at least that part of it which surrounds both the earth and the moon is irregular and variable, and liable to all manner of change. And if nothing comes into existence without a cause, and if the good cannot be a cause of evil, Nature then must be herself a source and origin of evil as well as of good.

46. This is also the opinion of the greatest and wisest portion of mankind. They believe that there are two gods, two rival workmen, as it were, one the maker of good things and the other of bad. Some call the better one God, and the other Demon, as did Zoroaster [5] the Magian, who, they tell us, lived five thousand years before the Trojan War. This Zoroaster called the first Oromazes, and the second Arimanius. He declared also that the first was more like light than like anything else perceptible to our senses and the second like darkness and ignorance; and that Mithras was in the middle between them. For that reason the Persians call Mithras the "Mediator." He taught mankind to pay vows and offerings of thanksgiving to Oromazes, and placating gifts of mourning to Arimanius. They pound a plant called *omomi* in a mortar and call on Hades and Darkness, and then mix with it the blood of a sacrificed wolf and take it out and throw it into a place where the sun never shines. Some plants, they believe, belong to the good god, and others again to the evil demon; among animals too they think that dogs, fowls, and hedgehogs belong to the good power, and water rats to the evil, and so they call him lucky who kills the largest number of them. . . .

---

[4] The reference is to the *Iliad*, XXIV, 527-8, where Zeus is described as having in his house two jars, one filled with good things, the other with bad.

[5] Zoroaster, also called Zarathustra, the almost mythical founder of the Persian religion, lived about 1000 B.C. In Plutarch's time the worship of Mithras the Mediator had spread through the Roman Empire.

48.   Such then is the mythology of the Magi. The Chaldeans [6] say that the planets are watchful gods, two of them beneficent, and two malignant, while the other three they call midway and indifferent. As for the Greeks, their beliefs are familiar to everyone—to wit, that the good part of the world belongs to Zeus of Olympus, and the hateful part to Hades. They have a tale too that Harmony was the child of Aphrodite and Ares, the former being sweet and protective, the latter rough and quarrelsome.

Note too how the philosophers agree with them. . . . Aristotle called the first of the two principles Form, and the other Formlessness. Plato in many passages expressed this in a veiled and ambiguous way, calling the first principle simply the Same, and the second the Other. But in his book of *Laws,* when he was old, he asserted, no longer in riddles and symbols but in plain words, that the world was moved not by one soul, but, perhaps, by many and certainly by not fewer than two, one of which was beneficent, the other contrary to it and the author of things contrary. Between the two he left also a third nature, which was neither without soul nor without reason nor devoid of power to move itself, as some suppose, but was dependent on both of the others, though it desired the better always and longed for it and pursued it, as I shall explain in the latter part of my essay. In that I shall try particularly to reconcile the religion of the Egyptians with this kind of philosophy.

49.   Now, according to the Egyptians, the frame and constitution of the world is complex, made up of opposing powers which, however, are not of equal strength, but the better is predominant. Yet it is impossible to eliminate the bad altogether, since much of it is innate in the body and much in the soul of the universe, where it carries on always a fierce battle with the better part. Now within the soul, the intelligence and reason which is the prince and master of all that is best is Osiris. And within the world, the wind, the water, the heavens, and the stars, whatever is orderly, stable, and wholesome, as shown in the seasons, the climates, and the revolutions of the stars, is an efflux and manifest image of Osiris. Again, the passionate, Titanic, irrational, and turbulent part of the soul

---

[6] "Chaldean" was a name applied by later classical writers to casters of horoscopes and other predicters of the future, whose lore was derived from the ancient astrologers of Mesopotamia. They taught the dependence of human affairs on the motions of the seven planets.

is Typhon,[7] and whatever in corporeal nature is precarious, diseased, and chaotic, as shown in irregular seasons, destructive temperatures, eclipses of the sun, and disappearances of the moon, is, as it were, an outbreak and devastation of Typhon. The name Seth, by which they call Typhon, indicates as much, for it signifies a domineering and compelling power, and often also an overthrowing and backward-turning power. Some say that Bebon was one of Typhon's companions, but Manetho [8] says that Typhon himself was also called Bebon, a name which means restraining and hindering, as if to imply that, while all things were marching on their course and moving steadily towards their natural end, the power of Typhon stood in their way. . . .

51. Osiris, on the other hand, they represent by an eye and a scepter, the one representing foresight and the other power. . . . They often denote him too by a hawk, because he excels in keenness of sight and speed of flying, and sustains himself on very little food. They say also that when flying over the earth he drops dust down on the eyes of unburied dead. And whenever he alights on a river bank to drink, he ruffs up his feathers, and then after he has drunk, lets them fall again, obviously because he is now safe and has escaped the crocodile. But if he happens to be caught, he keeps his feathers stiff as before.

They show us everywhere too Osiris' statue in the shape of a man, with phallus erect, as betokening his power of creation and nutrition. They dress up his image in a flame-colored robe, for they think of the sun as the body of the good power and the visible image of intellectual substance. Therefore we should despise people who assign the sun's orb to Typhon, since nothing of a luminous or healthful nature belongs to him, nor order, nor fertility, nor motion proceeding with measure and proportion, but everything that is perverse. Nor is the parching drought which destroys multitudes of living animals and plants to be counted as the work of the sun but of those winds and waters which in the earth and air are not moderated according to the season, during times when the principle of disordered and uncontrolled force is let loose, and stifles the exhalations which should be ascending. . . .

---

[7] See above, *Superstition*, ch. 37.

[8] Manetho was an Egyptian high priest who wrote a history of his country from mythical times to the year 323 B.C.

53. But we must go back to our proper subject. Isis is the female aspect of Nature, which is receptive of all forms of generation. In this sense she was called by Plato the Nurse and the All-receiver. The people have given her ten thousand names, because, as directed by reason, she takes on all manner of shapes and forms. But she has a natural love for the primal Head of all beings, which is the same as the Good, and yearns for it and pursues it and shuns and rejects her part in the evil one. For although she is indeed the abode and receptacle of both good and evil, of herself she inclines always to the Good, and offers herself to it to generate upon her and to sow in her its effluxes and likenesses. And she rejoices and is glad when she is impregnated and filled with its creations. For generation is the production of an image of real being in matter, and what is generated is thus a copy of true being.

54. Hence with entire consistency they tell us that the soul of Osiris is eternal and incorruptible, but that his body is often torn in pieces and destroyed by Typhon, and that Isis wanders to and fro searching for it, and when she finds it fits it together again. For the Permanent Being, the Intellectual Nature and the Good, is itself above chance and corruption, and the part that is sensual and corporeal receives certain images from it, and acquires certain proportions, shapes and resemblances. Yet these, like impressions on wax, are not permanent, but are obliterated by the disorderly and tumultuous element, which is driven down hither from the upper region and wars with Horus, the son of Isis, who is the sensible image of the intellectual world. . . .

64. To sum up all now in a word, it is wrong to believe that either the water or the sun or the earth or the sky is Osiris or Isis, or again that fire or drought or sea is Typhon. But we shall make no mistake if we ascribe to Typhon whatever in all these through excesses or defects is violent and disorderly, and on the other hand reverence and honor whatever is orderly, good, and beneficial as the work of Isis and the image, imitation, and reason of Osiris. . . .

65. Hence we should try to deal with the many vociferous persons who persist in identifying the persons of the gods with the seasonal changes which take place in the ambient air, or with the growing crops and the times of sowing and plowing, as also with those who say that Osiris is buried when the grain is sown and covered over by the earth, and that he revives again and reappears when the leaves begin to sprout. . . .

66. There would be no great harm in this if, in the first place, they would look on their gods as common to us too and not make them peculiar to the Egyptians, nor confine their names to the river Nile and the land which the river Nile waters, nor insist that their fens and their lotuses are the sole work of God's creation and refuse their great deities to the rest of mankind, who have neither a Nile nor a Buto [9] nor a Memphis. Yet all men have Isis and the other gods around her and are well acquainted with them, though it is not long since they learned to call some of them by their Egyptian names. But from the first they have known and honored that power which belongs to every one of them.

In the second place, what is of still greater consequence, they should take constant care and precaution lest, all unaware, they transform and dissolve their divinities into winds and streams and sowings and plowings, accidents of earth and alterations of seasons, as those do who make Dionysus wine and Hephaestus fire. Even Cleanthes [10] says somewhere that Persephone is the breath of air which blows through the crops and then dies. And a poet, speaking of reapers, says,

"Then when the youth are cutting the legs of Demeter."

But such men are no different from those who would take the sails and the ropes and the anchor of a ship for the pilot, and the warp and the woof for the weaver, and the cup of mead or of barley water for the doctor. They also breed in other men dangerous and atheistic opinions, when they give the names of gods to things that are senseless and lifeless, and are necessarily destroyed by the people who need them and use them.

67. No man can believe that these gifts of Nature are gods in themselves, because God is not mindless or lifeless or subject to human control. But the gifts have taught us to think of the gods as beings who use them themselves and bestow them on us and keep them permanent and continuous. And we think of the gods as not different in different countries, nor as barbarian and Greek gods, nor as southern and northern gods.

[9] Buto was a town situated in the Nile delta.

[10] Cleanthes was the philosopher and poet who succeeded Zeno as head of the Stoic school at Athens. For Persephone and Demeter, see *Lycurgus,* n. 44.

But as sun, moon, sky, land, and sea are common to all men, yet have different names in different nations, so the one Reason which ordains these things, and the one Providence which watches over them, and the subordinate powers which he sets over each, have received according to the laws of the various countries different honors and titles. And men employ consecrated symbols, some of them obscure and others clearer, and thereby guide their understanding to a knowledge of things divine, though not without hazard. For some go entirely astray and slip down into sheer superstition, and others, who shun the quagmire of superstition, fall as it were unwittingly over the precipice of atheism.

68.   For this reason, while considering these matters, we should take as our special guide through the mysteries the reasoned teaching of philosophy and regard with reverence also whatever is said or done in religion. Theodorus [11] once said that, though he held out his discourses in his right hand, some of his hearers received them in their left. So the wise ordinances of the laws on sacrifices and festivals we should not wrongly interpret otherwise than as they are meant. From the Egyptians themselves we learn that all such practices have a basis in reason. On the nineteenth day of the first month when they keep a festival to Hermes and eat honey and figs, they repeat while eating, "Truth is sweet." The amulet of Isis, which they say she hangs about her neck, means when interpreted, "A true voice." . . .

Nothing that man naturally possesses is more divine or leads to greater happiness than reason, especially when he reasons about the gods. Hence we lay a strict charge on anyone who goes down to the oracle [12] there, to think pious thoughts and speak words of good omen. But most people behave shockingly at processions and festivals. At the outset they give orders to speak only words of good omen, and then they both speak and think wicked words of sacrilege even about the gods. . . .

69.   . . . The Phrygians believe that God sleeps in the winter and wakes in the summer; so they sing lullabies to him in winter and rousing songs to him in summer, like Bacchic dancers. The Paphlagonians say that he is bound and imprisoned in winter, and walks abroad again at liberty in spring.

---

[11] Theodorus was a Greek teacher of rhetoric of the first century B.C.
[12] "The oracle" here means probably the oracle of Ammon in the Egyptian desert.

70. But the nature of the winter season makes us suspect that the rituals of mourning were prompted by the disappearance of grains and fruits. And yet the ancients did not actually believe that they were gods, but rather great gifts of the gods, essential for their preservation from a savage and bestial life. And when they saw the fruits dropping and disappearing entirely from the trees, and the grains which they had sown still starved and puny, they would scrape the soil away with their hands and lay it back again, thus committing the seeds a second time to the ground with uncertain hopes of their ever reappearing or coming to ripeness. Therein they did many things which were like what people do at funerals, when mourning for the dead.

But we used to say of one who had bought the books of Plato that he had bought Plato, and of one who was acting the comedies of Menander that he was playing Menander. So they too did not shrink from calling the gifts and creatures of the gods by the names of the gods and paying them honor and veneration for their usefulness to themselves. However, the men of after times took the practice up blindly and ignorantly and applied to the gods the vicissitudes of their crops, and the comings and goings of the gifts so necessary to them. They not only called them births and deaths of gods, but actually believed they were that. They filled their minds full of grotesque, unsanctioned, and distorted notions, even though they had plain before their eyes the absurdity of these irrational ideas. . . .

71. Men are not, however, altogether like this, fo. though they make lamentation for their crops, they pray to the gods, who are the authors and bestowers of them, to produce and bring up again other new harvests to take the place of those which are being consumed. But it is an excellent saying among philosophers that people who have not learned to understand correctly the sense of words go wrong too in their acts. Among the Greeks, for instance, there are persons who have not learned or trained themselves to speak of bronze and painted and stone images as statues and memorials of gods, but call them gods themselves. They are even silly enough to say that Lachares [13] stripped Athene, that Dionysius cropped off Apollo's golden locks, and that Jupiter Capitolinus was burned and destroyed during the civil wars at Rome. And before they

---

[13] Lachares made himself tyrant of Athens in 297 B.C. and stripped the gold from Athene's statue to pay his troops.

realize it, they have imbibed and absorbed the vicious opinions that go with such language.

The Egyptians have had much the same experience with regard to the animals they revere. About animals the Greeks speak and think correctly when they call the dove sacred to Aphrodite, the serpent to Athene, the raven to Apollo, and the dog to Artemis, as Euripides [14] says:

"Dog you shall be, and image of light-bringing Hecate." [15]

But the majority of Egyptians worship the animals themselves and adore them as gods, and have filled their religious worship with objects of ridicule and derision. This indeed is the least of the harmful results of their folly. Dangerous misconceptions arise therefrom, which plunge the weak and simple-minded into blind superstition, and drive sharper and bolder minds into atheism or brutish arguments. It seems therefore not inappropriate to describe what appear to be the facts of the matter.

72. Some Egyptians think that the gods, out of fear of Typhon, once changed themselves into these animals, and hid themselves as it were in the bodies of ibises, dogs, and hawks, which is foolery beyond all tales of miracles and legend. And their notion that all souls of the dead who go on existing are reborn into these animals is equally incredible. Some, however, assign a political ground for these beliefs. They say that Osiris on his great expedition divided his forces into many parts, which the Greeks call companies and squadrons, and gave them everyone a standard in the shape of an animal, each of which came to be looked upon as sacred and venerable by the descendants of those who received a share in that distribution. Others say that later kings, to terrify their enemies, put on gold and silver masks of wild beasts' heads when they appeared in battle.

Still others tell us that one of these clever and unscrupulous kings had observed that Egyptians were naturally frivolous and quick to grasp at a change or innovation, but when in sober mood and acting as a mass, they had a strength of numbers which was invincible and irresistible. He therefore taught them and planted among them a perpetual superstition,

---

[14] Fragment 968.
[15] Hecate, a goddess with magical powers, was often confused with the greater goddess Artemis. Both had associations with the moon.

which was to become the ground of endless strife among them. He commanded the different cities to honor and reverence different animals, and as these animals were at enmity and war with one another, and one of them by nature wanted one kind of food and another another, the several cities were always defending their own animals and fiercely resenting any wrongs done to them. Thus, without realizing it, they were drawn into the quarrels of their animals until they were actually at war. To this very day, the Lycopolitans [Wolf-town men] are the only tribe among the Egyptians who eat sheep, because the wolf, which they consider a god, eats them. And in our time, the people of Oxyrynchus [Pike-town] caught a dog and sacrificed and ate it like consecrated meat, because the Cynopolitans [people of Dog-town] ate a fish called *oxyrynchus,* or pike. From that incident they went to war and did much mischief to one another. Later they were all chastised and reduced to order by the Romans. . . .

74. I have yet to speak of the usefulness of these animals and of their symbolical value. Some possess one of these qualities and many possess both. It seems obvious that the Egyptians honored the cow, the sheep, and the ichneumon for their benefactions and usefulness to them, as the people of Lemnos did the lark for finding locusts' eggs and breaking them, and the Thessalians the storks, because when their soil was breeding swarms of snakes, the storks appeared and destroyed them all. For that reason they enacted a law that whoever killed a stork should be banished from the country. The Egyptians honored also the asp, the weasel, and the beetle, as seeing in them some faint reminders of divine power, like images of the sun in drops of water. Many of them to this day believe that the weasel copulates through its ear, and brings forth its young through its mouth, symbolizing in that way the genesis of speech. The race of beetles, they say, has no female, but the males all discharge their sperm into round pellets of earth, which they roll up by pushing them backwards with their hind feet, just as the sun apparently turns the heavens in the direction opposite to its own motion, that is, from west to east. The asp they compare to lightning for never growing old, and for moving with ease and smoothness without help of limbs.

75. Nor was the crocodile given his honor without plausible reason, for he was born, they say, an image of God, since he is the one animal without a tongue, and the divine Word has no need of a voice, but "moving on

its noiseless path it guides mortal affairs by justice." [16] They say too that he is the only animal living in water that has his eyes covered with a thin, translucent film, extending down from his forehead, so that he sees without being seen, which is a mark of the supreme God. And in whatever spot of the country a female crocodile lays her eggs, she knows that it marks the limit of the rise of the Nile that year. For she cannot lay eggs in water, and yet is afraid to lay far from it, but she has such exact foreknowledge of what is coming that she can make use of the approaching stream when laying and hatching her eggs, and yet have them dry and untouched by water. She lays sixty eggs and takes the same number of days to hatch them. The longest lived crocodile lives that many years. The number sixty is the first measure employed by men who study the heavens.

As for other animals honored on two counts, we have already mentioned the dog. The ibis, besides killing deadly reptiles, was the first to teach the people the use of medicinal purges, for they saw her employing clysters, and so purging herself. The strictest priests, when purifying water for lustration, take it from a place where an ibis has drunk, for she will not drink if the water is unwholesome or polluted, or even come near pollution. With her two legs standing apart from one another and her bill she forms an equilateral triangle, and the pattern and combination of her black feathers with her white make pictures of the curving moon.

76. Nor should we think it strange that the Egyptians took such pleasure in small symbolisms, for the Greeks too in both their painted and their carved portraits of gods worked out many of the same kind. In Crete, for example, there was an image of Zeus without ears, since he that is Ruler and Lord over all should hearken to no one. Phidias placed a snake by the statue of Athene, and a tortoise by that of Aphrodite in Elis, to show that maids needed guardians, and that silence and homekeeping were best for married women. The trident of Poseidon is a symbol of the third region of the world, which is occupied by the sea and designed to lie below the sky and the air. For which reason they gave Amphitrite [17] and the Tritons the names they did.

---

[16] Euripides, *Trojan Women*, 887-8.

[17] Plutarch attempts here to derive these two names, like the word "trident" from *tritos*, the Greek adjective meaning third. The Tritons were a race of lesser sea divinities who followed in Poseidon's train.

The Pythagoreans honored numbers and geometric figures with the names of gods. They called the equilateral triangle Athene Born-from-the-Head and Thrice-Born, because it is equally divided by three perpendiculars drawn from three angles. The number one they called Apollo because of the singleness of its unity and its refusal to be plural. The number two they called Strife and Audacity; the number three Justice, for whereas wronging and being wronged are caused by either deficiency or excess, justice, because it is equal, comes between them. The so-called sacred quaternion, which is the number thirty-six, made, we are told, the most binding of their oaths. It was given the name of World, since it is composed of the first four even numbers and the first four odd numbers added together.

77. If then the most distinguished philosophers, observing the riddle of the divine in lifeless and corporeal things, thought it not right to neglect or disparage anything that is, still more, I think, should we prize the peculiar features of natures which have perception and soul, feeling and character. We do not, however, revere them, but revere the Divine through them according as they are by nature clearer mirrors of him, and we should conceive of them as instruments or handiwork of the God who orders all things. In general too we must believe that nothing lifeless is better than something living, and nothing insensate than something with feeling—not even though one should heap together all the gold and emeralds in the universe, since Divinity lives not in colors or shapes or smooth surfaces. Things that never shared in living and by nature never will share have a portion of less honor than those that have lived and are dead. And a nature which still lives and sees, and has in itself a source of movement and a knowledge of what is its own and what belongs to others has drawn to itself an efflux and portion of beauty from that Mind "which," as Heraclitus [18] says, "controls the universe." Hence the Deity is no worse represented by animals than in works of bronze and stone, which suffer both discoloration and destruction and by their nature are totally devoid of perception and understanding. This is, I think, the best account to be given of the adoration of animals. . . .

---

[18] Fragment B 41.

Glossary

ACROPOLIS: the Greek name for any high eminence or citadel in a city. The most famous acropolis was the rocky height in Athens, sacred to the virgin goddess Athene, which, after its desecration by the Persian invaders in 480 B.C., Pericles beautified with a new Parthenon temple, walls, and entrance way, parts of which are still standing.

AEDILE: one of four officials elected annually at Rome charged with the duties of keeping the streets in order, supervising the water and grain supplies and the conduct of the markets, and organizing and to a large extent paying for public spectacles and games.

AFRICA: in Roman days the name meant northern Africa, eastward to Egypt, southward into the Sahara and westward as far as the mountains of Mauretania, modern Morocco.

AGORA: an open space in a Greek town, used first as a market place and then as a center for public activities of all sorts. It corresponded to a forum in a Roman town. The Athenian agora lay to the north of the Acropolis where recent excavations have uncovered remains of some public buildings.

ARCHON: the name given to chief magistrates in many Greek cities. In Athens of the 5th and 4th centuries B.C., there were nine archons, chosen yearly by lot, each representing one of the tribes into which the citizens were divided. At the head of the nine were the king archon, the polemarch, and the archon who gave his name to the year. See below under polemarch and thesmothetes.

AREOPAGUS or ARES' HILL: a rocky hillock west of the Acropolis in Athens; also the court composed of ex-archons which met there. It was a conservative and aristocratic body to which Solon, the lawgiver, assigned

428

the guardianship of the constitution. The democratic reforms introduced by Ephialtes in 460–461 B.C. stripped it of most of its power.

As: a Roman bronze coin, which when first cast in the early 3rd century B.C. weighed a pound and was worth in modern U.S. currency between 16 and 20 cents. Its weight and value were decreased with the growing demand for metals during the Punic Wars, and in 191 B.C. its weight was fixed by law at half an ounce and its value a little less than a cent. Meanwhile the silver denarius took its place as a coin of value.

Asia: to Greek geographers this was the land which spread eastward from the River Don in the north and the Suez in the south. To the Romans of a later time it usually meant the Roman province of Asia, which took in only the northern and western parts of Asia Minor.

Augur: a member of a religious college at Rome whose official function was to ascertain the will of the gods regarding any project under consideration by observing the flight, cries, and behavior of birds.

Campus Martius or Field of Mars: the low land stretching back from the Tiber, north of the Capitoline Hill at Rome, originally outside the city walls and used first for pasture. Later it was the site of army exercises, plebeian gatherings, and shrines to foreign deities. As the city expanded, a new forum, additional temples, a circus, and an amphitheater were built there; also Pompey's theater, in which Caesar was assassinated.

Censor: one of two Roman officers elected every four or five years to draw up a list of citizens marking each man's status or rank. As guardians of public morals, censors had the power to prosecute or strike from their lists any who had registered falsely or by misconduct had forfeited their right to offices or station.

Centurion: the officer in command of a century, the smallest unit in a Roman legion. There were sixty centuries to a legion, their size varying from seventy to a hundred men, as the size of the legion varied.

Choregus: a citizen of wealth and standing in a Greek city selected to bear the expense of training and costuming the chorus and defraying other incidental costs of producing a play or group of plays at a religious festival. The choregus who produced a successful spectacle was acclaimed almost as highly as the author of the play. A similar function was performed by an aedile at Rome.

CONSUL: the chief civil and military magistrate of the Roman republic. Two were elected yearly by the people, the candidates being nominated by the senate from its own members. Originally they were always patricians but by the Licinian Law of 367 B.C. the office was opened to plebeians. The consuls convened and presided over meetings of the senate and assemblies of the whole people and put into effect the decrees there enacted. In war they took command of the army, down to the time of the military dictatorships.

DACTYLI: fabulous beings of Greek mythology, who according to one story were wizard workers of iron in Crete, and according to another were skilled in medical magic and music.

DEME: an Attic township, which under Clisthenes (6th century B.C.) was organized into an autonomous unit of local government, but with a share in the central government at Athens. All registered members of a deme were members also of the citizens' assembly at Athens, and elected representatives of the demes composed the Athenian council or senate. Athens itself was divided into seven or eight demes; the total number in the 5th century was about 150.

DENARIUS: a Roman silver coin, counted as the equivalent of the Greek drachma. Its value in modern money is usually given as about 20 cents, but its purchasing power was much greater.

DICTATOR: a Roman magistrate with extraordinary authority, appointed by a consul at the request of the senate to deal with a crisis, civil or military, in the affairs of the state. He held office for not more than six months, but during that time his power was absolute. With Sulla, a new type of dictatorship for life was inaugurated; after Caesar's death the office was formally abolished.

DIVINER: a forecaster of future events by the interpretation of any one of a variety of portents, such as dreams, apparitions, celestial phenomena, and by the appearance of the entrails of animals slaughtered for sacrifice.

DRACHMA: a Greek weight equal to something over four grams; also a silver coin issued by many cities as a standard for exchange, its value given as between 15 and 20 cents in modern money but varying greatly at different times and places.

EPHORS: a board of executive magistrates in Sparta, five in number, elected annually by the citizens. They had a supervisory power over the two kings and could bring them to trial before the senate if found derelict in duty. They had rights of civil jurisdiction, saw to it that the citizens lived in accordance with Lycurgus' constitution, and conducted relations with foreign states. Down to the 3rd century B.C. theirs was the dominant authority at Sparta.

FASCES: bundles of elm or birch rods, bound by a red thong, out of which projected a naked axe. As emblems of Roman authority they were carried by the lictors who escorted high magistrates and the Vestal Virgins on their public appearances.

FETIALES: a college of Roman priests who performed the ceremonies incident to making a treaty or a declaration of war. In the first instance, they called upon Jupiter to visit Rome with his vengeance if she were the first to break the treaty; in the second, they appealed to Jupiter to witness that their cause was just.

FORUM: a public square in a Roman city, used as a market or a place of popular gathering. The Roman forum lay between the Palatine, the Capitoline, and the Quirinal Hills. It was drained, paved, and adorned with temples, basilicas or halls for the courts and for business transactions, rostra from which the people could be harangued, triumphal arches, and columns. The senate house opened on the forum, as did the house of the Vestal Virgins; through it ran the Sacred Way up to the great temple of Jupiter on the Capitoline. There were other forums in Rome for butchers, grocers, fishmongers, and craftsmen.

GALLEY: a long, slim ship without decks, propelled by oars, twenty-five commonly to a side; a mast and square sail could be hoisted if helpful. It had a high bronze beak or ram at the prow. Built primarily for war, the galley was not as sea-worthy as the broad, capacious sailing vessels of the merchants.

HELOTS: serfs of the Spartan state, descendants of the race which occupied the land before the Dorian Greeks conquered it. They worked as artisans and tilled the soil, and occasionally fought in the army. Because they outnumbered their masters, there was always a dread of a helot rising and a secret police used ruthless methods to keep them submissive.

IDES: the name given to what was called the middle day of a month. In the old Roman calendar, March, May, July, and October had 31 days. The Ides in those months therefore fell on the 15th. The other eight months had 29 days and the Ides were the 13th.

KNIGHT: originally one of the cavalry in the Roman army, serving for three times the pay of an infantryman. Later, when the allies furnished most of the cavalry, the knights made up a second rank of nobility, below the senators, and were given certain functions, such as service on juries, collection of taxes in Asia, etc. In time they became rivals of the senators for posts and privileges.

LEGION: the largest and most important unit of the Roman army. Polybius (3rd century B.C.) describes it as consisting of 4,500 men, 300 horse, 3,000 foot, armed with spears and swords, and 1,200 light-armed troops of various types. Under Marius the legion was enlarged to 6,000 foot and the cavalry section abolished. Drawn up in long open ranks, it was a more flexible tactical unit than the Greek phalanx and proved superior to it in battle. Like a modern regiment, it might develop a reputation and individuality of its own; Caesar's famous Tenth Legion is an example.

LICTOR: an attendant on a Roman magistrate who walked before him carrying the fasces, symbols of authority; the number of lictors in attendance depended on the rank of the magistrate.

LITUUS: a staff shaped something like a shepherd's crook which was the badge of an augur's office at Rome.

MEDIMNUS: a Greek dry measure, in Attica equivalent roughly to a bushel and a half in English measure, in Sparta to over two bushels.

MINA: a Greek weight equal to 100 drachmas, or a little under a pound avoirdupois; also a large coin of a possible value of $16 to $20.

MYSTERY: a secret religious cult into which applicants were admitted after purification and initiation. The greatest Greek mystery was celebrated at Eleusis in honor of the harvest goddess Demeter and her daughter Persephone. At the end of three stages of initiation the worshiper was assured of divine fellowship in this life and happiness in the next. The Dionysiac mysteries were ecstatic orgies in which only women took part. The Orphic mysteries were associated with a Thracian poet, Orpheus. Of the Cabirian mysteries little is known except that the Cabiri were protectors of seafarers.

NONES: the day of the month which by the Roman method of reckoning was the ninth before the Ides.

OBOL: the smallest Greek weight, one sixth of a drachma or about seven tenths of a gram; also the smallest Attic bronze coin, worth perhaps three cents.

OSTRACISM: an institution peculiar to Athens, the banishment for ten years, without disgrace or loss of civil rights, of a citizen whose power seemed to threaten the freedom or safety of the democracy. Every year the assembly was asked whether a vote to ostracize anyone should be taken. If a majority favored it, the voting took place and if any man's name appeared on more than 6,000 ballots, he went into exile. The prac·tice of ostracism was dropped after the 5th century B.C.

PARASANG: a Persian measure of distance, estimated usually as between three and three and a half miles.

PATRICIAN: a member of the old Roman aristocratic and wealthy class who under the early republic held all the important offices in the city, secular and religious, including membership in the senate. They gradually lost their special privileges and by the middle of the 3rd century B.C. in eligibility for office they were no better off than the plebeians.

PHALANX: a general name in early Greek literature for any infantry force drawn up for battle, but later denoting more particularly a body of foot and horse arrayed according to the methods of Philip II of Macedon. His phalanx consisted of about 25,000 men, armed with long, heavy pikes and disposed in solid ranks up to sixteen deep, protected by cavalry on their sides and rear. Eventually the phalanx was defeated by the more flexible Roman legion.

PLEBEIAN: one of the general mass of Roman free citizens, who in the first years of the republic were excluded from the magistracies, the senate, and the priestly class. Their struggle to attain political equality with the patricians, through organizing themselves into what amounted to a separate state, with its own assembly and protecting officials, the tribunes.

ended in their complete victory in 287 B.C. Thereafter the word plebeian meant little more than membership in a less aristocratic social class.

PNYX: a low hill to the west of the Acropolis at Athens, where the Athenian assembly held its meetings.

POLEMARCH: a Greek military commander. At Athens, by the 5th century B.C., the polemarch had lost his military functions and was simply the second of the nine archons, in charge of lawsuits involving foreigners.

PRAETOR: the Roman praetor was always the chief judicial magistrate of the city, responsible for the administration of justice in the courts. By the 3rd century B.C. the influx of foreigners necessitated the election of a second praetor, to judge cases in which one or both litigants were not Romans. Later, as provinces were conquered, the number of praetors was raised to eight and they officiated as representatives of Roman justice abroad, as assistants to governors and even as governors when necessary.

PROCONSUL, PROPRAETOR: under the later Roman republic, a supply of experienced men as governors for the provinces was created by the senate's appointment of consuls and praetors, who had finished their term of office, to go out as proconsuls and propraetors to govern one or more provinces for the ensuing year.

PRYTANIS: a board of magistrates in a Greek city who presided over meetings of the senate and assembly. At Athens they were a committee of the senate, 50 in number, who prepared the business for senate and assembly and summoned them to meetings. A new prytanis was elected about every five weeks, so that each of the 500 senators might have his turn on the board during the year. The members of the prytanis met daily and ate together at the prytaneum, a round building close to the senate house.

PYTHIAN: an epithet of the god Apollo after his slaying of the Python, the dragon which once guarded Delphi. Also called Pythian were the musical contest and games held every four years at Delphi in honor of Apollo's oracle there. The priestess who served as mouthpiece of the oracle was the Pythia.

QUAESTOR: a Roman treasury official. The two city quaestors were responsible for the management and safety of the state treasury, in which were stored both public funds and public records. As business increased, the number of quaestors was enlarged until under Caesar it reached forty. By then a quaestor was a necessary part of the staff of every provincial governor. He saw to the collection of local taxes and assisted his superior in other ways. The quaestorship was a training school for ambitious young Romans. It was a prerequisite for election as praetor or consul.

ROSTRUM: a speaker's platform; the rostrum in the Roman forum was a long, high platform to the front of which were affixed as trophies beaks of enemy ships captured in battle. The top was adorned with statues and a sun dial.

SATRAP: a Persian provincial governor who might be either hereditary king of a conquered territory or an appointee of the Great King himself. He had large powers, but by a system of checks was kept under control of the central authority. Alexander continued the method of government by satraps after his overthrow of the Persian monarchy.

SENATE: the senior deliberative and advisory or legislative council in a city state. At Athens the senate was a democratic body of 500, chosen by lot from the Attic tribes to serve for one year, no man being eligible for more than one re-election. It met every day and handled all kinds of public business, referring more serious matters to the assembly. At Rome the senate was composed of ex-magistrates, usually men of wealth and high birth, experienced in government and members for life. It was therefore aristocratic and conservative in its policies and possessed a strong sense of corporate dignity and authority. Nominally its duty was to advise the magistrates but actually its decrees had usually the force of law and for the two or three centuries before Christ, except under the dictatorships, its power was dominant in the Roman state.

SESTERTIUS: a bronze Roman coin, worth one quarter of a denarius, or about five cents.

STATER: a gold coin issued by the Persians and accepted as the principal gold medium of exchange in the Greek markets until the Macedonian stater began replacing it under Philip and Alexander. In modern currency its value has been reckoned as between $5.50 and $6.

SIBYL: a mysterious woman with a gift of prophecy. Such women are said to have appeared in various places in the ancient world and occasionally to have written their prophecies on leaves in the form of oracular verses.

STADIUM: a measure of distance, equal to about 600 English feet. It was also a track for footraces, in the form of a long narrow parallelogram with rounded ends, at each of which stood a pillar to serve as starting post or goal. Tiers of seats for spectators lined the sides and ends.

STRATEGUS: a Greek general or high military officer who might be commander of an army in the field or member of a board of strategy at home. At Athens such a board was responsible for the upkeep of garrisons and fleet, the protection of commerce from pirates, and the oversight of campaigns in war.

TALENT: as a measure of weight equal to sixty Greek minas, or between fifty-five and sixty pounds, considered a normal load for a man. As a sum of money, its value has been estimated as between $1,000 and $1,200 in modern currency.

TETRARCHY: a name given to one of the four political districts of Thessaly. Eventually it was used also for political subdivisions in Asia Minor and Syria. The petty prince or governor of such a subdivision was known as a tetrarch.

THESMOTHETES: the six junior archons at Athens, who sat as a board with broad judicial powers, as well as the duty of examining newly elected magistrates to ascertain if they were qualified for their offices.

TRIBE: a division of the people of an ancient city state along lines of either geographical location or of kinship, for purposes of civil administration. In Athens Clisthenes divided the citizens into ten tribes, basing the first enrolment on locality. Once enrolled a man bequeathed his membership to his son, regardless of where the latter lived. Rome began with three tribes, each from its own locality on the hills. In the 3rd century B.C. the number rose to 35, called urban and rural tribes, but went no further. When Roman citizenship was extended to all Italians at the beginning of the 1st century B.C., the new citizens were enrolled in one or another of the existing tribes.

TRIBUNE: an official elected by the plebeian assembly at Rome for the special duty of protecting plebeian lives and rights against the patricians.

He might call a meeting of their assembly, pass resolutions or plebiscites, use his authority to enforce them, and veto any act of a magistrate or decree of the senate that in his view might be injurious to plebeian interest. In the 3rd century B.C. plebiscites were accepted as binding on the whole citizen body and the tribunes were recognized as officials of the state rather than of a class.

TRIREME: a type of Greek warship which in the 6th century B.C. largely replaced the galley. It was longer and heavier, with a more formidable ram at the prow, and was propelled by upward of 200 oarsmen.

TRIUMPH: a gala procession escorting a victorious Roman general back from the wars on his way through the city to render thanks and honor to Jupiter Capitolinus. Permission for a triumph must first be obtained from the senate and until the day set the general must wait with his army outside the city walls. On that day the procession entered the city, magistrates and senators leading, followed by trumpeters, wagons laden with spoils, white oxen for sacrifice, captive leaders walking in chains, lictors, and at last the victor himself in his chariot, garlanded with laurel and holding a scepter. Behind him marched his army. Their road led them down through the forum and up to Jupiter's temple on the Capitoline, where the oxen were sacrificed, gifts offered to the god, and the laurel garland laid on his lap.

TRIUMVIRATE: any group of three men; in particular, the two groups who in the 1st century B.C. successively divided among them the supreme power over the Roman state. The First Triumvirate consisted of Pompey, Caesar, and Crassus; the Second of Octavian, Antony, and Lepidus. Both ended in wars between two of the triumvirs.

TYRANNY: an absolute rule set up by force, which might be either benevolent and enlightened or brutal and oppressive. This type of government rose out of incompetent oligarchies in many Greek cities during the 7th and 6th centuries B.C., and when circumstances were favorable tyrants appeared again afterward. The government they set up was usually short-lived, seldom lasting more than two generations.